RELIGION, ENLIGHTENMENT AND EMPIRE

In the second half of the eighteenth century, several British East India Company servants published accounts of what they deemed to be the original and ancient religion of India. Drawing on what are recognised today as the texts and traditions of Hinduism, these works fed into a booming enlightenment interest in Eastern philosophy. At the same time, the Company's aggressive conquest of Bengal was facing a crisis of legitimacy and many of the prominent political minds of the day were turning their attention to the question of empire. In this original study, Jessica Patterson situates these Company works on the 'Hindu religion' in the twin contexts of enlightenment and empire. In doing so, she uncovers the central role of heterodox religious approaches to Indian religions for enlightenment thought, East India Company policy and contemporary ideas of empire.

DR JESSICA PATTERSON is Lecturer in the History of Political Thought at the University of Cambridge.

IDEAS IN CONTEXT

Edited by DAVID ARMITAGE, RICHARD BOURKE and JENNIFER PITTS

The books in this series will discuss the emergence of intellectual traditions and of related new disciplines. The procedures, aims and vocabularies that were generated will be set in the context of the alternatives available within the contemporary frameworks of ideas and institutions. Through detailed studies of the evolution of such traditions, and their modification by different audiences, it is hoped that a new picture will form of the development of ideas in their concrete contexts. By this means, artificial distinctions between the history of philosophy, of the various sciences, of society and politics, and of literature may be seen to dissolve.

A full list of titles in the series can be found at: www.cambridge.org/IdeasContext

RELIGION, ENLIGHTENMENT AND EMPIRE

British Interpretations of Hinduism in the Eighteenth Century

JESSICA PATTERSON
University of Cambridge

Shaftesbury Road, Cambridge CB2 8EA, United Kingdom

One Liberty Plaza, 20th Floor, New York, NY 10006, USA

477 Williamstown Road, Port Melbourne, VIC 3207, Australia

314–321, 3rd Floor, Plot 3, Splendor Forum, Jasola District Centre, New Delhi – 110025, India

103 Penang Road, #05–06/07, Visioncrest Commercial, Singapore 238467

Cambridge University Press is part of Cambridge University Press & Assessment, a department of the University of Cambridge.

We share the University's mission to contribute to society through the pursuit of education, learning and research at the highest international levels of excellence.

www.cambridge.org
Information on this title: www.cambridge.org/9781009017688

DOI: 10.1017/9781009039192

First published 2022
First paperback edition 2023

A catalogue record for this publication is available from the British Library

Library of Congress Cataloging-in-Publication data
NAMES: Patterson, Jessica, author.
TITLE: Religion, enlightenment and empire : British interpretations of Hinduism in the eighteenth century / Jessica Patterson.
DESCRIPTION: New York, NY, USA : Cambridge University Press, 2022. | Series: Ideas in context | Includes bibliographical references and index.
IDENTIFIERS: LCCN 2021031096 (print) | LCCN 2021031097 (ebook) | ISBN 9781316510636 (hardback) | ISBN 9781009017688 (paperback) | ISBN 9781009039192 (ebook)
SUBJECTS: LCSH: Hinduism – History – 18th century. | Great Britain – Civilization – Hindu influences. | BISAC: POLITICAL SCIENCE / History & Theory
CLASSIFICATION: LCC BL1205 .P38 2022 (print) | LCC BL1205 (ebook) |
DDC 294.509/033–dc23
LC record available at https://lccn.loc.gov/2021031096
LC ebook record available at https://lccn.loc.gov/2021031097

ISBN 978-1-316-51063-6 Hardback
ISBN 978-1-009-01768-8 Paperback

For T. J. Fox

Contents

Acknowledgements page viii
A Note on the Text x
List of Abbreviations xi

Introduction 1

PART I RELIGION, ENLIGHTENMENT AND EMPIRE

1 European Letters, the Company and Hinduism 35

2 John Zephaniah Holwell and the Religion of the *Gentoos* 70

3 Alexander Dow and the *Hindoo* Shasters 113

4 Enlightenment and Empire 155

PART II FROM SCEPTICISM TO ORIENTALISM

5 Nathaniel Brassey Halhed and *Gentoo* Antiquity 207

6 Charles Wilkins and the *Gēētā* 239

7 William Jones, Vedānta and the 'Permanent Settlement' 263

Conclusion 309

Bibliography 320
Index 351

Acknowledgements

Writing this book has not been a solitary endeavour. I have gratefully accepted the generosity of friends and colleagues in aiding me through the journey to its completion. It therefore gives me great pleasure to be able to acknowledge them here. Above all, I must express my gratitude to Tom Scriven, who has read countless drafts and offered unending support. My greatest debts are also to those who have encouraged my interest in intellectual history and championed my endeavours to contribute to the field. Richard Bourke has been a constant source of inspiration and encouragement ever since I attended his brilliant classes as an MA student. As an examiner of the PhD thesis on which much of the work here is based, Richard's gift for formulating the right questions and his extraordinary knowledge of the field are what propelled that project forward. Likewise, I would like to stress my gratitude to Stuart Jones, whose steady stewardship, patience and brilliance of insight brought that PhD to completion. To my other supervisors at the University of Manchester, Jackie Hirst and Jeremy Gregory, I would also like to express my warmest thanks. Much of this book is built on Jackie's dazzling expertise in Indian philosophical traditions and Jeremy's encyclopaedic knowledge of eighteenth-century Christianity. I must also note my thanks to the Arts and Humanities Research Council for funding the research on which this work is based.

While writing this book I have found an academic home in a number of institutions, and in each of these I have met generous colleagues. At the University of Manchester, a special mention must go to both the supportive postgraduate community and the Ducie Arms. My first academic post was at Queen Mary, University of London, and I could not have hoped for a better start. In particular I must thank Barbara Taylor, whose teaching I covered; I learnt a great deal in the process. Barbara's support and generosity since have been invaluable. Likewise, Georgios Varouxakis, Quentin Skinner, Miri Rubin and Caroline Ashcroft have all encouraged my work and made my time at Queen Mary a particularly enriching experience. I must also mention the Eighteenth-Century Studies seminar, and in particular Miles Ogborn and Markman Ellis, for providing the ideal academic environment in which to learn from the research of others and present my own work. Likewise, the community around the History of Political Ideas seminar at the Institute of Historical Research has also been a source of inspiration and support. At King's College London I benefited immensely from the wisdom and encouragement afforded me by Hannah Dawson and Niall O'Flaherty, both of whom are exceptional scholars. Niall's work on political thought and theological debate in the eighteenth century has proved a vital resource. Finally, at Cambridge, I would like to thank Newnham College for welcoming me and providing such a wonderful environment in which to complete this book.

I would also like to express my thanks to Cambridge University Press, and in particular to Liz Friend-Smith, Atifa Jiwa and the two anonymous reviewers of the manuscript. Further thanks are also due to Ian Stewart, whose knowledge of William Jones has enriched this book immensely. Likewise, conversations with Joshua Ehrlich and Robin Mills have directed me to important arguments and ideas. I have also been grateful for the network of early career scholars in the fields of intellectual history and the history of political thought, who are too numerous to mention, though I would like to note Adeal Halo, Vanessa Lim, Conor Bollins and Shiru Lim for making me feel so welcome. A special mention must also go to the particular friends I made on the MA, who have stuck with me ever since: Signy Gutnick Allen, Lisa Kattenberg, Alexandra Ortolja-Baird, Sean Turnbull, Chris Berrisford and Joseph Biesterfield. In addition, I would like to thank the many archivists and librarians who have helped me find my way in unfamiliar territory.

On a personal note, I am especially grateful to those closest to me in life. My friends and comrades in Manchester are a constant source of inspiration, particularly our kid Josh, who we have sadly lost but whose kindness and commitment to solidarity we are all determined to learn from. My friends Kia Heron, Sara Woodward, Kiran Millwood Hargrave and Tom de Freston also deserve a mention for all the times they have told me to keep going. Finally, I thank Mary, Pam, Xavier, Rebecca, Xanthe and Orestes for their love and encouragement.

A Note on the Text

This book necessarily uses terms from Sanskrit, Persian and occasionally other South Asian languages. Except for where quoting source materials, I have chosen to use the International Alphabet of Sanskrit Transliteration (IAST) for the transliteration Sanskrit, and in the case of Persian terms, followed the models most frequently appearing in the academic secondary literature. Some words, however, have slipped into common usage in their anglicised versions, such as 'Brahmin' and 'pandit', and in these cases I have kept them the same. Likewise, place names have been left in their familiar, anglicised forms, so as to be consistent with the source material. I have not included a glossary of South Asian terminology used in this book, but have instead opted to offer rough equivalents and explanations of terms within the text itself.

Abbreviations

Add. MS	Additional Manuscripts
BL	British Library, London
FWIH	Fort William – India House Correspondence
HCSP	House of Commons Sessional Papers of the Eighteenth Century, Sheila Lambert (ed.), 145 vols. (Wilmington, DE, 1975)
IOR	India Office Records
MS Eur.	European Manuscripts, Oriental and India Office Collections, British Library
OIOC	Oriental and India Office Collections
OMS	Oriental Manuscripts
PRO	Public Record Office
TNA	The National Archives, Kew, United Kingdom

Introduction

In the middle of the eighteenth century, finding themselves with privileged access to Indian languages and advisors, servants of the East India Company became instrumental in delivering ideas about Indian religion to European audiences. This book is about the religion they decided to present, the intellectual frameworks that shaped their presentation of it, and some of the ramifications it had for Enlightenment thought, Company policy and contemporary ideas of empire.

*

In 1767 East India Company servant John Zephaniah Holwell described the central tenets of the *Gentoo* religion as 'short, pure, simple and uniform', arguing that the multiple gods associated with it were merely figurative.[1] A year later, another Company servant, Alexander Dow, declared that the *Hindoo* religion was oriented towards a belief in a singular 'Supreme Being'.[2] Following this, in two separate published works commissioned by the then governor-general of Bengal, Nathaniel Brassey Halhed controversially suggested that the *Gentoo* scriptures were of greater antiquity than the Bible, and Charles Wilkins described the ancient Brahmins as 'Unitarians'.[3] For these 'Company men', what they considered to be the ancient and original religion of India, which today we would recognise as Hinduism, was an unjustly maligned and essentially reasonable theology, insofar as each of them judged religion to be

[1] John Zephaniah Holwell, *Interesting Historical Events, Relative to the Provinces of Bengal, and the Empire of Indostan*, vol. 2 (London: T. Becket and P. A. de Hondt, 1766/1767), pp. 1, 111.

[2] Alexander Dow, *The History of Hindostan; From the Earliest Account of Time, to the Death of Akbar; Translated from the Persian of Mahummud Casim Ferishta of Delhi*, vol. 1 (London: T. Becket and P. A. de Hondt, in the Strand, 1768), pp. xxi–lxix, lv.

[3] Nathaniel Brassey Halhed, *A Code of Gentoo Laws, or, Ordinations of the Pundits: From a Persian Translation* (London [s.n.], 1776), p. xliv; Charles Wilkins, *The Bhăgvăt-Gēētā, or Dialogues of Krēēshnă and Ărjŏŏn* (London: C. Nourse, 1785), p. 24.

reasonable, the main tenets of which were compatible with Christian moral teaching. This was within a framework, however, where in common with all religions, the essential truths of this doctrine were liable to degeneration via the mutually reinforcing factors of vulgar superstition and priestly manipulation.

A decade before Howell's remarks, East India Company servant John Henry Grose offered a different account of what he saw as the religion of the *Gentoos.* In *A Voyage to the East-Indies, with Observations on Various Parts There,* Grose described his experiences in the regions of Bombay and Surat, as well as offering a recent history of the Mughal Empire, the Catholic missions, and a miscellany of social practices. In terms of the 'Gentoo religion', Grose thought that there was 'little or nothing to add' to the impressions of earlier travel writers and missionaries who had detailed its various polytheistic tendencies and so confined his discussion to 'those particulars of it that struck [him] the most.'[4] These 'particulars' were, namely, their religious toleration, 'their treatment of cows', and the 'practice of voluntary burning' among widows. By the second edition (1766), Grose evidently had a change of heart and decided to speculate about the origins of the religion of the ancient *Gentoos.* They were, Grose ventured, a people 'descended from Shem', the son of Noah.[5] This was a theory that followed biblical history and a notion made popular in the early modern period, that after the Flood Noah's three sons, Japheth, Shem and Ham, had repopulated the continents of Europe, Asia and Africa.[6] After this, claimed Gross, they were 'instructed by the Greeks in the worship of the heroes of fabulous antiquity', with the result that they eventually consecrated an elephant as their idol.[7] For Grose the *Gentoo* religion was a fantastical and idolatrous counterpoint to revealed Christianity.

The division between the ideas of Grose and those of Holwell reflect a broader change in approach to the interpretation of Hinduism[8] in the publications of East India Company authors in the eighteenth century. Grose understood Indian religion as a set of practices that could be understood in a general history of idolatry. In contrast, by the 1760s

[4] John Henry Grose, *A Voyage to the East-Indies, with Observations on Various Parts There* (London: S. Hooper and A. Morley, 1757), pp. 290, 295, 308.

[5] John Henry Grose, *A Voyage to the East-Indies, with Observations on Various Parts There,* 2nd ed., vol. 1 (London: S. Hooper, 1766), pp. 291, 293, 309, 327.

[6] Benjamin Braude, 'The Sons of Noah and the Construction of Ethnic and Geographical Identities in the Medieval and Early Modern Periods', *William and Mary Quarterly,* 54:1 (1997), pp. 106–8.

[7] Grose, *Voyage to the East-Indies,* vol. 1 (1766), p. 328.

[8] That is, the practices, beliefs and texts that are today commonly associated with the religious tradition known as Hinduism. For more on this, see the section 'Hinduism' in this Introduction.

other East India Company servants began to produce what were described by contemporaries as '*systematical* accounts of the doctrines of the Gentoos', based on appeals to scriptural sources (Persian and Sanskrit) and Brahmin instruction.[9] This book will explore the work of five such authors: John Zephaniah Holwell (1711–98), Alexander Dow (1735–79), Nathaniel Halhed (1751–1830), Charles Wilkins (1749–1836), and finally the better-known orientalist scholar, William Jones (1746–94). Firstly, it argues that their work advanced a philosophically inclined interpretation of what they saw as India's 'native religion', in which the emphasis was on its intellectual value, both in terms of its internal coherence, and in its potential as material for various European debates. Secondly, it suggests that this was a result of their engagement with heterodox Christian religious thought, as well as Enlightenment political thought regarding the nature of the relationship between religion, history and civil society. In turn, this philosophical interpretation of Hinduism will be shown to have played a significant role in the intellectual culture of the late eighteenth century. On the one hand, their works had major implications for arguments and ideas about religion and its role in society. On the other, it had ramifications for the ways in which East India Company policies were shaped, perceived and contested.

Contrary to what scholars have referred to as the 'ethnographic' or 'anthropological' approaches of missionaries and travel writers like Grose, which emphasised the external ceremonies and culturally unfamiliar practices, the interpretations of Hinduism forwarded by the authors in this study focused on the theological and philosophical content of what they saw as India's ancient and original religion.[10] A precursor to this shift in approach has been described by Joan-Pau Rubiés, who has marked the seventeenth century out as witnessing a transition from 'comparative antiquarian apologetics' to a 'comparative libertine anthropology of religion'.[11] This suggestion explicitly builds on Hunt, Jacob and

9 Luís Vaz de Camões, *The Lusiad: or Discovery of India. An Epic Poem. Translated from the Portuguese of Luis De Camoëns*, William Julius Mickle (trans.), 2nd ed. (Oxford: Jackson and Lister, 1778), p. 305.

10 The use of 'anthropological' and 'ethnographic' to describe this approach (which was grounded in the observation of customs and practice) takes its cue from two sources: Joan-Pau Rubiés, *Travel and Ethnology in the Renaissance: South India through European Eyes, 1250–1650* (Cambridge: Cambridge University Press, 2000), and Lynn Hunt, Margaret Jacob and Wijnand Mijnhardt, *The Book That Changed Europe: Bernard and Picart's Religious Ceremonies of the World* (Cambridge, MA: Harvard University Press, 2010).

11 Joan-Pau Rubiés, 'From Christian Apologetics to Deism: Libertine Readings of Hinduism, 1650–1730', in William J. Bulman and Robert G. Ingram (eds.), *God in the Enlightenment* (Oxford: Oxford University Press, 2016), pp. 107–8.

Mijnhardt's extensive study of Bernard Picart and John Frederic Bernard's best-selling *Religious Ceremonies of the World* (1723–37), which provided a compilation of known world religions and, according to the authors of the study, 'sowed the radical idea that religions could be compared on equal terms'.[12] To this Rubiés adds that John Frederic Bernard had aimed to demonstrate that religious life, across the spectrum, could be reduced to simple spiritual worship, and that corruptions of this through priestcraft, superstition and enthusiasm could just as easily be observed in Christianity as in pagan practices. This 'Deistic brand of religious libertinism' is thus taken to represent an important change in European accounts of Eastern religion.[13] This study builds on such a view, while at the same time challenging Rubiés' chronology, which jumps from the 'comparative libertine anthropology' of Bernard to the 'arrival of British orientalists such as William Jones' at the end of the eighteenth century.[14] This book will recover the overlooked, but contemporaneously important, body of thought that sits between these two polls. Bernard's study was an ethnological compendium of existing literature, arranged to encourage certain conclusions on the similarity between Christian and other more distant religions when it came to practices that expressed both rational devotion and superstitious excess. In the period 1760–90, however, British authors claimed to have penetrated the original principles of this 'symbolical religion', based on first-hand knowledge of texts, and advanced various interpretations of the philosophical and theological tenets of the *Gentoo* or *Hindoo* religion.[15] It therefore situates Jones in a longer history of British intellectual constructions of Hinduism, from the 1760s onwards – a period that was crucial in the East India Company's transformation from trading corporation to, controversially, possessing many of the features of a sovereign entity.

Prior to this study these earlier writers have received little historiographical attention, their work having been eclipsed by the emergence of orientalism as a defined category of scholarship at the end of the same epoch. Indeed, William Jones, and his founding of an 'Asiatick Society of Bengal' in 1784, are often considered definitive of eighteenth-century British understandings of Hinduism.[16] This is true of scholars across the interpretive divide of

[12] Hunt, Jacob and Mijnhardt, *The Book That Changed Europe*, p. 1.
[13] Rubiés, 'From Christian Apologetics to Deism', p. 127.
[14] Rubiés, 'From Christian Apologetics to Deism', p. 108.
[15] Dow, *History of Hindostan*, vol. 1 (1768), p. xxiii.
[16] See M. J Franklin, *Orientalist Jones: Sir William Jones, Poet, Lawyer, and Linguist, 1746–1794* (Oxford: Oxford University Press, 2011).

postcolonial studies, with Edward Said describing Jones as the 'undisputed founder' of orientalism,[17] as well as those tending towards a more apologetic emphasis on cultural exchange, invoking Jones as the embodiment of a sympathetic orientalism.[18] This latter approach pinpoints the transition from the eighteenth to the nineteenth century as the site of a 'new orientalism', or an 'Oriental Renaissance', in which Indological scholarship was born out of British and Indian encounters.[19] While this study disagrees that the relationship between orientalism and imperialism can be either satisfied or extenuated by an account of cultural attitudes, it does not dispute the placement of Jones as the primary representative of a certain kind of orientalism; indeed, it holds that his approach was distinct from the earlier British authors considered in this study on a number of counts. It does, however, object to the historiographical reduction of these earlier British authors to mere precursors, patchy in their scholarship and quickly outmoded by proper Sanskrit studies. Where Holwell, Dow, Halhed and Wilkins have been grouped together before, it has been under the banner of preparing the way for the Asiatick Society.[20] Instead, they ought to be accounted for according to the particular terms on which their work was predicated and received, which, it is the argument of this book, represented a distinctive and transformative moment in the diversity of European representations and constructions of Indian religion and philosophy, and in particular Hinduism. As such it represents the first comprehensive study of these authors and the political and intellectual milieus in which their ideas operated.

P. J. Marshall's *The British Discovery of Hinduism in the Eighteenth Century* (1970) has previously placed these authors alongside one another, hinting at the potential significance of viewing their works as a means to understanding 'Europeans and their beliefs'. He rightly assessed that such works were important 'not for the information which they give or fail to

17 Edward Said, *Orientalism* (London: Penguin, 2003 [1978]), p. 78.

18 Franklin, *Orientalist Jones.* In answer to Said's claim that Jones' ambition to obtain a perfect knowledge of India was complicit with imperialism, Franklin writes, 'Perhaps polemical postcolonialism might admit there can be no destruction of prejudice without the understanding that springs from knowledge' (p. 19).

19 See, for example, Thomas R. Trautmann, *Aryans and British India* (Berkeley: University of California Press, 1997), p. 64; Raymond Schwab, *The Oriental Renaissance: Europe's Rediscovery of India and the East, 1680–1880*, Gene Patterson-Black and Victor Reinking (trans.) (New York: Columbia University Press, 1984 [original German, 1950]).

20 Wilhelm Halbfass, *India and Europe: An Essay in Understanding* (Delhi: Motilal Banarsidass, 1990), pp. 54–68. Halbfass' 'philosophical essay' was originally published as *Indien und Europa Perspektiven ihrer Geistigen Begegnung* (Stuttgart: Schwabe & Co., 1981).

give about Hinduism, but for what they reveal about the authors and their contemporaries'.[21] Marshall's book, however, is not a study but an anthology of extracts from these authors, framed only by a general contextual introduction. The task of accounting for what exactly these works reveal about their authors and their readers was left to other scholars.[22] This book intends to take on this enterprise by offering an original study of these authors and their works.

As the following review of Dow's *History of Hindostan* shows, the work of East India Company writers was considered at the time to be a significant and new contribution to European knowledge:

> ... though India hath been much spoken of in ancient and modern ages, its real internal history hath hitherto been very imperfectly known, and still more imperfectly its philosophical and religious system. The curious and the learned will, however, have the pleasure and advantage of obtaining a fuller acquaintance with these things, in consequence of the great connections which the English have lately had with the East Indies, and the vast dominion they have acquired in that country. Several writers have favoured us with some account of the Indian affairs.[23]

Indeed, Holwell, Dow, Halhed and Wilkins each claimed to have delved into the mysteries of the mischaracterised *Gentoo* religion to an unprecedented degree. Significantly, this was a description with which many of their contemporaries agreed. Holwell was hailed by Moses Mendelssohn, an important thinker for both the German and Jewish Enlightenments, as the first author 'to see through the eyes of a native Brahmin'.[24] Dow was similarly highly regarded by Voltaire, who cited him as an authority in a number of works.[25] The work of Halhed and Wilkins followed in the two decades after, and was hailed as the first authentic and substantial translations of Brahminical scriptures into English, and thus accordingly as important contributions to European knowledge.[26]

[21] P. J. Marshall, *The British Discovery of Hinduism in the Eighteenth Century* (Cambridge: Cambridge University Press, 1970), p. vii.

[22] Some of these works have also been reproduced in a series, each with an introduction from Michael J. Franklin : *Representing India: Indian Culture and Imperial Control in Eighteenth-Century British Orientalist Discourse*, ed. M. J. Franklin, 9 vols. (London: Routledge, 2000).

[23] From a review of Alexander Dow's *History of Hindostan* in *Monthly Review, or, Literary Journal*, 39 (London, 1768), p. 377.

[24] Mendelssohn, quoted in Franklin, *Representing India*, vol. 1, p. xii.

[25] See Kate Marsh, *India in the French Imagination: Peripheral Voices, 1754–1815* (London: Pickering and Chatto, 2009), pp. 69–74.

[26] Bernard S. Cohn, *Colonialism and Its Forms of Knowledge: The British in India* (Princeton, NJ: Princeton University Press, 1996), p. 21.

The reconceptualisations of Indian religion offered by these authors were not carried out in a posture that was innocently aloof from power relations, moving in a world of benign cultural curiosity. They were the works of East India Company servants and were read as such. And yet, it would be a mistake to see these works as merely politics by other means. Instead, each was a product of complex intellectual engagement with Indian thought that related in diverse and intricate ways to dynamic arguments and ideas in Europe, and not entirely dictated by the interests of the East India Company. As recent works such as Sanjay Subrahmanyam's *Europe's India* have argued, the long history of European interactions with Indian culture were diverse and sometimes contradictory, the 'product of layered and intermittent conversations' and 'distinct asymmetries in perception', as well as the emergence of certain 'topoi'.[27] The British interpretations of Hinduism I explore in this book did play a significant role in the shaping of particular topoi, both in terms of the construction of ideas about India as possessing an ancient and sophisticated philosophical past, which played no small part in Enlightenment discourses on civilisation, as well as sharpening European distinctions of *Hindoo* as opposed to Muslim religion. And yet, these patterns emerged, as this book will demonstrate, from concerns more closely attached to religious Dissent than imperial policy, though they would come to be increasingly fixed to it towards the end of the eighteenth century. Particularly in the case of Holwell and Dow, this even entailed degrees of active invention for the purposes of intervening in debates about the origins and nature of religious truth.

This is a clear repudiation of scholarship which Subrahmanyam characterises as presenting Europeans as simply collecting 'information' about Asia to become better informed over time.[28] Of course, the most important criticism of this perspective has been Edward Said's conception of orientalism, the polemical force of which joined contemporary critiques of comparative religion, ethnography and cartography. In turn, Said's Foucauldian knowledge/power paradigm produced an array of studies on colonial discourse formation. Such a perspective has faced important challenges, among which has been the accusation that it results in a tendency to essentialise and homogenise diverse historical thought and action into a totalising thesis, often reduced to an abstract politics of domination.[29] Not all critiques have

[27] Sanjay Subrahmanyam, *Europe's India: Worlds, People, Empires: 1500–1800* (Cambridge, MA: Harvard University Press, 2017), p. 323.

[28] Subrahmanyam, *Europe's India*, p. 107.

[29] Sumit Sarkar, 'Orientalism Revisited: Saidian Frameworks in Modern Indian History', in Vinayak Chaturvedi (ed.), *Mapping Subaltern Studies and the Postcolonial* (London: Verso, 2012),

been equally sophisticated, however, and significantly less convincing is the stress on affective relations or sympathetic attitudes as rehabilitating European 'encounters' with India.[30] In the examination of the various religious ideas and concepts that these authors brought to bear on their interpretation of Indian religion, then, this book suggests that the pursuit of orientalist knowledge was not singularly an instrument of an abstract and homogenised imperial will to power, but neither was it unknowing and innocuous. These authors were commentators on the policies of the East India Company and its notorious conquests. Their accounts of the *Hindoo* or *Gentoo* religion were, therefore, necessarily embedded in the politics of British empire in India in the second half of the eighteenth century.

Like many Enlightenment authors who have been deemed 'critics' of empire, writers like Dow condemned the abuses of the East India Company, and some of the uses of empire, but not imperial government per se. Likewise, Enlightenment readers of these authors took the terms of their accounts of Indian civilisation and applied them to different arguments about empire and European culture. Self-consciously heterodox and tolerationist ideas were mobilised both in opposition to empire, and in the service of visions of its enlightened practice. The status of Brahminical scriptures as the locus of India's ancient customs was, for example, to prove a decisive feature in determining the nature of Company governance in terms of 'the administration of justice', which from the Hastings regime onwards necessitated the compilation and codification of Hindu law – tasks to which both Halhed and William Jones would devote themselves. Indeed, as studies such as Lata Mani's account of the debate on sati in the early nineteenth century has shown, such appeals to Brahminic scripture would become a defining feature of arguments about colonial policy well into the 1830s.[31] In addition, the interests of heterodox Christians in recovering the 'original purity' of ancient Hindu monotheism via the 'discovery' of ancient scriptures that stretched back to a golden age prior

p. 240. For a complicated critique of this at play in work on British imperialism in particular, see Andrew Sartori, 'The British Empire and Its Liberal Mission', *Journal of Modern History*, 78:3 (2006).

30 See, for example, the casting of William Jones as a spotless scholar in Garland Cannon, *The Life and Mind of Oriental Jones: Sir William Jones, the Father of Modern Linguistics* (Cambridge: Cambridge University Press, 1990), p. 82. For Subrahmanyam on this, see *Europe's India*, p. 215. See also William Dalrymple, *White Mughals: Love and Betrayal in Eighteenth-Century India* (London: Penguin, 2004).

31 The term 'sati' has come to be used for widows who burn to death on the funeral pyres of their husbands. See Lata Mani, *Contentious Traditions: The Debate on Sati in Colonial India* (London: University of California Press, 1998).

to Mughal rule would overwhelmingly cast Muslims as essentially foreign, and the practitioners of 'the Hindoo religion' as the ancient inhabitants of India. Combined in some cases with characterisations of Islam as fanatical and despotic, this laid the foundations for legitimatisations of Company rule that appealed to its status as the preserver of, or indeed an agent of regeneration for, India's ancient philosophy, religion and culture.[32] In the period covered in this study, however, this often sat alongside appeals to the principle that the Company was following precedents set by the 'ancient Mughal constitution', the example of which was, according to Dow, deist rather than Muslim.[33] As the following chapters will outline, then, the protagonists offering these accounts of *Hindoo* or *Gentoo* religion did so according to particular religious preoccupations, that were Dissenting and heterodox in nature, and in turn, these were married with differing and competing conceptions of empire.

In its account of the connections between British interpretations of Hinduism and the conquest of Bengal, this book offers a novel perspective, arguing that religion played a far greater role in the intellectual history of this period than has previously been assumed. Indeed, scholarship on British 'ideologies of empire' such as the great works of Ranajit Guha, as well as those following more recently by Robert Travers and Jon Wilson, has largely identified the various philosophical commitments underpinning British theories of empire as essentially secular or worldly concerns about sovereignty, law and political economy.[34] These were indeed central, and certainly shaped the commentaries of the several authors considered in this study, but what this book also demonstrates is that British ideas of empire were also closely intertwined with debates among Christians about reason and revelation, Trinitarian and Unitarian conceptions of the divine, as well as natural religion and priestcraft, all of which were refracted through conceptions of Indian society and of Hinduism in particular. In turn these arguments were utilised in a number of different ways, including

[32] See, for example, Halhed's poem 'The Brahmin and the Ganges', pp. 215–19 in Rosane Rocher, 'Alien and Empathic: The Indian Poems of N. B. Halhed', in Blair B. Kling and M. N. Pearson (eds.), *The Age of Partnership: Europeans in Asia before Dominion* (Honolulu: University Press of Hawaii, 1979).

[33] Robert Travers, *Ideology and Empire in Eighteenth-Century India: The British in Bengal* (Cambridge: Cambridge University Press, 2007); for Dow on this, see Jessica Patterson, 'Enlightenment and Empire, Mughals and Marathas: The Religious History of India in the Work of Company Servant, Alexander Dow', *History of European Ideas*, 45:7 (2019).

[34] Ranajit Guha, *A Rule of Property for Bengal: An Essay on the Idea of Permanent Settlement* (New Delhi: Orient Longman, 1982 [1963]); Travers, *Ideology and Empire*; Jon E. Wilson, *The Domination of Strangers: Modern Governance in Eastern India* (Basingstoke: Palgrave Macmillan, 2008).

as critiques of European orthodoxies, as well as in support of imperial policies.

In the early work of Holwell and Dow these arguments emerged outside of the perimeters of Company rule. By the 1790s, however, the distance between British knowledge of Indian religion and imperial governance was dramatically reduced. Part II of this book will therefore trace the gradual closing of this gap, and in particular locate the work of William Jones as a turning point in which concepts of a philosophical Indian religion were made to fit a more stable framework of British supremacy, situated in what C. A. Bayly described as the 'new imperial age'.[35] Indeed, following the French Revolution, these heterodox accounts of Indian religion, with their emphasis on its challenges to orthodox biblical chronologies and doctrines, grew increasingly out of favour. However, its traces continued on in the currents of nineteenth-century 'infidel' literature, German romanticism's vision of sublime Indian mysticism, and Hegel's *Lectures on the Philosophy of World History* (1822–30).[36]

Enlightenment

Of Holwell, Dow, Halhed, Wilkins and Jones, Holwell was the first to publish. He wrote first on Company politics, and then on Indian history and religion. His *Interesting Historical Events, Relative to the Provinces of Bengal, and the Empire of Indostan* appeared in three volumes during the years 1765–71.[37] Holwell's central position was that the *Gentoo* religion, in its ancient form, contained all of the essential truths of a reasonable monotheistic belief in the creator. Within his presentation of this thesis he also made several claims about the ability of *Gentoo* ideas to shed light on deficiencies within Christian theology, which through the volumes became more controversial. Following this, Alexander Dow (1735–79), who also operated independently from any official Company patronage, similarly described *Hindoo* religion as rational and monotheistic. His work *The History of Hindostan* was published in two volumes (1768–69, 1770), with an additional third volume appearing in 1772.[38] The projects of

35 C. A. Bayly, *The Imperial Meridian: The British Empire and the World, 1780–1830* (London: Longman, 1989).

36 Hegel, 'Lectures on the Philosophy of World History, Second Draft 1830', in L. Dickey and H. B. Nisbet (eds.), *Hegel: Political Writings* (Cambridge: Cambridge University Press, 1999), particularly pp. 144–5. For a fuller discussion, see Aakash Singh Rathore and Rimina Mohapatra, *Hegel's India: A Reinterpretation, with Texts* (Oxford: Oxford University Press, 2017).

37 Holwell, *Interesting Historical Events*.

38 Alexander Dow, *The History of Hindostan, Translated from the Persian*, 2 vols. (London, 1768), 2nd ed., 2 vols. (London, 1770), vol. 3 (London, 1772).

Nathaniel Brassey Halhed and Charles Wilkins, which appeared in the late 1770s and 1780s, continued to offer further insights into what they agreed were the essentially monotheistic and ancient tenets of an indigenous Indian religion. In contrast to Holwell and Dow, however, the work of Halhed and Wilkins was a result of the direct patronage of Governor-General Warren Hastings. It was at the request of Hastings that Halhed produced *A Code of Gentoo Laws* (1776), a digest of religious ordinances compiled by a panel of pandit scholars, rendered into Persian and subsequently by Halhed into English. Likewise, ensuring the publication of Charles Wilkins' *The Bhăgvăt-Gēētā, or Dialogues of Krēēshnă and Ărjŏŏn* (1785) was the design of Hastings. The prefaces and introductions that Halhed and Wilkins prepared for these literary contributions, however, were still oriented towards an interpretation of *Gentoo* religion that emphasised the relevance of its philosophical and theological content for debates relating to European religious Dissent and heterodoxy.

As well as admirers, because of the religiously liberal conclusions of their studies, these authors also had their critics. Their approach to Hinduism was one with which Charles Grant, three terms director of the East India Company's Court of Directors (1794, 1805 and 1816), did not agree. In response to Dow's claim that they worshipped the same 'Supreme Being' he wrote:

> It is doubtless very pleasing to discover the recognition of this grand principle, the foundation of all true religion, even under an immense mass of falsehood and superstition; but some persons seem to have thought, that in ascertaining the existence of this principle in the writings of the Hindoos, or in the opinions of their learned men, they had substantially vindicated and established the religious character of that people; making little account of their idolatry, which as practised by the Brahmins, they represent to be no more than a symbolical worship of the divine attributes.[39]

In fact, Grant and his circle of Anglican evangelicals centred around the so-called 'Clapham Sect' were anxious to make the opposite case to Dow, Holwell, Halhed and Wilkins. While the British were extending their influence in India, there had been no attempt to institute a missionary campaign. Yet, with the revival of evangelical Christianity towards the latter half of the century there were more and more calls for the Company to allow a Christian mission in its territories in India.[40] In 1797, for

39 Charles Grant, *Observations on the State of Society among the Asiatic Subjects of Great Britain* (London: Ordered by the House of Commons to be printed, 1813), p. 72. The text was written in 1792.

40 Penelope Carson, *The East India Company and Religion, 1698–1858* (Woodbridge: Boydell Press, 2012), pp. 25–31.

example, in order to convince the Company of the necessity of a mission Grant submitted a lengthy document designed to prove the moral depravity of the *Hindoos*. In it he chastised what he termed 'European apologists' for presenting a skewed picture of the *Hindoo* religion. The observations of writers like Holwell, Dow, Halhed and Wilkins were only made possible, according to Grant, because their proponents leaned to 'so latitudinarian an opinion, an opinion which falls below even the creed of deism' that such 'falsities' were a product of a general attack on religious truth.[41]

Grant's belief that these writers were so heterodox as to be 'below even the creed of deism' corresponds with their treatment by several historians of orientalism and South Asia, who have suggested that they all possessed 'deist leanings'.[42] For example, P.J. Marshall has described Holwell and Dow as 'writing from a deist point of view'.[43] German Indologist Wilhelm Halbfass adopted the same position in his celebrated 'philosophical essay' *Indien und Europa* (1981). In it Halbfass describes a 'deistic motif' as running through the early history of Indology, proximate to which was the almost 'deistic thinking' of William Jones.[44] In these cases, though, such assessments are based on an appraisal of general attitudes, supported by the odd quotation indicating a broadly universalist acceptance of different expressions of religion. There has been no sustained attempt to explain what exactly about their work was 'deist' and what that would mean in the context of eighteenth-century thought. Without this clarification these thinkers become distorted, reduced to the simplistic notion that they offered a more 'sympathetic' approach to Indian religion. There are important differences, for example, between the work of Holwell, who argued for the inherent rationality of reincarnation, and the presentation of Indian religion given by William Jones, whose work was welcomed by several Christian apologists.[45] Rather than presenting their views as coherent and superficially 'deist', this book traces the interaction of each writer with specific religious controversies and debates in shaping their account of an indigenous and ancient Indian religion. Not merely sympathetic, the

[41] Grant, *Observations*, pp. 65, 72.

[42] See, for example, Rosane Rocher, 'British Orientalism in the Eighteenth Century: The Dialectic of Knowledge and Government', in Carol A. Breckenridge and Peter van der Veer (eds.), *Orientalism and the Post-Colonial Predicament: Perspectives on South Asia* (Philadelphia: University of Pennsylvania Press, 1993), p. 219.

[43] Marshall, *British Discovery of Hinduism*, p. 27. [44] Halbfass, *India and Europe*, p. 56.

[45] In 1788 Richard Watson, Bishop of Llandaff, republished some of Jones' work on Hinduism, adding a note that Jones had proven (contra Halhed) that Hindu traditions confirmed the biblical Flood: *Sermons on Public Occasions, and Tracts on Religious Subjects* (Cambridge: J. Archdeacon Printer to the University, 1788), p. 221.

results were heavily invested with certain positions and suppositions relating to European intellectual debates, pertaining to religion, the history of human society and the politics of empire.

This approach acknowledges a recent historiographical challenge to the use of the term 'deism' to characterise a coherent system of historical thought.[46] Many have argued that such were the different shades of deism that the term could amount to anything from radical heresy to a moralistic theism that would not have been unpalatable to some liberal Christians.[47] As Hudson argues, the meaning of deism is often contextually specific, ranging from a term for 'mere theism' to a description of persons who rejected the need for revealed religion.[48] This has consequently prompted historians to talk of multiple 'deisms' and 'different kinds of heterodoxy', rather than use the term 'deism' as a simple signifier.[49] The authors in this study sit somewhere in the spectrum of deist thought identified by Hudson as ranging from the radically non-Christian deism of seventeenth-century deists influenced by classical theistic naturalism, and a more mild 'English deism' of the eighteenth century, which was closer to liberal Protestantism and centred on the idea of rational religion.[50] In this they shared some common concerns, such as the view that superstition and clerical influence were barriers to human progress. In and of itself this was not an essentially 'deist' position, except to the extent that it was intended as a wider critique of formalised, institutional religion in general; something which they each expressed to varying degrees. Likewise, most paid close attention to the question of God's providential capacities, positing variations on the preference for general over particular providence, an often shared though not unifying feature of deist thought.[51] Yet, these broad strokes of association do not do credit to the full scope and variety of religiously oriented discussions in their work. While Holwell was deeply concerned with theodicy, for example, Halhed forwarded a more fundamentally sceptical account of religion as a historically and anthropologically

46 M. Hunter and D. Wootton (eds.), *Atheism from the Reformation to the Enlightenment* (Oxford: Oxford University Press, 1992); R. D. Lund (ed.), *The Margins of Orthodoxy: Heterodox Writing and Cultural Response, 1660–1750* (Cambridge: Cambridge University Press, 1995); Ariel Hessayon and David Finnegan (eds.), *Varieties of Seventeenth- and Early Eighteenth-Century English Radicalism in Context* (Farnham: Ashgate, 2011).

47 'Introduction', in Wayne Hudson, Diego Lucci and Jeffry R. Wigelsworth (eds.), *Atheism and Deism Revalued: Heterodox Religious Identities in Britain, 1650–1800* (Farnham: Ashgate, 2014), pp. 6–7.

48 Wayne Hudson, 'Atheism and Deism Demythologised', in *Atheism and Deism Revalued*, p. 19.

49 Hudson, 'Atheism and Deism Demythologised', p. 13. See also Wayne Hudson, *Enlightenment and Modernity: The English Deists and Reform* (London: Pickering and Chatto, 2009), pp. 26, 38–9.

50 Hudson, 'Atheism and Deism Demythologised', p. 21.

51 Hudson, *The English Deists*, p. 81.

contingent phenomenon. Dow was concerned with contrasting rational and orthodox approaches to the deity, and Wilkins saw parallels with anti-Trinitarian theology. The final chapter of this book also offers a new perspective on the religion of William Jones, who has been referred to as both a deist and an Anglican, suggesting that his thought was more closely aligned with Unitarianism and Rational Dissent. Taking the suggestion that these authors were 'deist' as its starting point, then, this study details the theologies of each author to outline the complex role that European religious discourses played in their interpretation of Indian religion.

In turn, this has consequences for how we should think about religious thought in the Enlightenment, particularly in relation to the increasingly global dimensions of the period. As well as stressing the specific religious debates that shaped the work of these authors, the book will also demonstrate that the common result was an approach to Indian religion that centred on a discussion of its theological and philosophical aspects. While this was partly attributable to a Christian bias towards locating religious authority in text,[52] for these authors the importance of sourcing original scriptural evidence of Indian tenets should be more specifically located in their relationship with what a historian of English deism has described as 'primitive religion and the priestcraft hypothesis'.[53] This posited the idea that the original, pristine and universal religion of reason was gradually lost to humanity, largely because of the interested machinations of 'priests' who sought the consolidation of their unique social status through the manipulation of vulgar superstition.[54] This was implicit already in Christian accounts of pagan idolatry, with its origins lying in biblical accounts of the dispersal of peoples and the degeneration of worship from the fall of the Tower of Babel. For deists, this was reflected back on to contemporary Christianity, which was critiqued as having extended beyond the bounds of rational belief (variously defined) while also dogmatically insisting on conformity. Where some had advanced the idea that natural religion and revelation were mutually reinforcing, other Dissenting thinkers had taken the primacy of natural

[52] Indeed, this is a common argument used to characterise European encounters with non-Western religions. In the case of Hinduism specifically, see S. N. Balagangadhara, *'The Heathen in His Blindness . . . ': Asia, the West and the Dynamic of Religion* (Leiden: Brill, 1994).

[53] James A. Herrick, *The Radical Rhetoric of the English Deists: The Discourse of Scepticism, 1680–1750* (Columbia: University of South Carolina Press, 1997), p. 32.

[54] Justin Champion, *The Pillars of Priestcraft Shaken: The Church of England and Its Enemies, 1660–1730* (Cambridge: Cambridge University Press, 1992), pp. 133–68.

theology that this implied and used it to undermine the doctrines of the Church.[55]

More sceptical critics of religion went further, using similar formulations of natural reason to attack the premises underlying the basis of Christian claims to hold a monopoly on religious truth. For most of the authors in this study, tracing an original religion of reason back to Brahminical philosophy raised various vantage points from which to judge the rationality of European religious thought. This was also true of their readers. Diderot's contribution to the *Histoire des deux Indes*, for example, argued that the creation story of the 'Gentoux' (*Gentoos*) was no less fantastical than the biblical one, allowing the *philosophe* to launch an attack on revealed religion in general. Diderot's source for this was Halhed's *Code of Gentoo Laws*.[56] The accounts of what Holwell, Dow, Halhed, Wilkins and Jones saw as India's original religion are, therefore, features of larger history of religious debate within Enlightenment intellectual culture, wherein the communication of ideas from Eastern religions posed new challenges to traditional religion. China was the original focal point of these discussions, with Confucianism posing as a clear example of a simple moral philosophy, unencumbered by superstition and mystical theology.[57] From the mid-eighteenth century onwards, largely due to the dissemination of the work of the British orientalists discussed in this study, India played an increasingly prominent role in these debates.

This challenges visions of Enlightenment thought as primarily secular in orientation.[58] Certainly, conflicts between philosophy and theology resulted in various controversies about the authority of traditional religious doctrines and institutions. And yet, the consequences of alternative conceptions of religion were not always to fundamentally undermine the tenets of theism. Rather, there was a proliferation of arguments on the nature of religious belief, on the extreme end of which was the notorious scepticism of David Hume, while many others sought to reaffirm and revive the importance of religion for Enlightenment thought. While some of these accounts of Hinduism drew from sceptical and heterodox

[55] B. A. Gerrish, 'Natural and Revealed Religion', in Knud Haakonssen (ed.), *The Cambridge History of Eighteenth-Century Philosophy*, vol. 2 (Cambridge: Cambridge University Press, 2006), p. 644.

[56] Peter Jimack, 'Diderot and India', in David MacCallum and Terry Pratt (eds.), *The Enterprise of Enlightenment: A Tribute to David Williams from His Friends* (Berne: Peter Lang, 2004), p. 153.

[57] See, for example, Franklin Perkins, *Leibniz and China: A Commerce of Light* (Cambridge: Cambridge University Press, 2004).

[58] The classic text is Peter Gay, *The Enlightenment: An Interpretation*, vol. 1: *The Rise of Modern Paganism* (New York: Knopf, 1966).

discourses, this was sometimes in the service of arguments defending the fundamental rationality and coherence of religious epistemologies. This also runs contrary to Jonathan Israel's conception of a 'radical Enlightenment', characterised by expressions of atheist and Spinozist metaphysics, as distinct from a 'moderate' majority, still accepting of the fundamental tenets of religion. For Israel, it was exclusively the former that captured the true spirit of the Enlightenment, attaching radical scepticism to the liberal, egalitarian and democratic call for human emancipation that he sees as its programmatic core.[59] More recently several studies have questioned the assumptions on which this distinction has been built, particularly in relation to Enlightenment thought in England.[60] As Louise Hickman has stressed, for example, the links between Rational Dissent, a deeply God-centred theology, and radical thinkers like Richard Price and Mary Wollstonecraft means that it becomes 'difficult to separate a clearly secular reason from more theological ways of thinking', and that therefore the division between a radical Enlightenment and a theologically informed moderate Enlightenment obscures far too much.[61] To this the following study offers an additional perspective. For East India Company authors, religious heterodoxy was easily allied with imperial politics. And while it is not an account of the role of high theological debate in determining the epistemological and philosophical nature of the Enlightenment, it does consider the various ways in which heterodox perspectives, including sceptical and anti-Trinitarian beliefs, impacted other aspects of intellectual culture in Britain and Europe, such as engagement with overseas cultures and beliefs and the politics of empire.

This of course raises the further problem of what and which Enlightenment. We are now in possession of a vast number of different 'Enlightenments', broken down to specific discourses and contexts. A classic example was Pocock's 'Protestant Enlightenment' in England.[62] And while some have moved to recuperate the view of a distinctively European Enlightenment, focused on understanding and improving the

[59] Jonathan Israel, *Radical Enlightenment: Philosophy and the Making of Modernity 1650–1750* (Oxford: Oxford University Press, 2001).

[60] Niall O'Flaherty has challenged the binary between theology and the concern for human betterment, carefully reconstructing the 'man-centred theology' of William Paley: Niall O'Flaherty, *Utilitarianism in the Age of Enlightenment: The Moral and Political Thought of William Paley* (Cambridge: Cambridge University Press, 2019), pp. 23–4, 81.

[61] Louise Hickman, *Eighteenth-Century Dissent and Cambridge Platonism: Reconceiving the Philosophy of Religion* (Oxford: Routledge, 2017), p. 19.

[62] J. G. A. Pocock, 'Historiography and Enlightenment: A View of Their History', *Modern Intellectual History*, 5:1 (2008).

human condition,[63] others still have questioned these borders, arguing for transatlantic, transnational and global Enlightenments.[64] This book approaches the term from a different perspective. In it the idea of Enlightenment is used with reference an intellectual setting, of which these authors considered themselves and their audiences to be members. That is, they understood themselves as contributors to a culture of Enlightenment in terms of a contemporary trend in the elevation of the epistemological authority of experience and reason.[65] This was an entirely normative posture, signalling for them the emergence of mankind from barbarism, superstition and intellectual immaturity to the flourishing commercial society that was considered to characterise modern Europe and colonial America. As with other historiographic terms of convenience, this of course still groups together an extraordinarily diverse set of authors, arguments, dispositions, institutions and practices. It is also used, therefore, with the recognition that within the notion of an age of intellectual maturity, there were a variety of conflicting arguments and ideas as to what that meant. In fact, in this sense no one individual, ideological programme, party or movement had a monopoly on Enlightenment thus defined.[66] Indeed, this book makes the case that including the works of the thinkers like those considered in this study can vastly enrich our appreciation of the various contours of Enlightenment thought in this period. They were not theologians or philosophers. Nor were they, with the exception of Jones, major scholars. Holwell and Dow in particular were undisciplined thinkers, neither of whom had been formally educated beyond grammar school. And yet, they all saw and fashioned themselves as men of letters, concerned with the major intellectual preoccupations of their day. And indeed, they were widely read by thinkers and in corners of the European world that are associated with the Enlightenment, more typically defined.

63 John Robertson, *The Case for the Enlightenment: Scotland and Naples 1680–1760* (Cambridge: Cambridge University Press, 2005).

64 See, for example, Sebastian Conrad, 'Enlightenment in Global History: A Historiographical Critique', *American Historical Review*, 117:4 (2012).

65 In preferring to start from the premise that many contemporaries saw this as an 'enlightened age' I agree with Niall O'Flaherty in *Utilitarianism in the Age of Enlightenment*, pp. 27–8.

66 See, for example, how Richard Bourke positions Burke in the claim to enlightened thought, in Richard Bourke, *Empire and Revolution: The Political Life of Edmund Burke* (Princeton, NJ: Princeton University Press, 2015), pp. 68–9.

Empire

In the second half of the eighteenth century, the expanding presence of the British in India meant that the opportunities for greater knowledge of Indian religion and culture were mostly exploited by Company men. Holwell and Dow both independently began researching and publishing their discoveries of what they believed to be the original indigenous religion of India during their service in the Company, Howell as a surgeon and then administrator, Dow as a member of its militia, rising to the position of lieutenant-colonel. At the same time, they also published critical accounts of the Company, or factions within it, and their own recommendations on what an effective administration in India should look like. As the century progressed, the Company's gradual transformation into an entity possessing many of the attributes of a sovereign power pressed the question of how it would rule its non-Christian polity and prompted a deeper official engagement with the religious history, tenets and practices of India. These were the conditions in which the works of Halhed and Wilkins were commissioned by the governor-general of Bengal, Warren Hastings.

Halhed's reflections on *Gentoo* religion came in the form a preface to the *Code of Gentoo Laws*, a compilation of law composed by eleven highly regarded Brahmin scholars, translated from Sanskrit to Persian, and then from Persian to English by Halhed.[67] The purpose of this text had been administrative and propagandistic, although Halhed's speculations went well beyond these original objectives and ignited debate about the age and origins of Indian scriptures. The views of Wilkins on the *Hindoo* religion were likewise presented in the foreword to his translation of the *Bhagavad-Gītă*, published alongside which was a letter including his praise for Hastings' 'liberal sentiments' and policies.[68] Finally, the work of William Jones was composed in another qualitatively different period of British governance in India, and came from the relatively more independent perspective of his position on the bench of the Supreme Court in Calcutta. Pitt's India Act of 1784, the Regulating Act of 1786, and the appointment of Lord Cornwallis as governor-general all combined to renew the Company's image in a period of more assertive British imperialism.

[67] *A Code of Gentoo Laws*, p. 6. The Sanskrit names of these authors are Ramagopala, Viresvara, Krsnajivana, Banesvara, Krparama, Krsnacandra, Gaurikanta, Krsnakesava, Sitarama, Kalisankara and Syamasundara, as transliterated by Rosane Rocher in *Orientalism, Poetry and the Millennium: The Checkered Life of Nathaniel Brassey Halhed, 1751–1830* (Delhi: Motilal Banarsidass, 1983), p. 49.

[68] Wilkins' characterisation of Hastings' commission and justification of the work in a letter published with the translation, in Charles Wilkins, *Bhăgvăt-Gēētā*, p. 20.

It is important, therefore, not to take 'Company' interpretations and uses of Indian religion in the eighteenth century as monolithic, or as representative of an architecturally secure imperial project. In the decades that the work of these writers appeared (1760s–90s) the commercial East India Company took on more and more of the responsibilities of an administrative government. The period considered in this study contains three distinguishable stages in the evolution of the British presence in India. The first is the conflict and resolution surrounding the 1757 Battle of Plassey. This decisive encounter had been waged and won in response to the resistance of the Mughal governor of Bengal, nawab Siraj-ud-Daulah, who had attacked and captured the Company's base in Calcutta. Having asserted itself militarily the Company colluded with and installed as the new nawab the demoted army leader Mir Jafar. Robert Clive, the colonel credited with the victory at Plassey, went on to institute the system since described as 'double government' whereby the Company took control of revenue collection in Bengal, Bihar and Orissa, while abandoning other administrative responsibilities to the nawab.[69] The following decade was a time of crisis in British Bengal. The Company's finances stalled as it continued to extort revenues with a cruel disregard for the suffering of an Indian population experiencing a devastating famine.[70] News of an administration built on corruption, violence and plunder reached the metropole, and it is against this backdrop that the work of Holwell and Dow was produced and received.

The second shift in power is important for understanding the relative positions of Halhed and Wilkins, both of whom were directly engaged in the business of legitimising the new administration. It was on a tide of hostile public opinion that the question of the British presence in India became a matter for parliamentary debate.[71] The resulting Regulating Act of 1773 resolved that both the British government and the Company's Court of Directors would together appoint a council and a governor-general, upon whom it was incumbent to ensure that the Company's operations were to the benefit of Britain and the Company's stakeholders. It was into this role that Warren Hastings stepped, keen to affirm his commitment to ending the abuses that had both drained the Company's

69 Abbas Hoveyda, Ranjay Kumar and Mohammed Aftab Alam, *Indian Government and Politics* (London: Pearson, 2011), p. 50.

70 P. J. Marshall, *The Making and Unmaking of Empires: Britain, India and America c.1750–1783* (Oxford: Oxford University Press, 2005), p. 247.

71 Nicholas B. Dirks, *The Scandal of Empire: India and the Creation of Imperial Britain* (Cambridge, MA: Harvard University Press, 2006), p. 18.

profits and ruined its public image. How he chose to legitimise this project involved Halhed and Wilkins. For this reason, their work will be explored within the context of what have been described as the 'orientalist' policies of Hastings.[72]

Finally, the third stage, encompassing the impeachment trial against Hastings and its eventual failure, takes us to an account of the Company at the end of the eighteenth century. The need to tackle the metropolitan perception of a corrupt Company instigated a shift towards more regulated administration and a more assertive vision of imperial command.[73] With the appointment of Cornwallis as governor-general, the powers of the governor were vastly expanded, granting substantial discretionary powers independent of the Supreme Council in Calcutta.[74] Jones and his ideas regarding Indian religion and law had a more distant, but still important relationship with the shape that this pattern of governance took. Whereas these authors had in common a philosophical approach, the relationship of their work to empire and the policies and ambitions of the Company were different. This book therefore traces the practical implications of that approach from a starting posture of external critique, to contested policy, and finally as a branch of a new imperial power.

The subject of a rich historiography, the Company's metamorphosis in this period was typically viewed in early scholarship as a matter of practical politics, leaving its ideological foundations largely unexamined. While this was somewhat altered with the advent of postcolonial theory's critical excavation of the political present in terms of the colonial past, the intellectual origins of empire remained unappreciated among historians of seventeenth- and eighteenth-century European political thought. An important step towards examining how the particular intellectual dynamics of the eighteenth century shaped Company policy came from Ranajit Guha's influential study, *A Rule of Property for Bengal* (1963), which located the ideological origins of British India in debates about political economy and property law.[75] In Guha's footsteps followed a range of excellent histories of Company politics and policy in imperial India, most notably the work of C. A. Bayly which crossed a number of subdisciplines

[72] David Kopf, *British Orientalism and the Bengal Renaissance: The Dynamics of Indian Modernization 1773-1835* (Berkeley: University of California Press, 1969), pp. 13–21.

[73] P. J. Marshall, *'A Free Though Conquering People': Eighteenth-Century Britain and Its Empire* (Aldershot: Ashgate, 2003).

[74] B. B. Misra, *The Central Administration of the East India Company 1773–1834* (Manchester: Manchester University Press, 1959), pp. 33–4.

[75] Guha, *Rule of Property.*

including intellectual history.[76] Likewise, P. J. Marshall has long stressed the ways in which ideas underpinned the direction and shape of British imperialism.[77] Recognition of the intellectual dimensions of empire, however, remained largely peripheral to histories of political thought. Another generation of scholarship within the discipline, though, has sought to stress the ways in which the ideology of empire itself has a more varied and complex history, emerging from, as David Armitage has put it, 'the competitive context of political argument'.[78] In turn, the recognition that international commerce and exchange was the material context in which Enlightenment thought developed has underscored the importance of empire in shaping political ideas and practice more generally. Richard Bourke, for example, has challenged historical narratives about the thought of Edmund Burke precisely by restoring the centrality of questions about the politics of empire and conquest for him as a political actor.[79] Other scholars have turned their attention to the East India Company itself, as a case study for understanding historical conceptions of conquest, empire and corporate sovereignty. Philip J. Stern's *The Company-State*, for example, charts the long history of the Company's concern with sovereignty back to early modern political discourse.[80] Robert Travers' rich study of the East India Company's search for legitimacy in the remnants of Mughal power has illustrated the great extent to which Indian history and textual sources were utilised as materials for articulating different conceptions of a British administration in India.[81]

Although this book is not intended as an intellectual history of the Company, it does have an intimate relationship with that project. The work of authors like Stern and Travers provides an important setting for our enquiry into how the discussion of Indian religion presented by Holwell, Dow, Halhed, Wilkins and Jones related to the ideological and political contexts in which they were operating. The Company and figures within it were continually negotiating the terms on which its legitimacy

76 See, for example, C. A. Bayly, *Empire and Information: Intelligence Gathering and Social Communication in India, 1780–1870* (Cambridge: Cambridge University Press, 2000).

77 See Marshall, *Making and Unmaking of Empires*.

78 David Armitage, *The Ideological Origins of the British Empire* (Cambridge: Cambridge University Press, 2000), p. 5.

79 Richard Bourke, 'Edmund Burke and the Politics of Conquest', *Modern Intellectual History*, 4:3 (2007). For a detailed discussion of Burke's position on the Company in relation to Fox's East India Bill (1783), see chapters 11, 12 and 15 of Bourke, *Empire and Revolution*.

80 Philip J. Stern, *The Company-State: Corporate Sovereignty and the Early Modern Foundations of the British Empire in India* (Oxford: Oxford University Press, 2011).

81 Travers, *Ideology and Empire*, p. vii.

rested, and by the mid-eighteenth century, were increasingly turning to a sense of Indian history and religion to inform the ideas and arguments that underpinned its self-representation and policy. The discussions that shaped public consciousness of India, as well as knowledge of it within the Company, were oriented towards a broad Enlightenment intellectual context, which included speculation on the nature of civic society, empire and religion. Unlike Lucy Sutherland's Namierite vision of a Company led by political survival and short-term advantage, or sections of more recent historiography which tend to downplay ideology in favour of 'colonial anxiety', this book argues for greater attention to be paid to the wider intellectual frames that shaped policy and debate.[82] In particular, it examines how, ideas about the *Hindoo* religion became a heuristic through which to comprehend British empire in India.

By accounting for the ways in which religion preoccupied and informed British understandings of India in this period, this study moves our appreciation of the history of British empire in India from a focus on policy to a consideration of the intellectual frames and assumptions in which political action took place. While much Company policy and decision-making was shaped by pragmatism and circumstance, the language and ideas that informed, as well as were employed to reconcile and criticise, these decisions were a product of wider deliberations about the nature of civil society, legitimate governance and, crucially, their relationship to religious customs, sentiments and manners. In *Spirit of the Laws* Montesquieu had offered a sweeping survey of the world's different religions not as a theologian but as 'one who writes about politics'. Rather than their proximity to divine truth, each religious creed is assessed 'only in relation to the good to be drawn from them in the civil state'.[83] Elements of this approach, and various other asides on the nature of the relationship between religion and civil society, are laced through the work of the writers considered here, most obviously by Dow in his 1772 essay 'A Dissertation Concerning the Origin and Nature of Despotism in Hindostan'.[84] Moreover, contemporary debates that directly addressed Company governance often addressed religion along with the nature and possible

[82] Lucy Sutherland, *The East India Company in Eighteenth-Century Politics* (Oxford: Clarendon Press, 1952). For a criticism of arguments about 'colonial anxiety' in recent historiography, see Joshua Ehrlich, 'Anxiety, Chaos, and the Raj', *Historical Journal*, 63:3 (2020).

[83] Charles Louis Secondat, Baron de Montesquieu, *The Spirit of the Laws*, eds. Anne Cohler, Basia Miller and Harold Stone (Cambridge: Cambridge University Press, 1989 [1748]), part 5, book 24, chapter 1, p. 459.

[84] Patterson, 'Enlightenment and Empire'.

foundations for an 'enlightened' administration in Bengal. This is a concern to which all these writers turned their pen, be it in publications, correspondence or official documents. It also animated the trial of Warren Hastings. Throughout the prosecution, Edmund Burke claimed that Hastings' arbitrary and despotic practices were illegitimate because they patently failed to recognise the regularity of the existing Mughal settlement, in which the legal customs of both the 'Mahommedan' and *Hindoo* population were respected.[85]

Considering the relationship between these wider frameworks of thought and the practice of British empire in India necessarily raises questions about the relationship between Enlightenment and empire. The idea that Enlightenment thought and its legacy can be identified as the epistemological origins of nineteenth-century imperialism is pervasive. In Horkheimer and Adorno's *Dialectic of Enlightenment*, the essence of enlightenment rationality is 'the levelling domination of abstraction', which in the hands of the bourgeoise becomes the reified and unthinking 'principle of blind domination'.[86] In Said's *Orientalism* this epistemological domination is discursive, 'orientalism' defined as 'a cultural apparatus' that in its reduction of 'the Orient' is 'all aggression, activity, judgement, will-to-truth, and knowledge'.[87] This theoretical framework has produced an incredibly important set of critiques of Western imperialism in theory and practice as an 'epistemic violence'.[88] From the perspective of intellectual history, however, the causal connection between Enlightenment and imperial domination that such theories have implied elides the varied conceptions of both that were extant in eighteenth-century European thought. As we have seen, the notion of an 'Age of Reason' in any singular sense, characterised as it is by Horkheimer and Adorno's impulse to abstraction, is deeply contested by historical scholarship. Though an appeal to reason may have been common among eighteenth-century intellectuals, there was no such consensus on the knowledge that reason produced. Thus, in an attempt to restore complexity to Enlightenment thought in relation to empire, a spate of works in

85 See Bourke, *Empire and Revolution*, p. 551.

86 Max Horkheimer and Theodore Adorno, *The Dialectic of Enlightenment* (London: Verso, 1997 [New York, 1944]), pp. 7, 13, 42.

87 Said, *Orientalism*, p. 204.

88 For Gayatri Spivak, for example, this comes in the shape of the 'epistemic violence' of imperialism, whereby the dismissal of indigenous knowledge, and the projection of Western systems of thought onto the colonial subject, at once silence and essentialise the subaltern. Gayatri Spivak, 'Can the Subaltern Speak?', in Gary Nelson and Lawrence Grossberg (eds.), *Marxism and the Interpretation of Culture* (Urbana: University of Illinois Press, 1988), p. 281.

intellectual history have turned to offering accounts of various critics of empire and colonialism.[89] Sankar Muthu's *Enlightenment against Empire*, for example, is conceived of as a challenge to the reduction of Enlightenment thought to a coherent 'project', which ought to be extolled, or condemned as exposing its oppressive impulses in empire.[90] As such it examines what he terms the 'anti-imperialist' arguments of Enlightenment thinkers such as Kant, Diderot and Herder.[91] Similarly, Jennifer Pitts has looked at thinkers like Smith, Burke and Bentham as critics of imperialism and empire, contrasting their thought sharply with nineteenth-century liberalism's enthusiastic embrace of colonialism.[92]

These important studies have led the way in reassessing the diversity and complexity of eighteenth-century thought on empire. It is from this perspective that this study builds, while also challenging the clarity implied by the use of categories like 'anti-imperial' and 'critics of empire'. Many of the authors enlisted as critics of empire in this historiography had far more complex relationships with the politics of imperial expansion and its attachment to theories of commercial society, civilisation and international relations than such terms imply. Their arguments sat in a nexus of debates about how empire should be run that, although often denouncing certain practices in the strongest terms, tacitly accepted the legitimacy of foreign dominion itself. Chapter 4, therefore, adds richer detail to this picture by considering these debates alongside the criticisms of and recommendations for Company policy made by Holwell and Dow, and how in turn these were reflected in the concerns of writers like Smith, Burke and Diderot. Tracing the constructions and interpretations of Indian religion that shaped European knowledge of India in the period in which Britain violently established its empire in South Asia, this study seeks to historicise more fully the relationship between Enlightenment thought and empire. In interpreting the thought of these historical actors, it stresses the importance not of Enlightenment empiricism or rationalism, but of religious categories and debates.

It was religion, scepticism and heterodoxy that saw these authors shape and construct Indian religion to return to debates about the highly

89 This edited collection of essays assesses prominent modern European thinkers' writings about conquest, colonisation and empire: Sankar Muthu (ed.), *Empire and Modern Political Thought* (Cambridge: Cambridge University Press, 2012).

90 Sankar Muthu, *Enlightenment against Empire* (Princeton, NJ: Princeton University Press, 2003), p. 1.

91 Muthu, *Enlightenment against Empire*, p. 338.

92 Jennifer Pitts, *A Turn to Empire: The Rise of Imperial Liberalism in Britain and France* (Princeton, NJ: Princeton University Press, 2005).

contestable nature of truth and reason in Europe. The intellectual ramifications of this were various, and indeed, some worked and were explicitly used to reinforce systems of British imperial dominance in India, whereas others manifested a more critical posture. This is emphatically not, however, a denial that these ideas were utilised to underwrite and advance imperial ambitions. Nor is it aligned with an apologetic trend in some histories of early colonialism, that argue that mutual cross-cultural exchange was the defining characteristic of European interactions with foreign societies.[93] This requires a close consideration of the relationship between the knowledge of India that was constructed by Company servants and the conceptions of imperial power in which both were materially invested. There can be no doubt that as well as intellectual curiosity, scholarly translations of Hindu scriptures were commissioned by the likes of Governor-General Warren Hastings, precisely on the basis that such cultural exchange would, as he remarked in the prefatory letter to the publication of Charles Wilkins' *Bhăgvăt-Gēētā*, make more acceptable 'the weight of the chain by which the natives are held in subjugation'.[94] Instead, in recovering an overlooked body of knowledge by tracing the intellectual contexts that shaped British philosophical interpretations of Hinduism, this book aims to historicise the complex relationship between the genesis and the various uses of these different forms of Enlightenment knowledge, and their historical, commercial and political environment.

Hinduism

British interpretations of Hinduism significantly contributed to an important shift in the way that Indian theology and philosophy was understood in eighteenth-century Europe. It undermined what was seen as an undue emphasis on practice and custom, without the context of the religion's theological and philosophical centre. In accounting for what this centre was they articulated some common themes, such as an insistence that the *Gentoo* or *Hindoo* religion was essentially monotheistic, ancient and in many aspects essentially rational. In doing so, they also often pitted original theology against the corrupted practices of the vulgar, the main

93 For a discussion of this in the context of intellectual history, see Shruti Kapila, 'Global Intellectual History and the Indian Political', in Darrin M. McMahon and Samuel Moyn (eds.), *Rethinking Modern European Intellectual History* (Oxford: Oxford University Press, 2014).

94 Commenting on the publication of Wilkins' translation of the *Bhagavad-Gītā* as *The Bhăgvăt-Gēētā, or Dialogues of Krēēshnă and Ărjŏŏn* (1785) in his letter to Nathaniel Smith, Benares, 4 October 1784, published in Marshall, *British Discovery of Hinduism*, p. 189.

cause for which was identified as priestcraft. This new paradigm moved away from characterisations of the religion according to eye-witness accounts towards a construction of Indian religion based on the claim of British researchers that they were penetrating the original philosophical origins of a much maligned and ancient system of thought. The reality of this declaration was, however, tempered by the limits in their linguistic abilities, given that it was not until Wilkins' research in the mid-1780s that British scholars began to learn Sanskrit. Weighing the contents of their claims to authority against their sources, ideas and ways in which they presented this religion reveals the gap in which there was a degree not only of interpretation, but also elements of active invention, abstraction and plagiarism.

Both Holwell and Dow had claimed to have received instruction from Hindu scholars, the names of whom they declined to include or credit in their works. They also had access to Persianate scholarship, of which Dow appears to have made much use while again blurring the boundaries between his own commentaries and pieces of translation. Moreover, as Chapters 2 and 3 of this work will explore, both Holwell and Dow were less than forthcoming about the provenance of the texts with which they work and from which they quoted at length. In the case of Holwell, this has led others to wonder at the 'rather dubious' nature of his claims to have accessed genuine Hindu scriptures.[95] Halhed and Wilkins had more direct access to Brahmin scholarship and thought under the administration of Hastings as the patronage of educated elites, including particularly Brahmin Sanskrit scholars, became increasingly embedded in the practices of Company government. Jones in particular relied heavily on the intellectual labour of a network of Indian scholars, or what he described as 'my private establishment of readers and writers', aiding him in compiling a digest of Hindu law.[96] His network included a host of Persianate scholars, such as Tafazzul Husayn Khan, as well as Hindu pandits, including most prominently Jagannātha Tarkapañcānana and his student Rādhākānta Tarkavāgīśa.[97] The tendency among these British authors to not clarify or credit the importance of these scholars in making their own

[95] Franklin, *Representing India*, vol. 1, p. xiii.

[96] Jones to Cornwallis, Calcutta, 19 March 1788, in Garland Cannon (ed.), *The Letters of Sir William Jones*, vol. 2 (Oxford: Clarendon Press, 1970), p. 798.

[97] On Jones' use of Persianate scholarship, see Mohamad Tavakoli-Targhi, 'The Homeless Texts of Persianate Modernity', *Cultural Dynamics*, 13:3 (2001), and 'Orientalism's Genesis Amnesia', *Comparative Studies of South Asia, Africa, and the Middle East*, 16:2 (1996). On Rādhākānta Tarkavāgīśa, see Rosane Rocher, 'The Career of Rādhākānta Tarkavāgīśa, an Eighteenth-Century Pandit in British Employ', *Journal of the American Oriental Society*, 109:4 (1989).

works possible fits into a general pattern identified by Mohamad Tavakoli-Targhi, who points to the processes of translation and publication as means by which European orientalists obscured the extent of their reliance on the research of native scholars.[98]

Not taking the claims of East India Company authors to be original and unprecedented scholars at face value, this study proceeds on the grounds that the visions of Indian religion that they presented were a composite of existing sources, including Indian advisers and traditions of thought. Other choices in how to construct *Hindoo* religion were decidedly European in content and origin. In some cases, this was led by way of analogy and comparison. In others, they steered Hindu concepts towards European theological problems. Holwell, for example, brings ideas and arguments from Gnosticism, Cambridge Platonism and British medical discourses to bear on his account of what he sees as the origins of the *Gentoo* doctrine of metempsychosis. The emphasis in this study is primarily on these European preoccupations, both because of the difficulties in tracing the use of advisers and Indian sources in these British works, and because of specialisms of its author. That said, there are important connections across East India Company authors' attempts to interpret and present the philosophy and literature of Hinduism and the ways in which Islamic Persian writers, often influenced by Sufism, engaged in the translations from Sanskrit works – sometimes (for example in the famous cases of Akbar and Dara Shikoh) aiming at a kind of reconciliation of diverse theological traditions as sharing monotheistic truths,[99] not least because their use of Persian sources meant that British writers received information about Hindu philosophy and history that was mediated by the traditions of Mughal scholarship, which has a rich history of comparative religion.[100] This is particularly important in the cases of Dow and Jones. As such, this study is indebted to the recent work of scholars such as Shankar Nair, Manan Ahmed Asif and Supriya Gandhi on the precolonial history of Islamic political thought and scholarship in South Asia.[101] An account of

98 Tavakoli-Targhi, 'Homeless Texts of Persianate Modernity'.

99 Supriya Gandhi, *The Emperor Who Never Was: Dara Shukoh in Mughal India* (Cambridge, MA: Belknap, Harvard University Press, 2021).

100 For an account of Persian literature, including a brief look at how it was read by British orientalists, see Carl W. Ernst, 'Muslim Studies of Hinduism? A Reconsideration of Arabic and Persian Translations from Indian Languages', *Iranian Studies*, 36:2 (2003).

101 Shankar Nair, *Translating Wisdom: Hindu-Muslim Intellectual Interactions in Early Modern South Asia* (Oakland: University of California Press, 2020); Manan Ahmed Asif, *The Loss of Hindustan: The Invention of India* (Cambridge, MA; Harvard University Press, 2020); Gandhi, *The Emperor Who Never Was*.

these connections is limited here, and there is a great deal of potential for future research in this area. Rather, this study considers the uses made by these authors of Hindu philosophy, Persian texts and Brahmin instruction in a process of construction that was heavily shaped by their own religious preoccupations. In seeking to trace what these preoccupations were, its emphasis is on why they constructed Indian religion in the ways that they did and how these constructions were received by their European readers.

This is not, therefore, a book about Hinduism. It is about British interpretations and ideas of what today is recognised as Hinduism in the period before such a concept existed in European thought. This necessarily leads us towards existing debates about the nature and status of Hinduism as a singular religious tradition. This has become a particularly contentious point of conflict in the ideology of Hindu nationalism.[102] Within academic debates, though, the question has been as to what extent the notion of a unified indigenous Indian religion is a construct, the foundations of which were laid out in the work of European orientalists and the assumptions of Western thought in defining the category of 'religion'.[103] Alongside this exists the argument that Hinduism, although adopted and adapted by Hindus, was nevertheless rooted in a Western concept of religion.[104] Moreover, according to many within this position, British orientalism played a leading part in this process, not least in the priority it attached to scripture and the idea that the Hindu religion formed the basis of Indian civilisation.[105] Indeed, all the authors in this study have been recognised as having a degree of influence on the development of the term 'Hinduism', as a signifier of a unified religion that is native to India.[106] Moreover, the policies of the British Raj have been seen to have played a decisive role in shaping the modern dynamics on which certain religious identities, and particularly caste positions, operate.[107] For others, though, too much emphasis on the hand of colonialism in shaping modern Indian religion

102 For an overview of this development, see Katju Manjari, 'The History of Hindu Nationalism in India', in Torkel Brekke (ed.), *The Oxford History of Hinduism: Modern Hinduism* (Oxford: Oxford University Press, 2019).

103 For a detailed discussion, see Will Sweetman, *Mapping Hinduism: 'Hinduism' and the Study of Indian Religions, 1600–1776* (Halle: Franckesche Stifungen zu Halle, 2003).

104 Balagangadhara, 'Heathen in His Blindness'.

105 Catherine A. Robinson, *Interpretations of the Bhagavad-Gītā and Images of the Hindu Tradition: The Song of the Lord* (Abingdon: Routledge, 2006), p. 5.

106 Sweetman, *Mapping Hinduism*, pp. 56–7.

107 A strong articulation of this view comes in Sanjoy Chakravorty, *The Truth About Us: The Politics of Information from Manu to Modi* (Gurugram: Hachette, 2019).

downplays existing traditions and the limits of the agency of Indian actors. For example, some have stressed that those aspects of Hindu religion expressed in the theological and devotional practices surrounding the *Bhagavad-Gītā* and other texts acquired a sharper self-conscious identity much earlier.[108] Likewise, Indologists like Wendy Doniger have pointed to the diversity in Hindu identities, while also emphasising shared ideas, practices and Vedic traditions.[109]

It is outside the scope of this book to contribute to the debate on the origins of Hinduism. The argument pursued here, that the image of 'the religion of the *Gentoos*' painted by these authors was the product of idiosyncratic intellectual mythologies, is not to say that these and other European orientalists 'invented' the modern concept of Hinduism. It does, however, pay attention to the ways in which European narratives about Indian religion shaped colonial policy. It also calls to attention the actual degree of 'invention' in their work, which did indeed range from reinterpretation to suspected forgery. Thus, the starting point for our enquiry is located in the claim that a number of East India Company servants presented a version of Indian religion to European audiences that intentionally spoke to European intellectual culture and debate. More specifically, it takes the idea that these writers expressed opinions that were religiously heterodox and asks exactly what that means in context, in order to understand the version of *Hindoo* religion that emerged as a result. Its discussion of the 'construction' of Hinduism is specifically confined, therefore, to the manufacture of a particular European view of Indian religion in a particular historical period.

*

The book has two parts. Part I of the book focuses on John Zephaniah Holwell and Alexander Dow. Chapter 1 does two things: it charts the history of European interpretations of Hinduism from early modern travel accounts to the emergence of comparative approaches to the study of world religions in the late seventeenth and eighteenth centuries. Following this it offers an overview of the long history of the Company's policies on religion, as well as some of the significant turning points in the Company's political status and in its institutional approach to research on Indian languages, history and religion. Chapter 2 concerns Holwell's

108 David N. Lorenzen, 'Who Invented Hinduism?', *Comparative Studies in Society and History*, 41:4 (1999).

109 See, for example, Wendy Doniger, *On Hinduism* (Oxford: Oxford University Press, 2014).

religiously heterodox interpretation of Hinduism, which is at the core of the book's thesis, since his account would establish the ideas that would also run thematically throughout the works of Dow, Halhed and Wilkins. It outlines how Holwell's interpretation of 'the religion of the *Gentoos*' was shaped by his preoccupation with heterodox religious arguments, as well as some genuine insight into Indian philosophical concepts. Despite its idiosyncratic origins, Holwell's work captured some important tropes in deistic approaches to comparative religion, such as a narrative of original religion corrupted by priestcraft, which would come to dominate British constructions of India's original ancient religion throughout the century.

Chapter 3 offers the first sustained and systematic approach to understanding the ideas of Company servant Alexander Dow. It will outline how Dow's assessment of the origins of the *Hindoo* religion was grounded in the language and concepts of eighteenth-century rational religion, according to an account of Dow's treatment of the two primary schools of thought that he argued make up the *Hindoo* religion: the Bedang (Vedānta) and the Neadirsin (Nyāya). Chapter 4 ends this part of the book with an account of the reaction that Holwell and Dow's ideas received throughout Europe, pointing to how despite their differences, the common 'philosophical' quality of their enquiries is shown to have had a significant impact on numerous intellectual elements of the late Enlightenment period, including a discussion of debates on the legitimacy of Company governance and the significance for their work in debates on empire.

Part II considers British interpretations of Hinduism during the latter quarter of the eighteenth century. It argues that in the work of Halhed and Wilkins, which preceded these changes in the Company's ideological programme, we can trace elements of both the religious heterodoxy and scepticism present in the earlier work of Holwell and Dow, as well as a firmer sense of the practical uses of orientalist knowledge when it comes to establishing the legitimacy of a British presence in India. Chapter 5 turns to the work of Nathaniel Brassey Halhed, following the more fundamentally sceptical as well as deistic elements in his thought, to conclude that Halhed's particularly 'philosophical' interpretation of the *Gentoo* religion went well beyond the bounds of a project to legitimise Company policy. It then turns to an account of his involvement in Company politics, and more particularly his support for Warren Hastings throughout his impeachment trial. Chapter 6 situates Charles Wilkins' approach to his translation of the *Bhagavad-Gītā* in the longer history of British orientalism, highlighting how terms and ideas around which his 'philosophical' interpretation of *Hindoo* religion was oriented were rooted in the same

Enlightenment culture of religious debate that shaped the earlier work of Holwell and Dow.

Finally, Chapter 7 looks at the place of the recognised orientalist William Jones in this history. It argues that his work represents a significant turning point in the formulation and reception of British accounts of Indian philosophical religion. In the first instance his religious outlook, which it identifies as closest to the Rational Dissent of late eighteenth-century Unitarianism, preferred an account of Indian religion that posited it as mystical and sublime, and therefore more malleable to biblical scripture. This, in turn, made it particularly attractive to those seeking to redefine Britain's relationship with India in the wake of war with revolutionary France as one of paternalist guardianship of ancient customs and traditions. At the turn of the century, British interpretations of Indian religion were thus to be stripped of any heterodox implications, and aligned with the institutionalisation of orientalist knowledge as a branch of imperial governance.

PART I

Religion, Enlightenment and Empire

CHAPTER I

European Letters, the Company and Hinduism

In the period covered in this book British writers used two terms, *Gentoo* and *Hindoo*, to describe what they understood to be the native religion of India, until the work of William Jones, when 'Hindu' started to replace them. The use of these terms in describing some of the religious practices in India has a long and complex history. The term 'Hindu' has been traced to the Sanskrit *Sindhu*, used as 'river' as well as the River Indus in particular. This has also been identified as the origin for the Persian word *Hindu*, which in its usage came to denote the inhabitants of the geographical area surrounding the river Indus.[1] From early on its meaning was commonly fused with religious connotations as a descriptor of the region and its people. In the eighth century, for example, the Arab conqueror of the 'Sindh' region, Muhammad ibn Qasim, designated Hindus a distinct 'people of the book' so as to confer on them the status *dhimmi* (protected person), as non-Muslims living in an Islamic state.[2] There is also, however, evidence that the identification of a religious tradition with a particular place is also part of Hinduism's internal history. Wendy Doniger points out that while it does not use the term 'Hindu', the *Manusmṛti*, one of the central legal (dharma) texts in Hinduism, does contain a geographical definition of the people to whom it applies.[3] In eighteenth-century British use, the term *Hindoo* was again used to mean 'native' inhabitants of Hindostan, and from this we have references to the *Hindoo* religion: a definition which merged geography with religion, yet again, by implicitly excluding Muslims from this term for 'native' peoples, in distinction from their historically 'foreign' Mughal rulers.

By contrast, *Gentoo* was a derivative of the Portuguese word for gentile, *gentio*, stemming from the Latin word *gentilis*, and was therefore always

[1] Robinson, *Interpretations of the Bhagavad-Gītā*, p. 6.

[2] Arvind Sharma, 'On Hindu, Hindustān, Hinduism and Hindutva', *Numen* 49:1 (2002), p. 5.

[3] Wendy Doniger, *The Hindus: An Alternative History* (Oxford: Oxford University Press, 2009), p. 72.

a religious term in nature.[4] Its application to Indian religious traditions, and the related terms 'Gentilism' and 'Gentooism', was initiated by the significant Catholic missionary presence in Southern India from the sixteenth century onwards, the materials of which would prove a long-standing resource for European knowledge of Indian religion until the eighteenth century.[5] Inherent in both *Hindoo* and *Gentoo* was the assumption of a unified religious tradition native to a particular part of the world. While some thinkers, including Jesuit missionary Roberto de Nobili and Lutheran minister Bartholomäus Ziegenbalg, explicitly acknowledged the diversity in Indian religious practices, other attempts to identify the common beliefs of 'the gentiles of India' sought to generalise beliefs and practices as shared doctrine.[6] Sanjay Subrahmanyam, in his rich study of a vast array of sources on the subject of Europe's India, thus concludes that by the latter half of the seventeenth century it became 'common sense' to most European writers that India did indeed possess its own 'religion', in a sense comparable to more familiar European models of what a religion was.[7] The interchangeable use of these terms by Europeans in the period considered in this book thus continued a longer convention of homogenising Indian religious practices and culture in European thought.

The picture, as Carl Ernst has stressed, is more complicated in the case of Islamic perceptions of Hindu religions; he argues that it 'is only when the lens of the modern European notion of religion is applied that one can view premodern Muslims as having had a clear notion of Hinduism'.[8] Indo-Muslim scholarship on Sanskrit texts must therefore be seen in their specific contexts, one of which was imperial state building. In the case of the Mughals this often involved an attempt to interweave Persianate cultures with Sanskrit literature, such as the merging lineages of Muslim rule with Indian epic history drawn from the *Mahābhārata*. Nevertheless, the identification and translation of key texts like the *Mahābhārata* and the *Upanishads* (*Upaniṣads*) and their association in this literature with the

[4] Lorenzen, 'Who Invented Hinduism?' (1999). See also Sweetman, *Mapping Hinduism*, p. 56.

[5] See chapter 8, 'Archives and the End of Catholic Orientalism', in Ângela Barreto Xavier and Ines G. Zupanov, *Catholic Orientalism: Portuguese Empire, Indian Knowledge (16th and 18th Centuries)* (New Delhi: Oxford University Press, 2015), pp. 287–330.

[6] Will Sweetman, 'Unity and Plurality: Hinduism and the Religions of India in Early European Scholarship', *Religion*, 31:3 (2001). See, for example, *Das opiniões, ritos e cerimonias, de todos os Gentios da India* (Of opinions, rites and ceremonies of all Gentiles in India), attributed to Agostino de Azevedo, an Augustinian friar, included in a report to Philip III in Lisbon in 1603. Published in António da Silva Rego (ed.), *Documentação para a história das missões do padroado Português do Oriente, India*, vol. 2 (Lisbon: Centro de Estudos Históicos Ultramarinos, 1948).

[7] Subrahmanyam, *Europe's India*, p. 139. [8] Ernst, 'Muslim Studies of Hinduism?', p. 195.

'Brahmin religion', or in the case of Dara Shikoh (1615–59) 'the doctrines of the Indian monotheists', was read by British orientalists like William Jones as evidence of a distinctly original Hindu religion, which had been studied by their Muslim rulers.[9]

The term 'Hinduism' itself has been traced to the 1780s. Charles Grant, an evangelical and East India Company official, mentioned 'Hindooism' in a letter in 1787, and again in his proposals written in 1792.[10] The writers in this study, however, generally employed the terms *Gentoo* and *Hindoo* to describe the religion and the people they viewed as native to 'Hindostan' or 'Hindustan', as it was variously spelled. John Zephaniah Holwell, whose work was published first, from 1764 to 1779, adopted the term *Gentoo*. Alexander Dow, on the other hand, whose work was published shortly after Holwell's in 1768, used *Hindoo* for the same purposes. This was not merely a matter of the former going out of trend, as Halhed's 1776 *A Code of Gentoo Laws* shows with references to how 'the peculiar and national Prejudices of the Hindoo' are 'interwoven with the Religion of the country', as well as to 'the Hindoo religion'.[11] Charles Wilkins, however, preferred *Hindoo*, referring to the '*Mahabarat*' (*Mahābhārata*) as 'an ancient Hindoo poem'.[12]

One term that these writers did use in common was 'Brahmin'. Styled 'Bramin' by Holwell and Halhed, 'Brahmin' by Dow, and 'Brahman' by Wilkins, the idea of the Brahmin as the representative of Indian religion was a consistent theme in their work. Each cast the Brahmins as the priests of Indian religion, at once praising their learning and also blaming them for the superstitions of the vulgar. For Holwell and Dow, this depended on a distinction between learned Brahmins and lower, unscrupulous examples. This meant, as we shall see, that alongside the tendency to homogenise the religious beliefs and practices of India, these authors also shared a bias towards textual sources and Brahminical authority. This tendency to prioritise Brahmin knowledge, as well as 'scripture' in the form of religious manuscript sources, however, was not unique in the history of outside conceptions of Hinduism. The scholar Al-Bīrūnī (973–1048), for example, had seen an account of their beliefs and thoughts as the key to understanding the mysteries of Indian religion.[13] The Jesuits, too, singled out the Brahmins as the representatives of the beliefs of the *gentios*

[9] Ernst, 'Muslim Studies of Hinduism?', pp. 186, 189.

[10] For details of the 1787 usage, see Sweetman, *Mapping Hinduism*, p. 56.

[11] Halhed, *Code of Gentoo Laws*, pp. xi, xiii. [12] Wilkins, *Bhăgvăt-Gēētā*, p. 23.

[13] Sharma, 'On Hindu, Hindustān, Hinduism and Hindutva', pp. 7–8. For a discussion and translation of Al-Bīrūnī's Indological work, see Edward Sachau, *Alberuni's India*, 2 vols. (London: Kegan Paul, Trench, Tribner & Co., 1914).

in India.[14] For these Company writers, though, it had different implications and consequences. What those were, and how they shaped the particular accounts of Indian religion, will be explored in detail in the following chapters of this book, but first this requires an account of the situation as they found it. This chapter, therefore, is intended as an introduction to European thought regarding the identification of what is now termed Hinduism. This will begin with an overview of early modern European thought, turning to an account of what was distinctive about the British orientalists discussed in this book, before finally considering the specifics of the relationship between East India Company policy and Indian religion in the period covered by this study.

Europe and Hinduism

From the beginning, European interactions with India were always as much about religion as they were about trade. Not long after the Portuguese explorer Vasco de Gama travelled to India in 1498, the founder of the Jesuits and early missionary, Francis Xavier, followed in 1542. The Jesuit presence in India was continued by his successor, Roberto de Nobili, who began to record and interpret Indian religious ideas and concepts. Around the middle of the sixteenth century, in Goa, attempts were made to gain access and insight into Hindu texts. It was an Indian convert to Catholicism, under the name Manoel d'Oliveira, who provided Portuguese translations of some Marathi adaptations of Sanskrit texts, in the form of sections from the Marathi adaption of the *Bhagavad-Gītā* known as the *Jñāneśvarī* (also known as the *Dnyaneshwari*, *Jnaneshwari* or *Bhavartha Deepika*, and composed by the poet and saint Dnyaneshwar in 1290).[15] On the whole, though, the focus of translation was for the production of vernacular Christian texts. The earliest language to be translated for this purpose was Tamil, which was directed towards the translation of a Christian catechism for publication in India.[16] In 1579 the English Jesuit Thomas Stephens produced a grammar of the Konkani language of Goa, also with the intention of producing a vernacular catechism for Christian instruction. He also produced a work of 11,000 Christian

[14] Xavier and Zupanov, *Catholic Orientalism*, pp. 129–30.

[15] Stephen Neill, *A History of Christianity in India*, vol. 1: *The Beginnings to AD 1707* (Cambridge: Cambridge University Press, 1984), p. 237.

[16] The first Jesuit to do this was Henry Henriques. See Neill, *A History of Christianity in India*, vol. 1, pp. 241–4.

verses, the so-called *Christian Purāna*, or *Purāna of Biblical History*, in Marathi (1616).[17]

Despite their remarkable knowledge of Indian languages, most Jesuit writers were less concerned with understanding Indian religion itself. An exception is the Italian Jesuit Roberto Nobili, who had sought a more thorough understanding of Hindu religious concepts and associational practices, in order to harness these in service of communicating the Christian message. The products of this accommodationist strategy were two Latin treatises on Hindu customs and beliefs, *Informatio de quibusdam moribus nationis Indicae* (1613) and *Narratio fundamentorum quibus Madurensis Missionis institutum caeptum est et hucusque consistit* (1618–19). These works contained detailed information about 'Indian heathen' beliefs, with an emphasis on Vedānta (a prominent school of Hindu philosophy), as well as an account of the caste system and the identity of the Brahmins.[18] This served Nobili's missionary style of *accommodatio*, which had previously been adopted by Jesuit missionaries in China and Japan, and consisted of the assumption of local customs with the purpose of propagating Christianity in ways that were culturally intelligible to potential converts. Nobili himself adopted certain Brahmin customs and dress codes.

As well as customs, Nobili also sought to accommodate familiar Brahmin concepts and ideas that were, in his judgement, compatible with the Christian message. In this he was greatly aided by the Brahmin convert Bonifacio Xastri (Śivadharma).[19] In response another Jesuit, sceptical of Nobili's methods, produced an alternative to the *Informatio*, the *Tratado sobre o Hindúismo*, which listed those Indian beliefs and practices that were, in the author's view, demonstrably pagan and not compatible with Christianity.[20] These works would not, however, be published for a general audience until the 1970s.[21] Similar in this regard are the collected writings of the Lutheran missionary Bartholomäus Ziegenbalg, who lived on the Coromandel Coast between 1709 and 1714 and wrote numerous

[17] Neill, *A History of Christianity in India*, vol. 1, p. 240.

[18] Sangkeun Kim, *Strange Names of God: The Missionary Translation of the Divine Name and the Chinese Responses to Matteo Ricci's 'Shangti' in Late Ming China, 1583–1644* (New York: Peter Lang, 2004), p. 141.

[19] See Margherita Trento, 'Śivadharma or Bonifacio? Behind the Scenes of the Madurai Mission Controversy (1608–1619)', in Ines G. Županov and Pierre Antoine Fabre (eds.), *The Rites Controversies in the Early Modern World* (Leiden: Brill, 2018).

[20] Trento, 'Śivadharma or Bonifacio?', p. 105.

[21] Roberto Nobili, *Adaptation*, S. Rajamanickam (ed.), J. Pujol (trans.) (Palayamkottai: De Nobili Research Institute, 1971); Thomas More,*On Indian Customs*, S. Rajamanickam (ed. and trans.) (Palayamkottai: De Nobili Research Institute, 1972).

Christian texts in Tamil for dissemination among the Hindu population. Ziegenbalg's two books about Indian religion and culture, *Genealogie der Malabarischen Götter* (Genealogy of the Malabarian gods) and *Malabarrischer Heidentum* (Malabarian heathenism), were not published until 1867 and 1926 respectively.[22] Nobili's works were, nevertheless, copied and circulated in Rome and India by his supporters during the so-called 'Malabar rites' controversy, which was sparked by the accusations of the author of the *Tratado*, Gonçalo Fernandes Trancoso, that Nobili's accommodationist approach ceded too much ground to pagan idolatry.[23]

Despite the subsequent backlash, Nobili's work had a significant influence on the approach of French Jesuits, led by Jean-Venant Bouchet (1655–1732), in the Carnatic Mission of the early eighteenth century.[24] More generally, though, the earliest publications of missionary letters from India were part of the Society of Jesus' efforts to produce its own historiography. The letters were composed for the edification of its members, scattered as they were in institutions and on missionary projects across the globe. They were also compiled and published for a lay audience, to promote the methods and successful conversions of the missions abroad. To this end, letters by the missionaries in India, working exclusively under the Portuguese *padroado* (the royal patronage of the missions), appeared in print in the sixteenth century in Italian, Portuguese, Spanish, German, French and Latin.[25] And while these early letters did contain some descriptions of Indian beliefs and practices, such as those recounted by Francis Xavier in the widely read publication of his letters, *Copie d'une lettre missive envoyée des Indes* (Paris, 1545), these works contained few of the insights of Nobili. In many ways, the Jesuit understanding of Indian religion would not make a substantial impact on European audiences until the early eighteenth century, when the work of French Jesuit missionaries on Indian languages and religious beliefs was published as the *Lettres édifiantes.*[26]

Another genre dominated sixteenth- and seventeenth-century writings on Hinduism. Travel literature, often penned by merchants and voyagers travelling to the East for trade, was eagerly consumed by early modern

[22] Eric J. Sharpe, 'The Study of Hinduism: The Setting', in Arvind Sharma (ed.), *The Study of Hinduism* (Columbia: University of South Carolina Press, 2003), p. 24.

[23] Ines G. Županov, *Disputed Mission: Jesuit Experiments and Brahmanical Knowledge in Seventeenth-Century India* (New Delhi: Oxford University Press, 1999).

[24] For more on the Carnatic Mission, see Neill, *A History of Christianity in India*, vol. 1, p. 90.

[25] For the full list of these early letters, see John Correia-Afonso, *Jesuit Letters and Indian History: A Study of the Nature and Development of the Jesuit Letters from India (1542–1773) and Their Value for Indian Historiography* (Bombay: Indian Historical Research Institute, St Xavier's College, 1955).

[26] Will Sweetman makes a comprehensive case for this view in *Mapping Hinduism.*

readers, sometimes for their descriptions of odd and obscene customs attached to even more strange and confounding religious beliefs. Most approached Hinduism with their expectations shaped by classical accounts, often Ptolemy, and the Bible.[27] A favourite topic was the custom of sati, or suttee, the immolation of wives on the funeral pyres of their deceased husbands.[28] For some this was a diabolical ceremony, in which the victim is led by demonic forces 'into eternal flames to continue a never ending torture'.[29] Others, like Thomas Herbert, repeated a story which was scattered through a number of travel accounts, that the practice was a deterrent against husband poisoning.[30] This was so pervasive a claim that one of our Company authors, John Zephaniah Holwell, was very keen to refute it by linking the practice specifically to the importance of a theological conviction in reincarnation, and therefore consistent with the religion's own internal rationality.[31] When not repeating certain tropes, the reports offered by travel writers generally took what Rubiés has termed an 'anthropological or ethnographic approach', in that their main insight into Indian religion was a product of eye-witness observation.[32] In fact many seventeenth-century travel writers remarked on the difficulty of attaining more significant knowledge on account of the barriers of both language and Brahmin secrecy. As the Italian author Pietro della Valle, who had travelled in and around the regions of Surat and Goa in the early 1620s, testified, the difficulty of obtaining information about local religious beliefs was often due to the fact that trade was conducted in Persian, which limited their capacity to communicate outside the confines of business. He also stressed that the Indians with whom he came into contact were 'unlearned' and so limited in their own knowledge of theological concepts.[33] This is an assessment with which the writers explored in this study would have agreed. Each, by contrast, greatly stressed their ability to

[27] P. J. Marshall and G. Williams, *The Great Map of Mankind: British Perceptions of the World in the Age of Enlightenment* (London: J. M. Dent & Sons Ltd, 1982), pp. 7–11, 19.

[28] 'Suttee' is the anglicisation of 'sati', and both words may refer to the ritual itself, or to the woman who undergoes it. I use the term 'sati' rather than 'suttee', as is common among scholarship on the topic. For a comprehensive study, see Andrea Major, *Pious Flames: European Encounters with Sati, 1500–1830* (Oxford: Oxford University Press, 2006).

[29] Althanasius Kircher, *China Illustrata* (1667), as quoted in Kate Teltscher, *India Inscribed: European and British Writing on India, 1600 to 1800* (New Delhi: Oxford University Press, 1997), p. 56.

[30] Teltscher, *India Inscribed*, p. 52.

[31] Jessica Patterson, 'An Eighteenth-Century Account of Sati: John Zephaniah Holwell's "Religious Tenets of the Gentoos" and "Voluntary Sacrifice" (1767)', *South Asia: Journal of South Asian Studies*, 40:1 (2017).

[32] Rubiés, *Travel and Ethnology*.

[33] Sweetman, *Mapping Hinduism*, p. 75. Valle's account was only published posthumously in 1663, and was followed with French and English translations in 1664.

communicate with the 'learned' Brahmins, and their access to ancient texts, as the basis for their claim that they had penetrated the philosophical and theological tenets at the core of the religion, rather than just the external ceremonies of its practitioners.

In the seventeenth century, as well as the accounts of Jesuits and merchants, a number of Protestant missionaries wrote about India, offering their own judgements on its 'Gentile' religion. Henry Lord, the Anglican chaplain of the East India Company (1624–30), reported on what he termed the 'Banian religion', which Sweetman attributes to Lord taking the wide use of 'Banian' among Europeans to describe the merchant Vāṇiā caste, and applying it to religious practices associated with both Hindu and Jain traditions.[34] Lord's *Display of Two Forraigne Sects* (1630) was still very much confined to a description of certain ritual practices. Moreover, from Lord's perspective, the 'Banian' religion was nothing but a species of idolatry. Hence, in the opening of *Display* he describes its very practice as 'rebelliously and schismatically violating the divine law of the dread Majesty of Heaven'.[35] In a similar vein, but with a much wider impact, was the work of Dutch Reformed Church minister Abraham Roger, publishing under the name of Rogerius. His book *De open deure tot het verborgen heydendom* (The open door to the understanding of hidden paganism) was produced while in the employ of the Dutch East India Company in the 1630s. In the original edition, published in Leiden in 1651, Rogerius had suggested that Indian idolatry was comparable not only to ancient paganism, but also to corrupted Jewish and Christian rituals and doctrines.[36] The text was best known in Europe via a French translation by Thomas La Grue.[37] Another Dutch minister who produced a widely read work on Indian religion in this period was Philippus Baldaeus. His *Naauwkeurige beschryvinge van Malabar en Choromandel* was published in Amsterdam in 1672, and translated into English in 1703 under the title *True and Exact Description of the Most Celebrated East India Coast of Malabar and Coromandel.* The work itself was almost entirely derivative of earlier sources.[38] Nevertheless, *True and Exact Description* was a literary success. According to Joan Pau Rubiés, its

[34] Sweetman, *Mapping Hinduism*, p. 75.

[35] Henry Lord, *A Display of Two Forraigne Sects in the East Indies*, vol. 1 (London [s.n.], 1630), 'The Epistle', A2.

[36] Abraham Rogerius, *De Open-Deure tot het verborgen Heydendom ofte Waerachtigh vertoogh van het leven ende zeden, mitsgaders de Religie ende Gotsdienst der Bramines op de Cust Chormandel ende der landen daar ontrent* (Leiden: Françoys Hackes, 1651).

[37] Abraham Rogerius, *Le Theatre de l'Idolatrie, ou la porte ouverte pour parvenir à la cognoissance du paganisme caché*, trans. Thomas Le Grue (Amsterdam [s.n.], 1670).

[38] Sweetman, *Mapping Hinduism*, p. 90.

impact was enhanced by the antiquarian pretensions of its author and by the rich engravings featuring the different avatars of Vishnu.[39]

Popular though these works were, their accounts were limited to descriptions of various *Hindoo* customs. Little about the theology of the religion was known or understood. As Rubiés argues, the antiquarian knowledge of Baldaeus merely added speculation to the possible origins of those practices, resulting in the hypothesis that they had in some way descended to India from Ancient Egypt or the Near East.[40] Moreover, while Baldeus and Rogerius were less quick than Lord to dismiss Indian religious beliefs, their explanations were still governed by the rubric of biblical history. They were to be slotted into speculative histories on the origins of and connections between the disorienting assortment of pagan beliefs and rituals, as well as corrupted Abrahamic doctrines, but ultimately to also be regarded as the 'mysteries of heathendom' (Rogerius) or the beliefs of 'poor Wretches quite entangled in the Darkness of Paganism' (Baldaeus).[41] This was not so different from Lord's assessment of Indian practices as 'vaine Superstitions'.[42] Towards the end of the seventeenth century, however, works like Bernard Picart and John Frederic Bernard's *Religious Ceremonies of the World* (1723) announced a shift in perspective. This ambitious collection of information about religious practices across the increasingly known globe came in seven volumes, with 250 plates of engravings that depicted all of the religions known to Europeans in the early 1700s. The book, which castigated religious enthusiasm as a form of 'violent fanaticism', was a bestseller. Between 1733 and 1739 all seven volumes were published again in two sets of reprints, all of which sold rapidly. The first English edition was published in 1733 and seems to have amounted to around 800 copies, which was accompanied by a one-volume abridged version in 1741.[43] This compilation of religious traditions from

39 Joan-Pau Rubiés, 'From Christian Apologetics to Deism: Libertine Readings of Hinduism, 1650–1730', in William J. Bulman and Robert G. Ingram (eds.), *God in the Enlightenment* (Oxford: Oxford University Press, 2016), p. 109.

40 Joan-Pau Rubiés, 'From Antiquarianism to Philosophical History: India, China and the World History of Religion in European Thought (1600–1770)', in Peter N. Miller and François Louis (eds.), *Antiquarianism and Intellectual Life in Europe and China, 1500–1800* (Ann Arbor: University of Michigan Press, 2012).

41 As quoted in A. V. Williams Jackson (ed.), *A History of India*, vol. 9 (London: The Grolier Society, 1907), p. 240; Baldaeus, *True and Exact Description of the Most Celebrated East India Coast of Malabar and Coromandel*, trans. anon. (London: Awnsham and John Churchill, 1703), p. 901.

42 Lord, *Display of Two Forraigne Sects*, vol. 1, p. 93.

43 Lynn Hunt, Margaret Jacob and Wijnand Mijnhardt, *The Book That Changed Europe: Bernard and Picart's Religious Ceremonies of the World* (Cambridge, MA: Harvard University Press, 2010), pp. 271, 296–7.

within and outside of Europe, including the different variants of Protestantism, had explicitly invited a comparative perspective. Within it, religion appears a historically and geographically contingent aspect of human society, the competing truth claims of which seem ever more relative in relation to their volume. The authors of a masterfully detailed study of Picart and Bernard's enterprise hold off attaching to *Religious Ceremonies* 'one predetermined religious programme', and instead point to the confluence of Huguenot, Dutch Calvinist, deist, pantheist and even atheist influences in the thought of its creators. They are clear, though, that the work itself was intended to promote religious toleration through the invitation to reflect on the common truths that emerged across a diversity of practices and beliefs.[44]

More detailed information about the internal theology of Eastern religions came in the form of Jesuit reports, which were printed in the eighteenth century as the series *Lettres édifiantes et curieuses*. This was a collection of thirty-four volumes of letters from Jesuit missionaries in China, the Middle East, India and the Americas, published between 1702 and 1776. The letters demonstrated an unprecedented comprehension of Indian philosophical and scientific literature, and languages. They also included brief accounts of the doctrines of some of India's classical systems of philosophy, in particular those of Nyāya (mentioning Oudayanacarya, i.e. the scholar Udayana) and Vedānta. These commentaries still maintained their missionary standpoint, with disapproval most often being incited against the pagan monism of Advaita Vedānta philosophy, which holds that the self, or soul (*ātman*), is commensurate with the highest metaphysical reality (Brahmin).[45] That said, the letters of French Jesuit Jean Venant Bouchet (1655–1732) struck a different tone. Bouchet's first letter, published in 1711, argued that many of the doctrines of the Brahmins seemed to derive from Mosaic and Christian revealed traditions, and were not just an idolatrous set of practices elaborated from a primitive paganism.[46] Bouchet thus built on Nobili's claim that Christianity would amount to the restoration of a 'lost' fifth Veda (widely regarded as the religion's central scriptures), thereby restoring the original monotheistic religion of India that had been buried under idolatry. He also agreed that it was necessary to draw from local customs and doctrines in order to spread that Christian message, and that it was therefore essential that the Jesuits study their 'errors' by collecting information from Tamil Brahmins, as

44 Hunt, Jacob and Mijnhardt, *Book That Changed Europe*, p. 21.
45 Halbfass, *India and Europe*, p. 44.
46 Jean-Baptiste Du Halde, *Lettres édifiantes et curieuses*, vol. 9 (Paris: Chez Nicolas le Clerc, 1715), pp. 1–60.

well as reading texts such as the Puranas (*purāṇa*) and the *Ramayana* (*Rāmāyaṇam*).[47] As a result, John Frederic Bernard, one of the most appreciative readers of Bouchet, published the letters in *Religious Ceremonies of the World* in order to stress the antiquity of Indian religion.[48]

It was against this backdrop that the *Ezour-Védam* appeared in Europe. This text, it was claimed, was a lost French translation of one of the ancient Vedas, which had supposedly been discovered by Sir Alexander Johnston in Pondicherry. Although it was not published in its entirety until 1781, this 'French Veda' was introduced to Europe through the work of Voltaire from 1760 onwards. While the actual origins of the text are still a matter of debate, Rocher makes the case that the *Ezour-Védam* was likely composed by a Jesuit for the purposes of suggesting parallels between Christianity and Vedic theology, on the basis of which a missionary agenda could be fulfilled.[49] This, and the appeal of Bouchet's work for Bernard, suggests that the comparison of religious truths according to a Thomist appreciation of natural religion, which underpinned Jesuit *accommodatio* strategies, could also invite a more relativist conception of religious truth when approached from a different perspective. For Voltaire the *Ezour-Védam*, brought to him by the Comte de Modave, facilitated two particular arguments relating to Indian antiquity and philosophy that he would repeat again and again throughout his work.[50] In the first instance the apparent antiquity of its religious texts positioned Indian civilisation as a challenge to Judeo-Christian chronology. Moreover, in the *Hindoo* religion, Voltaire believed himself to have found a conception of faith which corresponded with universal reason and was thus able to satirically suggest that, based on the contents of the *Ezour-Védam*, Judeo-Christian mythology was merely a later imitation of Indian wisdom.[51] Independent of pontiffs or kings, the ancient 'Brachmanes', had established a 'religion according to universal reason'.[52] The authenticity of the *Ezour-Védam* was, however, called into question almost as soon as it appeared, and by the mid-1760s Voltaire had sought to distance himself from it. By 1769 John

[47] Joan-Pau Rubiés, 'Reassessing "the Discovery of Hinduism": The Jesuit Discourse on Gentile Idolatry and the European Republic of Letters', in Anand Amaladass and Ines G. Županov (eds.), *Intercultural Encounter and the Jesuit Mission in South Asia (16th–18th Centuries)* (Bangalore: Asian Trading Corporation, 2014).

[48] Hunt, Jacob and Mijnhardt, *Book That Changed Europe*, p. 229.

[49] Ludo Rocher, *The Ezourvedam: A French Veda of the Eighteenth Century* (University of Pennsylvania Studies on South Asia) (Amsterdam: John Benjamins Publishing, 1984), p. 72.

[50] Rocher, *The Ezourvedam*, p. 77.

[51] Voltaire, *Dictionnaire philosophique* (Paris: Gallimard, 1964 [1764]), pp. 25–6.

[52] Marsh, *India in the French Imagination*, p. 73.

Zephaniah Holwell became his principal source on India.[53] In the 1770s Voltaire also enlisted the work of Alexander Dow to challenge the monopoly of the Abrahamic religions on monotheism by denying that Hinduism was polytheistic, a point on which he and Holwell both agreed.[54]

Another early supporter of the *Ezour-Védam*, and contemporary of Holwell and Dow, was Abraham Hyacinthe Anquetil-Duperron (1731–1805). Anquetil was central to the emergence of French Indology. His interest in ancient religions began during his theological studies at the Sorbonne, and was sustained throughout his continued studies in Jansenist seminaries. This interest, and desire to recover genuine sources, would lead him to Southern India, where between 1754 and 1762 he travelled along the Malabar coast.[55] His account of his experiences while travelling was published in an abbreviated form in 1762, and then in English, in *The Annual Register* under the title 'A brief account of a voyage to India, undertaken by M. Anquetil du Perron, to discover and translate the work attributed to Zoroaster'.[56] Interestingly, the title belies a mythology that surrounds this trip, that it was inspired by the desire to uncover the origins of a fragment of the *Avesta*, which are the religious texts of Zoroastrianism. In fact, Anquetil had already planned to travel to India before this encounter, in search of works relating to the Brahmins, namely the Vedas. Serious illness interrupted these plans, and then the Seven Years' War further impeded his efforts. It was only then that Anquetil travelled to Pondicherry to study Zoroastrian texts. The full account of these, known as the *Zend-Avesta*, was first published in 1771.[57] William Jones ignited national rivalries with a scurrilous attack on this text, which claimed that Anquetil had been duped by modern forgeries. This inaccurate charge was as influential as it was vicious, and the reputation of both Anquetil and the text greatly suffered, mired by the possibility that it was a fake.[58] Anquetil's other major contribution to European orientalist knowledge was his *Legislation orientale* (1778), in which he endeavoured to prove that the nature of oriental despotism had been greatly misrepresented by Montesquieu and others.[59] It was not until 1787 that

[53] Urs App, *The Birth of Orientalism* (Philadelphia: University of Pennsylvania Press, 2010), p. 53.

[54] Marsh, *India in the French Imagination*, p. 118.

[55] App, *Birth of Orientalism*, pp. 363–5.

[56] *Annual Register* (London: J. Dodsley, 1762), pp. 103–29. The French report was published in *Journal des Sçavans* (June, 1762), pp. 413–29 and (July, 1762), pp. 474–500.

[57] App, *Birth of Orientalism*, pp. 406–7.

[58] William Jones, *Lettre à Monsieur A*** du P***. Dans laquelle est compris l'examen de sa traduction des livres attribués à Zoroastre* (London: Chez P. Elmsly, 1771). See M. J. Franklin, *Orientalist Jones: Sir William Jones, Poet, Lawyer, and Linguist, 1746–1794* (Oxford: Oxford University Press, 2011), p. 74.

[59] Jennifer Pitts, *Boundaries of the International: Law and Empire* (Cambridge, MA: Harvard University Press, 2018), p. 57.

he would successfully translate an authentic Hindu text, the *Upanishads* (*Upaniṣads*), via Persian, into French. Unhappy with that version, he prepared another in Latin, which was completed towards the end of 1796 and published in two thick quarto volumes at Strasbourg in 1801–2.[60] Throughout this time he maintained the authenticity of the *Ezour-Védam*.[61]

The reception that Anquetil-Duperron's work received in England, as well as the practical obstacles to his work, set the scene for explaining some of the reasons, despite the apparent abundance of demand in France, that British works dominated European understandings of Hinduism in the latter part of the eighteenth century. As the British presence in India expanded, and French commercial ventures faltered, Brahmin knowledge was more readily accessible to British authors. In common with the Portuguese, the Dutch and the English, France's encounter with India was occasioned by trade. Following the Seven Years' War French trade with Bengal and the Coromandel Coast steadily declined and the financial health of *La Compagnie des Indes* faltered, leading Voltaire, a shareholder, to bemoan France's 'grand ruinous trade with India'.[62] In contrast, the moves made by the Company in the same period would set them on the path to become an administrative power in Bengal, developing structures, policies and alliances that meant that British authors increasingly found themselves with unprecedented access to Indian sources and advisors, as well as a range of incentives, ideological and practical, for extending their collective knowledge of Indian culture and customs.

British Writers and 'Philosophical' Hinduism

The great antiquity of Indian civilisation was a common point of interest across Britain and France. Kate Marsh has pointed to how by the 1780s India's antiquity had become a necessary marker of its image in French literature.[63] This was true in Britain too, and to this we could also add the prevalence with which writers also emphasised the sophistication of Indian philosophy, as well as its great age. Both features meant that as well as lending ammunition to critiques that sought to challenge biblical chronology, orientalist knowledge was also enlisted in the Enlightenment endeavour of understanding 'man' and society. The mission of the

[60] George Sarton, 'Anquetil-Duperron (1731–1805)', *Osiris*, 3 (1937), p. 208.

[61] Rocher, *The Ezourvedam*, p. 15.

[62] Kate Marsh, *India in the French Imagination: Peripheral Voices, 1754–1815* (London: Pickering and Chatto, 2009), p. 11.

[63] Marsh, *India in the French Imagination*, p. 89.

Encyclopédie 'to assemble knowledge scattered across the earth' necessarily meant the inclusion of articles on the religions of the East. There were pieces on the 'Philosophie des Brachmanes', 'Sanscrit', the 'Shaster' and the 'Vedam' among others.[64] From another perspective, histories of human civilisation also required that attention be paid to Indian antiquity and the role of religion within its historical development.[65] Following Montesquieu, religion was an important category in any analysis of civil society, particularly for those interested in its relationship with social mores and institutions, as well as for tracing the connections between ancient peoples. By 1791, for example, William Robertson's *A Historical Disquisition Concerning the Knowledge Which the Ancients Had of India* loudly proclaimed the importance of an understanding of India for those concerned with the history of civil society.[66] Robertson's favourable view of what he perceived as the monotheistic beliefs underlying 'classical' Hinduism was a product of the surge of British orientalist writing at the end of the eighteenth century, and the work of William Jones in particular.

The same philosophical basis of Jesuit understandings of Asian religious thought, which had emphasised the similarities of its basic tenets according to the principles of the 'natural light' of God-given religious moral sense, or reason, also opened a path to challenging the authority of Christian doctrines.[67] The theology of Thomas Aquinas, which was central to both the Jesuits and Christian Humanism, had made an Aristotelian definition of our capacity to reason the basis for the possibility of knowing God, albeit imperfectly without the benefit of revelation.[68] In this conceptual paradigm alien religious cultures were judged on the degree to which they demonstrated evidence of a natural religion, according to reason. This was often expressed as the ability of pre-Christian societies to recognise and adhere to some basic moral precepts.[69] In Thomas More's fictionalised

64 Dennis Diderot, 'Articles from the *Encyclopédie*', in John Hope Mason and Robert Wokler (eds. and trans.), *Political Writings* (Cambridge: Cambridge University Press, 1992), p. 21. On these articles see Marsh, *India in the French Imagination*, p. 117.

65 Marshall and Williams, *The Great Map of Mankind*, pp. 133–41.

66 William Robertson, *Historical Disquisition Concerning the Knowledge Which the Ancients Had of India* (Dublin: John Ershaw, 1791).

67 Halbfass, *India and Europe*, p. 54.

68 See John W. O'Malley, *The First Jesuits* (Cambridge, MA: Harvard University Press, 1993); Ben Bradshaw, 'The Christian Humanism of Erasmus', *Journal of Theological Studies* (1982) 33:2, pp. 411–47; Thomas Aquinas, 'The Way in Which the Divine Truth Is to Be Made Known', in *Summa Contra Gentiles*, book 1, trans. Anton C. Pegis (Notre Dame, IN: University of Notre Dame Press), p. 63.

69 Richard H. Popkin and Mark Goldie, 'Scepticism, Priestcraft and Toleration', in Mark Goldie and Robert Wokler (eds.), *The Cambridge History of Eighteenth-Century Political Thought* (Cambridge: Cambridge University Press, 2006), p. 86.

pagan society of Utopia, for example, the native inhabitants 'believe that after this life vices will be punished and virtue rewarded' despite having received no Christian teaching.[70] In another example, Matteo Ricci, a Jesuit missionary in China, saw Confucianism as an important expression of natural religion on the basis that it 'contains a doctrine of reward for good done and punishment for evil'.[71] Throughout the seventeenth and eighteenth centuries, though, these examples of moral compatibility took an unintended turn by providing the conceptual foundations for a religious critique. Enlightenment thinkers increasingly cited the universality of these precepts in order to undermine the ultimate authority accorded to Christian orthodoxy.[72] While Christianity could accommodate comparisons between itself and some aspects of other faiths within an account of a common patriarchal religion before Babel, or the rational apprehension of God through nature, others used the same propositions to undermine orthodoxy. From a Dissenting perspective, the variety of expressions of faith according to natural religion surely begged the question of whether certain articles were necessary to Christianity, or whether these too were the products of historical degeneration. From a more fundamentally sceptical position, this plurality undermined the view that Christian revelation was the sole true expression of God's divine wisdom, particularly when religious traditions that were without it appeared to share a number of essential beliefs.

In England in the latter part of the seventeenth century, the 'latitudinarians' of the Anglican Communion welcomed the toleration of Protestant Dissent that was enshrined in the Toleration Act (1689), while also positing moderate reform of the rites and articles of the Church for the purpose of removing some of the barriers to conformity.[73] Historians are divided on whether this should be interpreted as an indication of the philosophical triumph of rationalism, natural theology, or whether it was a matter of political expedience.[74]

70 Thomas More, *Utopia*, trans. Robert M. Adams (New York: W. Norton and Company, 1975 [1516]), p. 80.

71 Matteo Ricci, *China in the Sixteenth Century: The Journals of Matthew Ricci, 1583–1610*, Louis J. Gallagher (trans.) (London: Random House, 1953), p. 94.

72 A focal point of this transition was the Rights controversy; see Jonathan Israel, *Democratic Enlightenment: Philosophy, Revolution, and Human Rights 1750–1790* (Oxford: Oxford University Press, 2011), pp. 558–9.

73 Martin I. J. Griffin Jr., *Latitudinarianism in the Seventeenth-Century Church of England* (Leiden: Brill, 1992); Isabel Rivers, *Sentiment: A Study in the Language of Religion and Ethics in England 1660–1780, vol.* 1 (Cambridge: Cambridge University Press, 1991), pp. 32–5. On the nuances and problems with the label, see John Spurr, '"Latitudinarianism" and the Restoration Church', *Historical Journal*, 31:1 (1988).

74 Richard Ashcraft, 'Latitudinarianism and Toleration: Historical Myth versus Political History', in Richard Kroll, Richard Ashcraft and Perez Zagorin (eds.), *Philosophy, Science and Religion in England, 1640–1700* (Cambridge: Cambridge University Press, 1992).

Moreover, despite the act, in the eighteenth century many features of the Clarendon Code remained in force to reassert the supremacy of the Anglican Church.[75] As the immediate threat of Catholicism diminished, however, the case for toleration resurfaced, many appealing to the Lockean principles that it was impossible to enforce conviction, that religion was a matter of private judgement and that, moreover, since improvement could only proceed on the basis of consensus, toleration was a basic constituent of enlightened practice.[76] For some thinkers, the principle that there were non-essential matters within the Church opened the door to speculation beyond internal theological disputes to pose the question of how knowledge of other religions shed light on those essential beliefs. Where some Anglican divines had advanced the idea that natural religion and revelation were mutually reinforcing, Dissenting thinkers had taken the primacy of natural theology that this implied and used it to undermine the doctrines of the Church.[77] More sceptical critics of religion went further, using similar formulations of natural reason to attack the premises underlying the basis of orthodox Christian claims to hold a monopoly on religious truth. This view was expressed in different ways across 'freethinking' religious criticism in Europe. In England Herbert of Cherbury published *De veritate* (On Truth) in 1624, which clearly set out five simple 'articles' to a universal and minimal religion: a belief in God, the duty to honour God, moral worship in the form of virtue, the pain of sin and finally, a belief in an afterlife that included punishment for evil and reward for goodness.[78] Following in this tradition, writers often associated with 'English deism', such as Toland and Tindal, constructed historical narratives in which contemporary 'religion' appears as the corrupt shadow of an original monotheistic faith already revealed to Confucius, Zoroaster, Socrates and Plato.[79] Studies of these 'deistical' writers have thus pointed to their significance in developing the radical intellectual culture of the Enlightenment. Moreover, and most relevant here, their promotion of critical biblical hermeneutics is seen

[75] Ashcraft, 'Latitudinarianism and Toleration', p. 152.

[76] John Locke, *A Letter Concerning Toleration and Other Writings*, Mark Goldie (ed.) (Indianapolis, IN: Liberty Fund, 2010), pp. 31–2. On this in the thought of Edmund Burke, see Richard Bourke, *Empire and Revolution: The Political Life of Edmund Burke* (Princeton, NJ: Princeton University Press, 2015), pp. 221–2, 274–9.

[77] B. A. Gerrish, 'Natural and Revealed Religion', in Knud Haakonssen (ed.), *The Cambridge History of Eighteenth-Century Philosophy*, vol. 2 (Cambridge: Cambridge University Press, 2006), p. 644.

[78] As summarised by David Edwards in *Christian England, from the Reformation to the Eighteenth Century* (Glasgow: Edermans, 1984), p. 366.

[79] Halbfass, *India and Europe*, p. 56. See also Wayne Hudson, *The English Deists: Studies in Early Enlightenment* (London: Pickering and Chatto, 2009).

to have prompted an alternative history and anthropology of positive religion.[80]

This was the inherited intellectual milieu that produced the conceptual parameters in which their interpretation of *Gentoo* religion, as a unified, original and natural religion, was formed and received. The discovery and interpretation of Indian religion in the eighteenth century was, consequently, related to debates about the nature and origins of religious belief. China was the original focal point of these debates, with Confucianism posing as a clear example of a simple moral philosophy, unencumbered by esoteric and mystical theology. Leibniz even floated the idea of introducing Chinese missionaries to Europe in order to instruct its inhabitants on the natural theology and 'practical philosophy' of Confucius.[81] In addition, despite his later position that India was the homeland of religion in its most ancient and purest form, Voltaire's initial interest in Eastern theology was also rooted in China.[82] With the expansion of the European presence in India, however, accounts of the Brahmin's religious philosophies similarly began to seep into the intellectual culture of the Enlightenment, and India became a focal point for discussion. Following the great extension of British military and commercial dominance in India via the East India Company's expansion, Company servants began to produce what were taken to be the most extensive and authentic accounts of India's original religion.

The French edition of Abraham Rogerius' *Porte ouverte*, published in Amsterdam in 1670 and annotated by an anonymous editor, contained additional notes which built on Rogerius' suggestion that Indian idolatry bore traces of corrupted Judaism to suggest that the core of the religion, lost to its vulgar practitioners, was in fact monotheistic.[83] The *Voyages de François Bernier* (1670–1) had approached Indian religion in a similar manner and took this argument a step further. Bernier dismissed Indian religious doctrines as superstitious, not on the theological basis that they contradicted Christianity, but rather as a general critique of the irrational components of all religious beliefs. As Rubiés has pointed out, taken in this sense Bernier's arguments 'could potentially be directed against

[80] Diego Lucci, *Scripture and Deism: The Biblical Criticism of the Eighteenth-Century British Deists* (Bern: Peter Lang, 2008), p. 260.

[81] Franklin Perkins, *Leibniz and China: A Commerce of Light* (Cambridge: Cambridge University Press, 2004), p. 155. This enthusiasm for China was continued by his follower, Christian Wolff: Donald F. Lach, 'The Sinophilism of Christian Wolff (1679–1754)', *Journal of the History of Ideas*, 14:4 (1953).

[82] See App, *Birth of Orientalism*, p. 37.

[83] Abraham Roger, *Le Theatre de l'Idolatrie, ou la porte ouverte pour parvenir à la cognoissance du paganisme caché*, trans. Thomas Le Grue (Amsterdam [s.n.], 1670).

Christianity no less than Gentilism'.[84] The works of Rogerius and Bernier therefore form the basis of what Rubiés has called the 'comparative libertine anthropology of religion' that emerged in the seventeenth century. This is certainly a crucial moment in this history of European approaches to Eastern religions. And yet Rubiés' subsequent jump from 'libertine' readings of Indian practices to the 'arrival of British orientalists such as William Jones' in the late eighteenth century is too sudden.[85] The transition from 'anthropological' comparison to the scholarly Indology of Jones misses out an important stage in which authority was more tentatively located in linguistic ability and the discovery of texts. While Rogerius, Bernier and Bernard's *Religious Ceremonies of the World* relied on the testimonies of others, and relayed the observed religious rites and customs of the Brahmins and their followers, the accounts of Holwell, Dow, Halhed and Wilkins presented what they claimed to be the theological and philosophical core of a religion that was unified, monotheistic, ancient and native to India.[86]

The authority of this interpretation was constructed on the claim of each author to have achieved a unique insight into Indian religious thought and texts on the basis of linguistic skill and contact with Brahmins. Though their effect on the public was powerful, these claims varied in authenticity. They all were known to have a proficient knowledge of Persian, which was the main administrative language of the Mughal Empire and so an important tool for those seeking advancement in the East India Company. The first English-to-Persian dictionary did not, however, appear until 1777, after the publication of Halhed's *Code of Gentoo Laws*.[87] This makes it difficult to trace their decisions in translation beyond local knowledge. This is similarly the case for Bengali, elements of which appear in the transliterations of Indian terminology presented by both Holwell and Dow. Bengali was the language of the Bengal region, and was therefore acquired by some Company employees in order to better conduct local affairs.[88] The first detailed study was in fact produced by Halhed, whose *A Grammar of the Bengal Language* was composed in 1778.[89] Halhed was also the first of these authors to make any strides in learning Sanskrit,

84 Rubiés, 'From Christian Apologetics to Deism', p. 111.
85 Rubiés, 'From Christian Apologetics to Deism', p. 108.
86 For Bernard's sources, see Hunt, Jacob and Mijnhardt, *The Book That Changed Europe*.
87 John Richardson, *A Dictionary, Persian, Arabic, and English* (Oxford: Clarendon Press, 1777).
88 Bernard S. Cohn, 'The Command of Language and the Language of Command', in Edmund Burke III and David Porchaska (eds.), *Genealogies of Orientalism: History, Theory, Politics* (London: University of Nebraska Press, 2008), p. 118.
89 Nathaniel Brassey Halhed, *A Grammar of the Bengal Language* (Bengal, 1778).

producing a glossary of terms in the *Code*, but it was Wilkins, followed by Jones, who became proficient.[90] Yet, despite the deliberate ambiguities surrounding Howell and Dow's sources, by claiming mastery of Indian languages and privileged access to texts, the claims of all four authors to unique insight were accepted by their audiences.

This emphasis on native languages as a gateway to important knowledge had a significant impact on the particular development of these ideas. Coupled with a European bias towards the authority of text, those enquiring into the nature of Indian religious institutions tended to see scripture as the ultimate standard by which to judge and determine the nature of the religion. It was this presumption that allowed the strong division, present in the work of all four writers considered in this book, between the original, pure and 'high' philosophical religion of the ancients, and the 'low', superstitious and largely practice-based faith of the vulgar. Thus, for those investigating native beliefs with the background of a classical education, like Halhed, their knowledge of Indian religion was usually foregrounded by the Greek conception of the Indians as the gymnosophists, or 'naked philosophers'.[91] Aligned with this was the discovery that *Gentoo* thought posited the existence of a Golden Age and a narrative of gradual deterioration to the present age (*kali yuga*), which was the most depraved and dissolute.[92] This complemented a thematic strand in Enlightenment critiques of religion, which saw it as a corrupt human institution that obscured the simple and rational ideas of natural religious belief. This has been summarised by Halbfass as the belief that 'Religion in general is derived and has degenerated from, the pure natural revelation of which the Indians were the first possessors.'[93] This idea of an original and rational religion is well illustrated by Halhed's poem 'An Ode on Leaving Banaras' (1784), which was written in a note to Warren Hasting, responding to Wilkins' translation of the *Bhagavad-Gītā*:

> Om! Veeshnu! Brahm! Or by whatever name
> Primeval Reshees have thy power ador'd:
> They worship'd thee, they knew thee still *the same*,
> One great eternal, undivided lord!
> Tho' now, in these worn days, obscur'd thy light,
> (Worn days, alas, and crazy wane of time!)

90 Halhed, *Code of Gentoo Laws.*
91 Rocher, 'British Orientalism in the Eighteenth Century', p. 215.
92 Trautmann, *Aryans and British India*, p. 73. 93 Halbfass, *India and Europe*, p. 58.

Tho' priest-craft's puppets cheat man's bigot sight.
With hell-born mockeries of things sublime.
Ages *have* been, when thy refulgent beam
Shone with full vigour on the mental gaze:
When doting superstition dar'd not dream,
And folly's phantoms perish'd in thy rays.[94]

Halhed's rendering of the idea that the various Indian deities were one 'undivided lord', but that this was a truth obscured by priestcraft, succinctly captures the themes of original purity and decline. These ideas are present in the work of all four writers studied in this book, and are often what underpin the assertion that they were deist and that they thus approached the interpretation of Hinduism from a deist perspective.[95] This assessment has often emerged from the view that the work of these authors was sympathetic to *Hindoo* religion in a way that more overtly religiously motivated writers, such as missionaries or evangelicals, were not. In many ways this is accurate. Where Claudius Buchanan, author of *Christian Researches in Asia* (1811), had written in 1799 that 'the character of the Hindoo superstition' was 'lascivious and bloody', these writers had sought to defend *Gentoo* religion against such views.[96] But far too much is extrapolated from this generalised contrast. This judgement of 'sympathy' in matters of religion sometimes uncritically extends to 'deism', via its association with Enlightenment toleration, to signify a milder, and from some perspectives more palatable, approach to empire. Much of this owes its provenance to a historiographical narrative that polarises 'orientalist' (eastward facing, scholarly and sympathetic) and 'Anglicist' (westward facing and Christian) cultural attitudes to India, outlined in David Kopf's *British Orientalism and the Bengal Renaissance* (1969). Kopf's account of the so called 'Bengal' or 'Oriental Renaissance' pitches British interaction with and promotion of Hindu scholarship and culture against more reactionary forces.[97] When it comes to understanding the role of European religious heterodoxy in shaping British interpretations of Indian religion in this period, however, these categories are too reductive.[98] These

[94] Nathaniel Brassey Halhed, 'An Ode on Leaving Banaras', as quoted in Rocher, 'Alien and Empathetic', pp. 224–5.

[95] Halbfass, *India and Europe*, p. 56.

[96] Hugh Pearson, *Memoirs of the Life and Writings of the Rev. Claudius Buchanan, DD, Late Vice-Provost of the College of Fort William in Bengal* (Philadelphia: Benjamin & Thomas Kite, 1817), p. 134.

[97] Kopf, *British Orientalism and the Bengal Renaissance*; see also Trautmann, *Aryans and British India.*

[98] In this I agree with Joshua Ehrlich, who similarly challenges this cultural thesis in obfuscating the political dimensions of the Company's approach to orientalist knowledge in this period. See Joshua

authors were perfectly capable of being, on the one hand, admiring of Indian religious doctrines and, on the other hand, perfectly contemptible towards Indian subjects. Their works were thus not necessarily 'sympathetic' in the sense that they denied the legitimacy of British domination in India, though they did sometimes invite critique. In fact, their approaches to *Hindoo* religion deliberately appropriated and reconstructed Indian ideas to suit a range of different ends. Their work was deistic not in the sense that it produced a benign cultural pluralism, but because it brought European religious heterodoxy to bear on their interactions with and assessments of Indian religion. The results were indeed complex accounts of Indian thought and history that certainly posited *Hindoo* religion as philosophically significant, but remained full of judgements and derision for various other aspects of Indian culture.

Moreover, without any sustained study of these works this assessment that they were writing from a 'deistic' perspective is naturally imprecise. Recent challenges to the broad historical usage of the term 'deism' have prompted historians to talk of multiple 'deisms' and 'different kinds of heterodoxy'.[99] While these authors certainly all express elements of some of the ideas that have been attached to 'deism', such as the view that superstition and clerical influence corrupted religion, they also offer differing approaches and priorities in their particular religious outlooks. Moreover, their common assent to the idea that *Hindoo* or *Gentoo* religion was ancient, monotheistic and in many ways a pure and rational expression of belief in a creator God still had different implications for each of them, and some were more radical than others. The following chapters will, therefore, trace the particularities of each author's approach, showing their accounts to be deeply embedded in their own personal engagements with European religious debate, heterodox thought and other intellectual influences. At the same time, though, this discussion will also call us back to the point that within this diversity was a consistent presentation of the idea that the original religion of India was not made up of strange rights and customs, but consisted of a series of philosophical and reasonable doctrines that could be traced through ancient scriptural texts. For them, and their enlightened readers, this was the starting point for all sorts of propositions on what this meant for various fields of knowledge, including

Ehrlich, 'The East India Company and the Politics of Knowledge', PhD diss., Harvard University, 2018, pp. 111–15, https://dash.harvard.edu/handle/1/39947190, accessed 2 July 2021.

[99] Hudson, *Enlightenment and Modernity*, pp. 26, 38–9; Wayne Hudson, 'Atheism and Deism Demythologised', in Wayne Hudson, Diego Lucci and Jeffry R. Wigelsworth (eds.), *Atheism and Deism Revalued: Heterodox Religious Identities in Britain, 1650–1800* (Farnham: Ashgate, 2014), p. 13.

political questions about empire, as well as arguments about the authority of biblical history.

The East India Company and Religion, 1600–1750

'A State in the disguise of a Merchant' was Edmund Burke's account of the East India Company as it stood at the time of the impeachment trial of Warren Hastings (1788–95).[100] Indeed, during the course of the eighteenth century the East India Company developed from a network of trading outposts to possessing many of the attributes of a sovereign and territorial power. Having been 'continually engaged in war' since 1745, as Company historiographer Robert Orme had put it in his 1763 *History of the Military Transactions of the British Nation in Indostan*, British prominence in India was by then well established in Bengal, Madras and Bombay.[101] But it was in Bengal that the British were first established as a territorial power. After the Battle of Plassey and various intrigues, the Treaty of Allahabad (1765) had transferred to the Company the right of *diwani*, which amounted to the right to collect territorial customs revenues in Bengal, Bihar and Orissa. In this arrangement the nawab's deputy remained responsible for territorial finances, and the actual collection of the revenues was devolved to a variety of intermediaries, while the Company's resident at the nawab's court oversaw these transactions. As a result, the Company had effectively taken hold of some of the responsibilities of government, albeit with many of the actual offices of administration entrusted to indigenous office holders. British interests in India had thus suddenly intensified. Not only did Company troop numbers in Bengal rise from 3,000 in 1756 to 26,000 by 1766, but the question of whether the Company possessed an adequate constitution to meet the demands of foreign dominion became increasingly pressing.[102]

Throughout this transition one of the major questions facing the East India Company was how to treat matters of religion. This had long been a source of contention. The 1698 charter that was granted to the new East India Company contained a clause that the ministers of each garrison 'were to

[100] Edmund Burke, 'Trial of Warren Hastings Esq: Third Day, 15th February, 1788', in *The Works of the Right Honourable Edmund Burke*, vol. 13 (London: F. C. & J. Rivington, 1822).

[101] Robert Orme, *A History of the Military Transactions of the British Nation in Indostan* (London: John Norse, 1763), p. 34.

[102] Huw V. Bowen, *Revenue and Reform: The Indian Problem in British Politics, 1757–1773* (Cambridge: Cambridge University Press, 1991), p. 12; Huw V. Bowen, *The Business of Empire: The East India Company and Imperial Britain, 1756–1833* (Cambridge: Cambridge University Press, 2006), p. 10.

learn the Portugueze and Hindoo languages, to enable them to instruct the Gentoos &c in the Christian religion'.[103] Roughly a century later (1793), William Wilberforce attempted to introduce a 'pious clause' into the Company's charter, a measure that he regarded as essential to promoting 'the Interests and Happiness of the Inhabitants of the British domains in *India*'.[104] Despite this continuity of intention from one faction, there were other, more influential, members of the Company who pursued an opposite policy. For many it was imperative that the Company should avoid both the trouble and the costs that Christianisation would incur. Despite the 1698 clause, the Court of Directors did not write despatches to India regarding the Christian terms of the charter until 1712. They had also successfully altered its wording to better suit their interests by replacing the demand that all *Gentoos* be instructed in Christianity with one that called for instruction of only those *Gentoos* that were 'servants or slaves of the Company's'.[105] The Company also utilised its power to refuse licenses to reside in its territories to effectively disbar missionaries.[106] When the Company reached a position whereby it had seized control of the region, these differences in approach required much more explicit justification.

Wilberforce's presentation of the matter as a question of public 'happiness' was not unique.[107] In this period the concept of public happiness became central to debates over who best represented the welfare of Britain's colonial subjects.[108] The 1781 select committee, set up to enquire into the affairs of the Company, included in its remit a consideration of 'how the British Possessions in The East Indies may be held and governed with the greatest Security and Advantage to this Country, and by what Means the Happiness of the Native Inhabitants may best be promoted'.[109] Evangelicals like Wilberforce regarded the eternal happiness of the immortal soul as

103 Document 30, in P. J. Marshall (ed.), *Problems of Empire: Britain and India 1757–1813* (London: Allen and Unwin, 1968), pp. 194–6.

104 *Journals of the House of Commons*, 48 (14 May 1793), p. 778.

105 Extract of General letter to Bengal, 1712/13, para. 195, BL, IOR, H. Misc. 59, pp. 195–7.

106 Carson, *East India Company and Religion*, p. 23.

107 See 'Part V, The Promotion of Public Happiness', in Mark Goldie and Robert Wokler (eds.), *The Cambridge History of Eighteenth-Century Political Thought* (Cambridge: Cambridge University Press, 2006), pp. 497–600.

108 A good discussion of this can be found in John Rosselli, *Lord William Bentinck: The Making of a Liberal Imperialist, 1774–1839* (Berkeley: University of California Press, 1974), pp. 123–7. See also Peter N. Miller, *Defining the Common Good: Empire, Religion and Philosophy in Eighteenth-Century Britain* (Cambridge: Cambridge University Press, 1994).

109 *Journals of the House of Commons*, 38 (31 October 1780–10 October 1782), p. 600.

a priority over material happiness, whereas for others, happiness meant leaving Indian institutions intact as far as possible.[110] Holwell represented an early formulation of this thinking. In the dedication to the second volume of his *Interesting Historical Events*, he states that his intention in writing about the customs of the *Gentoos* was to 'rescue the originally untainted manners, and religious worship of a very ancient people from gross misrepresentation.'[111] That this misrepresentation resulted in practical miscarriages of justice is expressed later in the volume (1767), when Holwell describes the rescuing of women from the controversial practice of what he terms 'voluntary sacrifice' (which came to be known as suttee and is often today denoted by 'sati') as an 'outrage' and recounts how the *Gentoos* considered it 'an atrocious, and wicked violation of their sacred rights and privileges'.[112] In the next decade, Edmund Burke echoed a similar sentiment when he stipulated that British government in India must ensure for the inhabitants of its territories 'enjoyment of all their ancient laws, usages, rights and privileges'.[113]

Within the Company, the reasons for rejecting the missionary cause were as much pragmatic as they were ideological. Since its inception some had assumed that it was the Company's moral duty to utilise its trade mission for the purpose of saving souls. From the 1770s onwards, there was once again mounting pressure from Evangelicals for the Company to pursue a missionary policy.[114] Most Company officials, however, held on to the idea that non-interference in native religions and institutions was the best means of achieving stability.[115]A clear example was the acknowledgement that the East India Company's military might was heavily dependent on sepoy troops. Fearing disaffection, administrators were not prepared to interfere with Indian religions. Hastings' predecessor, Lord Cornwallis, in a letter to the president of the Board of Control, stressed the need for good officers, 'perfect' in the appropriate Indian language, who would give 'a minute attention to the customs and religious prejudices of the sepoys', because 'you need not be told how dangerous a disaffection in our native troops would be to our existence in this country'.[116] We can certainly see this approach as a moment in the Company's history, at the height of

[110] Carson, *East India Company and Religion*, p. 126.
[111] Holwell, 'Dedication', in *Interesting Historical Events*, vol. 2. (1767).
[112] Holwell, *Interesting Historical Events*, vol. 1 (1767), p. 100.
[113] 21 Geo.III, c.70 sec. 1; as quoted in Marshall and Williams (eds.), *The Great Map of Mankind* (London: J. M. Dent & Sons, 1982), p. 161.
[114] Carson, *East India Company and Religion*, pp. 20–2.
[115] Carson, *East India Company and Religion*, pp. 4, 15.
[116] As quoted in Carson, *East India Company and Religion*, p. 23.

which were the policies of Warren Hastings. Hastings' administrative ideology was essentially underpinned by Montesquieu's legal geography, dictating that only where the demands of natural justice were at odds with custom should indigenous practice (including religious law) be overruled.[117] This principle was most clearly articulated in Clause XXIII of Hastings' 1772 Judicial Plan, which stipulated that 'the Laws of the Koran with respect to the Mahometans, and those of the Shaster with respect to the Gentoos shall be invariably adhered to'.[118] Religion and religious texts thus came to represent the very identity of the existing Indian 'constitution', to which British governance would claim to attach itself.[119] This was not, however, a forgone conclusion. From the declaration of the conquest of Quebec in 1763 to the decision in 1774 to allow French civil law to be maintained in the administration of the territory, the question of the status of English law in Britain's colonies was a live matter of intense parliamentary debate.[120] Questions about the suitability of English law for the Company's territories in India were also raised, and it was within this debate that Hastings set out his particular plan for Company governance as grounded in an existing Indian administration. This would continue to be debated, particularly when it came to the jurisdiction of the Supreme Court in Calcutta.[121] Nevertheless, it was this vision that largely won out: the consultation of Hindu and Muslim law officers in the various courts of British India was not abandoned until 1864, though this was in a vastly transformed system.

The 1770s–80s thus marked a significant turning point in terms of the Company's institutional approach to research on Indian languages, history and religion. In 1769, Robert Orme was appointed 'historiographer to the East India Company' at £400 a year. He was succeeded by John Bruce in 1801. As well as their published histories, both Orme and Bruce left to the library a large number of manuscripts relating to India.[122] In the same period the Company accumulated an ever-larger number of manuals on

[117] Travers, *Ideology and Empire*, p. 105.

[118] Clause XXIII, 'Plan for the Administration of Justice', *Reports from the Committees of the House of Commons*, 4 (1804), p. 350.

[119] Cohn even described this as modelling India as a 'theocratic state', though regrettably he does not elaborate much on this particular phrase: Bernard S. Cohn, 'Law and the Colonial State in India', in June Starr and Jane F. Collier (eds.), *History and Power in the Study of Law* (Ithaca, NY: Cornell University Press, 2018), p. 140.

[120] For a particularly rich account of the arguments in play, see Bourke, 'Edmund Burke and the Politics of Conquest'.

[121] See chapter 5 in Travers, *Ideology and Empire*.

[122] J. S. Grewal, *Muslim Rule in India: The Assessments of British Historians* (Oxford: Oxford University Press, 1970), pp. 24–5.

local dialects and translations of various different historical and legal texts, all by Company servants and all supported through subscriptions and other methods of financial support. In some cases, the Court of Directors resolved to subscribe for forty copies of works on India and often subscribed for more. The petitions or memorials of the writers as well as the 'dedication' of their work to either the directors or the governor-general also testify to some cases of direct patronage.[123] In the period that Wilkins and Halhed were writing, therefore, the Company was increasingly invested in the active discovery and use of knowledge about India, which in many cases included information about Indian religion.[124] The relationship between the Company and the works produced by these writers cannot be explained, therefore, without accounting for the particular role of Governor-General Warren Hastings.

Hastings' governorship was concerned with responding to the criticism of the Company that had mounted in the period under Clive. *The Annual Register*, for example, had greeted the victory at Plassey as 'affording a degree of triumph, unknown even to ancient Rome'. In the same volume it also reported on the discussions of a parliamentary select committee, one side of which had expressed the concern that 'luxury, corruption and the extreme avidity for making immense fortunes in little time, had totally infected the company's servants' and that 'nothing less than a general reform' could 'preserve the settlement'.[125] In redressing this the Regulating Act of 1773 resolved that both the British government and the Company's Court of Directors would together appoint a governor-general, and a council for Bengal, which would be responsible for a much more direct system of British rule. It was into this role that Warren Hastings stepped. Instead of the image of the plundering 'nabob', Hastings sought to erect a regime that could claim to be 'enlightened' and legitimate according to local customs. His approach bore a resemblance to some of the recommendations advanced by Dow, a copy of whose work Hastings had received from John Macpherson in 1772. Macpherson had forwarded it straight to Hastings having received it himself, 'reeking from the press', suggesting that it was 'the only Copy of it in India'.[126] Though Hastings' response to Dow's work was critical, mainly because it contained censure of the Company, he evidently shared Dow's admiration for the Mughal

[123] Holden Furber, *John Company at Work: A Study in European Expansion in India in the Late Eighteenth Century* (Cambridge: Cambridge University Press, 1948), p. 340.

[124] Bowen, *The Business of Empire*, p. 214.

[125] *Annual Register* (1767), pp. 22, 27.

[126] John Macpherson to Hastings, Madras, 12 October 1772, Warren Hastings Papers, BL, Add. MS 29133, f. 262.

Empire.[127] Hastings vigorously rejected depictions of India that cast nawabi officials as barbaric and instead preferred Dow's description of a benign Eastern despotism.[128] Like Dow, Hastings saw the benefits of emulating such a model for advancing company interests.[129] Indeed, despite the language of direct rule, Hastings was still very much depended on existing systems of Mughal governance in establishing his administration. Sending an early draft of his revenue reforms to the chairman of the Company, Hastings justified the changes on the basis that they did not include any measures which 'the original constitution of the Mogul Government hath not before established or adopted, & thereby rendered familiar to the People'.[130]

This approach has been described as a policy of 'conciliation', whereby Hastings sought to reconcile 'native sensibilities' to Company rule by taking account of Indian social norms and values.[131] Ever the pragmatist, Hastings certainly used Indology to shape his administration. He would personally fund the translation of Hindu and Islamic legal digests, as well as dozens of projects proposed by Indian and British scholars and administrators.[132] Moreover, Hastings was himself deeply attracted to Indian theology and some have speculated that Hastings' own beliefs had a deistic quality, which in turn underlined these interests and his policies. Penelope Carson, for example, suggests that Hastings was 'probably a deist', although he 'took care to attend church regularly'.[133] Likewise Stephen Neill argues that in India Hastings 'lacked any deep belief in the doctrines of the Christian faith', casting him instead as 'an eighteenth-century deist'.[134] Certainly Hastings' letters and patterns of patronage

[127] Hastings to Robert Palk, 11 November 1772, Warren Hastings Papers, BL, Add. MS 29127, f. 49.

[128] For example, Hastings' minute of 1 March 1763, printed in Henry Vansittart, *Narrative of the Transactions in Bengal from the Year 1760 to the Year 1764 during the Government of Henry Vansittart*, vol. 1 (London, 1766) pp. 302–4.

[129] Travers, *Ideology and Empire*, p. 106.

[130] Hastings to G. Colebrooke, 26 March 1772, Warren Hastings Papers, BL, Add. MS 29127, f. 13r, v. Also quoted in M. E. Monckton Jones, *Warren Hastings in Bengal, 1772–1774* (Oxford: Clarendon Press, 1918), p. 151.

[131] Michael. S. Dodson, *Orientalism, Empire and National Culture: India, 1770–1880* (Basingstoke: Palgrave Macmillan, 2007), p. 43. For a more developed discussion of conciliation in Hastings' approach, see chapter 1 in Ehrlich, 'East India Company'.

[132] As well as Halhed and Wilkins, among the Company servants who received Hastings' patronage were Francis Gladwin, translator of the *Ayeen Akbery* (Calcutta [s.n.], 1783–6), and Jonathan Scott, author of *A Translation of the Memoirs of Eradut Khan* (London: Stockdale, 1786). The pandit Radhakanta, who would go on to be an important educator of William Jones, wrote his *Puranaprakasha* at the request of Hastings. See Rocher, 'The Career of Rādhākānta Tarkavāgīśa'.

[133] Carson, *East India Company and Religion*, pp. 21–2.

[134] Neill, *A History of Christianity in India*, vol. 2, pp. 19–20.

demonstrate that he shared the view of Dow that the great Mughal ruler Akbar was to be admired for his impartiality on matters of religion.[135] It was after reading Dow that Hastings encouraged Francis Gladwin to translate the 'institutes' of Akbar,[136] resulting in the publication of the *Ayeen Akbery* (A'an-i Akbara) in 1783.[137] The work had actually been completed by Gladwin in 1777, but the directors were unwilling to bear the cost of ten guineas a copy and it was Hastings who eventually reimbursed Gladwin.[138] Hastings' commitment to the particularly secularised aspects of Akbar's government, or what Bayly has described as being understood by eighteenth-century British thinkers as Akbar's 'enlightened Islamic freemasonry', was thus reflective of the work of Dow.[139] Whether or not Hastings himself was a deist is difficult to determine, but he was certainly interested in ideas and arguments about Indian religion.

This policy of discrete law codes meant that a separation between the Islam of the Mughals and India's religious others became a central feature of the British administrative system. In turn this tended to categorise all non-Muslims as *Hindoo*.[140] This alienated and extracted Indian Christians from the system of native laws. By subsuming all other religions under the non-Muslim category, it also made the *Gentoo* majority seem even larger.[141] In fact, the most significant and certainly intended impact of the 1772 Judicial Plan was to discontinue the official monopoly that Muslim law had in the civil courts.[142] Indeed, more generally, eighteenth-century British sympathies tended to be on the side of *Hindoos*, as a category apart from Muslims. This was in part for political reasons: the great villain in the Company's recent history was the Mughal nawab Siraj-ud-Daulah, who in June 1756 had attacked and captured the Company's base at Calcutta, Fort William.[143] In more general cultural terms, although there were alternative depictions of the Muslims in the Enlightenment, the Ottoman Turk often stood as the archetypical Muhammadan, and the Ottoman Empire the seat of tyranny and barbarism.[144]

135 Dow, *History of Hindostan*, vol. 3 (1772), pp. xxv, 103.
136 Grewal, *Muslim Rule in India*, p. 25.
137 Reprinted in Franklin, *Representing India*, vols. 5–6.
138 Grewal, *Muslim Rule in India*, p. 25.
139 Bayly, *Empire and Information*, p. 53.
140 Rocher, 'British Orientalism in the Eighteenth Century', pp. 215, 222.
141 Duncan M. Derrett, *Religion, Law and the State in India* (London: Faber and Faber, 1968), pp. 542–5.
142 Rocher, 'British Orientalism in the Eighteenth Century', p. 222.
143 Michael Curtis, *Orientalism and Islam: European Thinkers on Oriental Despotism in the Middle East and India* (Cambridge: Cambridge University Press, 2009), pp. 29–30.
144 Humberto Garcia, *Islam and the English Enlightenment: 1670–1840* (Baltimore: Johns Hopkins University Press, 2012), pp. 2–3.

Indeed, eighteenth-century anti-Muslim sentiment was based in a certain set of assumptions about Islam that pervaded the intellectual and political culture of the period. On the one hand were critiques of the religion itself: both its doctrines and its historical manifestations.[145] On the other, was the theoretical alignment of Islamic polities with the concept of oriental or Asian despotism.[146] None of the four writers studied in this book discuss this first approach in any detail, aside for implicitly including Islam in their generalised comments about the universal features of religion. Dow elaborated his view of Islam slightly more in his 1772 'A Dissertation Concerning the Origin and Nature of Despotism in Hindostan', which will be discussed in more detail in Chapter 4. In it he considers those elements of the Qur'an that rendered Muslim polities despotic.[147] More accurate information about the theological contents of Islam had percolated into Europe via translations of the Qur'an into European languages. After Latin, the first translation was into French in 1647, which was then translated into English in 1649. The Qur'an was then directly translated into English, by George Sale, in 1734.[148] While there were dissenting voices, such as Mary Wortley Montagu (who resided in the Ottoman Empire from 1716 to 1718),[149] one of the most common approaches to Islam in the eighteenth century revolved around the idea that the prophet Muhammad was an imposter.[150] This is most clearly expressed in Voltaire's play *Le Fanatisme ou Mahomet le prophète* (1742), which was later translated into English as *Mahomet, the Imposter* (1744).[151] This served to support the second sphere of criticism, the idea that Islam was a historical mechanism by which despotism came to be the dominant political model in the Middle East. Though it has much older roots,[152] in the eighteenth century, Montesquieu's thesis that despotism was the essential characteristic of

[145] David A. Palin, *Attitudes to Other Religions: Comparative Religion in Seventeenth- and Eighteenth-Century Britain* (Manchester: Manchester University Press, 1984), pp. 81–104.
[146] Curtis, *Orientalism and Islam*, pp. 35–6.
[147] Alexander Dow, *The History of Hindostan, from the Death of Akbar, to the Complete Settlement of the Empire under Aurungzebe*, 2nd ed., vol. 3 (London: T. Becket and P. A. de Hondt in the Strand, 1772), pp. xv–xvi.
[148] Olive Classe (ed.), *Encyclopaedia of Literary Translation into English: A–L* (London: Fitzroy Dearborn Publishers, 2000), p. 63.
[149] Curtis, *Orientalism and Islam*, p. 62.
[150] David Allen Harvey, *The French Enlightenment and Its Others: The Mandarin, the Savage and the Invention of the Human Sciences* (Basingstoke: Palgrave Macmillan, 2012), pp. 18–19.
[151] Curtis, *Orientalism and Islam*, p. 35.
[152] Aristotle discussed despotic kingships as particularly prominent in Asia: *The Politics of Aristotle*, Peter L. Phillips Simpson (trans.) (Berkeley: University of California Press, 1997), 128a16, p. 106.

all Asian governments, had set the paradigm for the debate.[153] In Britain, Gibbon painted a portrait of Islam that was intolerant and conducive to despotism. In particular, he emphasised the perceived luxury and sensuality of its exotic Eastern kingdoms.[154] The French *philosophe* Volney (1757–1820), originally Constantin François de Chasseboeuf, pursued a sweeping generalisation that all of Asia was buried in an intellectual dark age, with a particular emphasis on the barbarity of the Turks and the tyrannical tribalism of the Arabs.[155] Yet again, these ideas also served broader discourses about the nature of European polities too; unflattering portrayals of the tyrannous sultan of 6the Ottoman Empire were, very often, barely implicit criticisms of autocratic France.

It is clear that despite their reflections of the sophistication and reasonableness of Indian religion, these authors reflexively adopt the position of assumed European superiority, if not supremacy. This is an unexamined perspective and, in this sense, cannot be located in any particular ideological commitment, and instead owes its manifestation to contemporary suppositions about Europe's unique status as a flourishing commercial society, in contrast to a stagnated East.[156] According to Colin Kidd, in the early modern period religion was the dominant intellectual paradigm in the Atlantic Protestant world and questions about 'racial Otherness' were primarily questions about 'pagan Otherness'.[157] Silvia Sebastiani has correctly added to this that as the eighteenth century proceeded, the construction of the idea of race itself increasingly featured arguments from the physical sciences, resulting in accounts of cultural difference that interlaced religious and political mores with arguments about climate and hereditary traits.[158] In turn, as Shruti Kapila has argued, towards the latter decades of the eighteenth century this understanding of India became increasingly entwined with the emergence of ethnology and its attention to developing typologies of race. While Jones' theory of what has subsequently come to be termed the 'Indo-European language family' and its

[153] Sharon Krause, 'Despotism in the *Spirit of the Laws*', in David W. Carrithers, Michael A. Mosher and Paul Rahe (eds.), *Montesqueiu's Science of Politics: Essays on the Spirit of the Laws* (Lanham, MD: Rowman & Littlefield Publishers Inc., 2001).

[154] See J. G. A. Pocock, *Barbarism and Religion: Barbarians, Savages and Empires*, vol. 4. (Cambridge: Cambridge University Press, 2005), pp. 24–6.

[155] Harvey, *The French Enlightenment and Its Others*, p. 59.

[156] Pitts, *Boundaries of the International*, pp. 28–67.

[157] Colin Kidd, *The Forging of Races: Race and Scripture in the Protestant Atlantic World, 1600–2000* (Cambridge: Cambridge University Press, 2006).

[158] Silvia Sebastiani, *The Scottish Enlightenment: Race, Gender, and the Limits of Progress* (London: Palgrave Macmillan, 2013).

attachment to the idea of common Aryan origins is implicated in this process, as Kapila acknowledges, this was largely to do with the use of his work by physician James Cowles Prichard in the early nineteenth century.[159] The thought of the authors considered in this book was more firmly rooted in these earlier frames of reference, making sweeping judgements about Indian temperaments and social mores on the basis of climate and geographical features, while also attributing certain assumptions about India's history and societal development to its religious customs, tenets and institutions. That is to say, these writers wrote in the dominant idioms of the day. For each of them their central focus was religion, and this was often the primary lens through which they judged Indian history and culture. Inherent in this, though, was a narrative of purity and decline that could complement conventional ideas about passive Hindus and despotic Muslims, which in turn would come gradually to dominate justifications of the necessity of British government in the region, to ensure the security of *Hindoo* subjects.

Often related to questions of British constructions in relation to religion and the structure of colonial Indian society is the topic of caste. Given its dominance in the ideology of the British Raj, however, caste is strikingly absent in the work of these Company authors. Thus, the lack of serious attention paid to it by these authors precluded its meaningful inclusion in the chapters on what they thought the *Gentoo* or *Hindoo* religion was that follow. Each author did mention some notion of caste, mostly referring to it as a feature of the ways in which Hindu society is structured into ranks or professions, and mostly with respect to the Brahmin caste, as a priestly grouping with the social hierarchy of India. Dow gave the most detailed account, which amounted to a few pages on the 'four great tribes, each of which comprehends a variety of inferior casts'. Again, this was primarily to emphasise the status of the Brahmins, 'who alone can officiate in the priesthood like the Levites among the Jews'. The information about the remaining 'tribes' offers an outline of the Hindu *varnas*, the four social classes referred to in a number of Sanskrit texts, most likely relayed to Dow by his unnamed pandit adviser. As well as the Brahmins, he lists the 'Sittris' (Ksatriyas), 'Bises' (Vaisyas), and the 'Sudders' (Shudras), whom he distinguishes from the 'Harri cast, who are held in utter detestation by all the other tribes'.[160] Beyond this, though, none of these authors offers any

159 Shruti Kapila, 'Race Matters: Orientalism and Religion, India and Beyond c.1770–1880', *Modern Asian Studies*, 41:3 (2007).
160 Dow, *History of Hindostan*, vol. 1 (1768), pp. xxxii–xxxiii.

serious reflection of the issue of caste in their construction of Indian religion and society, although Jones would provide one of the texts that would come to supply other British reflections on caste with its material, via the translation of the *Mānava-Dharmaśāstra*: from which James Mill took his account of the caste system.[161] This absence was possibly because of a particular bias in their presentation of Indian religion away from social customs and towards essential theological tenets, particularly those that could be deemed consonant with a universal religion of reason. Moreover, in general, as Dirks has argued, caste did not become a prominent colonial preoccupation until the mid- to late nineteenth century, though others have noted it as a feature of earlier Portuguese accounts and usages of '*casta*' in Indian society.[162]

More decisive were ideas about the ancient character of Brahmin philosophy and theology. The conceptual separation that this implied between the native *Hindoos* and their Muslim rulers in terms of religion was compounded by a distinction between ancient versus contemporary Hinduism as a matter of degeneration. Within this, though, they each expressed differing attitudes. Dow, for example, greatly admired the Mughal government and saw within it the possibilities of an enlightened treatment of the Hindoo religion. In contrast, Halhed depicted a romanticised narrative of it in which the morally virtuous *Gentoos* had suffered under their Muhammadan oppressors. In a poem titled 'The Bramin and the River Ganges', written for his patron, Warren Hastings, Halhed's river goddess implores a 'care-worn Bramin' to embrace 'The rule of reason' which had been exchanged for the Mughal 'rod of power' with the advent of British rule.[163] This poem, composed while Halhed was translating the Hindu law code, was more reflective of Halhed's thought than that of Hastings, who had also worked to commission and finance the translation of Islamic law codes and texts. Shortly after the composition of Halhed's panegyric, for example, Hastings obtained an Arabic text of Emperor Aurangzeb's *Fātwā al-ʿĀlmagīrī*, which he would have translated into Persian and then English.[164] Nevertheless, the notion of

161 This Sanskrit text is also known as *Manusmriti*. The translation appeared as *Institutes of Hindu Law; or the Ordinances of Menu* (Calcutta: Printed by the order of Government, 1794). James Mill, *The History of British India*, vol. 1 (Cambridge: Cambridge University Press, 2010), p. 109. For more on Jones and Mill, see Javed Majeed, *Ungoverned Imaginings: James Mill's The History of British India and Orientalism* (Oxford: Clarendon Press, 1992).

162 Nicholas B. Dirks, *Castes of Mind: Colonialism and the Making of Modern India* (Princeton, NJ: Princeton University Press, 2001), p. 15; Subrahmanyam, *Europe's India*, pp. 90–9.

163 Halhed to Warren Hastings, 22 May 1774. British Library, Add. MS 39899, ff. 2–3.

164 P. J. Marshall, 'Warren Hastings as Scholar and Patron', in A. Whiteman, J. S. Bromley and P. G. M. Dickson (eds.), *Statesmen, Scholars and Merchants: Essays in Eighteenth-Century History Presented to Dame Lucy Sutherland* (Oxford: Oxford University Press, 1973), p. 246.

India's decline under the Mughals would certainly facilitate all sorts of justifications for the rise of British dominion in its wake. Travers has even suggested that the scholarship of William Jones, with his evident preference for Sanskrit studies, marks a significant turning point in 'the hardening of attitudes towards the Mughal Empire and its officials', which he characterised as 'harsh and imperious'.[165] And yet, this had long been a popular trope. Before Dow and Burke's more nuanced accounts of Mughal government, Holwell had expressed similar sentiments to Jones and Wilkins when, in 1766, he had sympathised with those *Gentoos* 'labouring under Mahometan tyranny'.[166] Nevertheless, it was clear by the 1790s that the architecture of Mughal rule was being replaced by a more assertive Company administration.

In the 1780s increasing criticism of the government of Warren Hastings and his eventual impeachment trial meant that the question of Company administration and policy was once again publicly contested. An increasingly vocal faction in the conflict over suitable governance came from the Company's evangelical members. With the revival of evangelical Christianity towards the latter half of the century there were more and more calls for what one sermon referred to as 'the duty of attempting the propagation of the Gospel among our Mahometan and *Gentoo* subjects'.[167] Charles Grant, who after a career in India was an important member of the Company's home administration from 1794 to his death in 1823, was a strong advocate of a Christian mission.[168] An unrelenting advocate of the evangelical movement, belonging both to the Scottish Society for the Promotion of Christianity in the Highlands and Islands and the so-called 'Clapham Sect' of evangelical reformers and abolitionists, Grant saw 'the Hindoos' as practising nothing short of 'gross idolatry'.[169] In 1797, in order to convince the Company, Grant submitted a lengthy document outlining what he saw as the moral depravity of the *Hindoos* (composed in 1792, but not published until 1813). Although Grant's petitions were not in step with the general outlook of the directors at this time, he was an important figure in the Company and collected around him a circle of similarly minded evangelicals. He would raise the issue of missionary activity again when the Company's charter was up for renewal in 1813, this time publishing the

[165] Travers, *Ideology and Empire*, p. 246. [166] Holwell, *Interesting Historical Events*, vol. 1, p. 5.

[167] Joseph White, *The Duty of Attempting the Propagation of the Gospel among Our Mahometan and Gentoo Subjects* (London: Printed for G. G. J. and J. Robinson, 1785).

[168] Penelope Carson, 'Grant, Charles (1746–1823)', *Oxford Dictionary of National Biography* (Oxford: Oxford University Press, 2004); online ed., January 2008 [www.oxforddnb.com/view/article/11248, accessed 26 January 2017].

[169] Grant, *Observations on the State of Society*, p. 73.

tract for a wider audience. While the proposal was once again rejected, the attitudes to Hinduism that underwrote his concerns had become much more of a general consensus among his colleagues, and in evangelical circles.[170]

In the 1790s, following the conclusion of Hastings' trial and the appointment of Lord Cornwallis as governor-general, the question of administrative reform was raised once again. At the same time, a different conception of Britain's Asiatic empire was emerging, which P. J. Marshall describes as a more militaristic and absolute vision of imperial power, which harnessed the production of British knowledge about India's laws and customs to reduce the territory to a governable proposition.[171] Cornwallis' introduction of a 'new constitution' in 1793, which fixed land revenues and is otherwise known as the Cornwallis Code or 'permanent settlement', is widely regarded as instituting a rupture with earlier styles of governance.[172] The evidence for this has been found in the shift in the rhetorical framework surrounding property rights, with the kind of constitutional juridical language that located legitimacy in an interpretation of Indian religious and civic history being replaced by a discourse centred on the proper exercise of authority in India.[173] Grant's proposals were discounted by Company administrators like Cornwallis, who was the intended audience for the initial essay, and the 1793 Charter Act maintained that Britain would continue to govern India by Hindu and Muslim law. It was in providing the foundations for the judicial administration of this policy that William Jones was motivated to record Hindu legal thought, such as *The Institutes of Hindu Law; or the Ordinances of Menu*, which was based on translations of the *Mānava-Dharmaśāstra* (or *Manusmṛti*).[174] This pattern continued between 1795 and 1798 with the appointment of John Shore to the role of governor-general, who, despite his personal commitment to Christian evangelicalism, saw relationships of patronage between the Company and Hindu pandit elites as means to securing British interests in the territory.[175] Finally, in 1798 patterns of British governance in the Company's Indian territories changed once again. Taking the Lord-Lieutenancy of Ireland as his model, Richard Wellesley used orientalist

170 Ainslee Thomas Embree, *Charles Grant and British Rule in India* (London: George Allen & Unwin Ltd., 1962), pp. 155–6.

171 Marshall, *A Free Though Conquering People.*

172 Wilson, *The Domination of Strangers*, p. 46.

173 Mithi Mukherjee, 'Justice, War, and the Imperium: India and Britain in Edmund Burke' s*Prosecutorial Speeches in the Impeachment Trial of Warren Hastings', Law and History Review*, 23:3 (2005);Travers, *Ideology and Empire*, p. 236.

174 Jones, *Institutes of Hindu Law* (1794).

175 Rocher, 'The Career of Rādhākānta Tarkavāgīśa'.

scholarship to enhance what he saw as the necessary majesty of the position of governor-general.[176] The focal point of his administration became not the Sanskrit college at Benares that Cornwallis had committed the Company to support, but a college at Fort William, for the education of Company officials in 'the combined principles of Asiatic and European policy and government'.[177]

*

There are therefore two important contexts that shaped the formation and reception of British interpretations of Hinduism in the eighteenth century. The first is the long history of European attempts to understand and define Indian religion. What this history reveals has a twofold significance for understanding these authors. On the one hand, it demonstrates that knowledge can be produced and repurposed across competing intellectual traditions. Jesuits sought to find natural theology in Brahminical concepts in order to lay the foundations for a conversion of the *gentios* from above. These same materials provided the freethinkers of Europe with various grounds on which to criticise the demands of orthodox and dogmatic versions of Christianity. On the other hand, it also demonstrates that British interpretations of Hinduism in the eighteenth century represent a distinctive moment in that history, which marked a transition from comparative observation to the authority of claims to have penetrated the religion's theological core on the basis of translation and scriptural sources. The resulting idea of religion that they presented to the European world of letters as indigenous to India was ancient and philosophical, original and implicitly rational. The second context is eighteenth-century empire. This determined the conditions in which their interactions with Indian religion took place, and became the field in which they would have long-term practical ramifications. As the brief sketch in this chapter has aimed to illustrate, those conditions were changing, debated, and oriented to competing conceptions of what legitimate government in India should look like.

[176] Bayly, *The Imperial Meridian*, pp. 106, 111.
[177] R. G. Wellesley, 'The Governor-General's Notes with Respect to the Foundation of a College at Fort William', in Montgomery Martin (ed.), *The Despatches, Minutes, and Correspondence, of the Marquess Wellesley, KG, During His Administration in India*, vol. 2 (London, 1836), p. 340.

CHAPTER 2

John Zephaniah Holwell and the Religion of the Gentoos

John Zephaniah Holwell was described by one critic as having provided the best account 'of the religion of the *Gentoos* both in its original simplicity and in its present corruption'.[1] That this was the case is indicative of how little the reading public knew of India's varied religious traditions. Holwell's account included delinquent angels and, as we shall see, had deeply dubious origins. And yet, Holwell was nevertheless instrumental in presenting to European audiences the idea of a unified and ancient religion, native to India. These discoveries were offered over the course of three volumes in a work titled *Interesting Historical Events, Relative to the Province of Bengal*, each instalment making bolder statements about the significance of *Gentoo* doctrines than the last. In the first few pages of the first volume (1765, with a second edition in 1766), Holwell defended the *Gentoo* religion, which he saw as having been tarnished by 'imperfect and unjust' accounts.[2] In the second volume (1767) he declared the religion's 'principle tenets' to be 'satisfactory, conclusive and rational'.[3] Finally, in the third volume (1771), Holwell set out the significance of what he believed to be the 'Gentoo Bible', known as the *Shastah*, for resolving some of the obscurities and problems within Christian theology. This volume was met with less critical acclaim. In responding to Holwell's account of the importance of Indian thought for determining religious truth in general, one contributor to the highly influential *Critical Review* took particular exception. Of Holwell's enthusiastic endorsement of the *Shastah* they commented:

> After the specimens we have given of this production, it is almost superfluous to add, that it contains a system of religious doctrines, so extravagant and chimerical, as can be imposed only upon a people sunk in the grossest ignorance and credulity. We can pardon the uncultivated Gentoos for their

[1] *Annual Register* (1766), pp. 306–19: p. 307. Probably Edmund Burke.
[2] Holwell, *Interesting Historical Events*, vol. 1, p. 5.
[3] Holwell, *Interesting Historical Events*, vol. 2, p. 39.

> blind veneration of the Shastah; but the weakness of a contemporary British author, who maintains the authenticity of that spurious code of revelation, admits of no apology.[4]

The problem was not the accuracy of Holwell's account, but his validation of the doctrines contained in the *Gentoo Shastah*. This hostile reception reflects the radical swing from Holwell's liberal interpretation of the *Gentoo* religion in 1767 to what he described as his 'Christian Deist' conclusions in 1771.[5] The 1771 volume made great claims about the significance of *Gentoo* doctrines within a world history of religion. What Holwell meant by Christian deism requires some careful interpretation. This chapter will therefore provide an explanation through a detailed account of Holwell's thought in context. It will uncover Holwell's European sources, as well as his beliefs regarding the role of *Gentoo* theology within it, expounded through what he claimed to be the *Gentoo*'s primary and most original religious text, the *Shastah of Bramah*. It will explore the ways in which Holwell established the authority of these claims, before focusing on the main theological concepts around which Holwell's discussion of the *Gentoo* doctrines were oriented. These, in order, are the narrative of decline, the doctrine of metempsychosis (or transmigration of souls), theodicy and, finally, Christian deism.

J. Z. Holwell and the *Gentoo Shastah*

John Zephaniah Holwell was born in 1711 in Dublin, the son of a timber merchant in London. He was educated both at Richmond Green in Surrey and Iselmond, near Rotterdam. When his schooling ended he took up employment as a clerk in Rotterdam, but his interest waned and he decided instead to embark upon a medical career. He was thus apprenticed to a surgeon in Southwark and then, under Andrew Cooper, made senior surgeon at Guy's Hospital. In 1732 he sailed for India as surgeon's mate on an Indiaman. After spending some time serving as a surgeon on ships sailing to the Middle East, where he acquired skills in the Arabic language, he eventually settled in Calcutta in late 1736. There he became assistant surgeon to the hospital in 1740, and principal physician and surgeon to the presidency in 1746.

4 *The Critical Review, or Annals of Literature*, 32 (London, 1771), pp. 131–6: p. 136. *The Critical Review* had become an arbiter of literary taste in this period. See Frank Donoghue, *The Fame Machine: Book Reviewing and Eighteenth-Century Literary Careers* (Stanford, CA: Stanford University Press, 1996), p. 17.

5 Holwell, *Interesting Historical Events*, vol. 3, p. 91.

It was during this time that Holwell became increasingly involved in local administration, taking on a variety of civic roles within Fort William, the Company's base, such as acting as mayor in both 1747 and 1748. This involvement then extended into the administrative affairs of the Company, which would eventually lead to his embroilment in several controversies regarding its relations with the Mughal empire. The most audacious of his steps into Company administration was made on a brief sojourn in England in 1751, where he successfully convinced the Company's directors of the need to appoint him to the post of zamindar in Calcutta, making him responsible for revenue collection, as well as law and order. Holwell's subsequent efforts were met with enthusiasm, but in June 1756, the situation was dramatically altered when the nawab of Bengal, Siraj-ud-Daula, attacked and seized Fort William. Following the recapture of Calcutta by Robert Clive in January 1757, Holwell, who had survived the attack, became heavily entangled in several intrigues and further shifts of power, which left him serving briefly as governor in 1760. He was, however, quickly succeeded by Henry Vansittart, and in 1761 returned to England to turn his attention to literary pursuits.[6]

Accusations of corruption had overshadowed Holwell's departure from India, due to his involvement in a plan that deposed the nawab of Bengal, Mir Jafar, and replaced him with his son-in-law, Mir Qasim. Many supposed that Holwell had been motivated by some monetary reward in aiding the exchange of governance, and some claimed he was worth £96,000 upon his departure from office.[7] It seems that he had certainly amassed a substantial enough fortune, as on his return to England he had a grand mansion named 'Castle Hall' built as his residence. This great hall, built in Steynton (Pembrokeshire), is no longer standing, but was said to have been constructed in the 'Hindu style'.[8] In addition, some claimed that the designs included a pagoda-like structure, intended for the purposes of religious worship, at the far end of the estate.[9] The sense of mystery and religious subversion surrounding Castle Hall, even if contrived, is an appropriate epitaph to the life and work of Holwell (1711–98).

6 D. L. Prior, 'Holwell, John Zephaniah (1711–1798)', *Oxford Dictionary of National Biography* (Oxford: Oxford University Press, 2004); online ed., January 2008 [www.oxforddnb.com/view/article/13622, accessed 30 November 2016].

7 P. J. Marshall, *East Indian Fortunes: The British in Bengal in the Eighteenth Century* (Oxford: Clarendon Press, 1976), p. 236.

8 Thomas Hall, *The Lost Houses of Wales* (London: Save Britain's Heritage, 1986), pp. 68–9.

9 Tristram Stuart, *The Bloodless Revolution: Radical Vegetarians and the Discovery of India* (London: Harper Press, 2006), p. 275.

In many ways he was an impressive figure in Georgian society. His account of the events surrounding Siraj-ud-Daulah's conquest of the Company's base at Fort William, notoriously referred to as the 'Black Hole of Calcutta', was so widely read that it eventually became what Chatterjee has described as one of the most enduring myths of empire.[10] He was also made a member of the Royal Society, after publishing a treatise on smallpox inoculation.[11] Seemingly in contradiction with this image, though, were both the contents of some of his works and the reaction that they received. In particular, the final volume of *Interesting Historical Events* displayed some speculative ideas on the nature of the soul and the design of the universe which attracted both scorn and outrage. So outlandish were some of his claims for the essential similarity and common origins of Indian religion and Christianity that one reviewer jokingly hoped that Holwell might be a satirist, sarcastically suggesting that 'Mr. Holwell has evidently had an eye to the *Annus Mirabilis* of Dr. Swift' when it came to expounding his final thoughts on the significance of the *Gentoo* scriptures.[12]

Holwell's discussion of Indian theology appeared in *Interesting Historical Events Relative to the Province of Bengal*, which purported to be a much broader study of Indian history. The first volume (1765; second edition 1766) did indeed offer a snippet history of successive Mughal emperors, from Aurangzeb to Muḥammad Shah, as well as a more recent account of events in Bengal from 1711 to 1750. Both the second (1767) and third (1771) volumes, however, were dedicated entirely to conveying Holwell's thoughts and findings on 'the religious tenets of the Gentoos'. This was followed by a separate work in 1779, *A Review of the Original Principles, Religious and Moral, of the Ancient Brahmins*, which contained only the material on *Gentoo* religion from Holwell's previous works.[13] In them Holwell presented a new style and approach to Indian religion in this history of British writing. In the seventeenth century the religious practices and beliefs now associated with Hinduism were usually compared to the idolatrous gentiles of the Old Testament, or, on account of reports of a belief in reincarnation, as early precursors to Pythagorean ideas about the revolution of the soul through various forms and matter. Similarly, though

10 Partha Chatterjee, *The Black Hole of Empire: History of a Global Practice of Power* (Princeton, Princeton University Press, 2012).

11 Prior, 'Holwell, John Zephaniah (1711–1798)'.

12 *Critical Review*, 32 (1771), pp. 131–6: p. 135.

13 John Zephaniah Holwell, *A Review of the Original Principles, Religious and Moral, of the Ancient Bramins: Comprehending an Account of the Mythology, Cosmogony, Pasts, and Festivals, of the Gentoos, Followers of the Shastah* (London: Printed for D. Steel, 1779).

reports from the Jesuits and German-Danish Lutherans appeared in the early eighteenth century, British accounts of Hinduism were sparse and did not move beyond comparisons with European pagan idolatry.[14] Not long before Holwell, John Henry Grose, also a servant of the Company, had published *A Voyage to the East-Indies* (1757), which contained detailed descriptions of eighteenth-century India.[15] What made Holwell's account very different was a divergence in attitude to Indian theology that eventually led many to accuse Howell of having become seduced by Eastern religion.[16] Where Grose defined 'Gentoos' as 'Native Indians, who remain in a state of idolatry',[17] Holwell presented a rational religion, the tenets of which were 'short, pure, simple and uniform'.[18] Holwell claimed that writers like Grose had misrepresented the *Gentoos* because of a general ignorance of the true contents of its scriptures. It was up to him, therefore, to rescue them from such 'gross misrepresentation' by presenting to his readers the 'original' doctrines of the ancient Brahmins through a short translation from a mysterious manuscript, named the *Shastah*. The religion of the *Gentoos* was thus presented by Holwell as discrete from the 'complicated modes of worship' that travellers such as Grose had encountered, revealed in the original purity of their ancient texts.[19]

This self-styled mission 'to rescue distant nations'[20] from such misunderstanding has led some scholarship to align Holwell with a critical objection to Said's orientalist paradigm, on the basis that his work was motivated not by imperialist ideology, but an appreciation of Indian culture. Yet, this conceptual division falls foul of Holwell's deliberate ambiguity. Holwell was indeed deeply fascinated by and complimentary of Indian (though especially ancient) culture. This did not, however, mean that he was not also deliberately pursuing a different agenda. In fact, the authenticity of what Holwell presented as proof that previous accounts had been misconceptions points to a whole other form of misrepresentation. In short, there are many reasons to believe that his *Shastah* was not a genuine Indian text. Even if it was, in the form of some obscure manuscript, it was

[14] Marshall and Williams, *The Great Map of Mankind*, p. 103.

[15] Grose, *Voyage to the East-Indies* (1757).

[16] See, for example, *Critical Review*, 20 (1765), pp. 145–9, which compares Holwell's enthusiasm for Indian religion to Montesquieu's admiration for England.

[17] Grose, *Voyage to the East-Indies* (1757), p. xi.

[18] Holwell, *Interesting Historical Events*, vol. 2, p. 1.

[19] Holwell, *Interesting Historical Events*, vol. 2, p. 1.

[20] Holwell, *Interesting Historical Events*, vol. 1, p. 9. See, for example, Norbert Schürer's claim that Holwell was attempting to understand Hindu customs 'on Indian rather than European terms', in 'The Impartial Spectator of Satī, 1757–84', *Eighteenth-Century Studies*, 42:1 (2008), p. 24.

certainly not what he claimed it to be: one of the most important religious scriptures in Indian theology. If we accept that this was a deliberate misrepresentation, then Holwell was not offering a disinterested account of an unjustly maligned theology. Rather, he used the patchy but unprecedented knowledge of Indian religious ideas and texts to develop a new narrative about the origins of religious truth and thereby present a series of provocations to Christian thought.

Holwell claimed to have accessed the first and most original of three *Gentoo* scriptures, which were supposedly the core of the religion. This was the *Chartah Bhade Shastah of Bramah* (hereafter *Shastah of Bramah*), which he dated to 3100 BCE. He told his readers that he had spent 'eighteen months hard labour' translating the *Gentoo Shastah*, but that both the valuable manuscript and the translation he had laboured over for so long were lost in the sack of Calcutta of 1756. Miraculously, however, he was apparently able to recover 'some manuscripts' by an 'unforeseen and extraordinary event', the details of which are not explained in any of the three volumes of *Interesting Historical Events*. What is finally presented to readers is apparently Holwell's second attempt at conveying the contents of the *Shastah*, based on these recovered fragments. It is not clear whether the fruit of his 'researches' was a product of direct translation from an original manuscript, pandit instruction or a Persian translation of a Sanskrit text. That it was not a direct translation from Sanskrit, as Holwell seems to sometimes imply, we know because he shows no signs of having mastered this ancient language.[21] These layers of deliberate obfuscation have thus unsurprisingly been described by scholars as 'rather dubious', 'murky' and 'distorted'.[22] While some have attempted to suggest that Holwell's *Shastah of Bramah* may have been referring to the *Śatapatha Brāhmaṇa*, the two texts share few similarities aside from the title.[23] This is not to say that Holwell did not own antique Indian manuscripts, and in fact the Company did compensate him for those lost in the sack of Calcutta.[24] Yet, the *Shastah*, as described by Holwell, proves difficult to trace.

21 Holwell, *Interesting Historical Events*, vol. 1, pp. 3–4.

22 Franklin, *Representing India*, vol. 1, p. xiii; Trautmann, *Aryans and British India*, p. 69; Marshall, *British Discovery of Hinduism*, p. 18.

23 A. Leslie Wilson, *A Mythical Image: The Ideal of India in German Romanticism* (Durham, NC: Duke University Press, 1964), p. 24.

24 Holwell says this in *Interesting Historical Events*, vol. 1, p. 3. Those requesting compensation for losses sustained in the sack of Calcutta are listed in a letter written by council members at Fort William on 31 January 1757, in H. N. Sinha (ed.), *Fort William: India House Correspondence and Other Contemporary Papers Relating Thereto*, vol. 2, *1757–59* (Delhi: National Archives of India, 1957), pp. 192–3.

According to Holwell, the original *Chartah Bhade Shastah of Bramah* (3100 BCE) was transcribed by Bramah, an ancient 'legislator', to whom the *Gentoos* believe it was dictated by 'Birmah' (the deity Brahmā, or in Holwell's system, 'the spirit or essence of God').[25] This original was then followed by three other scriptures, each progressively declining in purity. After the original *Shastah of Brahmah*, the name of which Holwell says means literally '*four scriptures of the divine words of the mighty spirit*', came the *Chartah Bhade of Bramah* (or '*Six scriptures of the mighty spirit*'), in 2100 BCE. Here we see the obvious innovation of two additional 'scriptures of the mighty spirit' added. This had been followed, after another five hundred years (1600 BCE), by the *Aughtorrah Bhade Shastah*, or the '*eighteen books of divine words*'). The latter two were dismissed by Holwell as corrupt innovations. While the *Chartah Bhade of Bramah* was still ultimately rooted in the first, the *Aughtorrah Bhade*, with its additional fourteen books, was changed beyond recognition and the original *Shastah* was 'alluded to only'. In it, various allegorical tales, symbols and modes of worship were added, which the new commentators said were 'implied' by the original *Shastah*.[26] The introduction of this final text created, according to Holwell, 'a schism among the *Gentoos*', who had previously been of one religion 'throughout the vast empire of *Indostan*'. The Brahmins of the Malabar and Coromandel coasts had, after 'finding their brethren upon the course of the Ganges had taken this bold step in enslaving the laity' with this corrupted scripture, set about devising their own. This was the *Viedam of Brummah*, translated by Holwell as 'Divine words of the mighty spirit'. This, they claimed, was based on the second text, but according to Holwell in fact demarcated a 'new religious system'. Thus, 'the original, plain, pure, and simple tenets of the *Chartah Bhade of Bramah* (fifteen hundred years after its promulgation) became by degrees utterly lost'. That is, except 'to three or four *Goseyn* [presumably meant to indicate a caste] families', and then, apparently, Holwell, who had somehow managed to procure a manuscript copy of this forgotten text.[27]

The Indian origins of what Holwell is describing here are not at all clear. A quick analysis of the terminology used by Holwell to explain the various texts demonstrates his own creativity with Indian languages. What Holwell means by *Chartah* is difficult to determine. In the first text, *Chartah Bhade Shastah of Bramah*, which he translates as 'Four scriptures of the divine

[25] Holwell, *Interesting Historical Events*, vol. 2, pp. 3, 12, 7–8.
[26] Holwell, *Interesting Historical Events*, vol. 2, pp. 12–14.
[27] Holwell, *Interesting Historical Events*, vol. 2, p. 15.

words', it could signify 'four', and thus '*catur*' in Sanskrit. Its repetition in the title of the next text, *Chartah Bhade of Bramah* (Six scriptures of the mighty spirit), however, suggests instead that Holwell's explanatory footnote after *Bhade*, giving its meaning as 'a written book', applies to the complete phrase *Chartah Bhade*, in which case *Chartah* seems to be a different way of rendering *Sastah*, both which seem to signify the Sanskrit genre of text 'Shastra' or *śāstra*.

Trautmann has also pointed to the confusion of Bengali and Tamil in the title *Chartah Bhade Shastah*. Going with *Chartah* as meaning 'four', Trautmann suggests that in Sanskrit this would read something like *Catur Veda Śāstra*, which presents an odd combination of two distinct types of Sanskrit literature: the Veda and *śāstra*, suggesting that Holwell had misunderstood that *Bhade* and *Viedam* are transliterations of the same word, the first from Bengali and the second from the Tamil.[28] Thus, Urs App has even suggested that Holwell's basic source was not Indian in origin at all, but the 1612 work of Diogo do Couto, *Decada Quinta da Asia*. App offers a side-by-side analysis of the structure of the two authors' accounts of the different Indian scriptures and matches Holwell's *four scriptures of the divine words*, *six scriptures of the mighty spirit* and *eighteen books of divine words* with do Couto's report that there were four Vedas, six 'Xastras' and eighteen Puranas.[29] *Decada Quinta da Asia* was not an important source in the eighteenth century, but it is possible that in preparing *Interesting Historical Events* Holwell sought out other European sources. He certainly mentions others by name, such as Abraham Roger's hugely popular work *De open deure tot het verborgen heydendom* (The open door to the understanding of hidden paganism).[30]

Perhaps, though, in the purchase of Sanskrit manuscripts purporting to be the *Shastah*, Holwell had been the victim of fraud. Much later the infamous case of Francis Wilford's (1761–1822) remarkable discovery of several confirmations of biblical history in Sanskrit texts would come to serve as a cautionary tale about unscrupulous pandits. Wilford's researches were an attempt to reconstruct the ancient geography of Egypt and Ethiopia through a selection of Sanskrit sources, collected for him by his pandits. It seemed a remarkable discovery, then, that when selecting evidence from the Puranas he was able to identify a patriarchal figure, who had survived a great flood and had three sons, bearing a remarkable

[28] Trautmann, *Aryans and British India*, pp. 68–9.
[29] Urs App, *The Birth of Orientalism* (Philadelphia: University of Pennsylvania Press, 2010), p. 331.
[30] Rogerius, *De Open-Deure*.

similarity to the biblical progeny of Noah. The Japeth, Ham and Shem of *Genesis* appeared to be the Jya'Peti, C'harma and Sharma of the *Padma Purana*. In 1792 Wilford published these astonishing findings, but by 1805 was forced to retract these claims, having realised that his pandit had inserted these details into the manuscripts in order to satisfy his patron.[31] Such instances open up the possibility that Holwell was fooled, but there are some important differences in these examples, as well as discrepancies in Holwell's story. In Wilford's case, the passages were inserted over the course of an ongoing relationship with a pandit scholar, who adapted existing materials to meet the expectations of his patron. In contrast, Holwell claimed to procured two copies of the *Gentoo Shastah*, which he then spent considerable time translating. If Holwell had been sold a fake manuscript, the broker of which claimed was an authentic original, it seems a great coincidence that it happened to correspond with Holwell's already established convictions about the origins of the world and the state of human existence within it.

Indeed, the question of Holwell's use of indigenous knowledge and expertise raises further questions that point to inconsistencies in Holwell's explanation of what he was presenting to the public as the *Gentoo Shastah*. Holwell certainly suggests that he had conversations with pandit informants, though they go unnamed. Wilford's employment of pandit scholarship came at a significantly different point in the Company's rise to political power in Bengal, the administrative architecture of which increasingly rested on the patronage of indigenous scholarship.[32] Christopher Bayly thus explained Wilford's case as relating to the historical working practices of his pandits, who, used to creating new Sanskrit genealogies at the behest of their princely Maratha employers, were now negotiating offering alternative services to British patrons.[33] In contrast, Holwell, who gathered his materials in the 1750s, was writing much before this, in a period when in fact Brahmin instruction was regarded as generally inaccessible.[34] Principally, it seems he had sought assistance from members

[31] Francis Wilford, 'On Egyptand Other Countries, Adjacent to the Ca'li River, or Nile of Ethiopia, from the Ancient Books of the Hindus', *Asiatick Researches: Or Transactions of the Society*, vol. 3 (Calcutta: T. Watley, 1792). For more detail on this, see Trautmann, *Aryans and British India*, pp. 89–93; Nigel Leask, 'Francis Wilford and the Colonial Construction of Hindu Geography, 1799–1822', in Amanda Gilroy (ed.), *Romantic Geographies: Discourses of Travel 1775–1844* (Manchester: Manchester University Press, 2000).

[32] For a detailed overview of this process, see chapter 2 in Dodson, *Orientalism*.

[33] C. A. Bayly, 'Orientalists, Informants and Critics in Benares, 1790–1860', in Jamal Malik (ed.), *Perspectives of Mutual Encounters in South Asian History: 1760–1860* (Leiden: Brill, 2000).

[34] Dodson, *Orientalism*, p. 53.

of what he terms the *Koyt* (*kāyasth*), or 'tribe of writers', in determining the antiquity and varying standards of authority of the *Gentoo* scriptures. Conveniently for Holwell, these members of the laity were according to his judgement 'often better versed in the doctrines of their *Sastah* than the common run of *Bramins* themselves'.[35] He reports that they had confirmed for him 'in various conferences' that his text was the oldest and most original. The account he gives of the *Shastah*'s provenance, however, appears in quotation marks and is described as a 'recital' conveyed by 'learned *Bramins*'.[36] It is unclear whether this is in fact a reference to the *kāyasth* advisors, or whether Holwell had solicited a second opinion. Moreover, whether the quotation indicates a direct transcription or an approximation of a conversation is left unclear. This further confuses how we are meant to interpret the other sections of the text that are offered as quotations, implied by Holwell to be the fruit of his translation. It could be that they are similarly to be understood as a recital, although Holwell refers to them as a 'cited passage'.[37] Alternatively, are they a remembered account of the contents of his lost manuscripts, or a direct account of one of his 'recovered' manuscripts? If it was a translation, Holwell does not tell us from what language, though we are led, by his claims to have been 'drinking from the fountain head' of Indian religion, to believe that it must be from Sanskrit. Indeed, this is what many of his readers came to conclude. Voltaire assumed this, and so introduced Holwell as someone who had mastered 'not only the language of the modern Bramins, but also the Bracmans [sic] of antiquity' and who had 'translated some sublime passages of the first books composed in the sacred language' of ancient India.[38]

Moreover, this claim to unprecedented insight into Indian religion through linguistic knowledge, pandit consultation and access to original texts also allowed Holwell to successfully claim authority over previous accounts. With access to this supposedly ancient and therefore original and uncorrupted text, Holwell had discovered the source of Indian religious theology and was able to place it in competition with existing accounts of Indian religion based on alternative texts. Indeed, Holwell's presentation of the most corrupt and schismatic text as the *Viedam of Brummah* implied that the existing (and correct) notion that the Vedas were the most ancient

[35] Holwell, *Interesting Historical Events*, vol. 2, p. 21.

[36] Holwell, *Interesting Historical Events*, vol. 2, p. 9.

[37] Holwell, *Interesting Historical Events*, vol. 2, pp. 32–3.

[38] Voltaire, *Fragments Relating to the Late Revolutions in India, the Death of Count Lally, and the Prosecution of Count de Morangies* (London: Printed for J. Nourse, 1774), pp. 37, 82.

and important set of texts within the tradition of Indian religion had in fact been mistaken by a modern corruption.[39]

Holwell's desire to separate his textual authority from that of the *Viedam* becomes more significant when we view it in context. The notion that the Vedas constituted the religious scripture of India, in a model analogous to Europe and the Bible, had circulated in European intellectual culture since the seventeenth century.[40] Abraham Roger's hugely popular *A Door Open'd to the Knowledge of Occult Paganism* (1651) identified the 'Vedam' as 'the Heathens' Law-book' as well as the source of unity among the 'Bramines'.[41] In the early eighteenth century some awareness of the idea that several Vedic traditions existed was communicated to Europe via the *Lettres édifiantes* (1702–76), the published communiques of Jesuit missionaries in India.[42] Closer to Holwell, of course, was the *Ezour-Védam*, discussed in Chapter 1. This 'French Veda', likely the production of a Jesuit missionary, was introduced to Europe by Voltaire from 1760 onwards, but not long afterwards doubts about its authenticity began to surface and Voltaire moved on to Holwell's *Shastah* as his principal source on India.[43] In insisting on the centrality of the *Shastah* to *Gentoo* theology, and in claiming its greater antiquity, Holwell distanced himself from all the connotations associated with the Vedas in order to establish an alternative source of authority for his entirely new discovery. As Holwell put it, 'in place of drinking at the fountain head' like he had, these other authors had merely 'swallowed the muddy streams which flowed from' the later scriptures.[44]

Despite its crudity this approach was an apparent success, with Voltaire accepting Holwell's claim, and writing in 1769 that '*The Shastah* is older than the *Veda*'.[45] Indeed, Holwell's emphasis on the importance of linguistic expertise and the authority of original texts was a claim that all of the authors in this study would go on to repeat, as well as place at the centre of their own claims to expertise and exceptional insight. As Holwell put it, whereas previous authors had relied upon 'unconnected scraps and bits', he was able to offer a 'complete translation' of important *Gentoo* manuscripts.[46] Moreover, a basic colloquial grasp of the local language was not adequate;

39 Holwell, *Interesting Historical Events*, vol. 2, pp. 14–15.
40 Marshall and Williams, *The Great Map of Mankind*, p. 104.
41 Sweetman, *Mapping Hinduism*, p. 100. 42 Sweetman, *Mapping Hinduism*, p. 143.
43 Rocher, *Ezourvedam*, pp. 1–13. 44 Holwell, *Interesting Historical Events*, vol. 2, p. 63.
45 As translated by Marsh, *India in the French Imagination*, pp. 117–18. This comment appeared in Voltaire's 'Philosophie de l'histoire', which became the introduction to *Essai sur les mœurs* in 1769.
46 Holwell, *Interesting Historical Events*, vol. 2, pp. 7, 4.

the outsider must also be able to 'sufficiently trace the etymology of their words and phrases'.[47] Rather contradictorily, the main targets of his criticism were Catholic missionaries, who had in fact comprehended a number of Indian languages and dialects well before many others.[48] And yet, as Holwell's use of mainly Bengali vocabulary suggests, he had not mastered Sanskrit. Indeed, as it would be another two decades before sizable translations of Sanskrit would appear in published European accounts of Indian thought and language, critics were not equipped to challenge Holwell's claims. The actual authenticity of his account was never generally put in question, though his own enthusiasm for Indian religion was. Knowledge of India at this time was sufficiently limited for Holwell's vague linguistic authority to be convincing, and even those deeply critical of Holwell's conclusions admired his discoveries. The Scottish poet William Julius Mickle, for example, dismissed Holwell's enthusiasm for *Gentoo* tenets as a predictable cliché; like 'every liberal mind, who has conversed with the world' Holwell had become seduced by the mystical East.[49] Nevertheless, Mickle still summarised that of the existing studies of Indian religion, 'Mr. Holwell's account, upon the whole, is the most authentic'.[50]

In another ironic twist, Holwell's claims about language and textual authority also made his construction of *Gentoo* religion seem more authentic precisely on the basis that that afforded him a certain degree of objectivity. Despite the layers of confusion and dishonesty, Holwell's *Gentoo* religion appeared relatively untainted by European biases precisely because the *Shastah* and his access to it produced a format in which he was simply communicating ideas that had existed long before, in the recesses of extreme antiquity. Indeed, the appearance of objectivity was something that Holwell was careful to cultivate in his introductory remarks. He explicitly differentiated himself from the biases of his predecessors, claiming instead to have approached the *Gentoo* doctrines impartially. Previous accounts, swayed by prejudice, had been 'fallacious and unsatisfactory to an inquisitive searcher of truth'. Holwell, by contrast, had simply set out to rescue the *Gentoos* from misunderstanding.[51]

The first and most obvious targets of this polemic were the '*Popish* authors' that had preceded him. Holwell capitalised on popular anti-Catholic sentiment by summarily dismissing Jesuit authors on the basis

[47] Holwell, *Interesting Historical Events*, vol. 2, p. 9.

[48] Holwell, *Interesting Historical Events*, vol. 2, p. 7.

[49] De Camões, *Lusiad* (1778), p. 323.

[50] De Camões, *Lusiad* (1778), p. 327.

[51] Holwell, *Interesting Historical Events*, vol. 1, p. 5.

that their own religious orientation was 'more idolatrous than the system they travelled so far to stigmatize'.[52] Criticism of religious prejudice, however, was not reserved for Catholics alone. Holwell applied equally damning dismissals of Protestant writers, such as the Lutheran minister Phillipus Baldaeus (1632–71). Holwell accused Baldaeus, who had spent time in and written about the region of Malabar, of having produced 'a monster that shocks reason and probability' in his communication of the *Gentoo* doctrines. Note, too, that being located in Malabar, in Holwell's schema Baldaeus was encountering the corrupt religious practices inculcated by the schismatic *Viedam of Brummah*, not the original *Sastah* to which Holwell had access. More pointedly, though, it was the difference in their perspective that mattered most. According to Holwell, it was only the 'mistaken zeal of a Christian divine' that could excuse such a 'specimen' as Baldaeus had produced.[53] In contrast, Holwell deliberately constructed the persona of a detached observer, urging his readers to join him in divesting themselves of preconceptions. The 'ignorance, superstition and partiality to ourselves' that were commonly the cause of 'presumption and contempt of others' was to be left behind, the preserve of those 'whose knowledge of states and kingdoms extends no further than the limits of their native land'. Thus, as an extreme example, Holwell's treatment of the controversial practice of sati, or suttee, which involves immolation of widows on the funeral piers of their deceased husbands, implores readers to 'view it (as we should every other action) without prejudice' by dispensing with the tendency to regard things through the lens of '*our own* tenets and customs . . . to the injury of others'.[54]

The entirety of the introduction to the first volume of *Interesting Historical Events* is dedicated to setting up this polemic. Holwell, proficient in some languages and possessor of copies of the ancient *Shastah*, was writing to answer the 'injury and violence to letters, and the cause of humanity' done by the 'false zeal' and misrepresentations of former travellers.[55] This approach has meant that it is tempting to read Holwell as an archetypical Enlightenment thinker, and with that furnish a more apologetic interpretation of orientalist encounters with evidence of a sympathetic and impartial approach to Indian culture.[56] Such a view

[52] Holwell, *Interesting Historical Events*, vol. 1, p. 7.
[53] Holwell, *Interesting Historical Events*, vol. 2, pp. 33–4.
[54] Holwell, *Interesting Historical Events*, vol. 2, p. 97.
[55] Holwell, *Interesting Historical Events*, vol. 1, pp. 10, 7.
[56] In the matter of sati specifically, see Schürer, 'Impartial Spectator'. For this apologetic vein more generally, see Schwab, *Oriental Renaissance*, pp. 33–47.

takes Holwell's claims to be divested of prejudice too much at face value. Holwell certainly situates his enquiry in a wider project, in language widely associated with various aspects of Enlightenment thought. His calls for works on India that focus on the accumulation of knowledge in order to improve understanding, rather than those that injure 'the cause of humanity' through the propagation of ignorance, certainly echoes Diderot's description of the *Encyclopédie* project as an exploration of knowledge for the benefit of the next generation.[57] And yet, it was the goal of neither project to establish an absolutely impartial stance. In fact, as they themselves explicitly aver, this knowledge was to have some normative use; that was its value. Despite his claims to have abandoned prejudice, Holwell was viewing the *Gentoo* religion precisely with his own ends in mind. The difference was that he believed that this 'partiality to ourselves' should not colour European judgements against Indian religion, but that knowledge of other practices should instead enhance both perspectives. One of his ends was a superior understanding of all religion, and its common origins.

The Fall of the Delinquent Angels: A Narrative of Decline

We can also understand Holwell's emphasis on the importance of the *Shastah* as an authoritative basis for defining 'true' *Gentoo* doctrine as part of what religious studies calls the literary or textual bias in European conceptions of religion.[58] The fact that Holwell's discovery was referred to in reviews as the 'Gentoo bible' or 'Gentoo *Scriptures*' is a clear example of this.[59] Urs App, for example, uses Holwell's *Shastah* as an example in his overarching thesis about the significance of 'Ur-texts' in the development of orientalist discourses. In essence App suggests that in Holwell's case the creation of the *Shastah* was a means to an end, which was the propagation of a Christian 'reformist ideology'.[60] App bases this discussion on Holwell's confession that he had become 'a thorough convert' to the hypotheses of Jacob Ilive, a self-styled prophet who had been active in London between the 1730s and 1750s, during which time he had been imprisoned for blasphemy.[61] As we will see, Ilive certainly had an impact

[57] Diderot, *Encyclopédie*, p. 21.

[58] See, for example, Richard King, *Orientalism and Religion: Post-Colonial Theory, India and 'the Mystic East'* (Abingdon: Routledge, 1999), pp. 62–70.

[59] *Annual Register* (1766), pp. 306–19: p. 307; *Monthly Review*, 45 (1767), pp. 424–8.

[60] App, *Birth of Orientalism*, p. 363.

[61] Holwell, *Interesting Historical Events*, vol. 3, p. 143. For more on Ilive, see Herrick, *Radical Rhetoric*, pp. 181–204.

on the shape of Holwell's thought, but he was by no means the only influence that Holwell drew on to create the *Shastah*. As for the idea that Holwell was advocating a Christian reformism, a deeper appreciation of Holwell's engagement with a range of religiously heterodox European sources suggests that this was only part of what needs to be a much broader description of his thought. The idea that Holwell fabricated the *Shastah* to complement a certain religious agenda is, however, an important one. Understanding Holwell's journey from introducing the *Gentoo* religion in 1767 to his proclamation in 1771 that he was interpreting it as a Christian deist is the key to appreciating that agenda.

This section will introduce some of the key features of Holwell's *Shastah*, with a particular emphasis on those aspects of his interpretation that have led others to consider him a deist author. In the first instance this stems from Holwell's particular insistence that the *Gentoo* religion was essentially monotheistic, originally pure and had been corrupted by priestcraft. It is also an interpretation invited by his universalistic proposition that all practices that display reverence for the 'Deity' should be revered as 'divine worship'.[62] Holwell, who was educated in Rotterdam, a city considered by contemporaries to be the very example of religious toleration, thus argued that open-mindedness in matters of religion was an essential component to 'the cause of humanity'. As he put it, on being better informed about foreign beliefs and practices, 'we should find our minds opened, our understandings enlarged, and ourselves inspired with that benevolence for our species, without which the human form becomes rather a disgrace than ornament'.[63] It was these elements of Holwell's work that were the most conventionally deist in the moderate sense.

Holwell's insistence that monotheism was at the core of the *Gentoo* religion was not made subtle in the given extracts of the *Shastah*. The very first line of the supposed translation began with the declaration that 'God is ONE'. In a footnote Holwell explains that this statement was a translation of the word *Ekhummesha*, which he claimed literally translated as 'the one that ever was' and therefore becomes 'the eternal one' throughout the rest of the text.[64] Where Holwell has got this word from is unclear. A similar phrase, *ekam eṣa*, meaning 'this one' or 'the one is this', can be found in the

62 Holwell, *Interesting Historical Events*, vol. 1, pp. 8–9.

63 On Rotterdam, see Ernestine van der Wall, 'Toleration and Enlightenment in the Dutch Republic', in Ole Peter Grell and Roy Porter (eds.), *Toleration in Enlightenment Europe* (Cambridge: Cambridge University Press, 2000). Holwell, *Interesting Historical Events*, vol. 1, pp. 10–11.

64 Holwell, *Interesting Historical Events*, vol. 2, p. 31.

Upanishads.[65] Yet, as mentioned above, there is no substantial evidence, nor any direct claim made by Holwell, that he could grasp Sanskrit. Had Holwell been working with pandits they would have been very aware of this kind of vocabulary. The root of the word is essential to a whole host of Sanskrit terms related to singularity or unity, deriving from *eka*, simply meaning 'one'. A short list serves as illustration of this: *ekatva*, meaning unity or oneness; *ekantavada*, referring to monism; and finally *ekayana*, meaning union of thoughts and often used to describe monotheism.[66] Indeed, many of these terms hold connotations of theological significance. For example, the term *ekarasa*, primarily meaning homogeneous/uniform or 'of one essence', is an important concept in the *Upanishads*, and is occasionally used to refer to or denote *Brahman* (the essence of all being). Likewise, *ekamevadvitiyam*, meaning 'one alone' or 'without a second', also sometimes serves as shorthand for *Brahman.*[67] This was perhaps a clumsy transliteration of oral instruction rather than textual translation. Given his use of this word, it is possible that Holwell mapped an Upanishadic monism, one that held that all living things are elements of a single universal being (*Brahman*), onto his own construction of a monotheistic *Gentoo* religion.[68]

Also underlying Holwell's project 'to rescue distant nations from the gross conceptions entertained of them by the multitude' was the basic principle that all religions have a basis in natural and rational religion, and that all were equally vulnerable to corruption. This allowed him, especially with the example of the *Shastah*, to make a fundamental division between what he regarded as high and low religion. In the case of Indian religion, that was between the reasonable doctrines of the original Brahmins, those 'sacred and venerable sages', and the corrupted and superstitious practices of 'the vulgar'. Slightly complicating this was the accompanying trope that the agents of this corruption were also the Brahmins, forcing a distinction between 'the learned amongst the Bramins', who practise the tenets of the original *Gentoo* religion, and the 'common run of Bramins', who are less well versed in the original doctrines than Holwell's 'Koyt' advisors.[69] These latter examples of the priestly caste were unscrupulous in their exploitation

[65] S. S. Kapoor and M. K. Kapoor, *Hinduism: An Introduction [History, Scriptures, Prayers and Philosophy]* (New Delhi: Hemkunt Publishers, 2005), p. 36.

[66] Charles Rockwell Lanman, *A Sanskrit Reader: Text and Vocabulary and Note* (Delhi: Motilal Banarsidass, 1996), p. 136.

[67] John A. Grimes, *A Concise Dictionary of Indian Philosophy: Sanskrit Terms Defined in English* (New York: SUNY Press, 1996), pp. 124–5.

[68] Doniger, *On Hinduism*, pp. 12–13.

[69] Holwell, *Interesting Historical Events*, vol. 2, pp. 9, 21.

of the vulgar. The exclusive use of 'the *Sancrît character*' for religious matters, Holwell argued, was an invention of priestcraft, introduced by certain sects of Brahmins at the same time as '*they* first began to veil in mysteries, the simple doctrines of *Bramah*'. This deliberate obfuscation continued with the creation of the *Aughtorrah Bhade*, in which the pure *Gentoo* tenets were 'enveloped in impenetrable obscurity, allegory and fable', with the result of completely excluding the laity from that original knowledge. From that point onwards 'superstition, the sure support of priestcraft, took fast possession of the people'.[70] So different are the original and its corruption that should his study encompass, as Holwell suggests rhetorically, 'the whole of their modern ceremonials, and complicated modes of worship; the labour would be without end'. In contrast, the ancient tenets of the original *Gentoo* religion are defined as 'short, pure, simple and uniform'.[71] Holwell's own discussion of the *Gentoo* religion thus aligned itself with more deistical accounts of religious decline which tended to emphasise the role of priestcraft in the processes of degeneration.

In order to more immediately illustrate the corrupting effects of general religious decline, Holwell even provided a physical example of the purer elements of the original *Gentoo* religion in the shape of the city of 'Bisnapore' (Bishnupur). Bishnupur had been for almost one thousand years the capital of the Hindu Malla kings of Mallabhum and was a relatively independent kingdom in the time of Holwell's declared visit.[72] For Holwell, this region was untouched in a way that the regions under Mughal control were not. This thoroughly *Gentoo* region thus represented 'the only vestiges of the beauty, purity, piety, regularity, equity and strictness of the ancient *Indostan* government'.[73] Unsurprisingly, given this rather grandiose statement, some have singled out Holwell's account of 'Bisnapore' as being fictitious and a clear example of his general dishonesty.[74] Most have been led to this passage via Voltaire, who mentioned Holwell's description of the *Gentoo* city in the service of a similar claim that some areas of India had retained 'the purity of its ancient morality'.[75] Voltaire himself expressed some incredulity, accusing Holwell of 'some exaggeration'. Yet this appears to be a mistake on

70 Holwell, *Interesting Historical Events*, vol. 2, pp. 13, 14, 17.
71 Holwell, *Interesting Historical Events*, vol. 2, p. 1.
72 Trudy Ring, Robert M. Salkin and Sharon La Boda (eds.), *International Dictionary of Historic Places: Asia and Oceania* (London: Taylor & Francis, 1996), pp. 136–8.
73 Holwell, *Interesting Historical Events*, vol. 1, p. 198.
74 See, for example, App, *Birth of Orientalism*, p. 301.
75 Holwell, *Interesting Historical Events*, vol. 1, p. 212.

Voltaire's part, who claimed that Holwell relayed that it took sixty days to cross the territory, when the text in fact states that it took sixteen days.[76]

Aside from this and despite the exaggerated language, Holwell's account may not deserve so much incredulity. In this period Bishnupur was a distinctly Hindu settlement. Holwell's remark that 'There are in this precinct, no less than three hundred and sixty considerable Pagodas or places of public worship; erected by this Rajah and his ancestors' was in fact an accurate description of the famously unique and striking architecture of the city.[77] Bishnupur is famous for its prominent terracotta temples, constructed in the seventeenth and early eighteenth centuries, of which there are more than in any other city in West Bengal.[78] In fact, Holwell's emphasis on the distinctly 'Gentoo' character of the city was not unreasonable. A much-emphasised aspect of the city's history is that Gopal Singh, who ruled Bishnupur from 1730 to 1745, was considered to be deeply religious and committed to the worship of Vishnu (Vaishnavism). By the time Holwell visited this city, scholarship has suggested that it had a strongly blended culture of Brindavani Vaishnavism, Mughal and Rajput cosmopolitan traditions.[79] Gopal Singh's concern for the spiritual well-being of his subjects was channelled into the commissioning of public temples and festivals, the legacy of which shaped the character of the region.[80] That Holwell perceived there to have been something particularly unique about this province, which for him was evidence of its faithfulness to ancient doctrine, seems less of an extreme claim in this context.

Geographical examples of *Gentoo* worship had another important role in demonstrating Holwell's narrative of purity and decline. In contrast to 'Bisnapore', Holwell painted the southern regions of 'Indostan' as most deeply entrenched in superstition. As was mentioned earlier in this chapter, Holwell set up the authority of the *Shastah*, including its formulations of varying fidelity to the original, in direct competition with the *Viedam*. As well as wiping the slate clean for his own interpretation of *Gentoo* religion, this distinction was also related to the theme of doctrinal purity and corruption. After drawing a stark contrast between the 'purity and chaste manners of the *Shastah* with the great absurdities and impurities of the

[76] Holwell, *Interesting Historical Events*, vol. 1, p. 197.

[77] Holwell, *Interesting Historical Events*, vol. 1, p. 199.

[78] Ring, Salkin and La Boda, *International Dictionary*, pp. 136–8.

[79] Kumkum Chatterjee, 'Cultural Flows and Cosmopolitanism in Mughal India: The Bishnupur Kingdom', *Indian Economic and Social History Review*, 46:2 (2009).

[80] Holwell, *Interesting Historical Events*, vol. 1, p. 136; Binod Sankar Das, *Changing Profile of the Frontier Bengal, 1751–1833* (Bengal: Mittal Publications, 1984), p. 59.

Viedam', Holwell went on to claim that the '*Gentoos* of the *Mallabar* and *Cormandel* coasts' followed the *Viedam*,[81] whereas '*Gentoos* of the provinces of *Bengall*; and . . . all the *Gentoos* of the rest of *India*, commonly called *India proper*' were followers of the *Shastah*.[82] Holwell's decision to emphasise this geographical division was intertwined with his desire to establish an authoritative source outside of the previous productions of religiously motivated authors such as Baldaeus, who had written about Malabar, and the Jesuits in the south of India. Holwell's critiques of prejudiced ministers, '*Popish* authors' and his account of the various *Shastahs* neatly knitted into this grand narrative of decline as a result of priestcraft, as a universal phenomenon. Holwell thus paints an absurd picture in which the idolatrous Catholics are learning about *Gentoo* religion from the equally idolatrous and superstitious followers of the *Viedam*, placing Holwell in a position to to attack the impression given by the Jesuits, because it was based on 'hearsay from *Hindoos*, probably as ignorant as themselves.'[83]

This paradigm was universal. Holwell was not interested in the specific conditions that led to this particular corruption of *Gentoo* religion; instead, he intended to make a case for its significance for understanding religious truth in the abstract. Thus, Holwell reminded his readers, in this process of decline 'the *Gentoos* are not singular' and instead he poses the idea that 'the original text of every theological system, has, we presume, from a similar cause, unhappily undergone the same fate.'[84] Not only was this narrative of decline universal, so were the forms of superstition in which it was manifested. Obvious enough for most British authors were the parallels between popular conceptions of popery and the superstition of the idolatrous *Gentoos*. Yet, Holwell's critique extended further still, to a general distaste for the 'intemperate zeal of religious vanity' across the confessional divide. This, argued Holwell, was not a historical problem, but a contemporary 'fashion' which led to the unwarranted depreciation of other religions, with enthusiasts destroying 'the peace and tranquillity of their *poor* fellow Christians'.[85] Holwell's deism was an expression of the idea that not only were various religious traditions expressions of an essentially minimal rational religion, but that corruption through superstition and zeal was also part of a universal pattern of decline.

[81] Holwell, *Interesting Historical Events*, vol. 1, p. 12.
[82] Holwell, *Interesting Historical Events*, vol. 1, p. 11.
[83] Holwell, *Interesting Historical Events*, vol. 1, p. 6.
[84] Holwell, *Interesting Historical Events*, vol. 2, p. 1.
[85] Holwell, *Interesting Historical Events*, vol. 1, p. 8.

When we turn to the contents of Holwell's *Shastah*, though, his application of a paradigm of decline went much further than the simple label of deism would suggest. Conventionally enough, it was present in Holwell's grand narrative of the religion, which strayed from the purity of the original *Shastah* to an eventual schism and the production of the *Viedam*. Yet, decline was also central to the creation narrative presented within the *Shastah*; which conveyed how this earth was fashioned for the punishment of once pure 'delinquent angels'.[86] According to Holwell, this was the central truth of the *Shastah*, communicated from God to the 'Legislator' Bramah. It revealed that 'the Eternal One' had created angelic beings in the order of Birmah, Bistnoo, Sieb (Brahmā, Viṣṇu, Śiva) and then Maisasoor. Holwell's diabolical Maisasoor was taken from the 'buffalo demon' figure Mahīśāsura, who had used his gradually accumulated power to commit atrocities, most commonly depicted at the moment of his defeat at the hands of the goddess Druga (a manifestation of the combined powers of Brahmā, Viṣṇu and Śiva).[87] In Holwell's account, Maisasoor instigated a rebellion among the lower deities, the Debtah-Logue (*devatāloka*). In response to this failed coup, the 'Eternal One' condemned them to eternal punishment. With the intervention of Bistnoo, this was altered to offer the prospect of returning to grace by earning salvation through successive states of existence, transmigrating through eighty-eight different forms, the last two stages of which were *Ghoji* (cow) and *Mhurd* (man). It was in this final stage that the soul must show itself to be truly reformed in order to gain entry to the ladder of fifteen planets, or 'Boboons' (*navagraha*) until finally reaching heaven. Thus, according to Holwell's Eastern *Paradise Lost*, since its creation, the earth has been in a state of decline, in which the consumption of animal flesh and moral corruption has led these fallen spirits even further from their celestial origins.[88]

Holwell's account of what we would more commonly understand to be the concept of reincarnation was thus woven into a story that combined a mixture of Indian religion and Christian mythology. While the theology of reincarnation in the tradition of Hinduism is complex and varied among the schools of philosophy, the idea of rebirth is a central tenet to many key texts. Holwell was possibly exposed to these ideas through consultation with pandits, who appear to be the most likely sources for those broadly

[86] Holwell, *Interesting Historical Events*, vol. 2, p. 20.

[87] Charles Phillips, Michael Kerrigan and David Gould (eds.), *Ancient India's Myths and Beliefs* (New York: Rosen Publishing, 2012), pp. 98–100.

[88] Holwell, *Interesting Historical Events*, vol. 2, pp. 35–60.

correct aspects of Holwell's knowledge.[89] In addition, Holwell's attachment to the idea that a celestial revolt was the origin of evil does offer some interesting points of overlap. Wendy Doniger has suggested that the existence of similar ideas in Christian and Hindu mythologies means that the two were very easily fused and accommodated into tribal religious beliefs about 'the Fall'.[90] Referring specifically to Holwell's account, Doniger suggests that he extrapolated from Hindu beliefs about a set of demons cast out of heaven and sent to the earth. Moreover, in Holwell's narrative Śiva (Sieb) drives them out, which corresponds with some typical patterns in some Hindu mythologies.[91] Indeed, Holwell was touching upon an important discussion within Hindu theology itself, which also sought an origin of evil in the beginning of human action, while at the same time insisting on a cycle of rebirth. Holwell was possibly able to simplify these ideas into a general understanding of karma as free will and the origin of evil, thereby connecting a crude understanding of reincarnation with some notion of an original Fall.[92] Yet, although featuring a cast of Hindu deities, Holwell's angelic fall seems more likely to have been based on various Christian sources. The first and most obvious is the work of John Milton, although Howell twists this on its head, suggesting that Milton copied the idea of a heavenly rebellion from the Brahmins, via Greek and Roman 'Sages', with an 'extravagance of genius and invention'.[93] Diogo do Couto's *Decada quinta da Asia* (1612) also featured fallen angels, and App claims that Couto's report of his travels 'was used by Holwell who could handle Portuguese'.[94] Even if Holwell could grasp Portuguese (he nowhere claims to), he need not have had necessarily read this text to have formulated this idea. A firmer connection is the one directly referenced by Holwell, also identified by App, which were the ideas of Jacob Ilive, a neo-Gnostic prophet. Ilive's central message was that 'Man is an Apostate Angel and a Body' and that the earth was 'Hell', designed for their punishment.[95] As we shall see, though, there were several more immediate sources for Holwell's ideas, with the notion of a 'pre-existent lapse' of human souls in heaven as fundamental to his reinterpretation of many Christian concepts in the light of his *Gentoo* discoveries.

89 See Wendy Doniger O'Flaherty (ed.), *Karma and Rebirth in Classical Indian Traditions* (Berkeley: University of California Press, 1980).

90 Wendy Doniger O'Flaherty, *The Origins of Evil in Hindu Mythology* (Berkeley: University of California Press, 1976), p. 10, 69, 76.

91 Doniger O'Flaherty, *Origins of Evil*, pp. 68–9.

92 For discussion of karma and free will, see Doniger O'Flaherty, *Origins of Evil*, pp. 19–20.

93 Holwell, *Interesting Historical Events*, vol. 2, p. 45.

94 App, *Birth of Orientalism*, p. 330.

95 Jacob Ilive, *The Oration Spoke and Joyner's Hall* (London: T. Cooper, 1733), p. 59.

The Doctrine of Metempsychosis

Holwell's treatment of the doctrine of metempsychosis is the crux in understanding his work. Despite not appearing until the third volume of *Interesting Historical Events*, published in 1771, its inclusion in the full title of the 1765 edition demonstrates Holwell's intention to produce a dissertation on metempsychosis from the outset:

> *Interesting Historical Events, Relative to the Provinces of Bengal, and the Empire of Indostan. With a Seasonable Hint and Perswasive to the Honorable the Court of Directors of the East India Company as Also the Mythology and Cosmogony, Facts and Festivals of the Gentoos, Followers of the SHASTAH. And a Dissertation on the METEMPSYCHOSIS, Commonly, Though Erroneously, Called the PYTHAGOREAN Doctrine*

Yet, Holwell's conclusions about the implications of this 'doctrine' for a European religious landscape are not fully elaborated until the third and final volume of *Interesting Historical Events*, which was published much later in 1771. This delay was very likely attributable to its extraordinary content. But Holwell still had plenty to say about the significance of metempsychosis in the previous book (1767).

Metempsychosis, a term taken from Greek philosophy, refers to the movement of the soul between bodies after physical death. Among most European sources the metempsychosis expressed in Eastern religions was relegated to the realm of mysticism. In contrast, discussions of 'transmigration' as expressed in classical philosophy were designated ancient allegories for the principles of natural philosophy. In one of Holwell's sources, *Essay of Transmigration, in Defense of Pythagoras: Or a Discourse of Natural Philosophy* (1692), for example, an Aristotelian distinction between the rational soul and the sensitive (or vegetative) spirit allows its author, Bulstrode Whitelock, to conclude that Pythagoras was simply referring to the redistribution of the sensitive spirit into other material forms through the death of the body.[96] This is echoed in Toland's rationalist vindication of Pythagoras, who according to this account 'did not believe the Transmigration which has made [him] so famous to Posterity', since, 'he meant no more than the eternal Revolution of all Forms in Matter'.[97] Thus, when Holwell stated that '*Pythagoras* took the doctrine of *Metempsychosis*, from the *Bramins*', he was entirely reversing

[96] Bulstrode Whitelock, *Essay of Transmigration, in Defense of Pythagoras: Or a Discourse of Natural Philosophy* (London [s.n.], 1692), p. 79.

[97] John Toland, 'The History of the Soul's Immortality', in *Letters to Serena* (London: Bernard Lintot, 1704), p. 57.

this trope.[98] While most seventeenth- and eighteenth-century commentators had inferred that Indian ideas about reincarnation were derivative of classical concepts, Holwell attempted to convince his readers that the opposite was true.

As well as matters of natural philosophy, other attempts to separate classical accounts of metempsychosis from Eastern mysticism cast the former as a didactic tool, used to inculcate moral virtues. Whitelock suggests, for example, that Plato's moral pedagogy of punishment for effeminate men by way of transmigration into the body of a women, or lascivious people into swine, etc., is a story of 'good Design' born of moral necessity. Such 'pious lies' are transferred into social customs in the West, whereas they become literal errors in the East.[99] Again, Holwell reverses this paradigm, claiming instead that the literal truth of the *Shastah* was corrupted by the Greeks, '*Persian* and *Egyptian* Magi', who obscured its original tenets with the 'unintelligible jargon of divinity'.[100] In contrast, the original doctrine, as conceived of by the Brahmins, was 'simple and sublime'.[101] The spread and eventual obscurity of the doctrine of metempsychosis thus features as a parallel narrative of decline, outside India, to that of the *Gentoo* religion within. Just as the simplicity of the *Shastah* was gradually corrupted, the essential truth of metempsychosis, once known to humanity, was eventually lost due to the priestcraft of the Egyptian magi.

When using the term 'metempsychosis', Holwell is invoking not just the idea of transmigrating souls but also the creation story with which it is aligned. For Holwell, the *Shastah*'s key purpose was to communicate to humanity that 'mortal bodies were prepared by God, for rebel angels, in which they were for space to be imprisoned, and subject to natural and moral evils, more or less painful in proportion to their original guilt, and through which they were doomed to transmigrate under eighty-nine different forms, the last into that of man'.[102] Having set this out, Holwell confidently states that his readers 'are now possessed for the first time of a faithful account of the metempsychosis of the Bramins – commonly called the transmigration of souls'.[103] Holwell's portrayal of what we would more readily recognise as reincarnation was thus rooted in the idea

[98] Holwell, *Interesting Historical Events*, vol. 2, p. 26.

[99] Chi-ming Yang, 'Gross Metempsychosis and Eastern Soul', in Frank Palmeri (ed.), *Humans and Other Animals in Eighteenth-Century British Culture: Representation, Hybridity, Ethics* (Farnham: Ashgate, 2006), p. 23.

[100] Yang, 'Gross Metempsychosis and Eastern Soul', pp. 27–8.

[101] Holwell, *Interesting Historical Events*, vol. 2, p. 60.

[102] Holwell, *Interesting Historical Events*, vol. 2, p. 62.

[103] Holwell, *Interesting Historical Events*, vol. 2, p. 65.

that human suffering existed in proportion to the guilt accorded to the role played in Maisasoor's celestial rebellion. Though more tentative at this stage, Holwell still made some bold claims for the ability of the doctrines of metempsychosis, as expounded in this creation story, to solve some of the unanswered questions in Christian theology, before the eventual appearance of the *Dissertation on Metempsychosis* in 1771. The main theological problem to which it could supposedly provide an answer was no small issue. It was, for Holwell, a vital component of theodicy, the conundrum posed by the existence of evil in a perfect creation made by a benevolent God. To the question, as Holwell put it, 'Whence the origin and existence of *moral evil*?', the doctrine of metempsychosis provided an answer that was more 'satisfactory, conclusive, and rational' than any he had come across.[104] Thus, he reasoned accordingly, if original sin was committed by rebellious angels, prior to the creation of humanity, and their position on earth is determined in 'proportion to their original guilt', then souls do not enter the world as innocents and God is absolved of charges of unjust punishment. Holwell set this statement up in contrast to the argument of an unnamed author who had sought to explain that 'God would have made all things perfect, but that there was in matter an evil bias,' and so it was not God but his materials that were to blame.[105] This was in fact a direct quote, taken from a particularly unpopular work: *Free Inquiry into the Nature and Origin of Evil* (1756) by Soame Jenyns. Heavily criticised by Samuel Johnson in *The Literary Magazine* for its presentation of a superficial set of solutions to a complex theological problem, Jenyns' work was made notorious for its clumsy handling of the optimistic philosophy of suffering usually associated with Alexander Pope's *Essay on Man* (1733–4) and roundly critiqued in Voltaire's *Candide* (1759).[106] By also censuring Jenyns, Holwell aligned himself with the authoritative side of a relatively contemporary debate (despite obviously subverting that too), as well as positioning his theory as an alternative.

Holwell's full discussion of metempsychosis did not appear until the final volume of *Interesting Historical Events*, published in 1771. It is at this point that Holwell's thought takes a decidedly heterodox turn. The complete title of the dissertation included the suggestion that it would feature '*an Occasional Comparison between Them* [the doctrines of the *Gentoos*] *and the Christian Doctrines*'. This was, however, somewhat of a misnomer since

[104] Holwell, *Interesting Historical Events*, vol. 2, p. 39.
[105] Holwell, *Interesting Historical Events*, vol. 2, p. 39.
[106] For a discussion of Johnson's review, see Brian Hanley, *Samuel Johnson as Book Reviewer: A Duty to Examine the Labors of the Learned* (London: Associated University Presses, 2001 [1961]), p. 119.

this 'occasional comparison' actually spanned most of the 227-page volume. Among the deeply controversial ideas presented in the text was that Christianity was not simply compatible with early *Gentoo* doctrines, but in fact derivative of them. Holwell suggested that the doctrines 'preached first by *Bramah*', received from Brimah (Brahmā), were the same as those preached 'afterwards by *Christ*'. That is, for Holwell, what was true in the simple Christianity of Christ had already been part of the original tenets of the Brahmins and that, therefore, 'it is no violence to faith, if we believe that *Birmah* and *Christ* is one and the same individual celestial being'. Furthermore, Holwell suggested that this one celestial being had, in the style of a Hindu avatar, 'appeared at *different* periods of time, in *distant* parts of the earth, under *various* mortal forms' to deliver the primitive truths of religion. Similarly, the warlike archangel Michael was Shiva, and Gabriel was the benevolent Vishnu and together, these divine beings had made the original trinity.[107] Thus, in a clever twist of rhetoric Holwell suggested that it was therefore 'by the mouth of *Christ* (styled *Birmah* by the easterns)' that God delivered to creation the moral guides for their restoration.[108]

This equation of Christ and Birmah is not simply significant because of its potential connotations of blasphemy, but also for its more vital connection with a number of debates about the nature of the material body and the soul.[109] It is on the one hand the ultimate expression of Holwell's universalism, and on the other, the logical consequence of his adherence to a certain set of contemporary heterodoxies. For Holwell, this belief in 'the transmigration of souls' not only explains how there are several Hindu incarnations of different divine beings, 'in such ways as *Elijah* and St. *John* the Baptist' are 'one and the same spirit, from the intimation of the prophet *Malachi*', but also solved several other theological problems, principal of which was the question of human and animal suffering.[110] While this has much less to do with how Holwell's approach to Hinduism was read and received in the eighteenth century, the majority of responses to which were based on his 1767 account, the following section will consider the 1771 *Dissertation* in detail both because of what it tells us about how Holwell decided to construct the *Shastah* in 1767 and what it tells us about his own

[107] Holwell, *Interesting Historical Events*, vol. 3, pp. 72–3.

[108] Holwell, *Interesting Historical Events*, vol. 3, p. 80.

[109] James A. Herrick, 'Blasphemy in the Eighteenth Century: Contours of a Rhetorical Crime', in Wayne Hudson, Diego Lucci and Jeffery R. Wigelsworth (eds.), *Atheism and Deism Revalued: Heterodox Religious Identities in Britain, 1650–1800* (Farnham: Ashgate, 2014), pp. 102.

[110] Holwell, *Interesting Historical Events*, vol. 3, p. 82.

religious beliefs and attitudes in relation to the interpretation of Hinduism. What needs to be stressed as important here, though, is the fundamental departure that Holwell's 1767 interpretation of the doctrine of metempsychosis presented from already existing ideas about Indian philosophy and theology. While most took these 'Pythagorean' aspects of Brahmin thought to be derivative, it was Holwell's 'belief and conclusion' that 'the original tenets of *Brahma* are most ancient; that they are truly original, and not copied from any other system of theology, that had ever been promulged to, or obtruded upon the belief of mankind'.[111]

Theodicy

In the *Dissertation on Metempsychosis* Holwell reaffirms the creation story outlined in the previous volume, but this time as a summary with much of the specific 'Indianised' terminology removed. As Holwell himself put it, after having 'floated on the materials' left to him after the wreck of Calcutta, he was ready to 'launch out into the ocean of hypothesis and speculation'. Instead of reciting the *Shastah*, as in the previous volume, Holwell instead supplies a list of what he sees as being the 'Primitive Truths' common to all religion. These include the fairly conventional belief in 'the being of a God', as well as the not so conventional rebellion of angelic beings, leading to the idea that 'man is in a state of punishment and probation for a transgression committed in a prior state of existence'.[112] Holwell's primary commitment was, therefore, to the doctrine of metempsychosis and not the *Shastah*, which goes unmentioned until page sixteen. As was the case in the 1767 volume, the issue at stake was theodicy. Observing that 'the goodness of God stands most evidently impeached in the wild supposition that he could possibly create a race of beings subjected to misery, without some cause of offence on their parts', Holwell sets about finding an explanation for the existence of evil, setting out from the premise that since no cause on earth can present itself, the cause must have been an '*offence* in some *former state* of the soul's existence'.[113]

From this starting precept, the *Dissertation* details a complex engagement with a wide array of authors who had also posed the possibility of transmigrating souls and a pre-existent lapse as a potentially more satisfactory

[111] Holwell, *Interesting Historical Events*, vol. 2, p. 23.
[112] Holwell, *Interesting Historical Events*, vol. 3, pp. 1, 4–5.
[113] Holwell, *Interesting Historical Events*, vol. 3, p. 138.

theodicy. Among these was Jacob Ilive. Included by Herrick in his study of the English deists, Ilive argued for a religion of reason, while also affirming the pre-existence of human souls and maintaining that earth was devised for their punishment. In line with more conventional deist thinking, Ilive also held that Christianity, as it was practised, was a corruption of early rational religious truths.[114] The concept of imprisoned souls was not, however, an idea solely of Ilive's invention. In the seventeenth and eighteenth centuries, a revival of Gnosticism's focus on the cosmological origins of the world appealed to several different shades of radicals, including those dabbling in theories of metempsychosis and referred to as 'Pythagoreans'.[115] As well as Ilive's ideas, Holwell's *Dissertation* consisted of a wide-ranging discussion on metempsychosis and theodicy, in which he mentioned the positions of Locke and Leibniz, as well as exploring in greater detail the ideas of various theologians, such as Capel Berrow (1716–82) and the Cambridge Platonists.[116]

In early Enlightenment debates the radical separation of spirit from matter posed by Cartesian dualism opened up the possibility of a conceptual return to classical notions about transmigration.[117] It was in answering Descartes, who they nevertheless regarded as an ally in the conflict with materialism, that thinkers associated with the Cambridge Platonists articulated a philosophy of the soul that emphasised its pre-existence.[118] Seeking to counterbalance what they saw as the deprecation of human reason and agency in Reformed, and specifically Puritan, religious doctrine, these thinkers revived the theological legacy of church father Origen of Alexandria, which represented a viable rebuttal to the bleak orthodoxies of Augustinian anthropology.[119] It was in relation to this that the emphasis in theories of transmigration on the extraterrestrial existence of the soul proved useful for the construction of theological arguments.[120] Some Cambridge Platonists, most notably Ralph Cudworth (1617–88) and Henry Moore (1614–87), were, like Holwell, brought to consider transmigration as an aspect of theodicy. In particular, transmigration was posited

114 Herrick, *Radical Rhetoric*, pp. 181–2.
115 Herrick, 'Blasphemy in the Eighteenth Century', p. 144.
116 Holwell, *Interesting Historical Events*, vol. 3, p. 78.
117 Peter Harrison, 'Animal Souls, Metempsychosis, and Theodicy in Seventeenth-Century English Thought', *Journal of the History of Philosophy*, 31.4 (1993), p. 521.
118 Harrison, 'Animal Souls', p 532.
119 Rhodri Lewis, 'Of "Origenian Platonisme": Joseph Glanvill on the Pre-Existence of Souls', *Huntington Library Quarterly*, 69:2 (2006), p. 267.
120 Yang, 'Gross Metempsychosis and Eastern Soul', p. 16.

as an alternative to Calvinist conceptions of predestined election and the accompanying perceptions of injustice that such a harsh doctrine inspired. Rather than a God who had seemingly created humanity with the intention of condemning its majority to eternal damnation, the Cambridge Platonists looked to the work of Origen, and suggested that the apparent inequalities and injustices of this present life could be explained by his hypothesis of pre-existing souls.[121] Moreover, while the Cambridge Platonists generally stopped short of a full endorsement of transmigration as a pattern of reincarnation, there were tentative suggestions that tended towards this. Joseph Glanvill (1636–80), for example, suggested that the souls of deceased infants might await embodiment in another terrestrial vehicle, while others, more tangentially related to the Cambridge circle, suggested that transmigration was possible since one lifetime was too short an existence to achieve salvation. Most especially, revived Origenism, coupled with a theory of pre-existence, tended towards metempsychosis as the best possible explanation of why some of creation appeared to be, as Glanvill put it, 'faultlessly miserable'.[122]

Into the eighteenth century this controversial but not uncommon debate was taken up by a number of theologians grappling with the role of animal suffering in theodicy. In the strain of Cambridge Platonist thought, Cudworth paid the most attention to the status of animal souls. It was in grappling with Descartes' configuration of animals as mere 'beast-machines' that he developed his account of animal life. Bridging the gap between the Cartesian distinction of *res cogitans* and *res extensa*, Cudworth instead posited a concept of the soul that emphasised 'Internal Self-activity' or 'Vital Autokinesie', the essence of living creatures and part of providential design, stimulated as it was by some external force.[123] Incorporating this into the revival of Origenism, Cudworth thus proposed that it was possible that the souls of animals might also pre-exist.[124] Others expressed an interest in the idea that animals could express piety, following Pliny's suggestion that elephants demonstrated pious behaviours which was repeated by Henry More (and Montaigne) in his writings on natural history.[125]

[121] Anon [George Rust?], *A Letter of Resolution Concerning Origen and the Chief of His Opinions* (London, 1661).

[122] Letter reproduced in Charles Mullet, 'A Letter by Joseph Glanvill on the Future State', *Huntingdon Library Quarterly*, 1 (1937), p. 454.

[123] Ralph Cudworth, *The True Intellectual System of the Universe*, John Harrison (ed.), 3 vols. (London: Thomas Tegg, 1845 [1678]), vol. 1, p. 81; vol. 3, pp. 416, 438.

[124] Cudworth, *The True Intellectual System*, vol. 2, p. 357, vol. 3, p. 90.

[125] Peter Harrison, *The Bible, Protestantism, and the Rise of Natural Science* (Cambridge: Cambridge University Press, 1998), p. 188.

In the eighteenth century, Jesuit Father Guillaume Hyacinthe Bougeant's *Amusement philosophique sur le langage des bestes* (1739) was written as a 'letter to a Lady' and set out, with mock seriousness, the view that animals possessed the same passions, vices and morals as humans and that they were therefore also subject to the same system of justice and punishment for sin.[126] Skirting even more closely to heresy was his further supposition that they were perhaps inhabited by demons, suffering the torments of brute creation before their final judgement. According to Bougeant this explained both their misery, which they deserved, and their apparent intelligence.[127] In a further step, Bougeant reasoned that if these fallen creatures were merely animating animal forms, there was no reason they could not transmigrate after the death of their corporeal host, in the manner of the Pythagorean and Indian systems.[128]

Despite the popularity of the book, its sense of humour was apparently lost on Bougeant's colleagues and as well as being forced to retract a number of offending passages he was briefly exiled from Paris. Voltaire later commented that Bougeant had inadvertently revived 'an article of the faith of the most ancient oriental priests'. Notably, this comment came in an edition of Voltaire's *Philosophical Dictionary* which discussed 'The Metempsychosis of the Brahmins', the majority of which appears to have been taken from Holwell's 1767 edition of *Interesting Historical Events*, made particularly clear by his direct reference to Holwell's *Shastah* and the replication of terms used by Holwell, such as 'Mhurd' for man and 'Onderah' for Hell.[129] In turn, it is likely that Holwell will have been aware of Bougeant, whose thesis also excited controversy in Britain, where it appeared in two separate translations.[130]

Among those discussing animal suffering, metempsychosis and theodicy in the eighteenth century were two of Holwell's most cited sources, mentioned in the same passage as Ilive: Richard Dean and Capel Berrow. It was Holwell's contention that these authors were grasping at the general

126 Guillaume Hyacinthe Bougeant, *Amusement philosophique sur le langage des bestes* (Paris: Chez Antoine Van Dole, 1739).

127 Aaron Garrett, 'Human Nature', in Knud Haakonssen. ed.), *The Cambridge History of Eighteenth-Century Philosophy* (Cambridge: Cambridge University Press, 2000), vol. 1, p. 169.

128 Guillaume Hyacinthe Bougeant, *A Philosophical Amusement upon the Language of Beasts* (London: T. Cooper, 1739), pp. 23–6.

129 Translation taken from *A Philosophical Dictionary from the French of M. de Voltaire*, John G. Gorton (trans.), vol. 2, 2nd ed. (London: John & H. L. Hunt, 1824), p. 55. Voltaire also faithfully retells Holwell's account of the angelic fall in the *Shastah* in the section of the *Philosophical Dictionary* that was headed 'Angels', vol. 1, pp. 147–51.

130 Two London editions, printed for T. Cooper, appeared in 1739 and 1740, while another translation was published in Dublin, printed by Cor. Wynne, again in 1739.

truth of *Shastah*, without realising it. The Reverend Richard Dean, master of Middleton Grammar School, wrote and published *An Essay on the Future Life of Brutes, Introduced with Observations upon Evil, Its Nature and Origin*, shortly after Holwell's first two volumes of *Interesting Historical Events* in 1768. That this work provoked interest and discussion in the eighteenth-century world of letters is testified to by James Boswell's recounting of a conversation on the matter with Samuel Johnson in 1767.[131] Dean was wrestling with a similar problem to Holwell, which was 'the Nature and Origin of Evil', and more specifically, the question as to why in this context 'dumb Animals are liable to infelicity as well as Men'.[132] Dean's solution was to deny the idea that animals were unintelligent beings, and instead make the case that they too had a claim to immortality. Distinguishing between the different approaches to theodicy as Manichaean (dualistic cosmology of good and evil), Leibnizian (as caricatured in Voltaire's *Candide*) and 'Modern' (the work of thinkers like Jenyns), Middleton defines his own position as the belief that natural evil derives from moral evil, and that, therefore, animals were also suffering the consequences of the Fall.[133] To this, Holwell adds 'we wish he had said *the angelic fall*; possibly he meant it'.[134] It seems fairly certain that he did not; Dean had included a discussion of transmigration in the preface, describing it as a 'witty invention' and a 'noble device' that deterred the ancients from moral corruption, but went no further.[135] Nevertheless, Holwell goes on to conclude that had Dean known of the Brahmins' account of metempsychosis he would have surely embraced it, since it '*alone* rationally accounts for, and reconciles their existence as intelligent free agents doomed to misery'.[136]

Another of the works cited by Holwell in relation to theodicy and animal suffering was also authored by Anglican cleric rector of Finningley, Capel Berrow (1715–82). Berrow's *A Pre-Existent Lapse of Human Souls* was a more strident endorsement of the theory of a heavenly rebellion, and consequently presents an intriguing insight

[131] James Boswell, *The Life of Samuel Johnson*, vol. 1 (London [s.n.], 1791), p. 301. Boswell suggests that Johnson discourages the conversation, on account that he discouraged talk on matters outside of Christian orthodoxy.

[132] Richard Dean, *An Essay on the Future Life of Brute, Introduced with Observations upon Evil, Its Nature and Origin*, vol. 2 (London: Printed for G. Kearsly, 1768), pp. 1–3.

[133] Aaron V. Garret, 'Animal Language, Animal Passions and Animal Morals', in *Animal Rights and Souls in the Eighteenth Century*, vol. 1 (London: Thoemmes Continuum, 2000), p. xviii.

[134] Holwell, *Interesting Historical Events*, vol. 3, p. 139.

[135] Richard Dean, *An Essay on the Future Life of Brute*, p. iv.

[136] Holwell, *Interesting Historical Events*, vol. 3, p. 141.

into the extent to which such theological speculation was tolerated within the clergy, as long as it remained on the level of intellectual enquiry and not rhetorical polemic.[137] The take of *The Critical Review* was that this enquiry was a display of learning and erudition more than anything else.[138] Nevertheless, Berrow was strident that 'A pre-existent lapse of human souls' was 'as a truth equally demonstrable from scripture, as is the redemption of man by Jesus Christ'.[139] Deeply embedded in these ideas was the issue of theodicy and animal suffering. Berrow's discussion enlists quotations from a range of sources, principle among which were Holy Scriptures and Church divines, but also included chapters on the opinions of the ancients, and 'writers of a more modern date', such as Cambridge Platonists More and Glavnville and, rather audaciously, Joseph Butler, the Bishop of Durham from 1750 to 1752, claiming that his comments on the miserable state of the earth were an invitation to consider the 'reasons and circumstance of it'.[140] It was, therefore, with much relief, Holwell tells us, that he encountered Berrow's radical treatise, since 'it confirms, *from our own scriptures*, many leading and essential points of the Metempsychosis, as, the existence of angels, their rebellion, [and] their expulsion from blessed abodes'. So, while Berrow did not go so far as to support the idea of transmigration, his text had provided for Holwell 'every proof and confirmation from our own scriptures which we stand in need of to support the *Gentoo* doctrine', namely, 'the existence of angels, their fall, their expulsion and their punishments'.[141] That Holwell was very heavily influenced by Berrow is undeniable, and points to the more widespread intellectual presence of such ideas as those expressed by Ilive.

Holwell's ideas about animal spirituality are also closely interconnected with contemporary discourses on the moral imperative of abstinence from meat. To some extent this is a logical conclusion that stems from the Indian aspects of Holwell's interests and sources. Holwell was not the only European commentator to have theorised that the vegetarianism of the *Hindoos* was a rational consequence of accepting a theology of transmigrating souls.[142] As ever, though, Holwell chooses to put this in his own terms in relation to the *Shastah* and suggests that Moisasoor, the leader of the unholy rebellion, conducted a truly Machiavellian manoeuvre by

[137] Herrick, 'Blasphemy in the Eighteenth Century', pp. 116–7.

[138] *Critical Review*, 14 (1763), p. 97.

[139] Capel Berrow, *A Pre-Existent Lapse of Human Souls in a State of Pre-Existence, the Only Original Sin, and the Ground Work of the Gospel Dispensation* (London: Winston and B. White, 1762), preface.

[140] Berrow, *A Pre-Existent Lapse*, p. 37.

[141] Holwell, *Interesting Historical Events*, vol. 3, pp. 37–8.

[142] See Stuart, *Bloodless Revolution*.

persuading the early priests that animal sacrifice was a way to shorten one's earthly punishment. Likewise, this Satan-like figure presented alcohol, knowing that the inebriation it induced encouraged the wilful murder of humanity's fellow creatures. Thus, the introduction into the world of 'these two first-rate vices' is presented by Holwell as a 'master-piece of politics', designed to introduce further barriers to salvation.[143] Contemporary advances in anatomy also framed Holwell's understanding of the relationship between humans and animals. Most anatomists had confirmed the apparent similarity between human physiology and apes, as well as some other animals. A substantial sector of the scientific community further concluded that in its original state, the human body was designed to be herbivorous, a view that substantiated apparent scriptural detail that the primeval diet consisted of only fruit and vegetables.[144] It was on the basis of such findings that, despite their rivalry, both René Descartes and his principal critic, Pierre Gassendi, agreed that vegetarianism could be the most suitable diet for humans.[145] In conjunction with this new science of man as a natural herbivore, numerous vegetarian doctors appeared all over Europe, transforming these scientific arguments into practical dietary prescriptions for patients believed to be ailing from overconsumption of flesh.[146] That Holwell saw these theories as supporting his own is made clear when, in a later essay elaborating his commentary on metempsychosis (1779), he noted that eating meat was 'in opposition to the natural and obvious construction of the mouth and digestive faculties of Mhurd [man]'.[147] The difference was that Holwell's arguments against the consumption of animal flesh were also attached to a schema that supposedly recovered the lost and rational religious precept of metempsychosis.

This connection comes mostly clearly to the fore when Holwell, the former surgeon, cites throughout his work a very influential eighteenth-century medical text. Dr George Cheyne's *Essay of Health and Long Life* was published in 1724, went into multiple editions, and was still in print a century later.[148] According to Cheyne, God provided animal food after

[143] Holwell, *Review*, p. 160.

[144] 'And God said, Behold, I have given you every herb bearing seed, which is upon the face of all the earth, and every tree, in the which is the fruit of a tree yielding seed; to you it shall be for meat', *King James Bible* (Genesis 1:29). It was not until after the Flood that man was given leave to eat the flesh of other animals (Genesis 9:2–3).

[145] Stuart, *Bloodless Revolution*, p. xxi.

[146] Stuart, *Bloodless Revolution*, p. xxii.

[147] Holwell, *Review*, p. 79.

[148] Some twenty editions in fifteen years. See Roy Porter, *Bodies Politic: Disease, Death and Doctors in Britain, 1650–1900* (London: Reaktion Books, 2001), p. 84.

the Deluge only to shorten human life. Cheyne thus advocated the 'vegetable diet' as the most effective means of curing any major ailment.[149] While this may seem removed from the question of theodicy, for Holwell and Cheyne, the imperatives placed on meat consumption were as much moral as scientific. Dr Cheyne firmly situated his conception of bodily health within a context of sin and redemption. According to Cheyne's forceful invectives, health was the responsibility of the individual, and therefore contained within it a moral imperative. Those who overindulged themselves into sickness were guilty of crimes against God and nature.[150] Throughout the *Dissertation*, and in some parts of volume 2 of *Interesting Historical Events*, Holwell also invoked a causal relationship between moral corruption and the consumption of animal flesh by pointing out its deleterious effects. For Holwell this connection was a matter of inflammation. The Devil (or Moisasoor) knew that meat consumption would 'inflame and exalt the *desires of the flesh*, above the rule and dominion of the *spirit*'. For Holwell, then, the ill effects of animal flesh on the body had direct consequences for the soul: this 'inflamed state of the human body (from the continued accession of animal salts and juices, heated and fermented by the auxiliary force of spirituous liquors)' had a direct causal relationship with the various vices, including 'avarice, envy, hatred and malice'.[151]

Holwell had also encountered and written about such advice on a very practical level in India, when he observed that Indian physicians often prescribed vegetable diets to prepare patients for smallpox inoculation, a procedure that Holwell described in 1767, before it became standard practice in Europe.[152] We can see from the resulting publication of *An Account of the Manner of Inoculating for the Small Pox in the East Indies* (1767) that Holwell's own ideas about vegetarianism shared a kinship with the practices he described in India.[153] As Holwell explains in his treatise, certain foods are abstained from because they are thought to contain higher concentrations of *nigoda* and thus harm the body. This was a belief in Jainism that souls that have committed extreme crimes in previous lives are

[149] Anita Guerrini, 'A Diet for a Sensitive Soul: Vegetarianism in Eighteenth-Century Britain', *Eighteenth Century Life*, 23.2 (1999), p. 36.

[150] George Cheyne, *Essay of Health and Long Life* (London: George Strahan, 1724), pp. 4–5.

[151] Holwell, *Interesting Historical Events*, vol. 3, p. 161.

[152] *Asiatick Annual Register* (1800), pp. 25–31.

[153] John Zephaniah Holwell, *An Account of the Manner of Inoculating for the Small Pox in the East Indies. With Some Observations on the Practice and Mode of Treating That Disease in Those Parts* (London: T. Becket and P. A. De Hondt, 1767).

incarnated into airborne microscopic *nigoda*, which parasitically colonise other living beings.[154]

The entanglement between Cheyne's ideas about meat consumption and Holwell's conception of the doctrine of metempsychosis ran beyond medical theory and into heterodox theology. Cheyne, who was also listed as an authority by Berrow, had written his own sustained speculations about the nature of human and animal existence, the thematic heft of which touched on the same topics of a pre-existence lapse, suffering and the possibility of transmigration.[155] As well as his more popular works on diet, health and long life, Cheyne, whose personal beliefs and religious practices included Quietism and Millenarianism, also produced essays speculating in more detail on the relationship between the body, its health, morality and salvation.[156] Of these, his 'Philosophical Conjectures about the Nature and Qualities of the Animal Body, and of Its Progressive State in Several Stages of Existence', which appeared in *An Essay on Regimen, Together with Five Discourses, Medical Moral and Philosophical* (1740), dealt explicitly with the idea of transmigration.

Attached to his general belief that bodily suffering was a divine call and that the purification of one's diet was a moral duty, was a more complex theory of existence. Cheyne's theories built on the widely debated scientific notion of preformation, discussed by Leibniz among others, which suggested that organisms develop from microscopic forms of themselves in the form of homunculi or animalcules that have existed since the beginning of creation.[157] Taking this idea and running with it, fusing it with the notions of a pre-existent lapse, Chenye proposed that earth 'is really and literally a prison' and that as punishment the offending souls had been confined, in miniature, in the testes of the first generation of all male creation. Once released to animate their host, those who were able to purify themselves, of which Cheyne's medical advice concerning diet and abstinence were an integral part, would ascend to 'more pure, more happy' higher 'C*elestial Regions*', and those that were not would descend to 'dark *Dungeons*'.[158]

154 'Karma and the Problem of Rebirth in Jainism', in Doniger O'Flaherty (ed.), *Karma and Rebirth*, pp. 217–38.

155 Berrow, *A Pre-Existent Lapse*, p. 37.

156 See George S. Rousseau, 'Mysticism and Millenarianism: "Immortal Dr Cheyne"', in Richard Henry Popkin (ed.), *Millenarianism and Messianism in English Literature and Thought, 1650–1800* (Leiden: E. J. Brill, 1988).

157 For a thorough discussion of this, see Shirley A. Roes, *Matter, Life, and Generation: Eighteenth-Century Embryology and the Haller-Wolff Debate* (Cambridge: Cambridge University Press, 1981).

158 George Cheyne, *An Essay on Regimen, Together with Five Discourses, Medical Moral and Philosophical* (London: C. Rivington, 1740), pp. 26, 31, 32–3.

In this complex system of lapses, purification and probationary planetary stations animals are included, particularly in the second discourse in the same book, in which Cheyne suggested that they represented intelligent beings, lowered to a more base form of existence according to their position in this '*Progressive State*' of absolution.[159]

Again, this was a question of theodicy. The heart of the matter, as Cheyne explained to his readers, was the contention that since God would not let 'either *sentient*, or *intelligent* beings suffer, merely for suffering sake', all souls on earth must be the spirits who rebelled with apostate angels and were now reincarnating upwards from the 'animalcules' on the 'microscopical' level.[160] In other words, Cheyne was describing the same doctrine of metempsychosis that Holwell saw in the religion of the *Gentoos*, right down to distribution of purifying spirits to planets, or as they were in the *Shastah*, 'Boboons' (or *navagraha*).

A further thread in this tapestry of ideas connecting Holwell, the Cambridge Platonists, Berrow and Cheyne was the impact on Holwell's thought made by another admirer and friend of Dr Cheyne, Chevalier Andrew Michael Ramsay. Ramsay was known for an idiosyncratic blend of mysticism and deism, and was particularly infamous for his association with Cheyne's Quietist guide, the French mystic Madame Guyon.[161] Again, it is in this last dissertation of Holwell's, devoted to the topic of transmigration, that Holwell cites this source directly on at least two separate occasions.[162] The work Holwell appears to have been inspired by was Ramsay's *Travels of Cyrus* (1727), which recounted much of Cudworth's *True Intellectual System*.[163] Moreover, Ramsay was convinced that the Greeks, Persians and Chaldaeans had all derived their philosophies from the Brahmins. Significantly, he had also concluded that the souls inhabiting the physical bodies of earth's creatures were those of the rebellious angels, imprisoned here.[164] It seems that this book also had a profound influence on Holwell's account of the *Gentoo* scripture. Indeed, David Hume's description in *Natural History of Religion* (1757) of the beliefs of Ramsay could equally be a description of Holwell: 'having

[159] Cheyne, *Essay on Regimen*, p. 84. [160] Cheyne, *Essay on Regimen*, p. 30.

[161] C. J. Betts, *Early Deism in France: From the So-Called 'déistes' of Lyon (1564) to Voltaire's 'Lettres Philosophiques' (1734)* (The Hague: Martinus Nijhoff Publishers, 1984).

[162] Holwell, *Interesting Historical Events*, vol. 3, p. 40; Holwell, *Review*, pp. 40, 42.

[163] Urs App, 'William Jones's Ancient Theology', *Sino-Platonic Papers*, 191 (July, 2009), p. 9.

[164] Chevalier Ramsay, *Les voyages de Cyrus* (Paris [s.n.], 1727). English extract: Chevalier Ramsay, '"Of the Mythology of the Ancients," in Travels of Cyrus', in Burton Feldman and Robert D. Richardson (eds.), *The Rise of Modern Mythology, 1680–1860* (Bloomington: Indiana University Press, 1975).

thus thrown himself out of all received sects of Christianity, he is obliged to advance a system of his own, which is a kind of Origenism, and supposes the pre-existence of the souls both of men and beasts, and the eternal salvation and conversion of all men, beasts, and devils'.[165] Holwell's similar arguments are thus a reinforcement of, rather than an imitation of, a widespread heterodoxy that looked for alternative explanations of existence. Moreover, as we have seen, he was not alone in looking to ideas about metempsychosis to do this. Tied to this was the potential that a theory of pre-existence had in forging an alternative theodicy to more orthodox, or especially Calvinist, conceptions of predestination and sin. What was particular to Holwell was an experience of Indian philosophy and religion, including his practical medical experiences, which could be and were interpreted to support these alternative ideas. Theories of spiritual and physical health and their relation to the consumption of meat reinforced for Holwell the idea that metempsychosis was a prominent religious doctrine in what was evidently a very ancient theology.

A 'Christian Deist'

It is also in the *Dissertation on Metempsychosis* that Holwell describes himself as a 'CHRISTIAN DEIST'.[166] Holwell's statement comes in a section in which he defends himself against those who had 'unjustly' accused him 'of *Deism*'.[167] Such an accusation does not seem to have occurred in print, not, at least, in any of the notable reactions to Holwell's work, and is perhaps an anticipation of the response to this final and most controversial volume. What Holwell means by this is complex; yet it has often been cited as straightforward evidence of his 'deism' or taken for granted as a simple signifier of a recognisable theology.[168] Yet, to elucidate the actual signification of the term requires an analysis of the discussion surrounding it, as well as the contents and sources expounded in the rest of the *Dissertation on Metempsychosis.* More specifically, it necessitates an account of Holwell's Christology.

[165] David Hume, *Principal Writings on Religion Including Dialogues Concerning Natural Religion and the Natural History of Religion*, J. C. A. Gaskin (ed.) (Oxford: Oxford University Press, 1993 [London, 1757]), p. 93.

[166] Holwell, *Interesting Historical Events*, vol. 3, p. 91.

[167] Holwell, *Interesting Historical Events*, vol. 3, p. 90.

[168] See, for example, Siraj Ahmed, 'Orientalism and the Permanent Fix of War', in Daniel Carey and Lynn Festa (eds.), *The Post-Colonial Enlightenment: Eighteenth-Century Colonialism and Post-Colonial Theory* (Oxford: Oxford University Press, 2009), p. 177.

The term 'Christian deism' has been used by historians, as well as by some of Holwell's rough contemporaries, to denote a softening in the eighteenth century of the extreme separation between deism and orthodox belief that characterised the early radicalism of seventeenth-century scepticism.[169] In his study of what he terms the 'radical Enlightenment', Jonathan Israel has thus described this 'trend towards a "Christian deism"' as a consequence of attempts by Christian apologists in 'rationalizing theology' and as 'typical of the eighteenth century'.[170] In Israel's typology, separating the 'radical' from the 'moderate' or 'Christian' deists were varying degrees of commitment to certain doctrines, usually revolving around the role of God as a creator. Those considered radical are characterised according to their wholesale rejection of the doctrines of providence and the immortality of the soul. In contrast, many such self-declared Christian deists strongly affirmed their belief in the divine origin of morality and the special role of Christ (if not his divinity).[171] This is the conceptual scale that some writers are placing Holwell on when they refer to him as a Christian deist.[172] Further inspection of Holwell's work, though, indicates that although it was certainly this kind of moderate connotation that he was trying to invoke, what he actually meant when he described himself as a Christian deist, as well as other contemporary usages of the term, captured something quite different.

The term 'Christian deist' arises when Holwell defends himself against his invoked accusers on the basis that he has as 'indisputable right as Dr. *Clarke* and others, to extend and give *a new* signification to the word *Deist*'.[173] While exactly what Holwell meant by Christian deism is unclear, his reference to Samuel Clarke might provide an insight into how he would like his readers to approach it. Clarke was perhaps the principal promoter of Newtonianism in the eighteenth century, particularly according to a theological interpretation that saw Newton's discoveries as an argument for natural religion.[174] The resulting philosophy, which infused the world of scientific discovery with the powerful assertion of a creator God and the laws of general providence (as opposed to his intervention in particular affairs), simultaneously appealed to 'enlightened' Christians and what

[169] Joseph Waligore, 'Christian Deism in Eighteenth Century England', *International Journal of Philosophy and Theology*, 75:3 (2014).

[170] Israel, *Radical Enlightenment*, p. 470. [171] Israel, *Radical Enlightenment*, p. 471.

[172] See, for another example, Yang, 'Gross Metempsychosis and Eastern Soul', p. 18.

[173] Holwell, *Interesting Historical Events*, vol. 3, p. 90.

[174] Larry Stewart, 'Samuel Clarke, Newtonianism, and the Factions of Post-Revolutionary England', *Journal of the History of Ideas*, 42:1 (1981).

Israel has called 'moderate deists'.[175] Dr Cheyne, who, as we have seen, was an important source for Holwell's work, was also one of the writers associated with the new wave of Newtonianism precipitated by Clarke in the mid-eighteenth century.[176] Though it is clear that Howell's own scheme veers from Newtonian deism, his defence of Clarke's reinterpretation of the term suggests that he too seems to think he has a valid scheme for reinterpreting religion in a way that is neither atheistic nor heretical. It is in such a way as Clarke, Holwell explains, that 'a man may, with strict propriety, be *an orthodox Christian Deist*'.[177] This was his reply to the pre-empted accusation that he, along with the provocative names of '*Hobbes, Tindal, Bolingbroke* and others', was intending to 'injure the root of Christianity'. On the contrary, Holwell insisted 'our sole aim is to *restore* its purity and vigour.'[178]

Holwell clearly saw himself as adhering to the principal tenets of 'moderate deism'; that is, a belief that accepts the chief points of natural religion and the idea of an intelligent deity who had created the universe, maintained it, but was distant from it.[179] As Holwell put it, the Christian deist 'may, *consistently*, have a firm faith in *the unity of the Godhead, and in the pure and original doctrines of Christ.*'[180] Indeed, phrased like this, Clarke's natural religion does not seem an inappropriate bedfellow. Yet, when we remind ourselves that Holwell had also declared that Christ and Bramah were 'one and the same celestial being' the association becomes incongruous.

Holwell's 'Christian deism' is, therefore, Christian only in a restricted sense. To deduce where exactly Holwell draws the limits of this definition, it is necessary to examine the considerable portion of the *Dissertation* that he devotes to expounding a particular and idiosyncratic Christology. In it Holwell identified three positions regarding the status of Christ: that which determines Christ to be 'God himself', the position that regards Christ as 'God and man' and the last, which denies Christ any divinity whatsoever. After a section denying the equality of Christ with God, featuring extensive biblical quotation, we come to the third category. This is defined by Holwell as the position that conceives of Christ as a 'mere man, enlightened or inspired by God'. The great offence of this latter position is not, in

[175] Israel, *Radical Enlightenment*, p. 473.

[176] Margaret Jacob, *The Radical Enlightenment: Pantheists, Freemasons and Republicans* (London: George, Allen and Unwin Ltd, 1981), p. 94.

[177] Holwell, *Interesting Historical Events*, vol. 3, pp. 90–1.

[178] Holwell, *Interesting Historical Events*, vol. 3, p. 70.

[179] Israel, *Radical Enlightenment*, p. 473.

[180] Holwell, *Interesting Historical Events*, vol. 3, p. 91.

Holwell's eyes, the denial of the trinity, but the dismissal of 'the pre-existent state of his soul or spirit.'[181] Consistent with his idiosyncratic style Holwell thus at once takes a particular position in the Christian doctrinal debate, which is certainly anti-Trinitarian, while simultaneously attaching to it a completely unconventional hypothesis. Neither Socinian nor Arian, Holwell instead denied Christ's divinity on the grounds that not just Christ, but all humanity were once celestial beings.

The ontological pre-existence of Christ was already a feature of several different branches of Christology, but not in the sense that Holwell meant it. In dealing with a treatise targeted at the question of Christ's divinity, Holwell laments that the author, Paul Cardale, 'hurts the cause of Christianity' by denying not only Christ's divinity as traditionally conceived, but also his '*original divinity*' by contesting his pre-existence.[182] Holwell was also at pains to point out how in other respects he and Cardale, who was a Socinian, agreed.[183] First and foremost was their union on 'the evil tendency of the Athanasian Doctrine', a liturgical creed affirming Trinitarian Christology.[184] Holwell's position was thus more firmly in line with anti-Trinitarian authors like Cardale rather than with Christian orthodoxy, but always with the additional caveat of metempsychosis. Holwell's disappointment with Cardale was not his Socinianism, but his opinion on pre-existence in general. Referring to Cardale's outright rejection of Christ's pre-existence as a 'stumble' in an otherwise 'learned' book, Holwell suggested that if he would only give 'an unprejudiced hearing, and full force to the doctrines of Metempsychosis . . . he will, we flatter ourselves, receive full conviction that his doubts and disbelief of the pre-existent state and original divinity of Christ, were ill-founded'.[185] Indeed, it seems that it was Holwell's intention in this third volume to deliver precisely that message for writers like Cardale, whose *True Doctrine of the New Testament* was published in 1767, the same year as Holwell's second book in the *Interesting Historical Events* series, which had expounded the doctrine of metempsychosis as it was laid out in his *Shastah*. Cardale's inclusion in the 1771 volume thus points to the continuing evolution of Holwell's thought, as he layered atop the ideas

[181] Holwell, *Interesting Historical Events*, vol. 3, pp. 144, 145.
[182] Paul Cardale, *The True Doctrine of the New Testament Concerning Jesus Christ Considered* (London: Johnson and Davenport, 1767).
[183] On Cardale, see Helen Braithwate, *Romanticism, Publishing and Dissent: Joseph Johnson and the Cause of Liberty* (Basingstoke: Palgrave Macmillan, 2003), p. 11.
[184] Holwell, *Interesting Historical Events*, vol. 3, p. 145.
[185] Holwell, *Interesting Historical Events*, vol. 3, p. 146.

and philosophies he had gathered in India more and more material from contemporary European heterodoxy.

Referencing Tindal's *Christianity as Old as the Creation* (1730), Holwell proclaimed the issue raised by Tindal – whether or not Christianity could claim to be as old as the creation – ultimately resolved by the discovery of the *Shastah*. With this question Tindal had posed a radical challenge to religion based on revelation, and therefore biblical history, by positing that for Christianity to be true it must be coextensive with the truths that human reason can separately conclude for itself, and that consequently must be 'as old as the creation'.[186] Holwell's unique religious heterodoxy thus shines through when he concludes that 'Christianity is, *bona fide, as old as the creation*', because when what we mean by Christianity also incorporates the *Shastah*, a text that predates biblical chronology, then the origins of the truths it contains certainly seem to belong to the remotest antiquity of human reason.[187]

As well as allowing him to make this rather rhetorically ingenious statement, Holwell's decision to single out Tindal is interesting in another sense. Much of the secondary literature surrounding deism and the Enlightenment suggests that Matthew Tindal also described himself as a Christian deist.[188] While, as Stephan Lalor has pointed out, Tindal never wrote this, Holwell would nevertheless have been aware of this association, propagated by others who referred to Tindal as a Christian deist.[189] Holwell thus creates an interesting tension, using the same label as a writer he elsewhere describes as a 'libertine and free-thinker' and claiming it for himself. In doing so he sought to disavow the charge that he was seeking to injure Christianity by taking on Tindal's challenge and supplying the doctrine of metempsychosis in answer. He was a true Christian deist through linking both the universalism of deism and its critique of priestcraft with the precepts of Christianity by altering the latter to include the theodicy-solving theory of a pre-existent lapse and transmigrating souls. Thus, quoting the title of a work by clergyman Gregory Sharpe that 'the want of universality is no injury to Christianity', Holwell suggests that, though admirable, Sharpe's attempt to prove Christ was known in the

[186] Stephen Lalor, *Matthew Tindal, Freethinker: An Eighteenth-Century Assault on Religion* (London: Bloomsbury, 2006), p. 17.

[187] Holwell, *Interesting Historical Events*, vol. 3, p. 78.

[188] See, for example, Gerrish, 'Natural and Revealed Religion', p. 651.

[189] Lalor, Matthew Tindal, p. 148. See, for example, Benjamin Atkinson, *Christianity Not Older Than the First Gospel-Promise. In Answer to a Book, Entitled Christianity as Old as the Creation, &c* (London: Richard Ford and Richard Hett, 1730), p. 10.

East should be sidestepped because it was based on evidence 'utterly destitute of true chronology to support it', undermining more than it supported.[190] Rather, had Sharpe been aware of the *Gentoos*' original texts, he would have found the frequent visitation of angelic beings, including '*Birmah*, *Bistnoo* and *Sieb*', to corporeal forms on earth for the purposes of purification, like Christ's temptations in the desert, sufficient explanation for the exposure of Eastern cultures to the messages of Christ.[191] This, in fact, was the preamble to the observation that it was 'no violence to faith' to suppose that Christ and Birmah were indeed the same celestial being on such an excursion.

Conclusion

Once he had retired from the Company, Holwell continued to write about religion and metempsychosis in a way that was increasingly idiosyncratic and obscure. His last work, *Dissertations on the Origin, Nature, and Pursuits, of Intelligent Beings, and on Divine Providence, Religion, and Religious Worship* (1786), presented to the public a proposal for 'An essential Sketch for a more rational Form of Worship, and a New Liturgy'.[192] This is Holwell's clearest statement of his own particular brand of religious heterodoxy. He clearly rejected the doctrine of particular providence, i.e. God's intervention in earthly affairs, siding with the 'general providence' of Clarke and others. He also concluded that 'few parts of our established Liturgy are admissible in a rational worship of the Deity' to make the argument that they were in need of urgent reform.[193] Holwell's proposed liturgy thus consisted of short prayers and the occasional hymn, and is less than sixteen pages of large type long. Although the references to Indian religion, and Birmah, were removed, the doctrine of metempsychosis remained, with mentions of a 'great *original* transgression' and the 'present state of *punishment*' featuring prominently.[194] In fact, the only remnants of the religion of the *Gentoos* in the entire *Dissertation* is one allusion to 'the *most ancient Scripture*', as providing the answer to the question: 'why, and to what purpose, God created intelligent beings'.[195]

190 Gregory Sharpe, *The Want of Universality No Objection to the Christian Religion. Being the Substance of a Discourse Preached at the Temple Church the Tenth Day of November, 1765* (London: W. Richardson and S. Clark, 1766; Holwell, Interesting Historical Events, vol. 3, p. 79.

191 Holwell, *Interesting Historical Events*, vol. 3, pp. 79–80.

192 John Zephaniah Holwell, *Dissertations on the Origin, Nature, and Pursuits, of Intelligent Beings, and on Divine Providence, Religion, and Religious Worship* (Bath: R. Cruttwell, 1786).

193 Holwell, *Dissertations on the Origin*, p. 110.

194 Holwell, *Dissertations on the Origin*, p. 134.

195 Holwell, *Dissertations on the Origin*, p. 7.

The later thoughts of Holwell were undoubtedly highly idiosyncratic and increasingly eccentric. This was, of course, noted by reviewers, who nearly all considered the contents of his 'whimsical Dissertation on the Metempsychosis' to be nothing short of bizarre.[196] Nevertheless, this was the system of thought behind the 1767 discussion of metempsychosis, which did become an important part of the fabric of eighteenth-century intellectual culture. Voltaire, for example, had what Hawley has described as 'an enthusiasm for Holwell' that became 'more and more marked each time he cited him'.[197] Yet, we know that Holwell intended to publish the *Dissertation on Metempsychosis* from the beginning, given its prominent placement in the long title of *Interesting Historical Events.* Understanding Holwell's conclusion, in 1771, that he was a Christian deist is thus vital to understanding the make-up and the appeal of his interpretation of the *Gentoo* religion in 1767. For Holwell, the notion that the original tenets were 'short, pure, simple and uniform' was a product of an eighteenth-century anti-Trinitarian position, couched in a particularly heterodox set of solutions to theodicy.

What was 'deist' in the thought of Holwell was his belief in an original and universal religion, which disavows the specifics of Christian revelation. The final dissertation in *Interesting Historical Events* opens by echoing Montesquieu, with Holwell arguing that the number and variety of world religions could be explained by the fact that, owing to the impact of 'various soils and climates' on the 'dispositions of mankind', each 'mode of revelation' modelled by 'the supreme Being' also varies accordingly. This was further reinforced, believed Holwell, according to the evidence that while most nations diverge in their 'exterior modes of worship', there are some '*fundamental points* of every system, wherein *all agree* and profess unanimous faith'.[198] Yet, these 'deist' aspects are also given a distinct twist, specific to Holwell's own scheme, elements of which were drawn from sources across the spectrum of seventeenth- and eighteenth-century religious controversy.

While the particularly obscure direction that his later ideas took were not endorsed by most, Holwell's early account of Indian religious scripture according to this universalist interpretation was still used as an authoritative source into the nineteenth century. His theories were still passionately endorsed, for example, by German philosopher and anthropologist Carl

[196] *Critical Review*, 31–2 (1771), p. 131.

[197] Daniel Hawley, 'L'Inde de Voltaire', in Theodore Besterman (ed.), *Studies in Voltaire and the Eighteenth Century* (Oxford: Voltaire Foundation, 1974), p. 161.

[198] Holwell, *Interesting Historical Events*, vol. 3, pp. 2–4.

Josef Hieronymus Windischmann as late as 1832.[199] Similarly, in 1826 Friedrich Schlosser, Professor of History at the University of Heidelberg, declared that 'The best essay on the religion of Brahma is to be found in Holwell's work'.[200] Moreover, at the time of their publication, as we shall see, Holwell set the tone for a series of enquiries into Indian religion that followed a similar narrative of purity and decline. While scholarly standards did improve after Holwell's seemingly pioneering efforts, his claims to authority on the basis of textual analysis and unprejudiced objectivity created a paradigm for understanding Indian religious thought, set apart from earlier and later dismissals of its religious tradition as mere idolatry. While the 1771 *Dissertation on Metempsychosis* reveals a lot about the intellectual context in which his interpretation of *Gentoo* religion was constructed, the 1767 discussion of the *Shastah* introduced European audiences to a philosophical interpretation of the 'satisfactory, conclusive and rational' theology of the original Brahmins.

[199] Carl Josef Hieronymus Windischmann, *Die Philosophie im Fortgang der Weltgeschichte* (Bonn: Adolph Marcus, 1832), pp. 616–7.

[200] As cited in Stuart, *Bloodless Revolution*, pp. 283–4.

CHAPTER 3

Alexander Dow and the Hindoo *Shasters*

> The learned of modern Europe have, with reason, complained that the writers of Greece and Rome did not extend their enquiries to the religion and philosophy of the Druids. Posterity will perhaps, in the same manner, find fault with the British for not investigating the learning and religious opinions, which prevail in those countries in Asia, into which either their commerce or their arms have penetrated. The Brahmins of the East possessed in ancient times, some reputation for knowledge, but we have never had the curiosity to examine whether there was any truth in the reports of antiquity upon that head.
>
> Alexander Dow, *The History of Hindostan; From the Earliest Account of Time, to the Death of Akbar; Translated from the Persian of Mahummud Casim Ferishta of Delhi*

It is fitting in more ways than one that Alexander Dow should begin his 'Dissertation Concerning the Customs, Manners, Language, Religion and Philosophy of the Hindoos' by analogy to the Druids.[1] As Dow remarked, there had been a revival of interest in the lost wisdom of the ancient Celts, and enquiries into the Druids abounded, ranging from the visions of enlightened bards of nature presented in the poetry of the Warton brothers, to the polemical anti-clericalism of John Toland's *History of the Druids* (1726).[2] In fact, in the same year that he published the dissertation, Dow was living with the infamous author of various attempts to revive ancient Gaelic knowledge, James Macpherson.[3]

In 1760 Macpherson had published a slim volume entitled *Fragments of Ancient Poetry, Collected in the Highlands of Scotland, and Translated from*

[1] Dow, *History of Hindostan*, vol. 1 (1768), pp. xxi–lxix.

[2] James Sambrook, *The Eighteenth Century: The Intellectual and Cultural Context of English Literature, 1700–1789*, 3rd ed. (London: Routledge, 2013), pp. 211–12.

[3] As we are told by John Macdonald, Dow's servant and author of *Memoirs of an Eighteenth-Century Footman 1745–1779* (London: George Routledge and Sons, 1927), p. 38. The book was originally titled *Travels* and first published in 1790.

the Gaelic or Erse Language, under the encouragement of Hugh Blair, Chair of Rhetoric and *Belles-Lettres* at the University of Edinburgh. Blair was convinced that these fragments were parts of a lost whole and in his preface to the *Fragments of Ancient Poetry* attested to their authenticity, and suggested that more poetic remains were to be recovered. Blair, and members of the Edinburgh Select Society, thus commissioned and financed Macpherson's travels to explore the possible existence of a 'Scottish Homer' and recover the lost Scots national epic.[4] Within a few months Macpherson produced a translation of the six-book epic poem about a Scotch warrior *Fingal* (1762), narrated by Ossian, a blind bard of the Highlands. In his commentary, Macpherson stressed the simple natural religion of Ossian, not dissimilar to the tenets of a moderate eighteenth-century deism.[5] Living with Macpherson, preparing his dissertation on *Hindoo* religion, Dow was to also emphasise the natural religion of India's inhabitants, stressing that 'the polytheism of which they have been accused, is no more than a symbolical worship of the divine attributes' of God. Likewise, Dow's account of the Brahmins is similar to Macpherson's equivocal approach to the Druids, whom he casts as both priestly manipulators and symbols of the sophistication of Celtic culture.[6] In Macpherson's commentary on Ossian's poems he notes that the Druids were known for living 'after the Pythagorean manner, and philosophizing upon the highest subjects', including the 'immortality of the human soul'.[7] In Dow's version, this history has more of the flavour of Toland's suggestion that these Pythagorean doctrines may have originated with the Druids, with Dow stating that the belief that 'the soul, after death, assumes a body of the purer elements' is not unique to the Brahmins, and that in Europe, it 'descended from the Druids of Europe, to the Greeks, and was the same with the ἐιδωλον [eidolon, a spirit-image] of Homer'.[8] At the same time Dow is also a firm critic of the influence of the Brahmins 'and their characters as priests', just as Toland and Macpherson were of the

[4] Richard B. Sher, '"Those Scotch Impostors and Their Cabal": Ossian and the Scottish Enlightenment', in Roger L. Emmerson, Gilles Girard and Rosanne Runt (eds.), *Man and Nature: Proceedings of the Canadian Society for Eighteenth Century Studies*, vol. 1 (London, ON: University of Western Ontario, 1982).

[5] Burton Feldman and Robert D. Richardson Jr, *The Rise of Modern Mythology: 1680–1860* (Indiana: Indiana University Press, 1972), p. 202.

[6] Dow, *History of Hindostan*, vol. 1 (1768), p. xxi.

[7] James Macpherson, *The Poems of Ossian* (London: J. D. Dewick for Allen Lackington, 1803), p. 90.

[8] Dow, *History of Hindostan*, vol. 1 (1768), p. l. See R. Huddleston (ed.), *A New Edition of Toland's History of the Druids* (Montrose: James Watt, 1816), p. 209.

Druids, describing them as the 'History of Priestcraft' and 'cunning and ambitious priests' respectively.[9]

Dow lodged with Macpherson in 1768, when the debate about the authenticity of *Fingal* was still active. Questions concerning the epic's authenticity were raised very soon after its publication, led by Samuel Johnson who urged Macpherson to produce the original manuscript that he claimed to have translated. David Hume posed the alternative of transcriptions of oral sources, provided they were ancient and passed down through oral tradition.[10] Following Macpherson's death in 1796, the Highland Society of Scotland appointed a special commission to investigate the authenticity of the epic. After collecting testimonies and evidence, a final report was published in 1805, concluding that the poems were not a forgery, but that Macpherson had indeed amended and considerably altered his oral and written sources.[11] Despite the intention that this report be definitive, deliberation continues today. While a significant portion of scholarship now suggests that forgery is too strong an accusation to level at Macpherson, the layers of ambiguity in his presentation of the work mirror the same vagueness that surrounds Dow's account of his sources, particularly for the extracts of *Hindoo* 'scripture' provided in his texts.[12] Dow's discovery of ancient *Hindoo* religion, like Macpherson's rendering of a Gaelic epic, suggests a degree of ingenuity. Scholarship suggests that Macpherson built on Gaelic tradition to produce a text that was part translation of written fragments, part transcription of oral narrative, and part embellishment; though the degree to which his original sources were authentic is still in question.[13] Likewise, Dow was engaging with and describing some genuine Indian theological and philosophical concepts, but he fitted them to suit his own discussion, the audience for

[9] Dow, *History of Hindostan*, vol. 1 (1768), p. xxxv; John Toland, *History of the Celtic Religion and Learning* (Edinburgh: John Findlay, 1815), p. 48; James Macpherson, *An Introduction to the History of Great Britain and Ireland* (London: T. Becket and P. A. de Hondt, 1772), p. 6.

[10] Kristine Louise Haugen, 'Ossian and the Invention of Textual History', *Journal of the History of Ideas*, 59:2 (1998).

[11] Royal Highland and Agricultural Society of Scotland, *Report of the Committee of the Highland Society of Scotland, Appointed to Inquire into the Nature and Authenticity of the Poems of Ossian, Compiled by Henry Mackenzie* (Edinburgh: A. Constable, 1805).

[12] Fiona Stafford, *The Sublime Savage: A Study of James Macpherson and the Poems of Ossian* (Edinburgh: Edinburgh University Press, 1988).

[13] As well as Stafford, see Derek S. Thomson, *The Gaelic Sources of Macpherson's 'Ossian'* (Edinburgh: Oliver and Boyd, 1952). Thomas M. Curley has rekindled debate suggesting only a marginal correlation with original sources, in *Samuel Johnson, the Ossian Fraud, and the Celtic Revival in Great Britain and Ireland* (Cambridge: Cambridge University Press, 2009).

which was European, and his concerns with which were oriented towards the religious debates in that region.

Dow claimed that his introduction to the knowledge of the Brahmins was the result of a chance encounter. After finding himself 'conversing by accident, one day, with a noble and learned Brahmin', Dow learned, to his surprise, that he was 'perfectly acquainted with those opinions, which, both in ancient and modern Europe, have employed the pens of the most celebrated moralists.'[14] This direct comparison between the moral philosophy of India and Europe sets the tone for the rest of the dissertation, which hinges on Dow's commitment to the notion that 'common sense, upon the affairs of religion, is pretty equally divided among all nations'.[15] Throughout Dow details what he perceives to be the central tenets and texts of the religion of the *Hindoos*, saturating his reflections on the theological and philosophical concerns of the Brahmins with the language and concepts of eighteenth-century rational religion. Inviting his readers to join him in rejecting the 'stream of popular prejudice' against the religious practices of the *Hindoos* that is to be found in missionary and travel accounts, Dow's overriding thesis is that the Brahmins 'invariably believe in the unity, eternity, omniscience and omnipotence of God'.[16]

It is this defence of the reasonableness of 'the Brahmin religion' that has led scholars like Marshall and the German Indologist Wilhelm Halbfass to suggest that Dow was a deist.[17] And yet, as we have seen, more recent challenges to our understandings of what deism means have led historians to talk of 'multiple deisms and diverse heterodoxies', rather than designate 'deism' a simple signifier.[18] In this historiographical context Dow was certainly not a deist according to studies of notable English deists and their involvement in the complex interweaving of theological, political and natural philosophical discourses of eighteenth-century high intellectual culture. Yet, recognising that the changing social character of religion in the latter part of the century could mean that more people found an intellectual kinship with deist ideas, and particularly a critical bent towards Christianity, is useful when considering the work of Dow, who was neither an Enlightenment philosopher nor a theologian, but who was certainly an

[14] Dow, *History of Hindostan*, vol. 1 (1768), p. xxii.
[15] Dow, *History of Hindostan*, vol. 1 (1768), p. Ixxxvi.
[16] Dow, *History of Hindostan*, vol. 1 (1768), p. lxvii.
[17] Rubiés, 'From Christian Apologetics to Deism', p. 108; Halbfass, *India and Europe*, p. 56.
[18] Hudson, Enlightenment and Modernity, p. 7; Hudson, Lucci and Wigelsworth, Atheism and Deism Revalued; Jeffrey R. Wigelsworth, *Deism in Enlightenment England: Theology, Politics and Newtonian Public Science* (Manchester: University of Manchester Press, 2009).

important figure in shaping contemporary attitudes to a non-Christian religion.

This chapter will therefore focus on Dow's religious outlook and the ways that it shaped his construction of the *Hindoo* religion. It will outline how Dow's understanding of India's religious development centred on a basic division between what he saw as the two principal 'sects' of *Hindoo* religion, known as the Bedang and the Neadirsin. These refer respectively to two of the recognised six orthodox schools of Brahminical philosophy, Vedānta and Nyāya.[19] Vedānta is concerned with knowledge and insight and based its doctrines on interpretations of the final section of Vedic literature, such as the *Upanishads*. Nyāya, on the other hand, means 'that by which one is led to a conclusion' or 'correct reasoning' and is often referred to as 'the science of reasoning' (*tarkaśātra*).[20] It is in reflecting on these two philosophical schools that Dow concludes that 'in India, as well as in many other countries, there are two great religious sects; the one look up to the divinity, through the medium of reason and philosophy; while the others receive, as an article of their belief, every holy legend and allegory which have been transmitted down from antiquity.' [21] In this formulation we are to understand the Bedang (Vedānta), the older and more orthodox school, as those that receive their religion from 'every holy legend and allegory' of antiquity, whereas, the Neadirsin (Nyāya) arrive at an appreciation of the divinity founded on 'reason and philosophy'. And yet, we are reminded, such a pattern is not unique to India but universal, to be found in a different guise 'in many other countries'.

From the very beginning, then, Dow views Indian religious history and development as analogous to Europe's division between received and rational religion. Indeed, as this chapter will demonstrate, Dow's assessment of the origins of *Hindoo* religion was grounded in the language and concepts of eighteenth-century rational religion. Moreover, Dow's decision to focus on what he saw as the philosophical core of the religion, in order to illustrate its rational character, demonstrates a significant turning point in determining a new 'philosophic' approach to the interpretation of

19 This has also been recognised by Marshall, *British Discovery of Hinduism*, p. 119.

20 For a philosophical summary of both, see Richard King, *Indian Philosophy: An Introduction to Hindu and Buddhist Thought* (Edinburgh: Edinburgh University Press, 1988), pp. 53–62. See also Sibajiban Bhattacharyya, *Development of Nyaya Philosophy and Its Social Context: History of Science, Philosophy and Culture in Indian Civilization*, vol. 3, part 3 (Delhi: Centre for Studies of Civilizations, 2004), p. 106.

21 Dow, *History of Hindostan*, vol. 1 (1768), p. lxviii.

Hinduism. This chapter will begin by outlining Dow's immediate biographical and intellectual context, followed by an account of how Dow established his authority, his methodology and texts, before turning to an explanation of his treatment of the Bedang (Vedānta) and the Neadirsin (Nyāya). Finally, it will conclude with a consideration of how we can understand his philosophically focused approach to the interpretation of Hinduism to be a product of the above.

Dow's Literary Ambitions

Dow was born in Perthshire, Scotland (1735/6), and was set to be apprenticed for a mercantile career at Eyemouth. In 1757, however, he joined the *King of Prussia*, a private ship of war, as a midshipman. There are suggestions that this departure was the result of Dow's involvement in a fatal dual.[22] The will Dow drew up before leaving, which left everything to the brothers of the notorious smuggling family, the Nesbits, to whom he had been apprenticed, does indeed suggest an abrupt departure.[23] It is then thought that he went to Bencoolen in Sumatra before entering the Company's military service in Bengal in 1760, to be appointed captain in 1764.[24] After participating in the officers' protest against Clive's measure to abolish the double field allowance (1766), Dow found himself back in Britain in 1768.[25] His military career frustrated, after suffering these, as he put it, 'injuries in rank', Dow turned towards more intellectual pursuits.[26] In the first instance Dow wrote to the Court of Directors requesting a new position on the basis of 'the progress he has made in the oriental tongues, and his knowledge of the political state of Hindostan'.[27] Failing in this, he turned his attention to literary fame, first publishing *Tales Translated from the Persian of Inatulla of Delhi* (1768), a collection of extravagant and bawdy tales, presented to the public as 'a genuine specimen of oriental

22 Willem G. J. Kuiters, 'Dow, Alexander (1735/6–1779)', *Oxford Dictionary of National Biography* (Oxford: Oxford University Press, 2004); online ed., January 2008 [www.oxforddnb.com/view/article/7957, accessed 25 July 2016].

23 TNA: PRO, PROB 11/1091, no. 277. On the Nesbit family, see Derek James, *The Smugglers' Coast: The Story of Smuggling around Eyemouth* (Peterborough: Fast-Print Publishing, 2016).

24 V. D. K. Hodson, *Officers of the Bengal Army: 1758–1834*, vol. 2 (London: Constable, 1928), pp. 78–9.

25 Kuiters, 'Dow, Alexander'. Dow appeared as a witness for plaintiff Captain John Neville Parker in 1769, who brought the charge against Clive that he had illegally detained him to await court-martial following the protest: BL, MS Eur F128/117.

26 Dow, *History of Hindostan*, vol. 1 (1768), p. iii.

27 Dow's 'Letter to the Court of Directors', Letter 116 Memorial of Alexander Dow, 18 November 1768, IOR/E/I/51, ff. 232–232v.

composition'.[28] This was followed by his *History of Hindostan*, a loose translation of the *Tārikh-i-Firishta*, a history of the Mughal empire by Muhammad Qasim Hindu Shah (1560–1620), otherwise known as Firishta. To the first volume Dow attached 'A Dissertation Concerning the Customs, Manners, Language, Religion and Philosophy of the Hindoos', which is where Dow's thoughts on Indian religion that are the focus of this chapter can be found.[29]

There was also, from the beginning, a commercial and fashionable dimension to Dow's literary projects. Dow's first publication, *Tales Translated from the Persian of Inatulla of Delhi*, conformed to the standard tropes of exoticised and erotised eighteenth-century oriental fiction. Ballaster and others have identified the text as an extremely loose translation of the *Bahâr-e dâneš*, or 'Gardens of knowledge', by the seventeenth-century Persian writer Shaikh Inayat-Allah Kamboh (1608–71).[30] The tales feature ministers trying to cure the young Mughal prince Jehandar of his obsessive love for a Chinese princess by demonstrating the caprices and infidelity of women. The last six tales are delivered by a Brahmin, instructing the prince in moral restraint and virtue. It therefore features several of the themes to de developed in his more overtly political work, such as the wisdom contained in *Hindoo* philosophy, and the concealment of women as a facet of despotism.[31] Dow's text struck a different tone to other offerings of oriental tales, such as James Ridley's *Tales of the Genii* of 1764. Where Ridley weaved his pastiche into an instructive on honourable conduct and submitting to the will of God, Dow's collection was extravagant and morally dubious, revelling in the wit of its duplicitous wives and its fabulous setting. Dow was certainly no moralist.

An exoticised Orient was also to be the backdrop of his first play, *Zingis*. Purportedly taken from *Tarich Mogulistan* (History of the Mogul Tartars) and originally 'written in the Persian language', it was advertised as the story of 'perhaps, the greatest prince, that ever appeared in history', Zingis Chan (Genghis Khan).[32] In what would become a pattern in Dow's work, it appears there was a great deal of artistic licence applied in the formulation of such claims. No Persian original of this name exists (the most well-known

[28] Alexander Dow, *Tales, Translated from the Persian of Inatulla of Delhi* (London: T. Becket and P. A. de Hondt, 1768), vol. 1, p. iii.

[29] Dow, *History of Hindostan*, vol. 1 (1768), pp. xxi–lxix, lv.

[30] Ros Ballaster, *Fabulous Orients: Fictions of the East in England, 1662–1775* (Oxford: Oxford University Press, 2005), p. 35.

[31] A discussion of Dow's political dissertations features in Chapter 6 of this book.

[32] Contained in the advertisement; Alexander Dow, *Zingis. A Tragedy. As It Is Performed at the Theatre-Royal in Drury-Lane* (London: T. Becket and P. A. de Hondt, 1769), p. i.

Persian history of Genghis Khan is the thirteenth-century *Tārikh-i-Jahan-Gusha*), though most of what was known about Genghis at this time had been taken primarily from Persian and Arabic sources. A biography of the conqueror, Petis de la Croix's *Histoire du Grand Genghiscan*, had already been published in 1710 and was later translated into English in 1722.[33] The interest surrounding the great military leader and politician of the East proliferated, and preceding Dow's theatrical production there were a number of literary works, including a play by Voltaire on the same topic, *Orphelin de la Chine* (1755).

Dow's play obviously appealed to the excitement surrounding the newly rediscovered historical figure, capitalising on the fashionable demand for alternatives to the classics. Indeed, the prologue complains of the ubiquity of classical heroes left to 'languish on our stage' and bids its audience to turn to the excitement of Eastern conquerors, those 'Heroes, who like their gems, unpolish'd shine / The mighty fathers of the Tartar line; / Greater than those, whom Classic pages boast, /If those are greatest, who conquered most'. The prologue also goes some way to romanticising the author, Dow, by situating him in the same exotic context. The 'poet', as it describes him before adding the exciting qualification 'If a rough Soldier may assume that name', is presented as a warrior prosateur from 'India's burning shore', who 'In warlike toils, he pass'd his youthful years, / And met the Tartar, in the strife of spears'.[34] Dow's image as the brave and adventurous soldier sets him up perfectly as the translator of the conqueror's exploits, an approach that seems to have paid off since the play and Dow's abilities were well received by critics. John Macpherson, to whom Dow was connected via John's brother James Macpherson, wrote a piece for *The Monthly Review*, praising its 'ingenious Author' and offering several pages expressing his 'very high opinion of the tragedy Zingis'. In particular, Macpherson stressed the novelty of its dramatic characters as opposed to classical pieces, stressing that 'The character of Zingis is new'.[35]

Dow's later play *Sethona*, however, was less successful and in fact the source of some doubt about his literary abilities and authorship. Performed after his second return to Britain in 1774, the play was set some time in Egyptian antiquity and follows the heroine, Sethona, who is viciously pursued by the 'Tyrant Amasis'. In his *Biographia Dramatica* (1782), David Erskine Baker inferred that Dow's literary success was a product

[33] François Pétis de la Croix, *Histoire du Grand Genghiscan* (Paris: Chez la veuve Jombert, 1710); François Pétis de la Croix, *The History of Genghizcan the Great*, Penelope Aubin (trans.) (London, 1722).

[34] Dow, *Zingis. A Tragedy*, p. ii.

[35] *Monthly Review*, 40 (1769), pp. 50–5.

of 'the national partiality that Scotsmen labour for the promotion of each other', noting that 'Mr. Dow has been represented by persons who knew him well during his first residence at the East Indies, as a man utterly unqualified for the production of any work of learning or fancy, either in prose or meter'. According to Baker, his literary accomplishments were thought, therefore, to be a product of his 'strict intimacy with two of his own countrymen, one a translator, the other a dramatic poet' who took it upon themselves to assist 'a needy brother in trade'.[36] Though it is unclear who the second was, Baker was certainly referring to James Macpherson as one of these ghost writers. While the suggestion that these close companions assisted Dow in preparing these pieces for the stage is certainly plausible, particularly when one considers that the first was composed in a period in which the future of Dow's Company career was uncertain, *The History of Hindostan* and the essays it contained appear very much to be the work of Dow's own hand. Indeed, in the published memoirs of a footman, John Macdonald, who for a time was employed by Dow, there is a description of Dow writing the third volume of *The History of Hindostan* on his second voyage to India in 1769–70.[37] And in fact, in many ways the translation was itself a literary creation. Dow's decision to focus on what he judged to be the most interesting events, as well as his appeals to the literary trend of sensibility with vignettes such as Mamood I's (Mahmud of Ghazni) 'tears of resentment and compassion' at tales of injustice in his empire,[38] led one reviewer to reflect that Dow's history 'would better suit the fables invented by romance than the facts recorded by real history'.[39]

As well as the more popular and theatrical dimension to Dow's productions, it is no contradiction to say that Dow viewed all his literary projects as contributions to the Enlightenment 'Republic of Letters'. As well as Macpherson, Dow certainly had connections in this world. David Hume's surviving letters reveal that he and Dow were correspondents, who looked forward to 'a discussion over an evening fire'.[40] It appears that Dow first frequented Hume's lodgings in Brewer Street, London, during the same period that he returned to England and published *The History of Hindostan*, and continued an association.[41] It was on the *History* that

[36] David Erskine Baker, *Biographia Dramatica, or A Companion to the Playhouse*, 2nd ed., vol. 2 (Dublin: W. and H. Whitestone, 1782), pp. 335–6.

[37] Macdonald, *Memoirs*, p. 40. [38] Dow, *History of Hindostan*, vol. 1 (1768), p. 95.

[39] *London Magazine*, vol. 41 (London: May 1772), p. 242.

[40] Hume to Alexander Dow, 1772, in David Hume, *The Letters of David Hume*, J. Y. T. Greig (ed.) (Oxford: Clarendon Press, 1932), vol. 2, Letter 480, p. 267.

[41] Macdonald, *Memoirs*, pp. 37–9.

Dow's reputation as a man of letters would rest. As mentioned earlier, this work was a translation of a seventeenth-century Persian text, to which Dow added an appendix containing the last forty years of the history of the Mughal empire and several dissertations. It was the first general history of Muslim India to have been published in Britain. Before its publication in 1768, British knowledge of Mughal India had been confined to the accounts of European travellers, a few pages in James Fraser's *History of Nadir Shah* (1742), and some French articles in D'Herbolt's *Bibliotheque Oreintale*.[42] Thus, despite its imperfections, Dow's translation was used as the ultimate source of authority on Mughal history, guiding British perceptions of the Mughal empire, until it was replaced by John Briggs' *History of the Rise of Mahommedan Power in India* (also a translation of the *Tārikh-i-Firishta*) in 1829. Indeed, when it was published, Dow's work was responding to an increasing interest in the history of the Mughals, whose power the East India Company was rapidly entangled in and displacing. Just a few years before the publication of the first volume of *The History of Hindostan*, Robert Orme had complained that Muslim Indian history would remain obscure until Persian sources were translated.[43] Dow's work was a direct answer to that demand, and as such gained a wide reception. To give an example, one important work that made heavy use of Dow's translation, concerned as it was with the fate of empires, was Edward Gibbon's *The History of the Decline and Fall of the Roman Empire* (1776–89).[44]

The translation itself was loose. It seems that Dow had employed artistic license where he'd seen an opportunity to invigorate the text. In a passage in the third additional volume of *The History of Hindostan* (1772), Dow goes some way to explain why, noting that 'peace and public happiness afford few materials for history'. Dow suggests that periods of general tranquillity, though of importance to Indian history, 'would furnish no amusement in Europe'. Passing over times of peace, in favour of 'times abounding with revolutions and important events', Dow fashioned the original to suit the demands of the literary market place.[45] As J. S. Grewal has pointed out, Dow 'transformed his Persian sources into a new piece of historical literature' by liberally interspersing his own asides and offering commentaries on the cast of characters at play.[46] This, as well as his inclusion of romantic scenes, extraordinary characters and long diversions,

42 Grewal, *Muslim Rule in India*, p. 6. 43 Orme, *History of the Military Transactions*, p. 17.

44 See, for example, Edward Gibbon, *The History of the Decline and Fall of the Roman Empire*, vol. 4 (Dublin [s.n.], 1788), chapter 57, p. 280.

45 Dow, *History of Hindostan*, vol. 3. (1772), pp. 362–3. 46 Grewal, *Muslim Rule in India*, p. 13.

caused doubts to surface about the authenticity of the work. According to Briggs, whose translation of the *Tārikh-i-Firishta* was much stricter; both Samuel Johnson and Edmund Burke doubted it to be authentic until the East India Company's historiographer, Robert Orme, had a portion of the Persian original brought to London to be translated.[47] Likewise, Dow's qualities as a Persian scholar had been called into question by John Shore (governor-general of Bengal, 1793–98), who had argued that the looseness of the *Tales* suggested that it was far from a direct translation, and that Dow had employed a Persian interpreter to read and explain the stories, which he then freely wrote in English. Regarding the *History*, however, Shore conceded that Dow's translation of the *Tārikh-i-Firishta* was perfectly exact in some places, though not consistently.[48] As Dow explained it, he had attempted to work around the deficiencies of the 'writers of Asia', which he listed as 'too verbose' in diction and 'too florid' in prose. Despite reserving praise for the 'genius' of the history's original author, Dow concluded that the poetical style of his history was still not proper for European taste and so 'clipped the wings of Ferishta's turgid expressions'.[49] Such a characterisation of Eastern writing as less elegant than European prose was a common aside in orientalist works, asserting superiority even when appearing to be appreciative and admiring.[50] Thus Dow was able to simultaneously denigrate 'eastern writers' and advocate that 'there are many things in their works, worthy of the attention of literary men'. *The History of Hindostan* was to be particularly recommended, since contained within it was 'a minute and authentic history of a great empire'; empires being a topic that increasingly preoccupied British minds. It was for this reason, Dow explained, that he had worked to 'open the door to the literary treasures' written in Persian and deliver to Europe Firishta's history as 'a small specimen' of what could be found there.[51]

The first edition of *The History of Hindostan* was duly published in two volumes in 1768. This was followed by a second edition in 1770, which sought to revise the *History* to be more concise and offer better introductions and summaries of the different reigns.[52]A third volume was added in 1772, which updated the history to include more recent events, as well as

[47] John Briggs, *The History of the Rise of Mahomedan Power in India*, vol. 1 (London, 1829), p. vii.

[48] John Shore, Baron Teignmouth (ed.), *Memoir of the Life and Correspondence of John, Lord Teignmouth*, vol. 1 (London: Hatchard, 1843), pp. 105–6.

[49] Dow, *History of Hindostan*, vol. 1 (1768), pp. ix, xi.

[50] See, for example, Warren Hastings' letter to Nathanial Smith, published as a foreword to Charles Wilkins' *Bhăgvăt-Gēētā, or Dialogues of Krēēshnă and Ărjōōn* (London: C. Nourse, 1785).

[51] Dow, *History of Hindostan*, vol. 1 (1768), pp. i, ii, iii.

[52] Alexander Dow, 'Advertisement', in *History of Hindostan*, vol. 1 (1770).

offer a diagnosis of contemporary Bengal. Joining 'the current of public opinion' concerned with the Company's mismanagement of the region after the Bengal famine, Dow offered several dissertations proposing reforms.[53] Finally, in 1792 a third edition was published by John Murray in London and Luke White in Dublin, thirteen years after Dow's death from ill health at Bhagalpur.[54] The reason for this republication seems to be a renewed interest in the East India Company's affairs in anticipation of the Cornwallis Code of 1793, otherwise known as the 'permanent settlement' of Bengal. It was in the first edition, though, in 1768, that Dow included 'A Dissertation Concerning the Customs, Manners, Language, Religion and Philosophy of the Hindoos', which will be the focus of this chapter.[55] Its main concern is Dow's interpretation, and indeed deliberate construction, of the religion of the *Hindoos*.

Scripture and Authority

Despite its billing as a translation of Firishta's work, in the critical reception of *The History of Hindostan* a great deal of attention was paid to Dow's additional 'Dissertation Concerning the Customs, Manners, Language, Religion and Philosophy of the Hindoos'. The account given in *The Monthly Review*, for example, was focused entirely on Dow's summation of *Hindoo* doctrine, with only two of a total of ten full pages mentioning the translation. The rest of the review focused instead on how Dow had 'gained a more accurate knowledge of the religion and philosophy of the Brahmins, than any who have preceded him'.[56] It was solely the *Dissertation* that was immediately translated into French and published in Paris the following year (1769).[57] It was also reproduced again, much later in 1771, in another French-language study of transmigration by the Swiss savant Jean-Rodolphe Sinner, forming part of the library of Gotthold Ephraim Lessing.[58] Dow's insights into the religion of the Brahmins were, therefore, one of the most widely received aspects of his work on India.

[53] Dow *The History of Hindostan*, vol. 3 (1772), p. xl.

[54] William Zachs, *The First John Murray and the Late Eighteenth-Century London Book Trade* (Oxford: Oxford University Press, 1998), p. 118.

[55] Dow, *History of Hindostan*, vol. 1 (1768), pp. xxi–lxix, lv.

[56] *Monthly Review*, 39 (1768), pp. 377–87: p. 377.

[57] Alexander Dow, *Dissertation sur les moeurs, les usages, le langage, la religion et la philosophie des Hindous*, Claude-François Bergier (trans.) (Paris: Chez Pissot, 1769).

[58] Jean-Rodolphe Sinner, *Essai sur les DOGMES de la METEMPSYCHOSE & du PURGATOIRE enseignés par les Bramins de l'Indostan* (Berne: La Société Typographique, 1771); Hugh Barr Nisbet,

Central to understanding the dissertation is an account of Dow's methodological claims and sources. Dow appealed to a similar concept of 'authority' to that established by Holwell, the basis of which was an explicit rejection of travel accounts and missionary literature on two counts: their lack of objectivity and their insufficient grasp of native languages. While this was not an accurate or fair account of missionary literature in particular, it was a convincing assertion to those who associated the Jesuits with unsavoury machinations. Moreover, this contention was a part of a greater trend; Trautmann has, for example, described British engagement with oriental languages as precipitating a 'titanic shift of authority' from the Jesuit *Lettres édifiantes*.[59] Yet, while Trautmann focuses on the eventual discovery of Sanskrit by Charles Wilkins and the work of William Jones, Holwell and Dow were the first British authors to make such claims and should therefore be seen as instrumental in developing this altered orientalist framework. Thus, Dow imitates Holwell's dismissal of the existing literature by declaring it 'fiction', designating 'modern travellers' with a 'talent for fable' as the main culprits. Like Holwell, he also blamed misrepresentation of the *Hindoos* on religious prejudice, or what he called 'common partiality' for one's own religion. Finally, he underlined that these fallacies were the result of these authors' ignorance of Indian languages and texts, suggesting that they formed their judgements according only to the 'external ceremonies of the Hindoos'.[60]

Yet, also in alignment with Holwell, Dow's claim to unique authority on the basis of linguistic skill was not all it seemed. In the first instance Dow confessed that he had not been able to master Sanskrit. Relaying how he had hired 'a Pundit, from the University of Benaris [Banaras], well versed in the Shanscrita' in order to acquire it, Dow admitted that he had insufficient time to complete his studies. However, he did provide a key to the Sanskrit alphabet and noted that 'in regularity of etymology and grammatical order, it far exceeds the Arabic', suggesting that he had made some progress.[61] Instead, he had to rely on Persian and what he described as 'the vulgar tongue of the Hindoos' (Bengali). Undeterred from his quest to learn 'as much as possible, concerning the mythology and philosophy of the Brahmins', however, he still 'procured some of the principal

Gotthold Ephraim Lessing: His Life, Works, and Thought (Oxford: Oxford University Press, 2013), p. 581.

59 Trautmann, *Aryans and British India*, p. 30.

60 Dow, *History of Hindostan*, vol. 1 (1768), p. xx.

61 Dow, *History of Hindostan*, vol. 1 (1768), pp. xxx–xxxi.

SHASTERS'.[62] Dow claimed that it was from these texts that 'his pundit' advisor, who goes unnamed, explained numerous passages, so 'as to give him a general idea of the doctrine which they contain'.[63] Pandit instruction was to become an important part of the history of oriental scholarship, the reappraisal of which has become significant in histories aimed at restoring a fuller picture of the individual pandit scholars employed by orientalists in the Company from the late 1780s.[64] Nevertheless, this private appointment on the part of Dow was less usual at the time, and so it is difficult to determine who this could have been.[65] Indeed, most contemporary depictions of the Brahmins made much of the idea that they were secretive and mistrustful of European curiosity, including a reference by Dow to the 'impenetrable veil of mystery with which the Brahmins industriously cover their religious tenets'.[66] Somewhat incongruously with this statement, however, it seems that a good portion of Dow's genuine insights into Indian religion could reasonably have come from pandit instruction. And yet, as late as 1785, William Jones had great difficulty in securing a pandit scholar to aid his enquiries into the Sanskrit language. His first instructor was not a Brahmin but a vaidya Sanskrit instructor (a specialist in Ayurveda medical knowledge) at Nadia named Rāmalocana Kanthavarna.[67] As Jones relayed it, Rāmalocana had insisted on only disclosing the grammar of the language, staying away from theological precepts.[68] In this sense, Dow's instruction does seem unusual, though not completely implausible.

Another important set of sources for Dow were, of course, Persian texts. In the first instance his translation of the *Tārikh-i-Firishta* exposed him to the world view of its author, Firishta. As Manan Ahmed Asif's vivid reconstruction of the intellectual worlds of the *Tārikh-i-Firishta* in *The Loss of Hindustan* (2020) has shown, this was explicitly aimed at writing a comprehensive history of Hindustan through novel means such as the incorporation of details from texts like the *Mahābhārata*.[69] Dow had some disagreements with Firishta on the interpretation of this text, which will be dealt with in Chapter 4 of this book when we consider Dow's broader account of *Hindoo* history. What is clear is that Dow certainly took some cues from Firishta, while at the same time taking care to distance himself

[62] Dow, *History of Hindostan*, vol. 1 (1768), p. xxi.
[63] Dow, *History of Hindostan*, vol. 1 (1768), p. xxi.
[64] See, for example, Bayly, *Empire and Information*.
[65] Dodson, *Orientalism*, p. 53.
[66] Dow, *History of Hindostan*, vol. 1 (1768), p. xxii.
[67] William Jones to Charles Wilkins, dated 17 September 1785, in G. Cannon (ed.), *The Letters of Sir William Jones*, vol. 2 (Oxford: Clarendon Press, 1970), p. 682.
[68] See Dodson, *Orientalism, Empire and National Culture*, p. 53.
[69] Asif, *Loss of Hindustan*, pp. 89–101.

from his Mughal sources. His dissertation on the religion of the *Hindoos* begins, for example, with an explicit reference to the story of the attempts of the 'learned Feizi', that is, Faizi (Abu al-Faiz ibn Mubarak), the court poet for the Mughal emperor Akbar, to learn Sanskrit and access the knowledge of the Vedas. This takes its inspiration from Firishta's first chapter, which, as Ahmed Asif discusses in detail, recounts the story of Faizi's translation of the *Mahābhārata*.[70] In addition, Dow had clearly paid attention to the opening of Firishta's history, which he summarised as 'an extended introduction on the beliefs of the Indians, an account of Hindu kings' and 'a detailed description of the appearance of Islam in that land'. Thus Dow provides a truncated version of this at the start of his own translation and appears to base his own account of Hindoo chronology on Firishta's rendering of the *Mahābhārata*.[71] Moreover, in this section of the *Tārikh-i-Firishta*, Firishta argues that the original Hindus were monotheists, who had been induced to worship idols at some point in their ancient history, via encouragement from the Brahmins.[72] It is very likely that Dow's interest and confidence in the original monotheism of 'the Hindoo religion' stems from this source.

Despite these obvious connections, Dow was keen to set his authority apart from that of Firishta. He does this by contradicting him in several places. He argues, for example, that Muslim writers and 'some of the learned of Europe' had made a mistake in identifying the divinity 'Birmha' (Brahma) as 'some philosopher of repute in India' who they sometimes called 'Brumma, Burma and Brahma'.[73] This was not the case, argued Dow, because in the context of the Hindu religion Brahma was 'an allegorical person' only. According to Dow, Firishta had made this mistake. In contrast, Dow was explicitly siding with the Brahmins who he claimed 'deny, that any such a person ever existed'. Rather, in support of his vision of the Hindu deities as figurative, Dow clarifies that 'Birmha in the Shanscrita language allegorically signifies WISDOM, one of the

[70] Asif, *The Loss of Hindustan*, p. 195. Audrey Truschke on the other hand says that Firishta wrongly attributed the translation to Abu'l-Fazl, who wrote a preface: Truschke, *Culture of Encounters: Sanskrit at the Mughal Court* (Columbia University Press, 2016), p. 218.

[71] As quoted in Truschke, *Culture of Encounters*, p. 217.

[72] Truschke, *Culture of Encounters*, p. 220.

[73] This was possibly a reference to Holwell, who had also complained about these terms, while himself distinguishing Birmah the divinity (a mixture of Brahman and Brahma) from 'Brahma', as an earthly incarnation and lawgiver). Holwell, *Interesting Historical Events*, vol. 2, p. 6. Another possible target was Luke Scrafton, who had styled called 'Brumma' as a legislator figure: Luke Scrafton, *Reflections on the Government &c of Indostan, With a Short Sketch of the History of Bengal* (London: W. Richardson and S. Clark, 1763), p. 5.

principal attributes of the supreme divinity'.[74] Thus Dow sets up and vindicates his particular interpretation of *Hindoo* religion, as a pure monotheism, against Firishta as a faulty interpreter of Indian theology. To reinforce this Dow subsumes Persianate sources under the same criticism that he had launched at ignorant European travel writers and the accounts of biased missionary authors. That is, Persian authorities were unreliable sources both because of their 'ignorance of the Shanscrita' and because of the 'prejudices of the Mahommedans against the followers of the Brahmin religion'.[75] Nevertheless, the care taken to outline such disagreement is itself suggestive of the attention that Dow had paid to Firishta's account, which was no doubt an important source for his own construction of 'the religion of the Hindoos'.

Within the dissertation itself, however, there is a sleight of hand at play. Dow purported to provide two extracts from two different *Hindoo* scriptures, the origins of which are somewhat dubious. Dow first explains that 'the Bedas' (Vedas) are considered by the *Hindoos* to be the divine laws delivered by 'Brimha' (Brahma) at the creation of the world (an idea expressed in the *Mahābhārata*). Dismissing their divine origin, Dow turns to 'the first credible account' of the Vedas, correctly relaying that their collector or scribe is thought to be 'Beass Muni', by which he means Vyasa ('Muni' meaning ancient sage), also offering his alternative name, Krishna Dvaipāyana, as 'Krishen Baseo'.[76] He then gives an account of the four Vedas, more or less accurately listing them as the *Rug Beda* (*Rigveda*), the *Sheham Beda* (*Sāmaveda*), the *Judger Beda* (*Yajurveda*) and finally, the *Obatar-bah Beda* (*Atharvavedaḥ*).[77] His limited knowledge of these texts is excused by a elaboration of the comments in the preface to the *History* that the 'Bedas' are 'covered with a veil of darkness', as Dow adds that their extreme antiquity and the version of Sanskrit in which they were written made them obscure even to the Brahmins.[78] After some digressions, Dow suggests that the mystery surrounding the Vedas was, however, not such a problem, as in practice the *Hindoo* religion was in fact oriented around three different 'Shasters'; the *Dirm Shaster*, the *Bedang Shaster* and the

[74] Dow, *History of Hindostan*, vol. 1 (1768), p. xxviii.

[75] Dow, *History of Hindostan*, vol. 1 (1768), p. viii.

[76] This spelling may be a result of 'v' and 'b' having a similar pronunciation in Bengali; this also accounts for Dow's translation of Vedas as 'Bedas'. Dow, *History of Hindostan*, vol. 1 (1768), p. xxviii.

[77] Dow, *History of Hindostan*, vol. 1 (1768), pp. xxviii–xxix.

[78] Dow, *History of Hindostan*, vol. 1 (1768), pp. 3, xxix.

Neadirsin Shaster. It is from these texts that Dow presents several extracts and quotations, the origins of which are somewhat unclear.

By 'Shasters' Dow means 'shastras' or *śāstras* in Sanskrit, which he describes as a word signifying 'knowledge', commonly used to mean 'book that treats of divinity and the sciences'.[79] In this Dow was not too far off: *śāstra* does mean specialised or technical knowledge, and the different *śāstras* are philosophical texts or treatises on a specific field of knowledge.[80] There is, however, some confusion in Dow's terminology. By 'Neadirsin' Dow meant Nyāya, one of the six orthodox schools of Brahminical philosophy, which is most well known for its development of logical procedures as a means of establishing correct inferences.[81] '*Nyāyaśāstra*' is sometimes used to describe this as an area of specialised knowledge: the science of right reasoning. Its original text is usually considered to be the *Nyāya Sūtras*, which is possibly what Dow meant. Likewise, the *Bedang Shaster* seems mostly likely to have derived from the *Brahma Sūtras*, sometimes known as the *Vedānta Sutras*, which was, as Dow claims, associated with the Vedānta (Bedang) school. If it was this text, however, it is hard to reconcile Dow's attribution of the text to 'Sirrider Swami' (Sridhar Swami), as the author most widely associated with the *Brahma Sūtras* is known as Badarayana.[82]

It was the Shasters, Dow argued, that contained all of the essentials of the *Hindoo* religion, and it is from these texts that he draws all of his examples. His exact methodology, however, is ambiguous. He had informed his readers that his pandit advisor from Banaras had explained these texts so as to give him 'a general idea of the doctrine which they contain'.[83] And yet, we are presented with significant extracts from both the *Bedang Shaster* and the *Dirm Shaster*, as well as numerous quotations from the *Neadirsin Shaster*. Moreover, at various points Dow seems to suggest that he is indeed giving direct translations: for example, 'Before we shall proceed to the doctrine to the NEADRISEN SHASTER, it may not be improper to give a translation of the first chapter of the DIRM SHASTER'.[84] Elsewhere Dow also claimed to be offering extracts that were 'literally translated from the original SHASTER'. Though to confuse things further, he also described the

[79] Dow, *History of Hindostan*, vol. 1 (1768), p. xxxviii.
[80] King, *Indian Philosophy*, pp. 50–1; J. L Brockington, *The Sacred Thread: Hinduism in Its Continuity and Diversity* (Edinburgh: Edinburgh University Press, 1996), pp. 38–40.
[81] King, *Indian Philosophy*, p. 130.
[82] Dow, *History of Hindostan*, vol. 1 (1768), p. xxxviii; King, *Indian Philosophy*, pp. 53–4. By 'Sirrider Swami', Dow possibly meant Sridhar Swami, a fourteenth-century Sanskrit scholar known for his commentary on the *Bhagavad-Gītā*.
[83] Dow, *History of Hindostan*, vol. 1 (1768), p. xxiii.
[84] Dow, *History of Hindostan*, vol. 1 (1768), pp. l–li.

fragment of text offered as a 'commentary'.[85] We are left with the possibilities that perhaps these extracts were taken from Persian texts on the Sanskrit *śāstras* that Dow neglected to mention, or that perhaps they were sections of a text that was dictated to Dow by his pundit advisor. This is how William Robertson introduced Dow's Shaster, summarising that it was not made 'from the Sanskreet, but taken from the mouth of a Brahmin, who explained the Shaster in Persian, or in the vulgar language of Bengal'.[86] This is not implausible as a methodology. And yet, despite some important insights and correlations to Hindu traditions, the extracts themselves are difficult to trace.

Most decisive in placing a question mark next to the authenticity of Dow's texts is the material evidence left by Dow himself, who claimed to have possessed, and deposited in the British Museum, a manuscript copy of what he called the *Neadirsin Shaster*. This manuscript has subsequently been proven to be something else entirely. Bendall's catalogue of the museum's manuscripts refers to Dow's 'erroneous description' of the texts, concluding instead that the deposited item was 'A collection of Sanskrit MSS', with some pages in Bengali, that are 'more or less fragmentary'. Those fragments are now held at the British Library and bear the title 'The Neadrisen Shaster' with 'Alex Dow' written next to it.[87]

Dow may well not have known that the manuscript was not genuine, given his inability to read the text in the original Sanskrit. Nevertheless, this still leaves the origins of the translated excerpts unanswered for, suggesting that Dow's *Hindoo* scriptures were as much a construction as Holwell's *Shastah*, despite their stronger correspondence with actual Indian theological ideas. The most generous interpretation is that Dow's pandit may have translated something into Persian, claiming it to be a copy of the Sanskrit manuscript that Dow had procured and believed to be the *Neadirsin Shaster*, and that Dow then copied from this and deposited the Sanskrit fragments in the British Museum none the wiser. Alternatively, perhaps Dow wrote down these passages after his pandit gave an oral explanation of them in Bengali. Dow declines to explain this. In either case, Dow's claims to be presenting these texts as 'literally translated from the original' Shasters is somewhat duplicitous. Moreover, there are many ways in which Dow appears to have played an active hand in the

85 Dow, *History of Hindostan*, vol. 1 (1768), p. xxxix.

86 Robertson, *Historical Disquisition*, p. 359.

87 C. Bendall, *Catalogue of the Sanskrit Manuscripts in the British Museum* (London: British Museum, 1902), p. 147. Catalogued in the British Museum as Add. 4829; now in the British Library's Oriental MS collection as Add. 4830.

construction of these texts and their significance to fit a particular narrative about the religious composition of India, and the nature of religious belief in general, to which we will turn in the following section.

Dow used the explanations of his pandit advisor to fashion the Hindu traditions and ideas that were shared with him into the *Hindoo* religion, a monotheistic and 'symbolical religion'. As we have seen, central to this was the claim that the *Hindoos* were divided into 'two great religious sects', the beliefs of which were oriented around these texts. On the one hand were 'the followers of the doctrine of the BEDANG' (Vedānta) and on the other 'those who adhere to the principles of the NEADIRZIN' (Nyāya). This was not, however, a recognition of the religious pluralism of India. Rather, it was an explanation of different approaches to religion per se. The two 'sects' were differentiated not by core doctrines but by two different approaches to those doctrines, as expressed in a third unifying text, the *Dirm Shaster*. This text was 'common to both the grand sects of the Hindoos', the central tenet of which was 'the unity of the supreme being'.[88] United by a belief in a singular divine creator, the two sects merely differed in what Dow calls 'their philosophy': that is, according to his distinction between those who 'look up to the divinity through the medium of reason and philosophy' and those who 'receive, as an article of their belief, every holy legend and allegory' from antiquity.[89]

Dow's 'two great religious sects' are not just Indian, but represent a universal struggle between orthodox and rational religion. Indeed, Dow's comment that this was the case 'in many other countries' invoked a universal division between those who 'receive' their religion, in a manner akin to unquestioning faith in revelation, and those whose religion is a product of 'reason and philosophy'. When coupled with Dow's further statement, appearing in the final section of the *Dissertation*, that 'whatever the external ceremonies of religion may be, the self-same infinite Being is the object of universal adoration', the general application of this model is clear. Dow therefore requires that his readers see the followers of the Bedang as analogous to those who put their faith in revelation and tradition, and the Neadirsin as those forging a more rational form of religious belief.[90]

In summary, then, Dow's *Dissertation* on the Neadirsin and the Bedang is constructed from a complex mixture of pandit knowledge, Brahminical

[88] Dow, *History of Hindostan*, vol. 1 (1768), pp. xxxv, lx, lv.
[89] Dow, *History of Hindostan*, vol. 1 (1768), p. lxviii.
[90] Dow, *History of Hindostan*, vol. 1 (1768), p. lxxxvi.

tradition, Persian sources, untraceable texts and European religious frameworks and categories. Yet, this confused weaving of various sources and conjecture was skilfully presented as an unprejudiced account of genuine *Hindoo* scriptures. More importantly, it was received as such. One reviewer stated that Dow was better informed on Hinduism 'than any preceding writer'.[91] It was constructed in such a way not just to prove the genius of its author, but to press a particular interpretation of *Hindoo* religion. Far from the descriptions of various idolatries and ritual customs associated with previous accounts, Dow's description was centred on providing an exposition on two sects, which articulated two different epistemological approaches to religious truth.

Universal Religion and the *Dirm Shaster*

As mentioned in the previous section, Dow was insistent on the unification of the 'two great religious sects', the Neadirsin and the Bedang, through the doctrines of the *Dirm Shaster*. Dow's decision to present a text that unified 'both the grand sects of the Hindoos' was a conscious choice. Others had already recognised the possibility of seeing a great degree of plurality in Indian religious practices. Another employee of the company, Alexander Hamilton, for example, had already made the observation in the early eighteenth century that Indian religion was made up of 'above a hundred different Sects'.[92] Similarly, the Jesuit *Lettres édifiantes* remarked on a number of distinct groups and traditions within the fabric of Indian religion, pointing out differences in beliefs about the soul and its relationship with God.[93] In contrast, Dow's extract from the unifying *Dirm Shaster* was designed to throw 'a clear light on the religious tenets' shared by all *Hindoos*. It was his contention that the most central tenet contained within it, upon which all the *Hindoos* agreed, was 'the unity of the supreme being'.[94] It is unclear which Sanskrit text the title *Dirm Shaster* is supposed to refer to. It is possible that it is meant to be *Dharmaśāstra*, but Dow's description is ambiguous. The *Dharmaśāstra*, or Dharama-shastras, represents a genre of texts on the laws and procedures relating to the concept of 'dharma', which encompasses the particular set of obligations that position oneself in the alignment with right reality.[95] The most well known of these

[91] *Monthly Review*, 39 (1768), p. 387.
[92] Alexander Hamilton, *A New Account of the East Indies*, vol. 1 of 2 (Edinburgh: John Mosman, 1727), p. 162.
[93] Sweetman, *Mapping Hinduism*, p. 141.
[94] Dow, *History of Hindostan*, vol. 1 (1768), pp. li, lv.
[95] See King, *Indian Philosophy*, p. 40.

texts, in part due to the emphasis placed on it by Company administrators after its translation by William Jones in 1794 (as *Institutes of Hindu Law; or the Ordinances of Menu*), is the *Mānava-Dharmaśāstra*, or *Manusmriti*.[96] Dow's vague description of the text as containing 'the religious tenets common to both the grand sects of the Hindoos' in some sense captures the notion of *Dharmaśāstra* as a literature of duties.[97] It negates, however, the complexity of this body of work and the various ways in which different philosophical schools took to its interpretation. Moreover, Dow names another text, the 'NEA SHASTER', as the *Hindoo* 'code of laws', suggesting he was less understanding of this context than this interpretation of the title *Dirm Sashter* might suggest.[98]

The extract itself is presented as dialogue. There are two interlocutors: Narud, who represents 'human reason' (possibly from Manu), and Birmah, whom Dow claimed to be representative of 'Wisdom' and identifies as 'the genitive case of Brimh', which Dow takes to be Brahman (the highest universal principle), and describes as 'a primitive signifying GOD'. Throughout the dialogue both Birmah and Narud demonstrate the core doctrine of Dow's *Hindoo* religion by agreeing on the unity and singularity of God.[99] Narud asks questions such as 'Who is the greatest of all Beings?' to which Birmah replies, 'Birmh; who is infinite and almighty'. Likewise, to the question 'is he exempt from death?' Birmah provides the answer 'He is: being eternal and incorporeal'.[100] The dialogue form itself is of course a familiar one in European literature, especially in works dealing with philosophical and religious debate, ranging from classical literature and religious catechisms to contemporary philosophy.[101] It is also, however, a central feature of South Asian religious literature. In the traditions associated with Hinduism the dialogue form can be found in its earliest texts, such as the *Rigveda* and the *Upanishads*, and it became a central device for framing theological and philosophical discussion in texts such as the *Rāmāyana* and the Puranas.[102] Moreover, Dow's comments on *Hindoo* chronology suggest he was aware of the Persian translation of the

96 Jones, *Institutes of Hindu Law, or, the Ordinances of Menu* (London: J. Sewell, Cornhill & J. Debrett, 1796).
97 Dow, *History of Hindostan*, vol. 1 (1768), p. li.
98 Dow, *History of Hindostan*, vol. 1 (1768), p. xxxiv.
99 Dow, *History of Hindostan*, vol. 1 (1768), p. lv.
100 Dow, *History of Hindostan*, vol. 1 (1768), p. li
101 One of the most famous examples, of course, being Dow's correspondent David Hume's *Dialogues Concerning Natural Religion* (1757).
102 See the introduction in Brian Black and Chakravarthi Ram-Prasad (eds.), *In Dialogue with Classical Indian Traditions: Encounter, Transformation and Interpretation* (Oxford: Routledge, 2019).

Mahābhārata, known as the *Razmnāma*, which contained numerous sections of dialogue. The *Mānava-Dharmaśāstra* is very similar in style. Written in verse, it conveys a dialogue from an exalted being, in the role of teacher, to various students. The lessons are first delivered by Manu, and then his pupil Bhṛgu, a sage of Brahmin. Possibly this is where Dow took the names Narud (Manu) and Birmah (Bhṛgu).[103] The *Mānava-Dharmaśāstra*, however, is not a dialogue between these two, and the actual portions of text given by Dow are difficult to match up well to the text. The subject matter, however, is not too far off, in the sense that the *Mānava-Dharmaśāstra* does open with a discourse on the origin of the world, and touches on the nature of Brahman. Ultimately, however, they are very different texts and the exact origins of Dow's particular dialogue are obscure, if not rather dubious

The dialogue of the *Dirm Shaster* is didactic in nature. Emerging from Narud's questions about the nature of the divinity, it is an expression of the idea that religion may be understood differently according to the refinement of the mind in question. Thus, in answer to Narud's question 'What is his likeness?' Birmah replies, 'He hath no likeness: but to stamp some idea of him upon the minds of men, who cannot believe in an immaterial being, he is represented under various symbolical forms.'[104]

As well as the agreed unity of God, the *Dirm Shaster* is thus used to illustrate several important principles in Dow's presentation of the *Hindoo* religion. Most pressingly, these are the symbolical nature of the *Hindoo* deities and a fundamental distinction between the learned and the vulgar. At the heart of this distinction is a tension, similar to that expressed in the work of Holwell, between the idea that the natural, rational, original, simple and untainted religion of India was preserved only through the elite knowledge of the learned Brahmins. This is a tension that emerges in various expressions of Enlightenment thought, where reason was regarded as a natural faculty, but at the same time operated as a verb. Discourse and 'reasoning' were often exercised through knowledge and education, the precise relationship between which was the subject of varied opinion and philosophical critique throughout the period.[105] Indeed, in Dow's work, the tension between the natural religion of reason exhibited in these texts

[103] See Patrick Olivelle (trans.), *The Law Code of Manu* (Oxford: Oxford University Press, 2004), pp. xxiii–xxxi.

[104] Dow, *History of Hindostan*, vol. 1 (1768), p. li.

[105] Michel Marlherbe, 'Reason', in Knud Haakonssen (ed.), *The Cambridge History of Eighteenth-Century Philosophy*, vol. 1 (Cambridge: Cambridge University Press, 2006), p. 320.

and the tendencies of 'the vulgar' to slip into superstition is not a matter exclusive to *Hindoo* religion. In fact, as he puts it:

> To attentive inquirers into the human mind, it will appear that common sense, upon the affairs of religion, is pretty equally divided among all nations. Revelation and Philosophy have, it is confessed, lopped off some of those superstitious excrescences and absurdities that naturally arise in weak minds, upon a subject so mysterious: but it is much to be doubted, whether the want of those necessary purifiers of religion, ever involved any nation in gross idolatry, as many ignorant zealots have pretended.[106]

On the one hand, Dow firmly establishes a relative universalism that sees 'common sense', for which we can read natural reason, as the basis for religious belief. On the other hand, he at least rhetorically disavows pure deism by attributing some credit to '*Revelation* and Philosophy' (emphasis added). In this formulation, though, revelation is coupled and equated with philosophy, which was not typically attributed with the same infallibility as 'the Word'. Moreover, the added qualification that the absolute necessity of revelation was a construct of 'ignorant zealots' further affirms Dow's preference for a more minimalistic definition of religious truth.

This passing concession to revelation illustrates a pragmatic strand of thinking in Dow's approach to religion. He appears to consider the utility of religious doctrines in countering 'the absurdities that naturally arise in weak minds' a permissible necessity when it comes to practical religion of the vulgar. This was a not an uncommon stance in deist literature, which as well as decrying priestcraft and superstition, also considered the efficacy of a simple religious doctrine in ensuring the 'moral sense' of the general public.[107] The idea that religion could serve a social utility, as well as a social ill, was also of course part of the intellectual fabric of eighteenth-century comparative studies of different polities, established as it was by an author whose ideas Dow explores, as we shall see in Chapter 4, more thoroughly in his 'Dissertation Concerning the Origin and Nature on Despotism in Hindostan': Montesquieu.[108] From the above quotation it is clear that Dow viewed religious belief as a product of natural reason, hence generally equal in distribution, but that he also saw the corruption of that

[106] Dow, *History of Hindostan*, vol. 1 (1768), p. lxxxvi.

[107] Anthony Ashley Cooper, 1st Earl of Shaftesbury, *Characteristicks of Men, Manners, Opinions, Times. In Three Volumes. Vol. I. I. A Letter Concerning Enthusiasm* (London: John Darby, 1711).

[108] Montesquieu, *Spirit of the Laws*, part 5, book 24, chapter 1, p. 459. For more on the 'social utility of religion' in eighteenth-century thought, see S. Zurbuchen, 'Religion and Society', in K. Haakonssen (ed.), *The Cambridge History of Eighteenth-Century Philosophy* (Cambridge: Cambridge University Press, 2000).

faculty as a propensity in the vulgar. Through philosophy, though, natural reason could be conserved. It is on this basis that he establishes Brahmin learning as the location of the more 'elevated' ideas of Indian civilisation. And yet, for those whose, as Birmh puts it in the dialogue of Dow's *Dirm Shaster*, 'imagination cannot rise to devotion without an image', symbolical representations of the godhead could serve a didactic function.[109] Nevertheless, this is also carefully and significantly qualified with the idea that left unchecked, natural religion would still not descend into the 'gross idolatry' invented and, in the case of missionary literature on India, pronounced by 'ignorant zealots'.

Indeed, this was not an unequivocal celebration of the Brahmins. Dow, like Holwell, makes a careful distinction between 'learned Brahmins', like the one with whom an accidental conversation led to his enquiries, and the 'unlearned Brahmins'. While the former had helped to preserve the purest parts of the *Hindoo* doctrine, the latter were responsible for spreading misinformation about the religion.[110] Thus, in a repetition of the narrative established by the English deists to explain the process of religious corruption,[111] Dow blamed the loss of the pure and original tenets of the rational *Hindoo* religion on 'the influence of superstition and priestcraft'.[112] As evidence of active priestcraft in India, Dow discussed the notion of a *Hindoo* legal code. Arguing that although the Brahmins are not exempted from the laws they created, when it comes to capital punishment, 'the influence of the Brahmins is so great and their characters as priests so sacred, that they escape in cases where no mercy would be shewn to the other tribes'.[113]

In order to preserve the Brahmins as proponents of philosophical *Hindoo* religion, though, Dow reserved his harshest criticism for a different group of religious representatives. These were the 'idle and pretended devotees', known as the 'Fakiers'.[114] According to Lorenzen, the fakirs were religious mystics that largely modelled themselves on Hindu yogis and sannyasis.[115] In Voltaire's writings, the fakir is the epitome of religious corruption. In the *Dictionnaire philosophique* (1764) the fakir is offered as the personification of religion's worst traits: dogmatism and enthusiasm. Voltaire also includes them to typify *amour-propre* (self-love),

[109] Dow, *History of Hindostan*, vol. 1 (1768), p. lii.
[110] Dow, *History of Hindostan*, vol. 1 (1768), p. xxvii. [111] Herrick, *Radical Rhetoric*, p. 32.
[112] Dow, *History of Hindostan*, vol. 1 (1768), p. xxiv.
[113] Dow, *History of Hindostan*, vol. 1 (1768), pp. xxxiv–xxxv.
[114] Dow, *History of Hindostan*, vol. 1 (1768), p. xxxii.
[115] Lorenzen, *Who Invented Hinduism?: Essays on Religion in History* (Delhi: Yoga Press, 2006) p. 59.

via their displays of extreme suffering, motivated by the promise of a better fate in the next life rather than any higher spiritual ideal.[116] Dow will have understood them in the context of their relationship with the Company, where the fakirs who had the right to collect 'contributions' from official offices under the Mughal system were seen as a nuisance and a financial drain on the business of revenue collection. In 1763, a report of 'faquirs' taking over Dacca and wrecking the Company's factory reached Calcutta.[117] Dow's allegations thus consist of the fairly conventional claim that the fakirs were merely motivated by money, their pilgrimages laying 'whole countries under contribution'. He also adds an element of the dramatic with the more unusual accusation that they seduced the wives of the vulgar with mystical promises, and thus 'put on the character of sanctity, as a cloak for their pleasures'.[118] This more sensational illustration of the susceptibility of the vulgar to priestcraft may have been a product of information regarding the division of 'Left' and 'Right' tantric methods, within which there was a view that sexual intercourse can be considered a ritual offering.[119] Nevertheless, the more straightforward explanation for why Dow chose to present the fakirs as scandalous religious deviants was of course the pervasiveness of tropes of sexual transgression in European anticlericalism, long-standing since the Reformation.[120]

Like common sense, this manipulation of the vulgar was also universal. Dow's statement 'To attentive inquirers into the human mind, it will appear that common sense, upon the affairs of religion, is pretty equally divided among all nations' reads like an adaption of Descartes' phrase 'Good sense is, of all things among men, the most equally distributed'.[121] With it Dow affirms a deistic approach to natural religion that the essential elements of religious belief are knowable through reason, and therefore universal. Yet, similarly, if 'common sense, upon the affairs of religion' is equally divided among nations, so too is ignorance and superstition. To turn the common accusation that *Hindoo* religion was simply characterised by superstition on its head, Dow pointed to the parallels among Christian Europeans. Taking the idea that the 'more ignorant Hindoos' venerate subaltern divinities, for example, Dow argued that this was no different to

116 Voltaire, *Dictionnaire philosophique* (Paris: Gallimard, 1964 [1764]), pp. 112, 117, 38.

117 William R. Pinch, *Warrior Ascetics and Indian Empires* (Cambridge: Cambridge University Press, 2006), p. 87.

118 Dow, *History of Hindostan*, vol. 1 (1768), p. xxxiii.

119 Brockington, *Sacred Thread*, p. 129.

120 Katherine Crawford, *European Sexualities, 1400–1800* (Cambridge: Cambridge University Press, 2007), p. 66.

121 Descartes, *Discours de la method*, English translation in *Discourse on the Method and the Meditations*, John Veitch (trans.) (New York: Cosimo Incorporated, 2008 [Paris, 1637]), p. 11.

the fact that some 'Christians believe in Angels'. While Dow does stop short of making parallels between the *Hindoo* 'allegorical account of creation, for the purpose of vulgar theology' and anything Christian, the implication is clear when he reflects, just afterwards, that 'the vulgar of any country' do not require any aid to 'corrupt their ideas' on the subject of creation.[122]

While this might have established an equivalence between Christian and *Hindoo* religion in matters of superstition, for Dow, when it came to the more destructive crime of zealotry, the Christian had the potential to be much worse. As Dow put it, the *Hindoos* 'chuse rather to make a mystery of their religion, than impose it upon the world, like the Mahommedans, with the sword, or by means of the stake, after the manner of some pious Christians'.[123] This brazen equation of Christian zealots with the 'Mahommedans' would have had a great deal of rhetorical power. Anti-Islamic sentiment pervaded the intellectual and political culture of the period. On the one hand were critiques of the religion itself in both its doctrines and its historical manifestations.[124] On the other, was an intellectual alignment of Islamic polities with the concept of oriental or Asian despotism.[125] Indeed, elsewhere in *The History of Hindostan* Dow refers to Islam as a religion 'peculiarly calculated for despotism.'[126] In contrast, the tolerance of the *Hindoos*, juxtaposed with the violent irrationality displayed by the history of Christianity, completes the provocation. Following early eighteenth-century critics of religious fervour such as Shaftesbury and Hume, Dow is summoning a contemporary critique of religious excess as contrary to the spirit of reasonable thought.[127] This criticism was roused in the mid-century as a particular response to the rise of evangelical Methodism.[128] Absolutely integral to this critique of religious enthusiasm was the contrasting concept of religious toleration. Shaftesbury's 1708 *A Letter Concerning Enthusiasm*, for example, made an important distinction between piety and extravagance in religious expression which maintained that while piety, also termed 'serene' or 'reasonable enthusiasm', was not in contradiction with a tolerant attitude, extravagant enthusiasm was

122 Dow, *History of Hindostan*, vol. 1 (1768), pp. xlvi, xlix.

123 Dow, *History of Hindostan*, vol. 3 (1772), p. xxiii.

124 Palin, *Attitudes to Other Religions*, pp. 81–104.

125 Curtis, *Orientalism and Islam*, pp. 35–6.

126 Dow, *History of Hindostan*, vol. 3 (1772), p. xiii.

127 Patrick Müller, *Latitudinarianism and Didacticism in Eighteenth-Century Literature: Moral Theology in Fielding, Sterne and Goldsmith* (Frankfurt: Peter Lang, 2009), pp. 31–2.

128 For the interchangeable use of 'enthusiasm' for 'Methodism', see Misty G. Anderson, *Imagining Methodism in Eighteenth-Century Britain: Enthusiasm, Belief, and the Borders of the Self* (Baltimore: Johns Hopkins University Press, 2012), p. 37.

a form of irrationality that led only to the kind of violent fanaticism invoked by Dow's reference to the stake.[129] While Dow did not develop the nuance of later discussions, such as Hume's distinction between enthusiasm and superstition, the critique of fanaticism and zealotry is consistently at work throughout his essays.

Dow's observation that the *Hindoos* 'allow that everyone may go to heaven his own way' therefore contains an implicit critique of those enthusiasts, and worse, zealots, who do not.[130] Elsewhere in his work, he reserves praise for historical actors who appear the exception to the typical prejudices of religious bias. The Mughal empire's greatest stateman in Dow's judgement, for example, was Akbar (Jalal-ud-din Muhammad Akbar), whom he described as 'totally divested of those prejudices for his own religion'.[131] Likewise, in praising Firishta's accounts of the Mughals, he states, 'What is really remarkable in this writer is, that he seems as much divested of religious prejudices, as he is of political flattery or fear.'[132] Moreover, this critique is universal; both Dow's praise and criticism of religious culture is applicable to both *Hindoo* and Christian traditions. In effect, Dow was treating religion as a historical category, the fluctuating rationality of which was subject to the same mechanisms across the globe.

The Bedang and the Neadirsin

In his division between the Bedang and the Neadirsin, that is, between those who 'receive' their religion and those who arrive at it through reason, Dow is referring to the Vedānta and Nyāya schools of Hindu philosophy. This section of the chapter will deal with Dow's treatment of the Vedānta system, followed by an account of his understanding of Nyāya philosophy, tracing the ways in which Dow fused these two schools of thought with eighteenth-century European terminology and concepts to present a universal history of two different approaches to religion.

Vedānta/Bedang

There are a number of Vedānta traditions, but all schools accept the classical *Upanishads*, the *Brahma Sūtras* and the *Bhagavad-Gītā* as the

[129] Michael Heyd, *Be Sober and Reasonable: The Critique of Enthusiasm in the Seventeenth and Early Eighteenth Centuries* (Leiden: Brill, 2000), p. 226.

[130] Dow, *History of Hindostan*, vol. 1 (1768), p. xxiii.

[131] Dow, *History of Hindostan*, vol. 3 (1772), pp. xxv, 103–4.

[132] Dow, *History of Hindostan*, vol. 1 (1768), p. ix.

foundations of their tradition. In the nineteenth century Vedānta became an important focal point of the intellectual interest and codification of Hinduism.[133] But as this was not the case at the time Dow was writing, it seems that his assessment of the Bedang as 'the most orthodox, as well as the most ancient' was both a deliberate construction, and also probably a notion that he was led to by consultations with pandits of a particular tradition. Dow had already informed his readers that his knowledge rested on the authority of a pandit instructor and, if true, they would likely have been very well versed in Vedānta philosophy as one of the main branches of Indian philosophy.[134] Moreover, Vedānta is a prominent school of philosophy and theology, and Dow's decision to characterise it as the most orthodox may correspond with its particular exegetical method, the emphasis of which is the acquisition of metaphysical knowledge via Vedic literature.[135] If Dow's interest was in establishing the principle that the Brahmins 'invariably believe in the unity, eternity, omniscience and omnipotence of God', then Vedānta teachings would be an appropriate source.[136] The first chapter of the *Brahma Sūtras*, which Dow seems to mistake for the *Bedang Shaster*, does indeed establish a connection between certain texts and Brahman, variously thought of in the traditions of Hinduism as being the essence of all being, the goal of enquiry and the source of the universe.[137]

Dow cast the *Bedang Shaster* as a 'philosophical catechism', which explored several metaphysical concepts.[138] Just like the *Dirm Shaster*, this text is presented by Dow as 'a dialogue between Birmha, the Wisdom of the Divinity; and Narud or Reason', who here is described as 'the son of Brimha' (this is unlike the *Brahma Sūtras*, which consist of aphoristic verses). The first topic under discussion considers the relationship between God and the *Trimūrti*, that is, the trinity of deities that includes the main interlocutor, Birmha (Brahma), alongside Shiba (Shiva) and Bishen (Vishnu). The extract opens with Narud asking to be instructed on creation. Birmha insists that he is to be understood merely as 'the instrument of the great WILL' or 'a part of his being, who he called forth to execute his eternal designs'. Thus he responds, 'do not imagine that I was creator of the world, independent of the divine mover, who is the great original essence, and creator of all things'. In the footnotes Dow again explains, 'Brimha is the genitive case of BRIMH, which is a primitive signifying GOD'. In this sense he is called Birmha

[133] Andrew J. Nicholson, *Unifying Hinduism: Philosophy and Identity in Indian Intellectual History* (New York: Columbia University Press, 2013), pp. 2–4.

[134] Dow, *History of Hindostan*, vol. 1 (1768), pp. xxxv, xxi.

[135] King, *Indian Philosophy*, p. 53.

[136] Dow, *History of Hindostan*, vol. 1 (1768), p. lxii.

[137] Brockington, *Sacred Thread*, pp. 106–7.

[138] Dow, *History of Hindostan*, vol. 1 (1768), p. xlvi.

because this means wisdom, which is 'the first attribute of the supreme divinity'.[139] By 'Brimh', we can suppose Dow is referring to Brahman, which in some strands of Vedānta thought, can indeed capture the idea of a cosmic being, and could therefore plausibly be considered consummate to the more familiar concept of a 'supreme divinity', as offered by Dow.[140] While this dialogue could therefore reflect certain trends in theistic Vedānta, or even more widely the *Upanishads*, Dow's composition was designed to paint a very precise portrait of *Hindoo* religion as monotheistic according to a very strict distinction between a singular supreme deity and 'inferior divinities', which, as he claimed, 'the learned Brahmins, with one voice, deny'.[141] Thus, at the end of the dissertation Dow explains that in addition to Birhma, Bishen (Vishnu) is the symbolic representation of 'providential and preserving' qualities and Shiba (Shiva) is 'that attribute that tends to destroy'.[142] This understanding of the *Trimūrti* is not expressed in the *Brahma Sūtras*, but is explored in the *Mahābhārata* (3:272:47), which was perhaps where Dow had encountered these ideas via Persian literature, though it is difficult to trace this more precisely. Within the traditions of Hinduism, however, the actual configuration of the relationship between these gods has many variations, with Brahma sometimes in a position of subordination rather than pre-eminence.[143] Foremost for Dow, though, was the importance of the concept in illustrating his contention that the *Hindoos* 'were not polytheists' and that this was 'no more than the symbolical worship of the divine attributes'.[144]

In summarising the dissertation, reflecting on the teachings of the *Bedang Shaster*, Dow again stresses that pragmatic side of his religious thought, arguing that although the Brahmins affirm that God has no image, they consider 'it is necessary to strike the gross ideas of man, with some emblems of God's attributes' should the vulgar lose their 'sense of religion'.[145] For example, in explaining the image of the 'Birmha' as 'the first attribute of the supreme divinity' Dow gives us an idea of how he sees this as working. Birmha, he concludes, is 'figuratively represented' with 'one head, having four faces' in order to denote his 'all seeing abilities', as befitting of the attribute of wisdom.[146] Some features have a simple explanation: Birmha wears a crown, 'an emblem of power and dominion',

139 Dow, *History of Hindostan*, vol. 1 (1768), p. xxix.
140 Brockington, *Sacred Thread*, p. 54.
141 Dow, *History of Hindostan*, vol. 1 (1768), p. lxiv.
142 Dow, *History of Hindostan*, vol. 1 (1768), p. lxvii.
143 Doniger, *Hindus*, p. 681.
144 Dow, *History of Hindostan*, vol. 1 (1768), p. lxvii.
145 Dow, *History of Hindostan*, vol. 1 (1768), p. lxvii.
146 Dow, *History of Hindostan*, vol. 1 (1768), p. xxxvi.

whereas others are infused by Dow with a weightier meaning: Birmha's four hands, for example, indicate 'the omnipotence of divine wisdom'. In these hands, Dow tells us, he holds 'the four Bedas, as a symbol of knowledge', a sceptre 'as a token of authority' and a ring 'or a complete circle as an emblem of eternity'. There is nothing in the fourth hand, Dow claims, because 'the WISDOM OF GOD [that which Birhma represents] is always ready to lend aid to his creatures'.[147] In these explanations, just as in the extract from the *Bedang Shaster*, Dow presents a mixture of genuine knowledge and insight with degrees of distortion to fit his particular vision of *Hindoo* religion. While Brahma is often depicted as carrying various objects, Dow's interpretations of their meaning appear to be rather ad hoc. The sceptre is more likely a *sruk* or a *sruva*, two different kinds of spoons used to pour ghee within scared rituals. The ring that Dow had seen was most likely prayer beads (*aksamālā*), associated indeed with time. Moreover, providing an account of why the deity is often depicted as riding a goose, Dow explains that among *Hindoos* the goose is an 'emblem of simplicity'. He then adds that it is therefore 'intended to imply simplicity in the operations of nature', which as Dow explains 'is but another name for the wisdom of the divinity'.[148] In Hindu iconography the goose or swan (*hamsa*) is a *vāhana*, an animal or mythical entity that a particular Hindu deity uses as a vehicle, upon which they are often depicted. Dow is correct that the *vāhana* is often symbolic of certain concepts and considered to be emblematic of some aspect of their corresponding deity. In the case of Brahma, however, the goose is the 'mask of the creative principle, which is anthropomorphically embodied in Brahmā.'[149] Dow's explanation is within the bounds of this idea, but he interprets this imagery through a particular conception of God's wisdom, in the form that reverberated through eighteenth-century intellectual and religious discourses thanks to the work of Samuel Clarke, as evidenced by the faultless design at work in the operations of nature.[150]

The latter part of the dialogue becomes much more metaphysical in subject matter, providing an exposition of the *Hindoo* account of creation according to the Bedang. It is here that Dow presents an interpretation of *Hindoo* philosophy that came to have great appeal for certain strands of European intellectual culture in the nineteenth century.[151] This centred on

[147] Dow, *History of Hindostan*, vol. 1, p. xxxix.
[148] Dow, *History of Hindostan*, vol. 1 (1768), p. xxxix.
[149] Heinrich Zimmer, *Myths and Symbols in Indian Art and Civilization*, J. Campbell (ed.) (Princeton, NJ: Princeton University Press, 1972), p. 48.
[150] Stewart, 'Samuel Clarke'. [151] As discussed in Chapter 5 of this book.

the introduction of the idea of the 'Great Soul', which Dow translates in a footnote as 'Purmattima', and thereby introduces a significant concept in Vedānta philosophy, *Paramātmā* (sometimes translated as variations on 'Supreme soul/self' or 'Universal Self'). This idea is especially central to one of the oldest sub-schools of Vedānta thought, Advaita Vedānta, a non-dualist philosophy the central premise of which is that *ātman*, the individual self, and Brahmin, the highest reality, are one and the same.[152] This notion of the ultimate unity of reality is thus captured in the concept *Paramātmā*, a compound of *parama*, meaning 'highest', and *ātma*, the self/soul. Dow introduces the concept of the 'Great Soul' in response to Narud, asking the question 'What dost thou mean, O Father! by intellect?'[153] To this Birmah answers, 'it is a portion of the GREAT SOUL of the universe, breathed into all creatures to animate them for a certain time' and that after death 'it animates other bodies, or returns like a drop into that unbounded ocean from which it first arose'.[154] This is, of course, an explanation of reincarnation, the available literature on which, as we have seen in relation to Holwell, was abounding with Neoplatonist ideas, which is perhaps where Dow encountered them. We might understand Dow's use of 'intellect' in Narud's question, and thus the following interpretation of the 'Great Soul', therefore, as an application of the Neoplatonic notion of the intellect, or *nous*, which had been adapted by Christian thinkers to explore the relationship between matter and spirit.[155] While it is difficult to establish a direct connection between Dow and specific Christian Platonist thinking, the application of this word, in relation to the essential unity of matter and living beings, suggests some interaction with this tradition. And in fact, viewing Vedānta doctrines such as this as an expression of Neoplatonist Christianity would become a familiar approach in the later part of the century, with a special emphasis on the connections made by William Jones (see Chapter 7).[156]

In a footnote reflecting on the various terms used by 'the Bedang' to describe God, such as 'omnipotent' and 'eternal', Dow poses, 'Whether we, who profess Christianity, and call Hindoos by the detestable names of Pagans and Idolaters, have higher ideas of the supreme divinity, we shall leave to the unprejudiced reader to determine'.[157] In summary, according

152 Brockington, *Sacred Thread*, pp. 109–12. 153 Dow, *History of Hindostan*, vol. 1 (1768), p. xlii.

154 Dow, *History of Hindostan*, vol. 1 (1768), p. xliii.

155 John Rist, 'Plotinus and Christian Philosophy', in Lloyd P. Gerson (ed.), *The Cambridge Companion to Plotinus* (Cambridge: Cambridge University Press, 1996); Pauliina Remes, *Neoplatonism* (Abingdon: Routledge, 2008), pp. 117–21.

156 Cannon, *Oriental Jones*, p. 294. 157 Dow, *History of Hindostan*, vol. 1 (1768), p. xl.

to Dow, the *Bedang Shaster*, represented as the 'most orthodox' of the two sects, contained the *Hindoo* religion's most metaphysical doctrines.[158] Yet, this 'most ancient doctrine' was at its core a monotheistic religion, devoid of any objectionable doctrines, at least in Dow's 'unprejudiced' account. Despite its speculative quality, those elements of it that tended towards idolatrous polytheism were, when stripped back to their original meaning, ultimately only symbolical. Indeed, Dow supported this with some fairly accurate examples, such as Brahma's figurative embodiment. In this way Dow used fragments of Hindu symbolism and the authority of Vedānta, one of the more ancient schools and one primarily dealing with questions about the nature of existence, to argue for the philosophical integrity of *Hindoo* ideas according to European conceptions of monotheism as a core principle of natural religion.

Nyāya/Neadirsin

Where the Vedānta school was concerned with metaphysical knowledge, Nyāya was primarily a school of epistemology, principally logic.[159] Dow's account of Nyāya philosophy was broadly faithful to the main principles and tenets of the school. This may have been because the Nyāya Vaisheshika branch of philosophy was particularly cultivated in Benares, from where Dow's pandit was hired, in this period.[160] Yet, the language in which Dow chose to explain this school of thought deliberately invoked eighteenth-century European intellectual concepts. This is immediately evident in Dow's discussion of how the *Neadirsin Shaster* came to be. As in the case of the *Bedang Shaster* and the *Brahma Sūtras*, it seems that Dow was referring to the aphoristic work the *Nyāya Sūtras*. Indeed, he identified 'Goutam' as its author, which was a rendering of Akṣapāda Gautama or Gotama into Bengali dialect, who is indeed considered to be the founder of the Nyāya school (though not the creator of the *Nyāya Sūtras*, which have multiple authors).[161] The foundational similarity between the *Neadirsin Shaster* and eighteenth-century conceptions of rational religion is first alluded to in Dow's claim that Goutam, in contrast to the author of the *Bedang*, 'does not begin to reason, *a priori*'.[162] Instead, Dow suggests that the author of the *Neadirsin Shaster* 'considers the present state of nature, and the intellectual faculties, as far as they can be investigated by human

[158] Dow, *History of Hindostan*, vol. 1 (1768), p. xxxviii. [159] Brockington, *Sacred Thread*, p. 94.
[160] Bayly, 'Orientalists', p. 99.
[161] Theos Bernard, *Hindu Philosophy* (Delhi: Motital Banarsidass Publishers, 1996 [1947]), p. 20.
[162] Dow, *History of Hindostan*, vol. 1 (1768), p. lii.

reason; and from thence he draws all his conclusions', thus establishing a sharp parallel with Enlightenment epistemologies of natural philosophy, and its application in ideas of rational religion.[163] Indeed, Dow would not be the only British author to make a comparison between Nyāya and natural philosophy, but he was the first to do so, with Charles Wilkins, William Jones and Henry Colebrooke later expressing similar views regarding the school of logic.[164] Contrary to Dow, however, Jones favoured Vedānta, which he judged to be 'a system wholly built on the purest devotion' and one completely 'removed from impiety.'[165]

Dow presents the Neadirsin as defenders of rational religion against atheism. He argues that it is Goutam's fundamental proposition that 'By reason . . . men perceive the existence of God'. In fact, though, early Nyāya thought was reticent on the question of a divine being, and Gautama introduced the notion of God only casually.[166] Nevertheless, Dow shows an awareness of an important facet of Nyāya theism, since he correctly locates this defence of God's existence through reason within debates against 'The Boad', or Buddhists. Almost since its inception the Nyāya school was in conflict with Buddhist epistemology, and it is in fact out of those conflicts that the first expressions of Nyāya theism emerged. This was not a train of argument in the *Nyāya Sūtras*, but rather a result of defences of the concept of *Ishvara* or *Īśvara*, which in Nyāya denotes the notion of a creator god, against attacks by Buddhist thinkers like Dharmakīrti, such as those by the tenth-century Nyāya logician Udayana (also Udayanācārya).[167] Dow's retelling of these conflicts is in support of the central claim that Nyāya thought affirmed the existence of a Supreme Being 'through the medium of reason and philosophy'. According to Dow, the 'Boad' were 'atheists', who denied God 'because his existence does not come within the comprehension of the senses', and thus casts them as extreme materialists, holding the positions that 'there is no such thing as a soul' and 'all animals exist, by a mere mechanism of the organs, or by a fermentation of the elements'. In reply, Goutam offers 'a long train of arguments, such as have been often urged by European divines'. Yet again, Dow situates his account of *Hindoo* beliefs in a universal history of religion, casting Nyāya religious thought as an example of the conflict between

[163] B. W. Young, 'Newtonianism and the Enthusiasm of Enlightenment', *Studies in the History and Philosophy of Science*, 35 (2004).

[164] Bayly, *Empire and Information*, pp. 53–4.

[165] John Shore, Lord Teignmouth (ed.), *The Works of Sir William Jones, with the Life of the Author, by Lord Teignmouth*, vol. 1 (London: J. Stockdale and J. Walker, 1807), pp. 239–40.

[166] Brockington, *Sacred Thread*, p. 95. [167] Brockington, *Sacred Thread*, p. 95.

rational religion and the atheistical consequences of extreme materialism. As he puts it, 'Though superstition and custom my bias reason to different ends, in various countries, we find a surprising similarity in the arguments used by all nations, against the BOAD, those common enemies of every system of religion'.[168]

Udayana introduced the first systematic account of Nyāya theism, which was aimed at vindicating the existence of God through philosophical reasoning.[169] According to the tradition this work inspired, the divine being is the efficient cause of the world (*nimitta-kāraṇa*), that is, the initiator of the creation of the universe. This Nyāya position is known as 'the doctrine that the effect does not exist in the cause' (*asat-kārya-vāda*) or 'the doctrine of new production' (*ārambha-vāda*).[170] According to this position, causation involves a combination of three distinct types of causal factors: the inherent cause, the non-inherent cause, and the efficient cause. This final, efficient, cause refers to the agency that produces the effect from the first two causes. In the case of a cloth, for example, the inherent cause is the thread and the non-inherent cause is a property that belongs to the inherent cause, which has only a mediating effect (e.g. the colour of the thread). Finally, in this example, the efficient cause would be the weaver of the cloth. Working to this analogy, the creation of the universe requires an efficient cause, that is, an agency producing it, which was God (*īśvara*).[171] Primarily created as a system of secular logic, Nyāya thus became an effective tool for disputing against contrary schools, and eventually for establishing an argument for God as the efficient cause of existence. Dow was, then, correctly representing a strand of Nyāya argumentation that one can infer God's existence and status as an efficient cause by an analogous set of inferences. The similarity of this to contemporary physico-theology, which propagated the idea that evidence-based arguments for God's existence can be derived from a study of the intricacies of the natural world through similarly inferential reasoning relating to the concept of cause and effect, was marked by Dow's comment that many 'European Divines' had advanced similar trains of reasoning.[172]

One such area of similarity was on the question of God's providence. Acknowledging that 'Goutam, in another place, treats diffusely of providence

[168] Dow, *History of Hindostan*, vol. 1 (1768), p. lxiii. [169] Brockington, *Sacred Thread*, p. 95.

[170] King, *Indian Philosophy*, p. 207. [171] King, *Indian Philosophy*, p. 208.

[172] These arguments were most notoriously advanced through the Boyle Lectures of the period. See Katherine Calloway, *Natural Theology in the Scientific Revolution: God's Scientists* (Abingdon: Routledge, 2016 [2014]), p. 26; Dow, *The History of Hindostan*, vol. 1. (1768), p. lxiii.

and free will', Dow nevertheless goes on to summarise the matter in a single paragraph:

> He divides the action of man under three heads: The will of God, the power of man, and casual or accidental events. In explaining the first he maintains particular providence; in the second, the freedom of will in man; and in the third, the common course of things, according to the general laws of nature. With respect to providence, though he cannot deny the possibility of its existence, without divesting God of his omnipotence, he supposes that the deity never exerts that power, but that he remains in eternal rest, taking no concern, neither in human affairs, nor in the course of the operations of nature.[173]

The problem of denying God's active providence while at the same time not impeaching his omnipotence was a present one in Dow's intellectual context. Goutam's concession that it is possible that God retains the power to intervene in earthly affairs but that 'the deity never exerts that power' is similar to the Newtonian position articulated by Samuel Clarke, who used Newton's theories to support a general counterargument to the anti-teleological critique of final causes by distinguishing between general and special providence. General providence, God's beneficent provision of fully sufficient and unvarying natural laws, as opposed to special providence, God's extraordinary intervention, provided for the idea that Newton's well-ordered universe represented the design of an intelligent creator without necessitating his constant intervention.[174] This was a more complex matter in Nyāya philosophy. Gautama's aphorism 'God is the cause, because we find fruitlessness in the actions of men' in the *Nyāya Sūtra* was the main site of subsequent debate on the correct interpretation of providence and free will.[175] On the whole, though, most Nyāya thinkers argue that God limits his actions to those in accordance with the law of karma and that bad effects must therefore follow bad actions.[176] Dow's decision, therefore, to distinguish 'particular providence' from free will and the natural law is a faint reflection of this, while also being a direct imposition of the eighteenth-century division of 'general' and 'particular' providence.

As well as taking comparable positions in European theological disputes, Dow also presents Nyāya thought as a sophisticated system of natural

[173] Dow, *History of Hindostan*, vol. 1 (1768), p. lxv.

[174] J. C. D Clark, 'Providence, Predestination & Progress; or, Did the Enlightenment Fail?', in *Albion: A Quarterly Journal Concerned with British Studies*, 35:4 (2003), p. 576.

[175] Bhattacharyya, *Development of Nyaya Philosophy*, p. 295.

[176] Bhattacharyya, *Development of Nyaya Philosophy*, p. 294.

philosophy. He provides, for example, an account of the relationship between perception and reality according to the *Neadirsin Shaster*. Contrary to another 'system of sceptical philosophy',[177] which 'asserts that all nature is mere delusion', Dow reports that Goutam argues that 'imagination must be acted upon by some real existence, as we cannot conceive that it can act upon itself' and that we therefore 'must conclude, that there is something real, otherwise philosophy is at an end'.[178] Gautama did deal extensively with definitions of perception, the *Nyāya Sūtra* offering one of the most influential formulations of perception in Indian classical philosophy, although these discourses are grounded in a set of different concepts to those surrounding European notions of solipsism.[179] The idea of perception, *pratyakṣa*, for example, is heavily bound up with *ākāśa*, the intangible essence of material reality, often translated as space.[180] Gautama's arguments about perception are therefore predicated on a different set of criteria, but essentially put forward a theory of direct realism.[181]

Dow therefore correctly relays that Goutam contests that all things that fall under our comprehension are knowable. Dow also claims that Goutam distinguishes five things that are eternal: the first is 'the Great Soul', similarly conceived of as in the Bedang; the second is 'Jive Attima' (*jiva-atman*, which captures the idea of the individual soul, or as Dow puts it, 'the vital soul'); the third is 'time or duration'; the forth is 'space or extension' and the fifth is 'Akash', the concept of *ākāśa* named above, which Dow defines as a 'pure element, which fills up the vacuum of space'. When it comes to time, space and *ākāśa*, the *Nyāya Sūtra* makes the argument that because there is no perceptual evidence of the qualities either beginning or ending, they must be eternal.[182] Dow roughly communicates this, but with some subtle adjustments in framing to capture the language of European natural philosophical discourses, especially those surrounding Newton's conception of absolute space and absolute time. In the *Nyāya Sūtra* this inferential reasoning is captured in a simple aphorism, 'There is no denial of the eternal, as there is a regulation to the character of our perception'. Thus, as there is 'no perceptual evidence' of the

[177] Which Dow bizarrely names the 'Bedang', which seems like a mistake given all he has said of that 'sect', namely that it is the most orthodox in the *Hindoo* religion, in the section before.

[178] Dow, *History of Hindostan*, vol. 1 (1768), p. liii.

[179] 'Perception is that knowledge which arises from the contact of a sense with its object, and which is determinate, unnameable and non-erratic'; Satisa Chandra Vidyabhushana Mahamahopadhyaya (trans.), *The Nyaya Sutras of Gautama* (Allahabad: The Indian Press, 1913), 1.1.4, p. 3.

[180] Bhattacharyya, *Development of Nyaya Philosophy*, pp. 44–6.

[181] King, *Indian Philosophy*, p. 159. [182] *Nyaya Sutras of Gautama*, 4.1.28, p. 114.

production or destruction of these properties, they are eternal. Dow elaborates this into something different in his account of the *Neadirsin Shaster*. He claims that Goutam argues that 'space or extension, without which nothing could have been; and as it comprehends all quantity, or rather is infinite . . . it is indivisible and eternal'. Such an explanation of Gautama's argument couched it in the language of eighteenth-century natural philosophy, oriented as it was to arguments relating to Newton's conception of absolute space as ultimately characterised by infinite and indivisible extension, as an emanant effect of God.[183]

Dow relayed plenty of genuine Nyāya concepts. For example, the *Nyāya Sūtra*, outlines a five-membered argument or proof. The common example given to illustrate this in Nyāya teaching is: (1) The hill has fire; (2) Because it has smoke; (3) Since whatever has smoke has fire, like an oven; (4) This hill has smoke, which is associated with fire; (5) Therefore, this hill has fire.[184] Dow has obviously been exposed directly to this analogy, since he gives exactly the same one when he explains the Nyāya understanding of 'Onnuman' (*anumāna*), or inferential reasoning.[185] This, Dow explains, 'is that faculty of the soul which enables us to conclude that things and circumstances exist, from an analogy to things, which had before fallen under the conception of our bodily senses: for instance, when we see smoak [sic], we conclude that it proceeds from a fire; when we see one end of a rope, we are persuaded it must have another'. Furthermore, the relationship between this style of inference and formulation of an argument for God as an efficient cause of the universe is made clear by the fact that the next paragraph follows: 'By reason, continues Goutam, men perceive the existence of God'.[186]

In fact, Dow's discussion of Nyāya as 'the Neadirsin' possibly represents the most detailed and accurate account by a European writer, which was barely elaborated on in the nineteenth century beyond a few comments by Willian Jones.[187] Dow was certainly the first of the British writers to give such a nuanced account. Yet, in terms of understanding what Dow is trying to do in the broader context of the *Dissertation*, the 'Neadirsin' play a less straightforwardly authentic role. Dow calls on the Nyāya school by

[183] These arguments were presented in the *Principia* and the *General Scholium*; see Isaac Newton, *The Principia: The Authoritative Translation*, Bernard Cohen and Anne Whitman (eds.) (Berkeley: University of California Press, 1999), pp. 55, 587. They were popularised and made central to natural philosophy in Britain by Samuel Clarke; see Stewart, 'Samuel Clarke'.

[184] King, *Indian Philosophy*, pp. 130–1.

[185] John Vattanky, *A System of Indian Logic: The Nyāya Theory of Inference* (Abingdon: Routledge, 2003), p. 61.

[186] Dow, *History of Hindostan*, vol. 1 (1768), p. lxiii.

[187] See Chapter 7.

way of drawing a parallel to the complex ideas and discussions at play in contemporary eighteenth-century natural philosophy. Thus, when Dow declares that the Neadirsin hold that it is 'by reason . . . that men perceive the existence of God', he could equally be describing the notion of rational religion.[188] For Dow, the Neadirsin were the 'sect' who 'look up to the divinity through the medium of reason and philosophy'. Thus, from the start Dow presents the *Neadirsin Shaster* as a theistic text written according to inferences drawn from human reason and the 'present state of nature'. And yet, this was again in conflict with the capacity of the vulgar to comprehend this kind of rational religion. This is an idea foreshadowed by an analogy made at the outset of the *Dissertation*, in which Dow suggested that trying to understand the religion and philosophy of the *Hindoos* by discussing it with 'inferior tribes', just as previous authors had done, would be equivalent to asking a 'Mahommedan in London . . . to form his opinion of Newtonian philosophy, from a conversation with an English carman.'[189]

The Hindoo Religion

According to Dow, as well as a belief in the unity of a creator God, the doctrine of transmigration was also common to both the 'grand sects' of *Hindoos*. This was presented in a very different way to Holwell's *Dissertation on Metempsychosis*, and in even starker contrast still to those travel writers who had emphasised reincarnation as an example of Indian religion's pagan nature.[190] Rather, Dow integrates his discussion of reincarnation into the essential components of natural religion, which include a belief in an afterlife, as well as the punishment of sin and reward of good. In Dow's *Bedang Shaster* it is only the souls of the good that will be 'absorbed into the divine essence'. As Birmah explains to Narud, 'the souls of those who do evil' are for a time 'punished in hell' proportional to their 'inequities', after which they also 'rise to heaven to be rewarded for a time for their virtues'. Once this process is complete, they return to the world to 'reanimate other bodies'. It is not until they attain 'a state of purity' that they can be 'absorbed into God'. The Neadirsin hold a similar view: 'Goutam supposes, with the author of the Bedang', that only those souls 'purified by piety and virtue' are 'absorbed into the GREAT SOUL

188 Dow, *History of Hindostan*, vol. 1 (1768), p. lxiii.
189 Dow, *History of Hindostan*, vol. 1 (1768), pp. xxxiv, xxxv.
190 Bernier was particularly incredulous at the idea and the accompanying practice of vegetarianism. See Stuart, *Bloodless Revolution*, p. 56.

OF NATURE, never more to reanimate flesh'. Those who aren't purified will 'return to the earth, and wander about for new habitations'.[191]

The idea of reincarnation has roots in the *Upanishads* of the late Vedic period, bound up in the idea of karma. It is also central in the *Bhagavad-Gītā*, in which Krishna explains to Arjuna that *ātman* does not die when the body is killed, but transmigrates from body to body until it achieves final release.[192] Dow does not quite capture the concept of karma, but does correctly understand Indian philosophies of transmigration as relating to *ātman* and *Brahman*, although named the Great Soul. The emphasis, however, is on the point that the two 'sects' are united in the belief that moral action results in either punishment or reward, albeit within a system of reincarnation.

Within this discussion, in various footnotes, asides and qualifications, Dow reserves some sceptical remarks for this particular aspect of *Hindoo* religion. In Dow's extract from the *Bedang Shaster* Birmah describes the self's absorption into the 'Great Soul' as a state in which 'all consciousness is lost in bliss'. In a move that appears to be setting his extract up in opposition to common *Hindoo* belief and practice, Dow adds a footnote explaining that this state was most commonly understood as one of 'perfect insensibility'. He then reflects that it is 'strange' that the *Hindoos* should think of such a state of 'annihilation' as 'the supreme good', expressing a disapprobation usually reserved for the 'vulgar' in his hierarchy of religious reason. This is followed by an invitation to cast doubt on this standard interpretation, by way of a close reading of his very own *Bedang Shaster*. In contrast to an insensible unconsciousness, Dow points to how in the extract he has provided, Birmha seems to imply that this state 'is a kind of delirium of joy'.[193] This is noteworthy, given that Birmha's comments appear, in fact, to be an artefact of Dow's invention, at least certainly in the sense that they are presented as 'extracts literally translated from the original SHASTER'.[194] Nevertheless, the notion of this final state as one of release, or *mokṣa* as it is known in the traditions of Hinduism, is reckoned a state of bliss in the Advaita Vedānta school. In fact, it seems like Dow's advisor may have focused on this tradition, which Dow then took to be the Bedang. Within Vedānta this was a non-dualist tradition, a characteristic that Dow sees as fundamental to its division from the Neadirsin, who in contrast, according to Dow, insisted on the difference between the '*vital soul* and the *great soul*'.

[191] Dow, *History of Hindostan*, vol. 1 (1768), p. Ix. [192] Brockington, *Sacred Thread*, pp. 45, 56.
[193] Dow, *History of Hindostan*, vol. 1 (1768), pp. xliv–xlv.
[194] Dow, *History of Hindostan*, vol. 1 (1768), p. xxxviii.

As such the Neadirsin disavowed the monism of the Bedang, which maintained, as we have seen, the Advaita Vedānta notion of 'Purmattima', or *Paramātmā* (the idea that *ātman*, the individual self, and *Brahmin*, the highest reality, are one and the same). This is, therefore, a good example of where the accusation of deliberate construction in the work of Dow becomes complicated. Indeed, the words of Brimha that this was a state of bliss and not one of 'perfect insensibility', as many supposed, were in fact the words of Dow, but nevertheless infused with the genuine concepts and terms that had been relayed to him. On the other hand, we also see that his determination to assert his texts as definitive lead him so far as to set them against an alternative construction of common manifestations of the *Hindoo* religion itself, in a manner consistent with his disapproval of all vulgar expressions of religion.

Dow also weaves in comments and asides that convey some of the admiration he appears to reserve for especially non-dogmatic or more moderate expressions of religious thought. This is particularly the case when this discussion of transmigration pushes Dow to reflect on *Hindoo* theodicy. Having outlined this system of reward and punishment for moral actions, Dow adds that the followers of the *Bedang Shaster* 'do not allow that any physical evil exists', and instead hold that 'man, being a free agent, may be guilty of moral evil' but that this 'only respects himself and society' and 'is of no detriment to the general system of nature'. He meditates on this in some detail, adding that 'God . . . being possessed of no wrath . . . never punishes the wicked, but by the pain and affliction which are the natural consequences of evil actions'.[195]

As well as answering the question of evil by tying it to free will, the doctrine of transmigration itself also mitigates the problem. According to Dow, 'the Brahmins have no idea that all the sins that a man can commit in the short period of his life, can deserve eternal punishment'; rather, the successive process of purification and existence continually offer the possibility of returning to the Great Soul.[196] That Dow approves of this position is made clear by his alignment of this approach to the problem of evil with the 'more learned Brahmins'. Indeed, a little later on the dissertation adds 'the hell which is mentioned in the Bedang, was only intended as a mere bug-bear to the vulgar, to inforce upon their minds, the duties of morality'.[197] Even with those aspects of *Hindoo* religion that are less

[195] Dow, *History of Hindostan*, vol. 1 (1768), p. l.
[196] Dow, *History of Hindostan*, vol. 1 (1768), p. xliii.
[197] Dow, *History of Hindostan*, vol. 1 (1768), p. l.

familiar to a European conception of natural religion, such as reincarnation, Dow situates his account of them in relation to Christian theological problems, as well as more broadly within a framework that pitches the 'learned' against the 'vulgar'. Moreover, that this tension between the learned and the vulgar was not particular to the *Hindoos* was also reinforced throughout the dissertation. Most striking is the already mentioned comment that 'the more ignorant Hindoos' who, misunderstanding their symbolical nature, 'think that these subaltern divinities do exist' do so 'in the same manner, that Christians believe in Angels'.[198]

In presenting the religion of the *Hindoos* to a European audience, Dow was building on the controversial contribution of Holwell by emphasising the sophistication and significance of Indian religious concepts, which had previously been denied. Dow's claims to be motivated by the unprejudiced desire to rescue the *Hindoos* from misunderstanding were likely meant, but the outcome was far from impartial or dispassionate. Dow combined Indian and European concepts to argue for a universal concept of religion, the particular manifestations of which were subject to the same follies of human nature as each other.

Dow, like Holwell, consciously cast his discoveries as unique in the degree to which they penetrated the philosophical core of a previously 'veiled' religion. Furthermore, these discoveries were conveyed through language and concepts that belonged to eighteenth-century intellectual culture, inspiring an analogous status between Indian philosophy and Enlightenment thought. For Dow, 'common sense in the affairs of religion' was equally distributed, and so was superstition and enthusiasm. On the one hand, the vulgar *Hindoos* exhibited similar superstitions to those of the 'pious Christian'. On the other hand, there was the example of the Neadirsin, whose philosophical enquiries made them 'look up to the divinity through the medium of reason'; a method which included the rejection of the same irrational doctrines that Newtonian theology sought to overcome, such as particular providence. Dow's separation of the 'learned' from the 'vulgar' as well as the 'philosophical' from the 'allegorical' and the 'symbolical' thus articulated a view of religion that saw it as universal and natural, but that was nevertheless susceptible to corruption and degeneration. Moreover, that degeneration was unequivocally a product of priestcraft. Concluding his 'Catalogue of the Gods of the Hindoos' – a peculiar list – Dow reflected, 'Such is the strange system of religion that priestcraft has imposed on the vulgar, ever ready in all climes and ages to take advantage of superstitious minds'. And yet, as he continued,

[198] Dow, *History of Hindostan*, vol. I (1768), p. xlix.

'There is one thing however to be said in favour of the Hindoo doctrine, that while it teaches the purest morals, it is systematically formed on philosophical opinions.'[199] The sources for concluding this were varied, ranging from Persianate texts to theistic trends within Hindu thought, mediated by pandit instruction. Dow's presentation of these materials was, though, rooted in Enlightenment intellectual culture. Moreover, it was precisely this that would appeal to his European readers (see Chapter 4).

Dow deliberately constructed an account of *Hindoo* religion that fits into a particular narrative of purity and decline, as well as rational religion versus superstition. The case for this not only rests on the point that despite being infused with genuine insight his extracts were the product of literary licence, but also the fact that throughout *The History of Hindostan* Dow uses religion as a category of analysis, the proximity of which to either fanaticism or deism is grounds for condemnation or approbation. It is the third Mughal ruler in India, Akbar (Jalal-ud-din Muhammad Akbar), that Dow judged to have been both a deist and one of that empire's greatest stateman. Likewise, his son, Jahangir, who continued to uphold the most admirable aspects of the Mughal dynasty, was 'brought up a deist under the tuition of his father'.[200] By contrast, Dow argues elsewhere that it was 'the passive humility inculcated by Christianity' that led to the fall of Rome.[201] In the case of Islam, its promotion of public and private despotism meant 'that undefined something, called Public Virtue, exists no more'.[202]

For Dow, religion was at the centre of how a polity should be understood, and his discussion of *Hindoo* religion in the dissertation was therefore oriented towards a set of Enlightenment concerns regarding the nature of civil society, progress and social mores. Dow's work thus rested on the backdrop of Montesquieu's enquiries into the relationship between religion and civic society, treating it as a category of historical analysis. Dow's history of India was one of decline, rooted in an analysis of the division between the traditional but uncorrupted faith of Vedānta and the rational religion of Nyāya. This was further buttressed by his vision of the deist Akbar, as well as a bitter denunciation of Islamic zealotry, and by extension also Christian enthusiasm, as the most complete despotism. As we shall see in Chapter 4, these concerns fundamentally shaped his understanding of contemporary India and the Company's role within it.

199 Dow, *History of Hindostan*, vol. 1 (1768), p. lxxvi.
200 Dow, *History of Hindostan*, vol. 3 (1772), pp. xxv, 103–4.
201 Dow, *History of Hindostan*, vol. 1 (1770), p. 17. Gibbon also read and cited Dow; see Gibbon, *Decline and Fall*, chapter 57, p. 280.
202 Dow, *History of Hindostan*, vol. 3 (1772), p. xii.

CHAPTER 4

Enlightenment and Empire

Howell's and Dow's accounts of what they understood to be India's original religion were received widely across the world of European letters. Their writings on the history, politics and the religious culture of India were translated very quickly into other European languages after their publication in English. Holwell's 1767 *Interesting Historical Events* was translated into French in 1768, followed by Dow's 'Dissertation Concerning the Customs, Manners, Language, Religion and Philosophy of the Hindoos' in 1769.[1] Around the same time, *Interesting Historical Events* was also translated into German (1767 and 1778). A German translation of the three volumes of Dow's *History of Hindostan* then followed in 1772.[2] This chapter offers an account of the ways that they were read, and in particular the reception of their philosophical interpretation of Indian religious thought. This includes a consideration of why, despite the substantial differences in their descriptions of *Gentoo* or *Hindoo* beliefs, they were often considered in conjunction, as authors who had attained the most accurate knowledge of the origins of India's ancient religion to date. It also reconsiders them as critics of the Company and writers on empire. In particular, it points to the role of their accounts of Indian history and religion in shaping their proposals for how to conceive of a British administration in India, as well as how these commentaries were received by

[1] The French translation of Dow is Dow, *Dissertation sur les moeurs*. Holwell's work appeared as *Evénements historiques, intéressants, relatifs aux provinces de Bengale* (Amsterdam [s.n.], 1768).

[2] The first volume of Holwell's *Interesting Historical Events* was translated into German as E. Thiel and J. T. Koehler (trans.), *Sammlung neuer Reisebeschreibungen aus fremden Sprachen* (Gottingen and Gotha [s.n.], 1767–9). Holwell's work was translated into German by Johann Friedrich Kleuker: *Holwell's merkwürdige historische Nachrichten von Hindostan und Bengalen nebst einer Beschreibung der Religionslehren, der Mythologie, Kosmogonie, Fasten und Festtage der Gentoos und einer Abhandlung über die Metempsychose*, Johann Friedrich Kleuker (trans.) (Leipzig, Weygandschen Buchhandlung, 1778); Dow's was translated anonymously under the title *Die Geschichte von Hindostan aus dem Persischen von Alexander Dow*, 3 vols. (Leipzig: J. F. Junius, 1772–4).

readers in Europe in an intellectual culture saturated with debates about empire, civilisation, commerce, religion and decline.

Holwell and Dow in the World of European Letters

Holwell's and Dow's interpretations of the *Gentoo* or *Hindoo* religion, as they variously termed it, differed on a number of counts. Dow's essay appeared the year after Holwell's first dissertation on the *Gentoo Shastah* and in it, he explicitly distanced himself from the former's account. Referring to 'a late ingenious writer', Dow refutes Holwell's suggestion that the fourth Veda, 'the *Obatar-bah Beda*' (in Holwell the *Aughtorrah Bhade Shastah*) was a more recent text. A footnote naming Holwell elaborates that Dow found 'himself obliged to differ almost in every particular concerning the religion of the Hindoos, from that gentleman'.[3] Although Dow does not list all of the points on which they disagree, the clear separation in their accounts was the topic of transmigration. Where Holwell's 1767 essay introduced the doctrine of metempsychosis, including the punishment and reincarnation of rebellious angel souls, as a 'satisfactory, conclusive and rational' explanation of the existence of evil, Dow had provided a much less elaborate account of Indian philosophies of reincarnation, as well as ideas about death as a reunification of the self and 'the Great Soul' (for which we may read *ātman* and Brahmin).[4]

Nevertheless, despite this distinction there was much in style and tone to unite them, not least the untraceable nature of their sources in their presentation of extracts from the 'Shasters' or 'Shastahs' they presented as authentic and authoritative Indian scriptures. Likewise, both authors constructed a vision of Indian religion as an originally pure set of rational doctrines, preserved by learned Brahmins and simultaneously corrupted by less scrupulous members of the same priestly caste, to the general degradation of the religion. For each, the religion of the *Gentoos* or *Hindoos* hinged on a complex interplay of personal conviction, theological literature and some insight into Indian philosophical concepts, the origins of which were unclear. And yet, the reception of these texts centred on the question of the credibility of Indian religion itself, not of the authors presenting these accounts of them. Some reviewers were willing to accept the authenticity and antiquity of the scriptures

[3] Dow, *History of Hindostan*, vol. 1 (1768), p. xxix.

[4] Holwell, *Interesting Historical Events*, vol. 2 (1767), p. 39; Dow, *History of Hindostan*, vol. 1 (1768), p. ix.

presented to them, but not all embraced the conclusions of their translators that they were therefore evidence of some original and pure religious truth. Other readers, on the contrary, were inclined to use the same material in support of their own more pointedly polemical purposes.

Indeed, despite these substantial differences in their work, Holwell and Dow were regularly cited together as complementary sources on the obscure world of Indian religious beliefs. A good example can be found in Julius Mickle's translation of the Portuguese epic poem *The Lusiad*. The original poem, written by Luís Vas de Camões in 1572, presented the story of Vasco de Gama's voyage to India and incorporated information from various travel narratives. Mickle's 1776 translation tapped into a resurgent interest in both the work and its geographical subject, running into three editions before the turn of the eighteenth century, and many more in the nineteenth.[5] Attempting to provide readers with some explanation of the 'religion and philosophy of the Brahmins', Mickle discussed and cited extensively the work of both Holwell and Dow. Acknowledging their disagreements, Mickle nevertheless consistently referred to 'Mr Holwell and Mr Dow' together, and in the second edition (1778) their work appeared side by side as the basis of a separate essay on the religious tenets and philosophy of the Brahmins.[6] Crucially, Mickle regarded them as united by their methodology. In the first edition of *The Lusiad*, he introduced their work as 'Accounts much more to the honour of the Indian philosophy' precisely because they were produced by 'gentlemen, who, by conversing with some eminent Brahmins, have enjoyed the best opportunities of information'.[7]

Mickle thus endorses the impression which both authors took pains to convey when presenting themselves as unique authorities, conversant with the mysteries of Brahmin knowledge. Holwell, as we know, had denounced all previous authors as 'defective' on the basis that their evidence was only fragmentary and literal.[8] Dow had likewise dismissed 'modern authors' for presenting an 'unfair account' of the religion, having not investigated beyond its 'external ceremonies'.[9] Both Holwell and Dow

5 Luís Vaz de Camões, *The Lusiad: or Discovery of India. An Epic Poem. Translated from the Portuguese of Luis De Camoëns*, William Julius Mickle (trans.) (Oxford: Jackson and Lister, 1776). For more on the work, see S. George West and W. J. Mickle, 'The Work of W. J. Mickle, the First Anglo-Portuguese Scholar', *Review of English Studies*, 10:40 (1934).

6 See, for example, de Camões, *Lusiad* (1776), p. 298. In the second edition his discussion of their work appeared as a separate preparatory essay: de Camões, *Lusiad* (1778), pp. 305–32.

7 de Camões, *Lusiad* (1776), p. 294.

8 Holwell, *Interesting Historical Events*, vol. 1 (1766), pp. 5–6.

9 Dow, *History of Hindostan*, vol. 1 (1768), p. xxii.

were, then, united by their claims to be offering knowledge directly from scriptural sources. Ironically, though, owing to Dow's confession that 'he had neither the time nor leisure to acquire the Shanscrita language', whereas Holwell had left the extent of his linguistic abilities ambiguous, Mickle determined that Holwell's forged *Shastah* was 'the most authentic' and that although Dow's '*superior* knowledge' was unusual, it was also too '*partial*' since it was dependent on the 'truth of his pundit'.[10] That Mickle buys into this self-construction of authority is significant. While we can assert that, since much of their contents were greatly embellished, Holwell and Dow made a dubious contribution to eighteenth-century knowledge of India, the manner in which they presented their research explains how their ideas achieved a heightened degree of public attention.

Holwell's and Dow's claims to authenticity and authority were not just for their own sake, but also deployed in service of a particular reading of *Gentoo* or *Hindoo* religion. By accepting this paradigm of authority despite its shaky foundations, Mickle also gives credit to the more fundamental distinction that it was used to convey: between high philosophical and low allegorical religious traditions and thought. Both Holwell and Dow distinguished their work from previous authors on these terms, claiming that what had made earlier accounts so erroneous was precisely their failure to distinguish between what was 'philosophical' and what was purely 'allegorical'. Holwell thus attacked the Dutch traveller Baldaeus (1632–71) for not attending to allegory and consequently producing a translation of the *Viedam* (Veda) that was too literal. Despite his toils, 'which must have been great and intense', wrote Holwell, Baldaeus had produced 'a monster', the 'mis-representations' in which were nothing short of 'injurious to human nature', because of their tendency to obscure knowledge.[11] Likewise, Dow accounted for the sheer number of the 'many different accounts of the cosmogony of the Hindoos [that] have been promulgated in Europe' on similar grounds. According to Dow, while there is only one 'philosophical' account of creation in *Hindoo* doctrine, there are several 'allegorical' tales that the Brahmins made use of.[12] The exposure of travellers to these different systems, all of which ignored the philosophical core of the ancient theology, had thus resulted in a confusing picture. Mickle gives credit to this directly, agreeing that 'former travellers gave us a true picture of the popular religion of India, but they did not attend to the *gloss* and *refinement*

10 de Camões, *Lusiad* (1778), pp. 32, 310.

11 Holwell, *Interesting Historical Events*, vol. 2 (1767), p. 33.

12 Dow, *The History of Hindostan*, vol. 1 (1768), pp. lxvi–lxvii.

of the *recluse remnant* of the *Brahmins*'. He then goes on to quote Holwell directly, validating his comparison between 'the common run of the *Brahmins*' and the idea of an elite coterie of Brahmins who 'seclude themselves . . . in philosophic and religious retirement', representing 'the purest models of genuine piety that now exist'.[13]

Yet, while he tacitly accepted their assertion that these doctrines were 'more remote than that of any known writings', Mickle drew the line at the idea of a universal religion that both Holwell and Dow regarded as the logical conclusion of their research.[14] Mickle concedes to Dow's suggestion that many of the deities of the *Hindoos* are really allegorical representations of God's divine attributes, suggesting that this 'apology for the idolatry of the Brahmins is applicable to that of every nation'. But for Mickle, Dow's further assertion that consequently we might say 'that whatever the *external ceremonies* of religion may be, the self-same infinite being is the object of universal adoration' was a step too far. This 'ingenious refinement' of Dow's was, according to Mickle, the position of a 'metaphysician' rather than the more grounded considerations of a 'moral philosopher'.[15]

This owes much to the concerted effort made by Mickle, throughout the text, to assert a pious defence of Christianity, which since the first edition also manifested itself as a defence of the Crusades, and of the theological concept of particular providence. At least, this is what a reader wrote to *The Gentleman's Magazine* to mark as particularly worthy contributions.[16] Indeed, Mickle had already distinguished himself as a defender of Christianity in his 1770 work, *Voltaire in the Shades*. Set in purgatory, this had staged a dialogue between Voltaire and several other interlocutors, among them Rousseau, Socrates and Porphyry. *Voltaire in the Shades* was essentially a defence of revealed religion against the empty scepticism of the deists. In it, Voltaire and others are undermined by opponents who point to the unfolding contradictions in their arguments, occasionally aided by the testimonies of visiting characters like St Augustine. Mickle's design is to prick the pomposity of what he called the 'confidence of philosophical superiority which infidel writers assume' with examples of the efficacy of Christian morals.[17] Mickle's chastisement of Dow's transgression from moral philosophy into metaphysics might be seen in this light.

[13] *Lusiad* (1778), p. 323. [14] *Lusiad* (1778), p. 323. [15] *Lusiad* (1778), p. 313.

[16] *Gentleman's Magazine*, 47 (November 1777), pp. 532, 591.

[17] William Julius Mickle, *Voltaire in the Shades, or Dialogues on the Deistical Controversy* (London: G. Perch, 1770), p. A2. For a review praising this defence of revelation see *Monthly Review*, 44 (1771), pp. 27–33.

Mickle's use of and disagreement with Holwell and Dow marks a pattern of reception whereby some were willing to accept the authenticity and antiquity of the scriptures presented to them, but not the conclusion of their translators that they were therefore evidence of some original and pure religious truth that could facilitate the dissolution of some of the more restrictive forms of Christian orthodoxy. In its mildest form, criticism centred on the accusation that Holwell had spent too much time in India, becoming biased in its favour. One reviewer compared Holwell's 'admiration' of the *Gentoos* to Montesquieu's admiration of the English, as well as to a certain Scottish MP, 'who, after a long residence in Holland as a merchant', began every speech by referring to what the 'Dutch, a wise people', had to say on the matter.[18] By the time Holwell's more controversial observations appeared in 1771, this incredulity turned to offence, as one reviewer dismissed Holwell's 'Chartah Bhade Shastah, of Bruma, Bramma, Burma Brumma, Birma, Bramah, or Lord knows who', adding that in championing the *Shastah* Holwell had become a victim of 'the speculative errors of deluded superstition'. Yet, in claiming that the *Gentoo* religion was more 'a compound of Manicheism, vitiated Christianity, pagan idolatry, superstitious rites, and unintelligible jargon', than a rational creed, the reviewer was taking offence to Holwell's philosophical interpretation and endorsement of the *Shastahs*, not the credibility of his account or the authenticity of the text presented.[19]

The conclusions of Holwell and Dow also received a sustained denunciation in the work of the natural philosopher and Unitarian Joseph Priestley. Priestley used Holwell's work, contrary to its author's argument, to support his central thesis in *A Comparison of the Institutions of Moses with Those of the Hindoos* (1799) that Moses ought to be rescued as the author of the most original and divine theology. For Priestley this was of paramount importance in his version of Rational Dissenting theology, which, while it eschewed the supernatural elements of Christian religion, was deeply committed to biblical scripture.[20] Priestley was not convinced by the philosophical picture that either Holwell or Dow had painted of Hinduism, concluding that 'If the representations of Mr. Holwell may

[18] *Critical Review*, 20 (1765), pp. 145–9: p. 145. The reviewer is possibly referring to Patrick Craufurd, MP for Renfrewshire in 1761–8. Patrick's father was also a merchant in Holland, and his son was a friend of David Hume. See Lewis Namier and John Brooke, *The History of Parliament: House of Commons 1754–1790* (London: Secker and Warburg, 1985 [1964]), pp. 272–4. For details of the will, see William Maxwell Morrison, *The Decisions of the Court of Session: From Its Institution until the Separation of the Court into Two Divisions in the Year 1808*, vols. 11–12 (Edinburgh: Archibald Constable & Co., 1811), pp. 4486–9.

[19] *Critical Review*, 32 (1771), pp. 131–6.

[20] Hickman, *Eighteenth-Century Dissent*, pp. 24–5.

be depended upon, the most raised ideas of the Hindoos concerning the Supreme Being fall far short of those that were entertained by the Hebrews.'[21] Priestley also pointed to the various discrepancies between their accounts, noting in particular that 'the account of the fallen angels is peculiar to Mr. Holwell'.[22] In all other matters, though, he seemed to regard them as authoritative sources, and consistently cited both Holwell and Dow throughout in his assessment of the various aspects of *Hindoo* religious theology and practice. In the case of Holwell's assertion that the ancient *Hindoos* had no animal sacrifices, for example, Priestley was in fact outraged at what he was convinced was a 'mistake', precisely because Holwell otherwise 'had the means of the best information'.[23]

In general, Priestley was not questioning the authority of these authors, but rather their veracity. That is to say, he accepted that they had gathered correct and accurate information about Indian religion from important sources, but that the interpretive framework through which they had chosen to present them was in error. This was a theological disagreement about the possibility of a reasonable and pure Indian religion, without the benefit of revelation. This is a pattern repeated by other critics of their work, whose position could be best described as Christian apologist. Thomas Maurice, for example, joined Priestley in widely using these authors as sources in his *Indian Antiquities* (1793–1800), while at the same time roundly denouncing the heterodox conclusions they drew. He did this with the aid of William Jones' alternative chronology, which was much more favourable to a biblical interpretation of history.[24]

And yet, for other readers, it was precisely this heterodox and philosophical quality that accounted for the traction that their work gained. Both Holwell's discussion of metempsychosis and Dow's 'Dissertation Concerning the Customs, Manners, Language, Religion and Philosophy of the Hindoos' also featured in Jean-Rodolfe Sinner's *Essai sur les DOGMES de la METEMPSYCHOSE & du PURGATOIRE enseignés par les Bramins de l'Indostan* (1771). Sinner, who was the chief librarian at Berne, produced the *Essai* as the first critically annotated catalogue of important eighteenth-century works on the subject of reincarnation.[25]

21 Joseph Priestley, *A Comparison of the Institutions of Moses with Those of the Hindoos and Other Ancient Nations* (Northumberland: A. Kennedy, 1799), p. 34.
22 Priestley, *Comparison*, p. 57.
23 Priestley, *Comparison*, p. 174. Priestley objected to this both on the grounds that it was contradicted by other authorities (namely William Jones) and that it was simply too improbable.
24 Thomas Maurice, *Memoirs of the Author of Indian Antiquities*, 2nd ed., vol. 1 (London: Rivington, 1821), p. 102. See Chapter 7 of this book for an extended discussion of this.
25 Sinner, *Essai*.

Sinner had developed a fascination with the idea of reincarnation, and his extensive study traced the subject through more than twenty works appearing between 1699 and 1769. Like Holwell and Dow before him, he had become convinced that the theology of the ancient 'Brachmannes' had predated Egyptian and Greek ideas about transmigration. He also used their work to establish some similar connections between Indian philosophy and Christian doctrines, noting in particular parallels between the idea of a period of transmigration as purifying (alluded to by both Holwell and Dow) in Hindu theology and the notion of purgatory in Catholic doctrine.[26] Sinner also offered a particularly extended analysis of Dow's conversation between Narud (Reason) and Birmha (Wisdom) in the *Bedang Shaster*, taken to be the central text of Vedānta theology. Reproducing these extracts in French, Sinner stressed the commensurability between the loss of consciousness in bliss described by Brimha in Dow's questionable excerpt, and the 'bliss' of St Paul's Second Epistle to the Corinthians (12:2–4).[27] The *Essai* was also translated into German in 1773, furthering the wider dissemination of Holwell's and Dow's work, as well as the comparative speculations it invited.[28]

For others, the comparative lens, which implied an equivalence between European and Eastern religious thought and was wrought by Holwell's and Dow's interpretation of Brahminical Hinduism, was a particularly welcome addition to their own thought. Voltaire regularly deployed the work of Holwell and Dow in support of his ideas. Although Voltaire's understanding developed as he accumulated more reading on India, he tended to rely heavily on three sources in particular: the *Ezour-Védam*, Holwell's *Interesting Historical Events* and Dow's *History of Hindostan*. Like many others, Voltaire was initially reliant on Jesuit *Lettres édifiantes* for more recent information about Indian religious thought. Yet these interpretations, which generally characterised Hinduism as polytheistic, did not suit his purposes and he would come to follow Holwell and Dow in using them as examples of erroneous and biased misinformation.[29] Turning Jesuit denunciations of Indian superstition and irreligion on their head, he reminded European readers that 'if their customs were regarded by us as

26 Lieselotte E. Kurth-Voigt, *Continued Existence, Reincarnation, and the Power of Sympathy in Classical Weimar* (Rochester, NY: Camden House, 1999), pp. 56–7.

27 Sinner, *Essai*, pp. 80–5. This notion of bliss is in Dow, *History of Hindostan*, vol. 1 (1768), pp. xliv–xlv.

28 Kurth-Voigt, *Continued Existence*, p. 115.

29 He uses them in both the revisions of *Essai sur les mœurs* (1769) and elsewhere in the *Fragments sur quelques revolutions dans l'Inde* (1773). For more detail, see Marsh, *India in the French Imagination*, p. 181.

being ridiculous and idolatrous, ours seemed to them to be crimes', particularly after witnessing 'our monks' indulge in eating meat and sexual misconduct.[30] Moving on from the *Lettres*, Voltaire came to rely on the *Ezour-Védam*, brought to him by the Comte de Maudave in 1760. This forged 'Veda' was presented by Voltaire as a work of true antiquity.[31] He was its main champion and he described its unknown author as a 'vrai sage' (a true wise man).[32] Ironically, the text is thought to have been most likely written by a Jesuit missionary, who in an attempt to forge a way for a more accommodationist approach, sought to align Indian theology with Christian precepts.[33] Yet Voltaire also showed signs that he was aware that the text's origins were dubious. Some have even suggested that this was a deliberate coup and that Voltaire knowingly took it from its original intentions and appropriated it to the cause of anticlerical deism, in a calculated and even more ironic twist.[34] Voltaire himself provides a good summary of this reasoning when he suggests elsewhere that 'one praises the bracmanes in order to correct the [Christian] monks: and if Saint Ambrose had lived in India, he probably would have praised the monks to put shame on the bracmanes'.[35]

Later, and certainly because of the increasingly dubious status of the *Ezour-Védam*, Holwell and Dow became more central sources in Voltaire's work, informing some of his general philosophical works as well as those specifically devoted to India.[36] While their accounts of *Hindoo* or *Gentoo* religion contained significant differences, Voltaire was able to unify them in terms of several key positions that supported his broader polemical agenda, such as their insistence on the original purity and great antiquity of Indian religion, as well as its philosophical sophistication and compatibility with rational religion. Thus, he observed, on the basis of their work, that the ancient '*Brachmanes*', having neither a formalised ecclesiastical structure or a monarchy, could hardly fail to establish the religion according to reason ('ne pouvaient guère établir la religion que sur la raison universelle').[37] Voltaire's analysis thus utilised that which united Holwell

[30] As quoted by Marsh, *India in the French Imagination*, p. 119.

[31] Ludo Rocher, *The Ezourvedam: A French Veda of the Eighteenth Century* (University of Pennsylvania Studies on South Asia) (Philadelphia: University of Pennsylvania Press, 1984), pp. 16–19.

[32] Voltaire, Letter 9 of *Lettres chinoises, indiennes et tartares á M. Pawr par un bénédictin* (1776), in Louis Moland (ed.), *Œuvres completes de Voltaire*, vol. 29 (Paris: Garnier frères, 1877–85), p. 484.

[33] Rocher, *Ezourvedam*, pp. 16–19.

[34] See, for example, App, *Birth of Orientalism*, pp. 61–4, and Rocher, *Ezourvedam*, p. 16.

[35] As quoted by App, *Birth of Orientalism*, p. 61.

[36] See Rocher, *Ezourvedam*, p. 118.

[37] Voltaire, 'Essai sur les moeurs et l'esprit des nations', I–IV (1756–78), in *Oeuvres de Voltaire*, ed. M. Beuchot, 72 vols (Paris: Lefevre, 1829–34), vol. 15, p. 295.

and Dow, positing a theory in which the pure ancient monotheism of the ancient Brahmins (Brachmanes) had been corrupted by their modern successors, who had skilfully created a lucrative culture of superstition. Voltaire's principal work dedicated to India was *Fragments sur quelques révolutions dans l'Inde* (1773). In it he used the work of Holwell and Dow in conjunction to deny the monopoly of the Abrahamic religions on monotheism, arguing that India's ancient religion was not polytheistic. Indeed, acknowledging their differences, Voltaire pointed to how it was therefore even more striking that Holwell and Dow agreed on this point:

> That the Indians have always worshipped one God, in the same way as the Chinese, is an incontestable truth. One has only to read the first article of the ancient Shastah, translated by Mr Holwell. The faithfulness of this translation is recognised by Mr Dow, and this recognition is all the more convincing because these two differ over several other articles.[38]

Holwell's opening line of the *Shastah* is 'God is One- Creator of all that *is*'.[39] To say that Dow approved of this translation is somewhat of an exaggeration, given his scepticism about the authority of Holwell's text. Nevertheless, it seems that Voltaire was making an implicit connection between this line and Dow's own confirmation that the Brahmins believe in one god. Voltaire also joined Holwell and Dow together to affirm the antiquity of Indian scriptures, and to thereby assert that it was they that had influenced Western philosophy and theology, rather than vice versa. He certainly agreed with Holwell that the doctrine of metempsychosis had been transmitted to ancient Greece by the Brahmins via Pythagoras.[40] Their work thus perfectly served Voltaire's aim to challenge the idea of a universal history based in Judeo-Christian chronology and contest errors in biblical teaching.[41]

The philosophically inclined account of *Hindoo* religion presented by Holwell and Dow also had a significant impact on the intellectual culture of Germany, extending into the nineteenth century. Moses Mendelssohn had described Holwell as having attained the ability 'to see with the eyes of a native Brahmin'.[42] Mendelssohn had used Holwell's work in his

[38] As translated by Marsh, *India in the French Imagination*, p. 115.
[39] Holwell, *Interesting Historical Events*, vol. 2 (1767), p. 31.
[40] Voltaire, *Fragments sur quelques révolutions dans l'Inde, sur la mort du comte de Lally, et surplusieurs autres sujets* (1773), in *Œuvres complètes de Voltaire*, 20 vols (Paris: J. Bryainé [1858]), vol. 6, p. 226.
[41] Marsh, *India and the French Imagination*, pp. 116–17.
[42] (. . . mit den Augen eines eingborenen Braminen zu sehen); Moses Mendelssohn, *Jerusalem Oder Über Religiöse Macht Und Judentum* (Berlin: Maurer, 1783), p. 86. See the English translation in Moses Mendelssohn, *Moses Mendelssohn: Writings on Judaism, Christianity and the Bible,*

controversial *Jerusalem, or on Religious Power and Judaism* (1783), which argued that it was possible to conceive of the core of Judaism as a religion founded upon reason alone.[43] He cited Holwell's allegorical interpretation of the *Gentoo* creation story, and his explanation of the deities as symbolic attributes of 'the Eternal' and singular deity, to argue that all religions had begun with such symbolism, the true meaning of which had been lost in those ages in which 'real idolatry became the dominant religion in every part of the globe'.[44] This statement was at the core of Mendelssohn's argument, which separated Judaism from radical Spinozism on the one hand, and orthodox revealed religion on the other. Just as Holwell's philosophical interpretation of the *Gentoo* religion had concluded, Mendelssohn's rendition of Judaism put forward the argument that it was thus perfectly compatible with reasonable, enlightened and tolerant society. This work proved to be a pivotal text in the German Enlightenment.[45]

Mendelssohn's friend and intellectual collaborator Gotthold Ephraim Lessing also made use of the work of Dow. In 1771 Lessing had suggested that his brother Karl translate Dow's *History of Hindostan*, which he evidently thought was an important text.[46] Later, Dow appeared in his editor's commentary on the controversial fragments from the work of the deceased Hermann Samuel Reimarus, which Lessing had published as the work of an anonymous author in 1777. In these pages Reimarus had, to the surprise of his former colleagues, laid out a radical attack on orthodox Christianity, and in particular the idea of revelation. The publication of the fragments had led to a bitter dispute about the authority of revelation and the nature of religious belief among German philosophers and theologians, known as the *Fragmentenstreit*. Lessing's ironical commentaries were ambiguous, but at their centre was the suggestion that the idea of Christianity stood independently from the fallibility of the Bible. The truth of one could be independent of the other, or to put it another way, the truth of Christian faith was not dependent on the truth of Christian scripture.[47] Lessing had included Dow's account of 'the sacred books of the Brahmans' as evidence that the Old

Michah Gottlieb (ed.), Curtis Bowman, Elias Sacks and Allan Arkush (trans.) (Waltham, MA: Brandies University Press, 2011), p. 102.

[43] Allan Arkush, *Moses Mendelssohn and the Enlightenment* (New York: SUNY Press, 1994), p. 87.

[44] Mendelssohn, *Writings on Judaism, Christianity and the Bible*, pp. 102–3.

[45] Arkush claims that Mendelssohn was a deist who moderated his presentation of his own belief in order to 'construct a version of Judaism suitable for a time when Jews would take their places as citizens alongside their Gentile neighbours in a fully liberal polity.' Arkush, *Mendelssohn*, pp. 291–2.

[46] Kurth-Voigt, *Continued Existence*, pp. 53–4.

[47] On Lessing's approach to the fragments, see chapter 1 in Toshimasa Yasukata, *Lessing's Philosophy of Religion and the German Enlightenment* (Oxford: Oxford University Press, 2003).

Testament did not contain divine wisdom particular to Christianity, but presented the kind of 'worthy conceptions of God', or the 'truths of natural religion', that might be found 'in any other book of equal antiquity'. The truth of the particular divinity of the Bible must therefore lie elsewhere, not in its letter but in its spirit.[48] While this entailed a rejection of the rationalist deism of Reimarus' arguments, neither was it a defence of orthodoxy, leaving the Lutheran theologian Johann Melchior Goeze to declare Lessing's counter-propositions far worse.[49] The use of Dow in this context matches his intended presentation of Brahmin philosophy, and demonstrates how far that view had penetrated other Enlightenment discourses.

Howell and Dow's work also filtered into the intellectual movements that emerged out of the Enlightenment, such as German romanticism and German idealism. Johann Gottfried Herder, for example, came to an interest in Indian thought initially through the work of Holwell and Dow. This revelation then led him to translate fragments from Wilkins' *The Bhăgvăt-Gēētā, or Dialogues of Krēēshnă and Ărjōōn* (1785), as part of his wide-ranging attempt to capture world history in the development of a historicist philosophy of human nature.[50] Herder first encountered the works of Holwell and Dow indirectly, through Voltaire, but he did eventually acquire copies and read them for himself.[51] Most importantly it was their philosophical reading of *Hindoo* theology, couched as it was in the language of religious heterodoxy, that made Holwell's and Dow's works most attractive to his purposes. Particularly appealing to Herder was Dow's account of the presence of vitalism and monism in Indian philosophical thought. Where Voltaire had preferred to use their texts as evidence of a pristine monotheistic Brahmin philosophy, German romantics tended towards an understanding of Hindu thought as essentially a pantheistic monism.[52] Herder thus judged Dow's work to be a much more sophisticated investigation into Hinduism than Holwell's, focusing on Dow's depiction of the Hindu philosophy of a divine element, or the 'Great Soul', that was diffuse within all living things.[53]

[48] Gotthold Ephraim Lessing, *Philosophical and Theological Writings* (Cambridge Texts in the History of Philosophy), H. B. Nisbet (ed.) (Cambridge: Cambridge University Press, 2005), p. 77.

[49] Yasukata, *Lessing's Philosophy*, p. 19.

[50] Bradley L. Herling, *The German Gita: Hermeneutics and Discipline in the Early German Reception of Indian Thought* (London: Routledge, 2006), p. 62. On Herder's broader thought in the context of empire, see chapter 6 in Muthu, *Enlightenment against Empire.*

[51] Robert T. Clark Jr, *Herder: His Life and Thought* (Berkeley: University of California Press, 1955), p. 163.

[52] King, *Orientalism and Religion*, p. 124; Halbfass, *India and Europe*, pp. 70–1.

[53] Herling, *The German Gita.*

Indeed, Dow's emphasis on the belief that 'God is the animating soul of all living things', or 'the soul of nature', spoke to Herder's extensive engagement with the philosophy of Spinoza, which itself was generative of some of the most fundamental threads in the metaphysics of German idealism.[54]

It was through Herder that Holwell and Dow also appeared in the work of John Friedrich Majer, a follower of Herder who would become Germany's foremost expert in Indic knowledge. Majer quoted Holwell in particular as capturing the sublimity of the Hindu conception of God.[55] Georg Wilhelm Friedrich Hegel had also encountered Dow, whose work he enlisted in his description of the non-dualism of Advaita Vedānta philosophy (in Dow 'the Bedang'). He also quoted a passage from 'Colonel Dow' relaying the *Hindoo* creation story, which for Dow was an allegory 'for the purposes of vulgar theology' in which the attributes of God and 'the passions and faculties of the mind are personified'.[56] In Hegel, this story, in which the world emanates from Brahma, was taken to be indicative of how the subject is subsumed under and unified with the universal in Hindu thought. This particular interpretation, though, ran contrary to Dow's purposes. Where Hegel saw this non-dualism as a fundamental but stunted expression of pre-philosophical insight,[57] Dow cast 'the Bedang' as the more traditional account of *Hindoo* theology, which had been surpassed by 'the Neadirsin' (Nyāya) as a version of *Hindoo* rational religion. Instead, the emphasis on Advaita Vedānta concepts in German idealism would be shaped greatly by, as well as Wilkins' *Gēētā*, the work of William Jones. In fact, in ways explored in Chapter 7, Jones' work would prove an important point of departure from Dow's affirmation of *Hindoo* history, to Hegel's infamous proclamation that India sat outside of philosophical history.[58] Let it be noted, though, that Holwell and Dow played a significant role in the origins of German thought on Indian religion and philosophy, and that as late as 1832 Holwell was being defended as an authoritative source by notable German philosopher, anthropologist and disciple of Friedrich Schelling, Carl Joseph Windischmann (1775–1839).[59]

[54] Michael N. Forster, 'Herder and Spinoza', in Eckart Förster & Zithak Y. Melamed (eds), *Spinoza and German Idealism* (Cambridge: Cambridge University Press, 2012).

[55] Wilson, *Mythical Image*, pp. 96, 102.

[56] As it appears in Rathore and Mohapatra, *Hegel's India*, p. 209; Dow, *History of Hindostan*, vol. 1 (1768), pp. xlvi–xlix.

[57] For a more developed discussion, see Rathore and Mohapatra, *Hegel's India*, pp. 33–73.

[58] Hegel, 'Lectures', pp. 136–7.

[59] Windischmann, *Die Philosophie*, pp. 616–17.

In Britain too, in the first few decades of the nineteenth century, many had come to prefer William Jones' work on Hindu religion, which was both more scholarly and friendlier to biblical chronology. Nevertheless, Holwell's and Dow's works continued to circulate within the particular context of radical 'infidel' pamphlet literature.[60] Dow's discussion of the *Hindoo* conception of hell, for example, features widely in a work by George Ensor, an Irish political author and friend of Jeremy Bentham, James Mill and Daniel O'Connell. Ensor's work *The Principles of Morality* (1801) argued that morality is independent of religion, and instead a product of natural faculties such as sympathy and reason. Religion, on the other hand, was rife with priestcraft. One of the most pernicious Christian tenets was, according to Ensor, the doctrine of punishment for sin in hell, which had made virtue a matter of fear and so prevented cultivation of the conscience. While nearly all religions proffered some kind of punishment for vice, Ensor regarded Christianity as the most egregious for making it 'eternal'. To throw this into stark relief Ensor used the example of Dow's account of the learned Brahmins, which had discredited the idea of eternal punishment and regarded hell 'no more than the agonies of a reprehending conscience'.[61] For some of Ensor's detractors, it was precisely this comparative approach that was so objectionable. A commentator in the *Anti-Jacobin Review*, for example, decried Ensor's 'mischievous' lack of discrimination between 'the Greek philosophers and poets – our own Newton, and the Siamese and Hindu sages'.[62]

Holwell and Dow also appeared to have influenced some of the arguments appearing in the important 'freethought' journal *The Oracle of Reason* (1841). The first volume featured an essay on India which appears to take much of its information from Holwell and Dow, although they are not cited directly. Accounts of Hindu religion similar to theirs are explicitly invoked to counter the claims of Christian orientalist writers, such as Thomas Maurice, whose work *The Oracle* considered 'greatly disfigured by an unnecessary obtrusion of his religious opinions'. In particular, in defending Hindu chronology, the author took the position of Holwell, Dow and, as we shall see, Halhed, whose opinions were the ones Maurice explicitly sets out to correct on precisely this point in *Indian Antiquities*.[63] On the side of the authors in this study, *The Oracle* dismissed Maurice, whose particular

[60] For more on this, see chapter 1 in Tom Scriven, *Popular Virtue: Continuity and Change in Radical Moral Politics, 1820–70* (Manchester: Manchester University Press, 2017).

[61] George Ensor, *The Principles of Morality* (London: J. S. Jordan, 1801), p. 199.

[62] *Anti-Jacobin Review and Magazine*, vol. XI (London: R. Bostock, 1802), pp. 386–7.

[63] *The Oracle of Reason*, vol. 1 (London: Thomas S. Paterson, 1842), pp. 7–8.

Christian prejudices made him 'unfitted to treat fully and impartially' the antiquity of *Hindoo* scripture. References to Holwell also appeared in *A Few Hundred Bible Contradictions: A Hunt after the Devil, and Other Odd Matters* (1843), written by the railway worker Peter Lecount, and distributed by the radical campaigner and important figure in infidel print culture, Henry Hetherington.[64] This association with freethought was also affirmed as late as 1887 by the paper of the Social Democratic Federation, Britain's first organised socialist party, which listed Holwell in a catalogue of important freethinkers.[65]

A Crisis of Legitimacy: Holwell and Dow as Critics of the Company

Holwell and Dow were not only read as authorities on Indian religion and history, but also as commentators on the affairs of the East India Company and the politics of British interests in India. They were very much known as East India Company authors, and were often read accordingly. Indeed, the period in which Holwell and Dow published their works was pivotal in the history of British empire in India. Following the battle of Plassey and thus the Company's effective conquest of Bengal, both writers sought to intervene in the debates that followed. Each offered their own critique of the Company, or factions within it, as well as ambitious proposals regarding the future of British empire in India. Holwell's commentaries regarding Company affairs were mostly written as defences of his and his allies' conduct. They appeared in the period between 1758 and 1766, and addressed the circumstances of the Company's ascent to power, as well as his particular role in the various intrigues by which they sought to consolidate their position. The history of the Mughal empire supplied in *Interesting Historical Events* ought, therefore, to be seen in line with this project. Dow's literary interventions into Company affairs came a little later, between 1768 and 1771; that is, precisely the period in which its mismanagement had precipitated the first of many famines to come in Bengal, in which an estimated one-third of the Indian population starved to death. By 1772 the Company was thrown into deep financial crisis. As news of these events began to circulate, metropolitan attitudes took

64 P. Y. John, *A Few Hundred Bible Contradictions: A Hunt after the Devil, and Other Odd Matters*, vol. 3 (London: H. Hetherington, 1843), p. 876; Edward Royle, *Victorian Infidels: The Origins of the British Secularist Movement, 1791–1866* (Manchester: Manchester University Press, 1974), p. 109.

65 This appears in Joseph Mazzini Wheeler, *A Biographical Dictionary of Freethinkers of All Ages and Nations* (London: Progressive Publishing, 1889), p. 175.

a sharply critical turn.[66] A number of works denouncing the Company began to circulate, from Samuel Foote's satirical play *The Nabob* to the deeply serious *Political Essays Concerning the Present State of the British Empire* by Arthur Young.[67] Dow's essays in the 1772 edition of *The History of Hindostan* were intended as a contribution to this affray. As well as denouncing 'the ruin, which we have brought on an unfortunate country', Dow set out a series of proposals to curtail Company power and elevate the national interest in British affairs within India.[68]

Holwell and Dow have received some historiographical attention for these commentaries. Holwell has been most discussed for his dramatic first-hand account of the fall of Fort William in June 1756, and the imprisonment of the survivors in what came to be known as the 'Black Hole of Calcutta'.[69] This text, and the various other retellings it inspired, has been regarded as an important foundational myth for the British empire.[70] Very few of these studies, however, seek to explore this text in relation to Holwell's other works. Dow's place in the discussion surrounding the transformation of the Company's conception of itself as a sovereign power in the region has also received consideration. Some have positioned Dow as a humane 'whistleblower', appalled at the Company's tenure of Bengal.[71] Others have pointed to the more mercenary interests at play in his proposals. Ranajit Guha's *A Rule of Property for Bengal*, for example, supplies the most extensive study of Dow's speculative plans for the transformation of property relations in Bengal under the Company. Here, Guha, paints Dow as a 'philosopher mercantilist' and one of the first Company men, alongside Holwell in a minor role, who looked to property relations as the basis for establishing British rule in Bengal.[72] This would foreshadow the discussion leading up to the 'permanent settlement' of 1793, which fixed the revenues to be raised from the lands with the

[66] See Dirks, *Scandal of Empire*.

[67] Samuel Foote, *The Nabob: A Comedy in Three Acts* (London: T. Sherlock, for T. Cadell, 1778) (performed in 1773); Arthur Young, *Political Essays Concerning the Present State of the British Empire* (London: W. Strahan and T. Cadell, 1772).

[68] Dow, *History of Hindostan* (1772), p. lxxxiv.

[69] John Zephaniah Holwell, *A Genuine Narrative of the Deplorable Deaths of the English Gentlemen, and Others, Who Were Suffocated in the BLACK-HOLE in FORT-WILLIAM, at CALCUTTA in the Kingdom of BENGAL; in the Night Succeeding the 20th Day of June, 1756* (London: Printed for A. Millar, 1758).

[70] See, for example, Chatterjee, *Black Hole of Empire*.

[71] William Dalrymple, *The Anarchy: The Relentless Rise of the East India Company* (London: Bloomsbury, 2019), pp. 485, 878. However, the quotation attributed to Dow here ('The Bengal carcase is now bleaching in the wind and is almost picked to the bone') is not correct, and cannot be found in the place cited.

[72] Guha, *Rule of Property*, p. 21.

intention of creating a class of landowners, who would therefore be amenable to Company control. In different vein Robert Travers extends these insights towards recognising Dow's impact on contemporary disputes on the nature of the Mughal constitution, against which arguments about legal precedent could be attached and contested.[73]

Some studies of Holwell's and Dow's works on Indian history and religion have, however, often overlooked their roles in the Company as mere context. Indeed, some have tended to emphasise their broadly 'deist' attitudes as evidence of Enlightenment cosmopolitanism, in contrast to, or even as ameliorating, the networks of Company politics and interests within which they operated.[74] Siraj Ahmed has thought more carefully about their place in relation to later formulations of British orientalism and its relationship to Company politics. Taking his cue from Guha, Ahmed places them in a complicated thesis that argues that with the 'permanent settlement', Company orientalists helped fix a rule of property that answered to the fiscal imperatives of modern warfare, while simultaneously mystifying this with an appeal to ancient traditions. Holwell and Dow fit into this story by laying its foundations, according to the idea that 'both presupposed that colonial rule gains legitimacy to the extent that it appears to emerge out of the Orientalist study of native traditions'.[75] While this is a broadly correct characterisation of one approach to arguments about how to legitimise British rule in Bengal, which became more pronounced in the policies of Warren Hastings, Ahmed's study leaves little room for the particularities of how each conceptualised the relationship between 'native traditions' and colonial rule.

As Travers has shown, the use of orientalist work in the ideology of empire in this period was a nuanced field, not least of which was the distinction between Hindu and Muslim traditions. More recently, Manan Ahmed Asif's *The Loss of Hindustan* (2020) also looks to the role of Dow in what he calls 'the colonial episteme of European history'. The book's central aim is reconstruction of the intellectual worlds of the *Tārikh-i-Firishta*, which, according to Ahmed Asif, most meaningfully captured a pre-colonial idea of Hindustan as a diverse polity.[76] By contrast, Dow's

[73] Travers, *Ideology and Empire*, pp. vii, 62–5.

[74] See, for example, Trautmann's account of 'Indomania' in Trautmann, *Aryans and British India*, pp. 62–98.

[75] Ahmed, 'Orientalism', p. 181.

[76] Ahmed Asif's aim here is a genealogical history of the various acts of political forgetting that worked to erase the precolonial idea of Hindustan, in order to rediscover its history of political collective of diverse communities of belief: Ahmed Asif, *Loss of Hindustan*, particularly pp. 4–6.

translation of this text, and its consumption by Enlightenment authors, is positioned by Ahmed Asif as the original source for the denial of India's place in the emerging discipline of world history, itself a central plank of Europe's colonial knowledge project.[77] Yet again, this rich study of the Persianate India in which *Tārikh-i-Firishta* was composed leaves little space for a thorough account of the intellectual and political worlds shaping Dow's work, or the different in which it was interpreted and used. As such it both misses some of the particularities of Dow's thought, which in many ways vigorously affirmed the history of both Mughal and Hindu India, as well as the turns taken in European orientalism before we get to Hegel's denial of India's historical status in *Lectures on the Philosophy of History* (given in 1822–30, published in 1836). This chapter will address the former, while the latter will become an integral feature in the discussion of William Jones in Chapter 7, and in the Conclusion to this book.

Holwell and the Company

Holwell began his Company career as a surgeon, but would go on to pursue a contentious career in the administration of its affairs. Following a term as the mayor of the Company's settlement in Calcutta, Holwell returned to England between 1750 and 1752. During this period, he petitioned the Company's directors to consider what he saw as essential alterations to the operations of the Calcutta zamindari, a Mughal office of land-owning rights and revenues, which in Calcutta had been held by the Company since 1698.[78] Successful in his efforts, Holwell was appointed to the post, placing him twelfth in the Fort William council, but with the added stipulation that he rise no higher. Holwell duly introduced measures to increase revenues without the introduction of new duties. A degree of success in this endeavour meant that the restriction on his promotion was removed.

Things took a turn, however, when in June 1756 the nawab of Bengal, Siraj-ud-Daulah, captured Fort William, the Company's base in Calcutta. Holwell, who was caught up in these events, wrote a dramatic account for the reading public. Following the subsequent recapture of the fort, which in turn opened the field to Clive's aggressive conquests, Holwell's position on the council rose and fell with the political tide. The high point came when Clive resigned the governorship in January 1760 and Holwell acted as temporary governor until he was succeeded by Henry Vansittart in July of that year.

77 Ahmed Asif, *Loss of Hindustan*, p. 15.
78 The title of a Mughal landowning office which the company adopted in 1698.

It was during this brief period that Holwell became embroiled in some complicated political manoeuvres that would later come to be the topic of critical speculation. Holwell was instrumental in plotting to unseat Siraj-ud-Daulah's successor Mir Jafar, on the basis that he was incapable of raising sufficient revenues to meet the Company's costs.[79] In 1760 his successor, Henry Vansittart, did so and replaced him with his son-in-law Mir Qasim, on the terms set out by Holwell. Returning to England in 1761, Holwell took up his pen to defend his decisions in Bengal, as well as to denounce those of his opponents. This section will resituate these texts within the wider frame of his engagement with Company politics and his accounts of Indian history and religion.

Holwell was already well known before the publication of *Interesting Historical Events*, having made an impression on the reading public in 1758 with the publication of *A Genuine Narrative of the Deplorable Deaths of the English Gentlemen, and Others, Who Were suffocated in the BLACK-HOLE.* This was a first-hand telling of the fall and seizure of Fort William in June 1756 by the nawab of Bengal, Siraj-ud-Daulah. Its sentimental style and sense of jeopardy meant that it became a literary success both in this period, and long afterwards.[80] Given its impact, many have taken to reading it as a vindication of British conquest through the dramatisation of the horrors of Asiatic despotism. While indeed this was its legacy, Holwell had a somewhat different objective in mind. As Ian Barrow has emphasised, the true target of the critique was the East India Company, and in particular Howell's superiors, such as Robert Drake, who had abandoned the fort and left him as the most senior representative.[81] In this line of thought Partha Chatterjee has suggested that Holwell intended the tract as a commentary on the fragility of civilisation, reversing the racial relations between the European prisoners and their captors in order to critique the negligence of his superiors, as well as to provide a cautionary tale about the value of self-possession in the pursuit of the imperialist enterprise; as Chatterjee puts it, a 'pedagogical' call 'for the imperial nation to civilise itself before taking on the task of civilizing others'.[82] Likewise, Kate Teltscher suggests that Holwell mapped out a reversal of the natural

[79] For a fuller account of Holwell's career, see Prior, 'Holwell, John Zephaniah'.

[80] See Betty Joseph, *Reading the East India Company 1720–1840: Colonial Currencies of Gender* (Chicago: University of Chicago Press, 2004), pp. 64–73.

[81] Ian Barrow, 'The Many Meanings of the Black Hole of Calcutta', in Kate Brittlebank (ed.), *Tall Tales and True: India, Historiography and British Imperial Imaginings* (Clayton, Victoria: Monash University Press, 2008).

[82] Chatterjee, *Black Hole of Empire*, pp. 25–6.

order that, by implication, had to be restored.[83] Yet, while these appraisals astutely capture the allegorical nature of the narrative, which was indeed a moral corrective in tone and content, they also overlook some of the particularities of Holwell's religious thought. The narrative offers an account of the fragility of civilisation, not only according to the tropes of Asiatic despotism, but also as a feature of the generalised paradigm of purity and decline that permeates his wider idiosyncratic theology.

The *Genuine Narrative* places its author at its centre, as the dignified victim of incompetence and brutality. It sets off in an intimate tone, conveying its contents in the form of a letter written to a friend on the voyage home. As such Holwell recounts events in a serious and emotive register, consistent with the sentimental literary style of the day. At the climax of his description of that 'dreadful night', for example, Holwell informs the reader that tears have momentarily stopped his pen.[84] His ordeal is described in two parts. The first concerns his imprisonment, along with the remaining survivors of the siege, in a room at the back of the barracks 'commonly called the Black Hole prison'. Here he details 'the situation of one hundred and forty-six wretches . . . crammed together in a cube of about eighteen feet' without water or fresh air, the tragic result of which was, according to Holwell, the loss of 123 lives. The tale itself is peppered with vignettes of suffering, as Holwell describes the desperate scenes surrounding him in the airless chamber. The second part follows Holwell's arduous journey as a prisoner to Murshidabad, where he is eventually released by Siraj-ud-Daulah, who takes pity on the 'wretched spectacle' of his condition. A consistent theme is his own masculine fortitude. While others give way 'to the violence of passions', Holwell remains stoical and composed, urging his subordinates that their only hopes of survival rest on 'preserving a calm mind and a quiet resignation'.[85] Indeed, Holwell's imprisonment is itself a sign of his virtue. At one point in the narrative he is offered the chance of escape, but he resolves to stay, not wanting to 'ill repay the attachment the gentlemen and the garrison' had shown him, opting instead to 'share their fate, be it what it would'.[86] After this point, the specifics of the moral tale set out by Holwell bear a striking resemblance to the preoccupations that shaped his account of the *Hindoo Shastah* and the religious truths he attributes to it.

Holwell explains that after a certain period of time in the Black Hole, he came to regard death as inevitable. This, he maintained, was because he

83 Teltscher, *India Inscribed*, p. 120.
84 Holwell, *Genuine Narrative*, pp. 3, 33.
85 Holwell, *Genuine Narrative*, p. 11.
86 Holwell, *Genuine Narrative*, p. 7.

had 'seen this common migration in too many shapes' before, and that this knowledge allowed him to approach the fact 'with too much propriety to be alarmed at the prospect'.[87] Here, the use of the word 'migration' must be noted. From 1764 the doctrine of metempsychosis became a prominent feature of Holwell's work, that is, the belief in the *transmigration* of souls. In the 1767 dissertation on that topic, Holwell claimed to have been inspired with 'the first hints' of this thesis by the Gnostic Jacob Ilive, before acquiring knowledge of the *Gentoo Shastahs*.[88] Upon discovering the striking correspondence between Ilive's and the *Gentoo* system, Howell confirms that it is the doctrine of metempsychosis that constituted the lost knowledge of the *Shastah*, the manuscripts of which he claimed to have translated, but then lost in the sack of the fort.[89]

By his own chronology, then, he had been converted to the doctrine of transmigration before writing the narrative. That philosophical detachment is a by-product of this knowledge is attested to in other parts of his work. Describing the controversial practice of sati, for example, Holwell concludes that the self-immolation of widows on the funeral pyres of their husbands, though not necessarily original to *Gentoo* scriptures, was a result of 'heroic as well as rational and pious principles'.[90] This is not merely rhetoric: the unusual serenity of the widow in the throes of the act was, according to Holwell, a result of their knowledge of metempsychosis. When Holwell describes these women as 'raised to a soothing degree of dignity befitting *angelic beings*' (emphasis added) he chose these words very deliberately, and their literal meaning for Holwell has often been overlooked.[91] Moreover, he stressed that because of the doctrine of metempsychosis, 'a contempt of death, is not peculiar to the women of *India*, it is the characteristic of the nation; every *Gentoo* meets that moment of dissolution, with a steady, noble, and philosophic resignation, flowing from the established principles of their faith'.[92] The basis of his own composure in the Black Hole was therefore a system of knowledge, the beginnings of which he had explored before arriving in India, brought to full realisation by his supposed discovery of the original *Shastah*.

87 John Zephaniah Holwell, *India Tracts* (London: T. Becket and P. A. de Hondt, 1764), p. 259.
88 Holwell, *Interesting Historical Events*, vol. 3 (1771), p. 143.
89 Holwell, *Interesting Historical Events*, vol. 1 (1766), pp. 3–4.
90 Holwell, *Interesting Historical Events*, vol. 2 (1767), p. 97. Holwell refers to the practice as 'voluntary sacrifice'. In the later eighteenth century, the practice came to be referred to as suttee or sati.
91 Holwell, *Interesting Historical Events*, vol. 2 (1767), p. 98. Norbert Schürer, for example, sees these comments as evidence of Holwell's sympathetic impartiality: see Schürer, 'Impartial Spectator'. I have elaborated this argument further in Patterson, 'Eighteenth-Century Account'.
92 Holwell, *Interesting Historical Events*, vol. 1 (1765), p. 99.

For such an enduring myth of empire, we may expect to find a thoroughly unflattering portrait of Siraj-ud-Daulah, under whose command the Fort was captured and thereby returned to the control of the Mughal empire. And yet, Holwell makes a point of suggesting that his orders to secure the prisoners for the night 'had only been general' and that the decision to condemn them all to the Black Hole was 'the result of revenge and resentment' among the lower ranks of sergeants, owing to their losses in the siege.[93] Indeed, Holwell's official report to the Fort William council in 1756 also stressed that the incident was not a direct result of the nawab's orders.[94] Nevertheless, while the nawab is absolved of responsibility for the Black Hole itself, he is still portrayed as an opulent despot. After the prisoners are released, 'the tyrant' becomes so fixated on the treasure rumoured to be hidden in the fort that he barely acknowledges Holwell's desperate pleas for water.[95] Indeed, the dramatic heart of the tale is still dependent on the cruelties of its Indian characters. The most gratuitous example of this is Holwell's decision to include a female prisoner, 'Mrs Carey', who remains in the fort out of loyalty to her husband. She survives the 'Black-Hole', but was, we are told, 'too young and too handsome' to be let free.[96] What becomes of this sentimental heroine is left to the reader's imagination. Holwell thus crassly leads his readers to a stirring association between Asiatic despotism and sexual violence towards an idealised European femininity. Like some of the other characters in Holwell's published narrative, however, the name Mrs Carey is suspiciously absent from Holwell's official report.[97]

Such inconsistencies have caused many scholars to treat Holwell's account with suspicion, particularly in relation to his figures. Brijen K. Gupta's thorough analysis suggests that Holwell and others were indeed imprisoned in the Black Hole prison, but argues that according to records of the numbers of Europeans in Calcutta, accounting for those who fled, a more likely figure for the imprisoned would be a maximum of sixty-four, forty-three of whom died.[98] As Betty Joseph has pointed out, contemporaneous accounts from other outposts mention the prisoners, but not on a scale that corroborates Holwell's description. French communiqués

[93] Holwell, *Genuine Narrative*, p. 4.

[94] S. C. Hill, *Bengal in 1756–1757*, vol. I (London: John Murray, 1905), p. 186.

[95] Holwell, *Genuine Narrative*, pp. 34–5.

[96] Holwell, *Genuine Narrative*, p. 36.

[97] An inconsistency pointed out by J. H. Little in 'The Black Hole: Question of Holwell's Veracity', *Bengal Past and Present*, 11 (1915), p. 104.

[98] Brijen Kishore Gupta, *Sirajuddaullah and the East India Company, 1756–1757* (Leiden: E. J. Brill, 1966), p. 75.

surrounding the fall of Calcutta do not mention the Black Hole itself, though they do refer to various numbers being imprisoned and perishing in the fort, as do two Dutch accounts. And yet, these all came months after the incident itself, and it is possible that they originated with Holwell.[99]

Despite this, as is the case in his insistence on the veracity of his translations of the *Shastah*, Holwell presented his account as definitive, arguing that although the Company's Court of Directors 'will receive many different narratives and accounts of the causes of our misfortunes', his would be the most accurate, presented by an eyewitness, written for no other motive than 'to discharge this part of my duty' and with 'the strictest regard to truth'.[100] Yet, when in 1764 he published his account of the Black Hole alongside a set of other tracts pertaining to various controversies within the Company, it was clear that Holwell's version of events was indeed under question. Perhaps the clearest indication that Holwell's narrative was not considered credible was the decision by the directors not to honour Holwell, but another man, for the hardships endured during the siege.[101] Indeed, as Linda Colley has pointed out, the initial reception of Holwell's tale did not necessarily garner the sympathetic response he had hoped, with some blaming the Company's provocation of Siraj-ud-Daulah.[102] That said, after Clive's retaliations, writers supportive of the Company increasingly placed the 'Black Hole' in prime position as a justification for the military and political conquest that followed. In his *Reflections on the Government of Indostan* (1763), retired Company servant Luke Scrafton had decidedly 'given the Moors a detestable character', of which the Black Hole was cited as an illustrative example.[103] Once the uncertain position of the Company was redressed and subsequently secured to one of unprecedented dominance, the architectural epilogue to Holwell's narrative also condemned 'the Tyrannic violence of Surajud Dowla'. The monument, which Holwell had constructed as temporary governor in 1760, certainly struck a triumphalist tone, bearing the testimony that the 'Horrid Act of Violence' had been 'deservedly revenged' by 'his Majesty's Arms'.[104]

99 Joseph, *Reading the East India Company*, p. 69. See also Iris MacFarlane's account of how these reports can be traced back to Holwell's initial account, in *Black Hole, or, the Makings of a Legend* (London: George Allen and Unwin, 1975), p. 227.

100 Holwell, *India Tracts*, p. 268.

101 Little, 'The Black Hole', p. 102.

102 Linda Colley, *Captives: Britain, Empire and the World 1600–1850* (New York: Anchor Books, 2004), pp. 463–5.

103 Scrafton, *Reflections*, pp. 23, 53.

104 See the illustration of the monument in Holwell's *India Tracts*.

This depiction of '*Mahometan* tyranny' is a consistent feature of Holwell's historical conception of India. In *Interesting Historical Events* the province of Bengal was, in Holwell's estimation, a 'harassed country', not because of the Company's presence, but because of the likes of the 'Usurper' Alivardi Khan, who had become the nawab of Bengal (1740–57) after defeating Shuja ud-Din's successor, Sarfaraz Khan, at the Battle of Giria. After restoring some peace to the region's 'shattered constitution', Siraj-ud-Daulah, the 'succeeding young tyrant reduced it again'.[105] In stark contrast, when speaking of the *Maharattors* (Marathas), Holwell believed them to be representatives of uncorrupted *Hindoo* self-government. He compared them to 'the *Goths* or *Vandals* of the West', but with an 'essential difference'. Whereas the former 'were the barbarous invaders of the rights and property of others', the *Maharattors* were 'making justifiable efforts to recover *that* which their ancestors had been, for ages, in peaceable and just possession of'.[106]

Unfortunately, Holwell does not pause to reflect on where that leaves the East India Company's conquests. The result is thus a contrast between stable and regular *Hindoo* government in the Deccan, versus decline in Bengal, through a series of bloody Mughal intrigues. While in the dissertations on *Gentoo* religion much of what Holwell wrote demonstrated a commitment to heterodox religious ideas which strayed outside of Company concerns, in the context of the text as a whole this is thus complemented by a generalised juxtaposition between *Gentoo* ideals and *Mahometan* despotism. The first hints of this are given in a footnote in the introduction, following the justification of the history on the grounds that 'it is essentially necessary at this interesting period, that we should be able to form some clearer ideas of a people, with whom we have had such important transactions; and of whom so little is truly known'. Those people, the footnote explains, are the *Gentoos*, 'now labouring under *Mahometan* tyranny', but fated soon, he hoped, 'to feel the blessings of a mild *British* government'.[107] The decline of Bengal under Mughal rule and the discovery of ancient *Gentoo* philosophy was here, as well as in the *Genuine Narrative*, the basis upon which Holwell sought to legitimise Company rule.

This picture of Indian history belonged to the first volume in the *Interesting Historical Events* series, published in 1765. As we have seen, the

[105] Holwell, *Interesting Historical Events*, vol. 1 (1766), pp. 178–9.
[106] Holwell, *Interesting Historical Events*, vol. 1 (1766), p. 103.
[107] Holwell, *Interesting Historical Events*, vol. 1 (1765), p. 5.

latter two volumes are given over exclusively to a discussion of the *Shastah*. It is only in volume 1 that the reader is provided with anything approximating the promise of the work's main title. The 'historical events' promised are an account of 'the succession of the Mogull emperors from Aring Zebe' (Aurangzeb), in 1707, to the reign of Nader Shah, which ended in 1743. The text drew heavily on an earlier history by James Fraser, which Holwell references throughout.[108] The final section of the book then turns to a consideration of the particular transactions of the 'Subahdary of Bengal', by which Holwell meant the region and its nawabs, described from 1717 to 1750, ending with some final comments on Siraj-ud-Daulah. Throughout, Holwell's central claim is that the history of the Mughal empire, like all 'histories of the rise of states and kingdoms', was a history of cruelty, ambition and usurpation, from Aurangzeb's 'bloody example' onwards.

The overall narrative is thus that of decline, ending in a mercurial calculation of the potential profits to be made now that the Company had emerged triumphant from its recent military transactions with Siraj-ud-Daulah.[109] The final chapter of the book thus assesses the real 'value' of each province of Bengal.[110] Despite its billing as a history, therefore, the text is replete with references and asides on contemporary Company politics. Holwell even accused his political rival, Luke Scrafton, of plagiarising some of its contents before it had gone to print.[111] Indeed, the conclusion of this first book was that the Company was in an important but precarious position, at the end of a period of degeneration. It had secured the rights to *diwani* (understood as a branch of Mughal government pertaining to revenues and the administration of civil law), but this was, Holwell urged, a fragile settlement, particularly so long as they waged war in the region. To secure itself, the Company must come to an agreement with the nawab, the terms of which Holwell suggested should be the appointment of the Company's governor to the position of *soubha* (*subha* meaning province and title of governance) in Bengal, Bihar and Orissa, in exchange

[108] James Fraser, *The History of Nadir Shah, Formerly Called Thamas Kuli Khan, the Present Emperor of Persia; to Which Is Prefixed a Short History of the Moghol Emperors* (London: W. Strahan, 1742). On Fraser, see chapter 3 of Subrahmanyam, Europe's India.

[109] Holwell, *Interesting Historical Events*, vol. 1 (1765), pp. 17–19.

[110] Holwell, *Interesting Historical Events*, vol. 1 (1765), pp. 178–9. For arguments on land valuation, see Holwell, *India Tracts*, p. 178.

[111] Holwell, *Interesting Historical Events*, vol. 1 (1765), p. 14. The work that he claims features work plagiarised from him is Scrafton's *Reflections*. The offending section is the 'Second Epistle'. Details of the political dispute between them are given in John Zephaniah Holwell, *An Address from John Zephaniah Holwell, Esq; to Luke Scrafton, Esq* (London: T. Becket and P. A. De Hondt, 1767).

for which the Company could pay an annual fee to the treasury at twice the rate of their predecessor. In other words, the Company should take on the duties of government, but very firmly within the framework of Mughal rule. As he puts it, only this was 'eligible, honourable, or practicable'. Thus, he concludes, '*aut Soubah, aut nullus*' rather than *aut Caesar aut nullus* (either Caesar or no one).[112]

This is the argument that appeared in *Interesting Historical Events*, but Holwell had initially addressed these issues from the position of governor. After his involvement in deposing Mir Jafar in favour of Mir Qasim as nawab, Holwell had returned to England and took to offering his suggestions in writing, advocating for extensive administrative restructuring, particularly in relation to property rights. His central argument was that the current system of landholding needed urgent reform in order to raise the land tax of Bengal.[113] It was his view that the zamindars took an unfair share of the agricultural surplus, with the result that they both oppressed the local peasantry and cheated the central government.[114] The way to resolve this, he argued, was to dispossess the current zamindars and auction the lands to the highest bidders, thereby ascertaining their true value.[115] Holwell had already suggested something similar when, in the immediate aftermath of Plassey, the Company had first assumed fiscal responsibility for collecting Bengal's revenues. The most expedient measure, he argued, was to auction out the rights to revenue collection in certain districts. This is what the council did, and Holwell was among those to purchase some of those rights, deepening his personal investment in the Company's possession of Bengal.[116] The security of this investment, he believed, lay in positioning the Company within the fabric of the Mughal empire.

As early as the 1764 *India Tracts*, before the grant of *diwani*, Holwell had raised the idea that it should negotiate for itself the position of *subha*. This time it was made more tentatively, with Holwell hypothesising that although 'the times are not yet ripe for such a grasp', were the Company 'the Subas [rulers] of the provinces, the Emperor would regularly receive

[112] Holwell, *Interesting Historical Events*, vol. 1 (1766), pp. 186–8.

[113] For a detailed discussion of this position, see Robert Travers, '"The Real Value of the Lands": The Nawabs, the British, and the Land Tax in Bengal.' *Modern Asian Studies*, 38.3 (2004), p. 525.

[114] Holwell was able to cite evidence of such in the district of the 24 Parganas, where in 1758 the Company successfully used detailed revenue surveys to uncover a range of 'rent-free' lands that had been alienated in the rolls; it removed the existing zamindars and collected tax from farmers, one of whom was Holwell himself.

[115] Holwell, *India Tracts*, pp. 173–4.

[116] Subhas Chandra Mukhopadhyay, *The Agrarian Policy of the British in Bengal: The Formative Period, 1698–1772* (Allahabad: Chugh Publications, 1987), pp. 26–7.

more than double the revenues . . . and the East-India Company become, in a short time, the richest body of subjects in the world.'[117] The greatest threat to this, though, was, in Holwell's eyes, continuing military activity. The subsequent Treaty of Allahabad (1765) had tied the nawab to the support of its arms. Thus, Holwell testified to a parliamentary select committee on Indian affairs in 1767: 'a commercial Company and a military Company cannot long subsist at the same time'.[118]

There were two important propositions underlying Holwell's proposals. The first is that despite posing extensive interventions in the administrative governance of Bengal on the basis of property, he still envisioned, even in his most aspirational conjectures, that they would fall under the structures of the existing Mughal empire and the authority of its emperor. The Company would not become an independent sovereign power, but an 'English *Soubah*' or 'British *Soubah*', as he variously put it.[119] Second was the notion that this could be justified according to the history of purity and decline that pitted ancient *Hindoos* against a declining Mughal government. After repeating these proposals to the select committee, against their objections that Holwell's plan meant dispossessing the 'Hereditary Nobility of the Country', he retorted that only '4 or 5 of the Ancient Rajahs' remained in the region and that that most of the zamindars were 'Modern' appointments.[120] For Holwell, an 'Ancient Rajah' represented *Hindoo* government, and followers of the *Gentoo* religion, in contrast to 'modern' Mughal-appointed zamindars; though whether this placed limits on British intervention in relation to these rajahs is unclear. Less ambiguous, though, is the conclusion that in the context of Company affairs, Howell's more generalised conception of purity and decline in India, in the related categories of religion and government, could be marshalled to support British interests.

Dow and the Company

Dow believed himself to have discovered in the *Tārikh-i-Firishta* a 'minute and authentic history of a great empire.'[121] His prefaces and footnotes further suggest that it was his view that this empire had achieved something

[117] Holwell, *India Tracts*, p. 178.
[118] 'Evidence taken before the Committee [of the House of Commons] on the state of the East India Company 27 March to 13 April 1767', BL, Add. MS 18469, f. 12.
[119] Holwell, *Interesting Historical Events*, vol. 1 (1766), pp. 215, 220.
[120] 'Evidence taken before the Committee', BL, Add. MS 18469, f. 18.
[121] Dow *History of Hindostan*, vol. 1. (1768), p. ii.

of golden age under the reign of its third emperor, Akbar (1556–1605). Moreover, it was this example of empire that lay at the centre of his more immediate political commentary on the East India Company and the conquest of Bengal. Indeed, Dow attached a great deal of significance to both Sanskrit and Mughal histories of India. Dow's translation of the *Tārikh-i-Firishta* met an increasing appetite for Persian histories of the empire, which recognised their usefulness to those invested in 'Indian Affairs'.[122] It was less usual, however, to affirm the importance of Hindu history, of which little was known and which was often relegated to the status of religious mythology.

Indeed, from the time that Holwell and Dow were writing to the end of the eighteenth century, the question of the true antiquity of Hindu chronology would become a contentious debate. Dow's defence of Hindu history was rooted in the same critiques he had advanced against previous interpreters of the *Hindoo* religion, which accused previous authors of misrepresentation and prejudice. Rather than Christian missionaries, though, this time the culprits were Muslim scholars. According to Dow, 'The prejudices of the Mahommedans against the followers of the Brahmin religion, seldom permits them to speak with common candor of the Hindoos'. Indeed, the author of the *Tārikh-i-Firishta* had been thoroughly 'swayed' by religious prejudice, claimed Dow, 'when he affirmed, that there is no history among the Hindoos of a better authority than the Mahabarit' (*Mahābhārata*). This was, Dow explained, merely 'a poem and not a history', or as he elsewhere called it, a 'historical poem'.[123] Firishtah had, therefore, wilfully overlooked the fact that 'there are many hundred volumes of prose in the Shanscrita language, which treat of the ancient Indians'. Thus, Dow insists 'from his own knowledge' that 'the Hindoos carry their authentic history farther back into antiquity, than any other nation now existing.'[124] On what exactly this was based, however, Dow characteristically declines to give further detail. Nevertheless, he was adamant, Hindu history was vast and ancient.

In criticising Firishtah's dismissal of Hindu history, Dow was again challenging biblical chronology. Dow's translation of the section on Hindu history in the *Tārikh-i-Firishta* was written as follows:

> As the best and most authentic historians agree that Adam was the father of mankind, whose creation they place about five thousand years before the Hingerah, the sensible part of mankind who love the plainness of truth

[122] See, for example, Orme, *History of the Military Transactions*, p. 17.
[123] Dow, *History of Hindostan*, vol. 2 (1768), pp. viii, 1; vol. 1 (1770), p. 2.
[124] Dow, *History of Hindostan*, vol. 1 (1768), p. vi.

> better than the extravagance of fable, have rejected the marvellous traditions of the Hindoos, concerning the transactions of a hundred thousand years, and are of opinion that they, like other nations, are the descendants of the sons of Noo, who people the world. The Hindoos pretend to know nothing of the flood; however, as this event is supported by the testimony of all other nations, there is little room to doubt of its truth, and we shall, therefore, proceed to trace the Hindoos from that great aera, according to the best authorities.[125]

Ahmed Asif has stressed that opening with an account of *Mahābhārata* is a remarkable feature of Firishtah's history, for its departure from the norms of Arabic and Persian historiography that preceded him. These exclusively began with God's creation of Adam, continued to Noah's Flood and thus set Qur'anic time as historical time. In contrast to even the Persian translator of *Mahābhārata* (as the *Razmnama*), Abu'l-Fazl, who saw it as a work of religion, Firishtah, Ahmed Asif stresses, saw it as a work of history. Dow's dismissal of this as an act of prejudice is entirely ignorant of this context, as well as the subtleties of Firishtah's discussion. Nevertheless, as Ahmed Asif goes on to detail, Firishtah's intention was 'to intertwine the time from the Qur'an with the continuously unfolding time of the *Mahabharata*', through such efforts as insisting on Adam as the first man, and fixing Muhammad's migration from Mecca (Hijri, rendered 'Hingerah' by Dow in the above quotation) within the *kalyuga* (in Dow the 'Cal Jug', the fourth age in the Hindu Yuga cycle).[126] It was this that was precisely Dow's target, as part of a broader scepticism towards biblical history. Thus Ahmed Asif's claim that Dow had argued that Firishtah was wrong to consider Sanskrit texts history because they were poetry and not prose misses the thrust of Dow's point here.[127] As we have seen, Dow did not doubt the existence of a credible history in Sanskrit. Instead, he was objecting to the adaption of the *Mahābhārata* to fit within Abrahamic history. As he put it in a footnote to the above quotation:

> Though our author begins his accounts of Hindostan with the flood, yet like the annals of other nations, there is little to be depended upon in the history of that country, for some sages after that supposed period. This must rather be ascribed to the ignorance of the Mahommedans in the Sanscrita language, than to a real want of ancient monuments among the Hindoos themselves. In the first centuries of the Higerah, truth begins to beam forth with lustre in his accounts of India, and that with more precision

[125] Dow, *History of Hindostan*, vol. 1 (1768), pp. 7–8.
[126] Ahmed Asif, *Loss of Hindustan*, pp. 89–93. [127] Ahmed Asif, *Loss of Hindustan*, p. 17.

> and minuteness than any history we have of any European nation, in so early a period.[128]

Dow is indicating several things here: firstly, rather than assuming history begins with the Flood, which Dow casually dismisses as a 'supposed period', the absence of knowledge about India's ancient history is ascribed to the inability of outside enquirers to read Sanskrit texts; secondly, he supposes that these histories do exist; and thirdly, rather than dismissing Firishtah's history, he concludes by holding it up to be more precise than any accounts of Europe at the equivalent time, that is, the first few centuries of the Hijri era of the Islamic calendar (beginning in 622 CE). He therefore at once affirms the importance of Muslim records from this period, and the likelihood of *Hindoo* histories from before it. This was a feature and a direct result of Dow's religious heterodoxy, and is something that would separate him sharply from later orientalists who also sought to fix Hindu chronology in line with a biblical deluge.

Indeed, Dow's intellectual alignment with deist ideas also shaped the ways he saw religion and government interacting in his account of India's history. This was in alignment with a more common framework for asserting European supremacy in the period, which was accounts of the degenerative effects of climate and its demarcation of human typologies.[129] In Dow, this emerges as the product of the widespread influence of Montesquieu's *Spirit of the Laws* on European intellectual culture, and in particular ideas about political society and civilisation. In *Spirit of the Laws* Montesquieu sets up religion as a category of analysis that is to be understood 'in relation to the good to be drawn from them in the civil state'.[130] This is likewise the approach adopted by Dow in one of the essays appended to the 1772 volume of *The History of Hindostan*, titled 'A Dissertation Concerning the Origin and Nature of Despotism in Hindostan'. It begins, however, by rehearsing another of Montesquieu's analytical categories, specifically the contention that a country's climate and geography affects the temperament and customs of its inhabitants.[131] In Dow this is formulated as the not uncommon European proposition that 'The languor occasioned by the hot climate of India, inclines the

[128] Dow, *History of Hindostan*, vol. 1 (1768), p. 7.

[129] On this see Mark Harrison, *Climates and Constitutions: Health, Race, Environment and British Imperialism in India 1600–1850* (New Delhi: Oxford University Press, 1999).

[130] Charles Louis de Secondat Montesquieu, *The Spirit of the Laws*, Anne Cohler, Basia Miller and Harold Stone (eds.) (Cambridge: Cambridge University Press, 1989 [1748]), part 5, book 24, chapter 1, p. 459.

[131] On this see chapter 1 in Sebastiani, *Scottish Enlightenment*.

native to indolence and ease'.[132] This is one of the foundations for his claim, which again follows Montesquieu, that all Asian governments are despotic.

Second to climate in Dow's theory of causation, though, is religion. Dow's particular hypothesis is that the 'faith of Mahommed is peculiarly calculated for despotism'.[133] This was not dissimilar from the position of French *philosophe* Volney (1757–1820), who contrary to Montesquieu had argued that religion and style of government were more decisive in determining the character of a people than climate. The question of the origins of despotism in central Asia was not to be solved by such essential characteristics as climate, but through a historical analysis of the development of Islam.[134] It was the legal precepts of Islam that Dow judged to have had a significant effect on the social and political mores of its followers. In this he may have taken his cues from George Sale, whose 1734 English translation of the Qur'an frequently referred to the Prophet Muhammad as the 'legislator'.[135] Thus, like Voltaire in his play *Mahomet the Imposter*, which had been translated into English in 1744,[136] Dow cast 'Mahommed' as a charlatan. It was his ambition for power and 'politicking' that had 'effected a revolution and change in the human mind, as well as in states and empires'. This psychological transformation was rooted in theological doctrines such as the fatalistic 'absolute predestination', as well as the development of despotic customs, such as the 'unlimited power' conferred on the male head of each household, all of which habituated its followers to arbitrary rule.[137]

The view that Islam was inextricably linked to despotism was not unusual in eighteenth-century European political thought. Indeed, it was precisely the pervasiveness of this view that the French orientalist Abraham Anquetil-Duperron sought to refute in his *Législation orientale* (1778), which disputed the idea that all of the major Muslim polities were despotic or arbitrary, and in particular took aim at both Montesquieu and Dow.[138] Many of the uses of this idea of Islam were aimed at asserting the relative *superiority* of European civilisation and progress, but they could also have

[132] Dow, *History of Hindostan*, vol. 3 (1772), p. vii.
[133] Dow, *History of Hindostan*, vol. 3 (1772), p. xiii. [134] Harvey, *French Enlightenment*, pp. 38–9.
[135] Ziad Elmarsafy, *The Enlightenment Qur'an: The Politics of Translation and the Construction of Islam* (London: One World Publications, 2009), p. 24.
[136] Originally *Le Fanatisme ou Mahomet le Prophète* (1742). For more, see Curtis, *Orientalism and Islam*, p. 35. For an account of the widespread characterisation of the Prophet Muhammad as an 'imposter', see Harvey, *French Enlightenment*, pp. 18–19.
[137] Dow, *History of Hindostan* (1772), pp. xiii–xiv.
[138] See chapter 2 in Pitts, *Boundaries of the International.*

a more satirical edge. Some others had weaponised an imagined Eastern despotism in order to make an ulterior polemical point about the West. As Ziad Elmarsafy's impressive study, *The Enlightenment Qur'an* has traced, caricatures of Asian despotism often served as an effective ruse from which to launch ironical attacks on the hypocrisies of European Christendom.[139] In his dedicatory letter to Frederick the Great, Voltaire acknowledged that the play *Le fanatisme ou Mahomet le prophète* was not an accurate historical representation of the prophet's life. Instead it was an artistic invention which allowed him to represent 'the most awful actions of fanaticism' on the stage.[140]

No doubt Dow's criticisms of Islam's relationship to despotism were genuinely held beliefs, and were certainly related to his assertion of European superiority on the basis of climate. But they also operated within a general argument about the pernicious effects of religious inflexibility on political culture. In a similar vein to Voltaire's portrayal, Dow's essay was insistent on the wider polemic that religious hypocrisy was the 'great engine of political imposters'.[141] In the case of Islam, its promotion of public and private despotism meant 'that undefined something, called Public Virtue, exists no more'.[142] But the corrosive effects of religion on civic virtue were not exclusive to Islam. Before Gibbon, Dow argues elsewhere that it was Christianity that had led to the fall of Rome, as 'the spirit and power, and, we may say, even virtue of the Romans, declined with the introduction of a new religion among them'.[143]

The effects of religion on civic polities is a consistent feature of Dow's historical commentary. Indeed, it is the chief characteristic of his account of why, in the history of India's rulers, the 'Imperial house of Timur', that is, the line of the Mughal empire traced back through Barbur, represented despotism 'in its most engaging form'. The descendants of this line had 'rendered Hindostan the most flourishing empire in all the world', a feat that had much to do with the 'mild and humane character' of the Mughal empire, which in turn was related to their disavowal of religious dogmatism.[144] In particular, Akbar had displayed wisdom in disavowing the distractions of religious zeal. As Dow put it in the dissertation, 'He

139 Elmarsafy, *Enlightenment Qur'an*, p. 81.
140 As quoted in Harvey, *French Enlightenment*, p. 72.
141 Dow, *History of Hindostan*, vol. 3 (1772), p. 260.
142 Dow, *History of Hindostan*, vol. 3 (1772), p. xii.
143 Dow, *History of Hindostan*, vol. 1 (1770), p. 17. Gibbon also read and cited Dow: see Gibbon, *Decline and Fall*, p. 280.
144 Dow, *History of Hindostan*, vol. 3 (1772), p. xxiii.

regarded neither the religious opinions nor the countries of men: all who entered his dominions were his subjects, and they had a right to his justice'.[145] Elsewhere in *The History of Hindostan*, Dow's rendition of Firishtah again stressed that Akbar 'tolerated every religion'. Likewise, his son 'Jehangire' (Jahangir) was similarly 'imbibed with his principles' and was thus 'brought up Deist' according to the wishes of his father.[146]

Significantly, these comments came from the same 1772 edition of *The History of Hindostan* that also contained the dissertation on despotism. This portion of the history no longer represented a translation of *Tārikh-i-Firishta*, but instead picked up where Firishtah left off, accounting 'from the death of Akbar, to the complete settlement of the empire under Aurungzebe' (Arungzeb, 1618–1707). For this section, Dow claims to have used some European sources for what they had 'seen', but had mainly relied on 'domestic writers' for their accounts 'of what they heard'. He gives the names of six texts, which were 'in his hands', including the *Mir'at-i 'Alam* (The mirror of the world).[147] It is very difficult to tell, therefore, what comes from these sources and what is a product of Dow's own invention. It seems clear, though, that the use of the appellation 'deist' is certainly Dow's choice. Dow continues that while Akbar had considered a founding a new syncretic system 'which might reconcile the minds of all his subjects', he also foresaw the 'distractions which this arduous measure might occasion'. Thus, Dow tell us, he focused instead on the business of government and 'contented himself with giving no credit to any of the old systems of religion'. Jahangir had also briefly followed suit in considering founding a new creed, but likewise 'shewed more wisdom in relinquishing' the scheme.[148] In contrast, in the dissertation on despotism, the later influx of 'nobles from various kingdoms' into the imperial court, all of whom were 'followers of the Mahommedan religion', resulted in decline. For Dow, it was in 'the regulations and spirit of the Coran, [that] they lost their primary and characteristical ideas upon government'.[149] This narrative of decline in the dissertation was certainly a contribution to common tropes about Asiatic despotism, as well as a feature of his generalised narrative of Mughal decline in support of British interests in the region, but it was also a more general criticism of the ill effects of religious zealotry in the field of politics.

145 Dow, *History of Hindostan*, vol. 3 (1772), p. xxv.
146 Dow, *History of Hindostan*, vol. 3 (1772), p. 103.
147 Dow, *History of Hindostan*, vol. 3 (1772), 'Advertisement'.
148 Dow, *History of Hindostan*, vol. 3 (1772), p. 104.
149 Dow, *History of Hindostan*, vol. 3 (1772), p. xiii.

In the concluding section of the 'Dissertation on Despotism', Dow also applied this lens of analysis to a consideration of *Hindoo* government. In doing so he offered two contrasting visions. One the one hand, Dow began his comments on the *Hindoos* with the reflection that 'the system of religion which they profess, is only perfectly known in the effect which it has upon the manners of the people', that is, 'Mild, humane, obedient, and industrious' and because of that 'easily conquered and governed'.[150] Notions of Indian effeminacy were a consistent theme in British texts, with roots in the seventeenth century that stretched to the racial politics of British imperialist government in the nineteenth century.[151] In Dow's account this was a consequence of passive religious mores. It was also connected to contemporary debates about the political consequences of luxury, which in its crudest extremes was a question of whether commerce was beneficial to social development, or potentially effeminising and therefore injurious to civic virtue.[152] In the wake of accusations of Company corruption, this view of commerce also became intertwined with concerns about the effects of expansionist commercial enterprises on the politics of the metropole.[153] According to Dow's narrative, the combination of India's rich soil and the *Hindoo* religion, which encouraged both industry and asceticism, had rendered the region thoroughly 'opulent' and therefore too tempting for 'the fierce nations of northern Asia' to resist.[154] As Dow explains elsewhere in the 1772 *History of Hindostan*, it was in this imperial setting that the 'weed' of luxury, which 'takes root in prosperity', began to grow.[155] Even 'in the cool air' of Britain, Dow maintained that it was difficult 'to retain, in the midst of luxury and wealth, the vigour of mind necessary to keep us free'. Thus, in 'so rich a soil' as India, a heady mixture of religion, luxury and climate made it impossible for the *Hindoo* and Muslim polities of India to resist despotism.[156]

On the other hand, like Holwell before him, Dow makes the *Hindoo* polities beyond the Mughal empire stand in contrast to this picture of

[150] Dow, *History of Hindostan*, vol. 3 (1772), pp. xxxv–xxxvi.

[151] This trope became prevalent in the seventeenth century. See Kate Teltscher, '"Maidenly and well nigh Effeminate": Constructions of Hindu Masculinity and Religion in Seventeenth-Century English Texts', *Postcolonial Studies*, 3:2 (2000). On the nineteenth century, see Mrinalini Sinha, *Colonial Masculinity: The 'Manly Englishman' and the 'Effeminate Bengali' in the Late Nineteenth Century* (Manchester: Manchester University Press, 1995).

[152] Dow is discussed in this context by Jeng-Guo S. Chen, 'Gendering India: Effeminacy and the Scottish Enlightenment's Debates over Virtue and Luxury', *The Eighteenth Century*, 51:1/2 (2010).

[153] Dirks, *Scandal of Empire*, pp. 12–13, 281–2.

[154] Dow, *History of Hindostan*, vol. 3 (1772), pp. viii–ix.

[155] Dow, *History of Hindostan*, vol. 3 (1772), p. 55.

[156] Dow, *History of Hindostan*, vol. 3 (1772), p. cxxi.

submissive native subjects. Further entrenching the link between religious and civic identities in his account of Indian history, Dow suggests that despotism common to all Asian government is, in the *Hindoo* states, 'tempered by the virtuous principles inculcated by their religion' so that 'it seems milder than the most limited monarchy in Europe'.[157] The 'countries governed by native princes', that is, those that had not been conquered by the Mughals, were 'cultivated to the highest degree' and the source of India's manufactures. Dow's particular admiration is reserved for the nation of the *Mahrattor*s (Marathas), 'composed of Rajaputs [rajputs], or that tribe of Indians whose chief business is war'. Predominantly associated with the region of Maharashtra in the west of India, the Marathas controlled great areas of Western India at the time of Dow's writing.

Dow's claim to have recently visited these regions is corroborated by accounts of his time in and around Bombay in 1769–70.[158] His depiction of their domestic politics is strikingly idealised. While 'their armies carry destruction and death into the territories of Mahommedans, all is quiet, happy, and regular at home'. Within their territories 'No robbery is to be dreaded, no imposition or obstruction from the officers of government, no protection necessary but the shade. To be a stranger is a sufficient security.' Yet, he insists, this was 'no ideal picture of happiness' but based solely on 'the truth of his observations'.[159]

This bears an interesting resemblance to Holwell's description of the *Gentoo* polity living under the Malla kings in the city of 'Bisnapore' (Bishnupur), discussed in Chapter 2. For Holwell, this region was untouched by Mughal influence and thus represented 'the only vestiges of the beauty, purity, piety, regularity, equity and strictness of the ancient *Indostan* government'. Of particularly pronounced similarity to Dow's account of the Marathas was Holwell's claim that in Bishnupur 'no robberies are heard of, either private or public' and that 'the traveller ... on entering this district, becomes the immediate care of the government'.[160] This is no coincidence: both authors consistently distinguished Indian religious philosophy from its modern corruptions. In Holwell's case, this belief in the original simplicity of the *Gentoo* religion explains why the untouched city of 'Bisnapore' exemplifies the purity 'of the ancient *Indostan* government'. For Dow, too, the *Hindoo* polities that

157 Dow, *History of Hindostan*, vol. 3 (1772), p. xxxv.
158 Macdonald, *Memoirs*, pp. 45–9.
159 Dow, *History of Hindostan*, vol. 3 (1772), p. xxxvii.
160 Holwell, *Interesting Historical Events*, vol. 1 (1765), p. 198.

had avoided conquest represented the essential principles and virtues of what he considered to be central to India's ancient religion. Thus, the 'Dissertation on Despotism' concludes with Dow's statement that the Marathas were 'a great and rising people, subject to a regular government, the principles of which are founded on virtue'.[161]

In Dow's analysis, then, religion is one of the central categories in determining political virtue. On the one hand, it was a source of deceptive politicking, as in the case of religious charlatans like Muhammad, the consequences of which were a religious code peculiarly suited to despotism. Against this, he contrasts the enlightened despotism of the Mughals, the greatest rulers of which we are told were deists, as an illustration of the correspondence between religious latitude and political regularity. In the example of the *Hindoos*, a passive religion, like the Christians of Rome, undermined the necessary vigour to remain free. And yet, where married to martial virtues, as in the case of the Marathas, they also resulted in virtuous and regular government. In this sense, Dow was self-consciously cast himself as a contributor to contemporary speculation on the nature of civic society, luxury, empire and religion.

Some of his reflections were reminiscent of other better-known works in this oeuvre. As well as reasserting the categories of Montesquieu's climatic social theory, he can also be situated alongside the discourses on civilisation associated with the so-called Scottish Enlightenment, such as Adam Ferguson's observations in *An Essay on the History of Civil Society* (1767), for example, that India's climate and commercial arts 'can even assuage the rigours of despotical government'.[162] What was distinctive about Dow's intervention, however, was the decisive weight given to religion, relegating climate and commerce to the wider context. This approach was thus also brought to bear on his considerations regarding the more immediate politics of the Company, which accompanied the dissertation under the title 'An Inquiry into the State of Bengal and a Plan for Restoring that Province to its Former Prosperity and Splendor'. In this, Dow accused the British public of having previously approached the Company's conquest with a 'phlegmatic indifference' that was unworthy of their 'boasted humanity'.[163] As we have seen, this intervention was published in a period of increasing public criticism of the East India Company's malpractice, in both government and commerce. In the same year

161 Dow, *History of Hindostan*, vol. 3 (1772), p. xxxvii.
162 Adam Ferguson, *An Essay on the History of Civil Society* (Dublin: Boulter Grierson, 1767), p. 165.
163 Dow, *History of Hindostan*, vol. 3 (1772), p. xl.

William Bolts, an independent merchant in India, had published *Considerations on Indian Affairs*, which also sought to relay the Company's misdemeanours to a newly engaged domestic audience.[164] Thus, with 'hands free of rapine and depredation', Dow now turned to his audience newly 'rouzed into attention, with regard to a subject which concerns the welfare of the state'.[165]

For those aligned with Company interests, like Holwell, the blame for Bengal's rapid decline lay at the feet of the nawabs. It was a common argument that they had usurped the power of the Mughal emperor and thrown the empire into turmoil over their own bitter rivalries.[166] Dow's history partially supported this, arguing that since the reign of Muhammed Shah (1719–48) the political power of the empire had been undercut by these 'petty tyrants'.[167] And yet, this did not absolve the Company. In fact, Dow explicitly stated, 'We may date the commencement of decline, from the day on which Bengal fell under the dominion of foreigners; who were more anxious to improve the present moment to their own emolument, than, by providing against waste, to secure a permanent advantage to the British nation'.[168] Of course, according to this framing, the crime here was not one of conquest, but that of badly managed conquest. That said, Dow was also precise in his condemnation. In just six years, 'half the great cities of an opulent kingdom were rendered desolate', and men whose 'only object was spoil' found themselves 'wading through blood and ruin'. Not wanting to 'rend the veil that covers our political transactions in Asia' any further, Dow took the matter-of-fact position that the British presence in India was now 'an absolute conquest', which the 'thin veil' of *diwani* could not disguise. Dow insisted, therefore, that recent events be described as conquest, since 'to call them by any other name would leave them undefined'.[169]

Now that the dust had settled, the British government had a duty to both its British and Indian subjects. Of course, this duty was significantly weighted to the former, as it was to the benefit of Britain that Indian commerce should be restored. The rest of the essay is devoted to outlining Dow's proposals for how this should be achieved. The matter of government in Bengal was no small issue, and in fact Dow was writing on the

164 William Bolts, *Considerations on Indian Affairs, Particularly Respecting the Present State of Bengal and Its Dependencies*, 3 vols. (London: J. Almon & P. Elmsley, 1772).
165 Dow, *History of Hindostan*, vol. 3 (1772), p. xl.
166 P. J. Marshall, 'Indian Officials under the East India Company in Eighteenth- Century Bengal', *Bengal Past and Present*, 84 (1965).
167 Dow, *History of Hindostan*, vol. 3 (1772), p. c.
168 Dow, *History of Hindostan*, vol. 3 (1772), p. lxxvii.
169 Dow, *History of Hindostan*, vol. 3 (1772), pp. lxx, cxvi.

precipice of an intense debate about whether merchants could be sovereigns. This reached a crescendo in the furore that surrounded Fox's India Bill of 1783, that the better-known thinkers associated with eighteenth-century critiques of the Company, particularly in the history of political thought, such as Adam Smith and Edmund Burke, questioned the nature of Company rule.[170] At this point, in 1772, Dow was ahead of this direction of travel, presenting a plan that was unambiguously in favour of bringing the Company administration under the oversight of Parliament.

Like Holwell, Dow recommended that the Company's position be secured by acquiring the title of 'perpetual Nabob', and so still conceived of British rule as existing within the larger framework of the Mughal empire. And yet, he also explicitly acknowledged that this was more a matter of appearance, since really 'the sword is our tenure'.[171] As the work of Robert Travers has shown, such interventions existed in a developing discourse that sought to legitimise a British administration by drawing on the precedents of Mughal rule.[172] Dow's essays sit alongside the first wave of thought along these lines, prior to the 1772 Regulating Act. They bore some similarity, for example, with the work of Luke Scrafton, whose 1763 *Reflections on the Government &c of Indostan, with a Short Sketch of the History of Bengal* had also characterised the Mughal empire as a kind of limited despotism, which had maintained customary law for its *Gentoo* subjects.[173] Scrafton's pronouncements were on the whole, though, generally more negative, working to vindicate Robert Clive's conquest as a retaliation to Mughal provocation. Dow, on the other hand, was concerned more with its consequences.

To avoid the 'despotism which naturally sprung from the double government', that is, the division of Bengal's administration between the Nizamat and the Company acting as *diwani*, Dow argued that there needed to be a new system for the administration of justice. Next, lest there be a confusion of legislative and executive power, the Company's Governor and Council of Calcutta should produce an annual report of proposals, which was to be scrutinised by the Company's board in London,

170 Edmund Burke, 'Speech on Fox's India Bill', in David P. Fidler and Jennifer M. Welsh (eds.), *Empire and Community: Edmund Burke's Writings and Speeches on International Relations* (Boulder, CO: Westview Press, 1999); Adam Smith, *An Inquiry into the Nature and Causes of the Wealth of Nations*, R. H. Campbell, A. S. Skinner and W. B. Todd (eds.), 2 vols (Indianapolis: Liberty Fund, 1981), vol. 2, book IV: vii 'Colonies', pp. 556–641.

171 Dow, *History of Hindostan*, vol. 3 (1772), pp. cxv–cxvi.

172 See the introduction to Travers, *Ideology and Empire*.

173 Scrafton, *Reflections*.

and then put before Parliament to be framed into law. He also recommended severely restricting the power of the council, and the establishment of an independent judiciary, in the form of a 'supreme court of Bengal', which should be the counterpart of 'the king's bench in England'. At the same time, though, a balance had to be maintained, so that 'the ancient form of government remains in the lesser departments of the state'.[174] Fundamental to this was the premise that 'religion must never be touched'. This was with the added exception of those practices deemed offensive to moral norms, such as what has come to be termed the practice of sati.[175] The significance of this for Dow's scheme is often read as an extension of the Company's pre-existing pragmatism that non-interference in religious matters was the best means of sustaining tranquillity.[176] Travers, for example, suggests that Dow simply followed the rationale that India was firmly divided into two religious sects, 'Mahommedan' and 'Hindoo', neither of which would submit to the laws of the other.[177] Yet, given Dow's intense focus on the history of both, it seems reasonable to assume that Dow had meditated more deeply on the topic. Dow's commitment to maintaining the legal institutes of India's two religious groups (as he understood them) must be seen as a more deeply rooted ideological choice, related both to his outlook that 'common sense upon the affairs of religion' was equally divided among all nations, and his vision of Indian history, which paid close attention to religious mores and, in particular, pinned the success of the Mughal empire to the 'deism' of its greatest architects.

The other central feature of Dow's proposals was a plan for the 'establishment of property' by a general sale of land.[178] This has been written about most extensively by Ranajit Guha, who situates Dow's proposals at the beginning of a tradition of thought following the grant of *diwani*, that conceived of a permanent settlement for Bengal through the establishment of a system of property.[179] Indeed, where Dow's plan to return Bengal to prosperity centred on mercantilist proposals about the flow of specie, his design to use the sale of land to raise revenues had a larger purpose. As he put it, giving security of property to the native inhabitants of Bengal would

174 Dow, *History of Hindostan*, vol. 3 (1772), pp. cxxx–cxxxiii, cxv.

175 Indeed, this would become the subject of an intense debate, often with recourse to the the religious origins of sati, which resulted in by British officials banning the practice in 1829. See Mani, *Contentious Traditions*.

176 On East India Company policy, see Carson, *East India Company and Religion*, p. 4.

177 Travers, *Ideology and Empire*, p. 65.

178 Dow, *History of Hindostan*, vol. 3 (1772), p. cxlviii.

179 Guha, *Rule of Property*, p. 20.

be 'to bind them with stronger ties to our interest; and make them more our subjects', adding with a forceful clarity 'or, if the British nation prefers the name – more our slaves'.[180] This built on his earlier thinking about the relationship between luxury and despotism. As Dow notes in the following paragraph, whereas 'men who have nothing to lose' are enslaved only by disunion, and can be driven to freedom by despair, 'Men possessed of property are enslaved by their interest, by their convenience, their luxury and their inherent fears'.[181] The permanency of British rule was thus dependent on the ability of the administration to ensure property, and so secure the loyalty of a Bengal gentry.

Despite their innovations, as Guha suggests, Dow's actual plans were broached as a firming up of existing practices, in sharp contrast to the oppressions of Clive's 'double government'.[182] Dow had written that while the Mughal crown had retained the right to seize land, this had only ever been practised according to 'political necessity' and was not without compensation. Thus, while the foundation of the Mughal settlement had been that the empire retained property and rented it out annually, following the reign of Babur estates had be granted in perpetuity and 'descended in succession by will', and 'in equal division of his children, according to the law of the Coran'.[183] Thus Dow proposes that his system of property likewise follows the laws of Muslim and *Hindoo* inheritance, which in turn had the added benefit of distributing property more evenly. The result was an argument for dominion, through property, supported by reference to established conventions.

Dow was a critic of the Company, but he was no critic of empire. In the second volume of the 1770 edition of *The History of Hindostan*, Dow had boldly asserted that 'the immense regions of Hindostan might all be reduced by a handful of regular troops'. With just 'Ten thousand European infantry' and the sepoys in the Company's service, he suggests that all of India could be conquered and 'with proper policy' maintained as 'an appendage of the British crown'. This, he supposed, was 'not only practicable, but easy' on the grounds that the 'slavery and oppression, which Indians suffer from their native princes, make the justice and regularity of a British government appeal to them in a most favourable light'.[184]

By the 1772 volume, however, Dow's bluster had dropped, in favour of the more limited restoration of Bengal and Bihar. Indeed, his

[180] Dow, *History of Hindostan*, vol. 3 (1772), p. cxx.
[181] Dow, *History of Hindostan*, vol. 3 (1772), p. cxxi. [182] Guha, *Rule of Property*, p. 40.
[183] Dow, *History of Hindostan*, vol. 3 (1772), pp. xxvi–xxviii.
[184] Dow, *History of Hindostan*, vol. 2 (1770), pp. 401–2.

recommendations insisted that Allahbad be returned Siraj-ud-Daulah, and that the territories of Balwant Singh (the Maharaja of Benares) be ceded to the emperor.[185] This likely has a lot to do with the timing of the two publications. The 1770 second edition of *The History of Hindostan* was written by Dow while still in Britain, in response to complaints about the first edition (1768), such as the overuse of proper names.[186] This was revised before he sailed out once again for India in April 1769, prior to his experience of the territories of the Marathas.[187] The third additional volume of *The History of Hindostan*, published in 1772, was produced on his second return to London, after a period of two years based at Bombay. By this point it seems that Dow had changed his mind about the prospects of conquest beyond Bengal that he had made grand claims for in the 1770 edition. Indeed, the Maratha confederacy was to become the Company's fiercest adversary for the remainder of the century, with conflict between the Company and the Maratha empire stretching until 1818. Nevertheless, as Dow's plan made clear, Britain should secure the conquest of Bengal to its advantage. And his account of how to achieve this was fitted to a framework of constitutional geography, after Montesquieu, sharpened by Dow's own detailed consideration of how the historical regimes and religions of India had shaped its political landscape.

Critics of the Company

Recent scholarship on the Company's early modern foundations has emphasised the long history of its transformation into an imperial power, pointing to its ability to acquire rights within existing frameworks of governance, and thus gradually develop for itself 'a rich cloak of political and constitutional legitimacy'.[188] Holwell's suggestion that the Company dispose of the existing structures of the current zamindars while at the same time restricting the Company's ambitions to the acquisition of the role of *Subha*, was in line with this tradition. Likewise, so too were Dow's recommendations that the Company's possessions be brought under the purview of Parliament, while at the same time managing these according to existing customs and offices of state. Particularly striking in Holwell's and Dow's proposals for British governance in India is their emphasis on

[185] Dow, *History of Hindostan*, vol. 2 (1770), p. cxvii.
[186] See 'Advertisement', in *History of Hindostan*, vol. 1 (1770).
[187] This is when his footman says that they set sail; see Macdonald, *Memoirs*, p. 40.
[188] David Veevers, *The Origins of the British Empire in Asia, 1600–1750* (Cambridge: Cambridge University Press, 2020), p. 245.

property. From the conquests of the 1760s, how to manage the land and relations with an Indian propertied class was to become an essential feature of debates about Company administration.

Following Dow's proposals, Philip Francis, one of Hastings' fiercest critics (and a member of the Supreme Council of Bengal, 1774–80), likewise argued that the regulation of property rights was the solution to reforming the Company, as well as the best means of securing British interest through the creation of a landed class invested in its administration.[189] As Robert Travers has discussed at length, this was framed by Francis in the language of historical constitutionalism, as an impassioned defence of the ancient rights of Indian princes and landlords (in part because this is how zamindars had framed the matter themselves in their petitions to the Company).[190] On the other hand, so too did Hastings, who presented a counter-plan to make tax settlements with hereditary zamindars. This had also called on certain precedents within the historical 'constitution of the empire'.[191] In both cases, then, contesting policy proposals were grounded in appeals to existing customs. Holwell and Dow, as early presenters of such arguments for public debate, were thus pivotal in establishing the importance of ideas of Indian history and religion for those attempting to conceive of the possible foundations and limits to British governance in the region at a point when various competing visions vied for primacy. In fact, to further complicate this, whereas Travers has pointed to a turn from legitimising strategies grounded in Mughal constitutional history in the 1760s–80s to, by the end of the century, a preference for appeals to the ancient civilisation of the Hindus, Holwell's work suggests that both discourses coexisted throughout the period.[192]

In fact, it is in the light of such debates that we ought to reconsider our appreciation of the various critics of British rule in India, and by extension its imperial ventures elsewhere, that emerged in the latter part of the eighteenth century. For scholars such as Jennifer Pitts, this has been framed as a rising tide of critical challenges 'to European imperial conquest and rule', which stands in sharp contradistinction to the liberal imperialism of nineteenth-century thinkers like James Mill and John Stuart Mill. Among the list of these opponents to imperialism Pitts places Adam Smith, Edmund Burke and Denis Diderot, all of whom fiercely set the East India Company under their critical gaze.

[189] Guha, *Rule of Property*, p. 38. For more on Francis, see Travers, *Ideology and Empire*, pp. 141–80.
[190] Travers, *Ideology and Empire*, Chapter 4. [191] Travers, *Ideology and Empire*, p. 165.
[192] Travers, *Ideology and Empire*, p. 244.

And yet, if we situate these writers in the context of the reception of works like Holwell and Dow, and the active debates that emerged from them, it becomes clear that they were not straightforwardly the critics of 'European conquest and rule over peoples across the globe' that Pitts and others have declared them.[193] On the Anglophone side, Smith perhaps has the greatest claim to such an appellation. Despite the foundational importance of his theory of societal development through stages for various imperial arguments appealing to empire as a civilising force, Smith was himself sceptical about the advantages of colonies for either their possessors or their subjects.[194] Smith ventured some thoughts on the legitimacy of the East India Company's administration in Bengal in the 1784 edition of *Wealth of Nations*, noting that in the case of both Dutch and British settlements, 'the government of an exclusive company of merchants, is, perhaps, the worst of all governments for any country whatever'.[195] The debates leading to Fox's 1783 India Bill, which sought greater parliamentary oversight of the Company's administration, were the immediate critical tide upon which Smith's commentary floated. In what Smith termed his 'violent attack' on Britain's mercantile system in *Wealth of Nations*, one of his central targets was the Company's monopoly and the rule of merchants.[196] To Smith, 'Company government' was a contradiction in terms, its two components divided by irreconcilable interests. The designs of merchants answerable to shareholders would always be at variance with the local and general interest. The Company's tendency to restrict competition had, for example, supressed Indian markets and thus violated the principles of public finance.[197] Eager to leave with their own fortunes, no other sovereigns were, he remarked, 'so perfectly indifferent about the happiness or misery of their subjects, the improvement or waste of their dominions, the glory or disgrace of their administration'.[198]

And yet, this was not a rejection of the idea of British empire in India itself. According to Smith, the territorial acquisitions of the Company were 'the undoubted right of the crown, that is, of the state and people of Great

[193] Jennifer Pitts, *A Turn to Empire: The Rise of Imperial Liberalism in Britain and France* (Princeton, NJ: Princeton University Press, 2005), p. 1. See also Sankar Muthu, 'Adam Smith's Critique of International Trading Companies: Theorizing "Globalization" in the Age of Enlightenment', *Political Theory* (2008), 36: 2.

[194] See Emma Rothschild, 'Adam Smith and the British Empire', in Sankar Muthu (ed.), *Empire and Modern Political Thought* (Cambridge: Cambridge University Press, 2012).

[195] Smith, *Wealth of Nations*, vol. 2, book IV: vii, p. 570.

[196] Letter 208, October 1780, in Ernest Campbell Mossner and Ian Simpson Ross (eds.), *The Correspondence of Adam Smith* (Indianapolis: Liberty Fund, 1987), Letter 208, October 1780, p. 251.

[197] Smith, *Wealth of Nations*, vol. 2, book IV: vii, p. 632.

[198] Smith, *Wealth of Nations*, vol. 2, book IV: vii, p. 640. See also vol. 2, book V: i, p. 752.

Britain'.[199] The British government should, therefore, revoke the Company's charter, purchase its military institutions, assume responsibility for public administration in India and open trade 'to all the subjects of the state'.[200] They would also do well, he added, to prevent the misapplication of Indian finances to the benefit of the British treasury and attempt to ease the tax burden shouldered by Indian subjects. On balance, though, should such a venture prove to be of diminishing returns the purpose of maintaining it was questionable. Indeed, Smith continued, what were the American colonies but the expensive 'showy equipage of the empire', the costs of which ought to give Britain cause to 'accommodate her future views and designs to the real mediocrity of her circumstances'?[201]

Ironic in tone, these passages were certainly sceptical of empire. Smith did not reflect further on the details of what such a British administration would look like. In practice, although he would have preferred that Company's charter were removed, he supported Fox's bill. As others have pointed out, he wrote to MP William Eden, commending the success of the bill in the Lower House, predicting its smooth passage through the Lords (this proved too optimistic).[202] Thus, while Pitts and other have been correct to stress that for Smith, Europe's ascendency through empire was precarious and not owing to any inherent superiority other than circumstance, in practice this hardly amounted to a particularly forceful anti-imperialism. His reflections that when and if 'perhaps, the natives of those countries may grow stronger' or those of Europe weaker, then it may be possible to 'arrive at that equality of courage and force which, by inspiring mutual fear, can alone overawe the injustice of independent nations into some sort of respect for the rights of one another' were aspirational while remaining ambivalent.[203] Indeed, we me way well wonder whether Smith's incredulity regarding any innate European virtues or advantages is all that distant from Dow's reflections on the Mughal empire or the Marathas, and his acknowledgement that Britain's acquisitions were more the result of a 'revolution of fortune' than anything else.[204] As we have seen, Smith shared the view that the results of that accident were nevertheless

199 Smith, *Wealth of Nations*, vol. 2, book V: iii, p. 945.

200 Smith, *Wealth of Nations*, vol. 2, book V: i, p. 755.

201 Smith, *Wealth of Nations*, vol. 2, book V: iii, pp. 945–7.

202 Mossner and Simpson, *Correspondence*, Letter 233, 15 December 1783, p. 272. For a detailed account of Smith's thought on the Company and his response to the legislation, see Gregory M. Collins, 'The Limits of Mercantile Administration: Adam Smith and Edmund Burke on Britain's East India Company', *Journal of the History of Economic Thought*, 41:3 (2019).

203 Smith, *Wealth of Nations*, vol.2, book IV: vii, p. 626. Smith's particular reflections on the nature of Indian society seem to have been primarily gleaned from William Bolts; see Rothschild, 'Adam Smith', p. 190.

204 Dow, *History of Hindostan*, vol. 3 (1772), pp. xlii, lxxii.

one of legitimate conquest, following which Bengal ought to be secured to the British. That this was an impermanent advantage Dow was also well aware, rehearsing the common refrain that 'all empires seem to be subjected by Fate' to fall.[205] The question remained, then, what could make British government in India both durable, at least in the medium term, and legitimate?

This was the question to which Edmund Burke turned. Another of the thinkers associated with this eighteenth-century critical stance to empire, Burke differed in his position from Smith in that he was to defend the Company's charter while also strenuously asserting that in its misrule it had violated the trust on which it was granted.[206] Burke also shared with Smith a disquiet about the effects of the spirit of conquest, but as an active member of parliament he was more immediately concerned with how it could be disciplined and ameliorated with correct policy, rather than the hope of a future state of internationally balanced powers.[207] Like Dow, Burke judged that the Company's acquisition of territory in Bengal was a matter of fact, and that while the murky circumstances that had brought it about had certainly compromised the standards of justice, the matter in hand was how to reconcile it with the obligations of proper government.[208] The problem was that the Company had, in asserting the *rights* of conquest, established 'an oppressive, irregular, capricious, unsteady, rapacious, and peculating despotism', and had thus failed to also take account of its corresponding *duties*.[209] For Burke, these were the obligations of government, which were to rule ultimately for the benefit of those over whom it was established.[210] Like the Company's charter, such authority was originally granted in trust and thus likewise accountable. What was needed was a '*Magna Charta* of Hindostan'.[211] The proposed parliamentary Commission was thus intended to supply supervision that was detached from the voracious interests that currently governed Company policy, and so relieve the population of India from oppression. There was no question of abandoning empire in India altogether; for Burke this would both be impractical and leave the Indian population exposed to perhaps greater injustices at the hands of other warring factions, including both Indian powers and the French.[212]

[205] Dow, *History of Hindostan*, vol. 3 (1772), p. cl.
[206] Burke, 'Speech on Fox's India Bill', pp. 385–6.
[207] For Burke's evolving thought on the 'spirit of conquest', see Bourke, 'Politics of Conquest'.
[208] Edmund Burke, 'Speech on Secret Committee Resolutions', given on 15 April 1782, *Gazetteer* (16 April 1782). For a detailed discussion of Burke's position on the Company in relation to the bill, see Bourke, *Empire and Revolution*, pp. 550–67.
[209] Burke, 'Speech on Fox's India Bill', pp. 430, 425.
[210] Burke, 'Speech on Fox's India Bill', p. 385.
[211] Burke, 'Speech on Fox's India Bill', p. 386.
[212] Burke, 'Speech on Secret Committee Resolutions'.

With the failure of the bill, Burke's means for redressing these grievances became the impeachment of Warren Hastings. Gathering information on Indian religion, custom and culture had always played a role in informing Burke's approach to policy on India, collected as it was through the works of Dow and others, as well as the various pieces of testimony submitted to the select committee on the judicial arrangements in Bengal of which he was a part. This knowledge was to take a far more prominent role in the impeachment trial, one of the chief targets of which was Hastings' appeal to local norms as a pretext for arbitrary misdemeanours, or as Burke put it, his 'Geographical morality'.[213] In declaring his behaviour consistent with the customary practice of Asia, Hastings had called upon Dow, causing Burke to forcefully rebut that 'the History of Dow has no authority in the world'.[214] It is to this dispute that Uday Mehta attaches the claim that the British 'were insistent on denying the fact that India had a history of its own', holding Burke's appeal to existing laws to be an arresting exception.[215] And yet, this argument rested very much on the interpretation rather than the denial of history, the origins of which Dow, in his text, had sought to locate in both Persianate histories and the possibilities of Sanskrit records, to claim that both were essential to any understanding of how to apply correct political principles in India. Likewise, all three had called for the recognition of existing religious customs and laws. Indeed, it was the very law codes that Hastings had commissioned that Burke was able to ironically throw back at him in denouncing such claims.[216] Thus Burke concluded the impeachment trial with an appeal to the ideal of a tolerant empire, reiterating the same sentiments that had animated his speech on the Bengal Judicature Bill of 27 June 1781, that laws had to be adapted to the 'genius of the people' and that therefore local custom was to be the basis of a just settlement in Bengal.[217] The matter was, again, not one of relinquishing Bengal to its former rulers, and calling an end to British empire in India, but rather one of the means by which this initial conquest could be brought in line with the duties of the conqueror to govern in the interests of the governed, the answer to which at

[213] Edmund Burke, 'Speech on the Opening of Impeachment', in *The Writings and Speeches of Edmund Burke*, Paul Langford et al. (eds.), 9 vols. (Oxford: Oxford University Press, 1970–), vol. 4 (2015), p. 346.

[214] Edmund Burke, 'Speech in Reply', 5 June 1794, *Writings and Speeches*, vol. 7, p. 385.

[215] Uday S. Mehta, 'Edmund Burke on Empire, Self-Understanding and Sympathy', in Sankar Muthu (ed.), *Empire and Modern Political Thought* (Cambridge: Cambridge University Press, 2012), p. 178.

[216] Burke cited Halhed, *A Code of Gentoo Laws*, in Burke, 'Observations', *The Writings and Speeches*, vol. 5, p. 171.

[217] Speech on the Opening of Impeachment, 18 February 1788, Burke, *Writings and Speeches*, vol. 4 (2015), p. 459; Burke, Speech on Bengal Judicature Act, 27 June 1781, *Writings and Speeches*, vol. 5, p. 140.

least partly lay in the preservation of local custom, which was determined to be religious in nature and origin.

The debates into which Holwell and Dow had entered in Britain, then, were centred on the question of how to secure the conquests of the Company without also sharing in its disgrace, and ideas about Indian history, religion and custom were brought into the service of that endeavour. From a different perspective, though, Holwell's and Dow's essays on the philosophical nature of Indian thought, their rich accounts of its ancient history and their denunciations of Company misrule were indeed potent ingredients for a more fundamentally critical approach to empire. This came to be particularly significant in terms of their reception in France following on from Voltaire's promotion of their work. French and British rivalry in the territory had provoked the question of the legitimacy of either European power to wage conflict over Indian land, and consequently invited a period of what intellectual historians have defined as an anti-colonialist or anti-imperialist intellectual discourse in France in the 1770s.[218] For Pitts, taking the example of Diderot, this approach was categorical in its condemnation of empire since it was part of an uncompromising assault on the politics of the *ancien régime* more generally.[219] Though, as others have pointed out, this was not necessarily a critique of colonies per se, but the violent exploitation that had accompanied them. Diderot in particular had vociferously condemned the abuses of European empire, while at the same time exploring the idea that the improving benefits of commerce could be extended beyond Europe through more humane modes of colonisation, or *douce colonisation* (softer colonisation).[220] Others have suggested that critical French discourses on empire in the eighteenth century be seen in connection to support for American independence, physiocratic opposition to overseas expansion, and an idealisation of the 'noble savage'.[221] Indeed, scholars of French thought have pointed to how this also happened in a context in which the cause of American independence ignited a residual Anglophobia, which was then easily married to rising tensions between the two nations in India.[222] The moral implications of rule by the East India Company thus became

218 See, for example, the discussion of Abbé Guillaume-Thomas Raynal in Marsh, *India in the French Imagination*, p. 122.
219 Pitts, *Turn to Empire*, p. 165.
220 For a discussion of this, see Sunil Agnani, *Hating Empire Properly: The Two Indies and the Limits of Enlightenment Anticolonialism* (New York: Fordham University Press, 2016), pp. 32–45.
221 Sudipta Das, *Myths and Realities of French Imperialism in India, 1763–1783* (Bern: Peter Lang, 1993), pp. 23–4.
222 See Marsh, *India in the French Imagination*, p. 115.

a focal point for French debates about imperialism as well as a foil for various accounts of 'French values', be they republican or otherwise.

The *Journal Encyclopédique*, edited by Pierre Rousseau, to which Voltaire contributed several articles, provides an interesting insight into the development of these attitudes and discourses in relation to our authors throughout the course of the 1760s and 1770s. In 1768 an anonymous review of the French translation of Holwell's *Interesting Historical Events* welcomes the publication as a piece of scholarly research and, like Voltaire, accepts Holwell's explanation of the origin of the Brahmins.[223] In contrast, reviews of Dow's latterly published work focused their critique on the question of British government in India, and on what basis it could be justified. This evolved from a physiocratic objection to European expansionism to a condemnation of the Company in the language of despotism and tyranny. An important example of this was the Abbé Guillaume-Thomas Raynal's *Histoire philosophique et politique de l'établissement et du commerces de Européens dans les deux Indes* (1770–80).[224] Raynal, a renegade Jesuit, had indeed edited this extraordinary work, comprising a rich and uncompromisingly critical survey of the earliest colonial activities of the Spanish in the Americas down to the Dutch, Portuguese, French and British rivalries across 'the two Indies' of its time. Its most evocative condemnations of the inhumanity of the pursuit of empire and slavery were, however, the unattributed contributions of Diderot.[225] While there was, he acknowledged, a certain grandeur to imperial conquest, the horrors committed in its pursuit also nearly always inspired disgust and sorrow. Thus, in seeking to write a proper historical account of such transactions, Diderot admits, 'I almost always write it bathed in tears'.[226] One of the worst atrocities cited was the famine in Bengal (1769–70), for which Diderot holds the Company accountable in their failure to alleviate the suffering of the desperate population of its territories when it was in their power to do so.[227] Thus, he judged, the English had, in their conduct in Bengal, sacrificed one their usually essential characteristics: a sense of justice.[228]

223 Anon, 'Evénémens historiques, intéressans, rélatifs aux provinces de Bengale et de l' Indostan', *Journal Encyclopédique*, 2:2 (1769).

224 In English, 'Philosophical and political history of European settlements and commerce in the two Indies'. The *Histoire* was first published in 1772 (with an imprint of 1770). Diderot's contributions appeared in the 1780 edition onwards.

225 On this see Michèle Duchet, *Diderot et l'histoire des deux Indes ou l'ecriture fragmentaire* (Paris: Libraire Nizet, 1978).

226 As quoted in Muthu, *Enlightenment against Empire*, p. 90.

227 Guillaume Thomas Raynal, *A Philosophical and Political History of the Settlements and Trade of the Europeans in the East and West Indies*, J. O. Justamond (trans.), vol. 1, 2nd ed. (London: T. Cadell, 1776), book III, pp. 472–5.

228 On this see Marsh, *India in the French Imagination*, p. 128.

The work of Holwell and Dow were integral to these critics. Teltscher even suggests that the *Histoire* in particular 'plagiarizes a great many authors, including Holwell and Dow' in order to offer its rich account.[229] Most significantly, it was very often their presentations of the sophistication of Hindu philosophy and religion that were worked into the fabric of the 'anti-imperial' critiques in the *Histoire*. The two passages that Teltscher marks out as examples of this plagiarism both correspond to passages in Holwell and Dow that focus on the moral virtue and reasonableness of Indian religion. In the first instance, after a long retelling of Dow's story of a Mughal prince named Feizi who went in disguise to steal the secrets of the Brahmins, a passage attributed to Diderot shared Dow's admiration of *Hindoo* toleration. In the words of Dow, although they admit no converts, the *Hindoos* 'allow that everyone may go to heaven his own way'.[230] Mirroring this, Diderot likewise concluded that 'Brama delights in the distinct form of worship observed in different countries'.[231] The following chapter, on 'Religion, government, legislation, manners, and customs of Indostan', also relied heavily on the work of Holwell and Dow, with later additions adding in information from Halhed's *Code*. Holwell's *Shastah* and it account of the fallen angels featured prominently.[232]

Diderot also took from *Interesting Historical Events* Holwell's description of the *Gentoo* city of 'Bisnapore' (Bishnupur), which is utilised for the same purpose of illustrating a virtuous *Gentoo* polity. Diderot did add, though, that such an ideal place could be a fiction, since he found himself 'between two authorities', which were Holwell on the one hand, and possibly Dow, who simply did not mention it, on the other.[233] Far from undermining the important point that India possessed a virtuous religion, and so the social and political mores to match, however, this was part of a more general scepticism about the existence of any ideal society.[234] These examples were instead all part of a much wider purpose in the text which was an expression of, as Sankar Muthu puts it, Diderot's 'flexible moral universalism'. That is, they were evidence of his insistence on the dignity and inherent reasonableness of diverse cultural mores and practices, as

229 Teltscher, *India Inscribed*, p. 164.

230 Dow, *History of Hindostan*, vol. 1 (1768), pp. xxvii, xxv.

231 As quoted in Muthu, *Enlightenment against Empire*, p. 81.

232 Raynal, *Philosophical and Political History*, pp. 49–53.

233 Guillaume Thomas Raynal, *A History of the Two Indies: A Translated Selection of Writings from Raynal's Histoire philosophiqe et politique de l'établissement et du commerces de Européens dans les deux Indes*, Peter Jimack (trans.) (Farnham: Ashgate, 2006), p. 35.

234 As explained by Peter Jimack in his introduction to Raynal's, *A History of the Two Indies*, pp. xviii–xix.

expressions of a universal conception of the bounds of justice.[235] Indian religiosity as described by Holwell and Dow stands as an analogue of this position, according to its own tolerant nature wherein the Hindu 'is the intimate of the Muslim, and the friend of the Indian; the companion of the Christian, and the confidant of the Jew'.[236] In contrast, as Muthu stresses, prejudice and an aversion to pluralism are presented as the characteristics of the European imperialist.[237]

Writers like Marsh have attributed the development of a wider French 'anti-imperialist' discourse as precisely due to the popularity of Raynal's *Histoire*, which went into several editions throughout the latter part of the eighteenth century. Moreover, when, in 1776, the *Histoire* was translated into English, its notoriety soared yet again. Unsurprisingly it was widely cited in the British press during the trial of Hastings.[238] So while, indeed, Holwell and Dow were deeply involved and invested in the East India Company's colonial ambitions, the 'deist', or religiously oriented aspects of their work were not always in step with those same interests. While their diagnoses of Mughal decline formed the basis of claims for British dominion, their comments on Hindu religion and philosophy, as well as Indian history more generally, were also often the source of the more critical aspects of their engagement with Company politics. Moreover, their research into the *Hindoo* or *Gentoo* religion provided the source material for others intent on launching more radical attacks on the Company's imperialist exploits in India. This is something that Christian apologist writer and orientalist Thomas Maurice later recognised when writing his memoirs in the early part of the nineteenth century. Authors like Dow had, alleged Maurice, sowed the seeds for more radical attacks on religion and the Company by supplying 'infidel writers' such as 'Voltaire and others', grounds for the discussion of 'the uncounted ages during which the arts and sciences were asserted to have flourished amongst the Brahmins'. As a result, he lamented, India had become 'the *debateable ground* on which the fury of Jacobin hostility had reared her most triumphant banner'.[239]

235 Muthu, *Enlightenment against Empire*, pp. 72–3.
236 As quoted in Muthu, *Enlightenment against Empire*, p. 81.
237 Muthu, *Enlightenment against Empire*, pp. 81–2.
238 Marsh, *India in the French Imagination*, p. 128.
239 Maurice, *Memoirs*, p. 102.

PART II

From Scepticism to Orientalism

CHAPTER 5

Nathaniel Brassey Halhed and Gentoo *Antiquity*

Nathaniel Brassey Halhed's reputation went from that of an impressive young scholar in the 1770s to eccentric millenarian in the 1790s. Throughout, an interest in religion, which ranged from undercutting orthodoxy to endorsing prophecy, featured at the centre of his intellectual and personal endeavours. Another constant was his patron, Warren Hastings. In 1772 Hastings had returned to Bengal as the Company's governor, and in 1774 he was appointed governor-general by act of parliament, a post he filled until 1785. In 1772 he received orders from London to end Clive's system of 'double government' and replace it with a much more direct British involvement by 'standing forth as Dewan'. This was a mandate to establish a more direct system of British governance in India, with which came a more confident assertion of its status as a sovereign power in Bengal.[1] In navigating this task, Hastings made use of Indian and European scholarship. This was both to reconcile Company rule into local systems of governance and practice, as well as to British metropolitan opinion, by playing to lettered enlightenment discourses about the refinement of commerce. Halhed, and his *Code of Gentoo Laws* (1776), were to play a significant role in that project.

Prior to his engagement in India, Halhed had already demonstrated himself to be an able scholar of classical languages and had picked up some Persian and Arabic, possibly under the guidance of William Jones, his friend at Oxford.[2] Arriving in Bengal in August 1772 as a writer, it was not long before Halhed was put to work as a Persian translator, while resident in Cossimbazar.[3] It was at this time that Warren Hastings, who had

[1] P. J. Marshall, 'The Making of an Imperial Icon: The Case of Warren Hastings', *Journal of Imperial and Commonwealth History*, 27:3 (1999); Neil Sen, 'Warren Hastings and British Sovereign Authority in Bengal, 1774–80', *Journal of Imperial and Commonwealth History*, 25:1 (1997).

[2] Jones writes that Halhed had penned a letter to him, partly in Persian, on the voyage to Bengal: William Jones to Viscount Althorp, 18 August 1772, in Cannon, *Letters of Sir William Jones*, vol. 1, pp. 114–15.

[3] Rocher, *Orientalism, Poetry and the Millennium*, p. 38.

assumed the governorship in April 1772, was preparing and submitting what would come to be known as the Judicial Plan, which established the principle that British judicial decisions in Bengal should respect both Muslim and Hindu religious laws in general civil matters. With this came a series of practical administrative problems, foremost of which was the question of the origin and location of the Hindu legal principles that would advise English judges in their rulings. Warren Hastings selected and tasked Halhed with overcoming this obstacle, through the translation of a compilation of *Gentoo* laws into English. It was this endeavour that historian M. J. Franklin credits with transforming Halhed, formerly a composer of risqué Latin verse, 'from a libertine to an Orientalist'.[4] The several layers of translation meant that Halhed's code was somewhat removed from the original. Nevertheless, Halhed, who believed the text to have been 'translated literally into Persian', was unaware of this, and the comments in his rich preface offer an interpretation of *Gentoo* religion according to what he thought were the genuine insights of the original Sanskrit 'code'.[5] Most controversially, Halhed's insistence on the ancient and philosophical quality of the code levelled a series of ironic challenges to biblical orthodoxy. This chapter is principally concerned with the arguments supplied in this author's preface, which suggest a continuity between his self-styled 'libertine' tendencies at Oxford and his later orientalist thought, followed by the direction that this thought took later in his career.

Halhed went on to further distinguish himself as having a gift for Indian languages with the publication of *A Grammar of the Bengal Language* in 1778. This was an impressive work of scholarship which speculated on the relationship of Bengali to Persian, Sanskrit, 'Hindostanic' (Hindi) and 'Moors' (Urdu). Halhed thus formulated a comparative philology which pointed to the astonishing similarity between various Sanskrit terms and their equivalents in Persian and Arabic, as well as Latin and Greek – reflections, which would come to shape William Jones' account of the Indo-European linguistic family.[6] Ultimately, though, Halhed was not able to acquire Sanskrit, and his pursuit of it would be interrupted by

[4] Michael J. Franklin, 'Cultural Possession, Imperial Control, and Comparative Religion: The Calcutta Perspectives of Sir William Jones and Nathaniel Brassey Halhed', *Yearbook of English Studies*, 32 (2002), p. 2.

[5] Halhed, *Code of Gentoo Laws*, p. x.

[6] For a detailed account of Halhed's relation to developments in philology regarding the idea of an Indo-European linguistic family, see Rosane Rocher, 'Lord Monboddo, Sanskrit and Comparative Linguistics', *Journal of the American Oriental Society*, 100:1 (1980).

political events. In 1777 he had become a factor, but the prospect of any further advancement was dampened by the turning tide on Hastings' popularity.[7] Failing to secure promotion, Halhed resigned from the Company's service and returned to England in 1779. His first publication following this journey was a lengthy anonymous tract written in defence of Hastings, whose detractors were becoming increasingly vocal.[8] This continued when, under the pseudonym of Detector, he wrote a series of open letters and pamphlets, beginning in October 1782, all defending Hastings and his circle against the findings of a House of Commons select committee, instigated by Edmund Burke, on the administration of justice in India. These ended when, following the rejection of Fox's India Bill and the continued administration of Hastings, Halhed returned to India in the service of the Company between 1784 and 1785.

While back in India, Halhed followed closely the progress of Charles Wilkins in acquiring Sanskrit, but had little time for his own studies. Instead, as a firm member of Hastings' close circle, Halhed's efforts were spent mostly on the defence of his patron, in the wake of increased attacks. Indeed, he did not stay long in India, as Hastings devised a plan to have him return, along with some of his other confidants, so that he may prepare a defence for the charges Hastings anticipated would be brought against him. In compensation for the loss of the office he would have taken up in Calcutta, on the Company's revenue board, Halhed was set up as the agent to the nawab of Oudh, Wazir Ali Khan. This allowed him enough financial security and to return to England, under the pretext of acting as the nawab's agent, while also joining the preparations for the looming impeachment trial.[9]

When the official proceedings against Hastings commenced, it became clear that not only his patron, but also Halhed's construction and presentation of Indian religion and history, were to be under fire from Burke. Halhed was thought to be instrumental to one of Hastings' initial lines of defence in the trial, which had sought refuge in the idea that India's history was steeped in the arbitrary exercise of power.[10] This backfired when later,

7 Records of Service: Bengal Civil Servants, BL, IOR/L/F/10/2, pp. 318–19.

8 The particular issue in this case was Hastings' Maratha war. See Nathaniel Brassey Halhed, *A Narrative of the Events Which Have Happened in Bombay and Bengal, Relative to the Maharatta Empire, since July 1777* (London [s.n.], 1779). For more on this issue, see Rocher, *Orientalism, Poetry and the Millennium*, pp. 103–4.

9 Confirmed by the letters of Major William Palmer to Hastings, 22, 28, 29 October, 14 December 1784, in Warren Hastings Papers, BL, Add. MS 29166, ff. 321–2, 337, 339; Add. MS 29167, ff. 96, 122, 228–9.

10 Rocher, *Orientalism, Poetry and the Millennium*, pp. 132–3.

even after these statements were disavowed by Hastings, Burke used Halhed's *Code of Gentoo Laws* to not only undermine the claim, but also point to the great hypocrisy that it should be Halhed who produced both.[11]

During this period, Halhed continued to write about Indian history, philosophy and religion, but with limited resources he was confined to commenting on a number of Persian manuscripts which he had in his possession. It was in 1787 that Halhed completed a translation of some of the manuscripts from Dara Shikoh's (Dārā Shukoh) Persian translations of the *Upanishads* (*Upaniṣads*).[12] The notes and commentaries supplied by Halhed in relation to this work demonstrated, as Rosane Rocher has traced, a noticeable shift in his approach to Indian religion away from religious scepticism.[13] This corresponded with a dramatic change in his personal religious convictions too. In 1791 Halhed had become the MP for Lymington, standing as a Tory candidate, hardened in his opposition to the Whigs after the Hastings' trial. Four years later, after trying but failing to return to the employ of the Company, Halhed would join the cause of the millenarian prophet Richard Brothers. As he was later to testify in parliament, defending Brothers against charges of treasonable intent, he had been convinced of his authenticity after comparing Brothers' two-volume *A Revealed Knowledge of the Prophecies and Times* (1794) with biblical scriptures. In the course of studying both texts, the 'variety of connexions and coincidences' became so striking as to convince Halhed that Brothers' messages were divinely inspired.[14]

Along with this change in his personal beliefs, from scepticism to a highly charged millenarianism, Halhed's political views shifted and he became an avowed critic of Pitt and the war with revolutionary France.[15] When the impending Judgement Day failed to commence at the expected date, Halhed was left unelectable and alienated from his previous allies, his reputation as a scholar overshadowed by the ridicule that his publications on Brothers had inspired. After a decade as a recluse, Halhed was eventually coaxed out of isolation by his former Company colleagues, chief

[11] Edmund Burke, Speech of 28th May, 1794, in Edward Augustus Bond, *Speeches of Managers and Counsel in the Trial of Warren Hastings* (London: Longman, Brown, Green, Longmans & Roberts, 1859), vol. 4, pp. 359, 363.

[12] Halhed mentions that he has these fragments in the preface: Halhed, *Code of Gentoo Laws*, p. xviii.

[13] Rosane Rocher, 'Nathaniel Brassey Halhed on the Upaniṣads (1787)', *Annals of the Bhandarkar Oriental Research Institute*, 58/59 (1977–8).

[14] Speech to the Commons, 3 March 1795, in William Cobbett (ed.), *Parliamentary History of England*, vol. 31 (London: T. C. Hansard, 1818), col. 1419.

[15] For example, he voted with Charles Grey's motion for negotiations with France: Cobbett, *Parliamentary History of England*, vol. 32, col. 737.

among them Charles Wilkins. He secured a post in East India House, in the examiner's office, in the same building where Wilkins was working as custodian of the Company's library. Here Halhed once again turned to orientalist scholarship, labouring over notes on the personifications of abstract philosophical concepts in the *Mahābhārata.*[16]

The institutional shift towards the 'orientalist' policies of his patron Warren Hastings did indeed mean that in Halhed's writings, the relationship between knowledge and Company interests was more firmly established. Where the work of both Holwell and Dow can be described as independent and idiosyncratic, by the time that Halhed began publishing his thoughts on Indian religion, the implications of these reflections for the East India Company were much more closely felt. And yet, in the composition, construction and interpretation of the Indian religious ideas he laid out, Halhed, as much as the authors that went before him, was invigorated by a range of intellectual associations and implications that were not so clearly defined by Company interests. Indeed, his comments were received by some as an outright attack on Christian truth. This chapter will explore these moments in his work and the reception they were met with. It will then turn to a consideration of the intellectual shifts that accompanied Halhed's thinking on Indian religion following the vagaries of his life and outlook which resulted from the Hastings trial and his association with Richard Brothers.

The *Code* and Its Preface

Warren Hastings' administrative plan, set out in 1772, proposed that 'the Laws of the Koran with respect to Mahometans, and those of the Shaster with respect to Gentoos [Hindus] shall invariably be adhered to' in disputes regarding 'Inheritance, Marriage, Caste and all other religious Usages or Institutions'. This provision primarily rested on the consultation of 'Moulavies or Brahmins attending on the court', who would provide the judgements in these cases.[17] There has been much work interpreting the thought behind this clause. For J. D. M. Derrett, the use of religious law codes was designed to reflect English ecclesiastical courts, whereas Bernard S. Cohn attributes the clause to the perception that Indian society was fundamentally 'theocratic'.[18] Robert Travers has pointed to the immediate

[16] Rocher, *Orientalism, Poetry and the Millennium*, pp. 212–13.

[17] Clause XXIII, 'Plan for the Administration of Justice', *Reports from Committees of the House of Commons*, 4, p. 350.

[18] Derrett, *Religion, Law and the State in India*, pp. 233–4; Cohn, *Colonialism*, p. 65.

context of Company disputes over Mughal customs, connecting the clause to an exchange between the Calcutta council and the *naib diwan* (one of the highest administrative offices in Bengal), Muhammad Reza Khan, in the spring of 1772. Against the Company's preferred use of arbitration in settling civil disputes, Reza Khan had asserted that in the Mughal *adālats* (courts) matters concerning 'Inheritance, Marriages and other Disputes', which fall under the dictates of Islam, 'should be decided by a Magistrate, the Religious officers and men of Learning'.[19] As Travers points out, this exchange was referred to in 1773 by a House of Commons committee investigating judicial administration in Bengal, which suggests that it was understood to be part of the relevant background to the subsequent judicial plan. Where Hastings departed from Reza Khan's model, however, was in extending the principle to Hindu religious legal authorities, appointing Brahmin pandits as public officials for this purpose. From the perspective of Reza Khan this was in contravention of the current system, in which cases that came to the *adālats* (rather than those settled privately) were ultimately decided by Muslim magistrates.

As Travers suggests, this was not necessarily an accurate reflection of existing judicial practices, with the sponsorship and consultation of Hindu officials not appearing to be uncommon. The *naib diwan*, however, was obviously concerned that the appointment of Brahmin pandits to official positions by the British was a significant encroachment on the authority of the Mughal empire.[20] Indeed, the nawab had sponsored Brahmin scholarship, including that of the famed legal scholar Jagannātha Tarkapañcānana as well as of other Hindu groups such as *kāyasths* (scribes) and vaidyas (medical scholars).[21] Rather, the innovation was supplanting existing networks of sponsorship and patronage with British projects of cultural conciliation and influence. Alternatively, Nandini Chatterjee has also stressed that the clear distinction of Islamic law in this context was not what Reza Khan's interlocutors took it to be, and that existing practices were based on a permissive inclusion of India's diverse populace in the Islamic courts, which used multiple sources in a layered conception of the law. In either case, the British perspective of a divided religion-based distribution of legal authority was a distinct break.[22] In making his case for his plan to Lord Mansfield, Hastings acknowledged that pandits did

[19] 'Naib Duan's Representation', Factory Records Murshidabad, 4 May 1772, Murshidabad: Proceedings of Provincial Council of Revenue, BL, IOR/G/27/7.

[20] Travers, *Ideology and Empire*, pp. 119–22. [21] Dodson, *Orientalism*, p. 48.

[22] Nandini Chatterjee, 'Reflections on Religious Difference and Permissive Inclusion in Mughal Law', *Journal of Law and Religion*, 29:3 (2014).

not act as judges, but instead insisted that they did act as 'expounders of the Hindoo law', giving opinions to recognised magistrates. He also insisted, contra Reza Khan, that in the practice of their own religious law, the *Hindoos* had 'suffered no diminution from the introduction of Mohammedan government'.[23] In the judicial plan, the appointment of pandit court officers would thus ratify the notion that the British were acting as the benevolent stewards of Hindu customs, which were subsequently taken to be represented by a unified body law.

The necessity of a compilation of Hindu laws, translated into English, did not have as direct a relationship with these measures as it may at first appear. In the judicial plan, the authority of pandits or *maulavis* (Islamic scholars) as interpreters of Hindu and Muslim laws was more important to the working of the Company's courts than translated codes. Halhed's translation was instead commissioned to be published in London, for the purposes of laying down the intellectual foundations for the notion that Hastings and the judicial plan provided the most stable and legitimate means of managing the Company's new administrative settlement in India. The wording of the plan already intimated that there was a distinct body of law, under which the *Gentoos* were governed, by reference to the idea, inaugurated by Holwell and Dow and widely repeated in this period, that there was an authoritative 'Shaster'. Indeed, in the wording of the clause, the laws of 'the Shaster' are presented as parallel to 'the Laws of the Koran with respect to Mahometans'. This of course represented a misunderstanding of the *Dharmaśāstra*, a genre of Sanskrit legal thought made up of a number of texts and commentaries, rather than a singular codified system of law. Indeed, the report of Reza Khan's account of the Mughal legal settlement had stressed that 'the sect of the Gentoos' was made up of various groups. Ignoring his testimony that 'Each Tribe has its own distinct Customs and Laws', in the absence of a singular *śāstra* to translate, the *Code* stepped in to capture the idea of a singular textual authority for Hindu religious law.[24]

While Hastings was somewhat aware that this was an oversimplification, convincing the directors of the plausibility of the judicial plan required it. In his now well-known 1774 letter to the Lord Chief Justice, Lord Mansfield, Hastings sent a copy of Halhed's *Code* precisely to stress the

[23] Hastings to Lord Mansfield, Fort William, 21 March 1774, in R. G. Gleig, *Memoirs of the Life of the Right Hon. Warren Hastings: First Governor-General of Bengal; Compiled from Original Papers*, vol. 1, (London: Richard Bentley, 1841), p. 402.

[24] 'Naib Duan's Representations', 4 May 1772, Murshidabad: Proceedings of Provincial Council of Revenue, BL, IOR/G/27/7.

intelligibility of *Gentoo* law and its importance for effective governance. Rejecting the view that the people of 'Hindostan' were 'governed by no other principle of justice than arbitrary wills, or uninstructed judgements', he instead assured Mansfield that the *Hindoos*, whom he saw as the region's 'original inhabitants', were 'in possession of laws which have continued unchanged, from the remotest antiquity'. Moderating the earlier language of the judicial plan and its appeal to 'the Shaster', this knowledge, Hastings reflected, was preserved by the Brahmins, the 'professors of these laws, who are spread over the whole empire of Hindostan'.[25]

Thus, while Hastings acknowledged that pandits were indispensable to the interpretation and practical application of legal knowledge, the *Code* was intended to make intelligible the idea that British authority could be established on the foundation of the preservation of these legal norms. This was the model of enlightened and tolerant rule, the precedent for which had been established by Mughal systems of governance. The Sanskrit original, compiled between 1773 and 1775, was given the title *Vivādārṇavasetu*, the 'bridge across the ocean of litigation'. It was translated into Persian by Zayn al-Dīn 'Alī Rasa'i, which Halhed then translated into English. Compiled by some of 'the most learned pundits' who had been invited from 'different parts of the province' to Calcutta, the *Code* thus offered a bridge between the knowledge of the Brahmins and the idea of an enlightened British administration.

While Hastings well knew that in practical terms, the operation of the judicial plan meant the sponsorship of indigenous court officers, the notion of an authoritative code could bolster ministerial confidence in the Company courts, as well as 'prevent the ill effects' of any attempt to impose English laws. This, argued Hastings, would be 'misinformed', since the laws and customs of the *Hindoos* were 'interwoven with their religion' and were therefore 'revered as of the highest authority'. To impose anything else, Hastings insisted, 'would be a wanton tyranny'.[26] Rather than modelling the Mughal system exactly, however, standing forth as *diwan* meant the imposition of distinct categories of subject, based on a religious legal identity, according to which justice would be administered through the now sovereign Company's courts.

It was for the purposes of illustrating the viability and vindicating the judicial plan, therefore, that *A Code of Gentoo Laws* was commissioned. Halhed's 'translator's preface', however, and the reactions it engendered,

[25] Hastings to Lord Mansfield, Fort William, 21 March 1774, in Gleig, *Memoirs*, vol. 1, p. 400.

[26] Hastings to Lord Mansfield, Fort William, 21 March 1774, pp. 403–4, 400.

attached it to another set of intellectual and ideological conflicts, foremost of which was biblical history. As well as echoing Hastings' ambitions that the *Code* demonstrate that the *Gentoos* had 'long been misrepresented in the Western world', the essay also features a tangled network of bold assertions, equivocation and subtle raillery.[27] These were not, however, aimed in the direction of the avowed 'peculiarity' of some of the *Code*'s contents, but at the challenges that this much older set of scriptures posed to Christian orthodoxy and authority.[28] The whole preface is structured as a polemic against religious dogmatism, in favour of the idea that 'Diversity of Belief, which are Causes of Envy, and of Enmity to the Ignorant, are in fact a manifest Demonstration of the Power of the Supreme Being'.[29] This statement strongly echoes Holwell's claim that 'all divine worship' was directed towards 'the same Deity', as well as Dow's belief that 'common sense, upon the affairs of religion, is pretty equally divided among all nations'.[30] It was in this sense that Halhed's account of Indian religion registered with the philosophical readings of Holwell and Dow, who were emphatic that the original religion of India represented a rational approach to the worship of the Supreme Being.

And yet, Halhed's writings pushed beyond the moderate implications of this conception of universal religion, often to the effect of positioning himself in a more fundamentally sceptical posture. Generally, his rhetoric is considered and equivocal, making it difficult to pinpoint any singularly disreputable statement. But, by the end of the preface, the reader has been presented with numerous assertions that, taken together, offer an assertive challenge to orthodox Christian history and theology, as well as some foundational elements of religious faith in general.

Halhed worked, throughout the preface, to establish an equivalence between the premises of all religious belief in general. This is most boldly stated in his argument that the *Gentoo* faith is 'equally implicit with that of a Christian', since both have just as firm a faith in the 'supposed revelations of the Divine Will', and are as attached to their own system of worship as the other. Interwoven with such claims, however, there is always an equivocation, often with the inclusion of a bracketed caveat. Take, for example, the sentence 'The Faith of the Gentoo (misguided as it is and groundless as it may be) is equally implicit with that of a Christian.'[31] This

[27] Halhed, *Code of Gentoo Laws*, p. xi. [28] Halhed, *Code of Gentoo Laws*, p. xiii.

[29] Halhed, *Code of Gentoo Laws*, p. 3.

[30] Holwell, *Interesting Historical Events*, vol. 1 (1765), p. 9; Dow, *History of Hindostan*, vol. 1 (1768), p. ixxxvi.

[31] Halhed, *Code of Gentoo Laws*, p. xv.

careful balancing act was sustained in the following paragraph, which appeared below Halhed's discussion and insistence on the greater antiquity of *Gentoo* scriptures:

> Great, surely, and inexplicable must be the doubts of mere human reason upon such a dilemma when unassisted and uninformed by divine revelation; but while we admit the former in our argument, we profess a most unshaken reliance upon the latter, before which every suspicion must subside, and scepticism be absorbed in conviction: yet from the premises already established, this conclusion at least may fairly be deduced, that the world does not now contain annals of more indisputable antiquity than those delivered down by the ancient Bramins.[32]

This fragile and passive attempt to at once assert the antiquity of Indian civilisation while at the same time pay a manner of respect to Christian revelation did not go unnoticed. It was precisely this that had outraged his family friend, George Costard. Costard was a vicar and felt so strongly about Halhed's irreligious conclusions that he felt moved to publish a lengthy critical response. Of Halhed's conviction in the antiquity of the *Gentoo* 'annals', he asked, 'how will you reconcile this with that *unshakeable Reliance* on Revelation which you speak of in the Sentence immediately before?'.[33]

The challenge posed to biblical history by *Gentoo* scripture is the central feature of Halhed's preface to the *Code*. The above quotation followed a section in which Halhed had emphasised the absence of any record of the great biblical Flood in the annals of Indian history, 'which yet we must think infinitely too remarkable to have been even but slightly spoken of, much less to have been totally omitted, had it ever been known in that part of the world.'[34] The universality of the Flood as a challenge to biblical history was an established marker in sceptical polemics. Most famously, Charles Blount had suggested in *The Oracles of Reason* (1693), among other criticisms of the plausibility of the Scriptures, that the Flood must have been a localised phenomenon, according to its failure to account for, among others, the origins of Chinese civilisation.[35] This challenge

[32] Halhed, *Code of Gentoo Laws*, p. xlii.

[33] George Costard, *A Letter to Nathaniel Brassey Halhead, Esquire. Containing Some Remarks on His Preface to the Code of Gentoo Laws Lately Published* (Oxford: Clarendon Press, 1778), pp. 20–1.

[34] Halhed, *Code of Gentoo Laws*, p. xxxviii.

[35] Charles Blount, *The Oracles of Reason* (London [s.n.]: 1693), p. 11. This section appears as a defence of Thomas Burnet's *Archaeologiae Philosophicae* (1692), which had attempted a mechanistic account of creation, including the Flood, rather than literal interpretation of scripture. Blount thus repurposed this work to point to the dubious reliability of the Old Testament. For more on this, see

remained a mainstay of biblical criticism in the eighteenth century. Conversely, evangelicals like Johnathan Edwards had stressed the universality of the Flood as confirmation of Scripture's inherent truth, drawing on evidence from pagan histories and the natural sciences.[36] For Halhed, its absence from *Gentoo* records, considered alongside the equally 'plausible Accounts' of Chinese history, was enough to confirm that *Gentoo* chronology dated back 'to such antiquity the Mosaic creation is but as yesterday'.[37] Moreover, the latter was possibly a derivative of the former. Pointing to instances of 'wonderful correspondence with many parts of the institutes of Moses' in *A Code of Gentoo Laws*, Halhed suggested that 'it is not utterly impossible, that the doctrine of Hindostan might have been early transplanted into Egypt, and thus have become familiar to Moses'. Moreover, he argued for this on the grounds that it could not have happened the other way around, precisely because the contents of the *Code* were, evidently, much older.[38]

Halhed's comparison of the *Gentoo* and Christian religions takes an even more sceptical tone when he turns to consider the basis of each tradition's claim to religious truth. Holwell and Dow both did this by questioning those who approached the ultimately reasonable religion of other nations with prejudice because they believed their religion to be the only acceptable expression of adoration of the 'Supreme Being'. Halhed takes a far less subtle approach, arguing that since each religion's claim to truth was completely analogous, they were both, by implication, equally imperfect. Halhed did this by attacking the basis of those claims, and thereby positioning himself alongside freethinkers, deists and sceptics in one of the most contentious religious debates of the Enlightenment: the status of miracles. Having established that both the Christian and the *Gentoo* shared an equal conviction in 'the supposed revelations of the Divine Will', Halhed went on to remark that the *Hindoo* 'therefore esteems the astonishing miracles attributed to a Birhmā, a Raām, or a Kishen, as facts of the most indubitable authenticity, and the relation of them as most strictly historical'.[39] This, Halhed suggested, was equivalent to the Christian belief in a 'strictly historical' reading of the Bible: a flawed reasoning, as Halhed suggests a few pages later, when he pointedly remarks on the striking

Wayne Hudson, *The English Deists: Studies in Early Enlightenment* (London: Pickering and Chatto, 2009), pp. 67–8.

[36] Robert. E. Brown, *Jonathon Edwards and the Bible* (Bloomington: Indiana University Press, 2002), pp. 8, 156.

[37] Halhed, *Code of Gentoo Laws*, p. xxxvii.

[38] Halhed, *Code of Gentoo Laws*, pp. xlii–xliii.

[39] Halhed, *Code of Gentoo Laws*, p. xv.

absence of any mention of a global deluge in the thorough and more ancient *Hindoo* annals of history.[40]

Halhed was, therefore, resurrecting a debate that had raged throughout the first half of the eighteenth century, culminating in Hume's essay 'Of Miracles' (1748). In it, sceptical challengers of religion had increasingly ridiculed their opponents' use of miracles as evidence to support theological orthodoxy.[41] Though there were shades of difference between them, in general these writers were attacking the idea that the argument for orthodox Christianity could be established on supernatural foundations.[42] Although Halhed did not say this explicitly, by stating that the conviction of both the Christian and the *Hindoo* rested on the same assumptions, he implied that neither had ultimate authority over the other, since, as Hume had argued, supernatural arguments cannot be proven.[43] Halhed also pointed to the inherent circularity of arguments deriving from opposing scriptural authorities, observing that 'we are not justified in grounding the standard and criterion of our examination of the Hindoo religion upon the known and infallible truth of our own; because the opposite party would either deny the first principles of the argument, or insist upon an equal right on their side to suppose the veracity of their own scriptures incontrovertible'.[44]

This assertion of the relative value of both religions' claims to truth according to the imperfect logic of revelation was an implicit attack on the ideological foundations of religious dogmatism. This is what was most 'deist' in the thought of Halhed. His relativistic weighing up of scriptural authority implicitly endorses similar sceptical attacks on the idea that revelation was an adequate basis for religious belief.[45] It is a bolder expression of Holwell's sentiment that it is 'just' that every 'sect' has 'a high and superior opinion of the religious principles, under which they were born' as long as that does not lead to 'religious vanity'.[46] Rather, all are entitled to believe the veracity of their own scriptures, insofar as any can be proven to be conclusively true.

40 Halhed, *Code of Gentoo Laws*, p. xl.

41 R. M. Burns, *The Great Debate on Miracles, from Joseph Glanvill to David Hume* (London: Associated University Presses, 1981).

42 Jane Shaw, *Miracles in Enlightenment England* (London: Yale University Press, 2006), p. 161.

43 J. C. A. Gaskin, 'Hume on Religion', in David Fate Norton and Jacqueline Taylor (eds.), *The Cambridge Companion to Hume* (Cambridge: Cambridge University Press, 2009), p. 498.

44 Halhed, *Code of Gentoo Laws*, pp. xii–xiii.

45 M. A. Stewart, 'Revealed Religion: The British Debate', in Knud Haakonssen (ed), *The Cambridge History of Eighteenth-Century Philosophy*, vol. 2 (Cambridge: Cambridge University Press, 2006); David Hume, 'Of Miracles', in *Philosophical Essays Concerning Human Understanding* (London: A. Millar, 1748), Essay X.

46 Holwell, *Interesting Historical Events*, vol. 1 (1765), p. 8.

This difference becomes particularly clear when Halhed later points to some of the similarities he had observed between Indian and early Jewish mythology. The cause and foundations of this observation are markedly different from Holwell's and Dow's previous suggestions that each religion holds some essential truths in common. On the contrary, Halhed's equivalence is between the vulgar origins of each creed. Pointing to the 'scape-goat' of Leviticus, the animal that was cast into the desert with the sins of the community, Halhed remarks that there is a similar story, involving a horse, 'in a particular institute of the Gentoos'. Explaining that both of these stories were conceived of 'in a state of barbarism', Halhed insists that their originators were 'by no means fit subjects for the comprehension of mystery' and thus believed it a literal truth. The didactic meaning of the 'scape-goat', argued Halhed, had only developed subsequently.[47] Religion is thus subject to a reversal of the historical process described by Holwell, and to an extent Dow, whereby original purity is gradually corrupted by unrefined beliefs and practices. Rather, for Halhed, religion's rude origins are improved as 'the manners of a people become polished, and their ideas enlightened'. As society improves, 'attempts will be made to revise and resist their religious creed into conformity with the rest of their improvements'. So, as in the case of the 'scape-goat', those doctrines, which the ignorant ancestor received 'as the literal exposition of undoubted fact, the philosophic descendent, will strive to gloss over by *à posteriori* constructions of his own'.[48]

Rather than a critique of this stage in the historical development of religion, Halhed defends these allegorical interventions on this basis that they are an aspect of the general intellectual advancement of society:

> Hence it may be understood that what has been herein advanced does not mean to set aside the improvements of philosophy, or to deny the occasional employment of allegory, but merely to establish one plain position, that religion in general, at its origins, is believed as literally as it is professed, and that it is afterwards rather refined by the learned than debased by the ignorant.[49]

This was by far Halhed's boldest statement of the idea that theology was a matter of human artifice. Although different from Holwell's and Dow's assertion of universal truths in favour of universal contrivances, this retains the elitism of the narrative of decline, whereby refined religious sentiment is distinguished from the superstitions and practices of the vulgar. Halhed

[47] Halhed, *Code of Gentoo Laws*, p. xvi. [48] Halhed, *Code of Gentoo Laws*, p. xv.
[49] Halhed, *Code of Gentoo Laws*, p. xviii.

argues that we should see all early religious mythologies as they were literally meant, with the understanding 'that the Institution of a Religion has been in every Country the first Step towards an Emersion from Savage Barbarism, and the establishment of Civil Society' at a time when 'Reason is just beginning to dawn'.[50] In this sense religion becomes an abstracted concept: a stage in the successive progression of social states and a tool for instituting social development.

The scepticism of this position also bears a significant resemblance to Hume's 1757 essay *The Natural History of Religion*, which offered a bitingly satirical critique of the various assumptions underlying the concept of natural religion (i.e. the idea that a pure monotheism is innate, according to its inherent rationality), and instead offered an alternative naturalist explanation of the origins of religion. In this account, theism is reached not by reason, 'but by the adulation and fears of our most vulgar superstition'.[51] That is, rather than the product of rational speculation as to the cause of existence, early religious beliefs were the product of humanity's struggle for survival combined with their essential ignorance of the operations of nature, on which this survival depended. Like Halhed's summary above, Hume argued that it was the need of primitive polytheists to achieve order and simplicity that originated the belief of the refined monotheist. Like Halhed, Hume saw this as part of the process to actuate a civilised society.[52] No doubt Halhed took some of his sceptical cues from Hume, whom, as we shall see, he liked to cite in his letters to Sheridan. Like Dow's ideas about civic religion, then, much of Halhed's preface falls into a pattern of eighteenth-century thought which increasingly treated religious belief as a developmental stage in the history of society. Rather than point to original purity, though, Halhed suggests that all religions share a common history of literal primitivism, the refinement of which develops in conjunction with a general improvement in society, when manners 'become polished, and ideas enlightened'. Yet, while this approach is rooted in an ironical scepticism, its implications are similar. Halhed's history of religion still results in a universalism that sees the ancient and sophisticated system of the *Gentoos* as equally worthy of esteem as Christian teaching, as both represent the improvement of primitive religion through the art of philosophy.

[50] Halhed, *Code of Gentoo Laws*, p. xiv.

[51] David Hume, *Four Dissertations: I. The Natural History of Religion. II. Of the Passions. III. Of Tragedy. IV. Of the Standard of Taste* (London: A. Millar, 1757).

[52] Roger L. Emerson, *Essays on David Hume: Medical Men and the Scottish Enlightenment* (Farnham: Ashgate, 2009), p. 93.

Halhed's Religious Scepticism

Halhed's letters to his school friend, and co-writer in several literary enterprises, Richard Brinsley Sheridan, offer an important insight into his early intellectual formation while at Oxford. The letters were exchanged around the time of one such venture, a book of poetry, prompted by Sheridan's response to a series of bawdy literary compositions that Halhed had sent in the summer of 1770. Under Sheridan's apparent insistence that they work to produce some translations of 'a less sportive kind', Halhed thus promised to produce some compositions that were 'rather more shame face'd', and so a literary partnership ensued.

The same youthful letter, written at the age of nineteen, is full of pretensions regarding Halhed's risqué attitude and irreligious behaviour at Oxford. Boasting how his 'fame is up in college', Halhed regaled his friend with an anecdote of how he entertained his fellow students on a Sunday evening with songs parodied from a famous comic opera, *Love in a Village*, the response to which was apparently to exclaim, 'that never blasphemy and bawdy were so happily united before'. To this Halhed also added, with some evident pride, 'I shall be set up for an atheist in a little time.'[53] Indeed, throughout their correspondence, this irreligious attitude is a subject Halhed frequently returned to and flaunted. In one letter, after complaining that his studies were suffering due to a cycle of work followed by 'a month of riot and stupidity', Halhed added that his college had nevertheless 'in consideration no doubt of my frequent attendance at hall and chapel' made him 'a present of £20 per annum', precisely because his famous neglect of these places had 'long since been a proverb'.[54]

Later in his life this irreligious reputation seemed to have stuck: remarking on the news that Halhed had turned to supporting self-proclaimed prophet Richard Brothers, an East India Company colleague remarked, 'what shall I say of Halhed, who has lived his whole life as if he thought there was no God?'[55] Many indeed suggested that his testimony to be a supporter of Brothers must have been an elaborate joke on account of his reputation for irreligion. William Bennet, the then Bishop of Cloyne,

[53] Halhed to R. B. Sheridan, August 1770, in Rocher, *Orientalism, Poetry and the Millennium*, pp. 262–3.

[54] Halhed to R. B. Sheridan, 8 November 1770, in Rocher, *Orientalism, Poetry and the Millennium*, p. 265.

[55] John Shore, Baron Teignmouth, to Charles Grant, Bengal, 20 October 1795, in Shore, *Memoir of the Life and Correspondence*, p. 342.

wrote, 'he is only an unbeliever, and every word is in ridicule of scripture and prophecy.'[56]

While at Oxford, this affectation of an irreligious attitude also extended to mischievous references to the notable heterodox thinker David Hume. In one letter, in which Halhed was attempting to impress upon his more relaxed friend the urgency of their achieving literary fame and financial success, he brought up the topic of suicide. To his suggestion that if success eluded them for too long he might take a 'pretty leap from the top of the Abbey' in Bath, Halhed added that 'I have lately taken to wearing garters; which I never did, until I had guessed on what Hume's essays on suicide were about.'[57] Hume's *Essays on Suicide* offered an intricate argument against the theological position that taking one's own life was an act against God. It has been interpreted as both an attack on theological ethics, conceived of as duties towards God, and also a positive construction of the right to take one's own life as a matter of natural liberty.[58] Halhed's reference to this work is not very meaningful beyond his demonstration of his knowledge of it. The essay was a rare publication in 1770, when Halhed wrote this letter. Originally appearing as the fourth item in Hume's *Five Dissertations* (1757), Hume and his publisher soon changed their minds and removed it from the publication to quell the offence it had already caused, as well as the threat of prosecution.[59] It did not appear again until *Two Essays* (1777), published after Hume's death. Not all copies were destroyed, as is suggested by other contemporary literary allusions, most notably from the cleric William Warburton.[60] There was also a French version published in 1770, and evidence of a copied Dutch edition in circulation.[61] It is possible that Halhed had read the essays, yet it is more likely, as this quotation seems to suggest, that he 'guessed' its contents on the basis of the various outraged responses it inspired. Yet this certainly required some active interest in Hume's more controversial ideas on the part of the young

56 William Bennet to Samuel Parr, 4 March 1795, in Samuel Parr, *Works, with Memoirs of His Life and Writings, and a Selection from His Correspondence*, John Johnstone (ed.), vol. 1 (London [s.n.], 1828), pp. 468–9n.

57 Halhed to R. B. Sheridan, 8 November 1770, in Rocher, *Orientalism, Poetry and the Millennium*, p. 265.

58 Thomas Holden, 'Religion and Moral Prohibition in Hume's "Of Suicide"', *Hume Studies*, 31:2; Eugenio Lecaldano, 'Hume on Suicide', in Paul Russell (ed.), *The Oxford Handbook of Hume* (Oxford: Oxford University Press, 2016).

59 Hume, *Dialogues*, p. viii.

60 David Hume, *Essays and Treatises on Philosophical Subjects*, Lorne Falkenstein and Neil McArthur (eds.), (Toronto: Broadview Editions, 2013), p. 30.

61 David Hume, *David Hume: Essays Moral, Political and Literary*, Eugene F. Millar (ed.) (Indianapolis: Liberty Classics, 1985), p. 55, note 44.

Halhed. To invoke it in such a casual manner as part of this hyperbolic plea gives the impression that Halhed saw himself, and was keen Sheridan did too, as 'in-the-know' when it came to religious scepticism.

Halhed's ambitions of literary fame continued in Bengal. After being sent to India by his father, who had become increasingly frustrated at his son's lack of direction, Halhed quickly became involved in the intellectual and literary community. Upon arriving in Calcutta, Halhed stayed in the home of Charles Stafford Pleydell, who was married to Holwell's daughter, Elizabeth. Halhed, who had left England with a fragile pride, having lost the much sought-after affections of Elizabeth Linley to Sheridan, embarked on a rather flirtatious friendship with Elizabeth Stafford Pleydell.[62] It was through the connections made in Pleydell's home that Halhed settled into the British social scene in Bengal. Following the opening of the Calcutta Theatre in 1773, Halhed wrote several prologues, including one for a play given by the Freemasons which, according to Rocher, was replete with appropriate symbolism.[63] While there is no evidence that Halhed himself was a Freemason, since he would have been too junior to appear on the lists that have survived, we do know that Charles Stafford Pleydell was the deputy grand master for the Bengal lodge at that time.[64]

It was not until his appointment in 1773 as a translator of Persian, though, that Halhed began to acquire a reputation as a capable Company man. Throughout this time too, aside from an early appeal to his father to allow him to become ordained, as part of a series of attempts from the 'sufficiently humbled' Halhed to receive permission to leave Bengal, he showed no signs of permanent reformation towards a religious life.[65] That Halhed's preface to the *Code* was marked by the same cultivated unbelief and sceptical attitude expressed in his earlier years is testified to in its reception. Much as was the case for the other authors considered in this book, more than the translation itself, it was the interpretation of its author that proved the source of public interest and discussion. *The Critical*

[62] Lars E. Troide (ed.), *The Early Journals and Letters of Fanny Burney: 1768–1773*, vol. 1 (Oxford: Clarendon Press, 1988), p. 67; Rocher, *Orientalism, Poetry and the Millennium*, pp. 40–1.

[63] The prologue was dated February 1774. Taken from Rocher, *Orientalism, Poetry and the Millennium*, p. 42, Rocher appears to have viewed it in a private collection referred to as the 'Pilcher Papers', with the prologue appearing on pp. 162–3 of these papers. I have been unable to trace this collection, which formerly belonged to John Arthur Pilcher.

[64] Walter Kelly Firminger, *Early History of Freemasonry in Bengal* (Calcutta: Thacker & Spink, 1906), p. 11; Guy Robinson and Walter K. Firminger, *The Second Lodge of Bengal* (Mysore: Wesley Press, 1955), pp. 20, 59, 429.

[65] Halhed to Samuel Parr, 5 November 1773, in Parr, *Works*, vol. 1, pp. 469–71.

Review, for example, both praised Halhed's ingenuity and marked his sceptical attitude.[66] George Costard, vicar of Twickenham and family friend, felt it necessary to publish a letter refuting Halhed's claims.[67] His stated aim was 'to obviate the conclusions that might be drawn by the *unwary* or *ill-designing*' as a consequence of reading Halhed's preface.[68] Later on, Costard's letter itself was reviewed, thus expanding the public debate of the *Code* and its more controversial contents. One reviewer even declared that Costard deserved 'the thanks of every friend to revelation'.[69] Halhed's preface to the *Code* was, therefore, read and received as a religiously heterodox essay.

Reception of the *Code* and Its Preface

Halhed's *Code of Gentoo Laws* was largely received as an important contribution to the world of European letters, since it represented a firm step towards a more fixed knowledge of the perceived rules and ethics of Indian civilisation.[70] Historian and prominent figure of the Scottish Enlightenment William Robertson (1721–93) likewise viewed the *Code* as 'the most valuable and authentic elucidation of Indian policy and manners that has been hitherto communicated to Europe'.[71] But while the achievement of the *Code* was largely welcomed, Halhed's conclusions elicited a mixed reaction. There were two particular debates, already touched on in relation to Holwell and Dow, for which it had an immediate resonance: the questioning of biblical authority, and the question of colonial legitimacy. The *Code* offered controversial material which Halhed prefaced in a controversial way. Reactions were, therefore, married to the degree that the reader's ideological orientation was in tune with Halhed's approach. Those of a broadly liberal mindset received the book with sympathy, whereas for those whom the lack of Christian mission in India was a failing, the contents were a biting reminder. In turn, more radical anticlericals, such as Guillaume Thomas Raynal, advertised it as one more example to demonstrate the cunning of priestcraft.[72]

66 *Critical Review*, 44 (1777), pp. 177–90: pp. 188–9.
67 On his connection to Halhed, see Trautmann, *Aryans and British India*, p. 73.
68 Costard, *Letter to Nathaniel Brassey Halhead*, p. 47.
69 *Gentleman's Magazine*, 48 (March 1778), pp. 113–16.
70 In fact it was widely read by those not even especially interested in India, such as, James Boswell: diary entry, 16 November 1777, in *Boswell in Extremes, 1776–1778*, C. M. Weiss and Frederick A. Pottle (eds.) (New York: McGraw-Hill, 1970), p. 194.
71 Robertson, *Historical Disquisition*, pp. 273–5.
72 Rocher, *Orientalism, Poetry and the Millennium*, p. 54.

While some reviewers praised the preface for containing 'many ingenious observations', Halhed's critical stance on religion did not go unnoticed.[73] The most controversial aspect for Christian readers was his chronology, which unequivocally dated Hinduism as the most ancient philosophical system, and most others as therefore derivative. Halhed had known he was treading on dangerous ground, especially when bringing up the issue of the absent biblical Flood, as is evident in the convoluted justifications that both prefaced and concluded his calculations. Yet his interpretation was made clear in the general thrust of his arguments, evident in remarks such as 'when the line of implicit faith is once extended, we can never ascertain the precise limits beyond which it must not pass'.[74] Halhed was clear; the chronology of the *Gentoo* ordinations vastly eclipsed the timeline of biblical history and thus proved problematic for all its claims to authority. The controversy that Halhed thus deliberately courted came without fail.

The Critical Review praised Halhed's performance, as well as his liberal approach, while also noting the potential heterodoxy of his remarks. He had, it suggested, presented the dissertation 'from a scepticism of a Hume, or a Voltaire, as the world has not seen'.[75] The well-respected *Annual Register* suggested that Halhed would have been less prepared to accept the 'wild extravagant chronology of the bramins' had he 'given himself but a little time to reflect upon the absurdities of their geography', which is something Halhed himself referenced as 'deplorable' in the same preface.[76] *The Gentleman's Magazine* refuted Halhed's arguments at length, with a particular emphasis on chronology. The reviewer rightly pointed out the variation in opinion among other orientalists, and suggested that the common idea of a missing Veda, or 'Beids', meant that the problem was left open, suggesting that Halhed had been somewhat credulous in accepting *Hindoo* chronologies.[77]

As we have seen, the most sustained and public outrage at Halhed's remarks came from George Costard. Costard, a vicar and a friend of the Halhed family, had felt compelled to publish a letter refuting Halhed's assertions as 'totally void of truth, or at best precarious'. Costard's focus was on subverting Halhed's claims of the great antiquity of the *Gentoo* scriptures, so as to counter any heterodox conclusions that might be arrived at by readers who were naive, or worse, '*ill-designing*'. Halhed was castigated

[73] *Critical Review*, 44 (1777), pp. 177–90: p. 188. [74] Halhed, *Code of Gentoo Laws*, p. xxxvii.
[75] *Critical Review*, 44 (1777), pp. 188–9.
[76] *Annual Register* (1777), pp. 246–7; Halhed, *Code of Gentoo Laws*, pp. xlix–l.
[77] *Gentleman's Magazine*, 47 (Supplement, 1777), pp. 527, 636, 638.

in these terms, with Costard imploring him to reconsider his conclusions by turning away from his faith in the Brahmins and back to the perspective of 'Europe, the most enlightened part of the world'. He also disputed the validity of the *Code*, suggesting that the multiplicity of ordinances was a mark of modernity and corruption.[78] That this exchange took on the character of a fight between belief and unbelief, revelation and scepticism, is testified to in the critical reaction. *The Critical Review* characterised the debate according to the two protagonists, with Halhed on the one side representing 'the credulous pen of a young man of quick parts and lively genius' and Costard, on the other, 'in the character of a truly orthodox clergyman of the church of England'.[79] *The Gentleman's Magazine* likewise advertised Costard's letter as a welcome response to Halhed's aspersions, deserving 'the thanks of every friend to revelation'.[80] In a similar vein were the reactions of the Unitarian thinker Joseph Priestley. Again, it was Halhed's endorsement of *Gentoo* chronology, and his particularly controversial suggestion that Moses may have received the inspiration for his code of laws through the spread of Brahmin philosophy to ancient Egypt, that inspired the Dissenting thinker and natural philosopher Priestley to pursue his own researches into the *Hindoo* religion.[81] The outcome was, however, an inverse of Halhed's chronological suppositions. Priestley instead used Halhed, Holwell and Dow to make direct comparisons between Mosaic institutions and Indian thought, with a view to proving the superior 'wisdom of the Laws, and of the religion, prescribed in the writings of Moses'.[82]

In contrast, and widening the impact of Halhed's preface to the *Code*, the Abbé Raynal agreed 'without hesitation' with Halhed's supposition that *Gentoo* scriptures were of a greater antiquity than Western annals could account for. This, he suggested in his *Histoire des deux Indes*, was proven by the refinement of ancient Sanskrit, 'formerly in common use, but for a long time unknown', as well as the extent and sagacity of the contents of the *Code* itself. This interpretation also stressed, like Holwell and Dow, and Halhed to a degree, that the 'great number of ages' that had elapsed had been ones of decline, priestcraft and superstition, which had been a 'universal check on the progress of civilization'.[83]

As in the case of the setting of these comments in Raynal's *Histoire*, which was deeply critical of the East India Company, among the more

[78] Costard, *Letter to Nathaniel Brassey Halhead*, pp. 47, 17. [79] *Critical Review*, 36 (1778), p. 272.
[80] *Gentleman's Magazine*, 48 (June 1778), p. 277. [81] Priestley, *Comparison*.
[82] Priestley, *Comparison*, pp. 4–5.
[83] Raynal, *Philosophical and Political History*, book II, pp. 55–63, 73.

liberally minded press there was an ironic and deliberate intention to align Halhed's *Code* with the opposite position to that it had been intended to support, that is, the administration of Warren Hastings. *The Critical Review*, described by Sack as often tending towards a sceptical stance in religious matters, agreed with Halhed's account of the antiquity and sophistication of Indian civilisation in order to critique the Company.[84] After agreeing that some of the contents of the *Code* were no more ridiculous than 'European Codes', this reviewer goes on to make the mordant observation that:

> In this Code of Gentoo laws we have searched to no purpose for some passage declaring that, when, after a certain series of years, a nation of white people should come over the great water, bearing in their hands a message from their queen, requesting leave to trade in the country of the Gentoos; the Gentoos should grant them that leave, should trade with those people, and that it should be lawful for those people having so gained leave to trade, to begin to rob and plunder their hosts . . . that the white people should no longer be merchants in the land, but masters, legislators; that the natives should serve that people . . . In this code no such law appears; though it might properly have been made part of the chapter of *Theft*. It is to be found, however, we suppose, in the more enlightened codes of European laws, in the sacred Shaster perhaps of European faith.[85]

In line with this, perhaps the most iconic purpose to which the *Code* was put was in the course of the impeachment trial. When counsel mounted the defence that Asiatic governments had always been despotic, Burke brandished the *Code* as evidence to the contrary. He argued that in fact the duties of the magistrate were clearly spelled out, and the right of the people to property was well established.[86] In deciding to do so, it is very possible that Burke had remembered an earlier interaction during a debate in the Commons (1781) in which he had made a similar statement about the ubiquity of despotism in India, which John Courtenay had refuted by pointing to the example of the *Code*.[87]

In the sphere relating to the apparent cause for its composition, 'to assist the courts of justice in their decisions', however, the *Code* proved of limited use in the administration of law.[88] Soon after its completion, Elijah Impey,

[84] James S. Sack, *From Jacobite to Conservative: Reaction and Orthodoxy in Britain in c.1760–1832* (Cambridge: Cambridge University Press, 1993), p. 63.

[85] *Critical Review*, 44 (1777), pp. 177–90: pp. 180–1.

[86] Edmund Burke, Speech of 28 May 1794, in Bond, *Speeches*, vol. 4, p. 363.

[87] By John Courtenay [also Courteny] on 27 June 1781: 'Debate on the Bengal Judicature Bill', in Cobbett, *Parliamentary History*, vol 22 (1814), p. 559.

[88] Letter to Samuel Johnson, 7 August 1775, in Gleig, *Memoirs*, vol. 2, pp. 17–20: p. 18.

the chief justice of Bengal, ordered a copy to be deposited in the Supreme Court, which was to be treated as an authority, and a number of sitting judges attested to its use. In the years that followed, however, the reliability of the text was put into doubt.[89] William Jones' main contention was that the successive translations it had undergone had made it faulty, despite the Sanskrit original's fidelity to *Gentoo* legal principles.[90] Colebrooke, who continued Jones' attempts to produce a more useful digest of Hindu laws, agreed that the problem with the *Code* was the unfaithfulness of the Persian phase of translation to the original.[91] The *Code* also had an impact on British images of India, beyond the idea of impressive antiquity. It featured heavily in Charles Grant's call for a Christian mission in India on account of the cruelty of its customs.[92] Later, in contrast to the conclusions of Raynal that it was evidence of a great civilisation, James Mill would also take issue with Halhed's reasoning in the preface and instead use the *Code* to characterise Hindu society as thoroughly abject.[93] In the immediate term, though, Halhed's comments on the nature of Sanskrit would prove to have the most profound effect on European intellectual culture. Despite his admission that he had barely managed to penetrate the ancient language, so little was known among his European readers that even the small extracts and commentaries elicited a range of critical reactions. His accounts of the language and comments of the still mysterious Vedas, decorated with extracts from Sanskrit texts, made it an impressively authoritative source following the works of Holwell and Dow.[94]

Halhed, Hastings and Empire

The poetry composed by Halhed during the period when he was working on the *Code* provides an insight into his understanding of its role within the Hastings administration. One of the first poems, 'The Bramin and the River Ganges', follows a conversation between a 'care-worn Bramin' and

89 'Future government of British settlements in India', IOR/H/339, f, pp. 171–2.

90 Letter to John Macpherson, 6 May 1786, in Cannon, *Letters of Sir William Jones*, vol. 2, p. 699.

91 To his father, 21 June 1796, in Thomas Edward Colebrooke (ed.), *The Life of H. T. Colebrooke* (London: Trubner & Co., 1873), p. 84.

92 Grant, *Observations on the State of Society*, p. 110.

93 Mill's commentary focused on a feature that not many eighteenth-century readers discussed, which was the caste system. James Mill, *The History of British India*, vol. 1 (London: Baldwin, Cradock and Joy, 1817), pp. 142–4.

94 His comments on the nature of Sanskrit were used by, for example, James Burnett (Lord Monboddo) in *Ancient Metaphysics, or the Science of Universals*, vol. 4 (Edinburgh: J. Balfour, 1795), pp. 322, 332–3; and by Alexander Murray, *History of European Languages*, vol. 2 (Edinburgh: A. Constable & Company, 1823), pp. 396, 399.

the Ganga, 'the river's goddess', on the topic of Company governance. The poem casts the politics of British conquest with a Manichean simplicity, with the goddess chastising the lethargic Brahmin for his failure to recognise and celebrate the substantive difference between tyrannous Mughal rule and the enlightened administration of the British. This, she is given to voice, would be to swap 'The rule of reason for the rod of pow'r'. In this and other poems, Halhed thus reveals his own conviction and investment in the idea of Hastings, the dedicatee of the poem, as the benevolent steward of Indian culture and custom, as represented by the *Code*. Whereas Halhed's preface to the *Code* presents a more subversive account of religion's historical development, the poem reflects the more dominant narrative of India's decline, opening with the 'silent and sad' Brahmin, in the lethargic posture commonly attributed by Enlightenment geographies to peoples of a 'torpid' climate, 'Tracing his country's progress to decay'. Indian history is presented as violent oppression of the 'patient sage' by 'Tartar fury', the 'venal law' of the Qur'an and the 'extorted gold' of corrupt judges. A more complete picture of the tropes of oriental despots and meekly oppressed Hindus could not have been painted. Indeed, it was their religious mores, Halhed suggested in a similar manner to Dow, that secured their oppression. It is Ganga herself who suggests that 'superstition sanctified' this history of Muslim domination, and chastises the Brahmin for his lethargy, ordering him to 'Smile to obey (and hail the happy change)'. Whether this was an instruction Halhed vocalised to his scholarly colleagues compiling the *Code* we do not know, but the Ganga's reassurance to the Brahmin that 'no more ambitious spoilers range Thy labour's fruits relentless to devour' certainly suggests that this is how Halhed, the translator of their work into the language of their new benevolent rulers, thought they should view it.[95]

This poetical condemnation of the despotic tyranny of 'Muhammadan' rulers in India was, however, out of step with Hastings' own account of, and approach to, Mughal rule. As Travers has shown, much of the language and policy of his administration constructed itself on the basis that it was stepping into the existing Mughal structures, which were taken to have provided a tolerant settlement with regard to the various religions within its polity.[96] Alongside the work of the *Code*, Hastings had commissioned several projects relating to the translation of Islamic law codes.

[95] The poem is quoted here from Halhed to Warren Hastings, 22 May 1774, Warren Hastings Papers, vol. xxix, BL, Add. MS 39899, ff. 2–3.
For more on the poems, see Rocher, 'Alien and Empathic'.

[96] Travers, *Ideology and Empire*, chapter 3.

Records suggest that he personally invested in Francis Gladwin's translation of the *Ain-i Akbari*, or 'Institutes of Akbar', an extensive anthology of administrative, geographical and religious knowledge compiled by Abu'l-Fazl, the Emperor Akbar's chief minister.[97] From the early 1770s, Hastings also extended his patronage to educated figures from the Mughal nobility and intelligentsia, particularly to serve in the *adalats*. Nevertheless, foreshadowing the work of Wilkins and the development of Company scholarship at the end of the eighteenth century, Halhed lauded Hastings as exclusively bringing renewal to India via the sponsorship of *Gentoo* learning. As Ganga voices in the poem, his scholarly patronage would not be 'confin'd to legislation's sphere', but would also 'bid fair science too take root' and 'explore the mysteries concealed so long: To trace where learning's earliest sources lie,/ And ope the fountains of Sanscritian song'.[98]

Nevertheless, while Hastings may not have approved of the skewed opposition between to potential sources for establishing ideological legitimacy in his protegee's eager panegyric, as criticism of his administration rose, he would increasingly rely on Halhed's defence of his conduct in office. Between October and November 1782, under the pseudonym Detector, Halhed published several letters in the *Morning Herald*, addressing the findings of a Commons select committee, established to 'take into consideration the state of the administration of justice in the provinces of Bengal, Naha and Orissa'.[99] The letters began by agreeing with the importance of the general purpose of the select committee, but argued that in picking apart the details of certain policies and administrative arrangements, ministers had impetuously gone beyond its intended purview. A series of thirteen letters in total thus took to countering what Halhed determined to be inaccuracies or misrepresentations of Indian affairs, and in particular defended the decision-making of the governor. In January 1783, a much longer letter by the Detector was printed as a pamphlet of fifty pages, which took once again to defending Hastings' conduct, this time with particular reference to his handling of the Maratha wars and open revolt in Benares.[100]

97 Marshall, 'Warren Hastings', p. 246. 98 BL, Add. MS 39, 899, ff. 2–3.

99 Although it was widely known by both factions in the dispute over the Company that Halhed was the Detector, it was not publicly attributed to him until after his death. The first seven and the final two letters are dated (5, 6, 8, 12, 16, 18, 21 October; 2, 5 November), while numbers eight to eleven are not but seem to be from October. The letters were also published together as *The Letters of the Detector on the Reports of the Select Committee of the House of Commons Appointed to Consider How the British Possessions in the East-Indies May Be Held and Governed with the Greatest Security and Advantage to This Country and How the Happiness of the Natives May Be Best Promoted* (London [s.n.], 1782).

100 *A Letter to Governor Johnstone, &c. &c. on Indian Affairs* (London: S. Bladon, 1783).

Throughout 1783 the Detector kept writing, responding to each report by the select committee, maintaining the claim of an impartial observer. In response to Dundas introducing a bill 'for the better regulation of British possessions in India', Halhed produced six more letters for the *Morning Herald.* In these he strenuously opposed the use of the phrase 'British possessions' in the title of the bill, suggesting that it was intended to mean that the Company's Indian territories were possessions of the Crown. This outrage was again inherently linked to a defence of Hastings, and in pointing this out Halhed was stressing that the real intention of the bill was to depose the governor, and place control in the hands of the court of directors, who would in turn be subject to the approval of the king.[101] The bill aborted, the war of letters continued, with Halhed publishing in October of 1783 a letter addressed to Edmund Burke, which returned to the select committee reports and, once again, the revolt in Benares.[102] As pleased as the Hastings circle were with Halhed's productions, it was this particular defence that would come to be a problem, in which the tension between their visions of India, displayed by Halhed in his poems of the early 1770s, would become patently apparent.

In the proceedings against Hastings, which began in 1786, Burke brought forward twenty-two charges, which were read in April. Hastings, through John Scott, petitioned the Commons for leave to reply. This answer was prepared hastily by Hastings' circle, and later he would have to disown some of its contents, with Scott testifying that the former governor was only responsible for the general introduction and the answers to the first few charges. Among those it was suggested had composed the other responses was Halhed, who is thought to have played a central role in (and was certainly latterly blamed for) the preparation of Hastings' answer to what has been termed the Benares charge.[103] This charge demanded a justification of the process by which Benares, which had been an autonomous tributary state to Awadh in 1756, came to fall under the dominion of the East India Company while in the governance of Chait Singh, from 1775 onwards. Burke's complaint was that Hastings, from 1778, in demanding a special tribute from the Chait Singh, and in taking punitive action when it was left unpaid, had pushed the rajah to rebellion and exile in 1781.[104]

[101] Detector, *Morning Herald* (London), 28 April, 1 May, 5 May, 15 May 1783.

[102] *Letter to the Rt Hon. Edmund Burke, on the Subject of His Charges against the Governor-General of Bengal* (London: J. Johnson, 1783).

[103] Rocher, *Orientalism, Poetry and the Millennium*, pp. 132–4.

[104] For a detailed account of the Benares charge, see, P. J. Marshall, *The Impeachment of Hastings* (Oxford: Oxford University Press, 1965), chapter 5.

Burke's argument rested on the idea that Hastings had abrogated the sovereign's duty of protection, and had thereby licensed an appeal to natural right on the part of the subject. The wanton exaction of oppression on the part of Hastings meant that the Rajah's response to take up arms constituted an example of just rebellion.[105] The answers to this charge that particularly provoked Burke's ire were those that emphasised the despotic nature of Mughal governance, stressing that these were the confines within which Hastings had to act. This included the famed line, 'The whole history of Asia is nothing more than *precedents* to prove the invariable exercise of arbitrary power.'

Although Burke was unconvinced by Hastings' later attempt to distance himself from this position, according to Scott's protestations that Halhed had made last-minute amendments to the answer without the review of Hastings, scholars have verified that the handwritten copy of Hastings' defence before the Commons does include a great number of corrections, including this one, in Halhed's hand.[106] Changing their mind, Hastings' defence would make similar claims about Asiatic despotism again later in the trial. It was this decision that prompted Burke to bring out the *Code of Gentoo Laws* in retort.[107] The polarisation between this defence and Burke's particularly nuanced response in the trial was, however, less representative of the various ways in which the issue of the exercise of power in India was treated in political discourse in Britain. In considering impeachment on the Benares charge, William Pitt the Younger agreed with Hastings that the ruler has the right to tax subjects for the purposes of defence, including 'extraordinary resources for extraordinary dangers'; nevertheless, he conceded that in his treatment of the rajah, Hastings had transgressed 'the rules of justice and liberty' and voted in favour.[108] For others, the depiction of India's existing polity as rooted in arbitrary rule was already an all too convincing, and indeed familiar, argument.

By this time, the public imagination had, on top of Holwell's account of the 'Black Hole of Calcutta' and the crimes of Siraj-ud-Daulah, the example of the much-vilified despotic enemy of the British, the Tipu Sultan of Mysore. Indeed, towards the end of the trial, the victories of the new governor, Lord Cornwallis, over the Tipu Sultan were greeted with

105 Bourke, *Empire and Revolution*, pp. 665–6.

106 House of Lords Record Office: Main Papers, H. L., February 1788. See Rocher, *Orientalism, Poetry and the Millennium*, p. 133.

107 Speech of 28 May 1794, in Bond, *Speeches*, vol. 4, pp. 360, 363–4.

108 Pitt's speech, 13 June 1786, in Cobbett, *Parliamentary History*, vol. 26 (1816), p. 103.

much public applause.[109] Moreover, at the close of the trial Halhed had become an easy target onto which to deflect the less palatable arguments to which the defence had resorted, given his increasingly public association with the self-styled prophet Richard Brothers. Thus in summing up, the Lord Chancellor, Edward Thurlow, argued that he accepted Hastings' disavowal of the answers presented before the Commons since 'the defence of the Banares charge was entrusted to Mr Halhed, a gentlemen of splendid abilities, and great information, but of too high a genius to attend minutely to the strict accuracy of his facts' because he was 'certainly much better calculated to explain a prophecy' than offer a detailed account of the Company's affairs.[110] And yet, despite Burke's use of the *Code* and his mock incredulity that Halhed could be the author of both this and the Benares answer, indicative as that was of a general rot, Halhed's conceptual division between tyrannical Mughals and wise, but subjugated *Gentoos*, would prove to be more enduring. As Travers has mapped out, appeals to the existing fabric of the empire waned as British imperial ambitions became more assertive, and the ideological appeal to the preservation of *Hindoo* tradition gathered greater force.[111] The vision of Indian religion that Halhed had supplied, and then continued to weave into his arguments in support of his patron, was integral to a certain argument for empire in India, albeit a not very sophisticated one in the view of either Burke or Hastings.

Halhed's Symbolical Religion of the *Hindoos*

After finishing the *Code* and returning to England, Halhed continued his investigations into Indian religion. Without access to pandit advisors, his studies were necessarily confined to translating the Persian texts already in his possession. These included Abu'l-Fazl's *Ā'īn-i-Akbarī* and Persian copies of the *Mahābhārata*. The work produced by Halhed in this period included a translation of Dara Shikoh's Persian rendition of fifty *Upanishads*, referred to by Halhed as the 'the Opnekhets'. Although

109 P. J. Marshall, '"Cornwallis Triumphant": War in India and the British Public in the Late Eighteenth Century', in Laurence Freedman, Paul Hayes and Robert O'Neill (eds.), *War, Strategy, and International Politics: Essays in Honour of Sir Michael Howard* (Oxford: Clarendon Press, 1992).

110 Speech of 9 March 1795, in *Debates of the House of Lords, On the Evidence Delivered in the Trial of Warren Hastings, Esquire* (London: Printed by J. Debrett, 1797), p. 37.

111 Travers identifies this with William Jones, but as the analysis of Holwell and Halhed offered here has shown, this was of course a much more substantive train of thought in British accounts of Indian from the 1760s. Travers, *Ideology and Empire*, p. 245.

Halhed never published this translation, the manuscript, bearing the date of May 1787, was acquired by the British Museum in 1796.[112] As part of the oriental manuscripts collection, it was known to other scholars such as the Company's historiographer Robert Orme.[113]

Halhed's preface to the translation was left unfinished, containing blank spaces and various marginal and interlinear corrections.[114] Nevertheless, even in its unfinished form it offers an introduction to the translation that shows an enduring interest in *Hindoo* chronology and scripture. For Rocher it also demonstrates 'a significant departure in his approach to Hinduism', suggesting an endorsement of recourses to 'allegorical interpretations of Hindu concepts in order to reconcile them with Christian doctrines' that he'd previously criticised.[115] In the preface to the *Code*, though, Halhed's criticism was not directed towards the possibility of similitude between the different religions, but rather insisted that religious allegory, in both instances, was the polish applied to religion in line with the refinement of civilisation. Whereas in the preface of 1776 *Code* there was an implicit equality between both Hinduism and Christianity in the claim of each to truth, in 1787, in the introduction to his translation of 'the Opnekhets', there was an implicit equality in the truth contained in both. This change, of course, would correspond more generally with Halhed's transformation from sceptic to devoted follower of Richard Brothers.

Although Halhed mistakenly understood the *Upanishads* to be commentaries on the four Vedas, he came to some generally correct conclusions about its position in relation to the *Mahābhārata*. These were all part and parcel of his continuing concern with ascertaining the antiquity of Indian religious texts. Halhed insisted that because the *Upanishads* make no mention of the *Mahābhārata* and refer only to the first three *yugas* (the epochs of Hindu chronology), while the *Mahābhārata* refers to all four *yugas* and was written in the later *Kaliyuga*, the former must have been composed earlier, at the beginning of the *Kaliyuga*. Halhed also affirmed their great antiquity by again insisting on the anteriority of these scriptures to the Mosaic deluge, enlisting the work of French astronomer Jean Sylvain Bailly, who had also been convinced by the high antiquity of *Hindoo* annals.[116] Halhed also built on this reassertion of the great age of *Hindoo* scriptures to suggest that many foundational philosophies were derivative

112 Rocher, 'Nathaniel Brassey Halhed'. 113 Rocher, 'Nathaniel Brassey Halhed', p. 281, note 15.

114 The preface is now published, with an introduction, in Rocher, 'Nathaniel Brassey Halhed', pp. 283–9.

115 Rocher, 'Nathaniel Brassey Halhed', p. 282.

116 Rocher, 'Nathaniel Brassey Halhed', pp. 285–6.

of the ideas contained in the *Upanishads*. Repeating the idea that Pythagoras 'professedly travelled into India for instruction', Halhed suggested that the 'Manchean, Pythagorean, and other famous systems may clearly be deduced' in these scriptures, 'a book too which most indisputably must have been written before the earliest civilization of the western world'.[117] The text itself, argues Halhed, was actually aimed towards combating the 'Manichean heresy' or a 'resemblance of it' in order to establish 'not only the unity but the universality of the godhead'. To explain this concept, Halhed quipped that this was a system 're-invented the other day' by 'the learned Bishop of Cloyne'. This was a reference to George Berkeley's *Treatise Concerning the Principles of Human Knowledge*, published in 1710, which presumably was 'the other day' relative to 'the Opnekhets'. In this work Berkeley had put up a defence against Cartesian dualism by rejecting that anything exists independent of the perception the mind, an argument that Halhed here aligns with the Hindu concept of *Māyā*, which in the *Upanishads* refers to the material world.[118] He also suggests, in a marginal note added to the manuscript, that the text also contains the seeds of Plato's trinity and Epicurus' godhead.[119] As well as continuing to stress its greater age than Mosaic records, Halhed did then turn to a philosophical account of Indian religion that placed it as the source of many significant systems of thought.

The turn to symbolical interpretations of *Hindoo* religion related, in a manner not that dissimilar to Holwell and Dow, to Halhed's account of the various deities that featured in 'the Opnekhets'. Halhed suggests that in the text, the 'three great Angels, or Beings subordinate only to Brehma himself', that is Brahma, Vishnu and Shiva, are 'nothing more than personifications' of 'matter, space and time', with 'the three qualities of creation, preservation and destruction'.[120] This corresponds directly with a comment he would later write in his published affirmation of Richard Brothers' *Testimony to the Authenticity of the Prophecies and Mission of Richard Brothers and of his Mission to Recall the Jews* (1795). Here Halhed offered his own reasons for believing Brothers' claims to an impending millennium to be accurate, comparing the signs of the times with biblical passages. In defence of this method, Halhed reminds his readers that he was

117 Rocher, 'Nathaniel Brassey Halhed', p. 288.

118 For a discussion of *Māyā* and non-dualism, see King, *Indian Philosophy*, pp. 54–6. Halhed goes on to comment that despite this, the text could not but have helped encourage Manichean beliefs given that as an eternal substance it seemed to invite the reading that *Māyā* was 'the evil principle' and 'Brêhm' (Brahmin) was good.

119 Rocher, 'Nathaniel Brassey Halhed', p. 288.

120 Rocher, 'Nathaniel Brassey Halhed', p. 287.

well practised in 'the occupation of decyphering mysterious and allegorical modes of composition', and that if he had previously been 'negligent of our own sacred writing', he had bestowed an 'unwearied attention' on the Hindus. In the course of these studies, Halhed claimed, he had come to divine the 'true meaning' of the 'Hindú triad of Energies or Powers, called Brahma, Vishnu and Shiva' as 'nothing more than poetical personifications of *matter*, *space* and *time*'.[121] With this knowledge, Halhed supposed, the true meaning of the surviving scriptures could thus be interpreted. In neither this text, nor in his preface to the translation of 'the Opnekhets', does Halhed explicitly compare this to Christian theology. Rather, the inference is that *Hindoo* religion was allegorical and monotheistic.

Although his mission to testify on Brothers' behalf and the impact that this had on the following decade of his life meant that Halhed turned away from serious oriental scholarship, he returned to his interests when he began to emerge from his self-imposed isolation in 1809 to take a role in the Company's home administration. Halhed continued to take out oriental scholarship from the Company library, located in the same East India House as his offices, including Holwell's *Interesting Historical Events*.[122] His main focus in this period was to determine the nature of the *Mahābhārata*, on which he produced a manuscript of 700 pages. Again, using Persian copies, Halhed translated the text and added notes and comments.[123] Throughout his analysis Halhed identified personifications and allegories of philosophical concepts and metaphysical principles. He also drew parallels between biblical texts, Greco-Roman myths and Milton's poetry and the ancient epic.[124] This work, though, was never intended for publication, and it seems that by this point Halhed had given up on any kind of public life. His continued studies remained a personal pastime, shared mostly with his former patron turned correspondent, Warren Hastings. In his commentaries on the *Upanishads* and later the *Mahābhārata*, Halhed maintained his commitment to his belief in the greater antiquity of Indian scriptures and continued to search for the origins of significant philosophical ideas and principles in their contents, though this time aligning them with biblical scripture and prophecy.

[121] Nathaniel Brassey Halhed, *Testimony to the Authenticity of the Prophecies and Mission of Richard Brothers and of his Mission to Recall the Jews* (London: R. Faulder, 1795), p. 10.

[122] 'Records of the East India Company Library (1801–58)', BL, IOR: MS Eur F303/2. Entry dated 1 May 1818.

[123] See Rosane Rocher, 'Nathaniel Brassey Halhed's Collection of Oriental Manuscripts', *Annals of Oriental Research*, 25 (1975), pp. 279–89.

[124] Halhed to Hastings, 29 May 1800, in John Gran, 'Warren Hastings in Slippers. Unpublished Letters of Warren Hastings', *Calcutta Review*, 26:51 (1956), p. 133.

Conclusion

Halhed's interpretation of Indian religion, both in the preface to *A Code of Gentoo Laws* and in his later private writings on the *Upanishads*, maintained a consistent belief in their great antiquity and philosophical sophistication. The former was approached with a careful and shrewd scepticism, and the latter according to his conversion to Brothers' millenarianism; both were the product of a serious intellectual engagement with Indian and European religious ideas. Halhed's reading of the *Code* established an equivalency between *Gentoo* and Christian thought on the grounds that both were the products of historical process, whereby religion became more allegorical and refined, in tandem with the progress of civilisation. Both had an equal claim to truth, but one was irrefutably more ancient than the other, with potentially devastating implications for the authority claims of the younger text. Despite its apparent purpose and situation in the administration of Warren Hastings, Halhed's commentaries on *Gentoo* religious thought and the ordinances of the *Code* were as much oriented towards wider philosophical questions about the nature of religious thought and practice as they were towards government in India.

Halhed's presentation and commentary on the *Code* resulted in a series of critical responses that were forced to confront the implications of the great antiquity of *Gentoo* culture and religion for European knowledge. Much of this was focused on the issues that Halhed's scepticism had brought to the surface by pitting *Gentoo* chronology against Mosaic dispensation. The resulting exchanges were characterised as those defending Indian religion from a position of religious libertinism versus those who returned fire as friends to revelation. The more enduring reaction, particularly to Halhed's commentary on certain religious concepts and the character of the Sanskrit, was a continuing interest in Indian languages and ideas and their connections with European antiquity, which would be later developed most clearly by William Jones. The *Code* itself also provided further material for those wanting to either defend or contest the legitimacy of the Hastings administration, as both the circumstances of its commissioning and its uses in the later impeachment trial attest to. Likewise, for some it was a mark of the superiority of Brahmin tenets of religious toleration, and for others a source of evidence from which to call for missionary activity in India.

Halhed's *A Code of Gentoo Laws, or, Ordinations of the Pundits* was written in an effort to deliver Hastings' Clause XXIII, which upheld the importance of 'the Shaster' in line with 'the Laws of the Koran' for the purposes of maintaining 'native' laws and customs. The occasion for its production was Hastings' commission, both reasoned as a code to be used in the practical application of the clause and to be published in Britain to render knowledge of *Gentoo* laws and customs 'familiar to the inhabitants of this country'.[125] These conditions brought the interpretation of *Gentoo* religion by British authors securely into the framework of Company interests and administration. Within Halhed's preface, though, a variety of concerns and ideas were expressed, the reaction to which resulted in numerous ways of understanding and deploying knowledge of India. Here the relationship between knowledge and political argument was not aligned to one dominant ideology of empire, but contested understandings of the significance of the *Code* in relation to European religion and history, as well as the Company's debated policies.

[125] Letter to Lord Mansfield, 20 January 1776, in Gleig, *Memoirs*, vol. 2, pp. 20–5, p. 20.

CHAPTER 6

Charles Wilkins and the Gēētā

Comparatively little is known about the early life of the fourth central author considered in this study, Charles Wilkins. Born in 1749, Wilkins arrived in Calcutta in July 1770 to take up the position of writer, a junior clerk role, in the East India Company. Unlike most Company writers, Wilkins came from a modest family background of clothiers in Somerset, and apparently acquired the appointment through the intervention of a great-uncle, who was a London banker.[1] When he arrived in India, Charles Wilkins soon distinguished himself as a talented student of Indian languages. He first acquired vernacular Hindustani and Bengali, then, like most Company men interested in the business of administrative affairs and oriental scholarship, he turned to Persian. In the words of Halhed, Wilkins was also the 'metallurgist, engraver, founder, and printer' of the Bengali and Persian typefaces used in Halhed's *Grammar of the Bengal Language*.[2] Although unacknowledged at the time, this feat could not have been accomplished without the aid and expertise of local craftspeople, such as the blacksmith and engraver Panchanan Karmakara, who was undoubtedly instrumental to the whole endeavour.[3] Nevertheless, Wilkins would become most well known not for the typefaces, but as the first British scholar to master Sanskrit, which he studied under the instruction of Kāśīnātha Śarmā (sometimes Kasinatha Bhattacharya), one of the most esteemed pandits at Benares.[4] As an obituary in *The Asiatic Journal* of 1836 put it, Wilkins was 'the first adventurer on this literary ocean'.[5]

[1] Thomas R. Trautmann, 'Wilkins, Sir Charles (bap. 1749, d. 1836)', *Oxford Dictionary of National Biography*, 2004 [www.oxforddnb.com/view/10.1093/ref:odnb/9780198614128.001.0001/odnb-9780198614128-e-29416, accessed 7 April 2016].

[2] Halhed, *Grammar of the Bengal Language*, p. xxiv.

[3] Anindita Ghosh, *Power in Print: Popular Publishing and the Politics of Language and Culture in a Colonial Society, 1778–1905* (Oxford: Oxford University Press, 2006), pp. 109–11.

[4] Richard. H. Davis, 'Wilkins, Kasinatha, Hastings, and the First English Bhagavad Gītā', *International Journal of Hindu Studies* (2015), 19:1.

[5] Anon, 'Obituary: Kasinatha Bhattacharya', *Asiatic Journal and Monthly Register for British and Foreign India, China, and Australasia*, 20, May–August (1836), p. 166.

These studies eventually resulted in Wilkins' translation, *The Bhăgvăt-Gēētā, or Dialogues of Krĕēshnă and Ărjŏŏn* (1785). It is as a consequence of this direct translation that Wilkins is most often discussed in terms of his contribution to the development of Indological studies. Scholarship has thus tended to view him according to what came after the watershed translation of the *Gēētā* and not in relation to the work that preceded it. McGetchin, for example, places Wilkins alongside William Jones as being responsible for 'introducing Europe to the great works of Indian civilization' and thereby stimulating the growth of Indology.[6] Yet, at the core of Wilkins' interpretation of the *Bhagavad-Gīṭā* were the same concerns that animated the work of Holwell, Dow and Halhed before him. Rather than seeing the *Gītā* as making the case for a particular yogic discipline, as many Indian commentators had before and Sanskrit scholars have since, Wilkins saw it as a text designed to unify and reform the *Hindoo* religion around certain original and core principles. Declaring that the intention of its author was 'setting up the doctrine of the unity of Godhead, in opposition to idolatrous sacrifices, and the worship of images', Wilkins consciously cast his *Gēētā* in the language of European rational religion and reform.[7] In completing the first direct English translation from Sanskrit, from a text presented as an ancient, unifying and reforming scripture, Wilkins intended his *Bhăgvăt-Gēētā* to continue a philosophical account of Indian religion that presented it as an example of the universality of certain religious truths, as well as in some senses, equivalently rational to the basic tenets of Christianity.

Like the other authors considered so far, Wilkins has been identified with the suggestion that prominent eighteenth-century accounts of Indian religion were written from a 'deist' perspective. As P. J. Marshall's introduction to a compilation of extracts of their works puts it, 'there is no clear evidence about his religious beliefs, but he too seems to have had deist leanings'.[8] Likewise, Halbfass includes Wilkins, albeit 'to a lesser extent' than Holwell and Dow, in the category of 'deistic discussion' in his 'philosophical essay' on India and Europe.[9] Again, in the scope of the work in which these comments appear neither author is able to offer any sustained analysis in support of this claim. This chapter intends, therefore, to look more closely at Wilkins' religious thought. Indeed, within his commentary on the *Bhăgvăt-Gēētā*, as well as in some of his later

[6] Douglas T. McGetchin, *Indology, Indomania, and Orientalism: Ancient India's Rebirth in Modern Germany* (Madison, NJ: Fairleigh Dickinson University Press, 2009), p. 32.

[7] Wilkins, *Bhăgvăt-Gēētā*, p. 24. [8] Marshall, *British Discovery of Hinduism*, p. 29.

[9] Halbfass, *India and Europe*, p. 56.

productions, there are certainly hints that Wilkins aligned his favour with eighteenth-century conceptions of rational religion, which at times appears to include aspects of both *Hindoo* and *Seek* (Sikh) religiosity.

The following discussion, then, looks more closely at the identification of Wilkins with a particular religious outlook, examining the relationship between European and Indian theological debates and traditions in his presentation of the *Bhagavad-Gītā*, and by extension, the religion of the *Hindoos*. Moreover, as Wilkins was also a Company man, it also necessarily considers the translation's relationship with the British empire in India. Like the *Code of Gentoo Laws*, the work of Wilkins was commissioned and compensated at the behest of Governor-General Warren Hastings. This chapter thus argues that Wilkins was an important figure in the transition of British constructions of Indian religion from being the product of independent intellectual enquiry towards more institutional and instrumental approaches to orientalist knowledge. Like the work of Halhed, the commentary offered by Wilkins can be seen as addressing two debates: one concerned with the nature of enlightenment and religion, the other about the proper exercise of power in India.

The *Gēētā* and Its Preface

Charles Wilkins' *Bhăgvăt-Gēētā*, like Halhed's *Code*, was commissioned by Warren Hastings. Where the practical uses of the *Code* appeared more immediate, given Hastings' plan for the administration of justice and the call for a digest of *Gentoo* laws, the need for the *Gēētā* was less clear. It seems that from the beginning, Hastings' designs were that it would be produced 'for public notice', conceived of as part of a plan to bring to a home audience an illustration of the 'real character' of 'the inhabitants of India'. This would, Hastings claimed, 'conciliate distant affections' and imprint on 'the hearts of our own countrymen the sense and obligation of benevolence'. Indeed, these comments were themselves part of that plan; expressed in a letter to the chairman of the East India Company (Nathaniel Smith), they were published in the prefatory material to the translation.

In the letter, Hastings thus offers a clear articulation of the role of orientalist scholarship in his administration, at least as he wished it to be understood by the reading public. Such studies, Hastings wrote, would form 'the moral character and habits of service' among Company men, cultivate a 'generous sense of feeling' for the natural rights of Indian subjects at home, and 'lessen the weight of the chain by which the natives are held in subjection'. These were the benefits, he suggested, of a system of government that recognised that 'Every accumulation of knowledge, and especially such as is obtained by social communication with people over whom we exercise a dominion founded on the right of conquest, is useful to the state'. Though something of the impermanence of empires was acknowledged with the reflection that such writings 'will survive when the British dominion in India shall have long ceased to exist'.[10] The circumstance for Wilkins' commission, then, was the continuing and contested ex post facto legitimisation of Clive's conquest.

Ensuring the London publication of Wilkin's *Bhăgvăt-Gēētā* seemed to also be a personal cause for Hastings. In a letter to his friend Scott, asking for his assistance in passing it on to his publisher, Hastings suggested he would pursue its publication regardless of whether the Company would support the venture:

> If Mr Smith [the director of the East India Company], contrary to my expectation, and the ingenious opinion which I have conceived of him, should refuse his patronage to Wilkins' production, or the Court of D[irectors], refuse to give their consent to the publication; I devise that you will consequent Mr Smith to allow ... publication in my Name and under your inspection.

Acknowledging that not everyone would agree that the translation was so necessary, Hasting also implored his friend to 'Defend me if you hear me reproached with lavishing my time on these levities, as they may be termed by many, to the neglect of Business.'[11]

That the Company administration should require a translation of the *Bhagavad-Gītā* was certainly not obvious, and the circumstances of its production appear to have been the product of some opportunism on the part of Hastings. In his letter to the board requesting permission to support Wilkins' leave in Benares, Hastings explained that the writer had already begun translating 'a book called Mahbaurat' (*Mahābhārata*), but claimed that the principal reason for the trip was the restitution of his health. Hastings appears to have seen in these circumstances an opportunity, noting in his letter that in Benares, the 'professors of the Shanscrit learning' had become more favourable to cooperation with Company scholars.[12] Wilkins' subsequent instruction under the pandit Kāśīnātha

[10] Letter to Nathaniel Smith, Benares, 4 October 1784, in Marshall, *British Discovery of Hinduism*, pp. 186, 189.

[11] Most likely Major John Scott Waring (1747–1819), a political supporter and promoter of Hastings; BL Add. MS 29129, 1784, f. 270.

[12] Hastings to the Bengal Board of Revenue, 'Extract of Bengal Revenue Consultations, the 9th December 1783, No. 41', BL IOR: H/MISC/207, pp. 169–82.

Śarmā was integral to a policy in which the increasing appointment of pandit scholars to advise the Company in civil legal matters was part of a conscious effort to bolster Company rule by reference to existing political structures and established patterns of cultural patronage.[13] Indeed, Wilkins made much of this in his preface, claiming that while previously these texts had been shrouded in mystery, the Brahmins, following 'the liberal treatment they have of late years experienced from the mildness of our government', and the 'personal attention' paid by Hastings to learned men, now had sufficient confidence 'to remove almost every jealous prejudice from their minds' and share the secrets of their religion. Completing this picture of the success of his patron's enlightened administration, Wilkins also cited the Company's religious policies, listing 'the tolerating principles of our faith' as another reason for the cooperation of pandit scholars.[14]

And yet, if the choice of the *Bhagavad-Gītā*, in contrast to the *Code*, still remains less obvious when aligned with the practical business of administration, both Hastings' and Wilkins' framing of the text was even less defined by such demands. Hastings' interest in the *Gītā*, while certainly integral to his vision of an administration that used oriental scholarship as a means of conciliating itself to both local systems of rule and domestic scrutiny, also went beyond pragmatism. The letter published alongside Wilkins' preface clearly stressed that Hastings was also keen on a particular vision of the 'literature, the mythology, and morality of the ancient Hindoos'. With the caveat that many passages will appear obscure or incomprehensible because of their antiquity and 'sublimity', Hastings insisted that there was still very little in Wilkins' *Gēētā* that would 'shock either our religious faith or moral sentiments'. In fact, he then went on to declare the text 'a single exception, among all the known religions of mankind, of a theology accurately corresponding with the Christian dispensation, and most powerfully illustrating its fundamental doctrines'.[15] Hastings thus also voiced the idea that formed the underlying principle of Wilkins' presentation of his *Gēētā*: that within this text was an argument for monotheistic, rational religion, compatible with a minimalistic understanding of the core of Christianity.

The *Bhagavad-Gītā* forms part of the Sanskrit epic the *Mahābhārata*. It is written as a dialogue between Arjuna and the deity Krishna (*Kṛṣṇa*), in 700 verses. It captures the moments before a heroic battle between two

[13] Dodson, *Orientalism*, pp. 48–50. Kāśīnātha Śarmā would go on to also advise William Jones, and be appointed the first principal of the Company's Benares Sanskrit College in 1791.

[14] Wilkins, *Bhăgvăt-Gēētā*, pp. 23–4.

[15] Marshall, *British Discovery of Hinduism*, pp. 184, 189, 187.

rivals for control of a region in Northern India, one side of which is led by Arjuna, as the prince of the Pandava clan. Arjuna, beset by doubts about warring with those familiar to him on the other side, is counselled by his charioteer and adviser, Krishna, whose transcendent nature is finally revealed later in the text as the 'Lord of All Beings'. The dialogue consists of Krishna's counsel in the period between Arjuna's initial doubts and his ultimate decision to carry out his duties as a warrior. As with all sacred texts, the meaning of its contents has been interpreted in various ways, mostly revolving around the question of how to understand Krishna's account of dharma (duty) and *bhakti* (devotion), as well as other various philosophical and ethical questions.[16]

As in the case of Halhed's *Code*, it was primarily in the preface to the *Gēētā* that the translator set out his interpretation of its contents, and their particular signification for Indian religion. Wilkins' starting point is the claim that the '*Brahmans*' believe in a singular God. He therefore introduces the text as 'a dialogue supposed to have passed between *Kreeshna*, an incarnation of the Deity, and his pupil and favourite *Arjoon*'. This first hint, an opening reference to 'the Deity', singular, is developed into a bolder assertion that the very purpose of the literary scripture was 'setting up the doctrine of the unity of the Godhead'. In promoting that decided purpose, the modern followers of the *Gēētā*, whom Wilkins identifies as 'the most learned *Brahmans* of the present times', were, in his judgement, essentially 'Unitarians'. It was therefore, according to Wilkins, a reformist and rational corrective of 'idolatrous sacrifices, and the worship of images'.[17]

Although the *Bhagavad-Gītā* is considered important in the traditions of Hinduism, particularly for Vedānta philosophy, the commentaries and readings are various. These perspectives not only relate to different shades of theism, but also the ontology of dualist and non-dualist interpretations. While Vedānta commentaries all accept the divinity of Krishna, the signification of the claim in the text that he is the *brahman*, which in Vedānta designates the absolute or ultimate reality, is a matter of dispute, particularly for non-dualist thinkers, for whom *brahman* can have no attributes.[18] Within this, monotheism, as defined by Judaism, Christianity and Islam, fails to capture the various expressions of theism within Vedānta, and other schools, which can hold together the notion of

[16] See Richard H. Davis, *The Bhagavad Gita: A Biography* (Oxford: Princeton University Press, 2015), chapter 1.

[17] Wilkins, *Bhăgvăt-Gēētā*, pp. 23–4.

[18] Davis, *Bhagavad Gita*, pp. 60–1.

an ultimate or supreme being or reality and the idea of many other or lesser expressions of divinity.[19] Some Indologists have thus interpreted the *Bhagavad-Gītā* as a foundational text for turning Hinduism away from monism to a devotional theism, whereas others have stressed its contribution as presenting a singular path to liberation from the cycle of death and rebirth (*mokṣa*) through 'non-attached action' and an 'unswerving, single minded devotion to the lord of the universe', Krishna.[20]

Wilkins is not the only person to have interpreted the *Bhagavad-Gītā* as establishing a monotheistic system. And yet, though there is a long history of indigenous Hindu reformist movements, scholarship suggests that it was not until the nineteenth century that Hindu thinkers explicitly invoked Krishna's proclamations in the *Gītā* that he was the ultimate object of devotional aspiration in order to redefine Hinduism as a monotheistic creed.[21] According to Catherine A. Robinson, the interpretation of the *Bhagavad-Gītā* as presenting a monotheistic account of devotion is a product of modern interpretations of the text, central to which was the reading of Wilkins, followed by Raja Rammohan Roy and the formation of the monotheistic Brahmo Samaj movement, in the late 1820s. Robinson thus recognises that Wilkins and Hastings approached the *Bhagavad-Gītā* from a particular perspective, which would later appeal to these reform movements, understanding it to be 'a work of pure spirituality contrasted with the venality and corruption of vernacular religiosity and comparable with Christianity'.[22] What is particular about Wilkins' preparatory remarks, though, is not just his impulse to see the text as an expression of a monotheistic doctrine, but his extrapolation that followers of the theology expounded in the *Gītā* could be considered equivalent to Unitarians. Unitarianism had only become a formal denomination in the British religious landscape in 1774, eleven years prior to the publication of Wilkins' preface, when John Disney and Theophilus Lindsey, both former Anglican clergymen, founded the first Unitarian chapel in Essex Street, London. In invoking an association with Unitarianism, then, Wilkins

[19] Angelika Malinar, *The Bhagavad Gītā: Its Doctrines and Contexts* (Cambridge: Cambridge University Press, 2007), p. 238.

[20] Robert Charles Zaehner, *The Bhagavad-Gītā* (Oxford: Oxford University Press, 1969), pp. 38–40; Robert N. Minor, 'The "Gītā's" Way as the Only Way', *Philosophy East and West*, 30:3 (1980), p. 350.

[21] Sharada Sugirtharajah, 'Colonialism', in Sushil Mittal and Gene Thursby (eds.), *Studying Hinduism: Key Concepts and Methods* (London: Routledge, 2008), p. 82; M. V. Nadkarni, *The Bhagavad-Gita for the Modern Reader: History, Interpretations and Philosophy* (Abingdon: Routledge, 2017), pp. 79–83.

[22] Robinson, *Interpretations of the Bhagavad-Gītā*, pp. 16, 39.

attached the *Bhagavad-Gītā* to a complex and important movement within the landscape of contemporary English religious Dissent.

Unlike other heterodoxies, many of the prominent figures associated with Unitarianism in England moved within and around the Anglican Church, in line with the long history of latitudinarianism.[23] On the other hand, central to the doctrine of Unitarianism was a historical relationship with the heterodox anti-Trinitarian doctrines of Arianism and Socinianism.[24] Arianism was the much older heresy, which essentially held that Christ must be subordinate to God the Father. Socinianism, which was a much more present school of thought in the late eighteenth century, pushed the more radical conclusion that the trinity was logically incoherent. With this came a rejection of several doctrines deemed incompatible with reason, such as original sin, predestination and Christ's atonement.[25] However, unlike more radical uses of the Socinian heresy, such as John Toland's freethinking deism, the Unitarianism of Wilkins' period was more interested in prompting the Anglican tradition towards a more rational appreciation of the Godhead. While intellectual speculation on the trinity had been somewhat tolerated within the Anglican fold, Francis Blackburne's *The Confessional* (1766) once again reignited a debate about the need for clergymen to subscribe to the Thirty-Nine Articles of the Church of England (including an affirmation of the doctrine of the trinity), which Blackburne had attacked on the grounds of private judgement. This was followed in 1771 by the Feather's Tavern Petition, among the signatories of which were Disney and Lindsey, calling for an end to mandatory subscription to the Articles as a requirement for entering the clergy, for graduating from Cambridge or matriculating at Oxford.[26] Its failure to win assent in the House of Commons resulted in the departure of figures like Disney and Lindsey, and the development of Unitarianism as a denominational movement.

The Unitarians were therefore a decidedly Dissenting sect. Nevertheless, the early Unitarians were considered a respectable coterie,

[23] G. M. Ditchfield, 'Ecclesiastical Policy under Lord North', in John Walsh, Colin Haydon and Stephen Taylor (eds.), *The Church of England c.1689–c.1833: From Toleration to Tractarianism* (Cambridge: Cambridge University Press, 1993), p. 231.

[24] Earl M. Wilbur, *A History of Unitarianism: Socinianism and Its Antecedents* (Cambridge, MA: Harvard University Press, 1946).

[25] Douglas Headley, 'Theology and the Revolt against the Enlightenment', in Sheridan Gilley and Brian Stanley (eds.), *The Cambridge History of Christianity*, vol. 8 (Cambridge: Cambridge University Press, 2006), p. 33.

[26] For a full account of the crisis around Blackburne's text, see M. Fitzpatrick, 'Latitudinarianism at the Parting of the Ways: A Suggestion', in John Walsh, Colin Haydon and Stephen Taylor (eds.), *The Church of England c.1689–c.1833* (Cambridge: Cambridge University Press, 1993).

comprising of members such as the polymath Joseph Priestley, and were broadly united with liberal Anglicans in the opposition to the more extreme heterodoxies of radical deism and atheism. As Unitarianism spread in the 1780s, Unitarians were mostly members of a new merchant-gentry elite that dominated prominent industrial towns. Still, their denial of the trinity remained a doctrinal heresy and they were explicitly excluded from the Toleration Act until 1813.[27] In alluding to this movement for respectable Dissent, Wilkins was thus consciously associating his *Gēētā*, and its 'doctrines of *Kreeshna*', with a movement to reform the Christian religion towards a more rational and specifically anti-Trinitarian doctrine.

Like Holwell, Dow and Halhed, Wilkins presented this assessment of *Hindoo* religion within a framework that saw its development as a product of a conflict between purity and superstition, which could be viewed in terms parallel to the historical evolution of Christianity. The preface thus situates the *Bhagavad-Gītā* in the context of a religious reformation, identifying its explicit purpose as the unification of 'all the prevailing modes of worship of those days', through its insistence on the unity of the Godhead and its disavowal of idolatry. The resonance of this for certain moments in the history of Christianity would have no doubt struck Wilkins' readers. That the most learned followers of this doctrine are judged to be Unitarians certainly invites the reader to consider this in association with Christian attempts at rational reform. Moreover, throughout Wilkins' notes on the translation there are other tacit references to the struggle for rational religion within the history of Christianity. In one seemingly unnecessary footnote, for example, Wilkins annotates a moment where Krishna contradicts 'the bards' (i.e. the Vedas), to point to the commentary of '*Srēē-dhăr Swāmĕĕ*' (the fourteenth-century commentator, Sridhara Swami) on the same section of the *Gītā*. Wilkins judged Sridhara's explanation to be unnecessarily esoteric, and so provides an extract 'in order to shew that the commentators of India are no less fond of searching for mystery, and wandering from the simple path of their author' than the 'scholastic jargon' of 'those of more enlightened nations,

[27] For an account of the relationship between Unitarianism and Rational Dissent more broadly, see R. K. Webb, 'The Emergence of Rational Dissent', in Knud Haakonssen (ed.), *Enlightenment and Religion: Rational Dissent in Eighteenth-Century Britain* (Cambridge: Cambridge University Press, 1996); Ather Sheps, 'Sedition, Vice and Atheism: The Limits of Toleration and the Orthodox Attack on Rational Religion in Late Eighteenth-Century Britain', in Regina Hewitt and Pat Rogers (eds.), *Orthodoxy and Heresy in Eighteenth-Century Society: Essays from the DeBartolo Conference* (Lewisburg, PA: Bucknell University Press, 2002).

who for ages have been labouring to entangle the plain unerring clew of our holy religion'.[28]

In the same way that Holwell blamed the idolatry of *Hindoo* practices on the influence of 'the common run of *Bramins*' and Dow 'the unlearned part of the Brahmins', Wilkins also employed the notion of priestcraft to explain the conflict between the monotheism of the *Gītā* and idolatrous customs of *Hindoo* worship. Thus, despite their Unitarianism, Wilkins explains, some of the learned Brahmins of contemporary India still complied 'with the prejudices of the vulgar' by performing 'all the ceremonies inculcated by the *Veds*'. They do this, suggested Wilkins, 'for the support of their own consequence', choosing to manipulate 'the great ignorance of the people', instead of acting 'in compliance with the dictates of *Kreeshna*'. Such hypocrisy, however, Wilkins was clear to point out, was not particular to the Brahmins, adding that 'these ceremonies are as much the bread of the *Brahmans*, as the superstition of the vulgar is the support of the priesthood in many other countries'.[29]

In another imitation of Holwell and Dow, Wilkins used the idea of schism and division within the history of the *Hindoo* religion to explain those practices and beliefs which were not consistent the idea of an ancient, philosophical and rational religion. And again, like Holwell and Dow, this involved the contestation of the authority of the Vedas as the scriptural core of an indigenous Indian religion. The *Bhagavad-Gītā* had been calculated, Wilkins explained, 'to undermine the tenets inculcated by the *Veds*' in order 'to bring about the downfall of Polytheism'. To make this claim more comfortably align with the actual contents of the text, though, Wilkins explains that the author 'dared not make a direct attack, either upon the prevailing prejudices of the people or the divine authority with those ancient books', and instead encouraged monotheistic belief by 'offering eternal happiness' as the reward for the worship of *Brahm* (*Brahman*) as 'the Almighty'. The Vedas therefore occupy an interesting position in Wilkins' scheme, as 'the most ancient scriptures of the *Hindoos*', but also with contents that inculcated superstitious practices. Moreover, Wilkins posited that independent of the Vedas, the '*Brāhmăns* esteem this work [i.e. the *Gēētā*] to contain all the grand mysteries of their religion'.[30] Wilkins' reform text, therefore, gets to the core of the religion's doctrines, while cutting away from it any unnecessary ceremonies and practices.

[28] Wilkins, *Bhăgvăt-Gēētā*, p. 154. [29] Wilkins, *Bhăgvăt-Gēētā*, p. 24.
[30] Wilkins, *Bhăgvăt-Gēētā*, p. 23.

This was not entirely inaccurate. The *Bhagavad-Gītā* can indeed be interpreted as undermining elements of the Vedic texts, but is also imbued with essentially Vedic concepts. Indeed, the history of Sanskrit literature reveals the basic inadequacy of these British authors' attempts to identify the original and singular authoritative *Hindoo* or *Gentoo* text. While adherence to the authority of the Vedas is what classifies a philosophy as *āstika* (orthodox), knowledge, interpretation and use of the Vedic teaching varies widely between schools, most of which refer to later commentaries in conjunction with other textual canons. Vedānta, as we have seen, concentrates mostly on the Vedic *Upanishads*, from which, in turn, the *Bhagavad-Gītā* draws.[31] Thus, while the framing offered by Wilkins was an imposition of a particularly European interpretation, it did partially overlap with discussions within certain Hindu traditions themselves, to which it is possible that Wilkins was exposed through discussion with Indian Sanskrit scholars in Benares. As Davis has commented, the idea that the *Gītā* was an important text was 'the viewpoint not of all Hindus of all times but rather of a particular class of Sanskrit-teaching Brahmin pandits in northern India in the late eighteenth century.'[32] Wilkins appears to have taken the importance accorded to the *Bhagavad-Gītā* by his advisors, and with that claimed for it the status of containing the essentials of a reformed and rational religion of learned Brahmans.

This presentation of the *Gītā* as a reforming and rational expression of religion is also observable in some of the decisions that Wilkins made as a translator. Although he made no attempt to reproduce the poetical form of the Sanskrit original, Wilkins imbued the text with a literary tone with the addition of prepositions like 'thee' and 'thou', which, as Davis has observed, makes certain moments sound not dissimilar to the King James Bible.[33] In some cases, too, the translation of specific words and phrases betrays the influence of Wilkins' own religious context and preferences. In particular, certain terms are deployed to support the preface's constructed analogy between the purpose of the *Gēētā* and the European cause of rational religion. In the remainder of this section I give a comparative analysis of an extract taken from Wilkins' translation of the *Bhagavad-Gītā*, which examines the decisions he made in translation, in relation to both a modern translation and the original Sanskrit. This comparison of verses 15 and 16 of Discourse 5 begins

[31] Brockington, *Sacred Thread*, pp. 5–6, 56–7.

[32] Davis, *Bhagavad Gita*, p. 79.

[33] Davis, *Bhagavad Gita*, p. 80.

with the original Sanskrit verse, followed by Wilkins' translation, to be compared with a more modern English translation:[34]

> n'ādatte kasyacit pāpaṁ na c'aiva sukṛtaṁ vibhuḥ |
> ajñānen' āvṛtaṁ **jñānaṁ**; tena muhyanti jantavaḥ ||
>
> **jñānena** tu tad ajñānaṁ yeṣāṁ nāśitam ātmanaḥ |
> teṣām ādityavaj **jñānaṁ** prakāśayati tat param ||[35]

In Wilkins' translations this appears as:

> The Almighty receiveth neither the vices nor the virtues of anyone. Mankind are led astray by their reasons being obscured by ignorance, but when that ignorance of their souls is destroyed by the force of reason, their wisdom shineth forth again with the glory of the sun, and causeth the Deity to appear.[36]

Taking Wilkins' treatment of the Sanskrit neuter noun for 'knowledge/knowing', *jñāna*, and its inflected form *jñānaṁ*, as our focus, we can assess some of his choices in translation. Wilkins correctly translates *ajñānaṁ*, the antonym to *jñāna*, as 'ignorance'. Yet in this passage he translates the first *jñānaṁ* as 'their reasons', and then *jñānena*, another inflection, to 'force of reason'. In modern translations, *jñāna* is most commonly translated as 'knowledge' or 'cognition', and is meant here in the sense of self-realisation, or indeed 'wisdom', as Wilkins latterly identifies it in the final line. Modern translations thus resonate differently:

> The all-pervading Lord does not take on the merit or demerit of anyone's actions. Knowledge is concealed by ignorance – and in that way people are deluded.
>
> But for those whose ignorance of the self has been destroyed by knowledge, their knowledge is like the sun, flooding the highest reality with light.[37]

Here we see the term not only clearly translated as 'knowledge', but also as related to some kind of conception of self-realisation. In Advaita Vedānta, particularly in the commentaries of the eighth-century theologian Śaṅkara (Shankaracharya), these aspects of the *Gītā* are a confirmation of the

[34] For this purpose I have chosen to use the modern translation by W. J Johnson in the Oxford World's Classics series, since this is a good standard, rather than verse translation widely used by scholars: W. J. Johnson (trans.), *The Bhagavad Gītā* (Oxford: Oxford University Press, 1994).

[35] Bold emphases are mine. The Sanskrit verse is taken from a side-by-side Sanskrit-to-English translation: Zaehner, *Bhagavad-Gītā*, p. 209.

[36] Wilkins, *Bhăgvăt-Gēētā*, p. 59. [37] Johnson, *Bhagavad Gita*, p. 24.

philosophy of the identity of the self (*ātman*) with *brahman*.[38] Alternatively for non-dualist Vedānta thinkers, such as Rāmānujā (Ramanujacharya, 1017–37 CE), self-knowledge leads to interested action becoming disinterested, leading one to the discipline of devotion.[39] While not technically incorrect, then, Wilkins' decision to translate *jñāna* as 'reason' was a product of the same perspective that declared the text's Brahmin followers Unitarians in the preface, and thus apposite to a particular interpretation of the religious signification of the passage. His latter translation of *jñāna* as 'wisdom' was closer to its meaning, and shows that he was aware of the certain emphasis placed on it in this passage. The word 'reason' carried significant weight in contemporary religious discourse, not least in relation to Unitarianism and Rational Dissent. While eighteenth-century philosophy was as much characterised by critiques of reason as its exultation, it was broadly taken to be a natural faculty of human nature (the *lumen natural*) that could be corrupted by prejudices or obscured by passions, but in itself it was always true.[40] Within the context of eighteenth-century religious thought, the idea that this faculty would alone, when unobstructed, lead the possessor to both moral virtue and knowledge of 'the Deity', was a cornerstone of concepts of 'natural religion'.[41]

Wilkins also demonstrates the influence of contemporary British religious thought in his treatment of the concept of dharma. Modern attempts at translation present this variously as being captured in the terms 'duties', 'rights', 'laws', 'conduct', 'virtues' and the phrase 'right way of living'. In two passages of the the *Bhagavad-Gītā* the concept appears as the inflection *swa-dharmo*, meaning something like 'one's prescribed duty' (*swa*, own, and *dharma*, duty), as well as *para-dharmāt*, another's prescribed duties. These two verses are very similar, as they are both about performing one's particular dharma, over the duties of another. The first comes in the third discourse, and the second in the eighteenth and final discourse. Wilkins, however, translates them differently, in a manner that has a significant impact on the meaning of each verse. Again, this can be illustrated with a comparison with a more modern translation. In Discourse 18 (18.47), the verse appears as follows:

> śreyān **swa-dharmo** viguṇaḥ **para-dharmāt** svanuṣhṭhitāt |
> svabhāva-niyataṁ karma kurvan nāpnoti kilbiṣam ||[42]

[38] King, *Indian Philosophy*, pp. 53–4; Davis, *Bhagavad Gita*, p. 61; Alladi Mahadeva Sastri (trans.), *Bhagavad-Gita with the Commentary of Sri Shankaracharya* (Madras: V. Sadanand, 1977), pp. 169–71.

[39] Davis, *Bhagavad Gita*, p. 63.

[40] Marlherbe, 'Reason', p. 320.

[41] Gerrish, 'Natural and Revealed Religion', p. 647.

[42] Bold emphases are mine. Zaehner, *Bhagavad-Gītā*, p. 394.

A modern translation of this goes as follows:

> It is better to do **one's duty** inadequately **than another**'s well;
> no man is at fault performing an action enjoined by his own nature.[43]

In translating this verse Wilkins also makes some similar choices in phrasing, all centring on the translation of phrases deriving from dharma as duty:

> The **duties of a man's own particular calling**, although not free from faults, is far preferable to **the duty of another**, let it ever be so well pursued.

When it comes to the same phrase in Discourse 3 (3.35), however, Wilkins evidently chose to take a different path. The original is as follows:

> śreyān **swa-dharmo** viguṇaḥ **para-dharmāt** sv-anuṣhṭhitāt |
> **swa-dharme** nidhanaṁ śreyaḥ **para-dharmo** bhayāvahaḥ ||[44]

The modern translation presents this as:

> 'It is better to practice **your own inherent duty** deficiently than **another's duty** well.It is better to die conforming to **your own duty**; the **duty of others** invites danger.[45]

In this case Wilkins chose the words 'religion' and 'faith' instead:

> **A man's own religion**, though contrary to, is better **than the faith of another**, let it ever be so well followed. It is good to die in **one's own faith**, for **another's faith** beareth fear.[46]

In the latter case, it appears that Wilkins has made the decision to interpret this verse to be offering some wisdom on the topic of religious toleration, by preferring the words 'religion' and 'faith' to what he would later more accurately translate as 'duty'. Whereas modern translations capture the ideas of non-attached action and duty, which are consistent themes throughout the *Gītā*, the verse offered by Wilkins raises different concerns. For European readers, the notion of 'fidelity to 'one's own faith' will no doubt have evoked debates on the matter of private judgement in matters of religion.

Wilkins' preface was a mere five pages long. Yet within that space there features a comparison between Brahmins and Unitarians and, by implication, Unitarianism's Socinian predecessors, as well as the suggestion that

[43] Bold emphases are mine. Johnson, *Bhagavad Gita*, p. 79.
[44] Bold emphases are mine. Wilkins, *Bhăgvăt-Gēētā*, p. 131; Zaehner, *Bhagavad-Gītā*, p. 175.
[45] Bold emphases are mine. Johnson, *Bhagavad Gita*, p. 18.
[46] Bold emphases are mine. Wilkins, *Bhăgvăt-Gēētā*, p. 48.

the *Gēētā* was a reforming and Dissenting text, the main purpose of which was to establish a more rational and monotheistic worship. While the conditions for the existence of the translation were closely related to the policies of Warren Hastings, its heterodox contents had as much to do with the debate established in British interpretations of Indian religion initiated by Holwell and Dow.

Reception

In the various published reviews of the translation, as in the case of Halhed's *Code of Gentoo Laws*, it was the controversial religious content which caught the interests of reviewers, far more than the specifics contained within the text itself. Being the first translation of its kind, Wilkins' preface set the theological context in which the *Bhagavad-Gītā* was placed and understood. Some reviewers accepted wholeheartedly the vision presented by Wilkins. *The English Review*, which strongly identified with religious Dissent,[47] judged the *Bhăgvăt-Gēētā* to be an articulation of 'the principle of philosophical theism', concluding that it 'introduces a system of philosophical religion which a Christian will venerate'.[48] Acknowledging Wilkins' description of its author's intentions to 'erect a system of philosophic theism, in opposition to idolatry and superstition', the reviewer accepts Wilkins' decision to frame this text within the context of a universal struggle between the religiosity of the vulgar and 'the exertions of the enlightened' to join religion with 'the progress of philosophy'. In all, the reviewer agrees with the text that, 'Amidst the relics of an absurd superstition, of extravagant ceremonies, and puerile observances, we perceive the traces of a sublime morality, a philosophic religion, and a refined policy.'[49]

Following Wilkins' identification of the Brahmins with the Unitarians, others attached their philosophies to other heterodox sects. In its review of Wilkins' *Gēētā* in 1785, for example, *The Gentlemen's Magazine* faithfully relays that the Brahmins 'are all Unitarians'.[50] It also reflects on the esoteric sublimity of the text, taking its cue from Hastings' explanatory note in the published letter to Nathaniel Smith, on the 'spiritual discipline' of

[47] Robin Jarvis, *The Romantic Period: The Intellectual & Cultural Context of English Literature, 1789–1830* (Abingdon: Routledge, 2014), p. 68.

[48] 'Article III, The Bhagvat Geeta', *The English Review, or An Abstract of English and Foreign Literature*, vol. 9 (London: John Murray, 1787), pp. 94–110.

[49] 'Article III, The Bhagvat Geeta', pp. 95, 99, 96, 94.

[50] 'Remarks on the Dialogues of Kreeshna and Arjoon', *Gentleman's Magazine*, 55, part 2 (December 1785), pp. 955–7: p. 956.

contemplation practised by the Brahmins. Where Hastings refers to 'some of the religious orders of Christians in the Romish Church' to familiarise the idea of meditative contemplation, presumably thinking of Jesuit spiritual exercises,[51] the reviewer instead turns to a heterodox example to explain this 'conceptual abstraction'.[52] The reviewer thus compares the Brahmins to 'modern Behmenists', practitioners of a Christian theosophical devotion after the teachings of Jacob Boehme.[53] Boehme's mystical theology had been important in the seventeenth century, and was taken particularly seriously by the Cambridge Platonists. Their significance waned in the eighteenth century, except for something of a revival around the time of the publication of the *Gěětă*, particularly among the circles associated with German and English romanticism.[54] Although this association with Boehme's theology veered away from Wilkins' view of the Brahmins as believers in rational and natural religion, it perpetuated the association of the *Gēētā* with some kind of Dissenting text from what its composer saw as corrupt practices. Objecting to the inclination of both Hastings and Wilkins to draw parallels with Christianity, however, this reviewer insisted that the doctrine displayed in the pages of the *Gēētā* might be more properly compared to 'Jewish scriptures', given that it contains 'not a word of that provision made by his Grace in the Redemption of the world by Jesus Christ'. That is, it was not cognisant of Christian revelation. Of this truth, the Eastern religions, the reviewer points out, 'had not the faintest glimmering'.[55] In fact, in direct contravention of some Hastings' comments in the preface that the text contained 'a theology accurately corresponding with that of the Christian dispensation', the reviewer countered that it should be those 'who cannot comprehend the excellence of the Christian dispensation' that should be left to 'bewilder themselves on the divisions and subdivisions, the intricacies and the complexities, of Hindoo mysticisms'.[56] The extent to which these theologies were compatible clearly depended on what one considered to be essential to 'Christian dispensation'.

Indeed, in other publications, the religious speculation contained in Wilkins' preface was also received with some derision. On Wilkins'

[51] Hastings, in the *Bhăgvăt-Gēētā*, p. 8.

[52] *Gentleman's Magazine*, 55, part 2 (December 1785), p. 955.

[53] *Gentleman's Magazine*, 55: part 2 (December 1785), p. 955.

[54] See Khristine Hannak, 'Boehme and German Romanticism', and Elisabeth Engell Jessen, 'Boehme and the English Romantics', in Ariel Hessayon and Sarah Apetrei (eds.), *An Introduction to Jacob Boehme: Four Centuries of Thought and Reception* (Abingdon: Routledge, 2014).

[55] Hastings, in *Bhăgvăt-Gēētā*, p. 10.

[56] *Gentleman's Magazine*, 55, part 2 (December 1785), p. 957.

assessment that the *Gēētā* was designed to set up 'the unity of the godhead' a writer for *The Critical Review* remarked that this 'is perhaps "considering the matter too deeply"' and that Wilkins' suppositions had wandered too far into speculative territory. Wilkins' comments were, the reviewer argues, thus akin to 'the fancy of Warburton', who had traced ancient religions to uncover 'the secret which was revealed in the ancient mysteries, the important secret, that there was but one God'.[57] This was a reference to William Warburton's *Divine Legation of Moses* (1738–41), the second book of which had sought to prove that the 'ancient mysteries' of the Greeks and the Egyptians inculcated belief in one God, as opposed to polytheism.[58] The context of this was a complex and paradoxical attempt to refute the accusations of freethinkers that Moses was an impostor by using the same evidence of ancient 'mysteries' to argue that there was no hidden wisdom in these earlier texts.[59] Judging by this reviewer's comparison between Wilkins' excess and Warburton's 'fancy', they were not convinced by the validity of either, seeing instead the text of the *Gēētā* as a 'strange mixture between sense and nonsense'.[60] While scholars may now see Wilkins' translation as an important moment in the development of European Indology, it must be noted that contemporaries in England saw it and its author as intervening in a discourse about Christianity's place in an increasingly wider pool of sophisticated religious systems.

Wilkins and the Afterlives of the *Bhăgvăt-Gēētā*

After the publication of the *Bhăgvăt-Gēētā, or Dialogues of Krĕĕshnă and Ărjŏŏn*, Wilkins continued to enjoy Hastings' active support, but as the political landscape shifted once again, his research occupied a new status in relation to the Company. Wilkins was one of the cluster of Company scholars who set up the Asiatick Society in Calcutta in 1784. After Hastings had declined the presidency, this honour was taken up by William Jones, who had by then begun his own investigations into Sanskrit literature. Jones, who as an officer of the Supreme Court was appointed by the Crown, was sufficiently distanced from Hastings, who would soon face impeachment charges, that he lent the society some detachment from Company politics. Wilkins contributed articles, particularly on ancient

57 'Dialogues of Krĕĕshnă and Arjŏŏn', *Critical Review*, 61 (1786), pp. 1–8: p. 4.

58 William Warburton, *The Divine Legation of Moses Demonstrated, on the Principles of a Religious Deist, from the Omission of the Doctrine of a Future State of Reward and Punishment in the Jewish Dispensation*, 2 vols. (London, 1738, 1741).

59 Robertson, *Case for the Enlightenment*, pp. 280–1.

60 *Critical Review*, 61 (1786), pp. 1–8: p. 4.

Indian epigraphy, to the first two volumes of the society's journal, *Asiatick Researches*, which appeared in 1788 and 1790 respectively. After leaving the Company's service in 1786, he also published a translation of the *Hitopadeśa*, titled *The Hĕĕtōpădēs of Vĕĕshnŏŏ-Sărmā*, in 1787. This 'series of connected fables, interspersed with moral, prudential, and political maxims', catered to a growing market of interest in 'oriental curiosities', and was hailed as such by reviewers.[61] *The English Review* called it a 'curious monument to Asiatic Genius', and it was greeted by *The European Magazine* as a 'considerable acquisition to the stock of European literature'.[62]

Wilkins did not only write about the religion of the *Hindoos*, but also offered a preliminary account of Sikhism, about which very little was known in Europe in this period. Dow had managed a few passing remarks in 1768, but seemed to have confused some of its origin story with Buddhism, describing the 'Seiks' as 'followers of a certain philosopher of Thibet'.[63] Wilkins was writing in a period when British interest in Sikhism intensified, as Sikhs were becoming a real threat to Mughal Imperial possessions.[64] Appearing in the first volume of *Asiatick Researches* (1788), 'Observations on the Seeks and Their College' described his impressions of a Sikh gurdwara in Patna. In this essay, as well as the furnishings of the gurdwara, Wilkins detailed a religious ceremony, informing his readers that the congregation worshipped by reciting a hymn 'in praise of the unity, the omnipresence, and the omnipotence of the Deity'.[65]

While describing Sikh theology as monotheistic is an oversimplification which eschews pantheistic streams of thought, Wilkins was certainly capturing an important focus on the idea of a singular all-pervading divine essence (the difficulty of translating which is a much-expressed point in Sikh studies) in more familiar terms.[66] Whereas Dow summarised the Sikhs as followers of 'the pure doctrine of Deism, without any mixture of the Mahommedan or Hindoo superstitions', Wilkins offered a list of their

[61] Charles Wilkins, *The Hĕĕtōpădēs of Vĕĕshnŏŏ-Sărmā, in a Series of Connected Fables, Interspersed with Moral, Prudential, and Political Maxims* (Bath: R. Cruttwell, 1887).

[62] 'Art VII: The Heetopades', *English Review*, vol. 11 (London: J. Murray, 1788), pp. 114–19: p. 119; *European Magazine, and London Review*, 13 (London, 1788), p. 423.

[63] Dow, *History of Hindostan*, vol. 2 (1768), p. 82.

[64] Ganda Singh (ed.), *Early European Accounts of the Sikhs* (Calcutta: Indian Studies: Past & Present, 1962), pp. 53–69.

[65] Charles Wilkins, 'Article XII, On the Seeks and Their College', *Asiatick Researches; or, Transactions of the Society, Instituted in Bengal, for Inquiring into the History and Antiquities, the Arts, Sciences, and Literature, of Asia*, vol. 1 (London, 1799), p. 290.

[66] See Avind Pal Singh Mandair, 'Sikh Philosophy', in Pashaura Singh and Louis E. Fenech (eds.), *The Oxford Handbook of Sikh Studies* (Oxford: Oxford University Press, 2014).

beliefs. Correctly identifying a single book as the source of their religious teaching, Wilkins explains that 'this book teaches that there is but one God, omnipotent and omnipresent; filling all space and pervading all matter; and that he is to be worshipped and invoked'. It also teaches, he explains, that 'there will be a day of retribution, when virtue will be rewarded and vice punished', adding that he forgot to ask how. Wilkins also impresses readers with their moral doctrine, which 'not only commands universal toleration, but also forbids disputes with those of another persuasion' and calls for 'the practice of all the virtues' and particularly 'universal philanthropy'.[67]

In 1788 Wilkins was elected to the Royal Society in recognition of his achievement in unlocking oriental languages. Later he also published another portion of his work translating the *Mahābhārata*, the story of Shakuntala (Śakuntalā) in 1795, though this was overshadowed by the multiple editions of William Jones' more literary translation that had come in 1789. Jones had translated from Kālidāsa's dramatisation of this story (the Sanskrit original being *Abhijñānaśākuntalam*), and this would have a huge cultural impact, particularly among the German romantics.[68] In the 1800s, Wilkins returned to the employ of the Company. First, in 1800, he was appointed chief librarian of the Company's collections in India House. Then, on the establishment in 1806 of East India College at Hertford Castle (later Haileybury College), he accepted the offices of examiner and visitor, which held until his death in 13 May 1836.[69] In that time, he produced several lexicographical publications, for the purposes of instruction at the college.

Of all these productions, across his career, it was the 1785 *Gēētā* that would have the most lasting impact. Although it was of little practical importance in an immediate sense, Wilkins' *Gēētā* did play an important role in shaping future scholarship and perceptions of a homogenised Hinduism in the decades to come. Many have pointed to the role of Wilkins in the canonisation of the text as a key Hindu scripture.[70] What is most relevant here, though, is that like the other writers considered, Wilkins' work's most immediate impact was on the realm of European understandings of religion.

[67] Wilkins, 'Article XII, On the Seeks and their College', p. 292.

[68] Franklin, *Orientalist Jones*, chapter 7.

[69] For more on Wilkins' career, see Mary Lloyd, 'Sir Charles Wilkins, 1749–1836', in India Office Library (ed.), *India Office Library and Records Report* (London: Foreign and Commonwealth Office, 1978).

[70] Mani Rao, 'A Brief History of the Bhagavad Gita's Modern Canonization', *Religion Compass*, 7:11 (2013).

While scholarship might now be tempted to see Wilkins as ushering in a new 'Oriental Renaissance', contemporaries viewed the translation as very much sitting in the tradition of writers like Holwell, Dow and Halhed. Its impact was very much seen as continuing from and reinforcing the more controversial productions of these earlier authors. This situates Wilkins not only in the world of formal orientalism, but also in the ad hoc framework of eighteenth-century Enlightenment letters, where the emphasis was not simply on the mastery of language and the cataloguing of information, but on the religious implications and disruptions that the discovery of ancient philosophical thought encouraged.

Like the productions of our other authors, the *Gēētā* was also translated into French (1787).[71] In response, one French orientalist explicitly described how Wilkins had built on the work of his predecessors, 'MM. Holwell, Dow, et Halhed', from whom the French had 'received the most valuable part of our knowledge of Hindostan' ('la partie la plus précieuse de nos connaissances sur l'Hindoustan').[72] The work of Wilkins also had a particularly significant impact on what Wilson called the 'Indic ideal' in German romanticism.[73] This intellectual project, articulated by Herder and developed by various romantic artists, looked to India as the possible location of the origin of human culture. Rejecting the Kantian Enlightenment, Herder sided with an aesthetic, synthetic account of cultural reality which could only be understood through historical and anthropological enquiry. As we saw in Chapter 4, Herder's enthusiasm began with Dow's depiction of philosophical monism in Indian philosophy. Then, in his later work Herder translated passages directly from Wilkins' *Gēētā*. In his study of the German reception of the *Bhagavad-Gītā*, Herling has thus suggested that Herder's selective reworking of Wilkins' translations was inherently linked to his Spinozist interpretation of Dow, in response to the German *Pantheismusstreit*. In this 'pantheism controversy', Herder defended Spinoza and, in the process, developed a commitment to philosophical holism, which in turn pervades the pages of his rendition of the *Bhagavad-Gītā*.[74]

Finally, we can understand Wilkins as part of a tradition of transmitting a philosophical interpretation of Indian religious thought, with heterodox implications and consequences, by picturing him as he was described by the prophetic visionary William Blake. Wilkins appeared in an engraving by

[71] Charles Wilkins, *Le Bhaguat-geeta ou Dialogues de Kreeshna et d'Arjoon, contenant un précis de la religion & de la morale des Indiens*, J. P. Parraud (trans.) (Paris: Chez Buisson, 1787).

[72] Louis-Mathieu Langlès, *Fables et contes indiens, nouvellement traduits avec un discours preliminaire et des notes sur la religion, la littérature, les moeurs, etc. des Hindoux* (Paris: Royez, 1790), p. lix.

[73] Wilson, *Mythical Image*, p. vii.

[74] Herling, *German Gita*, p. 104, pp. 73–116.

Blake that was entitled *The Bramins*. Although no copy exists, the engraving was described in an exhibition catalogue as a depiction of Charles Wilkins consulting Brahmins while making the first English translation of the *Bhagavad-Gītā*, which Blake described as 'the Hindoo Scriptures'. Blake, the author of a manifesto outlining the belief that poetic inspiration was the source of all religious philosophy (*All Religions Are One*, 1788), could have been drawn to the *Gēētā* following its alignment in reviews to mystical and Dissenting religion. Blake scholars have suggested that in particular, the antinomian tone struck by Wilkins' rendering of the final discourse of the text will have certainly appealed to Blake's religious and philosophical sensibilities at the time, already cultivated by an interested in Boehme.[75] In the note in the catalogue accompanying the engraving, Blake described having dressed Wilkins in the manner of the Brahmin, thus suggesting his complete absorption into and understanding of the philosophy of his instructors. Blake admitted that his idea of what a Brahmin's clothing looked like was imagined, writing 'I understand that my costume is incorrect'.[76] However, it was the symbolism behind it that was more important. As Blake scholar David Weir suggests, this was a depiction of Blake's own feeling that Wilkins had in some sense 'gone native' in receiving the wisdom of the pandits.[77]

Blake's interest in the philosophical interpretation of Hinduism also alerts us to one final further setting which demonstrates the wider impact of all four of the authors considered so far. Well beyond their immediate context, these authors appear as sources and noted figures in the vast array of nineteenth-century radical pamphlet literature. As mentioned in Chapter 4, Dow's discussion of the *Hindoo* conception of Hell, for example, featured in a work by George Ensor, which examined the psychological foundations of natural religion and moral sense.[78] Moreover, the work of Halhed, Wilkins and Dow appears in the 1843 catalogue for the London Institute, founded in 1806 for Dissenters and which became the forerunner of the University of London.[79] Most striking is their association

[75] See Kathryn S. Freeman, *Blake's Nostos: Fragmentation and Nondualism in The Four Zoas*, (Albany: SUNY, 1997), p. 31; David Weir, *Brahma and the West: William Blake and the Oriental Renaissance* (Albany: SUNY, 2003), p. 21. For Weir's analysis of Blake's interaction with the *Gēētā*, see *Brahma and the West*, pp. 90–104.

[76] The drawing, now lost, is described in 'A descriptive catalogue of Pictures, no.x, exhibited by Blake in 1809', in William Blake, *The Complete Poetry and Prose of William Blake*, David. E. V. Erdman (ed.) (Berkeley: University of California Press, 2008 [1965]), p. 548.

[77] Weir, *Brahma and the West*, p. 21.

[78] Ensor, *Principles of Morality*, pp. 71, 77, 199, 214.

[79] *A Catalogue of the Library of the London Institution, Systematically Classed: Preceded by an Historical and Bibliographical Account of the Establishment*, vol. 3 (London: London Institute Library, 1843).

with nineteenth-century freethought.[80] As mentioned in Chapter 4, the ideas of Holwell and Dow appeared in publications like *The Oracle of Reason*, specifically to offer counterarguments to Christian apologists who used orientalist scholarship to support biblical scripture.[81] In one article in *The Oracle*, the author takes it upon themselves to challenge the argument of apologists like Thomas Maurice that one can dismiss the antiquity of the *Hindoo* scriptures because their account of antiquity 'flatly contradicts that furnished by the great Jehovah himself'. Such an argument was inadequate, because 'The assumption of the Indian or Egyptian priest is just as good, to our thinking, as the assumption of a Christian priest.'[82] This was a position very similar to Halhed's claim that 'we are not justified in grounding the standard and criterion of our examination of the Hindoo religion upon the known and infallible truth of our own', because the representatives of both religions hold steadfastly to the incontrovertible truth of each.[83] The appeal of Wilkins's translation to thinkers like Blake and Herder, though different, can likewise be seen in the context of the complex patchwork of heterodox and Dissenting freethought that proliferated at the turn of the nineteenth century.

Conclusion

The policies of Warren Hastings, and more specifically his patronage, were the conditions that led to the *Gēētā*. Such knowledge was, as Hastings made clear, intended to be 'useful to the state' and the dominion that the Company had obtained by 'the right of conquest'.[84] In the patterns of patronage nominally attached to the justification of practical necessity, however, it is clear that Hastings supported aspects of Indological research that extended beyond the strict confines of immediate political advantage. As the most detailed reader of the preoccupations that animated his networks of patronage has pointed out, Hastings was intellectually invested in promoting the 'Growth and Extension of liberal Knowledge' of and in India, as part of more sustained project of investment by India's new imperial rulers in the culture of the ruled, and vice versa.[85] Within this, Hastings strived to cultivate the image of himself as the custodian of Indian knowledge and its contribution to 'learning and reason' in Europe.[86] Hastings approached this by inserting himself as an enlightened interpreter

[80] See Royle, *Victorian Infidels*. [81] *Oracle of Reason*, p. 7. [82] *Oracle of Reason*, pp. 8, 9.
[83] Halhed, *Code of Gentoo Laws*, pp. xii–xiii. [84] Hastings, in *Bhăgvăt-Gēētā*, p. 12.
[85] Marshall, 'Warren Hastings'. [86] Marshall, 'Making of an Imperial Icon', p. 6.

of Indian culture and philosophy through his commentaries in prefatory material to productions of his sponsorship, such as the *Gēētā*. His praise for Indian theological principles displayed the tolerant attitude to religious difference in India, which he had already determined was fundamental to a functioning and justifiable administration, if the Company were to stand forth as *diwan*. Hastings thus saw a philosophical interpretation of Indian religion as vital to 'the accumulation of knowledge and social cultivation' that he argued were a means of softening the weight of dominion, both at home and abroad. This was why 'useful' knowledge could take the particular shape of a translation of the *Bhagavad-Gītā*, which had no direct or practical connection to the administration of the Company and its territories, but was essential to an appreciation of the 'obligation of benevolence' that was owed to Britain's new subjects, and which Hastings averred he be seen as upholding.[87]

Hastings had constructed around philosophical interpretations of Indian religion, and thus incorporated them into, the ideological architecture required to sustain British dominion in India. This circumstance in itself does not mean, however, that this was a schema to which it was confined. Hastings' appeal to enlightened learning with this material implied as much. In presenting this work the public, Wilkins was concerned with communicating the theological significance of the text. He chose to do this by aligning it with a movement for rational religious reform within the history of *Hindoo* religion, intended to set up 'the doctrine of the unity of the Godhead'. The 'learned *Brahmans*' who follow the dictates of this text are thus likened to 'Unitarians'. At the same time, they are held culpable for the continuation of idolatry, by performing associated ceremonies for the sake of 'their own consequence'. This is, however, to be judged to be a state of affairs not peculiar to the Brahmins, since such indulgence of vulgar superstition was 'the support of the priesthood in many other countries'.[88] The *Bhagavad-Gītā* is thus situated in a universal history of tension between the basic tenets of reasonable religion, and the corrupting embellishments of priestcraft and vulgar belief. Moreover, within the translation itself, Wilkins selected ways of translating verses and ideas that made them intelligible to European audiences familiar with the cadences of debate about rational religious reform in Britain. Thus at times the *Gēētā* featured teaching on the necessity of private judgement

[87] Letter to Nathaniel Smith, Benares, 4 October 1784, in Marshall, *British Discovery of Hinduism*, pp. 186, 189.

[88] Wilkins, *Bhăgvăt-Gēētā*, p. 24.

in matters of religion, and the role of reason in shaping one's faith. European audiences were alert to this presentation, and read the work accordingly, either accepting or rejecting Wilkins' vision according to their alignment within existing debates.

Often considered primarily for its significance as the first Sanskrit-to-English translation of the *Bhagavad-Gītā*, and therefore as leading the way for the Sanskrit researches of Jones, the reassessment of Wilkins' preface in relation to its own context demonstrates how his presentation of Indian religion and the relationship of these insights to the Company were intended as contributions to already established discourses, not ones yet to come. In their commentaries and observations, his and Halhed's philosophical interpretations of *Hindoo* religion were oriented towards the same Enlightenment culture of religious debate that shaped the earlier work of Holwell and Dow. And although the business of legitimising the policies of Hastings was the work to which their ideas were intended to be put, these authors also understood the relevance of Indian religion as part of a larger debate about the significance of comparative religion in the intellectual culture of the eighteenth century, and this was reflected in how they were received.

CHAPTER 7

William Jones, Vedānta and the 'Permanent Settlement'

At the very end of the eighteenth century, the work of William Jones came to dominate British interpretations of *Hinduism*. Much has been written on Jones and his achievements as a linguist, scholar, lawyer and poet, all of which had a significant impact on the intellectual culture of both Europe and India.[1] In particular, his famed 'Third Anniversary Discourse' (1786), which traced Sanskrit's affinity to Greek and Latin to posit the idea that they shared an earlier source, had an enormous impact on linguistic and ethnological theory in the nineteenth century.[2] Beyond this conception of the Indo-European language family, Jones' influence on eighteenth- and nineteenth-century letters was likewise significant. His poetical accounts of Hindu deities and translations of Sanskrit literature appealed to contemporary literary sensibilities, inspiring figures associated with the romantic turn at the dawn of the nineteenth century. In 1812, for example, Percy Bysshe Shelley ordered the complete thirteen volumes of Jones' *Works* (1807), which would, as many scholars have since noted, have a profound impact on his poetry.[3] His work would also become important for German philosophical and literary culture via its enthusiastic reception from Herder and Goethe.[4] And in India, the thought of the Indian reformer Rammohan Roy was sometimes expressed by reference to Jones' ideas about religion.[5] This chapter, however, is less concerned with discovering

[1] The three major biographies of Jones are: Garland Cannon's *Oriental Jones: A Biography of Sir William Jones 1746–1794* (New York: Asia Publishing House, 1964); S. N. Mukherjee, *Sir William Jones: A Study in Eighteenth-Century British Attitudes to India* (Cambridge: Cambridge University Press, 1968); Franklin, *Orientalist Jones*. Cannon also published a much-revised biographical examination of Jones in light of the discovery of more epistolary material: *Life and Mind of Oriental Jones*.

[2] See chapter 2 of Trautmann, *Aryans and British India*.

[3] See Kurt A. Johnson, '"Lisping Tongues" and "Sanscrit Songs": William Jones' Hymns to Hindu Deities', *Translation and Literature*, 20:1 (2011).

[4] V. de Sola Pinto, 'Sir William Jones and English Literature', *Bulletin of the School of Oriental and African Studies*, 11 (1946); on German thinkers, see Franklin, *Orientalist Jones*, pp. 259–64.

[5] Amit Ray, 'Orientalism and Religion in the Romantic Era: Rammonhan Roy's Vedanta(s)', in M. J. Franklin (ed.), *Romantic Representations of British India* (Oxford: Routledge, 2006).

the trajectories of Jones' work and instead takes as its focus the ways in which Jones understood and chose to present Indian religion in relation to his own political and intellectual context. In doing so it will also trace the continuities and breaks with what had come before in the works of Holwell, Dow, Halhed and Wilkins.

Jones has been taken to be the paradigmatic 'orientalist', according to two dominant meanings of the word. In his highly influential thesis on the role of cultural translation in establishing systems of colonial domination, Edward Said cast Jones as one of the first practitioners of this 'orientalism': a process of defining the ontological and epistemological distinction between 'orient' and 'occident' through 'codifying, tabulating and comparing' Indian culture.[6] Following this, scholars influenced by Said's account of the relationship between knowledge and power, captured in the linguistic apparatus of the 'discourse', have analysed this process of comparative definition between East and West as part of an ontological 'othering', which constitutes an imaginative and discursive subjugation.[7] On the other side of the cultural turn, some historians and literary scholars have emphasised cultural exchange and 'encounter' as an important mode of interaction between European and Indian peoples.[8] In this vein, scholarship on Jones has tended to stress his sensitivity as a translator of Indian thought, his empathetic admiration for India's cultural productions and his working relationships with indigenous scholars.[9] This has often been expressed in a terminology that has its origins in a framework set out by David Kopf's influential *British Orientalism and the Bengal Renaissance* (1969), which posited a conflict between 'orientalist' (Jones) and 'Anglicist' (imperialist and missionary) attitudes to India within British imperial ideology from the 1770s to the 1830s.[10] In both cases, though, to only see Jones' work as either a means to the ultimate end of domination or an artefact of sympathetic exchange obscures a thoroughly historicised interpretation of the specific political, intellectual and practical dynamics of British empire in India in this period.[11]

[6] Said, *Orientalism*, p. 77.

[7] The most influential usage of the term 'othering' in postcolonial studies can be located in the work of Gayatri Chakravorty Spivak. For its use in relation to Jones, see chapter 1 in Sharada Sugirtharajah, *Imagining Hinduism: A Postcolonial Perspective* (London: Routledge, 2003).

[8] See Jürgen Osterhammel, *Unfabling the East: The Enlightenment's Encounter with Asia*, Robert Savage (trans.) (Princeton, NJ: Princeton University Press, 2018).

[9] See Franklin, *Orientalist Jones.*

[10] Kopf, *British Orientalism and the Bengal Renaissance.*

[11] For a more nuanced account of the politics of knowledge in the Company in this period, see Ehrlich, 'East India Company'.

This chapter intends to recover an intellectual history of Jones' interpretation of Hinduism by an account of the particular ideas, relationships and political dynamics that informed it. It will also assess some of the ways that his account interacted with and shaped this landscape, continuing the book's focus on mapping the intellectual and ideological terrains in which British interpretations of Hinduism took place in the eighteenth century.

Where other studies have considered Jones' intellectual biography, it has been to stress the ambiguities, discontinuities and conflicts within his thought. Foremost in such an account is the apparent tension between his early sympathies for radical political ideas and his career interpreting Indian religion and law for the purposes of colonial administration. During the 1770s and early 1780s, Jones already had the reputation of a scholar for his translations of Persian literature and language. He was also a member of Samuel Johnson's Literary Club and a fellow at the Royal Society. Later in India, of course, he would become most well known as a great Sanskrit scholar and president of the Bengal Asiatick Society. And yet, less congruous with his later reputation was Jones' early notoriety as a political radical. Designated the 'second Wilkes' by the *Gentlemen's Magazine*, Jones had privately printed a speech, intended to be delivered in support of Wilkes in the 1780 Middlesex election, which had criticised parliament for its handling of the American war, its intransigence on the abolition of the slave trade and its mishandling of the East India Company.[12] Moreover the printer of Jones's pamphlet *The Principles of Government, in a Dialogue between a Gentleman and a Farmer* (1783) would be tried for seditious libel. This Socratic exchange, in which the farmer is educated on just and rational constitutional principles, promoted popular education and parliamentary reform.[13]

It is possible that this reputation was the reason that the Lord Chancellor, Edward Thurlow, delayed Jones' appointment to the judgeship in Calcutta by some six years. Indeed, once his appointment was

[12] William Jones, 'A Speech on the Nomination of Candidates to Represent the County of Middlesex, in September 1780'. This was reprinted in the second edition of William Jones, *An Inquiry into the Legal Mode of Suppressing Riots* (London: C. Dilly, 1782), pp. 43–60.

[13] This had originally been *The Principles of Government, in a Dialogue between a Scholar and a Peasant* (1782), and published as a free pamphlet by Major John Cartwright, and then was reprinted by William Shipley, dean of St Asaph at Wrexham (who would become Jones' brother-in-law), in January 1783, replacing the words 'scholar' and 'peasant' with 'gentleman' and 'farmer'. The high sheriff of Flintshire, Thomas Fitzmaurice, promptly prosecuted Shipley. See M. J. Franklin, 'Jones, Sir William (1746–1794), Orientalist and Judge', *Oxford Dictionary of National Biography* (Oxford: Oxford University Press, 2004); online ed., September 2004 [www.oxforddnb.com/view/article/15105, accessed 30 March 2021].

confirmed in 1783, through the intervention of Shelburne upon his departure as prime minister, others were quick to point out the potential conflict between Jones' political sentiments and his newly acquired responsibilities.[14] In 1784, the dean of Gloucester, Josiah Tucker, published a response to Jones' *The Principles of Government* with a mock sequel titled *Dialogue between a Freeholder of the County of Denbigh, and the Dean of Gloucester* (1784). In it, Tucker asked of Jones:

> I wish to know, whether he himself allows the consequences of his own doctrine, when put into practice against his own interest? Doth he or doth he not permit the poor enslaved Gentoos and plundered Indians to dispute his authority, and disobey his commands, by telling him to his face that they never chose him to be the judge of their country?[15]

In his own letters Jones also pondered this tension, insisting in 1782 on a necessary distinction between his 'speculative' thoughts on politics and his 'seat on the bench in India'.[16] That he considered the reformist principles he supported in Britain totally inapplicable in India was made clear by Jones when, reflecting on the possibility that his political reputation was proving a barrier to his appointment, he quipped in a letter to Edward Gibbon, 'I should hardly think of instructing the Gentoos in the maxims of the Athenians'.[17] Indeed, when in India, Jones increasingly treated the political issues that had earlier riled him as contingent on context. As Franklin has pointed out, his absolute condemnation of slavery slipped when in 1785 he defended the 1772 Supreme Council's justification of Indian slavery as radically different from the American model.[18] Like many others, he approached matters in the East with a relativism underpinned by the idea that despotism was the natural state of affairs in India. Thus Jones responded to Edmund Burke's queries on the best style of governance for Bengal with the recommendation that any British administration in India should have as its basis the Mughal constitution, since, as he explained to his correspondent, to force 'a system of *liberty*' on those 'invincibly attached to opposite *habits*' would in fact be 'a system of cruel *tyranny*' itself.[19]

14 Cannon, *Life and Mind of Oriental Jones*, p. 191.

15 Josiah Tucker, *A Sequel to Sir William Jones's Pamphlet on the Principles of Government, in a Dialogue between a Freeholder of the Country of Denbigh, and the Dean of Gloucester* (London: Cadell, 1784). This quotation comes from Mukherjee, *Sir William Jones*, p. 72.

16 Jones to Edward Gibbon, 30 June 1782, in Cannon, *Letters of Sir William Jones*, vol. 2, pp. 480–2. Hereafter *Letters*.

17 Jones to Edward Gibbon, 30 June 1782, in *Letters*, vol. 2, p. 482.

18 Franklin, *Orientalist Jones*, pp. 294–7.

19 Jones to Edmund Burke, Calcutta, 13 April 1784, in *Letters*, vol. 2, pp. 643–4.

The tendency of some scholars to emphasise the culturally sensitive attitudes expressed by Jones thus often sidesteps the political conditions in which his work was conceived, positing these expressions of admiration in contrast to, or even as ameliorating, the networks of Company power and patronage within which he operated.[20] These conditions did not mean that Jones' attraction to Indian culture was insincere, but then neither was his investment in the Company and its interests. Indeed, much of his oriental work was a product of the demands of those interests, such as the need, as he saw it, to produce a digest of Hindu laws that would lessen the monopoly of Hindu pandits over the knowledge required to administer it in the Company's courts.

For Jones, it would not have been contradictory to hold a sincere intellectual appreciation for Hindu religion, as well as to pursue the administrative efficacy of the Supreme Court of Calcutta, which at this time many ministers considered to be the main safeguard against Company abuses.[21] While we can criticise the simultaneous celebration of Indian culture and subjugation of Indian peoples as inconsistent, they were not irreconcilable for Jones or his colleagues. Even those contemporaries who have been singled out as eighteenth-century critics of empire, such as Edmund Burke, saw it as Britain's duty to improve the condition of its dependents, albeit acquired by conquest, by what was claimed to be enlightened practice and principle.[22] In fact, as we shall see, much of Jones' account of Indian religion, mirroring the narratives of purity and decline in the work of his predecessors, was designed to illustrate its fitting candidacy for protection under 'the toleration and equity of the BRITISH government', described in his poem 'A Hymn to Ganga' (1785).

Nevertheless, Company politics need did not determine the absolute limits of Jones' intellectual engagement with Hindu ideas, nor the uses to which his thought would be put. Like Halhed, whose construction of Indian religion was also produced as the result of an administrative venture, Jones' interpretation and construction of Hindu thought was

[20] For a more recent example, see chapter 2 in Andrew Rudd, *Sympathy and India in British Literature, 1770–1830* (Basingstoke: Palgrave Macmillan, 2011).

[21] On the politics of the Supreme Court, see chapter 5 in Robert Travers, *Ideology and Empire.*

[22] William Burke and Edmund Burke, *Policy of Making Conquests for the Mahometans* (1779), in P. J. Marshall and William B. Todd (eds.), *Writings and Speeches of Edmund Burke*, vol. 5 (Oxford: Oxford University Press, 1970), p. 114. For a discussion of this, see Bourke, *Empire and Revolution*, p. 537.

not entirely circumscribed by the parameters of political and commercial demands. Indeed, scholarship that talks of Jones as the architect of an 'orientalist project' suggests more strategic coherence on his part than the varied productions of poetry, unfinished legal codes and addresses to the Asiatick Society could confirm. Thus, as well as offering an account of the intellectual character of Jones' interpretation of Hindu religion, this chapter is also concerned with the place of that account in the wider history of philosophically and theologically oriented British interpretations of an ancient Indian religion in the eighteenth century that this book has made the case for.

The casting of Jones as the typical 'orientalist' has often meant the dismissal of earlier authors as failed attempts to produce work of the scholarly quality attained at the formation of the Asiatick Society. And yet, Jones and his audience were familiar with the ideas and arguments of these forerunners, which had established the authority of text, translation and chronology well before Jones. Nevertheless, while it is important to see Jones in relation to this tradition of scholarship, by the turn of the century the relationship between British accounts of Indian religion and Company policy had undergone some significant changes. Some of these were affected by the particular thought and approach of Jones. There is no doubt that in common with his predecessors, though, Jones saw the tradition of Sanskrit literature as philosophically sophisticated and theologically refined.

That Jones' view of Indian history, culture and religion was admirable, on the one hand, and yet consistent with British dominion on the other, was also underwritten by the same paradigm of purity and decline that structured the work of earlier writers like Holwell and Dow. Unlike Howell and Dow, however, this did not posit an implicit comparison with Christianity on an equal footing. As this chapter will argue, Jones' religious perspective was still heterodox, but in character more closely aligned with the Rational Dissent of fellow Royal Society member Richard Price. Jones was, therefore, much more invested in an account of Indian religion that was less antagonistic to scripture and biblical history than his antecedents. When Jones set *Hindoo* religion in a comparative framework, it was with other pagan religions. Part of what was particular about the view of Indian religion that this resulted in, this chapter will demonstrate, was Jones' preference for characterising the Indian theology as pious and sublime, rather than essentially rational. As he put it in a comparative essay on Indian and European ancient pagan religions, 'neither the Asiatick nor European system has any simplicity in it; and both are so complex, not to say absurd, however intermixed with the beautiful and the sublime'.[23]

Another major factor in the differences between the contents and reception of the work of Jones and the earlier examples of Holwell and Dow was, however, wider changes in both Britain and India regarding the politics and policies of the East India Company. The Company's political status underwent some significant shifts during Jones' ten years in India. From his arrival in 1783 to the end of the century, the terms of governance shifted from conciliation according to the pressures of preserving customs and Company interests, to a more assertive style of imperial rule and administration, tied up within which was the codification of Hindu law and plans for the College of Fort William. This chapter will, therefore, discuss Jones' account of Indian religion both in light of what came before and its situation within the changing administration of empire.

Rational Dissent and Mosaic Chronology

In his philosophical essay 'India and Europe', Halbfass separates Jones only slightly from the works of Holwell and Dow, declaring him not a deist but nevertheless someone who 'came close to deistic thinking'.[24] Others have used the term 'deist' more liberally to describe his general religious outlook.[25] Indeed, on the surface, 'deist' seems to be a useful designation of Jones' religious thought, in a broad and moderate sense. He appears to have adopted a public position of latitude on matters of religion, and despite his close alignment with Dissenting thinkers, such as fellow members of the so-called 'Club of Honest Whigs', he also managed good relations with his passionately evangelical colleagues, like John Shore.[26] Likewise, he appeared to consider his Christianity entirely consistent with an admiration for elements of Hindu and Muslim religiosity alike.

Scholarship has offered various descriptions of how Jones' religious outlook related to the motivations underlying his writing about Indian languages, philosophy and religious traditions. Most influential has been Thomas Trautmann's account of the 'ethnological' character of Jones' work, attaching his famous arguments about linguistic origins to a project to trace the descent of Noah through the recovery of the lost language of the post-diluvian period. In doing so, he has drawn our

[23] Shore, *Works of Sir William Jones*, vol. 1, pp. 272–3. Hereafter *Works.*

[24] Halbfass, *India and Europe*, pp. 56, 63. [25] Franklin, *Orientalist Jones*, p. 47.

[26] Indeed, Franklin presents Jones as engaged in strategically diplomatic relations in his dealings with Shore, particularly on the topic of religion. See Franklin, *Orientalist Jones*, pp. 219–20.

attention to Jones' interest in projects of Isaac Newton and Jacob Bryant, both of which were aimed at reconstructing the early history of mankind along lines that reconciled secular and mythical history.[27] To this Urs App has offered a different perspective, arguing that through similar methodologies and sources Jones was actually primarily in search of a *prisca theologia*, that is, 'mankind's primeval religion before Noah'. App stresses the significance not just of Bryant and Newton, but also Chevalier Andrew Ramsay's hunt for an original monotheism in *Voyages de Cyrus* (1728) as well as, more significantly, the influence of Sufi mysticism through Persianate sources such as translations of the *Upanishads* and the texts associated with the crown prince Dara Shikoh (Dārā Shukoh, 1615–59), the eldest son of the Mughal emperor Shah Jahan.[28] In conclusion, though, App still describes Jones as a deist.[29]

Contrary to this existing scholarship, the claim of this chapter is that rather than deism, Jones' religious thought ought to be framed particularly through his connections to Richard Price and the theology that centred around his ministry at Newington Green. Furthermore, while Trautmann's and App's works have been invaluable in accounting for the intellectual worlds that coloured Jones' scholarship, we ought to be more cautious of packaging this into a coherent and singularly focused 'project'.[30] Instead, the argument here is that we can understand the perspective that Jones brought to bear on these texts and ideas as being shaped more generally by his affinity with the theology of Rational Dissent.

Jones' connections to Richard Price were personal and intellectual. That Jones had an intimacy with Price's theology is suggested by the correspondence between Jones, Benjamin Franklin and Price, who, along with Joseph Priestley, were all members of the 'Club of Honest Whigs'. A letter from Franklin to Price, for example, indicates that Jones had discussed with Price and was aware of his thought beyond his published works. Writing to Price, Franklin noted that, 'I wish also to see the Piece you have written as Mr Jones tells me, on Toleration.' To this Price replied that although he had written a great deal on toleration he had not yet published on the subject.[31] In his letters, Jones mentions reading and agreeing with

[27] See chapter 2 in Trautmann, *Aryans and British India*.

[28] Urs App, 'William Jones's Ancient Theology', *Sino-Platonic Papers*, 191 (July, 2009), p. 9.

[29] App, 'William Jones's Ancient Theology', p. 76.

[30] In this I share the more circumspect position of Colin Kidd in *The World of Mr Casaubon: Britain's Wars of Mythography, 1700–1870* (Cambridge: Cambridge University Press, 2016), p. 120.

[31] Barbara B. Oberg (ed.), *The Papers of Benjamin Franklin*, vol. 33: *July 1 through November 15, 1780* (New Haven, CT: Yale University Press, 1997), pp. 389–90.

the works of his friend, or as Jones referred to him in a letter, 'good old Price'. Writing to George John Spencer (the Second Earl Spencer, styled Viscount Althorp from 1765 to 1783), whom he had tutored as a boy, Jones stated his approval of Price's recently published *Sermons on the Christian Doctrine* (1787).[32] These disquisitions contained the particulars of Price's Dissenting theology, by reference to biblical scripture. That is, he set forth an argument for his Unitarian Dissent by arguing that it was based on a more accurate and sturdy interpretation of scripture than those touted by Anglicanism, Catholicism and a different school of anti-Trinitarianism, Socinianism.[33]

This is an important distinction in our understanding of eighteenth-century Dissenting and heterodox religion, the implications of which for the case of Jones have been overlooked. As Louise Hickman has carefully demonstrated, simplified links between deism, itself a contested concept, and Rational Dissent are misleading. In particular, the latter had a deep commitment to biblical scripture and revelation in a way that disrupted the insistence on the division between received knowledge and reason that has been associated with English deism.[34] This, as we shall see, was an approach to Christianity that permeated Jones' thought, and in particular his account of Hindu philosophy and chronology.

In the first instance, Jones was no supporter of the Anglican establishment. In the same letter featuring his commendation of Price, Jones also approved of the idea that the established Church had become a barrier to reform, maintaining itself as a career path for the sons of the gentry. If the veracity of Price's sermons were more widely recognised, he suggested, 'the *Church of England*, as it is called, would inevitably fall, and *the Religion of the Gospel* be substituted in its place'. Such matters were of course, he shrewdly observed, not solely an issue of religious truth. Rational religion, after the manner urged by Price, would only be realised if 'it were not in the interest of so many thousands to profess belief in riddles for the sake of rectories, prebends, and lawn-sleeves'.[35]

His objections to Anglicanism were not, however, reserved to matters of practical episcopal reform. Jones' letters also suggest that his personal beliefs included a denial of the orthodox doctrine of trinity, in a manner consistent with Price's particular Unitarian theology. As well as citing his

[32] Letter 464 to the Second Earl Spencer, Chrisna-nagra, 4–30 August 1787, in *Letters*, vol. 2, p. 758.

[33] Richard Price, *Sermons on the Christian Doctrine, as Received by the Different Dominations of Christians* (London: Printed for T. Cadell, 1787).

[34] Hickman, *Eighteenth-Century Dissent*, pp. 19–20.

[35] Letter 464, to the Second Earl Spencer, Chrisna-nagra, 4–30 August, 1787, in *Letters*, vol. 2, p. 758.

approval of the *Sermons*, Jones also expressed a distaste for the tendency within orientalist scholarship to compare the triumvirate of Hindu deities (Brahma, Vishnu and Shiva) with the Christian trinity. Writing to another member of the Asiatick Society, for example, Jones expressed his exasperation with a work that had been submitted on Hindu astronomy. Evidently it had made some unsubstantiated speculations about the commonalities between Hindu and Christian theology by pointing to the trinity in each, prompting Jones to wish that the author would 'omit his Theology' from future work. Indeed, Jones continued, '[m]any pious Christians deny, that the doctrine of the Trinity is to be found in the Gospel'.[36] This was a point he would repeat in his published work too, dismissing what he saw as the 'absurd' idea, often presented by missionaries, that 'the Hindus were even now almost Christians, because their BRAHMÁ, VISHNU, and MAHÉSA [Shiva], were no other than the Christian Trinity'. For Jones, the temptation to draw such parallels not only represented a misreading of the Hindu religion, but also an incomplete picture of Christianity. While some 'pious *Christians*' had indeed deduced the doctrine of the trinity from the Gospel, others who were equally 'as pious' also 'openly profess their dissent from them'. In this division, writing for publication, Jones concluded, '[e]ach sect must be justified by its own faith and good intentions'.[37] In his private letters, however, his unequivocal endorsement of Price, and his insistence on this distinction, suggests that he considered himself one such 'pious' denier of the trinity.

Indeed, more specifically, Jones' anti-Trinitarian beliefs appear to match the Arianism of Price, rather than Socinianism or deism. There was a distinction in the theologies of Price and Joseph Priestley, Unitarianism's other most well-known proponent. Priestley would come to settle on a Socinian understanding of the relationship between God and Christ. Denying anything inconsistent with the dictates of human reason, he came to the view that the Christ of the Gospel was a mortal in receipt of God's grace and thus a profound moral exemplar rather than divine saviour. Price, on the other hand, rejected this position as strenuously as he rejected Trinitarianism.[38] Price viewed the subjection of revelation to

[36] Thought to be written to Thomas Dean Pearse, Letter 460, 17 June 1787, in *Letters*, vol. 2, p. 738. The work Jones was commenting on was written by Reuben Burrow, a mathematician and society member.

[37] Jones' essay 'On the Gods of Greece, Italy, and India', written in 1784 but revised before publication in the first volume of *Asiatick Researches* in 1788: *Works*, vol. 1, pp. 277–8.

[38] For a detailed account of their positions and their mutual basis in scriptural interpretation, see Hickman, *Eighteenth-Century Dissent*, pp. 24–9; quote is from pp. 27–8.

the tests of reason according to the Socinian method a misguided approach, maintaining that revelation remained true in and of itself. It was the role of reason to ascertain the teachings contained in the scriptures, rather than their veracity. Trinitarians, however, had gone beyond scripture and devised doctrines that did not align with the Gospel. Based on a close reading of the Bible, inspired by Samuel Clarke's own writings on the same topic, Price committed himself to a Christology which confirmed (contra the Socinians) the pre-existence of Christ and his subordinate divinity or 'peculiar dignity' as 'more than any human being', but lesser than God. Price also affirmed Christ's particular role as saviour through crucifixion.[39] We know that Jones approved of this approach from his remarks that he found himself 'confirmed in the opinions' which he had 'long formed from reading the Scripture' when reading Price's published sermons, one of the central enquiries in which was the nature of Christ as saviour.[40] Indeed, Jones wrote to Price to confirm the same.[41]

In his public works, however, Jones did not adopt a vigorous position of Dissent, but instead expressed the sentiments of latitude often associated with liberal Anglicanism in the period. In his letter confirming that Price's theology agreed most closely with his own opinions, Jones also emphasised that such differences should not be the source of serious division. Indeed, this was much the same position that Price adopted himself throughout the sermons, which urged that his congregation 'embrace with affection our fellow-christians of all persuasions, making allowances for their mistakes and prejudices'.[42] Indeed, Jones' own satisfaction in reading the sermons is presented as more of an intellectual commitment than a practical devotion to the cause of Dissenting religion. Reading Price was rewarding, he recounted, because 'there is something so pleasing in Truth, that it becomes interesting from its own charms independently from any advantage, that may be derived from it'. Such discussions were ultimately less important, Jones stressed, than the principle that 'all, who believe the *essentials* of religion and act according to the principles of virtue, must be happy'.[43] Happiness here has religious connotations. Reflecting the language of eighteenth-century Christian Platonism present in the work of

[39] Price, *Sermons on the Christian Doctrine*, pp. 84–6, 103, 108; Price, *Thoughts on the Progress of Socinianism; with an Enquiry into the Cause and the Cure* (London: J. Buckland and J. Johnson, 1787).

[40] Letter 464, to the Second Earl Spencer, Chrisna-nagar, 4–30 August, 1787, in *Letters*, vol. 2, p. 758.

[41] Letter 500, Chrishna-nagar, 26 September 1788, in *Letters*, vol. 2, p. 819.

[42] Price, *Sermons on the Christian Doctrine*, p. 26.

[43] Letter 463, 27 August 1787, in *Letters*, vol. 2, p. 758.

Price, it conveys a teleological conception of the soul's journey towards the eternal bliss of salvation.[44] What the essentials that one needed to believe were in order to achieve this were not specifically enumerated by Jones, though we can infer they were the minimal tenets common to all Christians, foremost of which was veneration of God, or as Price's sermons put it, 'the one Supreme Deity'.[45] Thus, while Jones held anti-Trinitarian beliefs, he did not consider open and oppositional Dissent to be a practical cause. This was a not uncommon stance by the late eighteenth century among liberal Anglicans sympathetic with various Dissenting opinions, but for whom a break with the Church was not practicable or necessary.[46]

That said, there were limits to his generosity towards other Christians. Jones evidently disliked the evangelist aspirations of Christian missions operating in India. Appearing right after his ameliorating remarks that it was only 'the *essentials* of religion' that mattered, Jones added that missionary activity was the 'one evil in the *corruptions* of our pure and rational religion, which, in this country [India], I often have occasion to deplore'.[47] The problem was not specifically missionary activity itself, which the Company actively discouraged by denying missionary societies licenses to settle in Bengal for practical and political reasons (see Chapter 1).[48] Rather, Jones' irritation was directed at the insistence of the '*Romanists*' and the '*Trinitarians*' in teaching 'their creeds as the religion of the Messiah', or in the words of Price, 'their mistakes and prejudices'.[49] By Trinitarians, we can suppose Jones was referring not only to the efforts of the Society for the Promotion of Christian Knowledge, whose sphere of activity was greatly restricted, but more generally to those of an evangelical bent who were campaigning for the Company's assent to a British Indian mission.[50]

This private complaint highlighted the stark difference between Jones and his friendly acquaintance Charles Grant, who in the years between hosting Jones at his home at Malda and this letter's composition, had been campaigning for a mission in Bengal.[51] Yet the offence was not only caused by missionary zeal, but more specifically by the propagation of

44 Müller, *Latitudinarianism and Didacticism*, pp. 182, 284.
45 Price, *Sermons on the Christian Doctrine*, p. 97.
46 Knud Haakonssen, *Enlightenment and Religion: Rational Dissent in Eighteenth-Century Britain* (Cambridge: Cambridge University Press, 1996), p. 21.
47 Letter 463, 27 August 1787, in *Letters*, vol. 2, p. 758.
48 See also Carson, *East India Company and Religion, 1698–1858*, p. 23.
49 Letter 463, 27 August 1787, in *Letters*, vol. 2, p. 758.
50 Carson, *East India Company and Religion*, pp. 12–16.
51 On Jones and Grant, see Franklin, *Orientalist Jones*, pp. 217–19; on Grant's plans, see Carson, *East India Company and Religion*, p. 30.

misinformation about the truths of the Christian Gospel, or as he put it, 'the religion of the Messiah'. In stark contrast, Jones continued, if 'Price's book be accurately translated into Persian, [Muslims] would not be shocked by the Christian doctrine' and indeed 'possibly convinced'.[52] This corresponded with his view of Muslims as 'a sort of heterodox *Christians*', which he had expressed in one of his earliest addresses to the Asiatick Society, 'On the Gods of Greece, Italy and India' (1784), citing Locke. This was a reference to Locke's *The Reasonableness of Christianity* (1695), which had relayed that Muslims believe in the 'divine character' of the Messiah, while also denying his 'equality, as God, with the Father'.[53] In this work Jones gives no hint as to his approval of this position, but his letter reflecting that Price's sermons might inspire conversion from Islam to Rational Dissenting Christianity reveals as much. The Hindus, on the other hand, he continued in the letter, 'would have less difficulty in admitting the Thirty Nine Articles, because if those articles were written in Sanscrit, they might pass well enough for a composition of a Brahman'. This was a rhetorical injunction against established Anglicanism by way of comparison between its list of central articles, and therefore the obstacles placed before Unitarians in the form of the Test Acts, and Brahmin priestcraft.[54] The comparison did no favours for the Hindu religion, but its ironic target was of course the Church.

Indeed, like Holwell and Dow, Jones' comments regarding the inherent reasonableness of certain Indian precepts were often as a counterfoil to what he judged to be lacking in contemporary Christianity. On the matter of transmigration, for example, Jones agreed that it provided a more satisfactory account of punishment for sin. While for Holwell this extended to the conviction that metempsychosis was a lost and original truth, Jones did not go so far. In his letter to George John Spencer, Jones stated, 'I am no Hindu; but I hold the doctrine of Hindus concerning a future state to be incomparably more rational, more pious, and more likely to deter men from vice, than the horrid opinions inculcated by Christians on punishments without end.'[55] Yet again, this was less to do with Hindu theology, and more a comment on the excesses of Christian conceptions of hell.

Price had likewise forcefully rejected the doctrine of original sin and Calvinist conceptions of 'the elect', again on the basis that they were not

[52] *Letters*, vol. 2, p. 758. [53] *Works*, vol. 1, p. 279.

[54] The 1779 Dissenters' Relief Act had freed ministers from the need to subscribe to the Thirty-Nine Articles of the Church of England as required by the Toleration Act, but most major reforms on the subject of religious toleration would have to wait until the nineteenth century.

[55] Letter 467, Krishnagar, 4 September 1787, in *Letters*, vol. 2, p. 766.

supported by scripture.[56] While Price acknowledged the presence of references to eternal punishment in the Bible, he stressed that they ought not to be taken as 'strictly literal', proceeding to outline a division between eternal death and eternal life that emphasised the benevolence of God, and human perfectibility towards the latter.[57] Indeed, Rational Dissent more generally posited a benign God who offered the hope of eternal joy in salvation, rather than the threat of torment in hell. Thus, in another letter Jones reports, 'We have just been reading an excellent discourse by that excellent man, Price. On the subject of future punishment he expresses himself inclined to think that it will be *temporary*, that is for a for *a length of time proportioned to the offence*.' Jones agrees that 'the contrary opinion is so horribly blasphemous, and so outrageous to the divine justice that I would give up Scripture rather than embrace it'. From such a conclusion he was, however, spared, as 'happily the language of Scripture confirms the former opinion beyond a doubt'. On this matter, the line between Jones remaining contentedly a Christian and becoming 'an apostle of infidelity' out of horror at God's injustice evidently rested on his agreement with Price's assessment of the Bible.[58]

Jones' early beliefs seem to have also centred around the idea of reconciling the nature of Christ and biblical scripture with reason. His notes while at Oxford reveal that this came to the forefront of his thinking while he was studying the Bible in Hebrew. In these he laboured to set out a series of logical propositions on which to base Christian belief. Proposition 1 begins by affirming the antiquity of the prophecies of Isaiah. Proposition 2 continues that these ancient prophecies foretold the coming of a Messiah. Proposition 3 adds that 'the life and death of Jesus, his virtues and doctrines, though not his miracles, are as much to be believed, as the life and death of Socrates, his virtues and his doctrine'. In other words, so far these were historical truths. Proposition 4 thus moves to synthesise these into the conclusion that 'Jesus was the subject of their writings, which are consequently inspired, and he a person of an extraordinary nature, that is, the Messiah.' The historical fact of Jesus' existence thus confirmed the authenticity of the prophecies of Isiah. From this, Jones continued, '[i]f this be just reasoning, we may believe his miracles, and must obey his law'.[59]

[56] Hickman, *Eighteenth-Century Dissent*, p. 28.

[57] Richard Price, *The Works of Dr. Richard Price, with Memoirs of His Life by W. Morgan*, vol. 10 (London: Richard Rees, 1816), p. 247.

[58] Letter 467, Krishnagar, 2 September 1787, in *Letters*, vol. 2, p. 764.

[59] John Shore, Baron Teignmouth, *Memoirs of the Life, Writings and Correspondence of Sir William Jones*, 2 ed., vol. 1 (London: John Hatchard, 1806), pp. 65–6.

While it is possible that this was exclusive to his thought at the time, the importance of the prophecies of Isaiah remain a consistent feature of Jones' reflections on religion. In 'On the Gods of Greece, Italy and India', for example, Jones repeated the conclusion of these early propositions by claiming that his own faith in the Messiah was founded on the 'undisputed antiquity and manifest completion of many prophecies, especially those of ISAIAH, in the only person recorded by history, to whom they are applicable.'[60] Moreover, although Jones disapproved of Trinitarian missionary efforts in India, the importance of the prophecies of Isaiah for validating the Christian faith is made clear when, in several places, he argues that the best prospect for spreading the religion would be through the translation of the book of Isaiah 'together with one of the Gospels, and a plain prefatory discourse containing full evidence of the very distant ages, in which the predictions themselves, and the history of the divine person predicted'.[61] Again, the proof lies in the convergence of prophecy and historical record. Likewise, in the 1787 letter to Spencer, Jones reflected that if he were 'to undertake a mission among them [the Hindus], I should begin by proving the antiquity of Isaiah, and showing the conformity of his prophecy with the life and death of Jesus, and of no other man recorded by History'.[62] This appears, therefore, to be the basis of Jones' own faith, the implications of which he appeared to think conformed with the theology of Price.

Jones did express a broad toleration for religion in general, and in particular voiced his admiration of pious expressions of devotion to the deity. On these counts the sublimity of Vedānta, and particularly Advaita Vedānta, fared well. Moreover, in contrast to Holwell and Dow, Jones somewhat eschewed a strict division between the learned and the vulgar versions of Indian belief, expressing approbation for popular religious devotion in India as well as its ancient textual culture. As Franklin has argued in numerous places, he was particularly inspired by the tradition of *bhakti*, and was fascinated by Vaishnavism (devotion to Vishnu, especially in his eighth avatar as Krishna), exploring its ideas and imagery throughout his poetry.[63] And yet, Jones also remained committed to the particular authority of the Bible. In fact, many of Jones' productions for the Asiatick

60 *Works*, vol. 1, p. 233. 61 *Works*, vol, 1, p. 280–1.

62 Letter 463, 27 August 1787, in *Letters*, vol. 2, p. 758.

63 See Franklin, *Orientalist Jones*, pp. 272–3; Franklin, 'Accessing India: Orientalism, Anti-"Indianism", and the Rhetoric of Jones and Burke', in Tim Fulford and Peter Kitson (eds.), *Romanticism and Colonialism* (Cambridge: Cambridge University Press, 1998); Franklin, 'Cultural Possession'.

Society were devoted to the defence of Christianity and the particular authority of its scriptures, especially in relation to *Hindoo* chronology.

A cornerstone of this endeavour became the search for the universal Flood of biblical history. Thus in 'On the Gods', Jones called on the *Bhāgavata Purāṇa*.[64] From this he pulls out a passage in which Manu is warned and saved from an impending deluge by Lord Vishnu, and uses this to fit the Sanskrit text into a biblical framework. In the story, Manu and seven sages board a boat, led by Vishnu in his fish incarnation (*kūrma avatāra*), and when the flood subsides, a new creation begins. This story, he declared, was evidently 'that of NOAH disguised by Asiatick fiction'. Consequently, rather than the dates given by the Brahmins, this text should be considered the 'epitome of the first Indian History', since it placed its setting, the first of the four *yugas* that make up the Hindu cycle of history (the *Satya Yuga*), within the diluvian age. Or as Jones put it, it confirmed the 'universal deluge described by MOSES', and therefore fixed 'consequently the time, when the genuine Hindu Chronology actually begins' to a point consistent with Genesis.[65]

In the same essay, Jones concluded that the similarities between the four Hindu *yugas* and 'the Grecian and Roman ages' indicated that 'the true History of the World seems obviously divisible into four ages or periods' – the antediluvian age and three post-diluvian ages – which included 'the mad introduction of idolatry at Babel', the rise of the patriarchs, the Mosaic age, and finally what Jones called 'the Prophetical age', which subsists 'until all genuine prophecies shall be fully accomplished'.[66] This conception of the final age also bears an affinity with Richard Price's account, which reasoned that since the fulfilment of past prophecies had come to pass, specifically those foretelling the coming of the Messiah, there were no grounds on which to question the validity of others, and that therefore it was correct to forecast the millennium some time in present history.[67]

Much of this account of *Hindoo* time seems to be directed at the controversy inspired in particular by Halhed's calculations in the preface

[64] This could be via a Persian translation, as in 1784 Jones could not read Sanskrit, and indeed, in a letter he wrote of being 'inexpressibly amused by a Persian translation of an old Sanscrit book, called Siry Bhāgwat [*Śrīmad Bhāgavatam* being another name for the *Bhāgavata Purāṇa*], which comprises almost the whole of the Hindu religion': Letter 390, to John Hyde, 14 May 1784, in *Letters*, vol. 2, p. 649. However, the text was much revised before its publication in 1788, so he could have been working from Sanskrit at this point.

[65] *Works*, vol. 1, pp. 237–42. [66] *Works*, vol. 1, pp. 243–4.

[67] See Jack Fruchtman, *The Apocalyptic Politics of Richard Price and Joseph Priestley: A Study in Late Eighteenth-Century English Republican Millennialism* (Philadelphia: The American Philosophical Society, 1983), pp. 34–6.

to *A Code of Gentoo Laws* (1776). Halhed's defence of *Hindoo* chronology, which suggested 'Mosaic Creation is but as yesterday', highlighted the absence of any mention of the Flood from the texts that Brahmins dated to a time before the Deluge, and, the consistency of this chronology across various *Hindoo* texts and schools of thought.[68] It was this argument that had provoked a response from George Costard, who countered that the *Gentoo* chronology was '*fictitious* and *absurd*'.[69] This was also sat against a general backdrop of intellectual debate regarding various challenges to biblical history, such as the geological age of the earth.[70] In 'On the Gods', Jones noted the importance of orientalist research in shaping this debate, noting how such work 'may even be of solid importance in an age, when some intelligent and virtuous persons are inclined to doubt the authenticity of the accounts, delivered by Moses, concerning the primitive world'. Lest he seem too prejudiced by interest, Jones clarified that it was not the truth of his 'national religion' that lay at the heart of these enquiries, but the pursuit of 'truth itself'. Thus, he added somewhat sceptically that 'if any cool unbiassed reasoner will clearly convince me, that Moses drew his narrative through Egyptian conduits from the primeval fountains of Indian literature, I shall esteem him as a friend for having weeded my mind from a capital error'.[71] In the earlier parts of the essay, however, Jones' own position was made clear. To 'the warm advocates for Indian antiquity', like Halhed, he apologised for any offence before insisting 'that the Vedas were actually written before the flood, I shall never believe'. There was 'no shadow' of a foundation, he insisted, for 'the adamantine pillars of our Christian faith be moved by the result of any debates on the comparative antiquity of the Hindus and Egyptians, or of any inquiries into the Indian Theology'.[72]

Fitting Indian chronology into biblical history remained a consistent feature of Jones' work. Again in 1786, in his famous 'Third Anniversary Discourse', Jones demarcated the age of the first three descendants of Vishnu as corresponding to a 'Universal Deluge', after which 'the second, or silver, age of the Hindus was subsequent to the dispersion from Babel'.[73] While his pursuit of Sanskrit shifted his perspective slightly

68 Halhed, *Code of Gentoo Laws or the Ordination of the Pundits*, pp. xxxix, xlii–xliii.

69 Costard, *Letter to Nathaniel Brassey Halhead*, p. 15.

70 Rhonda Rapport, 'Fossils and the Flood', in Roy Porter (ed.), *The Cambridge History of Science*, vol. 4: *Eighteenth-Century Science* (Cambridge: Cambridge University Press, 2003).

71 *Works*, vol. 1, p. 276.

72 *Works*, vol. 1, pp. 245, 277.

73 Michael J. Franklin, *Sir William Jones: Selected Poetical and Prose Works* (Cardiff: University of Wales Press, 1995), p. 364.

(he conceded that some of the texts, such as the *Yajurveda*, were older than the books of Moses), he still maintained the subordination of the Hindu *yuga* cycle to biblical history.[74] In discussing the origins of the misinformation that surrounds Hindu chronology, Jones offered some arguments sharply at odds with the image of him as a spotless admirer of Hindu culture.[75] In addition to challenging Hindu chronology according to textual analysis that positioned various Sanskrit texts in biblical history, Jones' position also rested on a general dismissal of the Brahmins as reliable informants on the accuracy of Hindu history. In an attempt to aggrandise themselves the Brahmins had, Jones claimed, 'designedly raised their antiquity beyond the truth'. In 'On the Chronology of the Hindoos' (1788), he explained that the fault of authors like Halhed had been to 'mistake enigmas and allegories for historical verity'. A central linchpin against the greater antiquity of Hindu history is yet again the comparison of a flood in the *Bhāgavata Purāṇa* with the story of Noah, though here Jones says he will leave his readers to decide whether it bears a resemblance to the biblical deluge.[76]

Jones is less even handed, though, when it comes to various accusations of priestly deception. Taking issue with Indian astronomical accounts of time, for example, he suggests that Indian astronomers had achieved more accurate calculations, 'but concealed their knowledge from the people'.[77] Likewise, he concludes that it was the 'dark enigmas' of astronomers and the 'heroick fictions' of Hindu poets that made up the first three ages of their history, which was strictly mythological.[78] Moreover, in general, it was precisely this 'fabling and allegorizing spirit' that Jones argues 'has ever induced the Bráhmens to disguise their whole system of history, philosophy, and religion'.[79] In a supplement to the original discourse, Jones goes into more detail, describing how when challenged on inconsistencies in the various accounts of time, Brahmins cannot answer without 'recourse to miracles or to prophesy'. And yet, elsewhere in his writings Jones affirmed the truth of both miracles and prophecy, albeit in a limited sense, in the case of Christianity. These are the limits of Jones' tolerating and universalising accounts of divine worship.[80] Miracle and prophecy are true in the case of the Bible, but not in their abundant necessity in justifying Hindu chronology.

[74] Jones, *Institutes of Hindu Law* (1794), p. viii.
[75] Cannon, *Life and Mind of Oriental Jones*, p. 82. [76] *Works*, vol. 1, p. 288.
[77] *Works*, vol. 1, p. 284. [78] *Works*, vol. 1, p. 309.
[79] Supplement to 'On the Chronology of the Hindoos', *Works*, vol. 1, p. 327.
[80] *Works*, vol. 1, p. 325.

While the result of Jones' religious outlook was a position of toleration that stressed an admiration for pious expressions of devotion to the deity, as well a deep interest in the relationship between the antiquity of Sanskrit literature and the Bible, the explanations that have been given for this before have been inadequate. Jones was not a deist. In the first instance, the precise meaning of this term in relation to Jones has been left unclear by those who have used it to describe him. Secondly, scholarship now keenly distinguishes deism from Rational Dissent, to which Jones had many connections, as outlined in this section. This affiliation itself explains his interest in asserting the integrity of biblical scripture. This also complicates Trautmann's picture of Jones' ethnological project as intended to defend 'the Bible against the skeptics upon their own, rationalistic terms' in order to make 'new orientalism' safe for Anglicans, allowing its antiquity to be welcomed by the 'orthodox' as corroborating biblical history.[81] Jones' belief was not orthodox in that it was anti-Trinitarian and dismissive of traditional orthodoxy, which itself deviated from an accurate interpretation of '*the Religion of the Gospel*'. This was what was behind Jones' investment in bringing the antiquity of Sanskrit scriptures in line with biblical time. The results, however, were different in important ways from the more heterodox positions of Holwell and Dow, and the scepticism of Halhed. Jones' affirmation of biblical history, and characterisation of *Hindoo* religion as qualitatively sublime but ultimately incomparable with the truth of the Gospel, appealed to the very sentiments that had previously been offended by these former authors. In this sense, the philosophically oriented engagement with Indian religion became divested of its subversive potential and consequently fitted more comfortably into paternalistic narratives about British stewardship of 'native' customs. To account for this, we need to turn to Jones' vision of 'the Hindu religion'. In particular, we need to turn to Jones' understanding of Vedānta philosophy, and the lenses through which he saw it: Persianate scholarship and the Neoplatonist theology of Rational Dissent.

Jones and Hinduism: Vedānta, a Poetic Muse

The version of the Hindu religion privileged in Jones' interpretation was mystical and esoteric. This was expressed in his presidential discourses for the Asiatick Society and the nine 'hymns' that he composed in lyrical celebration of Hindu deities. It was this mystical core that also formed the

[81] Trautmann, *Aryans and British India*, p. 74.

basis of Jones' comparative thought. Pointing again to shared origins, Jones stressed how 'the sacred poems of the Persians and Hindus', for example, 'seem to mean the same thing in substance, and differ only in expression, as their languages differ only in idiom!'[82] In particular, his writings expressed a deferential preference for Vedānta, one of the six recognised orthodox schools of Indian philosophy, which he sometimes called *vedanti*. Jones' attraction to Vedānta, and in particular the non-dualist strand of Advaita Vedānta, appears as early as 'On the Gods of Greece, Italy and India' (1784). A decade later, in the final eleventh anniversary discourse 'On the Philosophy of the Asiaticks' (1794), Jones still focused much of his discussion of *Hindoo* philosophy on the Vedānta school, which was to be compared to the philosophical insights of Plato, interpreted by Jones through the theistic lens of Christian Platonism and Sufi Neoplatonism.

Jones' account of Indian philosophy appears to have derived from several sources. Initially they were exclusively Persian. Jones' connection to Persianate scholarship predated his 1783 arrival in India, and it was through this language culture that he was initiated to conceptions of Hindu religion. The importance of this for Jones' thought has been stressed by Carl Ernst, Mohamad Tavakoli-Targhi and Urs App, the latter of whom has particularly stressed the significance of the works commissioned by Prince Dara Shikoh.[83] Jones' earliest impressions of 'the Hindu religion' were thus mediated through these texts. One of the first appears to have been what he writes down in his notebook in 1785 as the 'Jōg Bashest', which was the *Jūg Bāsisht*, a translation of the *Laghu-Yoga-Vāsiṣṭha*, which in turn is an abridged version of the *Yoga Vāsiṣṭha*. This text, as Jones jots down in the note, was being translated into English from a Persian copy by John Shore.[84] The teachings of this Sanskrit dialogue between Vasiṣṭha, a Vedic rishi (*ṛṣi*), and Prince Rāma have come to be closely associated with Advaita Vedānta, although it actually expresses different strains of non-dualist thought, including idealist Buddhism.[85] The Persian version that

[82] Jones, 'On the Mystical Poetry of the Persians and Hindus' (1792), *Works*, vol. 1, p. 415.

[83] Ernst, 'Muslim Studies of Hinduism?; Tavakoli-Targhi 'Homeless Texts of Persianate Modernity'; App, 'William Jones's Ancient Theology'.

[84] There were several versions of this text, which had a long history of translation. See chapter 1 in Nair, *Translating Wisdom*. M. J. Franklin appears to connect the Shore text to one of the original works in translation, made by by Nizām-al-Din Pānipati, with the aid of two two Hindu Sanskrit paṇḍits, Jagannātha Miśra Banārasī and Paṭhān Miśra Jājīpūrī, at the behest of Prince Salim Jahāngir in 1597; see M. J. Franklin, '"Harmonious" Jones and "Honest John" Shore: Contrasting Responses of Garden Reach Neighbors to the Experience of India', *European Romantic Review*, 27:2 (2016), p. 130.

[85] For a comprehensive account of the text, see chapter 12 in Surendranath Dasgupta, *A History of Indian Philosophy*, vol. 2 (Cambridge: Cambridge University Press, 1952).

Shore was dealing with was, however, a syncretic text that merged the metaphysics of the original with Sufiism and sat in a tradition of Mughal scholarship that aligned the *Jūg Bāsisht* with Advaita Vedānta specifically.[86] That Jones saw this through the lens of Platonism is clear from his notebook, which included the reflection that it contains 'Fine Platonism both in metaphysics and morals'.[87]

Jones was also drawn to Hindu theology through Dara Shikoh's translation of the *Upanishads*, known as *Sirr-i akbar* (The great secret).[88] This was rare for the time; while Anquetil-Duperron was working on a translation, Halhed only had a fragment.[89] According to Dara, the *Upanishads* represented an embodiment of the Vedas, and therefore contained the mystical secrets of the most original monotheism (the 'hidden book' of the Qur'an).[90] Jones thus renders them 'a compendium' of the Vedas, abounding 'with noble speculations in metaphysicks, and fine discourses on the being and attributes of God'.[91] Finally, Jones also appears to have studied two other of Dara's texts, the *Dabistan* and *Majma-ul-Bahrain*, translated as 'The meeting-place of the two oceans' (or 'confluence' or 'mingling'), and by Jones as 'The junction of the two seas', both of which Jones regards as containing the theology of the Sufis.[92] These have widely been regarded as syncretist texts, but scholars have warned against seeing this as a blending of two distinct traditions identifiable as Islam and Hinduism, stressing that Dara's emphasis was on mystical esoteric knowledge in general.[93] Nevertheless, in 'the pursuit of the doctrines of the Indian monotheists', it does fuse Vedānta with Sufism, and it seems that much of what Jones wrote about the similarities between the 'sublime' metaphysics of the two was shaped by Dara Shikoh's texts.

And yet, Jones only mentions these texts a few times in the body of his works, in particular in an essay explicitly comparing 'the mystical poetry of the Persians and the Hindus'. Alongside them he increasingly drew on

86 Nair, *Translating Wisdom*, pp. 33, 48–9.

87 Sir William Jones, Notebook (c.1785), p. 55: James Marshall and Marie-Louise Osborn Collection, Osborne c400, Beinecke Rare Book and Manuscript Library, Yale University.

88 He mentions this work in his commentary on 'On the Literature of the Hindus', an essay written by the pandit scholar Govardhan Kaul, which was published in the first volume of *Asiatick Researches* (1788), and 'The Third Anniversary Discourse' (1786): See *Works*, vol. 1, pp. 355, 33. App makes the case for him reading it in 1786: App, 'William Jones's Ancient Theology', p. 44.

89 Halhed, *Code of Gentoo Laws*, p. xviii.

90 Gandhi, *The Emperor Who Never Was*, p. 207.

91 *Works*, vol. 1, p. 33.

92 Jones, 'On the Mystical Poetry of the Persians and the Hindus' (1792), *Works*, vol. 1, p. 460.

93 Ernst, 'Muslim Studies of Hinduism?', p. 186; Gandhi, *The Emperor Who Never Was*, pp. 186–7.

a number of Sanskrit sources and the scholarship of Hindu pundits. For this reason, it seems App somewhat overstates the importance of the texts in leading Jones to emulate Prince Dara's search for the original 'primeval religion' as his main project. In 'On the Philosophy of the Asiaticks', Jones turns to a number of texts, all of which pointed to the multiplicity of Hindu philosophy. He begins with a treatise ascribed to 'Vyása' which he had 'leisure to peruse with a Bráhmen of the Védáti school'. Jones' suggestion that this text was 'the only philosophical Sástra' is obviously not correct. Given its attribution to Vyāsa (the compiler of the Vedas), and the mention of 'four chapters', we can infer that Jones was referencing the *Brahma Sūtras*, thought to be authored by Bādarāyana, who is also called Vyāsa (as a title). Unsurprisingly, Jones found this text rather obscure, and so turned instead to the commentary of 'the very judicious and most learned SANCARA'.[94] Jones was here referring to Adi Shankara/Sankara (or Śaṅkara), the eighth-century philosopher who is mostly closely associated with developing and compiling the Advaita Vedānta tradition.[95] His commentaries gave an account of the various orthodox (*āstika*) and unorthodox (*nāstika*) schools of philosophy, the latter of which Jones describes as 'modern hereticks'. In the context of Indian philosophy, 'modern' must be taken in a very relative sense, with the *nāstika* schools including, for example, both Buddhism and Jainism.

Jones reserved his commentary for the *āstika* schools, beginning with 'the oldest sect', attributed to 'CAPILA' (Kapila), which is described as the '*Sánc'hya*, or Numeral, philosophy'.[96] Here Jones was referring to the Sāṃkhya school, an enumerationist philosophy that upholds a radical dualism between consciousness and matter.[97] Jones compares the school to the 'metaphysicks of Pythagoras' and 'the theology of Zeno', but on what grounds is left unsaid. Little more detail is given, except that its doctrines were impugned by Kirshna himself in the *Bhagavad-Gītā*. This is followed by the discussion of Nyāya, which he identifies as 'a system of metaphysicks and logick', particularly suited 'to the natural reason and common sense of mankind'.[98] The pertinent question, then, becomes one of why, among this variety, Jones preferred and devoted so much of his writings on *Hindoo* thought to Vedānta.

That this school in particular was to be associated with Platonic philosophy was made plain by Jones in several instances. In 'On the Literature

[94] *Works*, vol. 1, p. 163. [95] Brockington, *Sacred Thread*, pp. 109–12.
[96] *Works*, vol. 1, pp. 163–4. [97] For an account, see King, *Indian Philosophy*, pp. 62–6.
[98] *Works*, vol. 1, p. 164.

of the Hindus', Jones offers his commentary on an essay written by the pandit scholar Govardhan Kaul.[99] Taking Kaul's survey of Sanskrit literature, Jones firmly describes 'Védánta' as analogous to 'the Platonick' school, adding that 'Vyása' could be likewise taken to correspond to Plato. This is, again, apparently on account of its rejection of reality independent of the mind. Jones doesn't explain this here, but the link is forged in references he makes elsewhere. One such example is the connection he makes between Platonism and a text called the *Yoga Vāsiṣṭha*, which he takes to be 'one of the finest compositions on the Philosophy of the Védánta'.[100] As we have seen, Jones came to know this text through the Persian name *Jūg Bāsisht*, or what he called the 'Jōg Bashest', which was a syncretic text exploring Advaita Vedānta specifically. As well as his comments on its 'Fine Platonism' in his notes, in a letter to Wilkins (1785) he also wrote 'A version of the Jōg Ba'shest was brought to me the other day, in which I discovered much of the Platonick metaphysicks and morality; nor can I help believing, that Plato drew many of his notions (through Egypt, where he resided for some time) from the sages of Hindustan.'[101]

As Jones mentions in his commentary for 'On the Literature of the Hindus', the *Yoga Vāsiṣṭha* takes the form of a dialogue in which, among other things, Vasiṣṭha instructs Rāma as to the means of attaining moksha (*mokṣa*).[102] To understand why Jones takes this text, and its association with 'Védánta', to be equivalent to Platonism, we must turn to Jones' extended discussion of 'Védánta' philosophy in both 'On the Gods' (1784) and 'On the Philosophy of the Asiaticks' (1794). In the first essay, Jones introduced readers to the '*Védántí* school', and with it the concept of *Māyā*. He explained that the pedestrian meaning of the term *Māyā* was 'delusion', but added that in Vedānta philosophy it had taken on 'a more subtile and recondite sense'. In this scheme of thought, it described 'the system of *perceptions*, whether secondary or of primary qualities, which the Deity was believed by EPICHARMUS, PLATO, and many truly pious men, to raise by his omnipresent spirit in the minds of his creatures, but which had not in their opinion, any existence independent of mind'.[103] This is also the dominant theme of the *Yoga Vāsiṣṭha*, and thus the *Jūg Bāsisht*, which emphasises that the phenomenal world is a construction of the mind. Jones' notebook entry on the *Jūg Bāsisht* makes this connection, jotting

99 The essay was translated by Jones from Sanskrit, and presented to the society in May 1787.

100 *Works*, vol. 1, p. 360.

101 *Letters*, vol. 2, p. 646.

102 For a comprehensive account of the text, see chapter 12 in Dasgupta, *History of Indian Philosophy*.

103 Franklin, *Sir William Jones*, p. 349.

next to its title the single word 'Myaya' (*Māyā*). In making this comparison, then, Jones in fact obscures an interesting difference, by placing God as the source of our perceptions. As Shankar Nair has put it in his masterful study of Muslim intellectual interactions with *Yoga Vāsiṣṭha*, 'both the Sanskrit and Persian versions of the text eschew giving credit to *brahman* for the world's appearance, but instead attribute it to *manas*, imagination (*saṃkalpa/khayāl*), and/or ignorance'. The imagination of the 'semblances' (*ābhāsas*) that constitute the objects of our perception are in fact products of *Brahman's* opposite, ignorance.[104]

Jones, however, is consistent in presenting *Māyā* as the understanding that perception of reality emanates from God. In 'On the Philosophy of the Asiaticks', he describes the core principle of the 'Védánta' school, and indeed of the Sufi theologians, as the belief 'that existence and perceptibility are convertible terms, that external appearances and sensations are illusory, and would vanish into nothing, if the divine energy, which alone sustains them, were suspended but for a moment'.[105]

This doctrine was, he wrote, not only 'an opinion, which EPICHARMUS and PLATO seem to have adopted', but also one that had 'been maintained in the present century with great elegance'.[106] This latter comment, we can infer, was a reference to George Berkeley, whose thought, as we saw in Chapter 5, was also likened to Hindu philosophy by Nathaniel Brassey Halhed. Jones had already written to Wilkins in 1785 making the comparison more explicit, claiming that the subject of his new poem, 'A Hymn to Náráyena' (1785), was also 'the doctrine of Parmenides and Plato, whom our *Berkeley* follows'.[107] This poem, as Jones later explained in its introduction, was about 'the perception of *secondary* qualities by our *senses*' which were, according to Indian religion, a production of 'the immediate influence of MÁYÁ [the illusion of creation]'.[108] For Jones, then, it was the notion of *Māyā* that made the 'Védánta' the Platonic school of India, or in fact, made Plato the Vedānta philosopher of Europe.

The next question is why. The most obvious answer is that Jones divined a connection between *Māyā* and Plato's theory of Forms, as well as a Neoplatonist or Christian Platonist rendering of the ontology of 'the One', and he would not be the last to do so.[109] The pairing of Vedānta with

104 Nair, *Translating Wisdom*, pp. 55, 35–3. 105 *Works*, vol. 1, pp. 165–6.

106 *Works*, vol. 1, pp. 163–6. 107 *Letters*, vol. 2, pp. 669–70.

108 Franklin, *Sir William Jones*, p. 107.

109 Daniel Soars, '"I Am that I Am" (Ex. 3.14): From Augustine to Abhishiktānanda – Holy Ground between Neoplatonism and Advaita Vedānta', *Sophia*, 60:2 (2020).

this trinity of authors, Plato, Epicharmus and Berkeley (with Parmenides being swapped with Epicharmus elsewhere), suggests that Jones saw them as sharing the view that perception of the world of material objects was dependent on and emanated from a divine cosmological unity. It is most likely that Jones would have understood this through the lens of Cambridge Platonism, given his association with Price, and in particular, the Platonic conception of ideas as active and originating in God, discussed by Price in his most popular work (running into three editions in his lifetime), *A Review of the Principal Questions in Morals* (1758).[110] In fact, in this text, Price grounds his discussion in commentaries on Plato and others, including references to Parmenides and Berkeley, which in turn he had taken from Ralph Cudworth's *True Intellectual System of the Universe* (1678).[111]

In volume 1, Cudworth depicted the mind of God as the archetypal intellect from which all particular created intellects are derived. Cudworth was himself drawing on Plotinus, for whom the intellect and individual souls derive from 'the One', but awareness of this is not possible in the noetic life of the soul.[112] It appears, though, that on the matter of Berkeley, Jones and Price did not agree. In *A Review*, Price had aligned Berkeley with the dangerous scepticisms of Protagoras about the relativity of perceptions of both matter and morality argued, against in Plato's *Theaetetus*. The 'extravagances' of the contemporary scepticism that the qualities of matter are 'nothing different from *impressions*' and thus that there is 'neither matter nor morality, nor Deity', were, in Price's mind, 'started by Bishop *Berkeley*' and carried to their extreme by David Hume.[113] Though Jones did not name Berkeley in 'On the Philosophy of the Asiaticks', it is probably safe to assume his learned audience would have made the association. Contra Price, Jones laments that despite its elegance, this more recent philosophy of perception had met 'with little publick applause', partly 'because it has been misunderstood' and partly because of this unfortunate association with Humean scepticism; or as Jones put it, 'because it has been misapplied by the false reasoning of some unpopular writers, who are said

110 Hickman, *Eighteenth-Century Dissent*, p. 23.

111 Richard Price, *A Review of the Principal Questions in Morals, Particularly Those Relating to the Original of Our Ideas of Virtue, Its Nature, Foundation, Reference to the Deity, Obligation, Subject Matter, and Sanctions* (London: T. Cadell, 1769), p. 83.

112 Douglas Hedley, 'Ralph Cudworth as Interpreter of Plotinus', in Stephen Gersh (ed.), *Plotinus' Legacy: The Transformation of Platonism from the Renaissance to the Modern Era* (Cambridge: Cambridge University Press, 2019).

113 Price, *Review of the Principal Questions*, pp. 85–6. On Price and Berkeley, see Colin Crowder, 'Berkeley, Price and the Limitations of the Design Argument', *Enlightenment and Dissent*, 8 (1989).

to have disbelieved in the moral attributes of God'.[114] For Jones, Berkeley was no Protagoras, but a Plato. Indeed, Berkeley had adopted much of Plotinus, albeit in a different system from Cudworth.[115] Jones was therefore keen to separate the concept that reality arose from 'the system of perceptions' from scepticism, and instead align it with the God-centred conception of the cosmos that he saw uniting Plato and Śaṅkara. The 'omnipresence, wisdom, and goodness' of God were also, he stressed, 'the basis of the *Indian* philosophy'.[116]

This discussion of Advaita Vedānta and the concept of *Māyā* was also, in Jones' mind, connected to the questions of contemporary physico-theology. While the systems of Berkeley and Price are very different, scholars like Colin Crowder have pointed to some overlap in 'their rational and non-fideistic insistence upon the immediacy of God's presence (in opposition to a variety of deistic and similar currents)' as part of and in relation to a design argument.[117] Although they resort to different answers, both sought to offer alternatives to a philosophy in which God is at the distant end of a long causal chain, leaving creation to operate according to mechanical laws of physics. Rather than resorting to miraculous intervention, both sought rationally to ground their conviction of God's propinquity in the metaphysical implications of our experience of the world, Berkeley with recourse to the inertness of ideas without God's active spirit, and Price with the argument that there can be no motion without God, on whom continuing creation is dependent.[118]

It is in precisely these ways that these ideas meet in the religious thought of Jones. In his letter to Wilkins, Jones claimed that he had become convinced that the ideas concerning perception common to Vedānta, Plato and 'our Berkley [Berkeley]' were 'the only means of removing the difficulties which attend the common opinions concerning the *Material* world'. [119] In returning to the theme in 'On the Philosophy of the Asiaticks', a few pages down from the allusion to Berkeley, Jones returned to the philosophy of Advaita Vedānta to make the connection between the

114 *Works*, vol. 1, pp. 165–6.

115 See, for example, Kevin Corrigan, 'Berkeley and Plotinus on the Non-Existence of Matter', *Hermathena*, 157 (1994).

116 *Works*, vol. 1, p. 166.

117 Crowder, 'Berkeley, Price and the Limitations of the Design Argument', p. 3.

118 Crowder, 'Berkeley, Price and the Limitations of the Design Argument', pp. 5–8. Hickman offers a nuanced account of how Price's position thus grew from both Cambridge Platonist theology and Newtonian physics, which both reject Cudworth's notion of 'Plastick Nature' while also resting on the idea of immutable morality, see chapter 4 in Hickman, *Eighteenth-Century Dissent.*

119 *Letters*, vol. 2, pp. 669–70.

idea that 'material substance is mere illusion' and the doctrine that 'there exists in this universe only one generick spiritual substance, the sole primary cause, efficient, substantial and formal of all secondary causes and of all appearances whatever' – that is, between perception and its origin. Crucially, this is not a distant first cause without attributes, but one endowed with 'sublime providential wisdom' of 'a constant preserver' and creator. This, Jones went on to state, must be differentiated 'as widely from the pantheism of SPINOZA and TOLAND, as the affirmation of a proposition differs from the negation of it'.[120] This vision of Vedānta, and in particular Jones' reference to 'a constant preserver', was thus neatly compatible with the view, in the case of Price, that God's providence could not be restricted to one creative causal act, but was continuous in upholding the operations of nature, or, according to Berkeley, the perceptions of the mind.[121]

Jones ended this discussion of Vedānta by expressing his contempt for Toland's use of a quotation from St Paul to support his '*insane philosophy*'. Though Jones doesn't name it, this was a reference to Toland's *Pantheisticon* in which he quotes, 'In him we live, and move, and have our being' (Acts 17:28).[122] St Paul's lines were not to be taken as a kind of pantheism, Jones insisted, but were instead better compared to a passage that Jones attributes to Varuṇa in the Veda and interprets as a sublime monotheism: 'That spirit, from which these created beings proceed; through which having proceeded from it, they live; toward which they tend and in which they are ultimately absorbed, that spirit study to know; that spirit is the Great One.'[123]

Similar ideas were expressed in Jones' poetry, through which his vision of Indian religion was received by the widest audience. The poem that he wrote to Wilkins about, and likened to Berkeley, 'A Hymn to Náráyena', was one of the most popular. The close of the hymn expresses similar sentiments to the passage from Varuṇa, depicting the soul's emanation and absorption into the divine: as perception of the material fades, its protagonist concludes, 'But suns and fading words I view no more: / God only I perceive; God only I adore.'[124] Its muse, Nārāyaṇa, is an incarnation of Vishnu sometimes termed a *vyūha*, or emanation of Vishnu.[125] As others

[120] All quotes from *Works*, vol. 1, pp. 172–3. [121] Hickman, *Eighteenth-Century Dissent*, p. 116.

[122] Isabel Rivers, *Reason, Grace, and Sentiment: A Study of the Language of Religion and Ethics in England, 1660–1780* (Cambridge: Cambridge University Press, 2000), vol. 2, p. 73.

[123] *Works*, vol. 1, pp. 173–4. [124] Franklin, *Sir William Jones*, p. 112.

[125] *Nārāyaṇa*, as Jones explains in the preface to the poem, means 'moving on the water' and refers to Vishnu's position in the creation myth, reclining on a snake on the celestial waters.

have pointed out, while in his hymns to goddesses Jones addresses their divine qualities (*sagua*), in 'A Hymn to Náráyena' the focus is on the non-personal absolute essence of the divine (*nirgua*).[126] Thus, rather than an expression of *bhakti* (devotion) to a particular deity, the poem is an exploration of mystical philosophy.

The poem begins with reflection on the origins of creation and a call for divine inspiration: 'Oh! raise from cumbrous ground/My soul in rapture drown'd, That fearless it may soar on wings of fire;/For Thou, who only knowst, Thou only canst inspire.' The stanzas then explore the primordial waters of the Hindu creation story, and, as Jones explains in his introductory note, 'the *Indian* and *Persian* doctrine of the Divine Essence', that is, the doctrines of 'Vedántì and Sùfi theologists' explored in 'On the Philosophy of the Asiaticks'. This connection features most prominently in the last two stanzas, which bring the poem back to its original call for divine inspiration on the nature of existence. That call is answered with the revelation that, as Jones explains in the introduction, 'the perception of *secondary* qualities by our *senses*' is a production of 'the immediate influence of MÁYÁ [the illusion of creation]'.[127] In the poem this is expressed as a mystical experience of fading perception, which concludes with the knowledge that God is the 'One abundant source,/When ev'ry object ev'ry moment flows', that is, that God is the cause of perception. Thus, at the climax of the poem, this sublime resolution to the issue of material reality is expressed as the removal of 'Delusive Pictures! unsubstantial shows!'. Apparent material objects, in this case 'dew-bespangled leaves and blossoms bright', thus vanish and leave the soul free to be absorbed by its creator.[128] It was this philosophy of perception (*Māyā*) and the mystical theology it inspired that Jones determined to be the essence of Vedānta thought, a subject in the letter to Wilkins about the poem he had described as 'the sublimest the human mind can conceive'.[129]

Of the nine hymns, it was 'A Hymn to Náráyena' that received a reputation as an important source of information on the nature of Hindu theology. In 1787, *The Critical Review* stated that to explain the contents of Jones' poetry would be to write a commentary on 'the religion, the mythology, and the customs of the Hindoos'. The reviewer thus resorted to concluding that 'A Hymn to Náráyena' was 'highly sublime', exploring as it did 'the active spirit of God'.[130] *The Monthly Review*

[126] This is also discussed in Sugirtharajah, *Imagining Hinduism*, p. 16.
[127] Franklin, *Sir William Jones*, p. 107. [128] Franklin, *Sir William Jones*, p. 112.
[129] To Charles Wilkins, 14 April 1785, in *Letters*, vol. 2, p. 669.
[130] *Critical Review*, 63 (1787), pp. 266–7.

presented a similar response. Describing the hymn as 'elegantly expressed', it goes on to say that to offer a proper introduction to the topic of the poem would be to offer 'no less than a full comment on the Vêds and the Poorans of the Hindoos' as well as 'the remains of the Egyptian and Persian theology'.[131] These are, of course, echoes of Jones' introductory words which claimed that there was no room for the vast disquisition that would be needed to introduce the poem fully.[132] The poem was therefore accepted as a full and reliable representation of core principles in Hindu theological thought and its many connections with other ancient systems of philosophy. Indeed, some later usages of the poem as an authoritative source on the core doctrine of the *Hindoo* religion took it to be a translation. One author would use the poem as evidence that the perceived idolatry of Hindu religion was a modern corruption, and that at its core was a 'system of pure and refined theism'. Referring to it as an 'ancient hymn', historian William Belsham seemed to think that the 'divine ode' was a translation by Jones and not an original work of poetical composition.[133] This is also true of Elizabeth Hamilton, who presents the work as a translation in her epistolary novel *Letters from a Hindoo Raja*. In this case it is used to express the religious sentiments of an Indian character. In a letter from the raja, which turns to the topic of the 'Omniscient Spirit', Jones' 'translation' of the poem, along with an excerpt from its introduction is provided as an explanatory footnote on *Hindoo* ideas of God.[134]

While Jones clearly saw in Vedānta and Sufi theology some of the ideas that he thought provided a suitable rebuttal to excessive materialisms, he was nevertheless clear to distance them from truths of Christian revelation itself. Both of these Asiatic philosophies were to be understood as 'blending uncertain metaphysicks with undoubted principles of religion'.[135] Indeed, Jones consistently characterised their theologies as sublime rather than rational; the product of a 'boundless imagination'.[136] In the 1791 essay 'On the Mystical Poetry of the Persians and the Hindus', Jones traced what he saw as the 'figurative mode of expressing the fervour of devotion' common to both Persian mystics and 'the *Védánta* school'. This was the direct product of his reading of Dara Shikoh's texts. While certainly sublime, both were characterised by Jones as being beset by

[131] *Monthly Review*, 76 (1787), pp. 418–19. [132] Franklin, *Sir William Jones*, p. 106.

[133] William Belsham, *History of Great Britain, from the Revolution to the Session of Parliament Ending AD 1793*, vol. 1 of 4 (London, 1798), pp. 445–7.

[134] Elizabeth Hamilton, *Translations of the Letters of a Hindoo Rajah: Written Previous to and during the Period of His Residence in England*, vol. 1 of 2 (London: G. G. and J. Robinson, 1796), pp. 170–1.

[135] *Works*, vol. 1, p. 173. [136] *Works*, vol. 1, p. 173.

a predilection for 'mystical religious allegory'. Much of this sat on the cusp of 'culpable excess', taken 'beyond the bounds of cool reason', and instead teetering between 'ardently grateful piety' and 'the brink of absurdity'.[137]

The mystical heights involved in expressing 'ardent love' for the creator were, however, not exclusively Asiatic. Jones also quotes at length from the mathematician and theologian Isaac Barrow, suggesting that his panegyric on pious love bordered on 'quietism and enthusiastic devotion'.[138] Indeed, many have taken Jones' comments that Barrow's text differed 'only from the mystical theology of the *Súfís* and *Yogis*, as the flowers and fruits of Europe differ in scent and flavour from those of Asia', as evidence of a syncretic tendency.[139] And yet, while indeed Jones conjures some examples of poetical tributes to divine love in the history of Christianity, these are also to be understood as examples of excess. The '*Védánta* school', presented as one of the most fundamental expressions of Indian religiosity, is thus aligned with the most mystical elements of Christian religiosity. Such devotion, while admirable in its piety, could also veer into absurdity. It could not be faulted, in the sense that 'nothing can be farther removed from impiety than a system wholly built on the purest devotion'. And yet, there was not sufficient evidence for the admiring Jones to fully endorse or believe a system which 'human reason alone could, perhaps, neither fully demonstrate, nor fully disprove', and which at times became 'wild and erroneous'.[140]

The enigmatic quality of Vedānta theology was to be contrasted with Nyāya philosophy. This was the second of four schools of Indian thought to which Jones devoted his attention in 'On the Philosophy of the Asiaticks', though Vedānta was still the predominant subject. Like Dow, Jones correctly identified 'GOTAMA' as the founder 'Nyáya'. He translated 'Nyāya' as 'logical', which he determined to be 'a title aptly bestowed', as it was to be understood as 'a system of metaphysicks and logick better accommodated than any other anciently known in India, to the natural reason and common sense of mankind'. Jones refrained, however, from attributing to the school any particular belief or theology, except to say that Nyāya was firmly based on 'admitting the actual existence of *material substance* in the popular acceptation of the word *matter*'. This was not to contrast it with '*Védántí*' theology, which 'consisted, not in denying the existence of matter', which Jones added 'would be lunacy', but

[137] *Works*, vol. 1, pp. 445–6. [138] *Works*, vol. 1, p. 448.
[139] *Works*, vol. 1. p. 448. See, for example, Franklin, *Orientalist Jones*, p. 274.
[140] *Works*, vol. 1, p. 166.

in 'correcting the popular notion of it' by making its existence dependent on God. Nyāya, on the other hand, was 'not only a body of sublime dialecticks', but essentially 'an artificial method of reasoning, with distinct names for the three parts of a proposition, and even for those of a regular syllogism'. Of Nyāya, however, Jones had little more to say, and overall the reader is left with the impression that it is primarily a technical system of logic, which accounted for 'the perfect syllogisms in the philosophical writings of the Bráhmens'. Thus, while it was Nyāya, or the 'system of GOTAMA', that Jones admitted 'the Bráhmens of this province [Bengal] almost universally follow', he nevertheless moved on to declare that overall, 'the most celebrated Indian school' was the Vedānta.[141]

For Jones, as it was for Holwell, Dow, Halhed and Wilkins, Indian religion was philosophical in its subject matter, composition and original insight. Nevertheless, the emphasis within Jones' philosophical portrait of the Hindu religion was firmly placed on the mystical and sublime. While he acknowledged the prevalence of the Nyāya school in his contemporary Bengal, it was the doctrine of the *Védánta* that both formed the core of his speculations on the common origins of early religious sects and captured his poetic imagination. Its doctrine, as Jones interpreted it, that perception of the material world was merely an illusory emanation from the divinity, and its implications for the possibility of unity with the divine, are what inspired Jones' grandest claims for the religion's weight and significance. And yet, while its ideas could be compared to the philosophies of Plato, as well as more modern debates on the nature of God's relationship to creation, it was ultimately mystical. Indeed, such a view was consistent with the pronouncement in Jones' 'Second Anniversary Discourse' (1785) for the Asiatick Society, 'that reason and taste are the grand prerogatives of European minds, while the Asiaticks have soared to loftier heights in the sphere of imagination'.[142]

Jones' knowledge and appreciation of India's scientific and philosophical traditions became much richer in the intervening years. Nevertheless, his 1794 'On the Philosophy of the Asiaticks' still reinforced elements of this view, placing the sublime, though sometimes absurd, theology of Vedānta as its central and 'most celebrated Indian school'.[143] Elsewhere, it was Vedānta that, in Jones' comparative system, was 'the source of that sublime, but poetical, theology, which glows and sparkles in the writings of the old Academicks'.[144] In this sense Jones retained the philosophical

[141] *Works*, vol. 1, pp. 166, 164, 165. [142] *Works*, vol. 1, p. 11. [143] *Works*, vol. 1, p. 165.
[144] *Works*, vol. 1, p. 445.

interpretation of Indian religion, but rather than revealing a lost truth, as it did for Holwell, or Dow's rational system, for Jones it was above all metaphysical and sublime. Without the prophecy of Isiah, and its fulfilment in the coming of the Messiah, they remained in the category of speculative metaphysics. Indeed, as Jones spelt out in 'On the Philosophy of the Asiaticks', while there was nothing more 'pious and sublime' than the tributes offered to the creator 'in Arabick, Persian and Sanscrit' languages, ancient Hebrew was to 'always be excepted'.[145]

The Company and the Law

In his 'A Hymn to Lacshmí' (1788), Jones associated the gifts often aligned with the goddess Lakmī, well-being and prosperity, with British government in India. This 'Ode to the Goddess of Abundance', we are reminded, is a poem about a prominent deity in a religion 'believed by many millions, whose industry adds to the revenue of *Britain*'.[146] The construction of that religion in relation to empire is revealed in the text of this poem, which laments the 'erring mind' of the Hindu, 'clouded by priestly wiles' and in need of the illumination brought by 'western skies'. For Jones, the Calcutta Supreme Court judge, the gift brought by 'the wand of empire' was the preservation of 'laws, by myriads long rever'd'.[147]

This is echoed an earlier poem, 'A Hymn to Ganga', which had been composed and published in 1785. In this work, which offers a lyrical description of the Goddess and the tributary rivers of the Ganges, Jones adopted the voice of a Hindu poet. With this voice he welcomed the arrival of British governance, greeting India's new rulers, 'a peerless race/With lib'ral heart and martial grace', as arriving to 'preserve our laws, and bid our terror cease'.[148] Given this thematic continuity, it will come as no surprise that between the composition of these two poems, and beyond, Jones had been busily employed in the production of what in 1786 he had announced to John Macpherson would be 'a complete digest of Hindu and Mussulman law'.[149] This was integral to his vision of empire, as a mild, liberal and enlightened dominion that preserved indigenous civil and religious laws.

Upon his arrival in 1783, Jones had asserted that a chief function of the Calcutta Supreme Court was to ensure 'that the natives of these important

145 *Works*, vol. 1, p. 173. 146 Franklin, *Sir William Jones*, p. 154.
147 Franklin, *Sir William Jones*, pp. 162–3. 148 Franklin, *Sir William Jones*, p. 132.
149 Letter 453, to John Macpherson, 6 May 1786, *Letters*, vol. 2, p. 699.

provinces be indulged in their own prejudices, civil and religious, and suffered to enjoy their own customs unmolested'. This was not merely a benevolent gesture. As Jones reasoned in the same address, it was by ensuring their Indian subjects' 'personal security, with every reasonable indulgence to their harmless prejudices' that the British would 'conciliate their affection, while we promote their industry, so as to render our dominion over them a national benefit'.[150] It was to this end that the digest would be put, the results of which only appeared with the publication of *Al Sirajiyyah: Or the Mohamedan Law of Inheritance* in 1792, and *The Institutes of Hindu Law; or the Ordinances of Menu* in 1794 (in Calcutta; 1796 in London). The final text, which was completed and published after Jones' death to much acclaim by Henry Colebrooke, was *A Digest of Hindu Law, on Contracts and Successions* (1798). This was a translation of a Sanskrit work commissioned by Jones and titled the *Vivādabhaṅgārṇava* ('The ocean of the resolution of litigation'), which had been compiled by the famed pandit Jagannātha Tarkapañcānana and his students.[151]

Jones' account of those 'native laws' and how they should operate in relation to the British courts was intimately related to his construction of Hindu religion. The beguiling 'wizard lore' mentioned in 'A Hymn to Lacshmí' is of course a reference to Brahmin priestcraft. Despite his digest being completely dependent on the instruction of pandit scholars, Jones did not hesitate to make plain that he saw them as potential manipulators of the vulgar and that he distrusted their role in the courts. Jones is not so clear, therefore, in repeating the separation, articulated by Holwell and Dow, between the 'common-run' of Brahmins and their 'learned' counterparts except by way of naming the merits of particular scholars. Instead, the suggestion that Brahmins were potentially dishonest is a pervasive theme in his poetry and, as we have seen, in his insistence that in their accounts of Hindu chronology they had 'rarefied their antiquity beyond the truth' so as to 'aggrandize themselves'.[152] In relation to the courts, it was the particular status of the Hindu pandits or Muslim *qazis* as interpreters of the varied sources of religious authority that Jones wanted to overcome. As others such as Jon Wilson have detailed, Jones' principal object in producing the digest was to undercut what he perceived to be the legal authority of the sacerdotal classes of Bengal.[153] As Jones stated the problem, 'If we give judgment only from the opinions of the native lawyers and scholars,

[150] Shore, *Works of Sir William Jones*, vol. 7: 'Charge to the Grand Jury at Calcutta, December 4th 1783', pp. 4, 21.
[151] See Rocher, 'Career of Rādhākānta Tarkavāgīśa'. [152] *Works*, vol. 1, p. 213.
[153] See Wilson, *Domination of Strangers*, pp. 75–83.

we can never be sure that we have not been deceived by them', especially 'in any cause in which they could have the remotest interest in deceiving the court'.[154] If his vision of empire was to be successful, Jones needed to produce an authoritative point of reference for British jurists administering the native laws that it was the duty of an enlightened administration to preserve, without compromising the court by relying on its native subjects.

If there is a tension in Jones' work, it is here. This digest, like Halhed's less successful *Code of Gentoo Laws* (1776), was to be the source of evidence for particular principles and practices in Hindu jurisprudence. On the one hand, it proposed itself as a final authority in matters of Hindu law to be administered in British courts. Jones suggested as much when in 1786 he described himself as the 'Justinian of India'.[155] Likewise, in his famous letter to Cornwallis in 1788, Jones argued for 'a complete Digest of Hindu and Mohammedan laws, after the model of Justinian's inestimable Pandects', which would ensure that the pandits and *maulvis* (Muslim legal scholars) 'would hardly venture to impose on us when their impositions might so easily be detected'.[156] On the other hand, Jones, disagreeing with Blackstone's characterisation of the municipal or civil law in terms of rules laid down by a superior power, had preferred to define law as 'The Will of the whole community as far as it can be collected with convenience'.[157] For Jones, as he remarked elsewhere, whereas written statutes were to be taken to be more representative of 'the whims of a few leading men', common law was to be defined as 'the collected wisdom of many centuries'.[158] This emphasis on custom presented a paradox in the context of India, where the preservation and observation of those customs were charged to a foreign power for whom they were unintelligible. Jones saw the digest as a compromise. Compiled to reflect the collective wisdom of the Indian judiciary, it nevertheless removed access to this knowledge from their exclusive grasp.

The result, however, was something quite different. Whereas Jones had wanted to emphasise the different customs belonging to the various regions of Bengal, his collaborator, Jagannātha, had seen the digest as an opportunity to synthesise different strands of Dharmaśāstra literature. The

[154] Jones to Lord Cornwallis, 19 March 1788, *Letters*, vol. 2, pp. 795–6.
[155] Jones to Sir John Macpherson, 6 May 1786, *Letters*, vol. 2, p. 699.
[156] Jones to the First Marquis of Cornwallis, 19 March 1788, *Letters*, vol. 2, p. 794.
[157] William Jones to Viscount Althorp, 21 November 1777, *Letters*, vol. 1, pp. 333–4.
[158] Jones too Thomas Yeats, Temple, 7 June 1782, in Shore, *Memoirs of the Life, Writings and Correspondence*, p. 212.

resulting Sanskrit original had employed the analogous reasoning of the Bengali Nyāya school to wed various different injunctions together. The result was an innovation rather than a reflection of historically determined current practice.[159] Moreover, in terms of practical application, it was to have very little impact. It assumed a familiarity with the reasoning that underpinned Dharmaśāstra principles in the first place. As Colebrooke commented in the introduction to a later edition, the digest was of 'little utility to persons conversant with the law, and of still less service to those who are not conversant with Indian jurisprudence'.[160]

It was this insistence on the importance of maintaining local customs that many have emphasised in designating Jones an example of a sympathetic orientalist, as opposed to an 'Anglicist', cultural attitude to India. This overlooks that for Jones, this was about British law and governance rather than a profound admiration for Indian law itself. Whatever he thought of Hindu law was not as relevant as the position that he articulated in the preface to *The Institutes of Hindu Law*, that 'It is a maxim in the science of legislation and government, that Laws are of no avail without manners.' This was not only a principle of the law, but the foundation of its practice. As Jones went on to elaborate, 'the best intended legislative provisions would have no beneficial effect . . . unless they were congenial to the disposition and habits, to the religious prejudices, and approved immemorial usages, of the people, for whom they were enacted'.[161] For Jones, this was the foundation of English law and therefore the basis of any just regime abroad. In this he was not alone: this was the precedent that had been established with the Bengal Judicature Bill of 1781, and later Act of 1782, which had made provisions for 'Native counsellors' to advise the Supreme Court, which had previously been accused of injuring the rights of Indian subjects.[162]

What Jones thought of Hindu law itself was an entirely different matter. The digest was intended to resolve an administrative problem, but Jones was of course interested in understanding Indian jurisprudence for its own sake, and the opinion that emerged out of his studies was not particularly

159 Wilson, *Domination of Strangers*, pp. 80–2.

160 H. T. Colebrooke (ed.), *A Digest of Hindu Law on Contracts and Successions, with a Commentary*, vol. 3 (London [s.n.], 1801), p. 276.

161 Jones, 'Institutes of Hindu Law', in *Works*, vol. 4, p. 75.

162 21 Geo.III, c.70, in Sheila Lambert (ed.), *House of Commons Sessional Papers of the Eighteenth Century*, vol. 33 (Wilmington, DE: Scholarly Resources, 1975), pp. 270–1. For an account of this conflict, and its relation to a particular case of Mughal inherence law (*patna cuase*), see Travers, *Ideology and Empire*, pp. 191–206.

favourable. In the introduction to *The Institutes of Hindu Law*, based on translations of the *Mānava-Dharmaśāstra*, Jones had summarised:

> It is a system of despotism and priestcraft, both indeed limited by law, but artfully conspiring to give mutual support, though with mutual checks; it is filled with strange conceits in metaphysicks and natural philosophy, with idle superstitions, and with a scheme of theology most obscurely figurative, and consequently liable to dangerous misconception; it abounds with minute and childish formalities, with ceremonies generally absurd and often ridiculous.[163]

The preservation of these laws was not inspired by their inherent value, but by the principle of custom that underwrote just and efficacious law. As Edmund Burke had put it in his speech on the Bengal Judicature Bill, enlightened government by consent meant respecting the local norms of administration, regardless of whether those customs 'resist the lights of philosophy'.[164] Indeed, it was after consulting Jones, who advised that to force liberty on Britain's Indian subjects would be a cruel tyranny,[165] that Burke defended the bill's protection of India law according to the view that the people of Bengal were 'familiarised to a system of rule more despotic'.[166]

As David Ibbetson has shown, Jones' early thoughts on the law were rooted in a natural law tradition of legal writing in the late eighteenth century. Through an analysis of Jones' *Essay on the Law of Bailments* (1781), Ibbetson suggests that for Jones, following George Turnbull and his English translation of the German jurist Gotlieb Heineccius (whose work was influential in University College Oxford, where Jones was a fellow at the time), law was a science, reducible to a set of identifiable principles, determinable by reason and by observation. Within this methodology he sought to reconcile first principles of natural reason with empirical evidence from developed legal systems, foremost of which were English and Roman law, thereby emphasising that common law was consistent with reason. Moreover, Jones also shared the view of Turnbull that while the principles of natural law were reflected in the practice of civilised nations, they could not be deduced from the general practice of nations. There was a clear hierarchy of developed legal systems. Jones'

[163] Jones, *Institutes of Hindu Law* (1974), p. xvii.

[164] Edmund Burke, Speech on Bengal Judicature Bill, 27 June 1781, in Burke, *Writings and Speeches*, vol. 5, p. 141. For a detailed account of Burke's thought on the bill, see Bourke, *Empire and Revolution*, pp. 542–59.

[165] See note 20 in this chapter.

[166] Speech on Bengal Judicature Bill, 27 June 1781, in Burke, *Writings and Speeches*, vol. 5, p. 141.

inclusion of Hindu laws in the essay, then known to him via Halhed's *Code of Gentoo Laws*, was precisely an example of how similar rules to those he was presenting as the reasoned approach to bailments could be found even in unsophisticated systems, which also included Gothic and Welsh law.[167] Jones thus upheld that though some areas of English and Hindu law intersected, where it deviated was consonant with its distance from the refinement that had been achieved in English law.

Later in his thought, this principle translated into Jones' view that while the Indians ought to be governed by their own substantive laws, English procedural norms should still prevail. In 1792, this was the emphasis of his 'Charge to the Grand Jury at Calcutta'. The English jury were, for Jones, the final defence of the British constitution, and it was in a commitment to fair process, something he had made clear could not be left in the hands of native pandits, that justice was to be done.[168] Jones' often-invoked compulsion to comparison was thus never at odds with his long-standing commitment to what he saw as the greater sophistication of English law.

What Jones thought of Hindu law is of course pertinent to understanding his presentation of Indian religion. The two were obviously deeply intertwined, ensuring that for him, the institutes were not just a system of 'despotism', but also 'priestcraft', the source of which were its 'strange conceits in metaphysicks', figurative theology and superstition. These had laid the foundations for its 'idle superstition' and 'absurd' ceremonies.[169] This depiction was complementary to, and not in contradiction with, his emphasis on the sublime metaphysics of Vedānta. Hindu religion and its attendant laws and customs were a feat of the imagination's encounter with the divine, not a catalogue of reasoned principles. Conversely, as Jones had elsewhere stressed, Nyāya, which was more compatible with 'natural reason and common sense of mankind' was still nevertheless a system of 'sublime dialectiks', as well as the preserve of the elite Brahmin class in Bengal.[170] It was the broader essence of Hindu religion, which Jones had aligned with Vedānta, that shaped the law. His commentary on *The Institutes of Hindu Law* thus continued, 'nevertheless, a spirit of sublime devotion, of benevolence to mankind, and of amiable tenderness to all sentient creatures, pervades the whole work'.[171]

[167] David Ibbetson, 'Sir William Jones and the Nature of Law', in Andrew Burrows and Alan Rodger (eds.), *Mapping the Law: Essays in Memory of Peter Birks* (Oxford: Oxford University Press, 2006), p. 631.

[168] Ibbetson, 'Sir William Jones', p. 636. [169] Jones, *Institutes of Hindu Law* (1794), p. xvii.

[170] *Works*, vol. 1, pp. 166, 164. [171] Jones, *Institutes of Hindu Law* (1794), p. xvii.

The sympathetic element of Jones' approach to Hindu law was, therefore, the same admiration for Vedānta that described it 'a system wholly built on the purest devotion', but which nevertheless fell into obscurity and the potential error of enthusiastic excess. The tenderness of its doctrines did nothing to undermine what Jones perceived as the 'childish' qualities of Hindu law. Indeed, the two were mutually reinforcing. Indian religion was indeed sublime, but it was not, as Holwell and Dow had suggested, essentially rational, except insofar as it had tended towards some great metaphysical insights in its ancient past. Reinforcing the separation between those philosophical heights and its contemporary adherents that Holwell and Dow had selectively employed, Jones' understanding of India's religious history, customs and manners was eminently suitable to his vision of enlightened British stewardship. As he had put in an address to the Asiatick Society in 1793, 'the religion, manners, and the laws of the natives preclude even the idea of political freedom; but their histories may possibly suggest hints for their prosperity, while our country derives essential benefit from the diligence of a placid and submissive people'.[172]

Where writers like Javed Majeed have correctly moved away from oversimplifying Jones as an admirer of India, Majeed still insists that there was a tension in Jones' thought, posed by the 'dilemma implicit in the attempt both to respect the uniqueness of cultures, and to define a neutral idiom in which cultures could be compared and contrasted'. To illustrate this dilemma, Majeed points to Jones' remarks on the *Mānava-Dharmaśāstra* contrasting his criticism of it as a 'system of despotism and priestcraft' with his praise for 'its spirit of sublime devotion, of benevolence to mankind' and the 'certain austere majesty' of its style. For Majeed, 'the sudden change from denigration to praise does not strike one as ironic' but rather as evidence of the dilemma posed by praising cultural distinctiveness while also pursuing comparison. While Majeed's perception of this problem is an entirely correct account of the basis for the criticisms that Jeremy Bentham and James Mill would level against the vision of Indian religion and law projected by Jones, for Jones himself, there was no such strain.[173] This judgement, as well as aligning with the religious preoccupations that animated Jones' thought, was also consistent with his pre-existing assumptions about the nature of law, and the nature and origin of Hindu philosophy.

[172] Jones, 'Tenth Anniversary Discourse' (1793), in *Works*, vol. 1, p. 150.
[173] Majeed, *Ungoverned Imaginings*, pp. 43–4.

Conclusion: Jones and the 'Permanent Settlement' of 1793

Scholars have coined an assortment of monikers to capture William Jones as a historical actor and thinker. For his first modern biographer, Garland Cannon, 'Oriental Jones', the 'father of modern linguistics', was primarily a 'humanitarian' who 'always resisted any political aspects of scholarship'.[174] Franklin, on the other hand, casts 'Orientalist Jones' as the scholarly realisation of Warren Hastings' orientalist governance, characterised as 'cultural empathy and Enlightenment relativity'. Jones, Franklin suggests, underscored Hastings' ideological vision of tempering 'short-term strategic utility by long-term cultural enrichment'.[175] Without denying the political aspects of Jones' works, then, Franklin's perspective nevertheless insists on the benign attitude of Jones himself and the comparatively empathetic approach of 'orientalist' governance. Shifting perspective yet again, for S. N. Mukherjee it was Jones the 'Liberal Imperialist'. Jones, who 'preached liberalism at home, but upheld authoritarian rule in India', was a precursor to the 'authoritarian liberal statesmen' of nineteenth-century British India. This, Mukherjee argued, was a direct consequence of his vision of India as a great civilisation which had nevertheless 'failed to produce a satisfactory system of government'. The consequence was not a flat endorsement of Asian despotism as an absence of law, but of a culture in which political freedom was an alien concept.[176] Taking issue with this, Majeed has questioned the accuracy of the label 'liberal imperialist' by pointing to the very different concerns underpinning Jones' approach to Indian laws and governance to those of other 'liberal imperialists' such as James Mill. Examining his 'attempt to define the cultural identity of a rejuvenated Hinduism', Majeed instead contends that the impact of Jones must instead be understood in relation to the 'revitalized conservatism of this period', in particular as a result of reactions to the Jacobin threat in Europe and India. In this context, Jones' emphasis on the ancient civilisation of India and its traditions was a bulwark against the disorienting spread of radical and revolutionary ideas, as well as a potential theory of legitimacy for a British administration that maintained customs.[177]

While Majeed's account does much to redress the oversimplification of Jones that rests merely on cultural attitudes by pointing to a wider political

[174] Cannon, *Life and Mind of Oriental Jones*, pp. xiii, xv. [175] Franklin, *Orientalist Jones*, p. 214.

[176] Mukherjee, *Sir William Jones*, pp. 72, 125, 141. Mukherjee's reference point for these 'liberal authoritarian statesmen' is Eric Stokes' *The English Utilitarians and India* (Oxford: Clarendon, 1959).

[177] Majeed, *Ungoverned Imaginings*, pp. 12, 45.

context, more attention needs to be paid to the specifics of the Company politics and policies that shaped that context. While many have tended to stress Jones' distance from the political scene in both London and Calcutta, more astute readers of his letters, particularly the newly available ones with John Macpherson, have stressed that he was not so distant from the networks of patronage politics that structured the Company as he was at pains to appear.[178] Jones, who certainly possessed a degree of remove as a result of his crown appointment, was still a British official in India, who was close enough to call on the Company's resources for certain projects.

Hastings was invited to become president of the Asiatick Society, but opted instead to become its patron, offering some distance from the Company, while nevertheless maintaining a connection with his policy of scholarly patronage as a means of reconciliation between ruler and ruled, commerce and sovereignty. Moreover, these links continued into the administration of Hastings' successors Macpherson and Cornwallis. This is important to note, particularly in the case of Cornwallis, who has often been taken as eschewing the 'orientalist' tack of Hastings. Certainly, with the impeachment trial of Warren Hastings ongoing, Cornwallis distanced himself from the system of local allegiances and patronage that was currently being marshalled by Burke as evidence of corruption. He is thus identified with a shift towards more regulated administration and a more assertive vision of imperial command.[179] Indeed, at his appointment the powers of the governor were vastly expanded, including the presidencies of Madras and Bombay, as well as substantial discretionary powers independent of the Supreme Council in Calcutta.[180] This does mean, however, that Cornwallis was an 'Anglicist', as he has sometimes been characterised.[181] Cornwallis and Jones established an effective working relationship, with Cornwallis endorsing the project to produce a digest of Hindu law. The terms of this arrangement were more cautious than the translations commissioned by Hastings, with Jones explicitly forgoing a salary. The principles behind the project, however, shared some of those animating Hastings' patronage of the *Code of Gentoo Laws*. Cornwallis' measured statement that 'the accomplishment of the

[178] Joshua Ehrlich, 'Empire and Enlightenment in Three Letters from Sir William Jones to Governor-General John Macpherson', *Historical Journal*, 62:2 (2019).

[179] For various perspectives on this shift, see chapter 1 in Marshall, '*A Free Though Conquering People*'; Sudipta Sen, *A Distant Sovereignty: National Imperialism and the Birth of British India* (London: Routledge, 2002), p. 11; Wilson, *Domination of Strangers*, p. 46.

[180] Misra, *Central Administration*, pp. 33–4.

[181] Kopf, *British Orientalism and the Bengal Renaissance*; Stokes, *English Utilitarians*, pp. 1–5.

Digest . . . would reflect the greatest Honour on our Administration' indicated that the continuing value of such knowledge was not limited to administrative practice, but also prestige.[182] Beyond this, the Asiatick Society remained appreciated, but untainted by too direct a connection to administration.

By the 1790s, metropolitan attitudes to the Company had softened, the reputation of Jones and the Asiatick Society having done much to secure the image of a learned and responsible regime. Pitt's India Act and the Regulating Act of 1786 were generally seen to have reformed the Company, and Cornwallis was largely viewed as a competent governor whose policies were aimed at shoring up British interests, while also rooting out the causes of corruption.[183] Increased financial management of the Company by Pitt's ministry, as P. J. Marshall has pointed out, had realigned the interests of the state and Company to run more closely together once again.[184] Moreover, after the French Revolution and the resultant divisions between Burke and his parliamentary allies, the pursuit of Hastings was increasingly viewed as ill-conceived and excessive, and Hastings was acquitted on all charges in 1794.[185] Finally, war with France and reaction in the wake of the French Revolution also shifted public narratives on the Company towards that of a bulwark of anti-Jacobin values abroad.[186]

It was this changing outlook on Indian affairs that was the setting for the so-called 'Cornwallis Code' of 1793. The code, which imposed a much more rigid British administration on its Indian territories and formalised relations with local officials, is widely regarded as having involved a significant and self-conscious rupture with earlier styles of governance.[187] As well as fixing property rights in the zamindari (landowning) class in Bengal, it punished illegal profiteering and placed firm restrictions on the channels of redress for aggrieved Indian rulers. The legal architecture of the code, motivated as it was by the design of subordinating Indian officials beneath a streamlined British administration, was supplied by Jones' continuing work on translating Indian legal codes. Jones' insistence that the means for determining judgements must be taken out of the exclusive control of indigenous advisers complemented the Company's efforts to distance itself from its lawless

[182] Governor-General in Council to Jones, 19 March 1788, in *Letters*, vol. 2, p. 801.

[183] Marshall, 'Cornwallis Triumphant'.

[184] P. J. Marshall, 'The Moral Swing to the East: British Humanitarianism, India and the West Indies', in K. Ballhatchet and John Harrison (eds.), *East India Company Studies: Papers Presented to Professor Sir Cyril Philips* (Hong Kong: Asian Research Service, 1986), p. 79.

[185] Travers, *Ideology and Empire*, p. 221. [186] Marshall, 'A Free Though Conquering People'.

[187] Wilson, *Domination of Strangers*, p. 46.

reputation not only via reforms, but also through the rhetoric of 'native corruption'.[188] It was in respect for the need to assert Company control without being perceived to violate Indian customs that Cornwallis would seek the guidance of Jones. Thus in 1790, Jones had studied the draft and supplements of Cornwallis' 'Minute on the administration of criminal justice in the provinces'. This would lead to the Judicial Plan of 1790, in which the Company formally took the administration of justice from the nawab, replaced Indian agencies with English ones, and introduced circuit courts. Despite his intention to write his objections unreservedly, Jones replied to Cornwallis that 'I found nothing to which I could object, and did not meet with a single paragraph to which, if I were a member of the Council I would not heartily express my assent'. Without any serious concerns, he signed off on the plan as 'just, wise and benevolent'.[189] Though Jones had previously rejected the idea of circuit courts, he was persuaded by the retention of indigenous legal advisers.[190] This precedent was established in 1790, and Jones then continued to consult with Cornwallis on the principles and details for the code. Jones' influence can be viewed in a range of its legal provisions, such as the principle that Islamic law will be followed in criminal cases, but that when it called for punishments like mutilation, English law should supersede it, or that in civil suits between Hindus, a pandit could assist the judge on matters of inheritance and caste. As Cannon put it, 'the code was consonant with Indian law, in harmony with Jones' feelings since his work on Indian judicature in 1781, but English agencies administered justice'.[191]

On the level of policy, then, despite the evident change in style by the 1790s, Jones' work on the legal interpretation of Indian religion continued to be perfectly compatible with imperial governance in India. Rather than see this as some kind of tension in Jones' thought, based on the perception that he had a sympathetic attitude to Indian religion, it is more appropriate to consider the ways in which his interpretation and subsequent construction of Indian religion fitted into this institutional context. While he benefited from expert instruction and possessed greater insight, scholarly discipline and linguistic knowledge than his predecessors, Jones was still at pains to privilege a particular view of Hindu religious thought. The version of the Hindu religion that pervaded Jones' writings, both poetry and prose,

[188] Travers, *Ideology and Empire*, p. 231.

[189] William Jones to Lord Cornwallis, Court House, 20 November 1790, in Charles Ross (ed.), *Correspondence of Charles, First Marquis Cornwallis*, vol. 2 of 3 (London: John Murray, 1859), p. 57.

[190] Cannon, *Life and Mind of Oriental Jones*, p. 325.

[191] Cannon, *Life and Mind of Oriental Jones*, p. 326.

was mystical and esoteric. That view picked up on many of the themes established by the philosophic approach, articulated by Holwell and Dow, and which had garnered British interpretations of Indian religion an international reputation. The Hindu religion was ancient and, moreover, probably the source of other heathen religions. It was philosophical and sophisticated, and as such contained both strains of religious truth and the corrupting effects of priestcraft. And yet where Holwell and Dow had posited a rational religion, compatible with, and in fact potentially illuminating of, Christian religion, Jones, the great pioneer of comparative linguistics, did not.

Above all, his focus on the mystical doctrine of *mokṣa*, or *māyā*, in Advaita Vedānta emphasised the sublime elements of religious belief, not its rational core. Such a religion, though affecting and transcendent, was not comparable with the truths of Christianity, except for the overlap where followers of the latter, such as Isaac Barrow, had also lapsed into enthusiastic mysticism. This was because of Jones' particular position within what has only previously been identified as a loosely 'deistic' thread that ran through British accounts of Indian religion that took it seriously. More specifically, Jones advocated and espoused a form of Dissenting Christianity that rejected the trinity, favoured a broad toleration, but defended a rational belief in revelation, based on what he saw as the evident fulfilment of the prophecies contained within the Bible. Jones' interpretation was still a product of a heterodox religious position, but one that removed the subversive potential of seeing the truths of Indian religion as rational, as had Holwell and Dow, or as equally implicit as any of those of Christianity, as was suggested by Halhed. Jones' comparison was between that of Hindu and other ancient 'heathen' religions, all of which were artefacts of biblical history.

This vision of Hindu religion, like its other British predecessors, was animated by religious concerns that were extraneous to the interests of the Company in India. The result was, however, still perfectly compatible with Jones' position on what an enlightened British government in India would look like. By the time Jones arrived in India, British conquest was an established fact, and public criticism was not centred on the question of empire, but on how best to manage it. The role of religion in determining this debate has often mistakenly pitted attitudes to Indian customs as indicative of more or less sympathetic approaches to governance, thereby attaching some kind of normative value to empire based on its cultural sensitivity. Franklin, for example, has offered the instance of Jones drawing his pen through the opening sentences of the first draft of the 'permanent settlement' of Bengal, which had argued that the two principal ends of government in India were 'to insure its political safety, and to render the possession of the country as advantageous as possible to the East India Company and the British nation'. Jones had added in the margin, 'Surely the principal object of every Government is the happiness of the governed.' This is recounted as evidence of a generalised contrast between Hastings and Cornwallis, as well as Jones and Cornwallis, according to which a value for 'oriental learning' is aligned with preferring the happiness of the governed.[192] Certainly, this is how it was presented by the likes of Hastings and Jones, but in real terms, this did not extend to Jones' rejection of the settlement, even if he sought to correct its framing.

In the early 1780s, the reform of Indian abuses was widely acknowledged as a necessary component in the political reconstruction following Lord North's resignation in March 1782. Jones' appointment coincided with this period. As the first attempt, Fox's India Bill, despite its defeat in the Lords, illustrated that parliamentary opinion supported measures of Indian reform. In 1784 Pitt's India Act was successful. In its establishment of a ministerial Board of Control to exercise supervisory powers over the Company, the act was set forth under the banner of 'doing the most good to India, & to the Company, with the least injury to our constitution'.[193] In this environment the courts were seen as a branch of that constitution in India, and as a potential bulwark against corruption, so long as it upheld the principle of preserving native laws set out in the 1781 Bengal Judicature Act. Jones, as a man of reputed oriental learning, had been consulted extensively on the bill before his appointment to the bench in India. Indeed, it was to aid British lawyers in the implementation of the act that his *The Mahomedan Law of Succession to the Property of Intestates* (1782) was written up.

When Jones arrived in India in 1783, these were the principles animating his enquiries into Sanskrit and his translation of the *Mānava-Dharmaśāstra*. The enquiries of the Asiatick Society went beyond these purposes, but did not interfere with them. The regard for Indian culture and for Indian customary law were intertwined, particularly where the interpretation of the latter needed, in Jones' eyes, to be wrested from the exclusive control of indigenous administrators. Thus, while the appointment of Cornwallis ushered in a more assertive imperialism, it is clear that in his support of

[192] Franklin, *Orientalist Jones*, pp. 309–10.

[193] 'Pitt's Speech on the India Bill, House of Commons, 6 July 1784', in A. C. Bannerjee (ed.), *Indian Constitutional Documents, 1757–1947* (Calcutta: A. Mukherjee & Co., 1961), p. 94.

Jones he also sought a certain continuity with those aspects of the Hastings administration that had been upheld in the 1782 Bengal Judicature Act. Between them, Jones and Cornwallis upheld the language of custom and, at the same time, restructured the administration in an effort to gain a certain amount of distance from the charges brought by Burke. Indeed, such was the perception of the metropole. As the *Public Advertiser* put it, 'With such a Governor General as Lord Cornwallis, reinforced by the wholesome authority of the newly amended act of Parliament, and with such a law chief as Sir William Jones, what should there be in reason to check the most thriving expectations of our Asiatick concerns?'[194]

Towards the end of Jones' career, and the turn of the century, outrage at Company servants' alleged misdemeanours was gradually replaced with a public discourse of pride in their supposed integrity and distinction. As well as the attempts to rebrand its image with parliamentary oversight and Cornwallis' reforms, opinions shifted due to war with Britain's imperial competitor, France, as well as widespread reporting on the crimes of the Company's South Indian enemy, Tipu Sultan of Mysore. Indeed, at the end of Hastings' trial, news of Cornwallis' victories over the French-aligned Tipu Sultan, who had taken the place of Siraj-ud-Daulah (made famous by Holwell's tale of the 'Black Hole') as the Company's chief antagonist, was greeted with public enthusiasm in Britain.[195] The work of Jones, and of the Asiatick Society, was closely aligned with this image of an improved and reputable Company, his scholarship seen as the evidential fruit of well-regulated Indian affairs.

That Jones' work was increasingly allied with a defence of British institutions, both religious and imperial, was nowhere more apparent than in the pages of orientalist writer and clergyman Thomas Maurice.[196] Maurice had studied at Oxford and in that time attracted the support of Samuel Johnson, through whose influence he was offered the curacy of Bosworth.[197] Having never travelled to India himself, his seven-volume book *Indian Antiquities* (1793–1800) was heavily reliant on the work of Jones. Maurice had in several works chastised 'infidel' writers who had allowed the supposed antiquity of India to become 'the *debatable ground*' for radical ideas. In his pamphlet *Brahminical Fraud Detected* (1812), for

[194] *Public Advertiser*, 27 March 1786, cited in Franklin, *Orientalist Jones*, p. 309.

[195] Marshall, 'Cornwallis Triumphant'.

[196] On Maurice's connections to mythography, see Kidd, *World of Mr Casaubon*, pp. 157–61.

[197] Nigel Leask, 'Maurice, Thomas (1754–1824), Oriental Scholar and Librarian' *Oxford Dictionary of National Biography* (Oxford: Oxford University Press, 2004) [www.oxforddnb.com/view/article/18387, accessed 29 March 2021].

example, Maurice attacked 'Messrs Bailly, Dupuis, Voltaire, Volney and the whole French infidel school' who had, he argued, 'hoisted their standard – the boldest standard of defiance – on the ground of the presumed unfathomable antiquity of India'.[198] Decrying 'the dangerous effect of republican principles' that had gripped both Europe and Asia, Maurice reflected in his memoirs that it was the correspondence and 'learned labours of Sir. W. Jones' that had allowed him to produce his own contrary corrective accounts of Indian history and culture.[199]

Like Jones, Maurice had gone to great lengths to insist on the authority of biblical history. In his use of Jones, though, Maurice managed to remove the distanced latitude on matters such as the importance of the trinity for Christian piety, and committed one of the most egregious sins in interpreting Hindu religion according to Jones' own writings, which was to compare Brahma, Viṣṇu and Śiva to the Christian trinity.[200] Maurice's *Indian Antiquities* thus appropriated the work of Jones for a polemic, designed to defend the Old Testament from the attacks of sceptical French mythographers who had weaponised Hindu religion, astronomy and chronology. For Maurice, Jones, whose 'intimate knowledge and acquaintance with the mythology and history of Oriental nations availed not to make a sceptic', had rescued Christianity, which Maurice reminded his readers was 'inseparably connected with the National Government', from such sceptical and radical attacks.[201]

198 Thomas Maurice, *Brahminical Fraud Detected, or, the Attempts of the Sacerdotal Tribe of India to Invest Their Fabulous Deities and Heroes with the Honours and Attributes of the Christian Messiah Examined, Exposed, and Defeated* (London W. Bulmer & Co., 1812), p. 6.

199 Maurice, *Memoirs*, p. 102.

200 Thomas Maurice, *A Dissertation on the Oriental Trinities* (London [s.n.], 1800).

201 Maurice, *Memoirs*, p. 111. This latter comment was a quotation of a passage from his *History of Hindostan; Its Arts, and Its Sciences*, vol. 1 (London: Bulmer and Co., 1795), p. 29.

Conclusion

> He spoke to me in the Persian language; of which, as well as the Arabic, and the different dialects of Hindostan, he was *perfect* master ... He had set out many months before, from Calcutta, with an intention of travelling through the northern parts of Hindostan, in order to trace the antiquities of the most ancient nations.[1]

The above is a description of the fictional character Captain Percy, given from the perspective of the eponymous 'Hindoo Rajah' in Elizabeth Hamilton's 1796 epistolary novel, *Translations of the Letters of a Hindoo Rajah*. This 'English officer' was modelled on Hamilton's deceased brother Charles (1753–92), who had authored several Persian manuscript translations. As Captain Percy, he thus represented what was by then the familiar archetype of the East India Company orientalist.[2] The account of India laid out in Hamilton's novel offers a literary reflection of British constructions of *Hindoo* religion and history, and their relationship to the politics of empire in India, as they stood towards the end of the eighteenth century.

The novel, which went into five editions between 1796 and 1811, follows a series of letters between the Rajah Zāārmilla and his two fellow *Hindoo* correspondents, a Brahmin and a zamindar, describing their experiences in India and England in the mid-1770s and early 1780s. The reader is guided through these epistolary exchanges with detailed footnotes, intended to educate them on ideas and terms pertaining to Indian religion and culture. In the composition of these didactic notes and references, Hamilton drew extensively from the writings of Dow, Halhed, Wilkins and Jones, as well as indirectly from Holwell, via her use of Thomas Maurice's *Indian Antiquities* (1793–1800). The image of *Hindoo* religion that emerges is of a theology founded on 'sublime and exalted notions of the Deity',

[1] Hamilton, *Translations*.

[2] Gordon Goodwin, 'Hamilton, Charles (1752/3–1792)', rev. Philip Carter, *Oxford Dictionary of National Biography* (Oxford: Oxford University Press, 2004) [www.oxforddnb.com/view/article/12054, accessed 2 July 2016].

characterised by the 'spirit of unbounded toleration'. Like her sources Hamilton insisted that the *Hindoos*' 'inferior deities' were merely symbolical. She also echoed the reflection that the vulgar, when left in ignorance, 'soon transfer their veneration to the symbol', and that in such a manner, *Hindoo* practices had indeed degenerated into 'the grossest idolatry'.[3] Nevertheless, their sublime conception of God was 'everywhere to be met with in their writings' which, Hamilton boldly claimed, were 'only to be equalled' by the Gospel. To illustrate this, Hamilton chose not a translation, but a series of excepts from Jones' 'A Hymn to Náráyena'.[4]

Hamilton's book has been described variously as a feminist critique, an anti-Jacobin novel, a satire and an apologia for imperialism.[5] Others have pointed to precisely the paratextual material on Indian religion and customs to suggest that the novel eludes any easy classification because in the footnotes and notes Hamilton appears to explore and appeal to various 'different aspects of Jacobin and loyalist thought'.[6] In particular, the novel follows Montesquieu's *Persian Letters* (1721) and Oliver Goldsmith's *Citizen of the World* (1762) in using the trope of the Eastern traveller to satirise European manners, and in particular Britain's treatment of women. To this assortment of definitions and ideas we might add that the novel's notes also offered an expression of the ways in which British interpretations of Indian religion had been adapted and applied at the end of the eighteenth century. In Hamilton's notes the ideas of Holwell and Dow are lifted out of their initial setting, stripped of their critical content and subsequently repurposed to suit a new set of conceptions regarding Enlightenment and empire in India. Hamilton's account of *Hindoo* thought and history is thus richly textured by their work, but reframed according to more recent events in Britain, Europe and India. The book was intended precisely as a monument to Company orientalism, and it was written, as its dedication made clear, not just in praise of Hamilton's 'much lamented brother' Charles, but also his 'honoured patron' Warren Hastings.[7]

[3] Hamilton, *Translations*, pp. xxv–xxvi.

[4] Hamilton, *Translations*, pp. xviii, xxi–xxiii, 170.

[5] For an account of the interplay between feminist readings and Hamilton's defence of imperialism, see Sonja Lawrenson, 'Revolution, Rebellion and a Rajah from Rohilkhand: Recontextualizing Elizabeth Hamilton's Translation of the Letters of a Hindoo Rajah', *Studies in Romanticism*, 51:2 (2012); for an account of Hamilton's politics in the text, see chapter 1 in Claire Grogan, *Politics and Genre in the Works of Elizabeth Hamilton, 1756–1816* (Burlington, VT: Ashgate, 2012).

[6] Alex Watson, 'Translating India: Geopolitical Identity in Elizabeth Hamilton's Translations of the Letters of a Hindoo Rajah', *Studies in English and American Literature*, 47 (2012), p. 68. See also Jeanne M. Britton, 'Fictional Footnotes, Romantic Orientalism, and the Remediated Novel: Elizabeth Hamilton's Translation of the Letters of a Hindoo Rajah', *European Romantic Review*, 26:6 (2015).

[7] Hamilton, *Translations*, Dedication, dated 6 June 1796.

In seeking to vindicate Hastings, who had recently been acquitted of the impeachment charges brought by Burke, Hamilton fitted this account of *Hindoo* beliefs and manners into a narrative of Indian history that had previously dressed the pages of her brother's *Historical Relation of the Origin, Progress, and Final Dissolution of the Government of the Rohilla Afgans* (1787). In the preliminary dissertation for the work, Charles Hamilton had sketched out 'a short view of the state of the provinces of Hindostan, subject to the Mussulman governments', which did not present a favourable depiction of Muslim rule. The 'petty tyrants' of these pages thus appeared again in Elizabeth's *Letters of a Hindoo Rajah*, which, despite its repeated celebrations of *Hindoo* toleration, does not hesitate to castigate the influence of 'the imposter of Mecca' over 'Musselman' governance in India.[8] In Hamilton's telling, the Muslim invaders of India realised, after much bloodshed, that they would have no hope of converting the 'mild and gentle' *Hindoos* and so 'relinquished the impracticable idea', opting instead for 'civil dominion'. Nevertheless, *Hindoo* laws and customs had been laid to waste: 'Mussulman courts of justice were erected' and, in an unintentionally ironic scene, 'haughty and voluptuous' lords began to greedily extract revenue from carved-up *Hindoo* lands. Thanks to Hastings and his successors, however, government under the 'milder spirit of Christianity' had meant that the *Hindoos*' 'ancient laws have been restored to them' and 'agriculture has been encouraged' by 'security of property' (i.e. Cornwallis' 'permanent settlement').[9]

This teleology of British rule, reiterated and confirmed through the letters of the Rajah, answered the aspirations set out in the poetry of Halhed and Jones, which had put into the mouths of Hindu deities various laments urging their followers to reconcile themselves to the benefits of Company governance. And yet, it also obscured the complex processes and various strategies of rule that had been advanced, rejected and pursued in these years preceding Clive's military conquests of the late 1750s. The idiosyncratic productions of Holwell and Dow had appeared in the immediate aftermath, and as such constituted a heady mixture of heterodox religious thought and criticism of the Company. They were not critics of empire, but their conceptions of what British government in India would look like were particular to this period, and to their accounts of Indian history and culture. Holwell, disparaging the expense of military ventures,

8 Hamilton, *Translations*, pp. xlviii, xlii. For this depiction of Muslim rule, see Charles Hamilton, *Historical Relation of the Origin, Progress, and Final Dissolution of the Government of the Rohilla Afgans* (London: G. Kearsley, 1787), p. 19; Hamilton, *Translations*, pp. xlviii, xlii.

9 Hamilton, *Translations*, pp. xliv, xlvii, li.

had argued that the Company should seize land from the existing zamindars and negotiate for itself the position of *subah* (a Mughal title for governor of a province), thereby securing its tentative advantage in the region. Dow, who wrote from the matter-of-fact position that conquest by arms was complete, had maintained that the best means of securing the Company's acquisition of *diwani* rights would be a 'permanent plan' to fix property revenues as well as judicial system based on the maintenance of existing laws. These projections of what was possible were limited to the Company's patchwork of acquisitions, and ultimately aspired to more secure integration into existing networks of sovereignty. Moreover, their understanding of Indian history and what they presented as the region's indigenous philosophy and religion appeared to limit the bounds of legitimate dominion to the displacement of Mughal authority. In advancing their claims about the inherent worth of Indian religion, both authors had regaled readers with accounts of distinctly *Hindoo* territories, which had preserved their ancient tenets, had enduring political settlements, and represented, in the words of Dow, a 'great and rising people'.[10]

In the work of Holwell and Dow, Indian thought was a store of knowledge which could challenge, correct and enhance European Enlightenment. For Holwell, Indian scriptures not only pointed to the purity of original natural religion, but also heralded the discovery of a lost original truth, which resolved many of the inherent inadequacies and contradictions in Christian theology: the doctrine of metempsychosis. For Dow, Nyāya bore all the hallmarks of the most reasonable accounts of a Supreme Being advanced in Europe. Moreover, the best example of foreign dominion in India was the reign of Akbar, precisely because of his deism. Consequently, readers took from them what best suited their own intellectual commitments, as well as condemning what was judged to be too irreverent. Much of this related to critical reflection on the Company, as well as the various religious debates to which these authors had deliberately addressed their work. In the eighteenth century their work was translated into other European languages, and used throughout the world of letters to support various sceptical and heterodox positions on religious topics, as well as in some cases as critiques of the Company. In the early nineteenth century, references to these writers continued to circulate in infidel and freethinking publications.

Some of the heterodox elements of Holwell's and Dow's works remained in the productions of Halhed and Wilkins, but in yet a new

[10] Dow, *History of Hindostan*, vol. 3 (1768), p. xxxvii.

setting. Halhed offered *Gentoo* chronology as a sceptical challenge to biblical history, and Wilkins situated the *Bhagavad-Gītā* in a contemporary framework of rational reform. The case for the production and presentation of these works to the public were, however, the prerogative of Governor-General Warren Hastings, 'a self-conscious builder of empire', the policies and position of whom they were intended to uphold.[11] Their reception was not straightforwardly aligned with these intentions though. Much of the commentary on the *Code* took to either refuting Halhed's scepticism, likening him to Hume and Voltaire, or pointing to the inherent contradiction between its contents and Halhed's promotion of them with the presumption of dominion. Wilkins' work no doubt added to Hastings' deliberate construction of himself as a governor-general who was a patron and interpreter of India to polite society in Europe. And yet, as the first direct translation of a major work of Sanskrit into English, his framing of the text as Unitarianism in principle also ensured the continued association between Indian religion and Dissenting positions within European theological debate.

The next incarnation of a British philosophical interpretation of Indian religion was the work of William Jones, conceived of in the turn towards the most confident assertion of British empire in India in the development of its claim to sovereignty in the eighteenth century. Jones' depiction of Advaita Vedānta as Indian philosophy's sublime centre, supported by his poetical depictions of its transcendent and devotional nature, was a much neater complement to an ideological account of the British administration as a benevolent guardian of 'native customs'. Likewise, though Jones has been aligned with a 'deistical' approach, a more thorough analysis suggests that his thought was more closely aligned with Rational Dissent, and with that came a focus on defending biblical scripture, which significantly distanced his presentation of *Hindoo* religion from the views advanced by Holwell, Dow and Halhed.

The difference between Jones and his predecessors is captured in his proclamation in the first publication of *Asiatick Researches* that 'Reason and Taste are the grand prerogatives of European minds, while the Asiatics have soared to loftier heights in the sphere of imagination.'[12] A properly historicised account of British interpretations and constructions of Indian religion in the eighteenth century must contrast this with the Nyāya of Dow,

[11] Marshall, 'Making of an Imperial Icon', p. 2.

[12] William Jones, 'The President's Second Anniversary Discourse, Delivered 24 February 1785' in *Asiatick Researches, or, Transactions of the Society, Instituted in Bengal, for Inquiring into the History and Antiquities, the Arts, Sciences, and Literature, of Asia*, vol. 1 (London [s.n.], 1799), p. 407.

who 'look up to the divinity, through the medium of reason and philosophy'.[13] While it could be argued that Jones' account of Indian thought became more sophisticated over the course of his researches than this quotation gives credit for, the idea, bolstered by Jones' authority as an orientalist scholar, had a wider appeal. The same line was quoted by Hamilton, in *Letters of a Hindoo Rajah*, as the affirmed opinion 'of one who must be allowed competent to the decision'. In this context, Jones' proclamation serves as evidence of her claim that the precepts of the *Hindoo* faith produced tranquillity rather than 'the paths of useful knowledge', though she allows them significant advancement on 'metaphysics, and ethics', as well as poetry.[14]

Another writer who also made liberal use of Jones' work on this topic was Thomas Maurice, for whom India's ancient history was mythological, not historical, because 'their empire was the empire of imagination', not terrestrial events. The proof for this was to be Jones' work tracing the conformity of Indian chronology with biblical history.[15] In Maurice's 1793 work *Indian Antiquities*, the same evidence from Jones was thus used explicitly to counter 'the daring assertions of certain sceptical French philosophers' in support of antiquity, which, as he would elaborate in his memoirs, was proving fuel to the fire of 'Jacobin fury' in Europe and India.[16] Indeed, as well as Cornwallis, and changes in India, there was another European perspective that accounts for the importance of Jones in developing a different thread for the use of the philosophical view of Indian religion. The French Revolution and attendant threat of radical atheism reverberated across the works of writers like Hamilton and Maurice.

The war with revolutionary France was a major theme in *Letters of a Hindoo Rajah*. As Nigel Leask has argued, in its depiction of Britain's relationship with India, Hamilton's novel 'is based on an analogy between the Islamic conquest of large parts of Hindu India and the impact of the French revolution on Europe'.[17] According to Hamilton, the ancient Rajahs possessed an 'amiable and benevolent character' characterised by the 'mild aspect of parental authority'. The only thing that had destroyed this was the 'resistless fury of fanatic zeal' brought by Muslim conquerors.

[13] Dow, *History of Hindostan*, vol. 1 (1768), p. lxv.

[14] Hamilton, *Translations*, pp. xxiv–xxvi.

[15] Maurice, *History of Hindostan*, pp. ii–iii.

[16] Thomas Maurice, *Indian Antiquities: Or, Dissertations, Relative to the Ancient Geographical Divisions, the Pure System of Primeval Theology, the Grand Code of Civil Laws, the Original Form of Government, and the Various and Profound Literature, of Hindostan* (London: W. Richardson, 1793), pp. 29–31; Maurice, *Memoirs*, p. 102.

[17] Nigel Leask, *British Romantic Writers and the East: Anxieties of Empire* (Cambridge: Cambridge University Press, 1992), p. 101.

That this was parallel to the revolutionary threat in Europe was implied by Hamilton's account of what had allowed *Hindoo* government to retain its mild character prior to its invasion: the system of caste. This was not a major feature in the works of earlier British orientalists, but Hamilton's usage echoes its assimilation into European notions of social hierarchies. It was 'the division of the Hindoos into four Casts, or tribes, to each of which a particular station was allotted, and peculiar duties were assigned', Hamilton argues, that had 'lent its aid toward the preservation of a general harmony'. The dissolution of rank and order by revolutionary turmoil in France was thus paralleled in her account of Islam's destructive rampage across Asia. Prior to this invasion, 'the separation of the different casts' had saved them from 'the murmurs of discontent' felt in other nations, since each individual followed in the footsteps of their forefathers and retained that station 'firmly believed to have been marked out for him by the hand of Providence'.[18]

While this particular framing would not have been familiar to the earlier authors cited by Hamilton, their conception of an ancient and philosophical original religion laid the foundations for ideas about the value of Indian culture as distinctively ancient and *Hindoo*, against which the Mughal regime could be placed as a despotic intruder. Moreover, it was Jones' work above all that satisfied Hamilton's depiction of the British preservation of the ancient customs as a bulwark against such dissolution. Likewise, for Maurice, where Holwell, Dow and Halhed could be more closely aligned with French opinions on the antiquity of India, Jones was to be enlisted in support of both the 'national Theology' and the 'national Government'.[19]

In addition to Jones, the institutionalisation of orientalism further obscured its more heterodox origins in the mid-eighteenth century. By the turn of the century, when the Company was undergoing rapid expansion and a formalisation of its system in recruitment and training, the idea that its servants ought to be well acquainted with local languages and customs became a standard expectation. Tied into this was the continuation of notions about Company patronage of learning and the stewardship of Indian culture as characterising a system of enlightened governance, while at the same time producing a much more deliberate imperial bureaucracy. The first step towards this in India was the establishment of a training college for Company servants at Fort William. The college had been founded by the governor-general succeeding John Shore, Richard Wellesley. The early history of the college consisted of a tense conflict between

[18] Hamilton, *Translations*, pp. ix, xi, xvi–xvii. [19] Maurice, *Memoirs*, p. 102.

Wellesley and the Company's court of directors, the causes of which have been the subject of a rich body of literature.[20] Much of this revolved around the notion that Wellesley was usurping the power of the directors, cultivating for himself a network of patronage and influence channelled through the college. Wellesley's notes highlighted the ways in which such an institution would complement the grand imperial aims of a British empire in India. In the first instance, the imposing building would stand as 'a public monument' to 'commemorate the conquest at Mysore', the scene of the Company's victory over the French-aligned Tipu Sultan.[21] Wellesley also envisaged it as a complement to 'the native Colleges', the Calcutta Madrasa and Benares Sanskrit College, in a system that would 'contribute to the happiness of our native subjects' and so 'qualify them to form a more just estimate of the mild and benevolent spirit of the British Government'.[22]

The college was also about discipling the minds of the Company's servants, which had become, in Wellesley's judgement, susceptible to 'erroneous principles' during 'the convulsions with which the doctrines of the French Revolution have agitated the Continent of Europe'. This 'dangerous tendency' had 'reached the minds of some individuals in the civil and military service of the Company in India', unsettling both political and 'religious opinions'. Such a situation, Wellesley argued, called for 'an Institution tending to fix and establish sound and correct principles of religion and government' in the minds of its young writers. This was, he judged, 'the best security . . . for the stability of the British power in India'. The foundations for this were an education in 'the history, languages, customs and manners of the people of India, with the Mahommedan and Hindoo codes of law and religion, and with the political and commercial interests and relations of Great Britain in Asia'.[23]

In the intervening years, the importance of these foundations was highlighted by the increasing advancements of the French in the acquisition of orientalist knowledge, displayed not only by the prestige of the exciting researches emerging from Napoleon's Commission of Science and Arts of Egypt, but also the number of French actors who were carrying out skilful diplomatic negotiations in Indian languages.[24] By 1800, the

20 See especially Kopf, *British Orientalism*; see also Trautmann, *Aryans and British India*.

21 Wellesley, 'Governor-General's Notes', p. 351.

22 Wellesley, 'Governor-General's Notes', p. 352.

23 Wellesley, 'Governor-General's Notes', pp. 346, 330.

24 'Report of the Committee Appointed to Enquire into the Plan for Forming an Establishment at Home' (26 October 1804), in Anthony Farrington (ed.), *The Records of the East India College Haileybury & Other Institutions* (London: HMSO, 1976), p. 18.

investigation of Indian religious and philosophical thought had been transported far away from the independent researches of Holwell and Dow, both of whom enlisted them in support of 'religious opinions' that were far from those of the established Church. Instead, they were part of a new conception of British empire, not just a trading company, which was in explicit competition with France. As Wellesley put it, the Company's servants 'can no longer be considered as the agents of a commercial concern. They are, in fact, the ministers and officers of a powerful sovereign'.[25]

*

This book began with the proposition that in the 1760s the claim among British authors that they had penetrated the original principles of India's ancient 'symbolical religion' prompted a distinctively philosophical approach to the interpretation of Hinduism. This perspective was rooted in their intellectual engagement with contemporary European religious and philosophical discourses, and in particular different varieties of heterodox theology. Common to each author was the notion that through pandit instruction, linguistic ability and access to ancient texts, they had penetrated the previously veiled doctrines of the original and ancient religion of India, and that this religion was philosophically sophisticated. They rejected previous authors on the grounds that eye-witness observation and antiquarian conjecture were inadequate and resulted only in very partial accounts. Although the Jesuits had collected an array of insights into Indian religious thought, for these British authors this was summarily rejected as prejudicial on account of their missionary agenda. In contrast, they presented themselves as disinterested men of letters, in pursuit of the truth. Further examination of the ideological commitments and intellectual preoccupations that these authors brought to bear on their work, however, reveals that they adapted and reconstructed Indian ideas to address various European concerns, just as much as their predecessors. The distinctive difference was that, rather than confirming the place of Indian religiosity in a biblical framework, in which heathen polytheism represented the depravation of the world without revelation, these authors posited the essential rationality and compatibility of Brahmin theology with the idea of a singular benevolent Supreme Being. Those practices that had previously been mistaken for the essence of the *Gentoo* or *Hindoo* religion were cast as in fact symbolical and allegorical expressions of the

25 Wellesley, 'Governor-General's Notes', p. 329.

various attributes of this singular deity. Moreover, while indeed the superstitions of the vulgar muddied these refinements, these authors insisted that this was no less true in the history of Christian theology and worship, since the ill-designs of priestly manipulation were in operation everywhere.

Indeed, this book also began by examining the common refrain in existing literature on British interactions with Hinduism in the eighteenth century, that these authors wrote about Indian religion from a deist perspective, taking note of the attendant implications that this observation has been intended to herald. Firstly, it noted that this claim, often made without substantiated analysis of their works, obscured the range of theological concerns, some similar, some different, that animated their conceptions of Indian religion and history. What was 'deist' in their thought pertained to some common assumptions about the universal nature of religious belief, and its origins in a pure natural religion of reason, the truth of which was gradually corrupted by priestcraft; a narrative which was in all of these thinkers supported by a rather robust contempt for the religiosity of the vulgar, prone as they were to superstition and enthusiastic excess. What constituted a more reasonable approach to religion, and the basic tenets of natural faith, however, differed from thinker to thinker.

Following this, this book has also challenged the idea that a 'deist' approach could be determined as shorthand for a 'sympathetic' or less prejudicial attitude to India and its peoples, pointing to how for many of these authors their religious concerns resulted in deeply invested agendas in their construction and presentation of Indian ideas. What complicated this further was that these philosophical accounts were related to the dual contexts of Enlightenment and empire, the nature of which were changing significantly over the last quarter of the eighteenth century. Their accounts of a 'native' philosophical Indian religion, often situated in narratives of decline from a pure golden age, supported various attempts to legitimise the status and policies of a shifting company-state, of which they were all interested members. In addition, and in ways that elude any straightforward connection, their philosophical engagements with Indian religion were also received by a European reading public, concerned not just with empire in India, the attempts to legitimise which were met with varying degrees of acceptance and scepticism, but also with the same religiously oriented debates that had inspired some of the more controversial statements advanced by these authors.

By the 1780s, the exploration and construction of Indian religion had become an activity that was sponsored by the Company's administration. In the 1790s the promulgation of new set of political and administrative relations also heralded new patterns for orientalism, scholarly patronage and ideas of Hinduism, which, with the aid of William Jones, further entrenched the idea that enlightened British government would be the benevolent guardian of Indian's ancient culture. By the turn of the century, Wellesley's East India College demonstrated how integral the construction and uses of ideas about India's customs, thought and mores had become to the simultaneous construction of a new conception of imperial sovereignty.

In returning to the 1760s, this study has offered a genealogy of British interpretations and constructions of Indian religion in the eighteenth century, often obscured by its culmination in such institutional forms, to recover its more critical and idiosyncratic origins. In doing so it has pointed to how historiographical accounts that subsume these intellectual histories under the broad categories of discursive dominance or cultural attitudes and encounters tend to obscure the complex relationship between the production and the various uses of knowledge, according to different intellectual and political environments. Some of these were decidedly about articulating particular conceptions of power, dominion and empire in India. Other ideas presented by the Company authors examined in this study also went beyond the requirements of practical knowledge, precisely so their work could be deployed in a European context to challenge particular orthodoxies and assumptions. In properly historicising and contextualising the origins and diverse uses of interpretations of the *Hindoo* religion, this book has revealed the importance of heterodox religious debate for the construction of such knowledge, as well as the multiple and varied ways in which it was understood and used.

Bibliography

Archival Sources

British Library, Additional Manuscripts (Add. MS)
- Warren Hastings Papers
- Wellesley Papers

British Library, Oriental and India Office Collections
- Bengal Law Consultations (BLC)
- Bengal Public Consultations (BPC)
- Bengal Revenue Consultations (BRC)
- Bengal Secret Consultations (BSC)
- Home Miscellaneous (HM)
- India Office Records (IOR)
- Murshidabad Factory Records (MP)
- Oriental Manuscripts (OMS)

European Manuscripts (MS Eur.)
- Philip Francis Papers
- Orme Papers

National Archives (Kew, United Kingdom)
- Public Record Office (PRO)

Journals and Periodicals

Asiatick Annual Register
Journals of the House of Commons
Public Advertiser
The Gentleman's Magazine
The Critical Review, or Annals of Literature
The Annual Register
The Monthly Review, or, Literary Journal
The Asiatic Journal and Monthly Register for British and Foreign India, China, and Australasia.

The Literary Magazine: or, Universal Review
The English Review, or an Abstract of English and Foreign Literature
The Anti-Jacobin Review and Magazine
The European Magazine, and London Review

Printed Primary Sources: Dow, Halhed, Holwell, Jones and Wilkins

Dow, Alexander

Tales, Translated from the Persian of Inatulla of Delhi, 2 vols. (London: T. Becket and P. A. de Hondt, 1768).

The History of Hindostan; From the Earliest Account of Time, to the Death of Akbar; Translated from the Persian of Mahummud Casim Ferishta of Delhi, 1st ed., 2 vols. (London: T. Becket and P. A. de Hondt, 1768).

Zingis. A Tragedy. As It Is Performed at the Theatre-Royal in Drury-Lane (London: T. Becket and P. A. de Hondt, 1769).

The History of Hindostan; Translated from the Persian. The Second Edition, Revised, Altered, Corrected, and Greatly Enlarged, by Alexander Dow, 2nd ed., 2 vols. (London:T. Becket and P. A. de Hondt, 1770).

The History of Hindostan, from the Death of Akbar, to the Complete Settlement of the Empire under Aurungzebe, 2nd ed., vol. 3 (London: T. Becket and P. A. de Hondt, 1772).

Sethona. A Tragedy. As It Is Performed at the Theatre-Royal in Drury-Lane (London: T. Becket, 1774).

The History of Hindostan; From the Earliest Account of Time, to the Death of Akbar; Translated from the Persian of Mahummud Casim Ferishta of Delhi, 3rd ed., 3 vols. (London: T. Becket and P. A. de Hondt, 1792).

Translations

Dissertation sur les moeurs, les usages, le langage, la religion et la philosophie des Hindous, Claude-François Bergier (trans.) (Paris: Chez Pissot, 1769).

Die Geschichte von Hindostan aus dem Persischen von Alexander Dow, 3 vols. (Leipzig: J. F. Junius, 1772–4).

Halhed, Nathaniel Brassey

A Code of Gentoo Laws, or, Ordinations of the Pundits: From a Persian Translation (London [s.n.], 1776).

A Grammar of the Bengal Language (Hoogly, Bengal: Charles Wilkins, 1778).

The Detector [pseud.]. *A Letter to Governor Johnstone, &c. &c. on Indian Affairs* (London: J. Johnson, 1782).

The Detector [pseud.]. *The Letters of the Detector on the Reports of the Select Committee of the House of Commons Appointed to Consider How the British*

Possessions in the East-Indies May Be Held and Governed with the Greatest Security and Advantage to This Country and How the Happiness of the Natives May Be Best Promoted (London [s.n.], 1782).

The Detector [pseud.]. *Letter to the Rt Hon. Edmund Burke, on the Subject of His Charges against the Governor-General of Bengal* (London: J. Johnson, 1783).

Testimony to the Authenticity of the Prophecies and Mission of Richard Brothers and of His Mission to Recall the Jews (London: R. Faulder, 1795).

Holwell, John Zephaniah

A Genuine Narrative of the Deplorable Deaths of the English Gentlemen, and Others, Who Were Suffocated in the BLACK-HOLE in FORT-WILLIAM, at CALCUTTA in the Kingdom of BENGAL; in the Night Succeeding the 20th Day of June, 1756 (London: Printed for A. Millar, 1758).

An Address to the Proprietors of East India Stock Setting Forth the Unavoidable Necessity and Real Motives for the Revolution in Bengal, in 1760 (London: T. Becket and P. A. de Hondt, 1764).

Important Facts Regarding the East-India Company's Affairs in Bengal, from the Year 1752 to 1760 (London: T. Becket and P. A. de Hondt, 1764).

India Tracts (London: T. Becket and P. A. de Hondt, 1764).

Mr. Holwell's Refutation of a Letter from Certain Gentlemen of the Council at Bengal, to the Honourable the Secret Committee. Serving as a Supplement to His Address to the Proprietors of East-India Stock (London: T. Becket and P. A. de Hondt, 1764).

A Narrative of the Events Which Have Happened in Bombay and Bengal, Relative to the Maharatta Empire, since July 1777 (London [s.n.], 1779)

An Account of the Manner of Inoculating Small Pox in the East Indies. With Some Observations on the Practice and Mode of Treating That Disease in Those Parts. Inscribed to the Learned the President, and Members of the College of Physicians in London (T. Becket and P. A. de Hondt, 1767).

An Address from John Zephaniah Holwell, Esq; to Luke Scrafton, Esq (London: T. Becket and P. A. de Hondt, 1767).

Interesting Historical Events, Relative to the Provinces of Bengal, and the Empire of Indostan, 1st ed., vol. 1 (London: T. Becket and P. A. de Hondt, 1765), vol. 2 (1767), vol. 3 (1771).

A Review of the Original Principles, Religious and Moral, of the Ancient Bramins: Comprehending an Account of the Mythology, Cosmogony, Pasts, and Festivals, of the Gentoos, Followers of the Shastah (London: Printed for D. Steel, 1779).

Dissertations on the Origin, Nature, and Pursuits, of Intelligent Beings, and on Divine Providence, Religion, and Religious Worship (London: R. Cruttwell, 1786).

Translations

Evénements historiques, intéressants, relatifs aux provinces de Bengale (Amsterdam [s.n.], 1768).

Sammlung neuer Reisebeschreibungen aus fremden Sprachen, E. Thiel and J. T. Koehler (trans.) (Gottingen and Gotha [s.n.], 1767–9).

Holwell's merkwürdige historische Nachrichten von Hindostan und Bengalen nebst einer Beschreibung der Religionslehren, der Mythologie, Kosmogonie, Fasten und Festtage der Gentoos und einer Abhandlung über die Metempsychose, Johann Friedrich Kleuker (trans.) (Leipzig: Weygandschen Buchhandlung, 1778).

Jones, William

*Lettre à Monsieur A*** du P***. Dans laquelle est compris l'examen de sa traduction des livres attribués à Zoroastre* (London: Chez P. Elmsly, 1771).

An Inquiry into the Legal Mode of Suppressing Riots (London: C. Dilly, 1782).

The Principles of Government, in a Dialogue between a Scholar and a Peasant (London [s.n.], 1782).

Al Sirajiyyah: or the Mohamedan Law of Inheritance (Calcutta: Joseph Cooper, 1792).

Institutes of Hindu Law; or the Ordinances of Menu (Calcutta: Printed by the order of Government, 1794).

Institutes of Hindu Law: Or, the Ordinances of Menu (London: J. Sewell, Cornhill and J. Debrett, 1796).

'The President's Second Anniversary Discourse, Delivered 24 February 1785', in *Asiatick Researches, or, Transactions of the Society, Instituted in Bengal, for Inquiring into the History and Antiquities, the Arts, Sciences, and Literature, of Asia*, vol. 1 (London [s.n.], 1799), pp. 405–32.

Edited Collections

Cannon, Garland (ed.). *The Letters of Sir William Jones*, vols. 1–2 (Oxford: Clarendon Press, 1970).

Franklin, Michael J. *Sir William Jones: Selected Poetical and Prose Works* (Cardiff: University of Wales Press, 1995).

Shore, John, Baron Teignmouth. *Memoirs of the Life, Writings and Correspondence of Sir William Jones*, 2nd ed., vol. 1 (London: John Hatchard, 1806).

(ed.). *The Works of Sir William Jones, with the Life of the Author, by Lord Teignmouth*, vols. 1 and 7 (London: J. Stockdale and J. Walker, 1807).

Wilkins, Charles

The Bhăgvăt-Gēētā, or Dialogues of Krēēshnă and Ărjŏŏn (London: C. Nourse, 1785).

Le Bhaguat-geeta ou Dialogues de Kreeshna et d'Arjoon, contenant un précis de la religion & de la morale des Indiens, J. P. Parraud (trans.) (Paris: Chez Buisson, 1787).

'Article XII, On the Seeks and Their College', in *Asiatick Researches; or, Transactions of the Society, Instituted in Bengal, for Inquiring into the History *and Antiquities, the Arts, Sciences, and Literature, of Asia*, vol. 1 (London, 1799), pp. 287–94.

The Hĕĕtōpădēs of Vĕĕshnŏŏ-Sărmā, in a Series of Connected Fables, Interspersed with Moral, Prudential, and Political Maxims (Bath: R. Cruttwell, 1887).

Other Printed Primary Material

Anon. 'Evénémens historiques, intéressans, rélatifs aux provinces de Bengale et de l'Indostan', *Journal Encyclopédique*, 2:2 (1769), pp. 202–16.

Anon. [George Rust?]. *A Letter of Resolution Concerning Origen and the Chief of His Opinions* (London, 1661).

Aquinas, Thomas. 'The Way in Which the Divine Truth Is to Be Made Known', in *Summa Contra Gentiles: Book 1*, Anton C. Pegis (trans.) (Notre Dame, IN: University of Notre Dame Press, 1975 [1259–65]), pp. 63–6.

Aristotle. *The Politics of Aristotle*, Peter L. Phillips Simpson (trans.) (Berkeley: University of California Press, 1997).

Atkinson, Benjamin, *Christianity Not Older Than the First Gospel-Promise. In Answer to a Book, Entitled Christianity as Old as the Creation, &c* (London: Richard Ford, and Richard Hett, 1730).

Baldaeus, *True and Exact Description of the Most Celebrated East India Coast of Malabar and Coromandel*, Anon. (trans.) (London: Awnsham and John Churchill, 1703).

Belsham, William. *History of Great Britain, from the Revolution to the Session of Parliament Ending AD 1793*, vol. 1 of 4 (London [s.n.], 1798).

Berrow, Capel. *A Pre-Existent Lapse of Human Souls in a State of Pre-Existence, the Only Original Sin, And the Ground Work of the Gospel Dispensation* (London: Winston and B. White, 1762).

Blake, William. *The Complete Poetry and Prose of William Blake*, David. E. V. Erdman (ed.) (Berkeley: University of California Press, 2008 [1965]).

Blount, Charles. *The Oracles of Reason* (London [s.n.], 1693).

Bolts, William. *Considerations on Indian Affairs, Particularly Respecting the Present State of Bengal and Its Dependencies*, 3 vols. (London: J. Almon & P. Elmsley, 1772).

Bond, Edward Augustus. *Speeches of Managers and Counsel in the Trial of Warren Hastings* (London: Longman, Brown, Green, Longmans & Roberts, 1859).

Boswell, James. *The Life of Samuel Johnson*, vol. 1. (London [s.n.], 1791).

Boswell in Extremes, 1776–1778, C. M. Weis and Frederick A. Pottle (eds.) (New York: McGraw-Hill, 1970).

Bougeant, Guillaume Hyacinthe. *Amusement philosophique sur le langage des Bestes* (Paris: Chez Antoine Van Dole, 1739).

A Philosophical Amusement upon the Language of Beasts (London: T. Cooper, 1739).

Briggs, John. *The History of the Rise of Mahomedan Power in India*, vol. 1 (London, 1829).

Burke, Edmund. 'Trial of Warren Hastings Esq: Third Day, 15th February, 1788', in *The Works of the Right Honourable Edmund Burke*, vol. 13 (London: F. C & J. Rivington, 1822), pp. 1–87.

The Works of the Right Honourable Edmund Burke, vol. 13 (London: F. C & J. Rivington, 1822).

The Writings and Speeches of Edmund Burke, 9 vols., Paul Langford et al. (eds.) (Oxford: Oxford University Press, 1970–).

The Writings and Speeches of Edmund Burke, vol. 5: *India: Madras and Bengal: 1774–1785*, P. J. Marshall and William B. Todd (eds.) (Oxford: Oxford University Press, 1981).

'Speech on Fox's India Bill', in David P. Fidler and Jennifer M. Welsh (eds.), *Empire and Community: Edmund Burke's Writings and Speeches on International Relations* (Boulder, CO: Westview Press, 1999), pp. 378–451.

Burnett, James (Lord Monboddo). *Ancient Metaphysics, or the Science of Universals*, vol. 4 (Edinburgh: J. Balfour, 1795).

de Camões, Luís Vaz. *The Lusiad: or Discovery of India. An Epic Poem. Translated from the Portuguese of Luis De Camoëns*, William Julius Mickle (trans.) (Oxford: Jackson and Lister, 1776).

The Lusiad: or Discovery of India. An Epic Poem. Translated from the Portuguese of Luis De Camoëns, William Julius Mickle (trans.), 2nd ed. (Oxford: Jackson and Lister, 1778).

Cardale, Paul. *The True Doctrine of the New Testament Concerning Jesus Christ Considered* (London: Johnson and Davenport, 1767).

Cheyne, George. *Essay of Health and Long Life* (London: George Strahan, 1724).

An Essay on Regimen, Together with Five Discourses, Medical, Moral and Philosophical (London: C. Rivington, 1740).

Cobbett, William (ed.). *Parliamentary History of England*, 36 vols. (London: T. C. Hansard, 1806–20).

Colebrooke, H. T. (ed.). *A Digest of Hindu Law on Contracts and Successions, with a Commentary*, vol. 3 (London [s.n.], 1801).

Colebrooke, Thomas Edward (ed.). *The Life of H. T. Colebrooke* (London: Trubner & Co., 1873).

Costard, George. *A Letter to Nathaniel Brassey Halhead, Esquire: Containing Some Remarks on His Preface to the Code of Gentoo Laws* (Oxford: Clarendon Press, 1778).

Cudworth, Ralph. *The True Intellectual System of the Universe*, John Harrison (ed.), 3 vols. (London: Thomas Tegg, 1845 [1678]).

Dean, Richard. *An Essay on the Future Life of Brute, Introduced with Observations upon Evil, Its Nature and Origin*, vol. 2 (London: Printed for G. Kearsly, 1768).

Debates of the House of Lords, on the Evidence Delivered in the Trial of Warren Hastings, Esquire; Proceedings of the East India Company in Consequence of His Acquittal: and Testimonials (London: Printed by J. Debrett, 1797).

de la Croix, François Pétis. *Histoire du Grand Genghiscan* (Paris: Chez la veuve Jombert, 1710).

The History of Genghizcan the Great, Penelope Aubin (trans.) (London, 1722).

Descartes, René. *Discourse on the Method and the Meditations*, John Veitch (trans.) (New York: Cosimo Incorporated, 2008 [Paris, 1637]).

Diderot, Dennis. 'Articles from the *Encyclopédie*', in *Political Writings*, John Hope-Mason and Robert Wokler (eds. and trans.) (Cambridge: Cambridge University Press, 1992), pp. 1–30.

Du Halde, Jean-Baptiste. *Lettres édifiantes et curieuses*, vol. 9. (Paris: Chez Nicolas le Clerc, 1715).

East India Company (British). *Preliminary Papers Respecting the East India Company's Charter* (London: Printed by the General Court, 1833).

Ensor, George. *The Principles of Morality* (London: J. S. Jordan, 1801).

Farrington, Anthony (ed.). *The Records of the East India College Haileybury & Other Institutions* (London: HMSO, 1976).

Fraser, James. *The History of Nadir Shah, Formerly Called Thamas Kuli Khan, the Present Emperor of Persia; to Which Is Prefixed a Short History of the Moghol Emperors'*(London: W. Strahan, 1742).

Gibbon, Edward. *The History of the Decline and Fall of the Roman Empire*, vol. 4 (Dublin [s.n.], 1788).

Gladwin, Francis. *Ayeen Akbery: Or, the Institutes of the Emperor Akber*, 3 vols. (Calcutta [s.n.], 1783–6).

Gleig, G. R. *Memoirs of the Life of the Right Hon. Warren Hastings: First Governor-General of Bengal; Compiled from Original Papers*, 3 vols. (London: Richard Bentley, 1841).

Gran, John. 'Warren Hastings in Slippers. Unpublished Letters of Warren Hastings', *Calcutta Review*, 26:51 (1956), pp. 59–141.

Grant, Charles. *Observations on the State of Society among the Asiatic Subjects of Great Britain* (London: Ordered by the House of Commons to be printed, 1813).

Grose, John Henry. *A Voyage to the East-Indies, with Observations on Various Parts There* (London: S. Hooper and A. Morley, 1757).

A Voyage to the East-Indies, with Observations on Various Parts There, 2nd ed., 2 vols. (London: S. Hooper, 1766).

Hamilton, Alexander. *A New Account of the East Indies*, vol. 1 of 2 (Edinburgh: John Mosman, 1727).

Hamilton, Charles. *Historical Relation of the Origin, Progress, and Final Dissolution of the Government of the Rohilla Afgans* (London: G. Kearsley, 1787).

Hamilton, Elizabeth. *Translations of the Letters of a Hindoo Rajah: Written Previous to and during the Period of His Residence in England*, vol. 1 (London: G. G. and J. Robinson, 1796).

Holwell, John Zephaniah. *An Account of the Manner of Inoculating for the Small Pox in the East Indies. With Some Observations on the Practice and Mode of Treating That Disease in Those Parts* (London: T. Becket and P. A. de Hondt, 1767).

Huddleston, R. (ed.). *A New Edition of Toland's History of the Druids* (Montrose: James Watt, 1816).

Hume, David. 'Of Miracles', in *Philosophical Essays Concerning Human Understanding* (London: A. Millar, 1748), Essay X, pp. 173–204.

Four Dissertations: I. The Natural History of Religion. II. Of the Passions. III. Of Tragedy. IV. Of the Standard of Taste (London: A. Millar, 1757).

The Letters of David Hume, vol. 2, J. Y. T. Greig (ed.) (Oxford: Clarendon Press, 1932).

Principal Writings on Religion Including Dialogues Concerning Natural Religion and the Natural History of Religion, J. C. A. Gaskin (ed.) (Oxford: Oxford University Press, 1993 [London, 1757]).

Dialogues Concerning Natural Religion, Richard Popkin (ed.) (Indianapolis: Hackett, 1980).

David Hume: Essays Moral, Political and Literary, Eugene F. Millar (ed.) (Indianapolis: Liberty Classics, 1985).

Essays and Treatises on Philosophical Subjects, Lorne Falkenstein and Neil McArthur (eds.) (Toronto: Broadview Editions, 2013).

Ilive, Jacob. *The Oration Spoke and Joyner's Hall* (London: T. Cooper, 1733).

Jarvis, Robin. *The Romantic Period: The Intellectual & Cultural Context of English Literature, 1789–1830* (Abingdon: Routledge, 2014).

John, P. Y. *A Few Hundred Bible Contradictions: A Hunt after the Devil, and Other Odd Matters*, vol. 3 (London: H. Hetherington, 1843).

Lambert, Sheila (ed.). *House of Commons Sessional Papers of the Eighteenth Century*, vol. 33 (Wilmington, DE: Scholarly Resources, 1975).

Langlès, Louis-Mathieu. *Fables et contes indiens, nouvellement traduits avec un discours preliminaire et des notes sur la religion, la littérature, les moeurs, etc. des Idons* (Paris: Royez, 1790).

Lessing, Gotthold Ephraim. *Philosophical and Theological Writings*, H. B. Nisbet (ed.) (Cambridge Texts in the History of Philosophy) (Cambridge: Cambridge University Press, 2005).

Locke, John. *A Letter Concerning Toleration and Other Writings*, Mark Goldie (ed.) (Indianapolis: Liberty Fund, 2010).

Lord, Henry. *A Display of Two Forraigne Sects in the East Indies* (London [s.n.], 1630).

Macdonald, John. *Memoirs of an Eighteenth-Century Footman 1745–1779* (London: George Routledge and Sons, 1927 [1790]).

Macpherson, James. *Fingal, an Ancient Epic Poem, in Six Books: Together with Several Other Poems, Composed by Ossian the Son of Fingal. Translated from the Galic Language, by James Macpherson* (London: T. Becket and P. A. de Hondt, 1762).

An Introduction to the History of Great Britain and Ireland (London: T. Becket and P. A. de Hondt, 1772).

The Poems of Ossian (London: J. D. Dewick for Allen Lackington, 1803).

Maurice, Thomas. *Indian Antiquities: Or, Dissertations, Relative to the Ancient Geographical Divisions, the Pure System of Primeval Theology, the Grand Code of Civil Laws, the Original Form of Government, and the Various and Profound Literature, of Hindostan* (London: W. Richardson, 1793).

The History of Hindostan; Its Arts, and Its Sciences, vol. 1 (London: W. Bulmer & Co., 1795).

A Dissertation on the Oriental Trinities (London [s.n.], 1800).

Brahminical Fraud Detected, or, the Attempts of the Sacerdotal Tribe of India to Invest Their Fabulous Deities and Heroes with the Honours and Attributes of the Christian Messiah Examined, Exposed, and Defeated (London: W. Bulmer & Co., 1812).

Memoirs of the Author of Indian Antiquities, 2nd ed., vol. 1 (London: Rivington, 1821).

Mendelssohn, Moses. *Jerusalem oder über religiöse Macht und Judentum* (Berlin: Maurer, 1783).

Writings on Judaism, Christianity and the Bible, Michah Gottlieb (ed.), Curtis Bowman, Elias Sacks and Allan Arkush (trans.) (Waltham, MA: Brandies University Press, 2011).

Mehta, Uday S. 'Edmund Burke on Empire, Self-Understanding and Sympathy', in Sankar Muthu (ed.), *Empire and Modern Political Thought* (Cambridge: Cambridge University Press, 2012), pp. 155–83.

Mickle, Julius. *Voltaire in the Shades, or Dialogues on the Deistical Controversy* (London: G. Perch, 1770).

Mill, James. *The History of British India*, vol. 1 (London: Baldwin, Cradock and Joy, 1817).

The History of British India, vol. 1 (Cambridge: Cambridge University Press, 2010).

Montesquieu, Charles-Louis de Secondat. *The Spirit of the Laws*, Anne Cohler, Basia Miller and Harold Stone (eds.) (Cambridge: Cambridge University Press, 1989 [1748]).

More, Thomas. *On Indian Customs*, S. Rajamanickam (ed. and trans.) (Palayamkottai: De Nobili Research Institute, 1972).

Utopia, Robert M. Adams (trans.) (New York: W. Norton and Company, 1975 [Louvain, 1516]).

Mossner, Ernest Campbell and Ross, Ian Simpson (eds.), *The Correspondence of Adam Smith* (Indianapolis: Liberty Fund, 1987).

Murray, Alexander. *History of European Languages*, vol. 2 (Edinburgh: A. Constable & Co., 1823).

Newton, Isaac. *The Principia: The Authoritative Translation*, Bernard Cohen and Anne Whitman (eds.) (Berkeley: University of California Press, 1999).

Nisbet, Hugh Barr. *Gotthold Ephraim Lessing: His Life, Works, and Thought* (Oxford: Oxford University Press, 2013).

Nobili, Roberto. *Adaptation*, S. Rajamanickam (ed.), J. Pujol (trans.) (Palayamkottai: De Nobili Research Institute, 1971).

Oberg, Barbara (ed.). *The Papers of Benjamin Franklin*, vol. 33: *July 1 through November 15, 1780* (New Haven, CT: Yale University Press, 1997).

Orme, Robert. *A History of the Military Transactions of the British Nation in Indostan* (London: John Norse, 1763).

Parr, Samuel. *Works, with Memoirs of His Life and Writings, and a Selection from His Correspondence*, John Johnstone (ed.), vol. 1 (London [s.n.], 1828).

Pearson, Hugh. *Memoirs of the Life and Writings of the Rev. Claudius Buchanan, D.D., Late Vice-Provost of the College of Fort William in Bengal* (Philadelphia: Benjamin & Thomas Kite, 1817).

Price, Richard. *A Review of the Principal Questions in Morals, Particularly Those Relating to the Original of Our Ideas of Virtue, Its Nature, Foundation, Reference to the Deity, Obligation, Subject Matter, and Sanctions* (London: T. Cadell, 1769).

Sermons on the Christian Doctrine, as Received by The Different Dominations of Christians (London: Printed for T. Cadell, 1787).

Thoughts on the Progress of Socinianism; with an Enquiry into the Cause and the Cure (London: J. Buckland and J. Johnson, 1787).

The Works of Dr. Richard Price, with Memoirs of His Life by W. Morgan, vol. 10 (London: Richard Rees, 1816).

Priestley, Joseph. *A Comparison of the Institutions of Moses with Those of the Hindoos and Other Ancient Nations* (Northumberland: A. Kennedy, 1799).

Ramsay, Chevalier. *Les voyages de Cyrus* (Paris [s.n.], 1727).

'"Of the Mythology of the Ancients," in Travels of Cyrus', in Burton Feldman and Robert D. Richardson (eds.), *The Rise of Modern Mythology, 1680–1860* (Bloomington: Indiana University Press, 1975), pp. 62–70.

Raynal, Guillaume Thomas. *A Philosophical and Political History of the Settlements and Trade of the Europeans in the East and West Indies*, J. O. Justamond (trans.), vol. 1, 2nd ed. (London: T. Cadell, 1776).

A Philosophical and Political History of the Settlements and Trade of Europeans in the East and West Indies, J. O. Justamond (trans.), vol. 2 (London: W. Strahan and T. Cadell, 1783).

A History of the Two Indies: A Translated Selection of Writings from Raynal's Histoire philosophiqe et politique de l'établissement et du commerces de Européens dans les deux Indes, Peter Jimack (trans.) (Farnham: Ashgate, 2006).

Reports from Committees of the House of Commons, 1715–1801, 15 vols. (London: Ordered by the House of Commons to be printed, 1803).

Ricci, Matteo. *China in the Sixteenth Century: The Journals of Matthew Ricci, 1583–1610*, Louis J. Gallagher (trans.) (New York: Random House, 1953).

Richardson, John. *A Dictionary, Persian, Arabic, and English* (Oxford: Clarendon Press, 1777).

Robertson, William. *An Historical Disquisition Concerning the Knowledge Which the Ancients Had of India* (London: A. Strahan and T. Cadell, 1791).

Rogerius, Abraham [Abraham Roger]. *De Open-Deure tot het verborgen Heydendom ofte Waerachtigh vertoogh van het leven ende zeden, mitsgaders de Religie ende Gotsdienst der Bramines op de Cust Chormandel ende der landen daar ontrent* (Leiden: Françoys Hackes, 1651).

Le Theatre de l'Idolatrie, ou la porte ouverte pour parvenir à la cognoissance du paganisme caché, Thomas Le Grue (trans.) (Amsterdam [s.n.], 1670).

Scott, Jonathan. *A Translation of the Memoirs of Eradut Khan* (London: Stockdale, 1786).

Scrafton, Luke. *Reflections on the Government &c of Indostan, with a Short Sketch of the History of Bengal* (London: W. Richardson and S. Clark, 1763).

Sharpe, Gregory. *The Want of Universality No Objection to the Christian Religion. Being the Substance of a Discourse Preached at the Temple Church the Tenth Day of November, 1765* (London: W. Richardson and S. Clark, 1766).

Sinha, H. N. (ed.). *Fort William: India House Correspondence and Other Contemporary Papers Relating Thereto*, vol. 2, *1757–59* (Delhi: National Archives of India, 1957).

Sinha, Mrinalini. *Colonial Masculinity: The 'Manly Englishman' and the 'Effeminate Bengali' in the Late Nineteenth Century* (Manchester: Manchester University Press, 1995).

Sinner, Jean-Rodolphe. *Essai sur les DOGMES de la METEMPSYCHOSE & du PURGATOIRE enseignés par les Bramins de l'Indostan* (Berne: La Société Typographique, 1771).

Smith, Adam. *An Inquiry into the Nature and Causes of the Wealth of Nations*, R. H. Campbell, A. S. Skinner and W. B. Todd (eds.), 2 vols. (Indianapolis: Liberty Fund, 1981).

Shore, Charles John, Baron Teignmouth (ed.), *Memoir of the Life and Correspondence of John, Lord Teignmouth*, vol. 1 (London: Hatchard, 1843).

The Oracle of Reason, vol. 1 (London: Thomas S. Paterson, 1842).

Toland, John. *History of the Celtic Religion and Learning* (Edinburgh: John Findlay, 1815).

'The History of the Soul's Immortality', in *Letters to Serena* (London: Bernard Lintot, 1704), pp. 19–68.

Troide, Lars E. (ed.). *The Early Journals and Letters of Fanny Burney: 1768–1773*, vol. 1 (Oxford: Clarendon Press, 1988).

Tucker, Josiah. *A Sequel to Sir William Jones's Pamphlet on the Principles of Government, in a Dialogue between a Freeholder of the Country of Denbigh, and the Dean of Gloucester* (London: Cadell, 1784).

Upcott, W., Thomson, R. and Brayley, E. W. *A Catalogue of the Library of the London Institution, Systematically Classed: Preceded by an Historical and Bibliographical Account of the Establishment*, vol. 3 (London: London Institute Library, 1843).

Vansittart, Henry. *Narrative of the Transactions in Bengal from the Year 1760 to the Year 1764 during the Government of Henry Vansittart*, vol. 1 (London, 1766).

Voltaire, *Fragments Relating to the Late Revolutions in India, the Death of Count Lally, and the Prosecution of Count de Morangies* (London: Printed for J. Nourse, 1774).

A Philosophical Dictionary from the French of M. de Voltaire, John G. Gorton (trans.), 2 vols., 2nd ed. (London: John & H. L. Hunt, 1824).

'Essai sur les moeurs et l'esprit des nations, I–IV (1756–78)', in M. Beuchot (ed.), *Oeuvres de Voltaire*, 72 vols. (Paris: Lefevre, 1829–34), vols. 15–18.

Fragments sur quelques révolutions dans l'Inde, sur la mort du comte de Lally, et surplusieurs autres sujets [1773], in *Œuvres complètes de Voltaire*, 20 vols. (Paris: J. Bryainé [1858]), vol. 6, pp. 167–262.

Letter 9 of *Lettres chinoises, indiennes et tartares á M. Pawr par un bénédictin* (1776), in Louis Moland (ed.), *Œuvres complètes de Voltaire*, vol. 29 (Paris: Garnier frères, 1877–85) pp. 451–98.

Dictionnaire philosophique (Paris: Gallimard, 1964 [1764]).

Warburton, William. *The Divine Legation of Moses Demonstrated, on the Principles of a Religious Deist, from the Omission of the Doctrine of a Future State of Reward and Punishment in the Jewish Dispensation*, 2 vols. (London: A. Millar and J. and R. Tonson, 1738, 1741).

Watson, Richard. *Sermons on Public Occasions, and Tracts on Religious Subjects* (Cambridge: J. Archdeacon Printer to the University, 1788).

Wellesley, R. G. 'The Governor-General's Notes with Respect to the Foundation of a College at Fort William', in *The Despatches, Minutes, and Correspondence, of the Marquess Wellesley, KG, During His Administration in India*, Montgomery Martin (ed.), vol. 2 (London, 1836), pp. 325–55.

Wheeler, Joseph Mazzini. *A Biographical Dictionary of Freethinkers of All Ages and Nations* (London: Progressive Publishing, 1889).

White, Joseph. *The Duty of Attempting the Propagation of the Gospel among Our Mahometan and Gentoo Subjects* (London: Printed for G. G. J. and J. Robinson, 1785).

Whitelock, Bulstrode. *Essay of Transmigration, in Defense of Pythagoras: Or a Discourse of Natural Philosophy* (London [s.n.], 1692).

Wilford, Francis. 'On Egypt and Other Countries, Adjacent to the Ca'li River, or Nile of Ethiopia, from the Ancient Books of the Hindus', *Asiatick Researches: Or Transactions of the Society*, vol. 3 (Calcutta: T. Watley, 1792), pp. 295–468.

Windischmann, Carl Josef Hieronymus. *Die Philosophie im Fortgang der Weltgeschichte* (Bonn: Adolph Marcus, 1832).

Secondary Sources

Agnani, Sunil. *Hating Empire Properly: The Two Indies and the Limits of Enlightenment Anticolonialism* (New York: Fordham University Press, 2016).

Ahmed, Siraj. 'Orientalism and the Permanent Fix of War', in Daniel Carey and Lynn Festa (eds.),*The Post-Colonial Enlightenment: Eighteenth-Century Colonialism and Post-Colonial Theory* (Oxford: Oxford University Press, 2009), pp. 167–206.

The Stillbirth of Capital: Enlightenment Writing and Colonial India (Palo Alto, CA: Stanford University Press, 2012).

Ahmed Asif, Manan. *The Loss of Hindustan: The Invention of India* (Cambridge, MA; Harvard University Press, 2020).

Anderson, Misty G. *Imagining Methodism in Eighteenth-Century Britain: Enthusiasm, Belief, and the Borders of the Self* (Baltimore: Johns Hopkins University Press, 2012).

Anon, 'Obituary: Kasinatha Bhattacharya', *Asiatic Journal and Monthly Register for British and Foreign India, China, and Australasia*, 20, May–August (1836), pp. 165–70.

App, Urs. 'William Jones's Ancient Theology', *Sino-Platonic Papers*, 191 (2009).

The Birth of Orientalism (Philadelphia: University of Pennsylvania Press, 2010).

Arkush, Allan. *Moses Mendelssohn and the Enlightenment* (New York: SUNY Press, 1994).

Armitage, David. *The Ideological Origins of the British Empire* (Cambridge: Cambridge University Press, 2000).

Baker, David Erskine. *Biographia Dramatica, or A Companion to the Playhouse*, 2nd ed., vol. 2 (Dublin: W. and H. Whitestone, 1782).

Balagangadhara, S. N. *'The Heathen in His Blindness ...': Asia, the West and the Dynamic of Religion* (Leiden: Brill, 1994).

Ballaster, Ros. *Fabulous Orients: Fictions of the East in England, 1662–1775* (Oxford: Oxford University Press, 2005).

Bannerjee, A. C. (ed.). *Indian Constitutional Documents, 1757–1947* (Calcutta: A. Mukherjee & Co., 1961).

Barrow, Ian. 'The Many Meanings of the Black Hole of Calcutta', in Kate Brittlebank (ed.), *Tall Tales and True: India, Historiography and British Imperial Imaginings* (Clayton, Victoria: Monash University Press, 2008), pp. 7–18.

Bayly, C. A. *The Imperial Meridian: The British Empire and the World, 1780–1830* (London: Longman, 1989).

Indian Society and the Making of the British Empire (Cambridge: Cambridge University Press, 1990).

Empire and Information: Intelligence Gathering and Social Communication in India, 1780–1870 (Cambridge: Cambridge University Press, 2000).

'Orientalists, Informants and Critics in Benares, 1790–1860', in Jamal Malik (ed.), *Perspectives of Mutual Encounters in South Asian History: 1760–1860* (Leiden: Brill, 2000), pp. 97–127.

Bendall, C. *Catalogue of the Sanskrit Manuscripts in the British Museum* (London: British Museum, 1902).

Bernard, Theos. *Hindu Philosophy* (Delhi: Motital Banarsidass Publishers, 1996 [1947]).

Betts, C. J. *Early Deism in France: From the So-Called 'déistes' of Lyon (1564) to Voltaire's 'Lettres Philosophiques' (1734)* (The Hague: Martinus Nijhoff Publishers, 1984).

Bhattacharyya, Sibajiban. *Development of Nyaya Philosophy and Its Social Context: History of Science, Philosophy and Culture in Indian Civilization*, vol. 3, part 3 (Delhi: Centre for Studies of Civilizations, 2004).

Black, Brian and Ram-Prasad, Chakravarthi (eds.). *In Dialogue with Classical Indian Traditions: Encounter, Transformation and Interpretation* (Oxford: Routledge, 2019).

Bourke, Richard. 'Edmund Burke and the Politics of Conquest', *Modern Intellectual History*, 4:3 (2007), pp. 403–32.

Empire and Revolution: The Political Life of Edmund Burke (Oxford: Princeton University Press, 2015).

Bowen, Huw V. *Revenue and Reform: The Indian Problem in British Politics, 1757–1773* (Cambridge: Cambridge University Press, 1991).

The Business of Empire: The East India Company and Imperial Britain, 1756–1833 (Cambridge: Cambridge University Press, 2006).

Bradshaw, Ben. 'The Christian Humanism of Erasmus', *Journal of Theological Studies*, 33:2 (1982), pp. 411–47.

Braithwate, Helen. *Romanticism, Publishing and Dissent: Joseph Johnson and the Cause of Liberty* (Basingstoke: Palgrave Macmillan, 2003).

Braude, Benjamin. 'The Sons of Noah and the Construction of Ethnic and Geographical Identities in the Medieval and Early Modern Periods', *William and Mary Quarterly*, 54:1 (1997), pp. 103–42.

Britton, Jeanne M. 'Fictional Footnotes, Romantic Orientalism, and the Remediated Novel: Elizabeth Hamilton's Translation of the Letters of a Hindoo Rajah', *European Romantic Review*, 26:6 (2015), pp. 773–87.

Brockington, J. L. *The Sacred Thread: Hinduism in Its Continuity and Diversity* (Edinburgh: Edinburgh University Press, 1996).

Brown, Robert E. *Jonathon Edwards and the Bible* (Bloomington: Indiana University Press, 2002).

Burns, R. M. *The Great Debate on Miracles, from Joseph Glanvill to David Hume* (London: Associated University Presses, 1981).

Calloway, Katherine. *Natural Theology in the Scientific Revolution: God's Scientists* (Abingdon: Routledge, 2016 [2014]).

Cannon, Garland. *Oriental Jones: A Biography of Sir William Jones 1746–1794* (New York: Asia Publishing House, 1964).

The Life and Mind of Oriental Jones: Sir William Jones, the Father of Modern Linguistics (Cambridge: Cambridge University Press, 1990).

Carson, Penelope. 'Grant, Charles (1746–1823)', *Oxford Dictionary of National Biography* (Oxford: Oxford University Press, 2004); online ed., January 2008 [www.oxforddnb.com/view/article/11248, accessed 26 January 2017].

The East India Company and Religion, 1698–1858 (Woodbridge: Boydell Press, 2012).

Chakravorty, Sanjoy. *The Truth about Us: The Politics of Information from Manu to Modi* (Gurugram: Hachette, 2019).

Champion, Justin. *The Pillars of Priestcraft Shaken: The Church of England and Its Enemies, 1660–1730* (Cambridge: Cambridge University Press, 1992).

Chatterjee, Kumkum. 'Cultural Flows and Cosmopolitanism in Mughal India: The Bishnupur Kingdom', *Indian Economic and Social History Review*, 46:2 (2009), pp. 147–82.

Chatterjee, Nandini. 'Reflections on Religious Difference and Permissive Inclusion in Mughal Law', *Journal of Law and Religion*, 29:3 (2014), pp. 396–415.

Chatterjee, Partha. *The Black Hole of Empire: History of a Global Practice of Power* (Princeton, NJ: Princeton University Press, 2012).

Chen, Jeng-Guo S. 'Gendering India: Effeminacy and the Scottish Enlightenment's Debates over Virtue and Luxury', *The Eighteenth Century*, 51:1/2 (2010), pp. 193–210.

Clark, J. C. D. 'Providence, Predestination & Progress; or, Did the Enlightenment Fail?', *Albion: A Quarterly Journal Concerned with British Studies*, 35:4 (2003), pp. 559–89.

Clark Jr, Robert T. *Herder: His Life and Thought* (Berkeley: University of California Press, 1955).

Classe, Olive (ed.). *Encyclopaedia of Literary Translation into English: A–L* (London: Fitzroy Dearborn Publishers, 2000).

Cohn, Bernard. S. *Colonialism and Its Forms of Knowledge: The British in India* (Princeton, NJ: Princeton University Press, 1996).

'The Command of Language and the Language of Command', in Edmund Burke III and David Porchaska (eds.), *Genealogies of Orientalism: History, Theory, Politics* (London: University of Nebraska Press, 2008), pp. 102–53.

'Law and the Colonial State in India', in June Starr and Jane F. Collier (eds.), *History and Power in the Study of Law* (Ithaca, NY: Cornell University Press, 2018), pp. 131–52.

Colley, Linda. *Captives: Britain, Empire and the World 1600–1850* (New York: Anchor Books, 2004).

Collins, Gregory M. 'The Limits of Mercantile Administration: Adam Smith and Edmund Burke on Britain's East India Company'. *Journal of the History of Economic Thought*, 41:3 (2019), pp. 369–92.

Conrad, Sebastian. 'Enlightenment in Global History: A Historiographical Critique', *American Historical Review*, 117:4 (2012), pp. 999–1027.

Cooper, Anthony Ashley, 1st Earl of Shaftesbury, *Characteristicks of Men, Manners, Opinions, Times. In Three Volumes. Vol. I. I. A Letter Concerning Enthusiasm* (London: John Darby, 1711).

Correia-Afonso, John. *Jesuit Letters and Indian History: A Study of the Nature and Development of the Jesuit Letters from India (1542–1773) and Their Value for Indian Historiography* (Bombay: Indian Historical Research Institute, St Xavier's College, 1955).

Corrigan, Kevin. 'Berkeley and Plotinus on the Non-Existence of Matter', *Hermathena*, 157 (1994), pp. 67–85.

Crawford, Katherine. *European Sexualities, 1400–1800* (Cambridge: Cambridge University Press, 2007).

Crowder, Colin. 'Berkeley, Price and the Limitations of the Design Argument', *Enlightenment and Dissent*, 8 (1989), pp. 3–24.

Curley, Thomas M. *Samuel Johnson, the Ossian Fraud, and the Celtic Revival in Great Britain and Ireland* (Cambridge: Cambridge University Press, 2009).

Curtis, Michael. *Orientalism and Islam: European Thinkers on Oriental Despotism in the Middle East and India* (Cambridge: Cambridge University Press, 2009).

Dalrymple, William. *White Mughals: Love and Betrayal in Eighteenth-Century India* (London: Penguin, 2004).

The Anarchy: The Relentless Rise of the East India Company (London: Bloomsbury, 2019).

Das, Binod Sankar. *Changing Profile of the Frontier Bengal, 1751–1833* (Bengal: Mittal Publications, 1984).

Das, Sudipta. *Myths and Realities of French Imperialism in India, 1763–1783* (Bern: Peter Lang, 1993).

Dasgupta, Surendranath. *A History of Indian Philosophy*, vol. 2 (Cambridge: Cambridge University Press, 1952).

Davis, Richard H. *The Bhagavad Gita: A Biography* (Oxford: Princeton University Press, 2015).

'Wilkins, Kasinatha, Hastings, and the First English Bhagavad Gītā', *International Journal of Hindu Studies*, 19:1 (2015), pp. 39–57.

Derrett, Duncan M. *Religion, Law and the State in India* (London: Faber and Faber, 1968).

Dirks, Nicholas B. *Castes of Mind: Colonialism and the Making of Modern India* (Princeton, NJ: Princeton University Press, 2001).

The Scandal of Empire: India and the Creation of Imperial Britain (Cambridge, MA: Harvard University Press, 2006).

DiSalle, Robert. 'Newton's Philosophical Analysis of Space and Time', inBernard Cohen and George Smith (eds.), *The Cambridge Companion to Newton* (Cambridge: Cambridge University Press, 2002) pp. 34–60.

Ditchfield, G. M. 'Ecclesiastical Policy under Lord North', inJohn Walsh, Colin Haydon and Stephen Taylor (eds.), *The Church of England c.1689–c.1833: From Toleration to Tractarianism* (Cambridge: Cambridge University Press, 1993), pp. 228–46.

Dodson, Michael S. *Orientalism, Empire and National Culture: India, 1770–1880* (Basingstoke: Palgrave Macmillan, 2007).

Doniger O'Flaherty, Wendy (ed.). *The Origins of Evil in Hindu Mythology* (Berkeley: University of California Press, 1976).

Karma and Rebirth in the Classical Indian Tradition (Berkeley: University of California Press, 1980).

Doniger, Wendy. *The Hindus: An Alternative History* (Oxford: Oxford University Press, 2009).

On Hinduism (Oxford: Oxford University Press, 2014).

Donoghue, Frank. *The Fame Machine: Book Reviewing and Eighteenth-Century Literary Careers* (Stanford, CA: Stanford University Press, 1996).

Duchet, Michèle. *Diderot et l'histoire des deux Indes ou l'ecriture fragmentaire* (Paris: Libraire Nizet, 1978).

Edwards, David. *Christian England, from the Reformation to the Eighteenth Century* (Glasgow: Edermans, 1984).

Ehrlich, Joshua. 'The East India Company and the Politics of Knowledge', PhD diss., Harvard University, 2018. https://dash.harvard.edu/handle/1/39947190, accessed 2 July 2021.

'Empire and Enlightenment in Three Letters from Sir William Jones to Governor-General John Macpherson', *Historical Journal*, 62:2 (2019), pp. 541–51.

'Anxiety, Chaos, and the Raj', *Historical Journal*, 63:3 (2020), pp. 1–11.

Elmarsafy, Ziad. *The Enlightenment Qur'an: The Politics of Translation and the Construction of Islam* (London: Oneworld Publications, 2009).

Embree, Ainslee Thomas. *Charles Grant and British Rule in India* (London: George Allen & Unwin Ltd., 1962).

Emerson, Roger L. *Essays on David Hume: Medical Men and the Scottish Enlightenment* (Farnham: Ashgate, 2009).

Ernst, Carl W. 'Muslim Studies of Hinduism? A Reconsideration of Arabic and Persian Translations from Indian Languages', *Iranian Studies*, 36:2 (2003), pp. 173–95.

Feldman, Burton and Richardson Jr, Robert D. *The Rise of Modern Mythology: 1680–1860* (Bloomington: Indiana University Press, 1972).

Ferguson, Adam. *An Essay on the History of Civil Society* (Dublin: Boulter Grierson, 1767).

Firminger, Walter Kelly. *Early History of Freemasonry in Bengal* (Calcutta: Thacker & Spink, 1906).

Fitzpatrick, M. 'Latitudinarianism at the Parting of the Ways: A Suggestion', inJohn Walsh, Colin Haydon and Stephen Taylor (eds.), *The Church of England c.1689–c.1833* (Cambridge: Cambridge University Press, 1993), pp. 209–27.

Foote, Samuel. *The Nabob: A Comedy in Three Acts* (London: T. Sherlock for T. Cadell, 1778).

Forster, Michael N. 'Herder and Spinoza', in Eckart Förster and Zithak Y. Melamed (eds), *Spinoza and German Idealism* (Cambridge: Cambridge University Press, 2012), pp. 59–84.

Franklin, M. J. 'Accessing India: Orientalism, Anti-"Indianism", and the Rhetoric of Jones and Burke', in Tim Fulford and Peter Kitson (eds.), *Romanticism and Colonialism* (Cambridge: Cambridge University Press, 1998), pp. 48–66.

ed.). *Representing India: Indian Culture and Imperial Control in Eighteenth-Century British Orientalist Discourse*, 9 vols. (London: Routledge, 2000).

'Cultural Possession, Imperial Control, and Comparative Religion: The Calcutta Perspectives of Sir William Jones and Nathaniel Brassey Halhed', *Yearbook of English Studies*, 32 (2002), pp. 1–18.

'Jones, Sir William (1746–1794), Orientalist and Judge', *Oxford Dictionary of National Biography* (Oxford: Oxford University Press, 2004); online ed., September 2004 [www.oxforddnb.com/view/article/15105, accessed 30 March 2021].

Romantic Representations of British India (Abingdon: Routledge, 2006).

Orientalist Jones: Sir William Jones, Poet, Lawyer, and Linguist, 1746–1794 (Oxford: Oxford University Press, 2011).

'"Harmonious" Jones and "Honest John" Shore: Contrasting Responses of Garden Reach Neighbors to the Experience of India', *European Romantic Review*, 27:2 (2016), pp. 19–142.

Freeman, Kathryn S. *Blake's Nostos: Fragmentation and Nondualism in the Four Zoas* (Albany: SUNY, 1997).

British Women Writers and the Asiatic Society of Bengal, 1785–1783: Re-Orienting Anglo-India (Farnham: Ashgate, 2014).

Fruchtman, Jack. *The Apocalyptic Politics of Richard Price and Joseph Priestley: A Study in Late Eighteenth-Century English Republican Millennialism.* (Philadelphia: The American Philosophical Society, 1983).

Furber, Holden. *John Company at Work: A Study in European Expansion in India in the Late Eighteenth Century* (Cambridge, MA: Harvard University Press, 1948).

Gandhi, Supriya. *The Emperor Who Never Was: Dara Shukoh in Mughal India* (Cambridge, MA: Belknap, Harvard University Press, 2021).

Garcia, Humberto. *Islam and the English Enlightenment: 1670–1840* (Baltimore: Johns Hopkins University Press, 2012).

Garrett, Aaron. *Animal Language, Animal Passions and Animal Morals* (London: Thoemmes Continuum, 2000).

'Human Nature', in, Knud Haakonssen (ed.), *The Cambridge History of Eighteenth-Century Philosophy* (Cambridge: Cambridge University Press, 2000), vol. 1, pp. 160–223.

Gaskin, J. C. A. 'Hume on Religion', in David Fate Norton and Jacqueline Taylor (eds.), *The Cambridge Companion to Hume* (Cambridge: Cambridge University Press, 2009), pp. 480–514.

Gay, Peter. *The Enlightenment: An Interpretation*, vol. 1: *The Rise of Modern Paganism* (New York: Knopf, 1966).

Gerrish, B. A. 'Natural and Revealed Religion', in Knud Haakonssen (ed.), *The Cambridge History of Eighteenth-Century Philosophy*, vol. 2 (Cambridge: Cambridge University Press, 2006), pp. 639–65.

Ghosh, Anindita. *Power in Print: Popular Publishing and the Politics of Language and Culture in a Colonial Society, 1778–1905* (Oxford: Oxford University Press, 2006).

Goldie, Mark and Wokler, Robert (eds.). *The Cambridge History of Eighteenth-Century Political Thought* (Cambridge: Cambridge University Press, 2006).

Goodwin, Gordon. 'Hamilton, Charles (1752/3–1792)', rev. Philip Carter, *Oxford Dictionary of National Biography* (Oxford: Oxford University Press, 2004) [www.oxforddnb.com/view/article/12054, accessed 2 July 2016].

Greene, Jack P. *Evaluating Empire and Confronting Colonialism in Enlightenment Britain* (Cambridge: Cambridge University Press, 2013).

Grewal, J. S. *Muslim Rule in India: The Assessments of British Historians* (Oxford: Oxford University Press, 1970).

Griffin Jr, Martin I. J. *Latitudinarianism in the Seventeenth-Century Church of England* (Leiden: Brill, 1992).
Grimes, John A. *A Concise Dictionary of Indian Philosophy: Sanskrit Terms Defined in English* (New York: SUNY Press, 1996).
Grogan, Claire. *Politics and Genre in the Works of Elizabeth Hamilton, 1756–1816* (Burlington, VT: Ashgate, 2012).
Guerrini, Anita. 'A Diet for a Sensitive Soul: Vegetarianism in Eighteenth-Century Britain', *Eighteenth Century Life*, 23:2 (1999), pp. 34–42.
Guha, Ranajit. *A Rule of Property for Bengal: An Essay on the Idea of Permanent Settlement* (New Delhi: Orient Longman, 1982 [1963]).
Gupta, Brijen Kishore. *Sirajuddaullah and the East India Company, 1756–1757* (Leiden: E. J. Brill, 1966).
Haakonssen, Knud. *Enlightenment and Religion: Rational Dissent in Eighteenth-Century Britain* (Cambridge: Cambridge University Press, 1996).
Halbfass, Wilhelm. *India and Europe: An Essay in Understanding* (Delhi: Motilal Banarsidass, 1990) (Originally published *Indien und Europa Perspektiven ihrer Geistigen Begegnung* [Stuttgart: Schwabe & Co., 1981]).
Hall, Thomas. *The Lost Houses of Wales* (London: Save Britain's Heritage, 1986).
Hanley, Brian. *Samuel Johnson as Book Reviewer: A Duty to Examine the Labors of the Learned* (London: Associated University Presses, 2001 [1961]).
Hannak, Khristine. 'Boehme and German Romanticism', in Ariel Hessayon and Sarah Apetrei (eds.), *An Introduction to Jacob Boehme: Four Centuries of Thought and Reception* (Abingdon: Routledge, 2014), pp. 162–79.
Harrison, Mark. *Climates and Constitutions: Health, Race, Environment and British Imperialism in India 1600–1850* (New Delhi: Oxford University Press, 1999).
Harrison, Peter. 'Animal Souls, Metempsychosis, and Theodicy in Seventeenth-Century English Thought', *Journal of the History of Philosophy*, 31:4 (1993), pp. 519–44.
The Bible, Protestantism, and the Rise of Natural Science (Cambridge: Cambridge University Press, 1998).
Harvey, David Allen. *The French Enlightenment and Its Others: The Mandarin, the Savage and the Invention of the Human Sciences* (Basingstoke: Palgrave Macmillan, 2012).
Haugen, Kristine Louise. 'Ossian and the Invention of Textual History', *Journal of the History of Ideas*, 59:2 (1998), pp. 309–27.
Hawley, Daniel. 'L'Inde de Voltaire', in Theodore Besterman (ed.), *Studies in Voltaire and the Eighteenth Century* (Oxford: Voltaire Foundation, 1974), pp. 139–79.
Headley, Douglas. 'Theology and the Revolt against the Enlightenment', in Sheridan Gilley and Brian Stanley (eds.), *The Cambridge History of Christianity*, vol. 8 (Cambridge: Cambridge University Press, 2006), pp. 30–52.
Hedley, Douglas. 'Ralph Cudworth as Interpreter of Plotinus', in Stephen Gersh (ed.), *Plotinus' Legacy: The Transformation of Platonism from the Renaissance*

to the Modern Era (Cambridge: Cambridge University Press, 2019), pp. 146–59.

Hegel, G. W. F. 'Lectures on the Philosophy of World History, Second Draft 1830', in L. Dickey and H. B. Nisbet (eds.), *Hegel: Political Writings* (Cambridge: Cambridge University Press, 1999), pp. 197–224.

Herling, Bradley L. *The German Gita: Hermeneutics and Discipline in the Early German Reception of Indian Thought* (London: Routledge, 2006).

Herrick, James A. *The Radical Rhetoric of the English Deists: The Discourse of Scepticism, 1680–1750* (Columbia: University of South Carolina Press, 1997).

'Blasphemy in the Eighteenth Century: Contours of a Rhetorical Crime', in Wayne Hudson, Diego Lucci and Jeffery R. Wigelsworth (eds.), *Atheism and Deism Revalued: Heterodox Religious Identities in Britain, 1650–1800* (Farnham: Ashgate, 2014), pp. 101–18.

Hessayon, Ariel and Apetrei, Sarah (eds.). *An Introduction to Jacob Boehme: Four Centuries of Thought and Reception* (Abingdon: Routledge, 2014).

Hessayon, Ariel and Finnegan, David (eds.). *Varieties of Seventeenth- and Early Eighteenth-Century English Radicalism in Context* (Farnham: Ashgate, 2011).

Heyd, Michael. *Be Sober and Reasonable: The Critique of Enthusiasm in the Seventeenth and Early Eighteenth Centuries* (Leiden: Brill, 2000).

Hickman, Louise. *Eighteenth-Century Dissent and Cambridge Platonism: Reconceiving the Philosophy of Religion* (Oxford: Routledge, 2017).

Hill, S. C. *Bengal in 1756–1757*, vol. 1 (London: John Murray, 1905).

Hodson, V. D. K. *Officers of the Bengal Army: 1758–1834*, vol. 2 (London: Constable, 1928).

Holden, Thomas. 'Religion and Moral Prohibition in Hume's "Of Suicide"', *Hume Studies*, 31:2 (2005), pp. 189–210.

Horkheimer, Max and Adorno, Theodore. *The Dialectic of Enlightenment* (London: Verso, 1997 [New York, 1944]).

Hoveyda, Abbas, Kumar, Ranjay and Alam, Mohammed Aftab. *Indian Government and Politics* (London: Pearson, 2011).

Hudson, Wayne. *Enlightenment and Modernity: The English Deists and Reform* (London: Pickering and Chatto, 2009).

The English Deists: Studies in Early Enlightenment (London: Pickering and Chatto, 2009).

'Atheism and Deism Demythologised', in Wayne Hudson, Diego Lucci and Jeffery R. Wigelsworth (eds.), *Atheism and Deism Revalued: Heterodox Religious Identities in Britain, 1650–1800* (Farnham: Ashgate, 2014), pp. 13–24.

Hudson, Wayne, Lucci, Diego, and Wigelsworth, Jeffery R. (eds.). *Atheism and Deism Revalued: Heterodox Religious Identities in Britain, 1650–1800* (Farnham: Ashgate, 2014).

Hunt, Lynn, Jacob, Margaret and Mijnhardt, Wijnand. *The Book That Changed Europe: Bernard and Picart's Religious Ceremonies of the World* (Cambridge, MA: Harvard University Press, 2010).

Hunter, M. and Wootton, D. (eds.), *Atheism from the Reformation to the Enlightenment* (Oxford: Oxford University Press, 1992).

Ibbetson, David. 'Sir William Jones and the Nature of Law', in Andrew Burrows and Alan Rodger (eds.), *Mapping the Law: Essays in Memory of Peter Birks* (Oxford: Oxford University Press, 2006), pp. 619–39.

Israel, Jonathan. *Radical Enlightenment: Philosophy and the Making of Modernity 1650–1750* (Oxford: Oxford University Press, 2001).

Democratic Enlightenment: Philosophy, Revolution, and Human Rights 1750–1790 (Oxford: Oxford University Press, 2011).

Jacob, Margaret. *The Radical Enlightenment: Pantheists, Freemasons and Republicans* (London: George Allen and Unwin, 1981).

James, Derek. *The Smugglers' Coast: The Story of Smuggling around Eyemouth* (Peterborough: Fast-Print Publishing, 2016).

Jessen, Elisabeth Engell. 'Boehme and the English Romantics', in Ariel Hessayon and Sarah Apetrei (eds.), *An Introduction to Jacob Boehme: Four Centuries of Thought and Reception* (Abingdon: Routledge, 2014), pp. 180–95.

Jimack, Peter. 'Diderot and India', in David MacCallum and Terry Pratt (eds.), *The Enterprise of Enlightenment: A Tribute to David Williams from His Friends* (Bern: Peter Lang, 2004), pp. 141–58.

Johnson, Kurt A. '"Lisping Tongues" and "Sanscrit Songs": William Jones' Hymns to Hindu Deities', *Translation and Literature*, 20:1 (2011), pp. 48–60.

Johnson, W. J. (trans.) *The Bhagavad Gita* (Oxford: Oxford University Press, 1994).

Joseph, Betty. *Reading the East India Company 1720–1840: Colonial Currencies of Gender* (Chicago: University of Chicago Press, 2004).

Kapila, Shruti. 'Race Matters: Orientalism and Religion, India and Beyond c.1770–1880', *Modern Asian Studies*, 4:3 (2007), pp. 471–513.

'Global Intellectual History and the Indian Political', in Darrin M. McMahon and Samuel Moyn (eds.), *Rethinking Modern European Intellectual History* (Oxford: Oxford University Press, 2014), pp. 275–94.

Kapoor, S. S. and Kapoor, M. K. *Hinduism: An Introduction [History, Scriptures, Prayers and Philosophy]* (New Delhi: Hemkunt Publishers, 2005).

Kidd, Colin. *The Forging of Races: Race and Scripture in the Protestant Atlantic World, 1600–2000* (Cambridge: Cambridge University Press, 2006).

The World of Mr Casaubon: Britain's Wars of Mythography, 1700–1870 (Cambridge: Cambridge University Press, 2016)

Kim, Sangkeun. *Strange Names of God: The Missionary Translation of the Divine Name and the Chinese Responses to Matteo Ricci's 'Shangti' in Late Ming China, 1583–1644* (New York: Peter Lang, 2004).

King, Richard. *Indian Philosophy: An Introduction to Hindu and Buddhist Thought* (Edinburgh: Edinburgh University Press, 1988).

Orientalism and Religion: Post-Colonial Theory, India and 'The Mystic East' (Abingdon: Routledge, 1999).

Kopf, David. *British Orientalism and the Bengal Renaissance: The Dynamics of Indian Modernization 1773–1835* (Berkeley: University of California Press, 1969).

Krause, Sharon. 'Despotism in the *Spirit of the Laws*', in David W. Carrithers, Michael A. Mosher and Paul Rahe (eds.), *Montesqueiu's Science of Politics: Essays on the Spirit of the Laws* (Lanham, MD: Rowman & Littlefield Publishers Inc., 2001), pp. 231–72.

Kuiters, Willem G. J. 'Dow, Alexander (1735/6–1779)', *Oxford Dictionary of National Biography* (Oxford: Oxford University Press, 2004); online ed., January 2008 [www.oxforddnb.com/view/article/7957, accessed 25 July 2016].

Kurth-Voigt, Lieselotte E. *Continued Existence, Reincarnation, and the Power of Sympathy in Classical Weimar* (Rochester, NY: Camden House, 1999).

Lach, Donald F. 'The Sinophilism of Christian Wolff (1679–1754)', *Journal of the History of Ideas*, 14:4 (1953), pp. 561–74.

Lalor, Stephen. *Matthew Tindal, Freethinker: An Eighteenth-Century Assault on Religion* (London: Bloomsbury, 2006).

Lawrenson, Sonja. 'Revolution, Rebellion and a Rajah from Rohilkhand: Recontextualizing Elizabeth Hamilton's Translation of the Letters of a Hindoo Rajah', *Studies in Romanticism*, 51:2 (2012), pp. 125–47.

Leask, Nigel. *British Romantic Writers and the East: Anxieties of Empire* (Cambridge: Cambridge University Press, 1992).

'Francis Wilford and the Colonial Construction of Hindu Geography, 1799–1822', in Amanda Gilroy (ed.), *Romantic Geographies: Discourses of Travel 1775–1844* (Manchester: Manchester University Press, 2000), pp. 204–22.

'Maurice, Thomas (1754–1824), Oriental Scholar and Librarian', *Oxford Dictionary of National Biography* (Oxford: Oxford University Press, 2004) [www.oxforddnb.com/view/article/18387, accessed 29 March 2021].

Lecaldano, Eugenio. 'Hume on Suicide', in Paul Russell (ed.), *The Oxford Handbook of Hume* (Oxford: Oxford University Press, 2016), pp. 660–72.

Lewis, Rhodri. 'Of "Origenian Platonisme": Joseph Glanvill on the Pre-existence of Souls', *Huntington Library Quarterly*, 69:2 (2006), pp. 267–300.

Little, J. H. 'The Black Hole: Question of Holwell's Veracity', *Bengal Past and Present*, 11 (1915), pp. 75–105.

Lloyd, Mary. 'Sir Charles Wilkins, 1749–1836', in India Office Library (ed.), *India Office Library and Records: Report for the Year 1978* (London: Foreign and Commonwealth Office, 1978), pp. 9–39.

Lorenzen, David N. 'Who Invented Hinduism?', *Comparative Studies in Society and History*, 41:4 (1999), pp. 630–59.

Who Invented Hinduism?: Essays on Religion in History (Delhi: Yoga Press, 2006).

Lucci, Diego. *Scripture and Deism: The Biblical Criticism of the Eighteenth-Century British Deists* (Bern: Peter Lang, 1997).

Lund, R. D. (ed.). *The Margins of Orthodoxy: Heterodox Writing and Cultural Response, 1660–1750* (Cambridge: Cambridge University Press, 1995).

MacFarlane, Iris. *Black Hole, or, the Makings of a Legend* (London: George Allen and Unwin, 1975).

Mahadeva Sastri, Alladi (trans.). *Bhagavad-Gita with the Commentary of Sri Shankaracharya* (Madras: V. Sadanand, 1977).

Mahamahopadhyaya, Satisa Chandra Vidyabhushana (trans.). *The Nyaya Sutras of Gautama* (Allahabad: The Indian Press, 1913).

Majeed, Javed. *Ungoverned Imaginings: James Mill's The History of British India and Orientalism* (Oxford: Clarendon Press, 1992).

Major, Andrea. *Pious Flames: European Encounters with Sati, 1500–1830* (Oxford: Oxford University Press, 2006).

Malinar, Angelika. *The Bhagavad Gita: Its Doctrines and Contexts* (Cambridge: Cambridge University Press, 2007).

Mandair, Avind Pal Singh. 'Sikh Philosophy', in Pashaura Singh and Louis E. Fenech (eds.), *The Oxford Handbook of Sikh Studies* (Oxford: Oxford University Press, 2014), pp. 298–315.

Mani, Lata. *Contentious Traditions: The Debate on Sati in Colonial India* (London: University of California Press, 1998).

Manjari, Katju. 'The History of Hindu Nationalism in India', in Torkel Brekke (ed.), *The Oxford History of Hinduism: Modern Hinduism* (Oxford: Oxford University Press, 2019), pp. 203–15.

Marlherbe, Michel. 'Reason', in Knud Haakonssen (ed.), *The Cambridge History of Eighteenth-Century Philosophy*, vol. 1 (Cambridge: Cambridge University Press, 2006), pp. 319–42.

Marsh, Kate. *India in the French Imagination: Peripheral Voices, 1754–1815* (London: Pickering and Chatto, 2009).

Marshall, P. J. *The Impeachment of Hastings* (Oxford: Oxford University Press, 1965).

'Indian Officials under the East India Company in Eighteenth-Century Bengal', *Bengal Past and Present*, 84 (1965), pp. 95–120.

(ed.). *Problems of Empire: Britain and India 1757–1813* (London: Allen and Unwin, 1968).

The British Discovery of Hinduism in the Eighteenth Century (Cambridge: Cambridge University Press, 1970).

'Warren Hastings as Scholar and Patron', in A. Whiteman, J. S. Bromley and P. G. M. Dickson (eds.), *Statesmen, Scholars, and Merchants: Essays in Eighteenth-Century History Presented to Dame Lucy Sutherland* (Oxford: Oxford University Press, 1973), pp. 242–62.

East Indian Fortunes: The British in Bengal in the Eighteenth Century (Oxford: Clarendon Press, 1976).

'The Moral Swing to the East: British Humanitarianism, India and the West Indies', in K. Ballhatchet and John Harrison (eds.), *East India Company Studies: Papers Presented to Professor Sir Cyril Philips* (Hong Kong: Asian Research Service, 1986), pp. 69–95.

'"Cornwallis Triumphant": War in India and the British Public in the Late Eighteenth Century', in Laurence Freedman, Paul Hayes and Robert O'Neill (eds.), *War, Strategy, and International Politics: Essays in Honour of Sir Michael Howard* (Oxford: Clarendon Press, 1992), pp. 57–74.

'The Making of an Imperial Icon: The Case of Warren Hastings', *Journal of Imperial and Commonwealth History*, 27:3 (1999), pp. 1–16.

'A Free Though Conquering People': Eighteenth-Century Britain and Its Empire (Aldershot: Ashgate, 2003).

The Making and Unmaking of Empires: Britain, India and America c.1750–1783 (Oxford: Oxford University Press, 2005).

Marshall, P. J. and Williams, G. (eds.). *The Great Map of Mankind: British Perceptions of the World in the Age of Enlightenment* (London: J. M. Dent & Sons, 1982).

McGetchin, Douglas T. *Indology, Indomania, and Orientalism: Ancient India's Rebirth in Modern Germany* (Madison, NJ: Fairleigh Dickinson University Press, 2009).

Miller, Peter N. *Defining the Common Good: Empire, Religion and Philosophy in Eighteenth-Century Britain* (Cambridge: Cambridge University Press, 1994).

Minor, Robert N. 'The "Gītā's" Way as the Only Way', *Philosophy East and West*, 30:3 (1980), pp. 339–54.

Misra, B. B. *The Central Administration of the East India Company 1773–1834* (Manchester: Manchester University Press, 1959).

Monckton Jones, M. E. *Warren Hastings in Bengal, 1772–1774* (Oxford: Clarendon Press, 1918).

Morrison, William Maxwell. *The Decisions of the Court of Session: From Its Institution until the Separation of the Court into Two Divisions in the Year 1808*, vols. 11–12 (Edinburgh: Archibald Constable & Co., 1811).

Mukherjee, Mithi. 'Justice, War, and the Imperium: India and Britain in Edmund Burke's Prosecutorial Speeches in the Impeachment Trial of Warren Hastings', *Law and History Review*, 23:3 (2005), pp. 589–630.

Mukherjee, S. N. *Sir William Jones: A Study in Eighteenth-Century British Attitudes to India* (Cambridge: Cambridge University Press, 1968).

Mukhopadhyay, Subhas Chandra. *The Agrarian Policy of the British in Bengal: The Formative Period, 1698–1772* (Allahabad: Chugh Publications, 1987).

Müller, Patrick. *Latitudinarianism and Didacticism in Eighteenth-Century Literature: Moral Theology in Fielding, Sterne and Goldsmith* (Frankfurt: Peter Lang, 2009).

Mullet, Charles. 'A Letter by Joseph Glanvill on the Future State', *Huntingdon Library Quarterly*, 1 (1937), pp. 447–56.

Muthu, Sankar. *Enlightenment against Empire* (Princeton, NJ: Princeton University Press, 2003).

'Adam Smith's Critique of International Trading Companies: Theorizing "Globalization" in the Age of Enlightenment', *Political Theory*, 36:2 (2008), pp. 185–212.

(ed.), *Empire and Modern Political Thought* (Cambridge: Cambridge University Press, 2012).

Nadkarni, M. V. *The Bhagavad-Gita for the Modern Reader: History, Interpretations and Philosophy* (Abingdon: Routledge, 2017).

Nair, Shankar. *Translating Wisdom: Hindu-Muslim Intellectual Interactions in Early Modern South Asia* (Oakland: University of California Press, 2020).

Namier, Lewis and Brooke, John. *The History of Parliament: House of Commons 1754–1790* (London: Secker and Warburg, 1985 [1964]).

Neill, Stephen. *A History of Christianity in India*, vol. 1: *The Beginnings to AD 1707* (Cambridge: Cambridge University Press, 1984).

A History of Christianity in India: 1707–1858 (Cambridge: Cambridge University Press, 1985).

Nicholson, Andrew J. *Unifying Hinduism: Philosophy and Identity in Indian Intellectual History* (New York: Columbia University Press, 2013).

O'Flaherty, Niall. *Utilitarianism in the Age of Enlightenment: The Moral and Political Thought of William Paley* (Cambridge: Cambridge University Press, 2019),

Olivelle, Patrick. (trans.). *The Law Code of Manu* (Oxford: Oxford University Press, 2004).

O'Malley, John W. *The First Jesuits* (Cambridge, MA: Harvard University Press, 1993).

Osterhammel, Jürgen. *Unfabling the East: The Enlightenment's Encounter with Asia*, Robert Savage (trans.) (Princeton, NJ: Princeton University Press, 2018).

Palin, David A. *Attitudes to Other Religions: Comparative Religion in Seventeenth- and Eighteenth-Century Britain* (Manchester: Manchester University Press, 1984).

Patterson, Jessica. 'An Eighteenth-Century Account of Sati: John Zephaniah Holwell's "Religious Tenets of the Gentoos" and "Voluntary Sacrifice" (1767)', *South Asia: Journal of South Asian Studies*, 40:1 (2017), pp. 24–39.

'Enlightenment and Empire, Mughals and Marathas: The Religious History of India in the Work of Company Servant, Alexander Dow', *History of European Ideas*, 45:7 (2019), pp. 972–91.

Pennington, Brian. *Was Hinduism Invented? Britons, Indians and the Colonial Construction of Religion* (Oxford: Oxford University Press, 2005).

Perkins, Franklin. *Leibniz and China: A Commerce of Light* (Cambridge: Cambridge University Press, 2004).

Phillips, Charles, Kerrigan, Michael and Gould, David (eds.). *Ancient India's Myths and Beliefs* (New York: Rosen Publishing, 2012).

Pinch, William R. *Warrior Ascetics and Indian Empires* (Cambridge: Cambridge University Press, 2006).

Pitts, Jennifer. *The Rise of Imperial Liberalism in Britain and France* (Princeton, NJ: Princeton University Press, 2005).

A Turn to Empire: The Rise of Imperial Liberalism in Britain and France (Princeton, NJ: Princeton University Press, 2005).

Boundaries of the International: Law and Empire (Cambridge, MA: Harvard University Press, 2018).

Pocock, J. G. A. *Barbarism and Religion: Barbarians, Savages and Empires*, vol. 4 (Cambridge: Cambridge University Press, 2005).

'Historiography and Enlightenment: A View of Their History', *Modern Intellectual History*, 5:1 (2008), pp. 83–96.

Popkin, Richard H. and Goldie, Mark. 'Scepticism, Priestcraft and Toleratio', in Mark Goldie and Robert Wokler (eds.), *The Cambridge History of Eighteenth-Century Political Thought* (Cambridge: Cambridge University Press, 2006), pp. 79–146.

Porter, Roy. *Bodies Politic: Disease, Death and Doctors in Britain, 1650–1900* (London: Reaktion Books, 2001).

Prior, D. L. 'Holwell, John Zephaniah (1711–1798)', *Oxford Dictionary of National Biography* (Oxford: Oxford University Press, 2004); online ed., January 2008 [www.oxforddnb.com/view/article/13622, accessed 30 November 2016].

Rao, Mani, 'A Brief History of the Bhagavad Gita's Modern Canonization', *Religion Compass*, 7:11 (2013), pp. 467–75.

Rapport, Rhonda. 'Fossils and the Flood', in Roy Porter (ed.), *The Cambridge History of Science*, vol. 4: *Eighteenth-Century Science* (Cambridge: Cambridge University Press, 2003), pp. 419–21.

Rathore, Aakash Singh and Mohapatra, Rimina. *Hegel's India: A Reinterpretation, with Texts* (Oxford: Oxford University Press, 2017).

Ray, Amit. 'Orientalism and Religion in the Romantic Era: Rammonhan Roy's Vedanta(s)', in M. J. Franklin (ed.), *Romantic Representations of British India* (Oxford: Routledge, 2006), pp. 259–76.

Rego, António da Silva (ed.). *Documentação para a história das missões do padroado Português do Oriente India*, vol. 2 (Lisbon: Centro de Estudos Históicos Ultramarinos, 1948).

Remes, Pauliina. *Neoplatonism* (Abingdon: Routledge, 2008).

Ring, Trudy, Salkin, Robert M. and La Boda, Sharon (eds.), *International Dictionary of Historic Places: Asia and Oceania* (London: Taylor & Francis, 1996).

Rist, John. 'Plotinus and Christian Philosophy', in Lloyd P. Gerson (ed.), *The Cambridge Companion to Plotinus* (Cambridge: Cambridge University Press, 1996), pp. 386–414.

Rivers, Isabel. *Reason, Grace, and Sentiment: A Study of the Language of Religion and Ethics in England 1660–1780* (Cambridge: Cambridge University Press, 2000), vols. 1–2.

Robertson, John. *The Case for the Enlightenment: Scotland and Naples 1680–1760* (Cambridge: Cambridge University Press, 2005).

Robinson, Catherine A. *Interpretations of the Bhagavad-Gītā and Images of the Hindu Tradition: The Song of the Lord* (Abingdon: Routledge, 2006).

Robinson, Guy and Firminger, Walter K. *The Second Lodge of Bengal* (Mysore: Wesley Press, 1955).

Rocher, Ludo. *The Ezourvedam: A French Veda of the Eighteenth Century* (University of Pennsylvania Studies on South Asia) (Amsterdam: John Benjamins Publishing, 1984).

Rocher, Rosane. 'Nathaniel Brassey Halhed on the Upaniṣads (1787)', *Annals of the Bhandarkar Oriental Research Institute*, 58/59 (1977–8), pp. 279–89.

'Nathaniel Brassey Halhed's Collection of Oriental Manuscripts', *Annals of Oriental Research, Madras, Silver Jubilee Volume*, 25 (1975), pp. 279–89.

'Alien and Empathetic: The Indian Poems of N. B. Halhed', in Blair B. Kling and M. N. Pearson (eds.), *The Age of Partnership: Europeans in Asia before Dominion* (Honolulu: University of Hawaii Press, 1979), pp. 215–35.

'Lord Monboddo, Sanskrit and Comparative Linguistics', *Journal of the American Oriental Society*, 100:1 (1980), pp. 12–17.

Orientalism, Poetry and the Millennium: The Checkered Life of Nathaniel Brassey Halhed, 1751–1830 (Delhi: Motilal Banarsidass, 1983).

'The Career of Rādhākānta Tarkavāgīśa, an Eighteenth-Century Pandit in British Employ', *Journal of the American Oriental Society*, 109:4 (1989), pp. 627–33.

'British Orientalism in the Eighteenth Century: The Dialectic of Knowledge and Government', in Carol A. Breckenridge and Peter van der Veer (eds.), *Orientalism and the Post-Colonial Predicament: Perspectives on South Asia* (Philadelphia: University of Pennsylvania Press, 1993), pp. 215–49.

Rockwell Lanman, Charles. *A Sanskrit Reader: Text and Vocabulary and Note* (Delhi: Motilal Banarsidass, 1996).

Roes, Shirley A. *Matter, Life, and Generation: Eighteenth-Century Embryology and the Haller–Wolff Debate* (Cambridge: Cambridge University Press, 1981).

Ross, Charles (ed.). *Correspondence of Charles, First Marquis Cornwallis*, vol. 2 of 3 (London: John Murray, 1859).

Rosselli, John. *Lord William Bentinck: The Making of a Liberal Imperialist, 1774–1839* (Berkeley: University of California Press, 1974).

Rousseau, George S. 'Mysticism and Millenarianism: "Immortal Dr Cheyne"', in Richard Henry Popkin (ed.), *Millenarianism and Messianism in English Literature and Thought, 1650–1800* (Leiden: E. J. Brill, 1988), pp. 81–126.

Rothschild, Emma. 'Adam Smith and the British Empire', in Sankar Muthu (ed.), *Empire and Modern Political Thought* (Cambridge: Cambridge University Press, 2012), pp. 184–98.

Royal Highland and Agricultural Society of Scotland, *Report of the Committee of the Highland Society of Scotland, Appointed to Inquire into the Nature and Authenticity of the Poems of Ossian* (Edinburgh: A. Constable, 1805).

Royle, Edward. *Victorian Infidels: The Origins of the British Secularist Movement, 1791–1866* (Manchester: Manchester University Press, 1974).

Rubiés, Joan-Pau. *Travel and Ethnology in the Renaissance: South India through European Eyes, 1250–1650* (Cambridge: Cambridge University Press, 2000).

'From Antiquarianism to Philosophical History: India, China and the World History of Religion in European Thought (1600–1770)', in Peter N. Miller and François Louis (eds.), *Antiquarianism and Intellectual Life in Europe and China, 1500–1800* (Ann Arbor: University of Michigan Press, 2012), pp. 313–67.

'Reassessing "The Discovery of Hinduism": The Jesuit Discourse on Gentile Idolatry and the European Republic of Letters', in Anand Amaladass and Ines G. Županov (eds.), *Intercultural Encounter and the Jesuit Mission in South Asia (16th–18th Centuries* (Bangalore: Asian Trading Corporation, 2014), pp. 113–55.

'From Christian Apologetics to Deism: Libertine Readings of Hinduism, 1650–1730', in William J. Bulman and Robert G. Ingram (eds.), *God in the Enlightenment* (Oxford: Oxford University Press, 2016), pp. 107–35.

Rudd, Andrew. *Sympathy and India in British Literature, 1770–1830* (Basingstoke: Palgrave Macmillan, 2011).

Sachau, Edward. *Alberuni's India*, 2 vols. (London: Kegan Paul, Trench, Tribner & Co., 1914).

Sack, James S. *From Jacobite to Conservative: Reaction and Orthodoxy in Britain in c.1760–1832* (Cambridge: Cambridge University Press, 1993).

Said, Edward W. *Orientalism* (London: Penguin, 2003 [1978]).

Sambrook, James. *The Eighteenth Century: The Intellectual and Cultural Context of English Literature, 1700–1789*, 3rd ed. (London: Routledge, 2013).

Sarkar, Sumit. 'Orientalism Revisited: Saidian Frameworks in Modern Indian History', in Vinayak Chaturvedi (ed.), *Mapping Subaltern Studies and the Postcolonial* (London: Verso, 2012), pp. 239–55.

Sarton, George. 'Anquetil-Duperron (1731–1805)', *Osiris*, 3 (1937), pp. 193–223.

Sartori, Andrew. 'The British Empire and Its Liberal Mission', *Journal of Modern History*, 78:3 (2006), pp. 623–42.

Sastri, Alladi Mahadeva (trans.). *Bhagavad-Gita with the Commentary of Sri Shankaracharya* (Madras: V. Sadanand, 1977).

Schürer, Norbert. 'The Impartial Spectator of Satī, 1757–84', *Eighteenth-Century Studies*, 42:1 (2008), pp. 19–44.

Schwab, Raymond. *The Oriental Renaissance: Europe's Rediscovery of India and the East, 1680–1880*, Gene Patterson-Black and Victor Reinking (trans.) (New York: Columbia University Press, 1984 [original German, 1950]).

Scriven, Tom. *Popular Virtue: Continuity and Change in Radical Moral Politics, 1820–70* (Manchester: Manchester University Press, 2017).

Sebastiani, Silvia. *The Scottish Enlightenment: Race, Gender, and the Limits of Progress* (London: Palgrave Macmillan, 2013).

Sen, Neil. 'Warren Hastings and British Sovereign Authority in Bengal, 1774–80', *Journal of Imperial and Commonwealth History*, 25:1 (1997), pp. 59–81.

Sen, Sudipta. *A Distant Sovereignty: National Imperialism and the Birth of British India* (London: Routledge, 2002).

Sharma, Arvind. 'On Hindu, Hindustān, Hinduism and Hindutva', *Numen*, 49:1 (2002), pp. 1–36.

(ed.), *The Study of Hinduism* (Columbia: University of South Carolina Press, 2003).

Sharp, Eric J. 'The Study of Hinduism: The Setting', in Arvind Sharma (ed.), *The Study of Hinduism* (Columbia: University of South Carolina Press, 2003), pp. 20–55.

Shaw, Jane. *Miracles in Enlightenment England* (London: Yale University Press, 2006).

Sheps, Ather. 'Sedition, Vice and Atheism: The Limits of Toleration and the Orthodox Attack on Rational Religion in Late Eighteenth-Century Britain', in Regina Hewitt and Pat Rogers (eds.), *Orthodoxy and Heresy in*

Eighteenth-Century Society: Essays from the DeBartolo Conference (Lewisburg, PA: Bucknell University Press, 2002), pp. 51–68.

Sher, Richard B. '"Those Scotch Impostors and Their Cabal": Ossian and the Scottish Enlightenment', in Roger L. Emmerson, Gilles Girard and Rosanne Runt (eds.), *Man and Nature: Proceedings of the Canadian Society for Eighteenth Century Studies*, vol. 1 (London, ON: University of Western Ontario, 1982), pp. 55–63.

Singh, Ganda (ed.). *Early European Accounts of the Sikhs* (Calcutta: R. K. Maitra, 1962).

Soars, D. '"I Am that I Am" (Ex. 3.14): From Augustine to Abhishiktānanda – Holy Ground between Neoplatonism and Advaita Vedānta', *Sophia*, 60:2 (2020), pp. 287–306.

Sola de Pinto, V . 'Sir William Jones and English Literature', *Bulletin of the School of Oriental and African Studies*, 11 (1946), pp. 686–94.

Spivak, Gayatri. 'Can the Subaltern Speak?', in Gary Nelson and Lawrence Grossberg (eds.), *Marxism and the Interpretation of Culture* (Urbana: University of Illinois Press, 1988), pp. 271–313.

Spurr, John. '"Latitudinarianism" and the Restoration Church', *Historical Journal*, 31:1 (1988), pp. 61–82.

Stafford, Fiona. *The Sublime Savage: A Study of James Macpherson and the Poems of Ossian* (Edinburgh: Edinburgh University Press, 1988).

Stephen, Leslie and Sir Sidney Lee (eds.), *Dictionary of National Biography*, vol. 5 (London: Oxford University Press [1949–50]).

Stern, Philip J. *The Company-State: Corporate Sovereignty and the Early Modern Foundations of the British Empire in India* (Oxford: Oxford University Press, 2011).

Stewart, Larry. 'Samuel Clarke, Newtonianism, and the Factions of Post-Revolutionary England', *Journal of the History of Ideas*, 42:1 (1981), pp. 53–72.

Stewart, M. A. 'Revealed Religion: The British Debate', in Knud Haakonssen (ed.), *The Cambridge History of Eighteenth-Century Philosophy*, vol. 2 (Cambridge: University of Cambridge, 2006), pp. 683–709.

Stokes, Eric. *The English Utilitarians and India* (Oxford: Clarendon Press, 1959).

Stuart, Tristram. *The Bloodless Revolution: Radical Vegetarians and the Discovery of India* (London: Harper Press, 2006).

Subrahmanyam, Sanjay. *Europe's India: Worlds, People, Empires: 1500–1800* (Cambridge, MA: Harvard University Press, 2017).

Sugirtharajah, Sharada. *Imagining Hinduism: A Postcolonial Perspective* (London: Routledge, 2003).

'Colonialism', in Sushil Mittal and Gene Thursby (eds.), *Studying Hinduism: Key Concepts and Methods* (London: Routledge, 2008), pp. 73–85.

Sutherland, Lucy. *The East India Company in Eighteenth-Century Politics* (Oxford: Clarendon Press, 1952).

Sweetman, Will. 'Unity and Plurality: Hinduism and the Religions of India in Early European Scholarship', *Religion*, 31:3 (2001), pp. 209–24.

Mapping Hinduism: 'Hinduism' and the Study of Indian Religions, 1600–1776 (Halle: Franckesche Stifungen zu Halle, 2003).

Tavakoli-Targhi, Mohamad. 'Orientalism's Genesis Amnesia', *Comparative Studies of South Asia, Africa, and the Middle East*, 16:2 (1996), pp. 1–14.

'The Homeless Texts of Persianate Modernity', *Cultural Dynamics*, 13:3 (2001), pp. 263–91.

Teltscher, Kate. *India Inscribed: European and British Writing on India, 1600–1800* (New Delhi: Oxford University Press, 1997).

'"Maidenly and Well Nigh Effeminate": Constructions of Hindu Masculinity and Religion in Seventeenth-Century English Texts', *Postcolonial Studies*, 3:2 (2000), pp. 159–70.

Thompson, Derek S. *The Gaelic Sources of Macpherson's 'Ossian'* (Edinburgh: Oliver and Boyd, 1952).

Trautmann, Thomas R. *Aryans and British India* (Berkeley: University of California Press, 1997).

'Wilkins, Sir Charles (bap. 1749, d. 1836)', *Oxford Dictionary of National Biography*, Oxford University Press, 2004 [www.oxforddnb.com/view/article/29416, accessed 7 April 2016].

Travers, Robert. '"The Real Value of the Lands": The Nawabs, the British, and the Land Tax in Bengal', *Modern Asian Studies*, 38:3 (2004), pp. 517–58.

Ideology and Empire in Eighteenth-Century India: The British in Bengal (Cambridge: Cambridge University Press, 2007).

Trento, Margherita. 'Śivadharma or Bonifacio? Behind the Scenes of the Madurai Mission Controversy (1608–1619)', in Ines G. Županov and Pierre Antoine Fabre (eds.), *The Rites Controversies in the Early Modern World* (Leiden: Brill, 2018), pp. 91–121.

Truschke, A. *Culture of Encounters: Sanskrit at the Mughal Court* (New York: Columbia University Press, 2016).

van der Wall, Ernestine. 'Toleration and Enlightenment in the Dutch Republic', in Ole Peter Grell and Roy Porter (eds.), *Toleration in Enlightenment Europe* (Cambridge: Cambridge University Press, 2000), pp. 114–32.

Vattanky, John. *A System of Indian Logic: The Nyāya Theory of Inference* (Abingdon: Routledge, 2003).

Veevers, David. *The Origins of the British Empire in Asia, 1600–1750* (Cambridge: Cambridge University Press, 2020).

Vidyabhushana, Mahamahopadhyaya Satisa Chandra (trans.). *The Nyaya Sutras of Gautama* (Allahabad: The Indian Press, 1913).

Waligore, Joseph. 'Christian Deism in Eighteenth Century England', *International Journal of Philosophy and Theology*, 75:3 (2014), pp. 205–22.

Watson, Alex. 'Translating India: Geopolitical Identity in Elizabeth Hamilton's Translations of the Letters of a Hindoo Rajah', *Studies in English and American Literature*, 47 (2012), pp. 67–78.

Webb, R. K. 'The Emergence of Rational Dissent', in Knud Haakonssen (ed.), *Enlightenment and Religion: Rational Dissent in Eighteenth-Century Britain* (Cambridge: Cambridge University Press, 1996), pp. 12–41.

Weir, David. *Brahma and the West: William Blake and the Oriental Renaissance* (Albany: SUNY, 2003).

West, S. George and Mickle, W. J. 'The Work of W. J. Mickle, the First Anglo-Portuguese Scholar', *Review of English Studies*, 10:40 (1934), pp. 385–400.

Wigelsworth, Jeffrey R. *Deism in Enlightenment England: Theology, Politics and Newtonian Public Science* (Manchester: University of Manchester Press, 2009).

Wilbur, Earl M. *A History of Unitarianism: Socinianism and Its Antecedents* (Cambridge, MA: Harvard University Press, 1946).

Williams Jackson, A. V. (ed.), *A History of India*, vol. 9 (London: The Grolier Society, 1907).

Willis, Arthur C. 'The Potential Use-Value of Hume's "True Religion"', *Journal of Scottish Philosophy*, 13:1 (2015), pp. 1–15.

Wilson, Jon E. *The Domination of Strangers: Modern Governance in Eastern India, 1780–1835* (Basingstoke: Palgrave Macmillan, 2008).

Wilson, Leslie A. *A Mythical Image: The Ideal of India in German Romanticism* (Durham, NC: Duke University Press, 1964).

Xavier, Ângela Barreto and Zupanov, Ines G. *Catholic Orientalism: Portuguese Empire, Indian Knowledge (16th and 18th Centuries)* (New Delhi: Oxford University Press, 2015).

Yang, Chi-ming. 'Gross Metempsychosis and Eastern Soul', in Frank Palmeri (ed.), *Humans and Other Animals in Eighteenth-Century British Culture: Representation, Hybridity, Ethics* (Farnham: Ashgate, 2006), pp. 13–30.

Yasukata, Toshimasa. *Lessing's Philosophy of Religion and the German Enlightenment* (Oxford: Oxford University Press, 2003).

Young, Arthur. *Political Essays Concerning the Present State of the British Empire* (London: W. Strahan and T. Cadell, 1772).

Young, B. W. 'Newtonianism and the Enthusiasm of Enlightenment', *Studies in the History and Philosophy of Science*, 35:3 (2004), pp. 645–63.

Zachs, William. *The First John Murray and the Late Eighteenth-Century London Book Trade* (Oxford: Oxford University Press, 1998).

Zaehner, Robert Charles. *The Bhagavad-Gītā* (Oxford: Oxford University Press, 1969).

Zimmer, Heinrich. *Myths and Symbols in Indian Art and Civilization*, J. Campbell (ed.) (Princeton, NJ: Princeton University Press, 1972).

Županov, Ines G. *Disputed Mission: Jesuit Experiments and Brahmanical Knowledge in Seventeenth-Century India* (New Delhi: Oxford University Press, 1999).

Zurbuchen, S. 'Religion and Society', in K. Haakonssen (ed.), *The Cambridge History of Eighteenth-Century Philosophy* (Cambridge: Cambridge University Press, 2000), pp. 779–814.

Index

Akbar, 27, 62, 127, 139, 154
Al Sirajiyyah: Or the Mohamedan Law of Inheritance (1792), 295
angels, 70, 161, 203, 235
  Capel Berrow's angels, 100
  Chevalier Andrew Michael Ramsay's angels, 104
  Diogo do Couto's angels, 90
  Dow on angels, 138, 153
  George Cheyne's angels, 104
  Holwell's fallen angels, 89, 92, 93, 100
Anglicist, 54, 264, 297, 302, *See also* Kopf, David
animal
  consumption, 89, 100–2
  sacrifices, 161
  souls, 97–8
  suffering, 94, 97, 98–100
  transmigration, 103
Anquetil-Duperron, Abraham Hyacinthe, 46–7, 185, 283
App, Urs, 77, 83, 270, 282
Arianism, 246, 272
Asiatick Researches, 256
Asiatick Society of Bengal, 4, 268, 275, 278, 281, 300, 303, 306
atheism, 16, 44, 107, 145, 146, 221, 247, 314
Aurangzeb, 66, 73, 179

Babel, 14, 49, 278, 279
Baldaeus, Phillipus, 42–3, 82, 88, 158
Barrow, Isaac, 292, 305
Battle of Plassey (1757), 56, 60, 169
Bayly, C.A., 10, 20, 62, 78
Benares charge, 231–2
Bengal Judicature Act (1782), 297, 306, 307
Bengal Judicature Bill (1781), 200, 297, 298, 306
Bengali, language, 52, 77, 81, 125, 130, 144, 208, 239
  Grammar of the Bengal language, 208, 239
  typeface, 239
Berkeley, George, 235, 286–9
Bernard, Jean Frederic, 4, 43, 44, 45, 52
Bernier, François, 51–2, 150
Berrow, Capel, 96, 98, 99–100, 103, 104
Bhagavad-Gītā, 18, 151, 241–62, 284, 313
Bhāgavata Purāṇa, 278, 280
Bishnupur (Bisnapore), 86–7, 189, 203
Black Hole of Calcutta, 73, 170, 173–4, 175–7, 232, 307
Blackstone, William, 296
Blount, Charles, 216
Boehme, Jacob, 254, 259
Brahmins, 6, 11, 37, 46, 51, 52, 65, 90, 113, 124, 127, 202, 204, 226, 237, 279
  ancient, 73–4, 104, 112
  as Unitarians, 1, 244, 252–4
  Dow's encounter with, 116
  drawn by William Blake, 258–9
  idolatry, 159
  in Halhed's poetry, 228–9
  in *Letters of a Hindoo Raja*, 309
  instruction, 3, 28, 52, 78, 130, 157, 214, 249
  Jesuit approach to, 39
  learned, 42, 134, 136, 141, 152, 156, 159, 168, 248
  monotheism of, 140, 163–4, 166
  priestcraft of, 85, 114, 127, 136, 156, 159, 248, 261, 275, 280, 295
  scholars, 18, 26, 211–12
  secrecy, 41, 126, 157, 203, 243, 299
Briggs, John, 122–3
Brothers, Richard, 210–11, 221, 233, 234, 235, 236, 237
Burke, Edmund, 21, 23, 24, 56, 58, 67, 70, 123, 192, 196, 199–200, 209–10, 227, 231–3, 266–8, 298, 302–3, 307, 311

Calvinist, Calvinism, 44, 97, 275
caste, 65–6, 85, 156, 211, 304, 315
Catholic emancipation, 259
Catholicism, 38, 50, 271
  accusations of idolatry, 88

Catholicism (cont.)
anti-Catholic, 81, 88
Popish authors, 81, 88
purgatory, 162
Romanists, 274
Romish Church, 254
Cheyne, George, 101–4, 107
China, 15, 39, 44, 49, 51
Christology, 105, 107, 108, 273
Clarke, Samuel, 107, 110, 142, 147, 273
Clive, Robert, 19, 60, 72, 118, 172, 177, 192, 194, 207, 242, 311
Code of Gentoo Laws, A, 11, 15, 18, 37, 207, 210, 232, 237, 241, 279, 296, 301, 302
circumstances of commission, 214
Halhed's preface, 214
reception of Halhed's preface, 224
Colebrooke, Henry Thomas, 145, 228, 295, 297
Confucianism, 15, 39, 49, 51
Cornwallis, Charles, 18, 20, 58, 68–9, 124, 232, 296, 302–4, 306–7, 311, 314
Costard, George, 216, 224, 225–6, 279
Cudworth, Ralph, 96–7, 104, 287–8

Dara Shikoh, 27, 37, 233, 270, 283–4
deism, 4, 12, 54, 104, 114, 135, 247, 288, 318
Dow, 116, 135, 137, 184
English, 50, 96, 116, 136, 246, 271
Halhed, 217, 218
historiographical revision of, 13–15, 55, 116
Holwell's Christian deism, 71, 84, 88–9, 105–10
Jones, 269, 272, 281, 305
of Picart and Bernard, 44
of the Mughals, 9, 62, 154, 187, 190, 193
of the Sikhs, 256
of Warren Hastings, 61
Reimarus, 165
secondary literature describing the authors in this study as deist, 12, 54, 116, 171, 240, 269–70
Voltaire, 159, 163
despotism, 192, 194, 199, 202
despotism, Asian, 22, 46, 61, 63–4, 119, 135, 138, 154, 173, 174, 176, 178, 184–90, 192, 227, 266, 298, 299, 300, 301
dharma, 35, 132, 244, 251–2
Diderot, Denis, 24, 83, 196, 201, 202–3
diwani, 56, 192, 193, 214, 261

East India
criticism of, 19
East India Company
Board of Control, 58, 306
Calcutta council, 176, 192
Charter (1689), 56
Charter (1712), 57
Charter (1793), 68
Charter (1813), 67
college, 69, 257, 269, 315
Court of Directors, 11, 19, 60, 67, 72, 118, 177, 192, 213
criticism of, 60, 67, 124, 173, 190, 191, 202, 227, 230, *See also* empire, critics of; impeachment, Warren Hastings
Fort William (Calcutta), 62, 69, 72–3, 170, 172–3, 176, 315
Revenue Board, 209, 243
Egypt, 43, 77, 78, 217, 225, 226, 285, 316
empire, critics of, 8, 24, 196–204, 268, 311
Encyclopédie, 48, 83
English laws, 304

Faizi (Abu al-Faiz ibn Mubarak), 127
fakirs, 136
Fātwā al-'Ālmagīrī, 66
Firishta (Muhammad Qasim Hindu Shah), 119, 123, 124, 139, 187, *See also Tārikh-i-Firishta*
Dow's disagreement with, 127–8, 182–3
Dow's use of, 126–8
Flood, biblical, 2, 77, 102, 183–4, 216–18, 225, 234, 278–80
Fox's India Bill (1783), 192, 198, 199, 209, 306
Franklin, Benjamin, 273
Fraser, James, 122, 179
French Revolution, 10, 303, 314, 316

Gama, Vasco da, 38, 157
Gautama, Akṣapāda, 144, 145, 147–9, 284, 292
Genghis Khan, 119
Gentoo, origin of the term, 35–6
Glanvill, Joseph, 97
Goethe, Johann Wolfgang von, 263
Grant, Charles, 11–12, 37, 67–8, 228, 274
Greece, 164, 253
Greek, 2, 53, 90, 91, 162, 168, 208, 263
Guha, Ranajit, 9, 20, 170, 171, 193–4

Halbfass, Wilhelm, 12, 53, 116, 240, 269
Hamilton, Elizabeth, 291, 309–11, 314–15
Hebrew, 276, 294
Hegel, Georg Wilhelm Friedrich, 10, 167, 172
Herbert of Cherbury, Edward, Lord, 50
Herder, Johann Gottfried von, 166–7, 258, 263
Hindoo, origin of the term. *See Gentoo*
Hume, David, 15, 104, 115, 121, 138, 139, 218, 220, 222–3, 225, 287–8, 313

Ilive, Jacob, 83, 90, 96, 98, 100, 175
impeachment, Warren Hastings, 20, 30, 56, 67, 200, 209, 232, 237, 255, 302, 311

Halhed's role in, 227, 230–2, *See* Benares charge
Institutes of Hindu Law; or the Ordinances of Menu, The (1794), 68, 133, 295, 299
Islam, 27, 35, 127, 283
Dow's comments on, 138, 154, 185–6
eighteenth-century European perceptions of, 9, 63–4
Elizabeth Hamilton on, 315
Islamic calendar, 184
Islamic perceptions of Hindu religion, 36
law, 61, 62, 66, 211–13, 229, 304, *See also* law, Muslim law
Prophet Muhammad, 185–6
Qur'an, 63, 183, 185, 186, 229, 283
William Jones' comments on, 275

Jacobin, 204, 301, 310, 314
anti-Jacobin, 168, 303, 310
Jesuit, 36, 37–40, 44–5, 48, 80, 81, 88, 98, 125, 132, 162, 202, 254, 334, 346, 350, *See also Lettres édifiantes*
Judaism, 164–5, 244
Judicial Plan (1772), 59, 208, 211–14, 237
Judicial Plan (1790), 304
Jūg Bāsisht, 282–3, 285

Kopf, David, 20, 54, 264

latitudinarianism, latitudinarians, 49, 246, 269, 273
law
adālats (courts), 212
administration of law in Mughal India, 172, 192, 211–14
British perceptions of Indian law, 211, 213–14, 304, 311
Burke's appeal to India's existing law, 200
common law, 296, 301
Dow's proposals, 192–4
English laws, 59, 211, 214, 301
French civil law (Quebec), 59
Hindu law, 8, 18, 26, 59, 66, 68, 80, 133, 208, 228, 238, 267, 269, 302
India's ancient laws, 58
Jones on Hindu law, 294–301
Muslim law, 59, 61, 62, 68, 194, 208, 211, 213, *See also* Islam, law
Leibniz, Gottfried Wilhelm, 51, 96, 103
Leibnizian theodicy, 99
Lettres édifiantes, 40, 132
liberal imperialism, 196, 301
Locke, John, 96, 275
Lockean, 50
Lord, Henry, 42

Macpherson, James, 113–15, 120–1
Macpherson, John, 60, 120, 294, 302
Mahābhārata, 36–7, 126–7, 128, 134, 141, 182–3, 211, 233, 234, 236, 243, 257, 293
Mānava-Dharmaśāstra, 66, 68, 133–4, 298, 300, 306
Marshall, P. J., 5, 21, 68
materialism, 96, 146, 290, 291
Maurice, Thomas, 161, 169, 204, 260, 307, 314–15
Māyā, 235, 285–9, 290
Mendelssohn, Moses, 6, 164
metempsychosis, 71, 91–7, 98, 99, 100, 101, 103, 104–5, 108–9, 110–11, 156, 161, 164, 175, 275, 312
Mickle, William Julius, 81, 157–60
Mill, James, 66, 168, 196, 228, 300, 301
Mill, John Stewart, 196
millenarianism, 103, 210, 237
Milton, John, 90, 236
Mīmāṃsā, 284
Mir Jafar, 19, 72, 173, 180
Mir Qasim, 72, 173, 180
mission, Christian, 11, 12, 36, 38–40, 45, 49, 58, 67
Catholic, 2, 36
criticism of, 237, 274, 277
missionary, authors, 39, 40, 44, 45, 80, 163
criticism of, 116, 125, 128, 136, 317
mokṣa, 151, 245, 285, 305
Montesquieu, Charles-Louis de Secondat, 22, 160
critiqued by Anquetil-Duperron, 185
in the thought of Dow, 135, 154, 184, 190, 195
in the thought of Hastings, 59
in the thought of Holwell, 111
oriental despotism, 46, 63, 185
Persian Letters (1721), 310
religion, 48
More, Henry, 97
Moses, 160, 217, 225–6, 255, 278–80
Muhammad Reza Khan, 212–13
Muthu, Sankar, 24, 203, 204

Noah, 269, 270, 278, 280
Nobili, Roberto de, 36, 38, 44, 163
Nyāya, 30, 44, 117, 118, 129, 139, 144–50, 154, 167, 284, 292–3, 297, 299, 312

Orme, Robert, 56, 59, 122–3, 234
Ossian, 113–16
Ottoman empire, 62, 64

pantheism, 258, 289
Picart, Bernard, 4, 43, 44
Pitt's India Act (1784), 18, 303, 306
Pitts, Jennifer, 24, 196–7, 198, 201
Plassey, 180

Plato, 50, 92, 288
Platonism
  Cambridge Platonism, 96–7, 100, 104, 254
  Christian Platonist, 143, 286
  Neoplatonist, 143, 281, 286
poetry
  'A Hymn to Ganga' (1785), 268, 294
  'A Hymn to Lacshmí' (1788), 295
  'A Hymn to Náráyena' (1785), 286, 289–91, 310
  Halhed's poems to Hastings, 228–9
Price, Richard, 16, 268, 270–5, 278, 287–9
priestcraft, 14, 26, 54, 84, 86, 88, 92, 109, 115, 135–8, 153, 224, 248, 275, 280, 295, 298–9, 300, 305, 318, *See also* Brahmins
Priestley, Joseph, 160–1, 226, 273
providence, 13, 106, 110, 146–7, 153, 159, 289, 315
Puranas (*purāṇa*), 45, 77, 133
Pythagoras, 91–2, 164, 235, 284
  Pythagorean, 73, 91, 95, 96, 98, 114, 235

Quietism, 103, 104, 292

race, 64
Ramayana (Rāmāyaṇam), 45, 133
Rammohan Roy, 263
Ramsay, Chevalier Andrew Michael, 104–5, 270
Rational Dissent, 14, 16, 31, 160, 251, 268, 269–77, 281, 313
Raynal, Guillaume Thomas, 202, 204, 224, 226, 228
Regulating Act (1786), 18, 303
Regulating Act(1773), 19, 60, 192
reincarnation, 12, 41, 73, 89, 92, 97, 143, 150, 153, 156, 161, *See also* metempsychosis
Robertson, William, 48, 130, 224
Roger (Rogerius), Abraham, 42–3, 51–2, 77, 80
Royal Society, 73, 257, 265, 268

Said, Edward, 5, 7, 264
Shakuntala (Śakuntalā), 257
Sāṃkhya, 284
Śaṅkara, 250, 284, 288
sati, 8, 41, 58, 82, 175, 193
scepticism, religious, 15–16, 24, 30, 106, 159, 216
  Halhed's, 210, 220, 225, 237, 281, 313
Schwab, Raymond, 5, 82
Secret Committee on Indian Affairs, 212
Select Committee (1766), 60
Select Committee (1767), 181
Select Committee (1781), 57
Select Committee on Indian Affairs, 209, 230, 231
Select Committee on Judicial Arrangements in Bengal, 200
sepoy, 58
Shastah, Holwell's, 70–1, 74–85, 87–105, 108, 109, 112, 130, 156, 160, 164, 174–5, 177, 179, 203
Shaster, Dow's, 126, 128–36, 140–54, 156, 162
Shelley, Percy Bysshe, 263
Sheridan, Richard Brinsley, 220–1, 223
Shore, John, 68, 123, 269, 282–3, 315
Sikhism, 256–7
Siraj-ud-Daulah, 19, 62, 173, 174, 176, 177–8
smallpox, 73, 102
Smith, Adam, 192, 196–9
Socinianism, 108, 246, 271, 272
Socrates, 50, 159, 276
Spinoza, Baruch, 167, 258, 289
  Spinozaism, 165
Sufism, 27, 270, 282–3, 286

Tafazzul Husayn Khan, 26
Tamil, 38, 40, 44, 77
Tārikh-i-Firishta, 119, 123, 126, 127, 171, 172, 181–2, 187
Tarkapañcānana, Jagannātha, 26, 212, 295
Tarkavāgīśa, Rādhākānta, 26
theodicy, 13, 71, 93, 95–100, 102, 104, 105, 109, 111, 152
Thirty-Nine Articles of the Church of England, 246, 275
Tindal, Matthew, 50, 107, 109
Tipu Sultan, 232, 307, 316
Toland, John, 50, 91, 113, 115, 246, 289
transmigration. *See* metempsychosis
Trautmann, Thomas, 5, 77, 125, 269, 270, 281
travel literature, 40–2, 82, 116, 122, 125, 128, 150, 157, 158
Travers, Robert, 9, 21, 67, 171, 192, 193, 196, 211–12, 229, 233
Treaty of Allahabad (1765), 56, 180, 181
trinity, doctrine of, 108, 246, 247, 305, 308
  anti-Trinitarian, 14, 16, 108, 111, 246, 247, 271, 272, 281
  comparison of Christian and Hindu trinities, 94, 271–2, 308
  Hindu trinity, 140
  Plato, 235
  Trinitarian, 9, 108, 273, 274, 277
  William Jones on, 270–4

Unitarianism, 1, 9, 14, 31, 160, 226, 244, 245–8, 251, 271, 272, 313
Upanishads (*Upaniṣads*), 36, 47, 85, 134, 151, 210, 249, 270, 283, 284
  Halhed, 233–7

vāhana, 142
Vedānta, 39, 44, 117, 118, 129, 139–44, 145, 154, 162, 244–5, 249, 251, 277, 281–90, 292–4, 299–300
  Advaita Vedānta, 44, 151, 152, 167, 250, 277, 282, 283, 284–5, 288, 305, 313
Vedas, 80
  Akbar, 127
  Dara Shikoh, 283
  do Cuoto, 77
  Dow, 128
  Ezour-Védam, 45–6, 80, 162–3
  Halhed, 228, 234
  Jones, 279, 283
  Vyāsa, 284, 293
  Wilkins, 248–9
Volney, Constantin François, 64, 185, 308
Voltaire (François-Marie Arouet), 6, 51, 202, 204, 225, 308, 313
  as critiqued by Mickle, 159
  Le Compagnie des Indes, 47
  on fakirs, 136
  on Holwell, 79–80, 111
  on Holwell's Bisnapore (Bishnupur), 86
  on Holwell's metempsychosis, 98
  on Islam, 63, 185, 186
  on the Vedas, 45
  Orphelin de la Chine (1755), 120
  theodicy, 93, 99
  use of Holwell and Dow, 162–4, 201
Vyāsa, 284, 293

Warburton, William, 222, 255
Wellesley, Richard, 68, 315–17, 319
Whitelock, Bulstrode, 91–2
Wilberforce, William, 57–8
Wilford, Francis, 77–8

Zamindar, 72, 172, 180–1, 195–6, 303, 309, 312
Ziegenbalg, Batholomäus, 36, 40
Zoroastrianism, 46